# THE
# KINGDOM OF AHMADNAGAR

THE

# KINGDOM OF AHMADNAGAR

*By*

DR. RADHEY SHYAM

M.A., D.PHIL (ALLAHABAD)

*Lecturer in History,*

*Hindu College, Delhi University, Delhi.*

*with*

A FOREWORD BY

Dr. BISHESHWAR PRASAD

*Prof. & Head of the Deptt. of History,*

Delhi University, Delhi.

MOTILAL BANARSIDASS

DELHI :: PATNA :: VARANASI

Bungalow Road, Jawahar Nagar, Delhi-7
Bankipore, Patna-4, (Bihar)
Nepali Khapra, Varanasi-1, (U.P.)

(THESIS APPROVED, FOR THE DEGREE OF DOCTOR OF PHILOSOPHY, BY UNIVERSITY OF ALLAHABAD)

*First Edition*, 1966

PRINTED IN INDIA BY SHANTILAL JAIN, AT SHRI JAINENDRA PRESS, BUNGALOW ROAD, JAWAHAR NAGAR, DELHI-7 AND PUBLISHED BY SUNDARLAL JAIN, MOTILAL BANARSIDASS, BUNGALOW ROAD, JAWAHAR NAGAR, DELHI-7

TO

MY FATHER

DR. BANARSI PRASAD SAKSENA

# FOREWORD

Indian history, in its long record, has witnessed the operation of two contrary phenomena, which may be characterised as integration and disintegration. In the course of ages these two forces have influenced the process of history and made deep impression on the emotional and intellectual build-up of the people. Integration has been a mighty element of motivation, and from the early centuries of the first millennium before Christ, the urge for the establishment of an all-comprehending, pervasive state, embracing the whole of India south of the Himalayan and Hindukush ranges, was powerful. The formation of the empires, such as those of the Mauryas and the Guptas, while encouraged by cultural unity and social uniformity, helped in its turn the emergence of politico-economic factors which provided stimulus for integration in the subsequent periods. But when political unity had been assured and divisive forces eclipsed, the processess of disintegration and division were active once again and the consequence was the creation of a plethora of local states, small in size and warring amongst themselves for territory or prestige. In the then known mechanism of reposition of power, where sovereignty resided in a despotic monarch and succession was dynastic, no other course was possible. A strong ruler or two was necessarily followed by a series of weaklings beset by vices of character and lacking in strong will or moral fervour. This was the invariable tale, and empires broke asunder in the reigns of do-nothing monarchs who were swayed by selfish courtiers and effete generals. Any one who showed and could muster a force under him could establish his independent principality, be he an official of the empire or a local chief and till a powerful leader could emerge to reactivise the centripetal forces and create a central organisation to raise another empire, these local sovereignties had their ephemeral effulgence in the regional firmament.

The malady of fissiparity and mutual warfare was universal throughout India in certain periods. The north had witnessed the rise of many provincial states on the extinction of the Gupta-Vakataka empire, and though the Pratiharas struggled to coalesce the mutually warring states by their superior military strength, they failed to stem the tide of disintegration. Thus when the Turks from the north-west, spurred by ambitions of territorial expansion and religious frenzy, strove for sovereignty in India, their advance met with little determined and united resistance, and the consequence was the foundation of Turkish sultanate in Delhi. Under the new sovereigns there were waves of integration which, when they had submerged the whole or major part of India, receded, enabling the local sovereignties to emerge once again. The Khaljis and Tughlaqs brought the Daccan and the South as well as the east and west under their sway, but with the death of Alauddin or Muhammad, the peripheral regions broke away and regained their independent existence to wallow in the mire of constant wars with their neighbours and faction-fighting within their boundaries.

The Daccan had found temporary peace under the Rashtrakutas but their wars with the Chalukyas or the northern states had devoured their vitality, and on the extinction of the Rashtrakuta state, the whole region became prey to internecine struggles and anarchy. The author has vividly described this condition in his introductory chapter. He writes very pertinently that "Broadly speaking the annals of this land constitute a record of the succession of minor kingdoms which rose on the ruins of the vanquished empires. On the one hand we are struck by their perpetual mutual antagonisms and on the other by the incidental promotion of all that is the best in the Hindu culture. These petty states had hardly any appreciation of the importance of peaceful coexistence, on the contrary, each of them tried to absorb as much of its neighbour's territory as it could at the expense of the others." This interminable dynastic warfare, reduced the vitality and the vigour of the people which ultimately paved the way for the Turkish conquest. But the Turkish conquest also failed to bring the remedy. The decline of the Delhi sultanate freeed the Daccan and the South from the imperial rule and resulted in the emergence of two large and relatively powerful states of Vijayanagar and the Bahmani kingdom. Territorial ambitions and religious dissimilarity prompted a state of perennial hostility between the two which ultimately weakened both of them and set once again the stage for the rise of conflicting local chiefships. It was in a situation as this that the Nizam Shahi kingdom of Ahmadnagar was founded by Malik Ahmad about the close of the 15th century. He was the son of a prominent official of the Bahmani kingdom and had enjoyed royal favour, which did not deter him from breaking into pieces the kingdom of his master. The state founded by him had a life of nearly two centuries before it was absorbed finally into the Mughal empire in the time of Shahjahan.

The Nizam Shahis met the same fate as the Bahmanis and the new kingdom had no peace from the aggressive intentions of its neighbours or the internecine wars fomented by disgruntled nobility, ambitious princes or intractable local chiefs. The largest preoccupation of the rulers of this kingdom, however, was the preservation of the integrity of the state and protection of its frontiers. The rise of the succession states on the break-up of the Bahmani kingdom brought into prominence the state of Golcanda, Bidar, Berar and Khandesh, of which the last three were contiguous to Ahmadnagar; and consequently the Nizam Shahis had almost continuously to fight them to avert their expansionist designs. These wars were directed at the creation of a united state, but each one of them was struggling to emerge victorious and establish its hegemony over the others. Similarly Gujarat had also broken away from the control of the Delhi Sultanate, and its rulers were employing their wealth and military strength to aggress and expand their territories by absorbing the states in the Daccan, Rajasthan and Malwa. The danger from the southern kingdom of Vijaynagar was no less acute. All these power-conscious new states were endeavouring to bring forth political unity in that region and thus give fresh impetus to the age-long tendency for integration of the country. But none of them had the resources adequate to vanquish local resistance and territorial separatism. However, in the process of mutual warfare each one of them was weakened and thereby unable to stem the tide of imperial unity which swept from the north in the time of Akbar and his successors. The Mughal Empire had favourable prospects and succeeded in absorbing Ahmadnagar even against the powerful resistance offered by Chand Bibi and Malik Ambar. Courage and devotion of a rare variety was exhibited in fighting the Mughal forces, but it is doubtful if in that struggle the people of that region had thrown themselves into the fight on the side of the ruler of the state. The Mughals managed to extinguish these Daccan states one by one and thereby brought the entire region upto the extreme south under one sway.

The kingdom of Ahmadnagar thus in its career had to withstand the opposition of its neighbours and ultimately to offer resistance to the mighty Mughal empire from whose blows it failed to recover. The history of the regional states, ruled by despotic chiefs, is thus essentially one of conflict between the forces of integration and disintegration. When central authority exhibited symptoms of weakness and decay, these states emerged into lime-light, but when it regained vitality, they disappeared to be absorbed and assimilated into the bigger whole. The unity of India was the powerful principle which history reveals and historians have the pious duty to unfold it. Regional histories, like the present one, have an important role but only if they are woven into the fabric of the history of India as a whole.

Dr. Radhey Shyam has narrated the story of the rise and fall of the kingdom of Ahmadnagar. His book opens with an analysis of the political situation in which the establishment of small local states had become a reality. In subsequent chapters he has narrated the tale of the struggles of the rulers of this kingdom with their neighbours and within their own territories. He then concludes the story by recounting the Mughal-Nizam Shahi wars and in that context has naturally been led to describe with admiration the heroic deeds of Chand Bibi and Malik Ambar's devotion to the State. He has given a chapter to describe the relations of the Nizam Shahis with the Portuguese. It may be said to the credit of the Nizam Shahis that they did not permit these foreigners to penetrate into the interior of the country which might have been the case if this state had not been vigilant. Finally he rounds off the story by discussing the political institutions and the cultural effulgence which was a great contribution of the Nizam Shahis. The story has been narrated with balance. The book will be a valuable addition to historical knowledge on a subject which had not so far been treated scientifically. It is a successful endeavour in local history without dimming the vision of India and its integrity.

*Bisheshwar Prasad*

Professor and Head of the History Department,
Delhi University, Delhi.

## PREFACE

Throughout the medieval period of our history, the people of the Daccan always displayed an urge to preserve their local cultural traditions, their individual characteristics and the territorial integrity of the region by overthrowing the central authority and setting at naught the concept of a unified empire. The Bahmani kingdom itself was the outcome of anti-imperial tendencies. And such feeling repeated itself at the close of the fifteenth century. Being supported by the local population, Ahmed Nizam-ul-Mulk-Bahri, carved out an independent principality, transformed it into a kingdom which aimed at safeguarding the interest of the region under his control. The subsequent pages narrate the story of this kingdom, which is known by the name of Nizam Shahi kingdom of Ahmadnagar.The story of it is chiefly a narration of its struggle for survival and expansion in the face of the rise of neighbouring powers in the north, west, south and east. It inherited all the virtues and the vices of the parent Bahmani kingdom and unlike it, as destiny intended, it also became the hub of the complicated politics of the Daccan. Its situation in the earlier stages brought it into conflict with the rulers of Khandesh and Berar in the north, Gujarat in the north-west, Bidar in the south-east, Portuguese in the west, Bijapur and Golkunda in the east and then, during the period of its decline, with the mighty power of the Mughal empire. Thus the history of this kingdom not only constitutes an unending record of the perennial wars waged for expansion, preservation and self-defence but it also represents the struggle between a kingdom and those political potentates, who cherished to be the masters of an empire, having wider dimensions and multiracial population under their control.

The picture of the struggle on this part of the Nizam Shahis may not be very exhilerating or instructive, but it is interesting in the sense that they did not allow the neighbouring powers to attain the status of imperial power and thereby they maintained proper balance between north and south. The details of the battles which, in pursuit of their objective they won or lost, are not only monotonous because of their wearisome repetitions, but are intensely complicated and confusing. Again the petty ambitions of the neighbouring rulers, the shifting alliances amongst them, their opportunism and occasional display of timidity have eclipsed the importance of the role played by the Nizam Shahi kings. In fact, the Nizam Shahis fought on every front, contesting for every inch of the soil of this region over which they ruled or which they claimed as their own. Although thrown in the welter of instability and uncertainity arising out of the rise of the other provincial states which by themselves were born from the ashes of the Bahmani empire, and the rise of the Hindu state of Vijayanagar, the kingdom of Gujarat under Sultan Bahadur Shah, the kingdom of Khandesh under the Faruqi kings, the Nizam Shahis pursued, with dogged determination the objectives for which they stood, often in the face of the heavy odds arrayed against them. The rulers of the neighbouring kingdoms always cast their eyes on the frontiers of this kingdom and seldom missed the opportunity of stepping into its territory, thereby forcing the Nizam Shahis to uncover their sword. It was the frequency of this peril which compelled them to be on this unavoidable path of war. The crisis was further accentuated by the absence of well defined natural boundaries, which led to the assertion of the claims and counter-claims on the disputed areas, by the rival parties which in turn produced a crop of misunderstanding and rivalries always resulting in armed conflicts. Be it said to the credit of the Nizam Shahis that, in spite of their internal and external difficulties, they continued to hold their own ground.

After the dreams of the rulers of Gujarat and Vijayanagar had been shattered, the kingdom of Ahmednagar found a chance to pursue the policy of territorial expansion. But no sooner did it occupy the kingdom of Berar, it was called upon to deal with another power i.e. the Mughals, who having captured and occupied Malwa and Gujarat, stood on its doorsteps. The pressure of the Portuguese from the west and of the rulers of Bijapur and Golkunda from the south placed them in a critical situation. Even so, its rulers, nobles and people successfully bore the brunt of the Mughal aggression and preserved the independent existence of this region for a long while.

When every thing appeared to be lost on account of the aggressive, expansionist policy of the Mughals, the valiant Malik Ambar, pulled out the Nizam shahi state from the jaws of total annihilation, gave it a new lease of life, revived the fortunes of the fallen dynasty and erected a strong bulwark against its fast approaching doom. This phase of the struggle, between the imperial power and protector of the other two kingdoms of the Daccan, was a unique phenomanon not only in the history of the Daccan but in the entire history of the Turkish rule in India. It is in this context that the full reaction of the policy of the Mughals towards the Nizam Shahis has been critically assessed.

Apart from the political role which the kingdom played on the political chess-board of the Daccan, its cultural contribution was by no means small or negligible. In spite of its pre-occupation with military activities, the Nizam Shahi Kings took genuine interest in promoting the various aspects of Indo-Muslim culture. Their court was the centre of poets, writers, theologians, artists, diplomats, and statesmen. Ahmadnagar, the capital of the Nizam Shahis, proved to be the cradle for the growth of the Madhvi movement, although the rulers patronised and professed Shiaism. The adoption of Shiaism by Burhan Nizam Shah I, brought the kingdom for a while in close touch with the Safvid kingdom of Persia and led to the flow of talent from Persia to Ahmadnagar. Learned, accomplished and pious men hailing from distant countries migrated to Ahmadnagar in the hope of improving their fortunes. They were welcomed, honoured, rewarded and elevated to high positions in accordance with their talents. Their works, which are mostly in Persian, enriched the contemporary Indo-Persian literature. The Nizam Shahis also set the precedent of religious discussions in the court, which broadened their outlook, made them and their nobles liberal-minded and generous. To them also goes the credit of having associated the garden pattern with buildings. They left to posterity their names in the shape of gardens, *dams*, and magnificent edifices. Their architectural monuments speak of their simplicity and interest in various fields.

This work is thus an humble attempt to assess the achievements and failures of the Nizam Shahis in correct perspective. While writing it I have tried my best to make use of the original Persian sources, published and unpublished, and the other material accessible to me. Every care has been taken to unravel satisfactorily the confused accounts to be found in some works which are deemed to be authoritative and the details have been adjusted in their proper places. Due attention has also been paid to determine the exact chronology. In certain cases inscriptions have been utilised to confirm it.

Words can not express my most profound sense of gratitude, which I owe to my father, *Guru* and guide, Dr. Banarsi Prasad Saksena, who not only created in me the urge for the deep and impartial study of history but inspired me to finish this work within eighteen months. At the same time I feel greatly indebted to Dr. Bisheshwar Prasad, Professor and Head of the History Department, University of Delhi, for giving the encouragement without which the work would never have seen the light of the day. The affection and love which he has for me, will always inspire me to learn and contribute my mite in unravelling and reinterpreting the sober facts of history. In course of my study I have also been encouraged by my teachers, Prof. O. P. Bhatnagar, Dr. M. A. Ansari and Dr. C. B. Tripathi. I am grateful to them for their suggestions, guidance, and kindness. I shall be failing in my duty if I fail to express my sincere thanks to Shri B. K. Trivedi, Assistant Librarian and Shri Pan Singh Adhikari, Chief Cataloguer, of Allahabad University Library for extending me all the facilities while I was working in its research hall.

I also wish to express thanks to Messers Moti Lal Banarsi Dass for accepting the thesis for publication. I can not resist expressing my feelings of appreciation for the great enthusiasm shown by Shri M. R. Suri, Manager Jainendra Press in printing this work promptly and the interest taken by Shri B. S. Sagar in correcting the proofs. I am grateful to both of them.

Inspite of my best efforts, there have remained some printing errors in the book, for which I crave the indulgence of the readers. I shall always welcome their criticism and suggestions which will make me feel amply rewarded for the labour I have put in writing this dissertation.

Radhey Shyam,
*Lecturer in History,*
Hin u College, Delhi.

March, 1966.

# CONTENTS

CHAPTER I

# INTRODUCTORY

## THE BIRTH OF THE NIZAM SHAHI KINGDOM

The land lying to the south of the Vindhyas is mostly rugged and rocky. On its northern side the slope being gentle, there are no well marked spurs or steep valleys; whereas on the southern side, the fall from the crest to the valley of Narbada is steep. The valley is protected by the chain of hills forming a wall covered with dense forests stretching to the Satpuras. Across the southern slopes of the latter flows the river Tapti westward parallel to the Narbada and Mahanadi, which together constitute another impregnable barrier. This double wall divides the peninsular south from the plains of northern India, but not in a manner as to have seriously hindered the inter-communication between them. Indeed from the prehistorical times to the present day, there was no period when the two regions did not influence each other politically, socially, culturally and economically.

**Geographical Background**

The greater part of the northern Daccan is known as Maharashtra. It is a tableland which has a general slope from the west to the east. The western side of Maharashtra which abuts on the Syhadris is the highest part in the Daccan. It forms a triangle, having for its base the sea from Daman to Karwar, the perpendicular being represented by a running line from Daman beyond Nagpur and the hypotenuse by an irregular line from beyond Nagpur to Karwar. This triangle has three distinct divisions. The seaboard below the Syhadris is known as the Konkan, which actually lies between the Ghats and the sea and extends along the coast from Swadeshgarh to the Tapti. Although it lies below the great chain of mountains stre ching parallel with the western coast of India, it is not a flat country. On the contrary in most parts it is rugged and broken, interspersed with the huge

**Physical Features of Maharashtra**

mountains and dense forests, intersected by rivers and innumerable rivulets. Notwithstanding its rough contour, in many parts it is fertile. Its breadth from the sea to the summit of the Syhadri is of unequal extent varying from twenty five to fifty miles. The upper tableland is called Konkan Ghat M hta or the upper Konkan or the Konkan below the Ghats. The breadth of the Konkan Ghat Mahta is about twenty to twenty-five miles. It comprises the mountainous tracts on the upper or eastern side including the valleys that lie between the smaller branches of hills.

The tract lying below the Syhadri is divided into Mawals, Khoras and Moras. These tracts are populous and the valleys are well cultivated. The inhabitants of this part have been known for their simplicity, their inoffensive demeanour and for their hard work and patience. In the north of Junnar as these valleys are not so well cultivated, the inhabitants for the most part, especially the Bhils and the Kolis were predatory tribes subsisting on hunting and plundering.

In the Ghats and along the hills, both above and below the great range, the summits are girded on the top by large rocks, capable of being formed into fortresses often impregnable or difficult of access. During the periodical rains when the rivulets turn into torrents, the region rocky and rugged as it is, becomes almost impassable to troop movements.

The wide rolling plains to the east, which succeed the Ghat Mahta, are known as the Desh. There are four great ranges of hills, running west and east extending far beyond the branches of the Syhadri mountains. In succession to the Satpura, there is the great chain of the Chandore range, extending from Rahora to the heart of Berar; the Ahmadnagar hills from Junnar to Bir; the range immediately to the southward of Poona and the Mahadeo hills to the north of Satara. This open country presents a variety of aspects. In the north, centre and east are the fertile alluvial plains of Kopargaon, Rahauri, Newasa, Shivgaon, Gavai, Majhalgaon, and Paithan lying in the valley of Godavari, where wheat and millets are grown. In the extreme south are the less fertile alluvial plains of Karjat, Parenda and Jeur, lying in the valley of river Bhima. Between the Godavari and the Bhima valleys are bare hills and cultivated dales in the subdivision of Sangamnir, Parner, Nagar and

Jamkhed. The general aspect of the Desh is desolate. It is only after the heavy showers that the hill slopes become green; but the green quickly turns to dull yellow, as the surface of the earth becomes heated and the tenderness withers away under the scorching sun.

In short, the general physical aspect of Maharashtra is hilly; the valleys are well watered by the rivers, Narbada, Tapti, Godavari, Bhima and the Krishna and their tributaries. For some distance along the banks of these rivers the soil is excellent but the crops are inferior.

After the process of Aryanisation had been completed in northern India, the Aryans began to spread southward. In the seventh century B.C. began a great forward movement which carried them over the Vindhyas, until it died away at the extreme south end of the peninsula. It broadened the geographical knowledge of the immigrants as much as their cultural outlook, and the old Vedic formula, that Aryavarata corresponds to the territory between the Himalayas and the Vindhyas :—

"आर्य्यावर्त्तः पुण्यभूमि मध्य विन्ध्य हिमालयोः" ॥[1]

was supplanted by another formula :—

"गंगे च यमुने चैव गोदावरि सरस्वति ।
नर्मदे सिन्धु कावेरि जलेस्मिन् सन्निधिं कुरु ॥"[२]

It also shows that the country lying to the south of Narbada was known to the Aryan settlers, who frequently called it Dakshinapath, Dakkhinabadh and Dakkhinabades, the names which appear in Markandya, Matsya, Vayu and the other Puranas besides the two great epics Ramayana and Mahabharata. It is in the Dakshinapath that Ahmadnagar is situated.

The early history of this region centers round the city of Paithan or Pratisthan,[3] situated on the left bank of the Godavari, about fifty miles north-east of Ahmadnagar city. The earliest references to Paithan appear to be in the fourteenth rock edict of the great Maurayan Emperor Asoka (B.C. 240) where mention is made of Patanikas, probably the people of Paithan.[4] Paithan is said to have been the scene of the miracles worked by Salivahan, the founder of the Saka era.[5] About 150 A.D. the Egyptian geographer Ptolemy notices Bathana, the capital of Sri Polemos or Sri Pulumayi the Satkarni or Andhbrihataya king, whose inscriptions have been found in Nasik and Karel.[6] About 247 A.D. the author of Periplus notes, Plithana as one of the two trading centers of Dakshinabades or the Daccan. The Andhbrihatyas ruled over the whole breadth of the Daccan from the mouth of Krishna to Sopara in the north Konkan (B.C. 90-300 A.D.) with their capital at Paithana.[7] They always appear to have held the territories lying round the later city of Ahmadnagar. During the four hundred years ending with 670 A.D. this part of the country remained in the possession of the Rashtrakuta dynasty (400 A.D.).[8] It then passed into the hands of the early Chalukyas and Western Chalukya kings (550-670 A.D.) who were in great power in the Karnatic. After the Western Chalukyas the region passed into the hands of the Yadava kings of Deogiri (1130-1170 A.D.) who reigned for about two centuries, with their capital at Deogiri.[9]

**Early History**

Broadly speaking the annals of this land constitute a record of the succession of minor kingdoms which rose on the ruins of the vanquished empires. On the one hand we are struck by their perpetual mutual antagonisms and on the other, by the incidental promotion of all that is the best in the Hindu culture. These petty states had hardly any appreciation of the importance of peaceful co-existence. On the contrary, each of them tried to absorb as much as of its neighbours territory as it could at the expense of the others. This interminable dynastic warfare joined to the pugnacious activities of the religious reformers and sectarian leaders, inevitably led to the political and social disintegration, reducing the vitality and the vigour of the people which ultimately paved the way for the Turkish conquest.

By the close of the 10th century A.D. the Turkish adventure s had began to hammer at the north-western gates of India, and within less than two centuries the Turks succeeded in reducing to submission the whole of northern India. But the problems of external aggression and internal insurrection in the central belt and in the distant corners; experiments in establishing new institutions and of popularising composite culture joined to the coercive character of the Turkish polity, left little time for the new rulers to divert their energies across the

Vindhyas, until the close of the thirteenth century of the Christian era. Plundering incursions in Malwa, in course of time were followed by a bold adventure on the part of Alauddin Khilji, who in 1294 A.D. dashed across the hilly ranges and launched a surprise attack on Ramdeo, the Yadava ruler of Deogiri, and forced him to submit. This was followed by a lull during which stirring events occurred in the north. Once stability had been restored there, the plan of systematic reduction of the south was relentlessly pursued. Malik Kafur over-ran the Kaktiya Kingdom of Warangal in 1309 A.D.; the Hoysala kingdom of Dwarsamudra in 1310 A.D.; and then the Chola and Pandya kingdoms of the far south. Henceforward, Deogiri became the headquarter of the Turkish expansion and the Turkish domination in the south. Often the chaos and confusion, rivalry among the nobles, murder and dethronements at the distant Turkish court in the north at Delhi gave opportunities to the local population and the Hindu princes of the Daccan and the far south to rise up in arms against the Turkish authority and to throw off the yoke of the Sultan of Delhi in order to save their local autonomy. But these attempts failed in the face of the organised might of the Empire.[10]

The era of Khilji imperialism was followed by the rule of the Tughlaqs. They too could not resist the temptation of annexing the Daccan into the Delhi empire, a process which had commenced since the later years of Alauddin's reign. To exercise effective control over his far flung empire Muhammad bin Tughlaq resorted to the experiment of establishing a second capital at Deogiri, which he renamed as Daultabad. He attempted to give a suitable administration to the Daccan and appointed able officers to look after the welfare of the people. But during the second half of his reign, the problems of the north arising out of the failure of his ambitious schemes, besides giving a blow to his prestige, up-set the machinery of government and accelerated the operation of fissiparous forces.[11] A group of nobles known as the *amiran-i-sadah*, rose in open rebellion against the central authority, which made the confusion worse confounded and gave birth to the Bahmani kingdom in 1347 A.D.[12]

Almost contemporareously the Hindu feelings of revolt gained momentum. Shankaracharya Madhav Vidrayana, the learned and influential head of the Shringarimath, associated religion with politics to liquidate the Turkish authority in the south. Hari Hara and Bukka established the Hindu Kingdom of Vijayanagara in 1336 A.D. which in course of time became the spearhead of the Hindu opposition to the Turkish dominance.[13]

The internal history of the Bahmani kingdom, with which we are at present concerned, is mainly a record of court factions, civil wars and extravagance; interspersed with some brilliant administrative experiments and a sustained desire on the part of its rulers to promote Indo-Turkish culture. In its external relations it found itself involved in perennial warfare with the kingdoms of Orissa and Vijayanagara on the one hand and Malwa and Gujarat on the other, which in the long run ate into the very vitals of the kingdom. But the basic cause of the disruption of the empire was party strife for which ambitious nobles found ground too fertile and they unscruplously engaged themselves in grinding their own axes. Alauddin Bahman Shah had laid the foundations of the kingdom with the support of the Daccani and Foreign nobles alike. To keep the hetrogenous group in control, he pursued a judicious policy of compromise and conciliation. There were three factions in the Daccan, each trying to get the best of the situation. There were those who stood for an independent Daccan under a new dynasty; others were the partisans of the Tughlaq house, and finally there were some local chiefs and *muqaddams*, saturated with the desire of their personal aggrandisement.[14] But Alauddin controlled these elements effectively and left a peaceful kingdom for his son and successor, Muhammad Shah I (1358-75 A.D.).

**The Bahmanides and the Party Strife**

The second ruler of the Bahmanide dynasty founded new institutions, promoted culture and strengthened the system of administration by specifying the powers and functions of the nobles according to their respective ability.[15] Muhammad I was succeeded by Mujahid in 1375 A.D. Henceforward there was a steady growth of forces culminating in determining the distinctiveness of the Bahmanide patterns in their varied phases.[16] By now the independent kingdoms of Gujarat, Khandesh and Malwa had come into existence and they divided Delhi from Gulbarga. Although, an attempt was made by the Rayas of Telingana and Vijayanagara to bring back the authority of the

Delhi Sultanate to the Daccan by soliciting the assistance of Firoz Tughlaq against Muhammad I, it did not materialise.

The moorings with the north having been cut off, the new rulers of the Daccan had to seek moral and material help from the other quarters. Luckily, a stream of new comers or the Foreigners began to flow into the Daccan from the coast round the Persian Gulf and from Iran, Iraq and Arabia. It included poets, authors, saints, artisans, merchants and soldiers, all of whom received patronage at the hands of the Bahmani sovereigns. The interregnum between the death of Muhammad I and the accession of Firoz Shah Bahamani represents the period of struggle between two outlooks, each associated with and drawing its inspiration from the group advocating it. The Foreign phase was represented by the Afaquis, who were mostly Iranians, and the indegenous tradition was represented by the Daccanis who had come from northern India. The latter had married the native women, raised the families of mixed descent, and like the early Aryans and had begun to look upon the country as their own, by virtue of their permanent settlement and association with the soil.[17]

Mujahid Shah reigned for three years only (1375-78 A.D.). While he was retreating from a campaign against Vijayanagara, Masud Khan, the son of Mubarak, the betel-bearer, whose collar bone the king had broken in his childhood, and Daud Khan who had been scolded for leaving his post at Adoni, conspired against him and murdered him, when he was sleeping in his tent (16th April 1378 A.D.).[18] Daud Khan now proclaimed himself sovereign, but his accession occasioned dissensions in every quarter. At the capital there arose two factions, one, which favoured the Sultan Daud Shah, while the other led by Mujahid's sister Ruhparwar Agha, refused to acknowledge the assassin as king.[19] She wanted to raise to the throne Bahman Shah's youngest son Muhammad II. She hired the services of the royal slave Bakah who had received promotion at the hands of the late king and stabbed to death Daud Shah on May 24th, 1378 A.D., when the latter was attending the Friday prayers in the great mosque in the Gulbarga fort.[20]

Now Muhammad Shah Bahmani II was proclaimed king. His long reign of nineteen years was one of the most peaceful in the whole of the Bahmani history.[21] He was succeeded by his son Ghyasuddin Tuhmatan a mere boy. His accession was followed by distribution of high officers among the Persian new-comers, a measure which was resented by a section of Gulbarga aristocracy, headed by the Turk, Taghalchin, himself an aspirant for the post of Prime Minister. But the Sultan rejected the claims of Taghalchin on the ground of his low birth. The disappointed noble became apprehensive of his safety and addressed himself not only to the task of avenging the insult which the Sultan had hurled at him, but even of removing him from the throne. He succeeded in his plan, inveigled Ghyasuddin into a trap, threw him into prison and seated on the throne his step-brother Shamsuddin Daud II. His desire was fulfilled, because he was appointed to the office of Malik Naib and Mir Jumla.[22]

The Bahamanide politics now took a new turn. When Ghyasuddin had been blinded and dethroned, the wives of Firoz and Ahmed Khan began to importune their husbands to exact vengeance for the wrong that had been done to their brother. Seeing that his power and influence were at stake, Taghalchin persuaded Shamsuddin Daud II, to imprison Firuz and Ahmad Khan. He then went to king's mother to ask her to have them murdered as they wanted to dethrone her son. On hearing of the plot the Prime Minister was maturing against them, they escaped to Sagar. Here they won over Siddhu, the officer-in-charge of the town, sent a representation to Gulbarga, protesting their loyalty to the king and demanding the dismissal of Prime Minister, who had played traitor to the late king. But on receipt of an unfavourable re ponse they marched to Gulbarga with a large force, arrived on the banks of Bithora, where Firuz proclaimed himself as king, appointing his younger brother Ahmad Khan as the Amir-ul-umra, Mir Fazl-ullah Anju as the Wakil or Prime Minister, and Siddhu as Sar-i-Naubat. Firuz now advanced towards the capital but was driven back to Sagar. The two brothers now sent Mir Ghyas-uddin, the son of Mir Fazl-ullah Anju, Sayyid Kamaluddin and others to Taghalchin and the Queen mother Makhdum Khwaja-i-Jahan with a message that they should be foregiven and allowed to return to Gulbarga. Having being promised security of their life they returned to the capital. But their wives informed them that they were still in the midst of danger. Firuz now allied himself with the party opposed to the court group, which consisted of men like Azhar Khan, Malik Shihab, Sayyid Tajuddin Jakajot and many others. He forced his way into the court with a contingent of twelve followed by hundred others, who were fully armed. After a free fight between the parties, Firuz ascended the throne. Taghalchin was arrested and killed and Shamsuddin Daud II was blinded and allowed to proceed with his mother to Mecca.[23]

With the accession of Firuz Shah there opened a new chapter of peace and prosperity (1397-1422 A.D.) in the Bahmanide empire. The sovereign encouraged the immigration of the foreigners from Persia and other countries, interested as he was in continuing and consolidating the traditions handed down by his predecessors, for making the Daccan, one of the greatest centres of culture in the East. The task had become comparatively easy owing to the decay of the kingdom of Delhi in the north. Firuz was fully alive to the danger, which his partiality for the Foreigners might provoke from the side of the Daccanis, who might feel the urge of either rising up in arms against him or otherwise of sabotaging his noble plans. To counteract such designs he invited the Hindu element of population to shoulder the responsibilities of the government. He gave offices to Brahmins, made Narsingh of Kherla, a peer of the kingdom and tried to make friends with the Hindu aristocracy of the Daccan. Moreover, he not only took wives from the Raya of Vijaynagara and the ruler of Kherla but included into his harem women belonging to different nationalities like the Arab, Circassian, Russian, Turk, Chinese, Afghan, Rajput etc. with the object of eliminating all possiblities of clash among the nobles, belonging to different races.[24] But the dethronement of Firuz Shah on 22nd September 1422 A.D. brought to a close the healthy tendencies which were being so assiduously fostered. He was succeeded by his brother Ahmed Shah Wali (1422-36 A.D.). He laid aside the policy of immediate predecessor and followed the age old policy of bestowing honours upon Foreigners alone.[25]

Let us now pause for a while to examine the factors which hence forward led to the formation of the parties in the court and the causes of clash among them on the basis of individual and group interests. Reference has already been made to the constant flow of the foreigners from their distant homelands to the Daccan and the patronage they received at the hands of the Bahmani sovereigns. Now they had merged into a bigger community and had become conscious of their separate entity, because they were handsome, energetic, enterprising, cultured and literate. They stood in striking contrast to the Daccanis, who were mostly dark, skinned, illiterate, lethargic and unimaginative. Naturally the lion's share of high offices in the state went to the Foreigners, much to the chagrin of the Daccanis, who found themselves superseded as much in the battlefield as in the council chamber. Moreover, the strain between the rival groups was further embittered by their conflicting religious beliefs. The Foreigners were mostly Shias while the majority of their rivals, the Daccanis and the Abyssinians were Sunnis. The Foreigners swayed by a feeling of superiority looked with contempt at the Daccanis and Abyssinians, which further intensified the discord between the two.

By the end of the fourteenth century the Daccanis began to realise that they were being gradually displaced from the power by the Foreigners. But they patiently bided their time. After his accession, Ahmad Shah changed his capital from Gulbarga to Bidar,[26] which proved to be signal for a revolution in the kingdom.[27] Whatever might have been the considerations which impelled him to take this step, but it by no means helped to smother the jealousy between the Foreigners and the Daccanis, which finally led to the fall of the kingdom. He appointed his old friend Khalaf Hasan Basari as his Prime Minister, conferring on him the title of Malik-ut-Tajjar, which in those days was considered the highest honour in the Daccan.[28] Naturally, it roused the jealousy of the Daccanis and they came into conflict with the Foreigners. In 1423 A.D. when Ahmad Shah had been surrounded by the enemy during a campaign against Vijayanagara, thanks to the courage shown by the Foreigners like Sayyid Husain Badakhshani, Mir Ali Sistani, Abdullah Kurd and others,[29] he succeeded in effecting his escape. In recognition of the timely help and skill of the Foreign archers, the Sultan ordered Malik-ut-Tajjar, "to raise a corps of 300 of them, a measure which was destined to have a deep and enduring effect on the history of the Muslims of the Daccan."[30]

The first reaction of Sultan Ahmad's favour towards the Foreigners became visible in 1430-31 A.D. when due to the lack of cooperation among its various sections, the Bahmani army was thrice defeated by the Gujarati forces. While Khlaf Hasan Basri attributed these reverses to the cowardice of the Daccanis, his rivals dwelt upon the incompetence of their Foreign adviser. The result was that the Daccanis were raised to power and the conduct of government was entrusted to a member of their faction *viz.* Mian Mahmud Nizam-ul-Mulk, surnamed Min-Allah, the wisest and the most learned of his contemporaries,[31] on whom was conferred the title of Malik-ut-Tajjar. In the second part of his reign the Sultan retired from the public affairs. To avoid clash between the two leaders, he sent Malik Hasan Basari to take over the charge of Dabul and the other towns of the western coast.[32] Further, he nominated his son Alauddin Zafar Khan as his heir. Though the Daccanis had been raised to power, but their party began to be entirely neglected by the king who died on 14th July 1436 A.D.[33]

Alauddin Ahmad succeeded his father, and he reverted to the policy of favouring the Foreigners. His capricious nature joined to the lack of firmness, rendered the conflict between the Daccanis and the Foreigners more acute than ever. When Nasir Khan of Khandesh attacked Berar,[34] the Sultan held a council of war to discuss a plan of throwing back the aggression. The Daccanis led by Mian Min-Allah and Khan-i-Zaman advised caution, but Malik-ut-Tajjar, Malik Hasan Basri in a spirit of bravado volunteered to fight the enemy provided all the foreign troops were placed at his disposal. His proposal was accepted and he succeeded in covering himself with glory on this occasion and in rehabilitating the prestige of his party. Indeed the Foreigners were deserving all honour and respect. Besides, being men of letters some of them were born statesmen and politicians. Moreover, their loyalty and intrepedity had enabled them to maintain family connections with the royal house; for three of the Sultan's sisters were married to Jalal Khan, Shah Nurullah and Shah Habibullah, and one of his daughters was married to Shah Muhibbullah and another to Shah Quli Sultan Changezi, who were all Foreigners, men of high repute and understanding.[35] Their accomplishments induced the Sultan to order that on all ceremonial occasions the

Foreigners should appear on his right and the Daccanis on his left.[36] This partiality shown by the Sultan enraged the Daccanis against their rivals, and in 1474 A.D. they treacherously massacred a large number of them. The same year a composite army of the Daccanis and the Foreigners was sent to subjugate the northern Konkan.[37] The Commander-in-Chief Malik-ut-Tajjar succeeded in reducing to submission a chief named Shirka, who persuaded the victor to lead the royal troops against the Raja of Samgameshwar. The latter taking advantage of the demoralisation which had befallen the invaders in the course of their laborious march through dense forests and pricipitious slopes, delivered a surprise attack on them slaying thousands of them including their leader. The Daccanis took a malicious delight in the disaster. They grossly misrepresented the affair to the Sultan, who without verifying the facts ordered that the remnant of the Foreigners who had taken shelter in the fort of Chakan should be put to death.[38] Luckily, however, two of them escaped to the Sultan to report the deception which had been practised on them. Further enquiry exposed the duplicity of the Daccanis and their sinister designs for the extermination of the remaining Foreigners. The Sultan laid an iron hand upon the leaders of the Daccani party. Mustafa Khan the author of the crime was executed; the properties of Mushir-ul-Mulk and Nizam-ul-Mulk were confiscated and the latter was dismissed from the post. Other Daccanis who were at Chakan were ordered to be brought to Bidar in chains and many of them were either put to death or confined to prison. On the other hand the Foreigners were promoted to high titles and offices. Qasim Beg was given the title of Malik-ut-Tajjar and was made Sar-i-Lashkar of Daultabad, in place of the deceased Khalaf Hasan Basari. Thus the Foreigners regained their ascendancy, but this did not mark the end of the trouble. On the other hand, deeper became and gloom on the political horizon of the Daccan.[39]

Ahmad II was succeeded by his son Alauddin Humayun Shah on 7th May 1458 A.D. He too like his predecessor bestowed high honours on the Foreigners and appointed Mahmud Gawan as Malik-ut-Tujjar and made him the Tarafdar of Bijapur and the Wakil-ut-Saltanat or Prime Minister of the kingdom, giving him full control over the military affairs.[40] The advent of Gawan in the politics of the Daccan gave a new shape to the long standing party strife, which entered its last phase. Had not the principle of balance and equilibrium been maintained between the two factions, the Bahmani kingdom would have disintegrated much earlier. Even then the exigencies of the political situation compelled Humayun Shah to resort to the one sided policy of his predecessors. Early in 1460 A.D. while he was campaigning in Orissa, his brother Hasan Khan effected his escape from the prison of Bidar and proclaimed himself king. Humayun Shah immediately returned to the capital, defeated the rebel, punished his adherents and had them thrown before the tigers. The tragic episode came to an end with the promotion of a number of Daccani converts.[41]

One of the Daccani converts who was fortunate enough to receive promotion on this occasion was Malik Hasan Bahri, the progenitor of the Nizam Shahi dynasty of Ahmadnagar.[42] His original name was Timma Bhat, and his father's name was Bhairon, a kulkarni Brahman of Pathri.[43] It is related that Timma Bhat with his father had come to the Karnatic owing to a severe famine which had taken place in their native place. While according to another version they had fled to Vijayanagara to escape the ruthless persecution let loose by the Muslims.[44] Ahmad Shah Bahmani in a campaign against Vijayanagara, in 1422-3 A.D. had captured many Hindus alive and among them was Timma Bhat who became a convert to Islam.

**Malik Hasan Bahri**

The story of Timma's rise to fame is very remarkable. Deprived of his patetnal love, he p ssed through many vicissitudes of fortune. By sheer dint of merit he rose from poverty to power. Sultan Ahmad Shah Bahmani III noticing his ability, intelligence, valour and literary aptitude sent him to a school with his eldest son Humayun. In a short time Timma learnt Persian and displayed his keen interest in the Arabic literature.[45] As the boy Prince Humayun could not correctly pronounce the word Bhairon, he called his class-mate Bahri.[46] Therefore, subsequently he came to be known as Malik Hasan Bahri. Humayun Shah honoured his friend with the title of Sarang Khan.[46]

The death of his royal patron in 1461 A.D. did not retard Malik Hasan's progress in any way. Shamudd'n Muhammad Shah Bahmani III (30-7-1463 to 26-3-1482 A.D.) who was very fond of hunting, appointed him as Mir-i-Shikar, so that he could remain constantly in attendence upon him.[48] When he visited the harem, it was the duty of Mallik Hasan to keep watch at the palace door, till his master retired to bed.[49] He soon ingratiated himself into the favours of his master, who promoted him to the rank of amir, by giving him the mansab of 2000 horse and granting him the privilege of kettle drum.[50] Later, he was distinguished with the insignia of the Mahi Miratib, and was appointed to the post of Qush Begi or falconer.[51]

While the fortunes of Malik Hasan were making long strides, Mahmud Gawan,[52] described as, "pearless in courage, intelligence and diplomacy", was also rapidly gaining influence and popularity by introducing many benevolent reforms which raised the kingdom to the pinnacle of glory. During his period of ministry, the frontiers of the kingdom extended from sea to sea; the Konkan was occupied, the Godavari and the Krishna Doab was annexed; expeditions were led into the very heart of Orissa and Kanchi, and the ambitions of Malwa, Orissa and Vijayanagara were reduced to shreds. These results were achieved in spite of the rivalry between the Daccanis and the Foreign factions at the capital. Gawan succeeded where others had failed. He maintained political equlibrium by an equitable distribution of the places of honour among the nobles of the two parties.

Being a Daccani by birth, Malik Hasan's robust vigour and bubbling energy could not but urge him to champion the cause of the sons of the soil, who had not been getting a fair deal from the Foreigners. True that the Bahmani sovereigns were very cosmopolitan in their outlook and liberal in their behaviour towards their subjects, but in their administrative set-up they did not assign honourable places to the Daccanis. It was mainly manned by the Foreigners and run by fortune seekers. The Daccanis who derived their moral and material support from the natural patriotism of the people had a more decisive claim to conduct the government than their rivals. Malik Hasan saw this. What disturbed the peace of his mind was the thought that his countrymen had been deprived of their rightful share of the honour and control in the affairs of the kingdom.

In 1471 A.D. the Raya of Orissa died and the throne was usurped by Mangal Rai, a Brahman, who expelled the lawful heir Hamvira, the late Raya's cousin.[53] In sheer despair Hamvira solicited help from the Bahmani Sultan, who directed his favourite Malik Hasan to lead the expedition. The latter succeeded in expelling the usurper and in restoring the throne to Hamvira. After this he conquered Rajamundari and the forts of Kondavidu, which created much suspicion in the minds of the Foreigners, who did not see an eye to eye with Malik Hasan. However, with flying banners he returned to Bider, where he was graciously received by the Sultan, who granted him a robe of honour. But Mahmud Gawan was not slow to penetrate into the ambitious designs of Malik Hasan and on his suggestion the Sultan appointed the latter as Sar-i-Lashkar of Telingana and honoured him with the title of Ashraf-i-Humayun Nizam-ul-Mulk.[54] But this move of the Prime Minister had a purposeful motive behind it. It gave him an opportunity to elevate other Foreigners with the awoed object of maintaining a balance between the rival parties. At his instance, Fathullah, the wisest of the subordinates of Khawaja Jahan Turk was created Imad-ul-Mulk and was made Sar-i-Lashkar of Berar. Had Gawan stopped here nothing untoward would have happened, but he went further and promoted Yusuf Adil Khan, whom he regarded as his son, as Sar-i-Lashkar not only of Daulatabad but also of Chakan and Junnar, placing other Foreigners like Darya Khan and the Tarkish nobles like Qasim Beg, Shah Quli and Khan Sultan and others under him.[55] Thus inadvertently he provided a pretext to the rival party to rise in opposition to him. Malik Hasan was not slow to react to the plan of the Prime Minister, which unmistakingly pointed to the conclusion that his future was at stake. He was touched to the quick, when Yusuf Adil Khan was given precedence at the court. Where lay the justification for Gawan to accord a step-motherly treatment to the Daccani noble? This proved to be a link in the chain of subsequent events which brought about the fall of that wise minister. Smarting with the sense of despair, disgust and disgrace, Malik Hasan joined hands with his brother Daccanis and the leaders of the Habshi party. He became their popular and respected leader and in collaboration with them formed plans for the ruin of the Foreigners.

While Gawan was busy in the western campaigns, Malik Hasan made Rajamundari his headquarters and in the next three years subjugated the whole of Telingana, strengthened the frontier outposts and completed his preparations to invade the Karnatic. Suspecting the intentions of his rival and therefore to cripple his growing influence and power Mahmud Gawan persuaded the Sultan to separate from Malik Hasan, the latter's son Malik Ahmad, who by now had become young and was showing signs of a promising career. Another reason which was given out for removing Ahmad from the court was that he had been married to a lady of the royal seraglio. Accordingly Malik Ahmad was sent to Mahur as the commander of three thousand horse (1478 A.D.). Malik Hasan now threw off the mask and began to oppose Gawan openly.

In 1480 A.D. the army stationed at Kondavidu mutinied. It put itself under the protection of Narsimha, the virtual ruler of Vijayanagara and siezed the entire eastern coast of the peninsula, south of river Krishna. The Sultan marched against the rebels, laid siege to Kondavidu and compelled the garrison to surrender. He made over the citadel to Malik Hasan Nizam-ul-Mulk and granted him the high sounding titles of Masnad-i-Ali and Ulugh-i-Azam. Narsimha retired to the South, but the Sultan made up his mind to pursue and punish him.[56]

At the time of his departure from the capital the Sultan enquired of Gawan as to who should be appointed governor of Rajamundari. The minister suggested the name of Malik Hasan. The suggestion was pregnant with sinister motives. If implemented, it would give a blow to the growing influence of Malik Hasan for it would mean his removal from the court to a distant place, besides his being deprived of the governorship of Telingana, which along with Warangal was intended to be assigned to Prince Azam, son of Sikandar Khan.[57] Malik Hasan saw through the game of his rival. To circumvent it, he begged the Sultan to appoint his son Ahm d to act as his deputy at Rajamundari and allow him to accompany the royal army on the expedition against Vijayanagara.[58] As Malik Ahmad stood high in favour of the Sultan, it did not prove difficult for him to persuade his master to grant his request, much against the wishes of Gawan, who did not relish the idea of handing over the important charge of Rajamundari to a young man like Malik Ahmad, who was summoned from Mahur and was appointed as his father's deput with the rank of 1000 horse.[59]

As the boundaries of the Bahmani Kingdom now touched the Bay of Bengal in the East and Arabian sea in the West, Gawan resolved to introduce some administrative reforms. It was after the Maharashtra campaign that he had made out a plan for it. Abul Muzaffar Bahman Shah, the founder of the kingdom had divided the kingdom into four provinces, termed as *tarafs*, for the convenience of the administration. Each *taraf* was placed under a separate governor, designated as *Tarafdar* or governor. These provincial governors enjoyed great power. Within their respective jurisdictions they were almost autonomous. They collected revenue, raised and commanded the army and made all appointments, both civil and military. The system worked well so long as it had behind it the force of strong personality, either of the king or of the minister, failing that, they acquired local prestige and made it difficult for the central authority to control them. To meet the situation Mahmud Gawan divided the kingdom into eight Sar-i-lashkarship or provinces of equal size.[60] He also revolutionised the system of military administration.[61] He recruited an equal number of Habshis, Daccanis and foreigners to keep a balance between the rival factions and to raise the glory of the kingdom.[62] But in the end the Daccanis and the Habshis combined, gained an upper hand of the politics and wrought the downfall of the author of these reforms.[63]

**Malik Hasan's Ascendancy**

After Gawan's assassination, Malik Hasan Nizam-ul-Mulk Bahri became the Prime Minister, with the title of Wakil and Peshwa;[64] his friends and associates Quiwam-ul-Mulk the elder and the younger being given governments of Rajamundari and Warangal. Struck with terror Foreigners withheld their cooperation from the the Central government, with the result that the political affairs were thrown into confusion.[65] Sultan Muhammad III, appointed his son Mahmud, as his heir and to drown his anxieties he took to excessive drinking and other incontinent habits. He died on 27th March 1482 at the age of twenty nine, leaving behind the memory of a ghastly tragedy and an empire heading to a fall.[66]

Mahmud now became Sultan (26.3.1482—7.12.1518) of the Bahmani kingdom to witness its disruption. As the Daccanis were in ascendancy, Malik Hasan became the Regent of the kingdom, with the title of Malik Naib. On the eve of the royal coronation, when all the nobles were in the capital, Malik Hasan formed a plot to assassinate his other rivals like Yusuf Adil Khan, now the leader of the Foreign party, along with his followers. But unfortunately, the plan was miscarried and the entire ceremony passed off peacefully. The procession went to the Takht Mahal, where precedence was given to Yusuf Adil Khan over Malik Hasan; after him came Darya Khan and Malik Ahmad, who had recently been appointed governor of Chakan and Junnar. After the robes of honour had been conferred on the nobles by the new Sultan, the leaders of the rival factions left the place hand in hand as if nothing had ever occurred between them.[67]

Malik Hasan now invited Yusuf Adil Khan, who was encamping out side the city, to come in to live there as a good friend and help him in carrying on the administration. But Yusuf Adil Khan, having no faith in his words, excused himself saying that being essentially a man of arms, he had neither the interest in nor the aptitude for civil government and the other affairs of the state. But Malik Hasan found it difficult to run the administration so long as Yusuf Adil Khan remained at the court.[68] He, therefore, resolved to destroy his influence either by supplanting him from the governorship of Bijapur and by appointing in his place Adil Khan Daccani, or by removing him by violence. Accordingly, he requested the Sultan to hold a review of the provincial levies before they left for their respective places. At its conclusion the Sultan was persuaded to say to Yusuf Adil Khan and Fathullah Imad-ul-Mulk that he was by no means pleased with the conduct of their Turkish entourage.[69] Adil Khan Daccani was ordered to punish the foreigners for their insolence. The gates of the city were closed and a gruesome tragedy was enacted. For twenty days Bidar witnessed a scene of bloody conflict between the rival factions and as many as four thousand men were killed on either side. Realising that Bidar was not a safe place for him, Yusuf Adil Khan left for Bijapur, leaving Malik Hasan supreme at the capital.[70]

**Conflict between Foreigners and Daccanis**

Having thus gathered all power in his hands, Malik Hasan conferred high honours and estates on the Daccanis. He assigned Bir, Dharur and many other districts to his son Malik Ahmad. Fakhr-ul-Mulk Daccani was raised to the rank of a thousand horse and his son received the title of Khwaja Jahan. Fathullah Imad-ul-Mulk was created Wazir and his son Shaikh Alauddin was appointed as his father's deputy in Berar. Qasim Barid, another Daccani noble, who had showed great activity against the Foreigners, was appointed Kotwal of the city of Bidar, with the office of Mir-i-Naubat.[71]

For the next four years Malik Hasan ruled the kingdom successfully and efficiently. But when the Sultan attained the age of discretion, he began to lend his ears to unscrupulous men, who began to conspire against the Prime Minister. Dilawar Khan Habashi, the leader of the Habashi party, who had alienated himself from the Daccani faction, and had grown envious of Malik Hasan's power and influence, persuaded the young Sultan into the belief that he was being neglected by the regent.[72] The Sultan therefore, ordered him to kill both Malik Hasan and Fathaullah Imad-ul-Mulk. But the plot failed; for the ministers had fled from the city before it could materialise. Qasim Barid closed all access to the Sultan, reduced him to such distress that he had to write to the ministers apologising for his conduct and inviting them to come back. Tables were now turned on Dilawar Khan, who might have met the same fate as he had planned for his rivals; but he escaped to Khandesh and sided with the Sultan, later on against Qasim Barid. However, Malik Hasan returned with his son to the capital; but Fathullah Imad-ul-Mulk saw the danger in associating himself with Malik Hasan and therefore, he left for his own province of Berar, never to return to take part in the politics of the capital.[73]

**Malik Hasan rules the Bahmani Kingdom**

Now to strengthen his party, which was on the decline, Malik Hasan, showered his favours on Malik Wuji and his brother Malik Ashraf, formerly the dependants of Mahmud Gawan. Of the two, the elder was appointed governor of Daultabad and the younger as his deputy. The new incumbents had to pledge fidelity for the Prime Minister's son Malik Ahmad, who three months later was appointed as his deputy at Junnar.[74] Perhaps Malik Hasan planned to unite Daultabad and Junnar into a single province, which had been split into two units by Mahmud Gawan. It is unmistakably clear that henceforward

Malik Hasan was aiming at carving out a principality for himself, to overthrow the feeble Bahmani Sultan, and then declare himself independent, a process which gradually gained momentum. To complete his plan he entrusted the two strong fortresses of Parenda and Sholapur to Khwaja Jahan Daccani, exacting from him similar promises of fidelity and devotion to him and his son as had been taken from Malik Wuji and his brother.

It would, however, be very uncharitable to presume that only Malik Hasan was actuated by ambitious designs. In fact the entire political atmosphere was surcharged with fissiparous forces in which every adventure was trying to make the best of the opportunity or opportunities which came in his way. It proved difficult, almost impossible, for Malik Hasan either to check the internal disorder, or machinations of neighbouring states, which were but too anxious to create trouble on the frontiers of the Bahmani Kingdom, and equally keen to ally themselves with one or the other of the contending factions inside it. But for sometime nothing untoward happened. Though the provincial governors had become virtually independent, the Bahamanide Sultan still enjoyed a halo of glory, however unreal it might have been. The independent governors were jealous of their own position, but they were equally zealous for preserving the fiction of the Bahmani supremacy and of guarding it from outside enchroachments. The Bahmanide kingdom had disintegrated, but the extinction of the Bahmanide house was yet to come.

In 1486 A.D. Adil Khan Daccani, the governor of Warangal died.[75] Qiwam-ul-Mulk the governor of Rajamundari occupied the whole of Talingana and Warangal. This offended Malik Hasan, who in order to put an end to his ambitious designs marched against him.[76] The latter complained to the Sultan Mahmud Shah against the aggressive conduct of the Prime Minister.[77] Events began to move fast. On the one hand Malik Ahmad accused Yusuf Adil of abetting Bahadur Khan Gilani in seizing Dabul, Kolhapur and creating insurrection at Goa; on the other Zain-ul-Abdin the governor of Panhala, Sarnalah, Belgam and Chakan refused to recognise Malik Amhad as governor of Junnar.[78] Whereupon an army was sent against him. Yusuf Adil Khan sent a contingent of five or six thousand to the assistance of the rebel. This large scale defiance undermined the authority of the Prime Minister, who was with the Sultan at Warangal. To add to his consternation his friend Qasim Barid also turned against him and joined hands with Dastur Dinar the Habshi leader, and succeeded in procuring a firman from the Sultan that Malik Hasan should be done away with. The latter having got an inkling of the conspiracy, relying upon his friend Dilpasand Khan fled towards the capital to join him and sent urgent summons to his son Malik Ahmad to hurry back with his army and save him from the perilous situation. He seized all the wealth stored in the royal treasury and broke out into open rebellion. On being apprised of the turn the events had taken the Sultan appointed Qutb-ul-Mulk Daccani as the governor of Telingana and himself returned to Bidar. Malik Hasan was betrayed by his friend Dilpasand Khan, who fell upon the aged and the defenceless minister, seized him by the neck and strangled him to death. He chopped off his head and exposing it to the public view cried out, "such is the reward of traitors to their sovereign."[79] Later on, it was presented to the Sultan Mahmud Shah on his arrival at the capital. The feeble monarch considered the minister's assassination as on act of final deliverence and gave himself up to the pleasures of wine, women and music. (1586 A.D.)

To avenge the insult and injury so caused, the Daccanis once more allied themselves with the Habshis, for a concerted attempt to overthrow the power of the Foreigners.[80] They planned to put an end to the life of the Sultan himself. But thanks to the loyalty of the Foreigners, they arrived at the opportune moment and saved the Sultan. The failure of the plot, gave a severe blow to the cause of the Daccanis. Many of them were put to sword. In sheer fright most of them fled to distant places. It became patent to the provincial governors and the jagirdars that the fall of the kingdom was approaching fast and therefore they began to assert their autonomy in their respective jurisdictions. When Qasim Barid declared himself independent, the Sultan sent Dilawar Khan against him but he was defeated and killed. Qasim Barid having gained victory over the royal forces, marched straight to the capital and forced the feeble Sultan Mahmud Shah to appoint him as Prime Minister and assign to him Daultabad, and Balaghat in jagir.[81] He was now keen to play the role of the former Prime Minister and to rule the entire kingdom in the name of the Sultan. But the provincial governors would not tolerate his dominance. Hence they marched together against him and defeated him and put him to flight in the battle of Deoni. The Sultan fell from the horse in the field of battle, but the nobles restored him to the Bahmani throne. Sometime later Qasim Barid again returned to Bidar, recovered his lost position and began to assert his authority. Henceforward he spent his time in fishing in the troubled politics of the Daccan, rendering confusion worse confounded.[82]

As to Malik Ahmad, he could never excuse the Bahmani Sultan for the murder of his father. He withdrew from the politics of the court, but maintained outward loyalty to the throne. He chalked out a different line of action, which after the death of the last of the Bahmanide Sultan culminated in the formation of the Nizam Shahi kingdom of Ahmadnagar.

---

*Notes and References*

1. See, "The Fundamental Unity of India".
2. Ibid.
3. See, "The Early History of the Daccan", pp. 9.
4. Ibid. pp. 9.
5. Reports of Archeological Survey of India, III. pp. 55-56.
6. Bombay Gazetteer, Vol. XVI. pp. 620-23.
7. Ahmadnagar District Guzetteer, pp. 350.
8. Ahmadnagar District Guzeteer, pp. 350; Bombay District Guzetteer, Vol. XII. pp. 412.
9. For the details see, "Early Muslim Expansion in the South" : "Early History of the Daccan," and Ahmadnagar District Guzetteer, pp. 352.
10. For the detailed study see, "Southern India and her Muhamadan Invaders" and, "The History of the Khiljis".
11. For the Daccan Policy of the Tughlaqs, see, "Rise and Fall of Muhammad bin Tughlaq" and "The Qarunah Turks".
12. For the birth of the Bahmani kingdom, see "The Bahmanis of the Daccan".
13. For the origin and growth of the Vijayanagara Empire, see, "Forgotten Empire".
14. The Bahmanis of the Daccan. pp. 50-51; A history of the Maratha People. pp. 60-61.
15. The Bahmanis of the Daccan, pp. 76-101; A history of the Maratha People. pp. 61-62.
16. The Bahmanis of the Daccan. pp. 113-14; A history of the Maratha People, pp. 63-64.
17. The Bahmanis of the Daccan, pp. 113-4.
18. The Bahmanis of the Daccan, pp. 117-18; A history of the Maratha People, pp. 64.

19. The Bahmanis of the Daccan, pp. 123; A history of the Maratha People, pp. 64.
20. The Bahmanis of the Daccan, pp. 124-5; A history of the Maratha People, pp. 64.
21. The Bahmanis of the Daccan, pp. 125-27; A history of the Maratha People, pp. 64.
22. Taghalchin resorted to a stratagem to avenge the insult hurled upon him by the young king. He had a pretty daughter who was accomplished in music and other arts. Her talents were brought to the notice of the king, who was much intrigued by what he had heard about her. As Taghalchin knew it, he invited the king to a feast and a arranged that nothing should be spared in the shape of wine and merriment which should increase his sexual appetite. He appointed one of his slaves Tarab to see that the king was served as much as wine as he asked for. When the king almost lost all his senses, Taghalchin whispered to him to send away others so that he may bring his daughter to him. The traitor now went upstairs came back not with his daughter but with a dagger, blinded the king and put to death the amirs one after the other on the pretext that the king wanted to see them. He then sent the blind king to Sagar as a prisoner and raised his step brother Shamsuddin to the throne. See, The Bahmanis of the Daccan, pp. 128-9.
23. The Bahmanis of the Daccan. pp. 129-32; A history of the Maratha People, pp. 66.
24. The Bahmanis of the Daccan, pp. 143-6.
25. Ibid. pp. 191.
26. Ibid. pp. 180-84.
27. Ibid. pp. 180.
28. Ibid. pp. 191-2.
29. Ibid. pp. 192-3.
30. Cambridge History of India, Vol. III, pp. 398.
31. Ahmad's inclination towards the Sufi principles and the Shia religion encouraged the influx of the Foreigners. Two episodes reveal the great regard which the king had for them (i) He sent 30,000 silver *tankas* to be distributed to the needy Sayyids of Karbala, (ii) when a member of the Daccani party Sher-ul-Mulk insulted one Sayyid Nasir-ud-din Karbalai, the king had the culprit trampled to death by a mad elephant. See, The Bahmanis of the Daccan, pp. 194 and 210.
32. The Bahmanis of the Daccan, pp. 210.
33. The Bahmanis of the Daccan, pp. 233-35; A history of the Maratha People, pp. 71.
34. The Bahmanis of the Daccan, pp. 210.
35. Ibid. pp. 224.
36. Ibid. pp. 224.
37. The Bahmanis of the Daccan, pp. 224-5; A history of the Maratha People, pp. 73.
38. The Bahmanis of the Daccan, pp. 225.
39. Ibid. pp. 240-4.
40. For the rise of Mahmud Gawan, see, H.K. Sherwani's, "Mahmud Gawan" and "The Bahmanis of the Daccan".
41. The Bahmanis of the Daccan, pp. 262-64; A history of the Maratha People, pp. 74.
42. Ferishta, Briggs. III, pp. 190; Muntakhab-ul-Lubab, III, pp. 140; A history of the Marathas, Vol. I, pp. 67.
43. Ferishta, Briggs. III, pp. 190; Mantakhab-ul-Lubab, III, pp. 140; Masir-i-Rahimi, II. pp. 413; A history of the Marathas, Vol. I pp. 67; Gribble, A History of the Daccan, pp. 150.
44. Ferishta Briggs. III, pp. 191; Muntakhab-ul-Lubab, III, pp. 140; Masir-i-Rahimi. II, pp. 413; A history of the Marathas, Vol. I pp. 67; Gribble, A History of the Daccan, pp. 150.

45. Ferishta Briggs, III, pp. 191; Muntakhab-ul-Lubab, III, pp. 140; A history of the Maratha People, pp. 78; Gribble, A history of the Daccan, pp. 150.
46. Ferishta, Briggs. III, pp. 191; Muntakhab-ul-Lubab, III, pp. 140; According to Nizamuddin Ahmad, his name was Bholu, see, Tabaqat-i-Akbari, Vol. III, pp. 67. While according to the others, as he was subsequently given the charge of the royal falcony (bahr), from which he seems to have derived his surname Bahri.
47. The Bahmanis of the Daccan, pp. 264.
48. Muntakhab-ul-Lubab, III, pp. 140-41.
49. Ibid. pp. 141.
50. Ibid.
51. Ibid.
52. See note no. 40.
53. The Bahmanis of the Daccan, pp. 308-9.
54. Ferishta, Briggs. III, pp. 190; Mantakhab-ul-Luabab, III, pp. 141; The Bahmanis of the Daccan, pp. 309; A history of the Maratha people, pp. 78; Gribble; A history of the Daccan pp. 150.
55. The Bahmanis of the Daccan, pp. 325-6.
56. The Bahmanis of the Daccan, pp. 331; Mahmud Gawan, pp. 164.
57. The Bahmanis of the Daccan, pp. 331.
58. The Bahmanis of the Daccan, pp. 332; Mahmud Gawan, pp. 164.
59. The Bahmanis of the Daccan, pp. 332; Mahmud Gawan, pp. 165; A history of the Marathas, Vol. I, pp. 67.
60. The two provinces of Gawil and Mahur were carved out of the old Berar; Daulatabad and Junnar formed the *taraf* of the old Daultabad; Bijapur and Ahsanabad replaced Gulbarga; while Telingana and the new ad ditions to it were divided into two charges, Rajamundari and Warangal.
    (i) Gawil was placed under Fathulah Imad-ul-Mulk (ii) Muhur under an Abyssinian Khudawand Khan; (iii) Daultabad was entrusted to the charge of Yusuf Adil Khan, (iv) Junnar which included Konkan and the districts as far as south of Goa and Belgam was given to the charge of Fakhrul-Mulk, (v) Mahmud Gawan himself held Bijapur which included many best districts as far as Bhima, the Raichur and Mudgal, (vi) Dastur Dinar was placed incharge of Ahsanabad Gulbarga, Sagar, Naldurg and Sholapur, (vii) Malik Hasan was appointed as governor of Rajamundari, which included Masulipatam, Pielconda, Oreah and other adjoining districts (viii) Azam Khan was appointed as governor of Warangal. In each Taraf, land was reserved for the Sultan's expences, and special collectors were appointed by the central authority to manage them, which proved to be a source of resentment to the old Tarafdars. Their sphere of authority was curtailed; their power was snatched away; they themselves were reduced to miserable plight. Naturally they had no other alternative but to rise against such reforms. See. The Bahmanis of the Daccan, pp. 322-5; A History of the Marathas, Vol. I, pp. 65-66.
61. Mahmud Gawan laid down that only one fort in a *taraf* should be under the control of a *tarafdar*, the remaining forts were to be incharge of the officers directly appointed by the Sultan. (ii) that each commander was to be paid at the rate of one lac huns annually for every five hundred men kept under arms, and if a *jageer* was granted in lieu of the cash payment provision was made whereby the *jageerdar* was to be compensated to the extent of the expence incurred in the collection of the rent. If the jageerdar failed to maintain the stipulated number of soldiers, he had to refund the proportionate amount to the royal treasury. These reforms curtailed the powers of the tarafdars which they resented. See, The Bahmanis of the Daccan, pp. 324; Mahmud Gawan, pp. 156-60;
62. The Bahmanis of the Daccan, pp. 325.

63. The Sultan marched into the Vijayanagara territory up to Nalore pursuing Narsimha, the ruler of Vijayanagara, who soon after tendered his submission. At Nelore the Sultan heard of the wealth stored at Kanchi. He marched thither and seized it. He asked Gawan to remain with the Crown Prince at Nellore and while travelling homeward, he halted at Kondapalli. Here the Daccanis taking advantage of the absence of Yusuf Adil Khan, who kept Gawan informed about the daily affairs of the court, poisoned the ears of the Sultan against the minister. Further they purchased the support of Miftah Habshi, Zarif-ul-Mulk and others. One evening when the keeper of the seals, an African was drunk, the conspirators placed before him a blank sheet of paper purporting to be a petition for the reprieve of an innocent friend. On the paper, were the seals of the other ministers and high officials. They pursuaded the tipsy officer to affix the Khwaja's seal on it. This having been done, they forged a letter purporting to have been written by Gawan to Purushottam of Orissa, inviting him to invade the Daccan. The forged letter was placed before the Sultan by Zarif-ul-Mulk in the presence of Malik Hasan. The Sultan in his indignation summoned Gawan and without making enquiries into the facts ordered his slave Jauhar to kill him. See, Mahmud Gawan, pp. 166-171; The Bahmanis of the Daccan, pp. 333-36.
64. Ferishta, Briggs, III, pp. 190; The Bahmanis of the Daccan pp. 342; Mahmud Gawan, pp. 202.
65. The Bahmanis of the Daccan, pp. 342; Mahmud Gawan, pp. 202-3.
66. The Bahmanis of the Daccan, pp. 342-3.
67. The Bahmanis of the Daccan, pp. 362; Mahmud Gawan, pp. 202-4; Gribble, A history of the Daccan.
68. The Bahmanis of the Daccan, pp. 363.
69. Ibid.
70. The Bahmanis of the Daccan, pp. 363; Mahmud Gawan, pp. 205, A History of the Maratha People, pp. 78.
71. Mahmud Gawan, pp. 205; A history of the Marathas, Vol. I, pp 71.
72. The Bahmanis of the Daccan, pp. 364-6; Mahmud Gawan, pp. 205-6.
73. Muntakhab-ul-Lubab, III. pp. 142; A history of the Marathas Vol. I, pp. 71.
74. The Bahmanis of the Daccan, pp. 364.
75. Ibid.
76. Ibid.
77. Ibid.
78. Cambridge history of India, III, pp. 424.
79. Burhan-i-Masir (I, A. 1920) pp. 85-6; The Bahmanis of the Daccan, pp. 365; A history of the Marathas, Vol. I pp. 71; Mahmud Gawan pp. 206.
80. The Bahmanis of the Daccan, pp. 366-7; Mahmud Gawan, pp. 207;
81. The Bahmanis of the Daccan, pp. 367-8.
82. The Bahmanis of the Daccan, pp. 368.

## CHAPTER II

# AHMAD NIZAM SHAH BAHRI

Sober history records that Malik Ahmad, who later on styled himself as Ahmad Nizam Shah Bahri was the son of Malik Hasan, Malik Naib of the Bahmani kingdom.[1] But there is little authentic record with regard to the date of his birth or his early education. Sayyid Ali Azizullah Tabataba, the historian of the Nizam Shahis, makes a bare reference to Ahmad's early life. Malik Hasan who was not only literate and educated, but was also interested in the promotion of learning, it may be presumed, must have made suitable arrangements for the education of his son Malik Ahmad. It is related that he used to send large retinues to his jagirs of Mahur and Ramghir, which he had selected for his child's residence. The arrival of well dressed soldiers, created an abiding impression on the mind of the child, and he began to take delight in talking of feats of bravery and military skill. And when Ahmad reached the age of discretion he devoted himself to literary and cultural pursuits.[2] By his 12th year he became as much proficient in learning as in the art of warfare, and "kingship seemed to blossom in him and to be evident in his speech and actions"[3]. It was during his stay with his father in Telingana that Ahmad gained an insight into the working of administration.[4]

**His Early Life**

As a young man he was married to one of the princess of the Bahmani house, which offended most of the Foreign nobles. Add to this, his restless energy, his charming manners, his penetrating intellect, quick grasp of details, all this excited the enmity and jealousy of his rivals. But in the end it paved the way for his success. Mahmud Gawan too could not fail to foresee his bright future. Getting suspicious of the loyalty of Malik Hasan and alarmed at the promising career of his son, he persuaded the Sultan Muhammad Shah Bahmani III, to separate the two, by appointing Ahmad to Mahur as a commander of three hundred horse (1475 A.D.).[5] Here he remained for five years till he

**His youth**

was appointed as his father's deputy at Rajamundari and was the rank of raised to 1000 horse[6] (1480 A.D.).

Ahmad's fortunes brightened up after the murder of Mahmud Gawan, when his father Malik Hasan Nizam-ul-Mulk became the Prime Minister of the Bahmani Kingdom.[7] Muhammad Shah Bahmani III died on March 7th 1482 A.D. to be succeeded by his minor son Mahmud Shah.[8] Malik Hasan gathered the reins of authority into his own hands, and thanks to the pusillanimity of the boy king that the minister's power increased daily.

**His early activities**

He added to his estates, the provinces of Bir and other adjoining districts round about Daultabad and Junnar.[9] For the administration of these territories Malik Hasan summoned his son Ahmad to the court and appointed him as his deputy in the aforesaid provinces. Accordingly, Ahmad took up his residence at Junnar.[10] He found the entire region in the grip of Maratha oppression. Within a short time he supressed the aggressors and curbed their ambition so that, "all the inhabitants of the country and all the travellers therein, the Daccanis and Khurasanis, Hindus and Muslims, passed their lives in peace and contentment, and gladly submitted to him." In short Malik Ahmad fully justified the trust reposed in him by his father, and he managed the affairs of the province with justice and efficiency.[11]

**Honoured at the Bahmani Court**

Later, when Malik Ahmad came to the capital to participate in the coronation ceremony of Mahmud Shah, he remained there to second his father's attempt to crush the Foreigners headed by Yusuf Adil Khan of Bijapur.[12] It occasioned a bloody conflict which continued for twenty days, causing tremendous loss of life. In the end the rival factions concluded peace and Yusuf Adil Khan returned to Bijapur. When, on the eve of his departure, Malik Ahmad came to pay his respects, the Sultan embraced him affectionately, bestowed on him the high title of Ashrif-i-Humayun Nizam-ul-Mulk Bahri, clothed him with a robe of honour and put on his head a royal cornet. Thereafter, he was permitted to leave for Junnar.[13]

It has already been mentioned that the Bahmani capital was passing through the death pangs of party strife, mutual jealousy and endless conflict. Naturally the affairs of the kingdom fell into a fatal confusion. It gave an opportunity to the Prime Minister Malik Hasan Malik Naib, to realise his dream of carving out an independent principality. Therefore, he directed his son Malik Ahmad, who had now become very popular in the Konkan area, to reduce the hill forts held by the Marathas. For the last five years they had been with-holding the payment of revenue and refusing to submit to authority on the pretext that the Sultan was a minor. Such a situation called for a decisive and effective line of action.[14] (1485 A.D.).

**Malik Ahmad carves out independent principality**

Malik Ahmad opened the campaign by launching an attack on the hill fort of Junnar, which was outside the pale of his authority.[15] After a prolonged siege the garrison tendered its submission. Ahmad occupied the fort wherein were stored rich treasures representing the collection of revenue of all the Mahals of the Konkan. The windfall whetted the territorial appetite of Malik Ahmad further and he began to plan more daring projects. Like his father, he too was fully alive to the fast declining politics at the court, the dwindling prestige of the crown and the mounting ambitions of the other nobles. He was not the man to lag behind. He could visualise to himself a vista of bright prospects. He lavishly rewarded his soldiers and his followers for their gallant services, purchased the loyalty of others and thus collected a large army.[16] Now he addressed himself to the task of raiding and reducing the neighbouring hill forts of Shivanir (Shivnari)[17] Jond, Lohgarh,[18] Tung,[19] Nikona,[20] Kondana,[21] Purandhar,[22] Bhorap,[23] Morabdes, Judhan,[24] Khej, Kherdurg,[25] Muranjan,[26] Tungi and Taroni, Maholi and Pali,[27] which he captured and occupied within a short time. Having thus strengthened his position he attacked the fortress of Danda Rajpuri,[28] surrounded it and laid siege to it.[28]

These events synchronised with a general uprising in the empire. Yusuf Adil Khan, who was keenly watching the activities of Malik Ahmad, instigated Bahadur Gilani to rise up against the central authority. The latter seized the port of

Goa, captured Dabul, Kolhapur, Panhala, Sirala etc., and became more obnoxious than ever, delivering attacks on the port of Chaul and other adjoining areas. On the other hand, Zain-ul-Abidin, the governor of Chakan refused to recognise Malik Ahmad as the governor of Junnar. Realising the precariousness of his position, Malik Ahmad pressed the siege of Danda Rajpuri very vigourously and compelled the garrison to capitulate on terms. The occupation of the fort, completed the object with which the campaign had been opened. Now Malik Ahmad was the undisputed master of all the forts and the districts of Konkan, both below and above the Ghats, from Shivanir to Purandhar on the main line of the Syhadris.[30] But while he was busy in organising the affairs of the recently occupied forts, he was directed by his father Malik Hasan to reduce Zain-ul-Abidin.[31] Orders were issued to Khwaja Jahan Daccani and Malik Wuji to assist Malik Ahmad. In the face of this distress, Zain-ul-Abidin appealed for help to Yusuf Adil Khan, who sent a large force to his succour.[32] The commander was instructed to encamp near the fort of Indapur and from there to watch the movements of Malik Ahmad and to entrap him in the event of his marching towards Chakan.[33] Just at this juncture Malik Hasan ordered his son to return to Junnar with his entire army. But before he could reach there, he received the news of the murder of his father at the hands of Dilpasand Khan.[34]

**Slow dismemberment of Bahmani Kingdom**

The tragic end of his father alarmed Malik Ahmad, but soon he regained his composure and began to make plans for future. He assumed the appllation of his father and styled himself as Ahmad Nizam-ul-Mulk Bahri.[35] After some time, he reopened his aggressive campaigns against the nobles of the Bahmani kingdom, siezed their lands and annexed them to those of his own, a process which was also later on imitated by other powerful and resourceful leaders. He conquered Bir, Shivgaon, Mahur and the whole country as far as the Godavari.[36] Like a rebellious governor, he bent his energies to the task of carving out a kingdom for himself by over-throwing all such officers who were still faithful to the Bahmanide house. He assembled a large army with which he manned the forts, and became ready to wreak vengeance on his father's enemy. This did not make him oblivious to his responsibility to the people. He assiduously promoted good administration in his country and earned the gratitude and loyalty of the masses and the classes, who had long been exposed to suffering, because of the rot which had set in the centre.[37] In the words of Sayyid Ali, such was the justice of Ahmad Nizam-ul-Mulk that, "without the sanction the loadstone dared not attract iron and kahrooba lost all its power over the grass."[38] He was universally respected and feared by Hindus and Muslims, Daccanis and the Khurasanis alike.

**Ahmad's bold stand against the rival forces**

Malik Ahmad's success became an eyesore to the nobles of the court, particularly Qasim Barid who had succeeded Malik Hasan as *maire de palais*.[39] He was loth to sit and gaze at others who were carving out principalities for themselves. He reduced the authority of the Sultan, gained complete control over administration, looked askance at other nobles and began to wield unlimited authority in the political affairs. Firstly, he sent an army against his Foreign rival Yusuf Adil Khan, but being unable to achieve anything against him, he turned his attention against Ahmad Nizam-ul-Mulk. The result of this policy was that the more sober tarafdars, to ensure their personal security for the moment, allied themselves with the most powerful among them and threw off the yoke of the central authority. But no sooner was their aim accomplished then they again professed their loyalty to the Sultan and endeavoured their best to become autonomous in their respective provinces.

At the instance of Qasim Barid, Sultan Mahmud Shah Bahmani sent a firman to Yusuf Adil Khan, the governor of Bijapur, to march to Junnar along with Khawaja Jahan Daccani and Zain-ul-Abdin of Chakan and destroy the rising power of Ahmad Nizam-ul-Mulk.But Yusuf Adil Khan instead of marching against him, sent him his messenger to express his grief on the death of Malik Hasan and assuring him of good will and consideration. Moreover, he secretly encouraged Ahmad to mature his ambitious design and to remain firm against the dominance of Qasim Barid. He also withdrew his own forces which he had sent to the succour of Zain-ul-Abidin and evacuated the fort of Indapur.[40]

Having failed to enlist the support of Yusuf Adil Khan in his nefarious project of destroying the power of Ahmad Nizam-ul-Mulk, Qasim Barid now selected Shaikh Muaddi, an Arab entitled Nadir-uz-Zaman,[41] known for his valour and intrepidity. With 12000 horse, the Shaikh was sent against Ahmad Nizam-ul-Mulk in the hope that, "A lamp could remain alight in the storm wind and that a crafty fox would prevail against the teeth of a raging tiger".[42]

Ahmad Nizam-ul-Mulk now appointed Zarif-ul-Mulk Afghan, his Amir-ul-Umra and conferred the post and title of Mir Jumla on Nasir-ul-Mulk Gujarati.[43] He removed his family from Junnar to the fort of Shivaneri and himself retreated a few miles from his headquarters.[44] He then opened negotiations with Zain-ul-Abidin the governor of Chakan, who had already marched to attack him. Ahmad asked him to join hands with him in the impending struggle against the Bahmani forces. At first Zain-ul-Abidin gave a favourable response to the proposal, and even promised to meet Ahmad but later he changed his mind when he heard that the royal army under Shaikh Muaddi had reached Parenda.[45] He now decided to join the latter. Thereupon Ahmad Nizam-ul-Mulk assembled his army, distributed money among the soldiers, and sent for Nasir-ul-Mulk Gujarati to seek his advice for meeting the crisis.[46] It was planned that Mir Jumla should stay where he was with the main body of the army, to check the advance of Shaikh Muaddi, whereas Ahmad should fall upon Zain-ul-Abidin before he should be able to join his ally. After having dealt with the latter, Ahmad Nizam-ul-Mulk would join the main army and in concert with Mir Jumla fall upon Shaikh Muaddi.[47] Accordingly, Ahmad with his picked body of men set out at night and by forced marches appeared before Chakan early in the morning. He surrounded the fort, scalded the walls and took the garrison by surprise.[48] The enemy put up a brave fight, but the game was up. Zain-ul--Abidin and his seven hundred men were killed, and much booty fell into the hands of the victors.[49] After occupying the fort, slaying and plundering the enemy, Ahmad Nizam-ul-Mulk hastened back to complete the second part of the plan. But before he could arrive Nasir-ul-Mulk Gujarati had opened the attack on the royal army in spite of his small following. He was defeated twice and was compelled to retreat to his former position. His action having been in contravention to the preconcerted plan, the Mir Jumla was censured for his conduct by his master, but was forgiven for his error of judgement.[50]

On the other hand, this initial success made Shaikh Muaddi over-confident. He gave up the idea of resuming the fight, and threw himself into a life of pleasures and enjoyment. Ahmad Nizam-ul-Mulk watched the development for a few days. Finding that the Shaikh was negligent of his duties, he launched a night attack on him, and took him completely by surpirse. The royal troops were routed with heavy losses. Their commander with many officers of distinction lost their lives in the action. A few survivors escaped to Bidar with much difficulty. But all their camp-bargage, horses and elephants fell into the hands of the victors. Ahmad Nizam-ul-Mulk returned to Junnar, where he devoted himself to the organisation of the civil administration of his government.[51]

The news of the defeat and the death of the Shaikh Mauddi and Zain-ul-Abidin proved very distracting to Sultan Mahmud Shah Bahmani and his Prime minister Qasim Barid, who had underestimated the power and resources of Ahmad Nizam-ul-Mulk.[52] It was clear that the leaders of the royal army were sadly lacking in unity of action, not to speak of the foresight which could have enabled them to win the support of other nobles opposed to Ahmad Nizam-ul-Mulk, and thus make a joint effort against the latter. Repenting their folly many of the military leaders deserted the royal cause and joined Ahmad Nizam-ul-Mulk, which strengthened his position still further. By making an appeal to his sense of self respect and pointing out the necessity of rehabilitating the imperial prestige, Qasim Barid once more succeeded in persuading the Sultan to send against Ahmad another large army led by experienced generals under the command of a daring and discreet officer. Accordingly an army of 18,000 men with eighteen experienced officers under the command of Azmat-ul-Dabir was organised and sent against Ahmad Nizam-ul-Mulk.[53] In view of the superiority of numbers of the royal forces, the latter avoided pitched battle. He left Junnar, and encamped in the hilly region of Qadirabad. When the royal army reached Ghat Miri, Ahmad Nizam-ul-Mulk with three thousand men came out and cleverly dodged them by rapidly changing his movements. He made a dash for Bidar.[54] Arriving there he overcame the guards of the city, entered it by night, and effected the rescue of the female members of his father's family, whom he sent to Junnar.[55] Next morning he seized the women of all such officers as had been sent against him; taking them along with him, he moved towards Parenda, giving instructions to his officers to treat them with respect.[56] When he arrived near the army, the Bahmani officers sent word to inform him that they could not possibly think of fighting with him as enemy, because he had behaved so nobly towards their wives and children.[57] Later, they also ridiculed Ahmad for his unworthy conduct in fleeing from the field like a thief and falling upon their unprotected women and children. The remarks touched Ahmad Nizam-ul-Mulk to the quick. He forthwith sent back to the nobles their wives and children and himself retired to Parenda.[58]

The Sultan now wrote to Azmat-ul-Mulk Dabir bitterly reprimanding him for allowing Ahmad to make such a daring raid on the capital and inflict such a disgrace on the imperial troops.[59] The Commander-in-Chief was asked to bring Ahmad to the court, failing which he was threatened with severe punishment. The royal army encamped near Bir.[60] Here the officers openly remonstrated against the slur cast upon their conduct by the Sultan, and they sent a message to the latter saying that they had always been ready to attack the enemy but they could not do it because of the incompetency of Azmat-ul-Mulk Dabir, who had failed to obtain intelligence about the movements of the rebel. They also requested the Sultan to recall Azmat-ul-Mulk and to send another general to lead them.[61] The Sultan now sent Jahangir Khan, the governor of Telingana, with 3000 horses to assume the command of the royal army at Bir. Jahangir Khan moved towards Parenda. Its commandant Makhdum Khwaja Jahan was unwilling to oppose Ahmad Nizam-ul-Mulk openly, and therefore, he sent his son Azam Khan to join the Commander-in-Chief and himself retired into the fort.[62]

Upon the advance of the royal army under Jahangir Khan, Ahmad Nizam-ul-Mulk fled from Parenda to Junnar and thence to Paithan.[63] He importuned Imad-ul-Mulk of

Berar to come to his assistance.[64] Jahangir Khan moved on, whereupon Ahmad retreated further and took up his position in the hilly country of Jeur. Here he was reinforced by his minister Nasir-ul-Mulk Gujarati with a body of troops and convoy of provisions from Qadirabad. Having secured the pass of Jeur, he remained moving among the hills. Meanwhile, Jahangir Khan crossed the hills at Tisgaon and encamped at Bhingar with the two fold object of cutting the supplies of the enemy and closing their path of retreat to Junnar.[65] The rival armies though encamped within a distance of six kos, remained inactive for a month.[66] When the rains set in, Ahmad's troops began to suffer severely. On the other hand the royal officers labouring under the belief that Ahmad would be unable to effect his escape, not only neglected to take the necessary precautions, but took to a life of gaity and merry-making.[67] This gave a splendid opportunity to Ahmad Nizam-ul-Mulk, who marched by night to Nikapur, arrived there early in the morning of June 19th, 1490 A.D.[68] He fell upon the enemy at a time when most of the soldiers were fast asleep, and wiped out almost the entire army.[69] Among the generals who were slain, were Jahangir Khan, Sayyid Lutfullah, Nizam Khan and Fathullah. Those who were taken prisoner were mounted on buffaloes and stripped down to their knees and paraded in Nizam-ul-Mulk's camp. They were then sent back to Bidar.[70] The battle is known as the battle of Bagh from the garden which Ahmad laid out on its site to commemorate his victory. Afterwards Ahmad Nizam-ul-Mulk built here a palace which was beautified by his successors who having made fortifications round it, renamed it as Bagh-i-Nizam.[71] A village in the neighbourhood was assigned as Waqf for the maintenance of the holy men in residence there. Ahmad now returned to Junnar with flying banners.

**Ahmad declares his independence**

Ahmad Nizam-ul-Mulk began to give serious thouglt to the situation with a view to clarifying the relationship between the weak sovereign and his powerful vassal. We have seen that he had twice been hit by the dirty politics of the Bahmani court, but inspite of severe opposition he had emerged out victorious. In fact, there were only three courses open to him viz. (1) either to declare himself independent of the central authority or (2) otherwise to form a coalition of the disgusted and disappointed nobles and overthrow the dominance of Qasim Barid, depose the feeble Bahmani Sultan and thus wipe off the existence of the Bahmani kingdom for all time or (3) to openly defy the politicians of the court at Bidar, to continue to profess his loyalty to the Bahmani house, while retaining his own independence. He decided to adopt the third alternative. He omitted the name of the Bahmani Sultan from the Khutuba, struck coins in his name and entitled himself as Ahmad Nizam Shah Bahri.[72a] At the same time he continued to profess loyalty to the Bahmani house in his own interests.[72b] According to Ferishta, when his action was resented by the local nobility headed by Khawaja Jahan Daccani, apprehending lest he should lose their support, Ahmad upon their suggestion restored the name of the Bahmani Sultan in the Khutba. In a similar way, when he begun to use white umbrella, the emblem of royalty, the people who still professed their loyalty to the Bahmani house remonstrated, and once again Ahmad had to yield to their wishes by putting forward a weak plea that he was doing so in order to keep off the sun from him. But no sooner did he find himself powerful than he returned to his old ways and styled himself as an independent ruler of the recently carved out territory. (1490 A.D.).

Complete was the dismemberment of the Bahmanide empire. Ahmad held Junnar and its dependencies, viz. Poona, Chakan, Chamargunda and the fort of Dandarajpuri etc. His contemporaries Yusuf Adil Khan held the governorship of Bijapur. Bahadur Gilani held the territory, west of Bijapur to the sea, including Mirza-Gulbarga, Kalahar and strong forts of Panhala and Kavli. Dastur Dinar held the territory south of Bijapur, between the river Banswara and the capital Bidar, which included the best parganas of Kanjoti, Aland, Ashanabad-Gulbarga, Bakhyl-i-Yeli, and Jajoti; another noble Khwaja. Jahan Daccani held Parenda, Sholapur and its neighbouring territory; the fort of Daultabad was held by Malik Wuji; one half of Berar was in the hands of Fathullah Imad-ul-Mulk, and the other half which included the forts of Mulher, Timmar, Kalan and Mahur was in the hands of Khudawand Khan. The governorship of Telingana was held by Qutub-ul-Mulk, and the prime ministership of Bidar was in the hands of Qasim Barid. After 1490 A.D. every one of these nobles made an attempt to seize the possession of other's territory and to carve out an independent principality for himself. In this struggle the weaker had to bow before the stronger. So finally there arose five independent kingdoms, namely, the Nizam Shahi kingdom of Ahmadnagar, the Adil Shahi kingdom of Bijapur, the Barid Shahi kingdom of Bidar, the Imad Shahi kingdom of Berar and the Qutb Shahi kingdom at Golkunda, in the Daccan out of the Bahmani kingdom. The founders of these kingdom believed that they would open a new era in the history of the Daccan, but in fact, this was not to be. During the next two hundred years instead of restoring peace and order in the country, the rulers of these states were constantly in the grips of deadly contest for the absolute supermacy which drove them one by one into the limb of oblivion.

**His attempts to enhance the territorial limits of his principality**

Ahmad Nizam Shah lost no time in reorganising his army on new lines, doing away with tyranny and oppression, reorienting the values of justice and equality, which immensely enhanced his prestige besides adding to his strength and ressources. To increase the territorial limits of his infant kingdom, he opened his first campaign to sieze the fort of Daultabad.[73] It was held by Malik Wuji and Malik Ashraf, formerly in the service of Mahmud Gawan; but after his murder, they had enrolled themselves into the corps of *Silahdars* of Mahmud Shah Bahmani.[74] In course of time they attained the rank of nobles in the time of Malik Hasan, who had appointed the former as the governor of the fort of Daultabad and the latter as his deputy. The two brothers conducted their administration very efficiently. They suppressed highway robbery and rendered safe, the roads leading to the frontiers of Sultanpur, Nandubar, Baglana and Gujarat so that the merchants and travellers moved freely and fearlessly and the people heaved a sigh of relief. In gratitude for the patronage of Malik Hasan they continued to be friendly with him and subsequently with his son Ahmad. To cement these ties further, soon after the battle of Bagh, the latter gave his sister Bibi Zainab in marriage to Malik Wuji, who was a scholar and a virtuous man.[75] A son was born to him in the very year of his marriage and Malik Wuji requested Ahmad Nizam Shah to name the child and he suggested the name Moti. Unfortunately the birth of the child, strained the relations between Malik Wuji and his brother Malik Ashraf, who began to form malicious designs. His ambition goaded him to murder his unsuspecting brother and to poison his nephew. The widow, Bibi Zainab instead of shedding tears on the loss of her husband and son, escaped to her brother to save her life and to seek revenge for the wrong that had done to her.[76]

Distressed at the double tragedy, Ahmad left his capital in 1493 to avenge the murder of his brother-in-law. But when he had reached Bagh-i-Nizam, he halted there for a while to enjoy and take rest.[77] Here he received pressing invitations from Qasim Barid and Sultan Mahmud Shah for help against the common enemy Yusuf Adil Khan[77a] who was closely besieging the capital. The message was delivered by Tajjuddin and Deoras Pandit, who pointed out the necessity of relieving the capital immediately.[77b] In return, Qasim Barid promised to help him in reducing the fortress of Daultabad and to assign him Goa, Konkan, Panhala and Kalahar which at the moment were in the hands of Bahadur Gilani. Partly tempted by the offer and partly buoyed up with the hope of putting an end to the growing power of Yusuf Adil Khan, Ahmad Nizam Shah changed his mind and marched to the relief of Sultan; but before he could arrive at Bidar, Qasim Barid had been defeated in a battle with heavy losses and Ahmad's hopes were completely blasted, and he in sheer disappointment came to Daultabad and opened its siege which continued for two months but without any success. Upon this he thought of gaining his object with other means. To decide their shape he held a consultation with his amirs and officers.[78] Nasir-ul-Mulk Gujarati suggested that every year at the harvest time the district adjoining the fort should be laid waste, which would seal off the supply of provisions to the garrison, and in the end they would be compelled to surrender. The suggestion was approved by Ahmad Nizam Shah and he started on his return journey to his capital.[79]

Once more the Sultan and his prime minister Qasim Barid dangled before Ahmad the prospects of territorial gain and the rehabilitation of his prestige when they asked him for help to put down Bahadur Gilani, who after the death of Nizamuddin, the kotwal of Goa, (1491 A.D.) had occupied Debul, Kalahar, Panhala, Belgam, Miraj, Kolhapur and had began to harass the people inhabiting the country as far as Chaul. His depredations had become a source of grave anxiety to the rulers of Gujarat and Bidar alike. Ahmad complied with the request and sent an army. The joint forces crushed the rebel, who was killed. The Sultan honoured his promises and handed over to Ahmad some portions of the territory of Bahadur Gliani.[80]

On his way back from the recent campaign when Ahmad arrived at Bhingar, a village between the two towns of Junnar and Daultabad, he decided to lay foundations of a town from whence he could detach his forces every year against the fort of Daultabad. For this purpose he selected "a tract in which climate and greennees of its hills and plains may be compared with paradise". Here arose the future capital of the kingdom which the founder named after himself as Ahmadnagar.[81] He asked his astrologers to select an auspicious day for commencing the building operations. He summoned surveyors, architects and builders to beautify the city with palaces, gardens and houses. Within two years the new city rivalled the cities of Cairo and Baghdad in splendour and magnificence.[82]

**The foundation of the city of Ahmadnagar 1494 A.D.**

In 1495 A.D. some changes were made among the provincial governors of the Bahmani kingdom on the death of Qutb-ul-Mulk Daccani, the governor of Western Telingana. Dastur Dinar who had been granted the fiefs of Gulbarga, Aland and Gangawati etc. succeeded him. But after some time he was transferred to his former fiefs in order to make room for Qutb-ul-Mulk Hamdani, who had to be rewarded for his loyal services.[83] This offended Dastur Dinar, who resolved to make a bid for autonomy. He allied himself with Ahmad Nizam Shah, who directed Khwaja Jahan of Parenda to march to his aid. The two expelled the royal officers from many places, whereupon the Bahmani Sultan asked Yusuf Adil Khan to help him in supressing his rebellion. A battle took place at Mahendri in which Dastur Dinar was

**Minor activities to enhance his power**

defeated, captured and produced before the Sultan who ordered him to be beheaded, though subsequently he was pardoned and Gulbarga and Aland were granted to him in jagir for the second time.[84] But Yusuf Adil Khan was keen to annex this part of the Bahmani kingdom into his principality with the object of not allowing Dastur Dinar to live in peace.

In 1498 Yusuf Adil Khan once more marched against Dastur Dinar and compelled him to fly to Ahmad Nizam Shah. Yusuf Adil Khan now wrote to Sultan Mahmud Shah Bahmani that Ahmad was helping a rebel. But Ahmad appealed to the Sultan on behalf of Dastur Dinar, requesting him to let him remain in possession of the fiefs which he had held for such a long time, and which Yusuf was coveting for himself. Accordingly, the Sultan ordered Yusuf Adil Khan not to proceed any further against Dastur Dinar. Thus, Ahmad Nizam Shah acted as a check on the fast growing ambitions of Yusuf Adil Khan, who was making constant efforts to seize the truncated possessions of the Bahmani kingdom and to absorb them into his own. And yet he had no scruples in coming to terms with Yusuf Adil Khan and Imad-ul-Mulk for partitioning among themselves the territories which once belonged to the decaying empire.

Ahmad Nizam Shah now resumed his operations against the fortress of Daultabad. The destruction of the adjoining districts drove the garrison to the narrow straits.[85] In utter helplessness, the commander Malik Ashraf solicited the assistance of Mahmud Shah Bageda of Gujarat promising to hold the fort on his behalf and to recite the Khutba in his name. Finding to be a good opportunity to fish in troubled waters, the Sultan of Gujarat marched towards the Daccan, firstly, with idea of humbling the power of Adil Khan Faruqi, the ruler of Khandesh, who had neglected to pay tribute and allegiance to him and secondly, to help Malik Ashraf against Ahmad Nizam.[86] On his approach Adil Khan Faruqi made an alliance with Ahmad, and sent him two thousand men to assist him in his campaign against Daultabad. Further, to secure himself against the ruler of Gujarat he made friends with Fathullah Imad-ul-Mulk, of Berar.[87]

When the Gujarati forces arrived at Sultanpur, Adil Khan

requested Imad-ul-Mulk and Ahmad Nizam to send their forces to assist him. Ahmad Nizam, who was besieging Daultabad, raised the siege, and marched towards Burhanpur with 15,000 cavalry.[88] Similarly, Imad-ul-Mulk responded to Adil Khan Faruqi's call for help. The confederates encamped near the city of Burhanpur, while the Sultan of Gujarat Mahmud Shah Bageda took up his position at Asir.[89] Seeing that the the number of men under the command of the enemy was overwhelmingly large, Ahmad Nizam Shah resorted to strategem.[90] He sent his minister Nasir-ul-Mulk Gujarati as an envoy to the enemy's camp, ostensibly for negotiating peace, but really to bribe the elephant keepers, and persuade them to let loose drunken elephants at a pre-arranged signal.[91] In a dark night Ahmad Nizam with five hundred infantry including archers, rocketeers, and matchlockmen and five thousand cavalry moved towards the camp of the enemy and fell upon it.[92] At that very moment according to the pre-concerted plan the elephant-keepers released the elephants and drove them towards the royal harem. The officers were completely taken by surprise, whereas when the elephants entered into the female apartments, the ladies stricken with fear began to shriek loudly. The Sultan of Gujarat thought that the enemy had made his way into his camp and were committing great slaughter. In sheer fright, he fled along with his officers, not pulling his reins till he had covered six miles. Having thus harassed the Gujarati forces, Ahmad withdrew to his camp, and the confusion soon after subsided. When some of the officers came to Mahmud Shah Bageda's camp to congratulate him, not finding him there, they too were overtaken by fright took to their heels. Next morning Ahmad Nizam Shah and his allies took up their position on the ground where the Sultan of Gujarat had previously disposed his men. The armies faced each other for a while, after which a treaty was concluded between the two parties. Ahmad Nizam Shah returned towards Daultabad, ascending the Ghats from Berar side. He encamped at Ellora, where he gave himself to all sorts of pleasure and amusements.[93]

**Gujrati forces put to flight**

Malik Ashraf was again reduced to narrow straits, he again solicited help from the Sultan of Gujarat, promising him the same condition as before.[94] The Sultan of Gujarat once more tempted by the offers moved from his capital and arrived on the banks of river Tapti. Upon this Ahmad raised the siege, and withdrew to Ahmadnagar.[95] Malik Ashraf was now asked to fulfil his promise, and he recited the *Khutba* in the name of the Sultan of Gujarat in the Friday prayers in the mosque of Qutbuddin Mubarak Shah Khilji in the Daultabad fort.[96] He also went to pay his respects to the Sultan, offered him valuable presents and promised to pay to him annual tribute like a vassal.[97] Mahmud was satisfied with his conduct, went to Khandesh, collected tribute from Adil Khan Faruqi II and then returned to his dominions.[98]

No sooner was the report of the retreat of the Sultan of Gujarat communicated to Ahmad Nizam than he marched again to Daultabad. On his way he was informed that the Maratha garrison of the fort bitterly resented the conduct of Malik Ashraf in recognising the suzerainty of the Sultan of Gujarat. Subsequently, they sent word to Ahmad offering their submission to him. From the banks of Godavari, Ahmad made a forced march towards Daultabad, surrounded it early next morning and opened the siege. Malik Ashraf was shocked at the duplicity of the Marathas, in whom he had placed much confidence. He fell ill and died five or six days afterwards.[99] There was none to oppose the invader and the gates of the fort were opened to him. Ahmad Nizam entered it, installed his own garrison in it, and after giving necessary instructions for its repairs, he returned to his capital.[100] (1499 A.D.). The occupation of the fort of Daultabad enhanced the prestige of Ahmad Nizam. His strength and power was now unrivalled. The very same year he reduced the forts of Antur and other places in Khandesh and compelled the chiefs of Galna and Bagalna, to pay to him annual tribute and acknowledge his suzerainty.[101]

**Daultabad captured 1499 A.D.**

In the political arena of the Daccan now restless rivals like Ahmad Nizam Shah, Yusuf Adil Khan, Ali Barid, who had succeeded his father Qasim Barid as *maire de palais*, and Alauddin Imad-ul-Mulk who too had succeeded his father Fathullah Imad-ul-Mulk in the governorship of Berar, faced one another, constantly forming combinations and counter-combinations, changing friendships as quickly as they were formed. In 1504, Yusuf Adil Khan finding himself to be the most powerful of the *tarafrars* of the Bahmani kingdom, proclaimed the public profession of the Shia creed in his dominions. The discontentment and confusion which followed the order, furnished a pretext for his rivals, especially Ali Barid to instigate Sultan Mahmud to ask Alauddin Imad-ul-Mulk, Khudawand Khan, Sultan Quli Qutb-ul-Mulk and Ahmad Nizam Shah to join the league against the heretic. Ahmad Nizam Shah had a personal grudge against Yusuf Adil Khan. He was the first to respond to the call and join Ali Barid to curb his growing power. Ali Barid opened the campaign by seizing Gangawati. His ally Ahmad Nizam Shah sent messengers to Bijapur demanding the surrender of Naldurg. Yusuf Adil Khan could bear no more. He sent a respectful reply to Ahmad and humbled Ali Barid by recovering Gangawati. Ali Barid now sent his son Jahangir Khan to Ahmadnagar with pathetic appeals for speedy help. Upon this, Ahmad Nizam moved out with 10,000 horse and train of artillery together with the troops of other allies. To ward off the approaching storm, Yusuf Adil Khan resorted to a strategem. He marched northward laid waste the territory of Ahmad Nizam Shah near Bir, but being hotly pursued by the allies entered Berar. Here in concert with Alauddin Imad-ul-Mulk he contrived to create disenssions among the allies whose plan ended in smoke. Feeling secure in his position he reestablished the *shia* faith in his province. Nor did he fail to convince Ahmad of the risk involved in making common cause with Ali Barid, who, he pointed out, wanted first to seize Bijapur, and then the territories of Ahmadnagar. Realising that the friendship with Ali Barid would not yield him any dividends, Ahmad Nizam Shah withdrew to his capital.[102]

**Ahmad joins the league against Yusuf Adil Khan 1504 A.D.**

Baulked of the prospects of aggrandisement in the Daccan, but burning with ambition to enhance his prestige and increase his possessions, Ahmad Nizam Shah turned towards Khandesh.[103] Adil Khan Faruqi II the ruler of Khandesh died on September 28th, 1501 A.D. and was succeeded by his brother Daud Khan. Hismauddin one of the worthless amirs of Daud Khan invited Ahmad Nizam to assist him in deposing the king. Thus, on the pretext of supporting the claims of Alam Khan,[104] a scion of the Faruqi house, who had been expelled from Khandesh and had taken refuge in Ahmadnagar, Ahmad responded to the invitation, and attacked Khandesh in 1504 A.D.[105] Daud Khan appealed for help to Nasiruddin Shah the ruler of Malwa, who sent an army under one of his amirs Iqbal Khan, who put to flight Ahmad Nizam Shah and his protege Alam Khan from Khandesh. But the trouble did not end here. Daud Khan died in August 28th, 1508 A.D. and he was succeeded by his son Ghazni Khan, who was poisoned after a brief reign of ten days.[106] With Ghazni Khan's death the direct line of the Faruqi house became extinct. Two parties now arose in Khandesh; one under Hisamuddin, supporting Alam Khan, the candidate of Ahmad Nizam Shah and the other under Malik Ladan Khilji who held in his possession the other half of Burhanpur and supported the cause of another Alam Khan, the candidate of Sultan Mahmud Shah of Gujarat.

**A few set backs**

Being invited, this time by Hisamuddin, Ahmad Nizam Shah once more marched towards Burhanpur. On this occassion he had allied himself with Alauddin Imad-ul-Mulk.[107] The allies succeeded in proclaiming Alam Khan as king and in seating him on the throne of Khandesh.[108] Ladan Khilji finding that he had lost the game, shut himself in fort of Asirgarh. Ahmad Nizam Shah and Alauddin Imad-ul-Mulk along with Hisamuddin opened the siege of the fort. Meanwhile arrived the Sultan Mahmud Shah of Gujarat, with his protege and encamped at Thalnir. The unexpected turn in the events frightened Ahmad Nizam Shah and his ally Alauddin, and they fled towards the frontiers of their kingdoms, leaving behind forty thousand troops for the assistance of Alam Khan and Hisammuddin. Upon this, Sultan Mahmud Shah ordered Sayyid Asaf Khan and Aziz-ul-Mulk, the fief holders of Sultanpur and Nandurbar, to march jointly against Hisamuddin and drive him out of the country. He also sent messages to Malik Ladan Khilji saying that if he would help him against his rival, he would appoint him to his place. When the joint forces reached near Ranubar, considering opposition to be futile Hisamuddin came to Thalnir and tendered his fealty to the Sultan of Gujarat. He was followed by his rival Malik Ladan Khilji. The Sultan now placed his protege Alam Khan, the son of Hasan Khan, on the throne ennobling him with the title of Adil Khan Faruqi III. (April 1509 A.D.). Malik Ladan Khilji was given the title of Khan Jahan and the village of Bansal which was his birth place. The Sultan brought about a reconciliation between the two nobles, promoted many other officers, rewarded them and exacted promise of fidelity to the new king and thereafter he returned to Gujarat.[109]

The cup of Ahmad Nizam's humilitation was not yet full. More of it was in store for him. On reaching the frontiers of his kingdom, he wrote a letter to the Sultan Mahmud Shah of Gujarat, suggesting to him that Alam Khan should inherit at least a share in the territories of Khandesh. When the letter, which had been written in the style of one king addressing another, reached Mahmud Shah, he was so bitterly offended that he kept mum for a while and then he gave vent to his anger, telling the envoy, "How dare the son of a slave of a Bahmani king, write as though he were a king? A humble petition is the only communication that a slave can address to a king. Let Ahmad not repeat the insolence, lest he should come to grief." Disgraced and mortified, the ruler of Ahmadnagar returned with his protege to his capital. To add further to the insult, he was warned by Sultan Mahmud Shah of Gujarat that he would have to rue the day he thought of reopening the aggression. In token of his determination to implement his threat, Mahmud Shah made a gift of 12,00000 of tankas to Adil Khan Faruqi III and ordered the mobilisation of a large force under the command of Dilawar Khan. In these circumstances Ahmad Nizam Shah gave up the idea of reviving the conflict and of supporting the claims of his protege.[110]

**Ahmad Nizam Shah Humiliated**

It would be clear from the foregoing account that Ahmad Nizam Shah could not make a correct assessment of the power of Sultan Mahmud Shah of Gujarat abroad; nor of the strength of the Foreign and Daccani factions at home. He had to struggle incessantly against heavy odds and in conditions subject to rapid change. He could not depend on the loyalty or the promise of his neighbours and friends. But ambition urged him on to restless activity. The failure of his projects and indignities hurled at him by the ruler of Gujarat must have touched him to a quick. And in the end he found himself no better than a soldier thrown on his knees, with no energy to avenge the insult or strength to win fresh laurels to retrieve the lost honour. Even so he succeeded in carving out a principality which included the country from Bir to Chaul and Ravadanda on the sea coast and from the frontiers of Khandesh to the south of Poona.

**The death of Nasir-ul-Mulk Gujrati**

Ahmad's career of adventure came to a sudden end in 1508-9 A.D. when his most wise, faithful trustworthy minister and experienced general Masnad-i-Ali Malik Nasir-ul-Mulk Gujarati died, which grieved him most. At the various turns of fortunes in the life of his master Nasir-ul-Mulk had helped him very skilfully with his intelligence, bravery, and superior statescraft. He was succeeded by Mian Chandu, an old servant of Ahmad Nizam Shah, whose intelligence acumen and benevolence had attracted the attention of his master. On him was conferred the title of Mukammal Khan.[111]

**Death of Ahmad Nizam Shah**

Ahmad Nizam Shah in the later part of his life nominated his son Burhan as heir-apparent and died after a short illness in 1510 A.D.[112] He was one of the foremost personalities of the age in which he lived. He possessed a high sense of discipline and appreciation for the standard values. Though born and brought up in an atmosphere of chaos and confusion caused by the intrigues and party strife at the Bahmani court, he did not fail to profit by the example of Mahmud Gawan. His early campaigns against the Marathas of Konkan, his method of guerilla warfare rveal his keen intelligence, bubbling energy, high ambitions and unquenching thirst for power. Although a Brahman by blood, he gave unmistakable proofs of daring and courage, rising superior to every general of the Bahmani kingdom sent against him to put him down. True that in the later part of his life, he failed to achieve his objectives; but this was not surprising because of the circumstances in which he was placed.

Of strict morals as he was, Ahmad Nizam Shah never cast his eyes either right or left while passing in a procession in the streets of the city.[113] When he was asked by one of his courtiers as to why he did so, he replied, "lest his eye should fall upon a beautiful damsel and he should try to possess her." It was a lesson which he had taken from the pleasure seeking blood-thirsty Bahmani sovereigns, who were mostly addicted to drink, and debauchery. Once the Wazir, Nasirul-Mulk Gujarati pressented a beautiful woman captured from the fort of Rawil as *peshkash* to Ahmad Nizam Shah. When she was brought to the royal bed-chamber, the Nizam Shah enquired of her parentage. In reply she mentioned the name of her husband and other relatives, who had been made captive by his troops. Ahmad Nizam Shah refused to touch her, handed her over to her husband and released all her relatives. This reflects the greatness of the man, his sense of justice and above all the purity of his character.[114]

In the field of battle if Ahmad Nizam Shah found any soldier behaving cowardly and turning his back on the enemy, he would go to him and would ask him to explain his conduct. If he apologised for his reprehensible conduct and promised not to repeat it again he was forgiven and Ahmad would give him a quid of betel and allow him to return to his post.[115] At the close of the campaign honours and rewards were not only distributed to those who had distinguished themselves, but consideration was also given to such cases in which the individuals could not come up to expectations.[116] Mainly because of this attitude of generosity no Indian leader, save Shivaji was better served by his officers than Ahmad Nizam Shah.

Ahmad was a skilful gladiator. He introduced the custom of duelling.[117] When the young men came before him with their mutual complaints, he used to order them to fight in his presence, deciding in favour of the one who first wounded his adversary. In course of time unfair advantage was taken of this custom. A crowed of young men would attend the hall of audience every day, in expectation of winning fame and distinction in the presence of Ahmad Nizam Shah.[118] At length these combats became an every day affairs and many lives were lost.[119] Upon this Ahmad ordered that combats should not take place in his presence in the audience hall, but in the plains out side the city.[120] He laid down rules and regulations for such duels. Bystanders and relations were not allowed to interfere. All blood feuds, in consequence of death of one of the combatants were strictly prohibited. Very soon the practice spread among the people and rings were established in every street and muhallah of the city. Women also used to witness these duels and when a man of sound physique was defeated, they used to run to their houses, crying all along, "Khan Bhai Jeete, ham hare". This custom did not remain confined to Ahmadnagar, but spread in the whole of the Daccan, where noblemen were specially skilled in the use of sword.[121]

---

*Notes and References*

1. Like all other historians of his age, who trace the lineage of their sovereigns from one or the other of the royal house, the author of Burhan-i-masir, Sayyid Ali bin Azizullah Tabataba has also traced the genealogy of the Nizam Shahi kings from Bahman the son of Isfandiyar and takes it as far as back as Kaymurs. To impart authenticity to his statements he has invented two stories with regard to the date of birth and parentage of the founder of the Nizam Shahi kingdom. Though full of human interest, they fail to carry conviction. He relates that during the reign of Muhammad Shah Bahmani III (1463-82) his noble in one of Vijayanagara compaigns captured a beautiful damsel worthy of the royal bed-chamber. Unlike other ladies of the harem she not only excelled in beauty and other outward manifestations of physical appearance, but she was gifted with charming modesty and unusual fidelity. She became the object of attraction for the Sultan who showered unlimited favours on her. Intense love and close affection brought in its train the desire for biological process which gave birth to a prince whom he named Moti Shah and later on called him Ahmad. The royal astrologers cast the horoscope of the child and prophesied that the stars indicated royal destiny for him, but for the time being he should be sent away from the capital. The Sultan was much depressed, but bowed to destiny. He decided to send the Prince and his mother to Malik Hasan Humayun Shahi, entitled Majlis-i-Ala mansab-i-iMualla Malik Naib, who was holding the fief of Mahur and Ramghir. Like a devoted servant Malik Hasan took pains for the education and upbringing of the Prince. When he grew young, after the death of the Sultan he came to be known as the son of Malik Hasan. See, Burhan-i-Masir (I.A. 1920) pp. 67-8.
   Another story related by the author is also interesting. According to it once, the Sultan Muhammad Shah Bahmani III presented a slave girl from his harem to Malik Hasan who took her into his harem where soon after he found her in a state of pregnancy. In a state of perplexity, he rushed to the Sultan to bring the matter to his notice. The latter simply remarked, "that as it was decreed with the connivance of the slave girl, but since the royal offshoot has first seen the light in Malik Hassan's house henceforth he should be his tutor." But after the death of Sultan Muhammad Shah, when Mahmud Shah ascended the throne, the young child Ahmad was believed to be the son of Malik Hasan. See, Burhan-i-Masir (I.A. 1920—pp. 67-8).
   But these stories give no clue to the historical truth, for none of the historical works except the Burhan-i-Masir mention that Ahmad was

the son of Muhammad Shah Bahmani III, whose geneology had been traced by the historians to Bahman, the son of Isfandiyear. In this way Sayyid Ali has tried to conceal the facts under the garb of fiction. Sir Wolseley Haig had rejected his version on the following grounds :—

(i) that Sayyid Ali has cited no authority for the source of his versions, except some unnamed historical work and the oral testimony of some old man.

(ii) that the statement of Burhan Nizam Shah I in his own handwriting is cited by Ferishta, that he was the grand-son of Malik Hasan.

(iii) that there is circumstancial evidence also. In 1518 Burhan Nizam Shah demanded from Alauddin Imad-ul-Mulk of Berar the cession of the town of Pathri in exchange for another district yielding an equal revenue, on the plea that Pathri was his ancesteral home and many of his relations still lived there. Upon the refusal of Imad-ul-Malk, Burhan Nizam Shah I made war against him, annexed and occupied the town and the districts as well.

(iv) that had he been a Prince of the royal house he would have called himself as Bahmani rather than Bahri.

(v) that we know that after the death of Malik Hasan, Sultan Mahmud Shah Bahmani was completely dominated by Qasim Barid and later on by his son Ali Barid, and had Ahmad been a scion of the royal house of Bahman Shah, he must have certainly claimed the throne of his ancestors or at least would have made some claim to the Regency, but he did not.

(vi) that had he been a Prince, he would have commanded due allegiance of Yusuf Adil Khan, or of Imad-ul-Mulk or at least of Qutb-ul-Mulk; but they were all hostile to him.

2. According to Sayyid Ali, when Ahmad assumed independence, his age was only twenty years, which he had underestimated. We know that in 1478 he had been considered sufficiently dangerous to be sent to a distant place from the court, and thus at that time he must have not been less than twenty-five years of age. His father was then at least fifty-five years of age and it is probable that Ahmad was thirty or thirty five or even more so that he was probably now about forty or forty five in 1490. Therefore it seems that he must have been born about the year 1455-56 A.D.

3. Burhan-i-Masir (I. A. 1920) pp. 68.

4. Ibid. pp. 68-9.

5. Ibid, pp. 69 n.

6. Ibid. pp. 69 n; The Bahmanis of the Daccan pp. 321-22.

But Sayyid Ali has misrepresented the circumstances which impelled the Sultan to appoint Malik Ahmad as Malik Hassan's deputy at Rajamundri. According to him, while Ahmad (whom he calls Prince) was living at Mahur and Ramghir, war broke out between Mahmud Shah (It should be Muhammad Shah III) and the Raya of Orissa (whereas it should be Raya of Vijayanagara). The Sultan resolved to put down the Hindus, therefore he set out; but was defeated in a battle, so that he lost all his baggage and also some ladies and female servants of the harem. When Ahmad heard of the defeat and the pursuit of the Sultan, he marched from Mahur, took up his position in a mountain pass, blocked the way of the Hindus, defeated them and put them to flight. The Sultan was over-joyed to hear of the victory. But Ahmad's enemies poisoned the ear's of the Sultan and persuaded him to keep the latter away from the court reminding him of the predictions of the astrologers See, Burhan-i-Masir (I.A. 1920) pp. 69. The story of the defeat of the royal army is incorrect. Besides the author is guilty of having committed other errors. He has confused Sultan Mahmud Shah with Muhammad Shah Bahmani III, and has wrongly mentioned his flight. Moreover at this time (1480) in fact no fight occured with the ruler of Orissa. It was the army stationed at Kondavidu, which had mutinied by joining the inhabitants, putting themselves under the protection of the ruler of Vijayanagara, who enjoyed undisputed sway over the eastern coast of peninsula, south of the river Krishna. The Bahmani Sultan marched against the rebels, laid siege to the fort and forced Narsimha to retire. Soon after the rebels were pardoned. See, The Bahmanis of the Daccan, pp. 330-1.

7. The Bahmanis of the Daccan. pp. 342.
8. The Bahmanis of the Daccan, pp. 361.
9. Ferishta, Briggs III, pp. 190.
10. Burhan-i-Maasir (I.A. 1920) pp. 69-70; Ferishta, Briggs III, pp. 190.
11. Burhan-i-Maasir (I.A. 1920) pp. 70-1; Farishta, Briggs. III, pp. 190; Gribble, A history of the Daccan, pp. 151.
When Ali Balish Dihi (Zain-ul-Abidin), who had been one of the dependants of Mahmud Gawan, and was at this time the governor of the fort of Chakan and its dependencies, heard of the obedience and loyalty of the inhabitants of Junnar towards Malik Ahmad, he was moved by envy and jealousy. He poisoned the ears of the Sultan who summoned the latter to the court. Malik Ahmad marched with his forces to Bidar, where he was favourably received. He was accorded the honour of Istaqbal (reception) which was performed by the officers of the state, the Sayyids, Shaikhs and the learned men. He succeeded in clearing suspicion from the mind of the Sultan, who treated him with much consideration and affection, shovering high honours on him. When the Sultan came to know of the manner in which Ahmad had behaved towards his subjects in Junnar, in consultation with Malik Naib, he appointed him as governor of that place, conferring on him a robe and the title of Nizam-ul-Mulk. It was ordered that any fort which he would conquer from the hands of the Hindus will be added to his jageers.
12. The Bahmanis of the Daccan, pp. 363-64.
Sayyid Ali gives a different account. According to him the amirs of the kingdom, with the real object of breaking into open rebellion, assembled together and marched against the capital Bidar. The Sultan in all perplexity summoned Malik Ahmad to his assistance. The latter immediately marched towards Bidar. On his arrival, he presented a peshkash to the Sultan consisting of rich clothes, merchandise, horses and elephants etc. Thereafter the Sultan entrusted to him the duty of supressing the rebellion. Malik Ahmad fought the rebels valiantly and drove them away from the capital. See, Burhan-i-Maasir (I.A. 1920), pp. 85.
13. Burhan-i-Maasir (I.A. 1920) pp. 85.
14. Ferishta, Briggs, III, pp. 191; A history of the Marathas, Vol. I, pp. 73; Gribble, A history of the Daccan, pp. 151.
Sayyid Ali has failed to appreciate the object of these campaigns which Malik Ahmad undertook. He says that, "Prince (Ahmad) was ever desirous of raising the standard of Islam and propagating the Faith and Sacred Law of Muhammad, by engaging in a holy war and stamping out strife and wickedness of the infidels without faith and righteousness and the most of the forts of the Konkan and hilly country of the Daccan were in the hands of the polytheists and idolators", See, Burhan-i-Maasir (I.A. 1920) pp. 71.
15. Ferishta Briggs, III, pp. 191; Tabqat-i-Akbari, III, pp. 68.
16. Burhan-i-Maasir (I.A. 1920) pp. 71-3; Ferishta, Briggs. III, pp. 191.
17. Shivneri is the hill fort of the town of Junnar, situated in $19^0$ 12′ N and $73^0$ 52′ E.
18. Lohgarh is a fort of some antiquity and importance, situated in $18^0$ 42′ N and $73^0$ 29′ E. The fort was used as state prison by the Nizam Shahi kings.
19. The fort of Tung is situated five miles to the south-west of Lohgarh.

20. The fort of Nikona is situated twelve miles south-east of Lohgarh.
21. The fort of Kondhana is situated 18° 22′ and 73° 45′ E.
22. The hill fort is situated in 18° 17′ N and 73° 57′ E.
23. A fort situated fifteen miles south-west of Lohgarh.
24. About thirteen miles north-west of Junnar.
25. About twelve miles south of Poona.
26. A fort about forty seven miles south-west of Junnar.
27. The hill fort of Mahauli is situated forty miles west by north of Poona.
28. "The fortress of Dandarajpuri is situated on the shores of the Indian ocean, waters of which roll on the two sides of it. It is approached on the third side by a road across the dry land, but in front of this road runs a deep and artificial ditch connecting the two branches of the Sea. The ramparts and bastions of the fort are of stones and are very high". See. Burhan-i-Maasir (I.A. 1920) pp. 74.
Danda and Rajpuri are the two forts standing on either bank of the Rajpuri creek on an island at the entrance of which now stand the fort and village of Janjira, situated in 18° 18' and 73° East, forty four miles south of Bombay island.
29. Burhan-i-Maasir (I.A. 1920) pp. 71-4; Ferishta, Briggs. III, pp. 191.
30. Burhan-i-Maasir (I.A. 1920) pp. 74; A History of the Marathas Vol. I, pp. 73.
31. According to Sayyid Ali after occupying the fort of Dandarajpuri, Ahmad returned to Junnar, from where he sent to the Sultan a report of his victories together with offerings from spoil, whereupon the latter sent him a robe of honour and a jewelled waist-belt, through a messenger and bestowed on him in Jageer, all the forts which he had captured. See, Burhan-i-Maasir (I.A. 1920) pp. 74.
32. Cambridge History of India, III, pp. 424.
33. Ibid, pp. 424.
34. Ferishta Briggs. III, pp. 191-2; Gribble, A history of the Daccan, pp. 151; According to Burhan-i-Maasir, Ahmad was sent away by the Sultan to pacify the Konkan territory. See (I.A. 1920) pp. 70-74.
35. Muntakhab-ul-Lubab, III, pp. 143.
36. Muntakhab-ul-Lubab, III, pp. 143; The Bahmanis of the Daccan, pp. 368.
37. Ferishta, Briggs. III, ppl 192; The Bahmanis of the Daccan, pp. 369.
38. Burhan-i-Maasir (I.A. 1920) pp. 74; Ferishta Briggs, III, pp. 192.
39. Muntakhab-ul-Lubab, III, pp. 143; The Bahmanis of the Daccan, pp. 369.
40. Ferishta, Briggs, III, pp. 192; Mutakhab-ul-Lubab, III, pp. 144 The Bahmanis of the Daccan, ppl 369.
41. Gribble has mentioned his name as Nadir-ul-Zaman, see pp. 151.
42. Ferishta, Briggs, III. pp. 193; Burhan-i-Maasir (I.A. 1920) pp. 86-7.
43. Ferishta, Briggs, III, pp. 192; Muntakhab-ul-Lubab, III, pp. 144; The Bahmanis of the Daccan, pp. 369.
44. Ferishta, Briggs, III, pp. 193; Muntakhab-ul-Lubab, III, pp. 144; The Bahmanis of the Daccan, pp. 369.
45. Ferishta, Briggs, III, pp. 193.
46. Burhan-i-Maasir (I.A. 1920) pp. 87; Ferishta, Briggs. III, pp. 193.
47. Burhan-i-Maasir (I.A. 1920) pp. 88; Ferishta, Briggs. III, pp. 193.
48. Burhan-i-Maasir (I.A. 1920) pp. 88; Ferishta, Briggs. III, pp. 194.
49. Burhan-i-Maasir (I.A. 1920) pp. 88; Ferishta, Briggs. III, pp. 194.
50. Burhan-i-Maasir (I.A. 1920) pp. 88; Ferishta, Briggs, III, pp. 194.
51. Burhan-i-Maasir (I.A. 1920) pp. 88; Ferishta, Briggs. III, pp. 14; Gribble, A History of the Daccan, pp. 151; The Bahmanis of the Daccan, pp. 369.
52. Ferishta, Briggs. III, pp. 194; Khafi Khan has confused the sequence of events. He mentions this campaign, while narrating the conquest of Daultabad—see, Muntakhab-ul-Lubab, III, pp. 146-47

53. Ferishta, Briggs. III, pp. 194; The Bahmanis of the Daccan pp. 370; Gribble, A History of the Daccan, pp. 151.
Sayyid Ali wrongly says that Yusuf Adil Khan took the field against Malik Ahmad on this occassion. Moreover, he gives an entirely different account of the whole affair. According to him, Sultan Mahmud Shah sent 18 ministers with a large army against Malik Ahmad. Ali Talish Dihi (Zain-ul-Abidin) also came from the fort of Chakan to assist them. The royal army encamped near Wagaon and Malik Ahmad's forces were also there. Some nobles were sent with the advance guard of the army to deal with Malik Ahmad, but the latter sent Rumi Khan and Chalak Khan to repulse them. These officers overcame the advanced guard of the royal army, slew many of them and captured three elephants. Next day, Ahmad marched from Wagaon to Kopan, where his spies reported that the royal army was engaged in drinking and merriment and in their pride had even forgotten to take the military precautions against the enemy. Accordingly Ahmad marched at mid-night with his army to attack the nobles and with Ali Talish Dihi fell upon them, before morning broke. The amirs were captured and stripped to the waist and were then mounted on buffaloes and paraded in the army. After this they were allowed to go. Malik Ahmad highly honoured Ali Talish and conferred on him the fortress of Chakan. Later, Ahmad asked for the hand of his daughter in marriage, but Ali Talish put him off with excuses. Malik Ahmad then led an army against him, captured the fort, put Ali Talish and principal officers to death, but laid no hands on his daughter.
Burhan-i-Maasir (I.A. 1920) pp. 89.
It seems that Sayyid Ali has confused the whole account by piecing together all the conflicting versions he could find, of a campaign, and has thus offered different accounts of the same.
54. Ferishta, Briggs. III, pp. 195; Muntakhab-ul-Lubab III, pp. 146.
55. Ferishta, Briggs. III, pp. 195; Khafi Khan has mentioned this campaign after the declaration of independence by Malik Ahmad—see, Muntakhab-ul-Lubab III, pp. 146.
56. Ferishta, Briggs. III, pp. 195; Muntakhab-ul-Lubab, III, pp. 146-47.
57. Ferishta, Briggs, III, pp. 195; Muntakhab-ul-Lubab, III, pp. 146-47.
58. Ferishta, Briggs. III, pp. 195; Muntakhab-ul-Lubab, III, pp. 147.
59. Ferishta, Briggs. III, pp. 196; Muntakhab-ul-Lubab, III, pp. 147.
60. Ferishta, Briggs. III, pp. 196; Muntakhab-ul-Lubab III, pp. 147.
61. Ferishta, Briggs. III, pp. 196; Muntakhab-ul-Lubab III, pp. 147.
62. Ferishta, Briggs. III, pp. 196; Muntakhab-ul-Lubab, III, pp. 147.
63. Ferishta, Briggs. III, pp. 196; Muntakhab-ul-Lubab, III, pp. 147.
64. Ferishta, Briggs. III, pp. 196; Muntakhab-ul-Lubab, III, pp. 147.
65. Ferishta, Briggs. III, pp. 196; Muntakhab-ul-Lubab, III, pp. 148.
Sayyid Ali gives another version, which materially differs from Ferishta, who gives the entire credit to Malik Ahmad. According to Sayyid Ali, Ahmad halted at Parenda. He sent for Jalal Rumi Khan to tell him that the Bahmani forces had been weakened; for one detachment had gone to escort the harem, while the other was tired because of the forced march from Bidar. And he asked him to keep the enemy engaged till he had secured his own position. To entice away the imperialists Ahmad feigned retreat from Parenda and the enemy in hot pursuit of him advanced. When the royal army arrived near Alat river, which flows near Parenda, it halted there to await the reappearance of Ahmad Nizam-ul-Mulk. When the latter was not to be seen, they gave themselves to drinking and feasting, unmindful of Jalal Rumi Khan's presence in the fort of Parenda. When the night had far advanced, Jalal Rumi Khan assembled his troops and swooped down upon the sleeping enemy. Many of them were slain and eighteen amirs were taken prisoner. They were sent to Ahmad's camp. see—Burhan-i-Maasir (I.A. 1920) pp. 102-3.

66. Ferishta, Briggs. III, pp. 197; Muntakhab-ul-Lubab III, pp. 148.
67. Ferishta, Briggs. III, pp. 197; Muntakhab-ul-Lubab III, pp. 148.
68. Ferishta, Briggs. III, pp. 197; Muntakhab-ul-Lubab III, pp. 148; Kincaid had mentioned 28th May 1490 A.D.—see, A History of the Maratha People, pp. 88-89.
69. Ferishta, Briggs. III, pp. 197; Muntakhab-ul-Lubab, III, pp. 148; The Bahmanis of the Daccan, pp. 370.
70. Ferishta, Briggs. III, pp. 197; Muntakhab-ul-Lubab III, pp. 149 Gribble, A History of the Daccan, pp. 152;. A History of the Maratha People, pp. 88-89.
71. Ferishta, Briggs. III, pp. 197; Muntakhab-ul-Lubab, III, pp. 148.
72. (a) Burhan-i-Maasir (I.A 1920) pp. 105; Ferishta, Briggs. III pp. 198; Dalpat Rai, the author of Narsimha-prasad (which was written about the year 1499 A.D.) mentions Ahmad with him royal title of "Shah" in the following conplet :—

"दिल्ली शाधुपरिः समभव न्नैजाम साहो महान्"

(b) See. Prof. H.K. Sherwani's article, "Independence of the Bahmani governors;" published in the proceedings of Indian History Congress, Session 1945. pp. 159; The Bahmanis of the Daccan, pp. 391-93.
(c) Referring to the dismemberment of the Bahmani Kingdom, John Frayer an English traveller, who visited India in 1673, remarks, "as far as back the time of Ramras (Ram Raya) about two hundred and fifty years ago, the sole monarch of India intra Gangem, and the last Emperor that was Gentile, nourished three slaves that were Chias Moore and advanced them to the principal employ both of court and Empire to wit, Cutube Can (Qutub Khan) Master of hunt; Nitam Maluka (his chief treasurer) Adul Can (Adil Khan) Cutwal or High constable; from these officers they rose to be commanders of greatest provinces in the Realm with as Absolute power and authority as would be transferred on subjects being kings; only wanting the appellation. The first Baganaga now Golkunda; the second of Dawltabad Alead and all the country from Gujarat to Bengal and great part of the Daccan with all the continent on this side of the Ghats, till it conclude in the cape of Comora. Thus they were seated and by the sequel not minded to be dismounted; wherefore they jointly combined against their supreme master; whilst he too credulously relied on their fidelity and ousted him; and so many of his Heathen nobles only such as were befriended by strong Gurrs or Fastness upon the mountains, who are those that retain the name of Rajas to this day; who are still not with standing so numerous, that would they stand up unanimously for their ancient freedom, the Mohemetans could not stand in competition with their idolaterous tribe. After the conspiracy every one be took himself to the government then being no more to possess themselves of; the imprudent king having given all away even his person, which they scrupled not to rotate. Extinguishing the very lineage or leaving them so defencible, that they are only said to be pretty Rajaship in the plain and thereby easily prevented to aspire to their lawful sovereignity; the supremacy being established in their own hands and shared to their mutual conteste; they took upon without control of Regal dignity, title of Pedeshwas and exercised their functions very amicably some years and so long they kept themselves safe enough from the Mughals, who began to make inroads into the country, without any notable success, till they had found means to make them break with Nisam Shaw, who maintained the frontiers against them; for all that he was beset before and abandoned behind he held them play a long while................." see, "A new account of East India and Persia", pp. 48-49; Also, see, "The Voyage of John Huyhen Van Linschoten to East Indies", Vol. I, pp. 165-174.
73. Burhan-i-Maasir (I.A. 1920) pp. 105; Muntakhab-ul-Lubab III, pp. 145; According to Ferishta he renewed the siege of Daudarajpuri—Briggs. III, pp. 198-199.

74. Ferishta, Briggs. III, pp. 199-200; Burhan-i-Maasir (I.A. 1920) pp. 107; Muntakhab-ul-Lubab, III, pp. 145.
75. Ferishta, Briggs. III, pp. 199-200; Muntakhab-ul-Lubab, III, pp. 145; Burhan-i-Maasir (I.A. 1920) pp. 107; Gribble, A History of the Daccan", pp. 153.
76. Burhan-i-Maasir (I.A. 1920) pp. 107; Ferishta, Briggs. III, pp. 200; Muntakhab-ul-Lubab III, pp. 145.
77. Ferishta, Briggs. III, pp. 200; The Bahmanis of the Daccan, pp. 371-72.
(a) Ferishta, Briggs. III, pp. 200; Muntakhab-ul-Lubab, III, pp. 145.
(b) Ferishta, Briggs. III, pp. 200; Muntakhab-ul-Lubab III, pp. 145.
78. Burhan-i-Maasir (I.A. 1920) pp. 107; Muntakhab-ul-Lubab, III, pp. 148.
79. Burhan-i-Maasir (I.A. 1920) pp. 107; Ferishta, Briggs. III, pp. 200 201; Muntakhab-ul-Lubab, III, pp. 148.
80. The Bahmanis of the Daccan pp. 372-76.
81. Ahmadnagar is in north latitude 19° 40′ and East longitude 70° 40′ and is situated in the plains of the river Sena, about 12 miles from its source and on its left bank. The city is surrounded by an earthen wall about 12 ft. high having numerous bastions and 9 gates. See, Imperial Guzetteer, pp. 76-86.
82. Sayyid Ali has also related a story about the foundation of the city of Ahmadnagar. He says that Ahmad was very fond of hunting. One day he saw a fox in the plain, on which Ahmadnagar now stands and ordered that hounds should be let loose after it. The fox tried to save itself, but when it became impossible, it turned round and began to face the hounds. The scene astonished Ahmad Nizam Shah, who decided to found a new city on that spot. When the question of naming the city came up, Ahmad named it after himself. It was a strange coincidence that the name of his wazir and Qazi was the same. see, Burhan-i-Maasir (I.A. 1920) pp. 108; Ferishta, Briggs. III, pp. 153; Tabqat-i-Akbari III, pp. 68; Gribble, A History of the Daccan, pp. 153; Wondors of Ellora, pp. 520-21.
83. The Bahmanis of the Daccan pp. 377.
84. Ibid pp. 377.
85. Sayyid Ali gives a very cursory account of the capture of the Daultabad fort. According to him, "when some years passed in this manner, most of the cultivators and labourers of that country were reduced to sore straits by want of food and by the attacks of the royal army and every day bands of men from the fort, girded by divine grace into the path of the wisdom, truth and righteousness, used to desert the fort and came to royal court, where, when their affairs were bettered and they lived free from the anxieties of the times and under king's protection, those misguided fools who turned their backs on the good fortunes and sought no refuge at the court had their recompense from the world consuming." Burhan-i-Maasir (I.A. 1920) pp. 123.
86. Ferishta, Briggs. III, pp. 201; Muntakhab-ul-Lubab, III, pp. 149.
87. Ferishta, Briggs. III, pp. 201; Muntakhab-ul-Lubab, III, pp. 149.
88. Ferishta, Briggs. III, pp. 201; Muntakhab-ul-Lubab, III, pp. 149.
89. Ferishta, Briggs. III, pp. 201; Muntakhab-ul-Lubab, III, pp. 149.
90. Ferishta, Briggs. III, pp. 202; Muntakhab-ul-Lubab, III, pp. 149.
91. Ferishta, Briggs. III, pp. 202; Muntakhab-ul-Lubab, III, pp. 149.
92. Ferishta, Briggs. III, pp. 202; Muntakhab-ul-Lubab, III, pp. 149.
93. Ferishta, Briggs. III, pp. 202; Muntakhab-ul-Lubab, III, pp. 149.
94. Ferishta, Briggs, III, pp. 203-3; Muntakhab-ul-Lubab, III, pp. 148-52.
95. Ferishta, Briggs. III, pp. 203; Muntakhab-ul-Lubab, III, pp. 153; Mahmud Gawan, pp. 210.
66. Ferishta, Briggs. III, pp. 203; Muntakhab-ul-Lubab, III, pp. 153; Mahmud Gawan, pp. 210.

97. Ferishta. Briggs. III, pp. 203; Muntakhab-ul-Lubab, III, pp. 153; Mahmud Gawan, pp. 210.
98. Ferishta, Briggs. III, pp. 203; Muntakhab-ul-Lubab, III, pp. 153; Mahmud Gawan, pp. 210.
99. Ferishta, Briggs. III, pp. 204; Muntakhab-ul-Lubab, III, pp. 153.
100. Khafi Khan attributes Ashraf's death with greater probability to poison. See—Muntakhab-ul-Lubab III, pp. 154.
101. Ferishta, Briggs. III, pp. 204; Muntakhab-ul-Lubab, III, pp. 154. After the conquest of the fort, Dalpat Rai, the author of Narsimha-prasada, calls his patron Ahmad Nizam Shah as "देव गिरि पूर्ण धीशवर:"
102. Ferishta, Briggs. III, pp. 204; Muntakhab-ul-Lubab III, pp. 154; Mahmud Gawan, pp. 210.
103. The Bahmanis of the Daccan, pp. 377-78.
104. Khandesh is situated in the valley of the river Tapti, bounded on the north by the Vindhya, and Satpura ranges and in the south by the Daccan plateau, in the east by Berar and in the west by the province of Gujarat. It was formerly a part of Muhammad Tughlaq's empire and continued to be a feudatory of Delhi during the reign of Firoz Shah Tughlaq, who entrusted it to the care of Malik Raja Faruqi in 1370 A.D. After the death of Firoz when the Delhi empire broke up, Malik a man of ambition, in possession of a fertile province far from the capital, declared his independence and laid the foundations of an independent kingdom. Once his ambitions brought him in canflict with the ruler of Gujarat, but at last peace was concluded between them. He died in 1397 A.D. and was succeeded by his son Malik Nasir, who died in 1494 A. D. leaving to his successors a unit.d Khandesh.
105. Alam Khan is said to have been a scion of the Faruqi family, born of the daughter of Ahmad Nizam Shah. See, Bird's History of Gujarat, pp. 246 (n).
106. T.W. Haig, "The Faruqi Dynasty of Khandesh." (I.A. 1918) pp. 121; Ferishta, Briggs. III, pp. 204-5; Commassariat, "The History of Gujarat", pp. 205.

Sayyid Ali gives a different account of the whole affair. According to him after the death of Adil Khan Faruqi, Muhmud Shah succeeded to the throne. In those days there were friendly relations between the ruler of Gujarat and the ruler of Khandesh. The former being puffed up with pride was much enraged when he heard that the ruler of Khandesh had styled himself Shah. He summoned his officers, told him "what power has the ruler of Burhanpur to make himself a partner in our name and title and compare himself with us?" At this time the brother of Mahmud Shah, the king of Khandesh sent letters to the Sultan of Gujarat professing obedience and soliciting friendship, holding out the promise that whenever the army of Gujarat would invade his brother's country, he would cause the fortress of Asir to be surrendered to him. The Sultan of Gujarat thinking it a good opportunity to annex the kingdom set out with a force towards Asir and Burhanpur. When the ruler of Burhanpur heard this he appealed is to Ahmad Nizam Shah for assistance, complaining of the high-handedness of the ruler of Gujarat. Ahmad Nizam Shah upon receiving the letter refrained from taking advice from his minister Nasir-ul-Mulk, for he was doubtful if he would ever support him in his designs against the ruler of Gujarat, to which country he belonged. But Nasir-ul-Malik got an inkling of the matter and indirectly pointed out to his master the danger that lay ahead in the undertaking. But Ahmad Nizam Shah paid not need to his warning. Ahmad Nizam Shah marched to Burhanpur and encamped there. Nasir-ul-Mulk tried to allay the strife by checking out plans so that no harm should come to the country. Accordingly, he decided to open negotiations with one of the trusted officers of the Gujarati Sultan

in order to bring about a peaceful solution. But before the letter could reach the Sultan of Gujarat, Ahmad Nizam Shah with the help of one of his Mahauts won over the Gujarati Mahawat who held the charge of Biri Sal the biggest and the strongest of the elephants in the stable of the Gujarati army. He promised to let loose Biri Sal at the dead of the night when the Sultan and his men were sleeping. The Mahawats began to plunder the camp. In the confusion so caused they thought that Ahmad Nizam Shah had delivered a surprise attack. Sultan Mahmud Shah, the ruler of Gujarat and his army abandoned their camp and fled; they did not halt until they had covered a distance of nearly twenty miles. Next day Ahmad received the news of their flight, he came from Burhanpur and tookup his position at the place where the Sultan of Gujarat had encamped. Meanwhile the Sultan of Gujarat received the letter of Nasir-ul-Mulk to which he replied asking him to request his master to withdraw, and thereupon he too will retire to his country. At last it was agreed that the Gujaratis should first march two stages towards Ider whereupon the Daccani army would also march two stages towards Imad-ul-Mulk's country. When proposal was accepted and the Gujaratis first marched towards Ider and then the Daccanis too withdrew two stages and thence retreated towards their homeward journey. See, Burhan-i-Maasir (I.A. 1920) pp. 124-5.
In this account Sayyid Ali has committed two errors; firstly, that there was no such person as Mahmud Shah, the king of Khandesh but Daud Khan, who had succeeded his brother Adil Khan Faruqi II; secondly, that he has mixed up this account with the one which is connected with Ahmad Nizam Shah's siege of Daultabad.

107. Ferishta, Brigg. II, pp. 204-5; According Zafar-ul-Walih, Ghazni Khan had been poisoned during the life time of his father. It is said that Ghazni Khan never actually reigned and almost immediately after the death of Daud, Ahmad Nizam ul-Mulk reappeared in Khandesh with his protege Alam Khan.

108. Ferishta, Briggs. III, pp. 205.

109. Ibid, pp. 205.

110. Ferishta, Briggs. III, pp. 205; Mirat-i-Sikandari, pp. 76-77; T.W. Haig, "The Faruqi Dynasty of Khandesh" (I.A. 1918) pp. 121; Bird's, History of Gujarat" pp. 216-17; Beylay, "The History of the Muhamadan Dynasties" pp. 224-25; Commissariat, "A History of Gujarat" pp.305-6.

111. Ferishta, Briggs. III, pp. 205; T.W. Haig, "The Faruqi Dynasty of Khandesh (I.A. 1918) pp. 122.

112. Ferishta, Briggs. III, pp. 206; Burhan-i-Maasir (I.A. 1920) pp. 128; Mantakhab-ul-Lubab III, pp. 156; According to some historians Ahmad Nizam Shah predeceased Malik Nasir-ul-Mulk who poisoned him in a quid of betel leaf and the latter was executed for his treason.

113. Ferishta, has given 1508 as the date of Ahmad's death. Burhan-i-Maasir records 1505 A.D.; Duff's "The Chronology of India from the earliest times to the beginning of the 16th Cen.", mentions 1508; James Burges also mentions 1508; Beale in his "Dictionary of the Oriental Biography", also gives 1508 as the date of Ahmad's death; Ferishta mentions that Ahmad successfully intervened in the quarrel between Yusuf Adil Khan and Dastur Dinar, which took place in the last part of 1509 which means that Ahmad lived up to the end of 1509. But a letter of Affenso de Albuquerque, the Portuguese Viceroy in India to the king of Portugal dated 15th Oct. 1510 A.D. makes reference to Ahmad Nizam Shah, which shows that he must have lived up to the month of Oct. 1510 A.D. See, V.S. Bendre's article, "Death of Ahmad Nizam Shah I," New Indian Antiquary 1941, pp. 242.

114. Burhan-i-Maasir (I.A1920) pp. 157; Ferishta, Briggs. III pp. 206; Muntakhab-ul-Lubab III, pp. 166.

115. Burhan-i-Maasir (I.A. 1920) pp. 157; Ferishta, Briggs. III, pp. 206; Muntakhab-ul-Lubab III, pp. 156.

116. Burhan-i-Maasir (I.A. 1920) pp. 157.
117. Ibid pp. 157.
118. Ferishta, Briggs. III pp. 207; Muntakhab-ul-Lubab III, pp. 157-58.
119. Ferishta, Briggs. III, pp. 207; Muntakhab-ul-Lubab, III, pp. 157-58.
120. Ferishta, Briggs. III, pp. 207; Muntakhab-ul-Lubab, III, pp. 157-58.
121. Ferishta, tells us that he had been an eye witness·to such duels and mentions that on one occassion six grey beared men were killed in one of the streets of Bijapur. He condemns the custom calling it, "abominable". Ferishta, Briggs. III, PP. 208-9; Muntakhab-ul-Lubab III, pp. 158.

CHAPTER III

## BURHAN NIZAM SHAH I (1510-1553 A.D.)

The speedy conquests and the stormy life of Ahmad Nizam Shah had no doubt given birth to the small kingdom of Ahmadnagar, but consolidation was still far away from its horizon. A few of his contemporaries with whom he had measured his dazzling sword, were still in the field, perhaps not to allow respite to his son and successor Burhan Nizam Shah I. Thus it was left to the latter to increase the territorial limits of his infant kingdom, to consolidate it; to make it so strong so that it may bear every onslaught of the enemy, and to promote the cultural traditions of the land. With an steady eye on his constructive plans, Burhan Nizam Shah never hesitated to bow before the storm, but no sooner did it pass away, he would stand aga in inall his vigour and vitality and resplendent with glory and greatness.

**Burhan Nizam Shah ascends the throne**

Al Muwayyad Min-ud-daullah Abul-Muzaffar Burhan Nizam Shah, succeeded his father at the age of seven in 1510 A.D.[1] Mukammal Khan Daccani who had the posts of Wakil and Amir Jumla during the time of Ahmad Nizam Shah was confirmed in them. His son Mian Jamâluddin was honoured with the title of Aziz-ul-Mulk and the office of Sar-i-Naubat was assigned to him.[2] Within a short time, both father and son taking advantage of the minority of Burhan Nizam, gathered all power in their hands, obtaining control of the royal household. Mukammal Khan is said to have begun to govern the kingdom like an independent king, exercising authority over all the affairs of the government.[3] In the early period of the regency much attention was paid to the education of the child Burhan. In his tenth year, it is related that he could read poetry with facility and could write exceedingly well.[4]

Nearly three years had now elapsed since the dominence of the Daccani minister. The harsh behaviour of his son Aziz-ul-Mulk joined to his vanity and insolence became intolerable to a section of nobility, headed by the foreign leaders like Rumi Khan Arabi, Karim Khan, Munir Khan, and Qadam Khan, who had served Ahmad Nizam Shah with loyalty and devotion.

They formed a plan of removing Burhan Nizam Shah from the throne and placing on it his brother Rajaji instead. But their conspiracy failed, and they had to flee with eight thousand horse towards Berar where they sought protection with Alauddin Imad-ul-mulk.[5]

From Berar, these refuge nobles, under the leadership of Rumi Khan made every possible effort to stir up strife in Ahmadnagar.[6] They instigated Alauddin Imad-ul-Mulk to invade the Nizam Shahi country, on the pretext of the minority of Burhan, the dominance of Mukammal Khan and the hateful behaviour of his son towards the masses, and the prevailing discontentment among all sections of society.[7] They painted to him a picture of thundering success in the enterprise. Beguiled by their sweet words, Imad-ul-Mulk who had stood in good relations with Ahmad Nizam Shah, now collected his troops from all parts of his country, and marched from Elichpur to open an era of constant warfare.[8] But the regent Mukammal Khan rose equal to the occassion. He summoned his men and despatched them towards Berar to intercept the advance of the enemy. Taking with him the army of Khwaja Jahan of Parenda and the young Burhan, the regent marched towards Bir, and encamped near the town of Ranubari.[9] The following morning the rival armies drew up in the full battle array.[10] Mukammal Khan disposed his army into two divisions; the first under the command of Mian Kala Azdar Khan, who was ordered to protect the person of infant Burhan.[11] He placed Burhan in front, tied a belt round his waist and fastened the belt with that of own, so that he may fight with ease. Mukammal Khan himself commanded the second division.[12] Imad-ul-Mulk also arranged his army in the same way. A fierce battle ensued. In the thick of the fight, two of the fiercest elephants of Burhan namely, Barkhurdar and Buzurgwar, were led by their Mahawats to the neighbouring river to give them a drink. By chance they began to fight each other. They ran towards the enemy in full heat. Precisely at this moment the Nizam Shahi army delivered a fierce attack on the Imad-ul-Mulk's forces. Confusion began to rage among the rank and file of the enemy. The nobles who had brought Imad-ul-Mulk into the field deserted him. Imad-ul-Mulk himself fled from

**Battle of Rahauri (1510-11 A.D.)**

the field and did not take breath until he had reached Elichpur. He was hotly pursued by the Nizam Shahi forces who seized his horses, elephants and the entire camp equippage,[13] compelling him to take refuge with Adil Khan Faruqi III, the ruler of Khandesh. He importuned the Faruqi ruler for mediation and for restoring peace between him and Burhan Nizam. At his intervention, peace was concluded between Imad-ul-Mulk and Burhan, after which they retired to their respective capitals.[14]

Though for all practical purposes the Bahmani Kingdom had ceased to exist, but it had become extinct. The provincial governors had declared themselves autonomous; yet they continued to profess loyalty to the throne. In 1514 A.D. Ali Barid the protector of the Sultan, conferred the title of Dastur-ul-Mulk on Jahangir Khan the son of Dastur Dinar and appointed him governor of Gulbarga with the ostensible object of preventing Ismail Adil Khan the successor of Yusuf Adil Khan from molesting him but with the real intention of crushing the power of Bijapur. Ali Barid in the name of the feeble Sultan Mahmud Shah Bahmani formed a confederacy consisting of Sultan Quli Qutb-ul-Mulk, the governor of Telingana and Burhan Nizam, and launched an attack on Bijapur. Ismail Adil Khan inflicted a crushing defeat upon the allies, captured Sultan Mahmud Shah and his son Prince Ahmad. He treated the royal prisoners with courtsey. He handed over Bibi Satti to her husband Prince Ahmad and appointed five thousand horsemen to escort the Sultan honourably to Bidar. Upon the approach of this force, Ali Barid in sheer fright fled to Ausa, but soon after he returned to Bidar again and obtained control of the person of the Sultan with the assistance of Burhan Nizam, and compelled the Bijapuri cavalry to retire.[15]

The helpless Bahmani Sultan, deprived of power and devoid of prestige, now made a frantic effort to free himself from the thraldom of Ali Barid, who had reduced him to a mere cypher. He fled and took refuge with Imad-ul-Mulk, who marched against Ali Barid. But the latter cleverly enlisted the support of Burhan Nizam Shah. The two advanced to meet Imad-ul-Mulk in the field. Before the battle started Imad-ul-Mulk sent word to Sultan Mahmud Shah, requested him to be by his side because he was fighting for him. The message was delivered to the Sultan while he was taking his bath. In sheer fright he quickly dressed himself, but instead of marching to assist his ally, he rode towards Ali Barid's camp and joined him. Naturally Imad-ul-Mulk had to abandon the struggle and to retire from the field of battle, after having been befooled by the Sultan.[16]

Imad-ul-Mulk rightly concluded that Burhan was the main prop of the strength of Ali Barid. Therefore, he decided first to make an end of him and then deal with Ali Barid. The rival forces joined issues twice; once at Boregaon[17] and then near the Deonati river,[18] but on each occasion they withdrew to their respective capitals without gaining any decisive results. Burhan Nizam Shah having grown weary of the struggle with Imad-ul-Mulk opened a vigorous offensive against him. He marched from Ahmadnagar, gave him a severe defeat at the village of Veloran,[19] put him to flight and pursued him for a considerable distance. Imad-ul-Mulk instead of going to his capital at Elichpur, went to take refuge with the ruler of Gujarat.[20]

Soon after there arrived the message of the inhabitants of Pathri, requesting Burhan Nizam Shah to take possession of the town. His recent successes against Imad-ul-Mulk encouraged him to take the forward step in this direction, with the ultimate object of annexing Berar. Accordingly, at his instance, his minister Mukammal Khan opened negotiations with Imad-ul-Mulk asking him to cede the district of Pathri, adding that, he had every right to annex it; firstly, because that it lay close to the frontiers of his territory and secondly, because it was the ancestoral home of his master. He also promised to give in exchange to Imad-ul-Mulk some other district yielding equal revenue. But the latter refused to comply with the demand and in fear of his own safety, he begun to construct a fort there. Mukammal Khan remonstrated with him, and warned him that his action would further embitter the relations between the two rulers. But Alauddin Imad-ul-Mulk was obdurate and he continued his operations. One day, Mukammal Khan taking Burhan and some light cavalry with him left the capital on the pretext of a pleasure trip to the caves of Ellora and Ajanta. He arrived at Pathri, surrounded the fort and opened its siege. The garrison made strenuous efforts to defend it, but could not resist the invaders for long. Batteries were set up against the fort and a breach was made in the

**Annexation of Pathri (1520 A.D.)**

wall. The assailants entered the fort from all sides, put the whole garrison to the sword and occupied it. This was followed by the occupation of the whole district. Thus Pathri was annexed to the kingdom of Ahmadnagar. Muhammad Khan, who had shown great valour on this occassion was appointed to hold charge of the newly conquered district and was honoured with the title of Kamil Khan.[21]

Early in his youth Burhan Nizam Shah fell in love with a dancing girl, name Ameena, married her and placed her above other ladies of the royal seraglio.[22] Her enchanting love, wild passion and bewitching beauty led the young Burhan to drink the purple wine and to engross himself in all sorts of pleasures, and enjoyments. To extricate his master from the clutches of a women, and to remind him of the responsibilities towards his people Mukammal Khan, who had grown old, requested Burhan Nizam Shah to take the reins of administration into his own hands, because he had now attained the age of discreation and was capable enough to rule the country.[23] Burhan who had been on the look out for an opportunity to free himself from the dominance of his old minister, accepted his resignation,[24] raising his worthless son Aziz-ul-Mulk to this post of honour and responsibility.[25] Mukammal Khan for some time led a retired life after which he died.

Arrogant, unscruplous and turbulent as he was, the new minister opened his regime with tyranny and injustice. The young sovereign, who passed his time in drinking, hardly ever looked to the affairs of the state, which gave an opportunity to the minister Aziz-ul-Mulk to gather power into his own hands and to entertain vain hope of assuming an autonomous position like the other nobles of the Bahmani Kingdom.[26] To implement these designs, he gradually removed all the close attendants of Burhan except three eunuchs and old nurses, who had served the latter's father. He went to the length of making an attempt at the life of Burhan by administering poison to him, by mixing it with milk which he was fond of drinking. Fortunately, the suspicion of the wet nurses was roused and they gave a little of the milk to an animal, which died forthwith. Thus they succeeded in saving the life of their master. Within a short time Burhan and his nobles became sick of the prime minister's arrogance and they began to look eagerly for the time when his downfall would occur. At this stage Jai Singh Ji Dannaya, the governor of the fort of Antur arrived at the court to pay his respects to his liege lord. He was fully acquained with the state affairs in Ahmadnagar. He suggested to Burhan a plan to bring about the fall of that minister. According to it he was to be allowed to retire to his charge, where he would feign rebellion. He would inveigle Aziz-ul-Mulk into a trap, if the latter was sent to put him down. As planned Jai Singh ji Danayya left Ahmadnagar, and after his arrival at Antur, he unfurled the banner of revolt. But Aziz-ul-Mulk instead of heading the campaign against him personally, sent his brother Jahangir Khan to suppress the outbreak. When Jahangir Khan arrived near the fort, Jai Singh withdrew his men from the walls and bastions and let the imperial commander advance within striking distance. Then he suddenly opened fire upon the army of Jahangir Khan. It broke up and took to flight. Now Jai Singh's sons emerged out of the fort, pursued the fugitive and made him prisoner. He was paraded in the army and there after his nose was cut off, and then he was allowed to return to Ahmadnagar.[27]

**Fall of Aziz-ul-Mulk**

When Aziz-ul-Mulk heard the fate of his brother and of the disgrace and disaster which had befallen on the royal forces, his anger knew no bounds. Now he himself marched to suppress the rebellion. While he was on the way to Antur, the advisors of Burhan Nizam Shah suggested to him to recall from exile such nobles as had fled in fear of Aziz-ul-Mulk's power and dominance. They hastened to meet Burhan, but before they could arrive the latter entered the camp of his prime minister, seized him by the neck and blinded him with red hot iron. Thus ended the hateful and intolerable regime of Aziz-ul-Mulk. Burhan Nizam now took the whole administration into his own hands. Mir Ruknuddin, a pious and learned man was appointed as prime minister. His prime companions like Shaikh Jafar and Maulana Pir Muhammad Sherwani were taken into imperial service. But unfortunately, after some time the behaviour of the Mir, bred dissatisfaction among the people. Therefore, he was removed from the office and Shaikh Jafar was appointed in his place.[28]

Now appeared in the political arena of Ahmadnagar a

very outstanding personality named Shah Tahir. His unrivalled genius, his vast learning, his skilful statesmanship, wrought a welcome change in the political and cultural atmosphere of the country of his adoption. He was a descendant of the Fatimaid Caliphs of Egypt, and his ancestoral home is said to have been was in Khurd, a village in Qazwin, a district of Persia on the borders of Gilan. Here his ancestors had lived for about three hundred years. He surpassed his predecessors both in spiritual and secular attainments, and his fame had spread far and wide.

**Arrival of Shah Tahir in the Daccan[29] (1520 A.D.)**

He attracted students from Egypt, Bokhara, Samarqand and other countries far and near. They not only benefitted themselves from his scholarship, but they also accepted his faith, and turned Shia. His proselytising activities attracted the attention of Shah Ismail Safvi, the ruler of Persia, and a staunch supporter of the Shia faith, and a crusader against the Kashwandiah sect which he was keen to root out from his country. The Shah extended an invitation to Tahir through Shah Husain Ispahani, his Nazir and the Diwan. But though Tahir was reluctant to give up his profession, the Diwan successfully persuaded him to come to Sultania in 926 A.H. where he was introduced to the Shah, who was so impressed with him as to include him among his intimate courtiers. He was given a place of honour in the royal circle. But the growing popularity and influence of Shah Tahir, became an eye-sore to the Shah, who began to repent the step he had taken. At length, to keep him away from politics, on the suggestion of his Diwan, Shah Ismael appointed Shah Tahir as the principal of a school at Kashan. Here too students and scholars began to crowd round him in ever increasing numbers, and Kashan was transformed into a great centre of learning. His activities unfortunately, excited the jealousy of local officers who, in their keenness to ruin him, wrote to the Shah saying that Tahir was promoting and propagating the Ismailia faith which was held in abomination by the Shias and the Sunnis alike. They further charged Shah Tahir with the guilt of being in correspondence with the neighbouring kings with whose support he was setting at naught the Muslim Law. These allegations gave to the Persian ruler the long sought for opportunity and he issued orders for his execution. But his friend, the Diwan, being interested in him, managed to send him a note of warning asking him to leave Iran as soon as possible. In great consternation, Shah Tahir abandoned his wealth and home in Iran and taking with him his children and a few dependents left the country in the mid-winter. He arrived at the port of Gazrun, where he luckily found a boat ready to sail for India. After saying his Friday prayers he got into the boat and exactly after a week he arrived at Goa (19th April 1520 A.D.).[30]

From Goa[31] Shah Tahir went straight to Bijapur to seek his fortune there, but as Ismail Adil Khan was unable to give him a suitable place, he left the country and formed a plan of performing a pilgrimage to Mecca. Accordingly he embarked at the port of Chaul. On his return from Mecca he took up his residence at Parenda,[32] where Makhdum Khwaja Jahan, went to pay his respects to him and to request him to impart religious instruction to the people. After some time Pir Muhammad Sherwani came from Ahmadnagar on a diplomatic mission to Makhdum Khwaja Jahan Daccani. Being himself a learned man he went to meet Shah Tahir. He was so deeply impressed with his learning that during the whole period of his stay at Perenda, he went daily to attend the Shah's lectures and was much profitted by them. On his return to Ahmadnagar he gave an account to Burhan Nizam Shah of Shah Tahir's excellence and attainments in all branches of learning, emphasising in particular the effective eloquence of his religious discourses. It excited Burhan's keenness to meet the learned saint. Accordingly, express messages were sent to him requesting him to come to the court. After making a show of reluctance, Shah Tahir arrived at Ahmadnagar, where a cordial and respectful welcome was accorded to him. Burhan was so much deeply impressed with his ready wit, his ponderous scholarship and his charming manners, that he appointed him to give discourses twice in a weak in the Jami-Masjid. Large number of students and scholars flocked here from distant corners of the country to benefit themselves from the Shah's learning. Sometimes even Burhan Nizam Shah himself would go and sit in the mosque, listening to Tahir's lecture and would not leave his place till it was over.

Babar's eventful triumphs in northern India had country wide reaction. In the Daccan Kalim-ul-llah,[33] the last of the

**Kalim-ul-llah honourably received by Burhan Nizam Shah (1526 A.D.)**

Bahmanides, began to dream of reviving the fortunes of his dynasty by throwing off the galling dominance of his prime minister Ali Barid and by recovering the territories which had been usurped by autonomous nobles. Accordingly, he addressed a letter to Babar, promising him to cede to him the provinces of Berar and Daulatabad in lieu of his support for fulfiling his ambitions. But even before any scheme could take shape, news of the correspondence leaked out. In sheer fright of his prime minister, Kalim-ul-llah fled to Bijapur; where Ismail Adil Khan refrained from extending to him a hearty welcome. Thus, being disappointed Sultan Kalim-ul-llah Bahmani left Bijapur and came to Ahmadnagar with high expectations. Thinking that he would be able to use him for the eventual conquest of Bidar, Burhan received him with all possible hospitality, promising him to recover Bidar for him. To assure him of his *bonafides* Burhan went one step further, requested Sultan Kalim-ul-llah to sit on the throne, himself standing with folded hands before him. But Shah Tāhir warned Burhan of the fateful consequences, in case he repeated his homage to the Bahmani Sultan again. After this Burhan never let Kalim-ul-llah come in the open court. Finding the political atmosphere of Ahmadnagar uncongenial, Sultan Kalim-ul-llah again repaired to Bijapur where, he died in 1538 A.D. Now the autonomous rulers of Bijapur, Golkunda, Bidar and Berar, for all the practical purposes threw off the mask they had wore. They cast off the titles granted to them by the Bahmani rulers and declared themselves independent sovereigns, by assuming the royal title of "Shah".[34]

In the politics of the Daccan events were now moving fast. The Hindus of Vijayanagara had given a serious blow to the power and prestige of Ismail Adil Khan by defeating him in the battle of Raichur. Ismail Adil Khan thereupon abandoned his designs of further expansion in the south and he turned his attention towards the remnants of the Bahmani kingdom, which had fallen into utter ruin. It was clear to him that it was impossible to gain anything by himself singly. Conditions pointed to the necessity of forming an alliance with one or more of his neighbours with the object of eliminating the weak and absorbing their territory, which would also check the growing power of the Hindus of Vijayanagara and prevent them from swollowing the entire Daccan. His immediate aim, however, was to inflict punishment on Amir Ali Barid, who had instigated the Raya of Vijayanagara against him. With the result that henceforward Raichur and Mudgal became the bone of contention between the two.

At the instance of Asad Khan Lari, it was decided to form alliance with the ruler of Ahmadnagar. Accordingly Sayyid Ahmad Haravi was sent from Bijapur to conduct the negotiations for an everlasting peace.[35] Upon his arrival at the court of Ahmadnagar, he was introduced by Shah Tahir to Burhan, and it was agreed that the two rulers should meet to decide the future course of action. The meeting took place at Sholapur, where Ismail Adil Khan gave his sister Bibi Maryam in marriage to Burhan Nizam.[36] The nuptials were celebrated amidst much pomp and rejoicings. But cordiality soon changed into bitterness and permanent hostility, when Burhan demanded the cession of five and half district, together with the fort of Sholapur,[37] which had been promised by Asad Khan Lari to be given to him in dowry. Ismail Adil Khan, being unaware of such a promise, refused to comply with the demand. Burhan Nizam repeated it, saying that it was the main plank of alliance between the two. The situation would have taken a very ugly turn but for Shah Tahir, who succeeded in persuading Burhan to drop the demand for the time being and to return to Ahmadnagar. Though the crisis had been averted, but Sholapur became the bone of contention between the rulers of Bijapur and Ahmadnagar.[38]

**Marriage of Burhan Nizam. (1523 A.D.)**

The relations between the two rulers were further strained, when Ameena gave birth to a son named Muhammad Hasan and the began to treat Bibi Maryam contemptuously. Unable to tolerate the superiority of a dancing girl, and encouraged by the influence she wielded, Bibi Maryam complained to her brother Ismail Adil Khan of her miserable and pathetic plight in the royal harem. The latter was so enraged that he remonstrated with Burhan Nizam for his reprehensible conduct and abused his ambassadors in residençe at Bijapur.[39]

Offended by the behaviour of Ismail Adil Khan, Burhan

sent messages to Amir Ali Barid and Imad-ul-Mulk requesting them to join him against their common enemy, the ruler of Bijapur. In 1526 A.D. the allies assembled and marched against Ismail Adil to humble his pride and to wrest the fortress of Sholapur from him.[40] Ismail took the challange in right earnest. He advanced with 10,000 foreign troops to defend the town and to throw back the aggressor. In the field of battle, the forces of Imad-ul-Mulk were opposed by Asad Khan Lari, the Bijapur commander, who soon broke through his ranks and compelled him to quit the field and to retire to Gawilgarh. As to Burhan partly, because of the intolerable heat of the day, and partly because of the fear of being defeated, he returned in his palanquin to Ahmadnagar. Asad Khan Lari pursued him up to Parenda where he took Khwaja Jahan Daccani prisoner and captured twenty elephants and other heavy baggage.[41]

**Hostilities against Bijapur**

Ismail now in his turn instigated Alauddin Imad-ul-Mulk to rise against Burhan. The two succeeded in seizing Pathri. Upon this Burhan allied himself with Ali Barid and recovered Pathri after a siege of two months. Then they marched to Mahur which was occupied. After this they proceeded towards Elichpur to teach a lesson to Imad-ul-Mulk. Unable to resist the invader Alauddin took refuge with Muhammad Shah I, the ruler of Khandesh. The two marched with 25,000 horsemen to fight Burhan and his ally, but they were defeated in a battle, losing 300 elephants. They retreated to Burhanpur from where they sent messages to Bahadur Shah of Gujarat entreating him to help them.[42]

Bahadur Shah seized the opportunity of intervening in the affairs of the Daccan, and with this object set out from his capital in the middle of the rainy season (14th zilhajj, 934 A.H., 1528 A.D.)[43]. At Halol, he assembled his forces and in the month of Muharram, 935 A.H. he moved to Baroda where he stayed, for about a month. Then he marched straight towards the Deccan. On the way he was met by Jafar Khan, the son of Alauddin Imad Shah, and at Nandrbar by Muhammad Shah I and his ally, Alauddin Imad Shah. Now Sultan Bahadur Shah and

**Bahadur Shah's invasions on the Daccan (1528 A.D.)**

his confederates, with 100,000 horsemen and 900[44] elephants advanced via Galna, arrived at Daulatabad and pitched their camp in the vicinity of the town. At the sight of overwhelming odds the garrison lost heart;[45] but the sudden appearance of a contingent of Nizam Shahi troops, which lay behind the bush, and which opened an attack on the enemy's van, encouraged their spirits. Though the contingent was defeated, but during the affray it killed two of the enemy's nobles e. g. Mukhlis-ul-Mulk, Muhibb-ul-Mulk.[46] Bahadur Shah now opened the siege of the fort and invested it closely. The valour of his soldiers began to cause anxiety to Burhan. To gain time he sent an embassy to Bahadur Shah, expressing his readiness to wait upon him, provided he was guaranteed safe conduct.[47] The Sultan gave the necessary assurance, and the envoy took leave promising that his master would attend the court within ten days[48]. On the expiry of the stipulated period Burhan Nizam-Shah sent another envoy requesting respite for another ten days.[46] This aroused the suspicions of Bahadur Shah, who warned the envoy saying that, "if he fails in his promise this time, I will lay Daultabad even with dust and uproot its foundations." But the threat had no effect on Burhan. Enraged at the deceitful conduct of the enemy, Bahadur Shah ordered his soldiers to attack the fortress from all sides. For twenty days fighting went on, but success seemed to be as remote as ever. Disappointed, Bahadur Shah marched towards Bidar to punish Ali Barid.[50]

While he was on the way to Bidar, the envoys of Burhan, Ali Barid, Ismail Adil Shah and Khudawand Khan Banthri waited on Bahadur Shah. They laid before him presents on behalf of their masters, and pleaded for Burhan. They convinced him that in reality it was Imad Shah who was the aggressor, because he opened the dispute by seizing the fort of Mahur from the officers of Burhan, who was compelled to act in self-defence. Impressed with the version of the incident, Bahadur Shah changed his mind, restored peace between Burhan and Alauddin Imad Shah, and returned to his own country.[51]

In 1529 A.D. Jafar Khan, son of Alauddin Imad Shah went to the court of Bahadur Shah to represent that Burhan had failed to fulfil the conditions of the recent pact. He had neither restored his elephants, nor had ceded the town and the district of Pathri.[52] He requested the Sultan to undertake another expedition against the defaulter and help his father in wresting the lost territory. Accordingly Bahadur Shah marched from his capital on 2nd Muharram A.H. 935. (1529 A.D.). He first encamped at Dabhoi, and thence he marched to Daharavali, where Muhammad Shah I of Khandesh waited on him. On the way Alauddin Imad Shah also met him and joined him. At Mulher Raja Bahar Jui of Beglana, came and meekly submitted to the authority of the Sultan of Gujarat. He gave one of his sisters in marriage to the Sultan and another to Muhammad Shah I. After crossing the Baglana frontiers, the Sultan honoured the Raja with the title of Bahar Khan and sent him towards the port of Chaul, ordering him to ravage and plunder the country of Burhan, and prevent the Portuguese from extending any assistance to the latter; while the Sultan himself moved towards the city of Ahmadnagar.[53]

The approach of the Gujarati forces alarmed Burhan, and he appealed to Ismail Adil Shah and Sultan Quli Qutbūl-Mulk to help him in repelling the invaders.[54] He even wrote to Babar soliciting his assistance. But the Mughal Emperor was too preoccupied with his own problems in the north to spare any time to involve himself with the politics of the Daccan. Nor could Sultan Quli Qutb-ul-Mulk send his army to the help of Burhan, because he was busy in the campaigns against the Hindus of Telingana. But thanks to the foresight of the other two rulers of the Daccan viz. Ismail Adil Shah and Ali Barid that they were able to make a correct estimate of the consequences of the approaching storm.[55] But for their assistance to Burhan on this occassion, Bahadur Shah would have conquered the whole of the Deccan. Amir Ali Barid came with 6000 foreign horses of Ismail Adil Khan and three thousand of his own.[56]

Bahadur Shah, entered Berar to recover Mahur and Pathri. He liked the country so much that he tarried there for some time and expelled Burhan from there.[57] But his prolonged stay excited the apprehensions of Alauddin Imad-Shah, who persuaded him to proceed towards Burhan's country and seize some parts thereof from him.[58] Accordingly, Bahadur Shah marched thither and pitched his camp in the hilly district of Bir. Amir Ali Barid attacked a part of the enemy's forces which had been separated from the main army, stationed between Bir and Paithan.[59] He killed 3000 men and seized seventy camels laden with treasure. When Bahadur shah received intelligence of this defeat, he sent his wazir Kundawand Khan with 20,000 horses to avenge the disgrace, but he too met with no better fate and had to suffer heavy losses.[60] But a third detachment under the command of Alauddin Imad-Shah which was coming to reinforce Khudawand Khan compelled Burhan to fall back on Parenda and then retire to Junnar.[61]

Bahadur Shah reached Ahmadnagar without further opposition, and took up his residence in the palace of Burhan where he remained for forty days.[62] He built a large platform known as Kala Chbutra to commemorate the victory.[63] He left Alauddin Imad-ul-Mulk to continue the siege of the fort, and himself moved towards Daultabad. Burhan again appeared before the Gujaratis and tried to cut off their supplies. He sent another letter to Ismail Adil Khan to come to his help. In response Ismail Adil sent a suitable reply and one hundred chosen horsemen under the command of Haidar-ul-Mulk Qazwini. Burhan was disappointed at this poor gesture of friendship.[64]

He now thought of putting his own house in oder. He removed from the post of Peshwa Shaikh Jafar who had become unpopular among all the classes, and appointed in his place Kunwar Sen a Brahman, known for his penetrating intellect as much as for his fidelity and integrity.[65] On his minister's suggestion Burhan collected all his available troops from Junnar and Ahmadnagar and took up his position in the hills near Daultabad within eight miles of the Gujarat army. From this point of vantage he harassed the enemy for three months with frequent skirmishes and night attacks.[66] Now Ali Barid and Khwaja Jahan joined Burhan and the combined army marched towards Asir and Burhanpur. Bahadur Shah sent Qaisar Khan and Muhammad Shah I to oppose the enemy. A battle occurred near Burhanpur in which the Deccanis were defeated and driven back with heavy losses.[68]

On the other hand Bahadur Shah pressed the siege of Daultabad more vigourously than ever.[69] But the commandant of the fort, Khanjar Khan, son of Khairat Khan, rose equal o to the occassion. He valiantly organised the defence, remaining alert and active all the time. But the recent defeat near Burhanpur laid low the spirit of Burhan Nizam. Being unable to contend against the Gujarati forces, Ali Barid made peace with Imad-Shah, by giving the hand of his daughter to him. Whereupon the latter begged the Sultan Bahadur Shah to forgive him. Bahadur Shah overlooked his fault, upon which Ali Barid agreed to read his name in the Khutuba and strike coins in his name. Now Bahadur Shah moved from Bir to Pathri. The Deccanis shut themselves up in the fort. The fort was besieged and fighting went on for some days. As the place was strong and its reduction was impossible, the Sultan left Alp Khan to assist Imad Shah in carrying on the siege.[70]

Being unable to bear the pressure of the Gujarati forces Burhan Nizam Shah started overtures for peace with Imad-Shah through Muhammad Shah I, promised to restore to Imad-Shah the forts and elephants which he had seized from him during the war. They now told Khudawand Khan that they had called in the aid of Bahadur Shah only to recover Mahur and Pathri, and in return for which they had agreed to read Khutba in his name both in Berar and Ahmadnagar and pay annual tribute, but Sultan Bahadur Shah's desire to make himself the master of the whole country was becomming a source of much anxiety to them. Khudawand Khan too had grown weary of the campaign and impressed by the arguments advised them to break up the league. Accordingly, Alauddin Imad Shah permitted the supply of provisions to pass through his line into the fortress of Daulatabad and at the commencement of the rainy season he retreated to Elichpur.[71]

On having been deserted by his most active ally, the position of the Sultan of Gujarat and Muhammad Shah I, the ruler of Khandesh became too critical, especially in a country which was not their own. They had nothing to gain by prolonging hostilities. Add to it, the approach of the rainy season which created grave anxiety in the mind of the invaders. Such were the considerations which pointed to the urgency of opening negotiations for peace. But the terms on which it was concluded, were very humilitating to Burhan. He and his friend Alauddin Imad Shah agreed to have the Khutuba recited in the name of Sultan Bahadur Shah, in their kingdoms. After the conclusion of the peace Bahadur Shah returned to Gujarat. Before Bahadur Shah retired from the Daccan, Burhan Nizam Shah met him in a village near Daulatabad on the advice and intervention of Khwaja Ibrahim and Sabaji. After the meeting Burhan honoured Khwaja Ibrahim with the title of Latif Khan and Sabaji with that of Partab Rai.[72] Burhan Nizam Shah, however, fulfilled only partially the stipulations he had made. He restituted the elephants of Muhammad Shah I of Khandesh, only when he was asked to do it, but he retained those of Alauddin's. Muhammad Shah I having obtained what he had wanted, made no further attempt to compel Burhan to fulfil other conditions of the pact. On the contrary he entered into a close alliance with him and thus Pathri and Mahur remained for all time in the hands of the ruler of Ahmadnagar.[73]

**Cordial Relations with Bahadur Shah of Gujarat**

The following year Burhan Nizam sent Shah Tahir to Bahadur Shah with costly presents consisting of cloth, elephants and horses, as a token of friendship towards him.[74] But as Burhan had the Khutba recited only once in Bahadur's name, the latter delayed to give audience to the envoy and wrote to Muhammad Shah I about it.[75] The latter assured the Sultan of the loyalty of Burhan, and even justified his conduct on the ground of the necessity of retaining his honour in the eyes of other nobles of the Daccan, and also on the ground that Sultan Kalim-ul-llah was passing his last days at Ahamadnagar. Bahadur Shah being satisfied with the explanation received Shah Tahir, but in the beginning showed him scant regard. When Khudawand Khan acquainted him with the qualities of learning and piety of Shah Tahir, Bahadur Shah conferred upon him high honours and at the end of three months gave him leave to depart.[76]

Once again at the suggestion of the ruler of Khandesh, Burhan Nizam sent Shah Tahir and Narsu Pandit to congratulate Sultan Bahadur Shah upon his recent achievement in conquering and annexing Malwa to his own kingdom.[77] In 1531 A.D. at the close of the rainy season Bahadur Shah went towards Burhanpur and Asir. Upon his arrival at the capital of Khandesh, Muhammad Shah I introduced Shah Tahir into his presence. As, in his court there were many men of learning like Shah Mir, Shah Kamaluddin, and Shah Abu Turab, who enjoyed the privilege of sitting in the presence of the Sultan, Shah Tahir was also accorded the same privilege, on condition that on the first occassion he would have to deliver the message of his master standing, then he would be allowed to sit according to the practice of the court.[78] Accordingly, Shah Tahir delivered his master's message of good will and friendship to Sultan Bahadur Shah, and like a shrewed politician and diplomat requested him to confer on Burhan the title of "Shah", assuring him that such a gesture on his part would cement permanent friendship between the two.[79] Upon this Bahadur Shah asked Shah Tahir, if Nizam-ul-Mulk is to be styled Nizam Shah, what difference would be here between me and him ?", to which Shah Tahir gave an intelligent reply, saying, "there would still be a great difference. Up to this time the august Sultan was the king of the nobles only, now he would be the king of the kings".[80] It was a wise move on the part of Shah Tahir to have suggested the elevation of Burhan to the position of a monarch. It was seconded by the ruler of Khandesh, who represented to the Sultan the need of establishing amicable relations with Burhan, because of the changing political conditions in northern India and the prospects of a race for power between him and the Mughals. The argument went home to the mind of Bahadur Shah and, he loaded Shah Tahir with favours and allowed him to return to Ahmadnagar and asked him to persuade his master to come to meet him at Burhanpur to enter into the bond of friendship.[81]

At first Burhan was reluctant to meet Bahadur Shah to receive the royal title at his hands, imply as it did loss of prestige and humilitation in the eyes of his compeers.[82] Thanks however to the persuasive genius of Shah Tahir, that he succeeded in convincing Burhan to accept his suggestion for two reasons; firstly, it would free him from the danger from the north and secondly, the title of Shah will raise his dignity and enable him to rise still higher than the other rulers of the Daccan. Leaving his son Husain in the charge of the government under the care of Kunwar Sen, Burhan marched to Burhanpur with a contingent of seven thousand horse.[83] He sent in advance Shambhuji Chitnavis and Khwaja Ibrahim as his envoys to Burhanpur, to arrange a grand reception for him there.[84] When he arrived at Changdev, on the banks of the river Tapti, he was received by Muhammad Shah I, the ruler of Khandesh, who told him that Sultan Bahadur Shah

**Meeting with Sultan Bahadur Shah (1532 A.D.)**

would receive him seated on the throne. On his either sides would be pious men of learning who had privilege to sit in his presence, others would remain standing with their arms folded across their breasts.[85] Burhan said nothing in reply, but no sooner did Muhammad Shah I leave his camp, than he called in his confidential officers and nobles and told them he would not go to meet Bahadur Shah, stressing further that he was no more a noble of the Bahmani house, but an independent ruler.[86] Shah Tahir discussed the matter once again with him, assured him that Sultan Bahadur would accord to him a dignified reception, warned him against hasty action and the impropriety of loose talk in future.[87] For the moment, Burhan Nizam Shah was carried away by arguments of Shah Tahir who told his master that he had a plan to avert any indignity or insult, if it was ever intended at all. It would not only protect his honour, but would also enhance the cordiality between the two. He said that he had a copy of the Quran in the handwriting of Ali, which Sultan Bahadur Shah was very eager to see, and that he would carry it with him, which would compel Bahadur Shah to descend from his throne, partly to satisfy his curiosity to have a look on it, and partly out of reverence for Holy Book.[88]

On the following day Burhan started with his attendants and arrived at Burhanpur for the proposed meeting.[89] Shah Tahir hastened to the garden of Muhammad Shah I where Bahadur Shah was staying, and informed him of the arrival of his master. Bahadur Shah said that he would meet him in the evening[90] and he asked Muhammad Shah I to arrange a grand banquet for the guest in which he could receive him. About sun-set Burhan with some of his learned courtiers and a contingent of troops left his place to call on Sultan Bahadur Shah.[91] The moment Shah Tahir entered Bahadur Shah's camp he put the Quran at the head of Burhan. Upont his Bahadur Shah enquired of his Wazir Khudawand Khan as to what Shah Tahir was holding in his hands. When he was told about the Holy Book in the handwriting of Ali, he descended from his throne, stepped towards him, took Quran from his hands, kissed it three times and then placed it upon his forehead.[92] He then received Burhan with all kindness, love and friendship. After this, presents consisting of horses, elephants and valuable articles were laid before the Sultan Bahadur Shah, who bestowed all of them on the guest.[93] Then Bahadur Shah asked in Gujarati, about his welfare, to which the latter replied in Persian. Bahadur Shah now mounted the throne, leaving Burhan and Shah Tahir standing. When the Sultan saw Shah Tahir standing, he asked him to sit down; but the latter excused himself saying that how he could do it so long as his master was standing. Bahadur Shah then asked Burhan Shah also to sit.[94] Again he asked him in Persian as to how he had passed his time during the recent vicissitudes of fortune, to which Burhan replied "afflictions which lead to prosperity, and absence which ends in happy union remove the memory of the past", adding that, "the present moment was a sufficient recompense for all the trials he had experienced in series of years".[95] Bahadur Shah was highly pleased at this reply and turning to Muhammad Shah I he said, "Did you hear what Burhan Nizam-ul-Mulk said?", to which the latter replied that he did not.[96] Bahadur Shah then again put the same question to Burhan and received the same reply. In a loud voice the Sultan praised Burhan Nizam Shah.[97] Shah Tahir got up exclaiming, "May such proofs of royal favour increase daily." At the end of the dinner according to Farishta Bahadur Shah removed the sword and the dagger set with jewels from his own belt and girded them on the waist of Burhan Nizam saying, "May the title of Shah prove auspicious to you." He ordered that the green *Chhatra* and *aftabgir* which he had captured from the king of Malwa be brought. He presented them to Burhan and conferred on him the title of Burhan Nizam Shah Bahri.[98] It is however difficult to accept this version that the Nizam Shahi sultan of Ahmadnagar who had assumed all the titles and insignia of royalty as early as 1490, should have so late as 1531 sought and obtained confirmation of their sovereignity from a neighbouring ruler of almost equal dignity. Turning to Maulana Pir Muhammad Sherwani, Bahadur Shah asked in a spirit of light heartedness, "Tumhari bazan kya karti hai ?" to which the Maulana replied in his sweet language, "Tumhari anewali ki dua karti hai ?" For this the Sultan gave him in reward two horses, one Turki and one Arab.[100] Burhan Nizam Shah now took leave to return to his camp. Bahadur Shah ordered his wazir Khudawand Khan and Muhammad Shah I to accompany him to his camp.[101]

The Sultan asked from Shah Tahir, "Does your master know the game of Polo ?"[102] If so, let him come in the field tomorrow morning, and watch the game." Next morning arrangements were made by Bahadur Shah for entertaining Burhan Nizam Shah. The two kings now met in the open plain. Bahadur Shah seated his guest in a golden chair which was placed in front of the throne. Thereafter both of them played the game. Burhan Nizam Shah showed remarkable skill in playing the game and was the recipient of popular applause. Sultan Bahadur Shah and his party were amazed at the suppleness of his movements, dexterity of his hand, and boldness and dash of his strokes. In fact Bahadur Shah left the field to admire and watch Burhan Nizam Shah, cheering him vociferously.[103]

At the end of the game Bahadur Shah presented to Burhan Nizam Shah five horses, two elephants and twelve fighting *cheetahs*.[104] Burhan Nizam Shah thereafter accompanied Bahadur Shah to his camp, where he ordered his attendants to bring numerous gifts in the form of cash, goods, horses, elephants and other valuables, all of which were presented to Burhan Nizam Shah.[105] The latter in return also offered presents to Bahadur Shah, who returned them all except the Holy Quran and the sword on which was engraved the name of one of the Abasside Caliphs, four elephants and two horses.[106] Burhan Nizam Shah then asked for leave to depart. Bahadur Shah embraced him and gave him permission to return saying, "I give you back all the rest of your offerings and all the country of the Daccan." Burhan Nizam Shah returned to his camp, where he was entertained to music by the artists[107] who had been sent by Sultan Bahadur Shah. He handsomely rewarded them and sent them back. Thereafter Burhan Nizam Shah proceeded towards his capital via Daulatbad. On his way he visited the shrines of saints, halted at Hauz-i-Kutlu, where he was received by his son, his minister, and the ambassadors from Bijapur and Golkunda, who had come to congratulate him.[108]

The meeting between Burhan Nizam Shah and Bahadur Shah was expected to prove a truning point in the history of the Nizam Shahi Kingdom. It appeared that the strained relations between the two rulers had come to an end. Each of them expected to get moral and material support from the other, to strengthen his position in times of peace and to avert the crisis in the time of war. The sky seemed to have been cleared of the clouds of hostility. But the peace so made turned out to be a temporaty truce; the parties having entered into it with reservations in mind. Bahadur Shah's conciliatory attitude towards Burhan Nizam was motivated by the desire of making him an ally, to enable him to oust the Mughals from northern India. He had conquered and annexed Malwa; Muhammad Shah I was his vassal; the rulers of Berar and Ahmadnagar were his allies. He could now heave a sigh of relief and satisfaction and expand his ambitious projects further. On the other hand Burhan Nizam Shah had his own designs. He had entered into the alliance to exploit it in reducing his rivals in the Daccan and making himself undisputed power in that region. No wonder, therefore, that the moment Bahadur Shah had turned his back and arrived in Gujarat, Burhan Nizam Shah threw off the mask. His example was followed by Alauddin Imad Shah also, who too, had bowed before the storm, and had meekly acknowledged the suzerainty of the Sultan of Gujarat.

Bahadur Shah's restless ambition and the imperialistic pattern of his plans brought him into conflict with the Mughal emperor Humayun, who drove him out of Malwa and ejected him from Gujarat. Bahadur Shah the conqueror was reduced to the unfortunate plight of Bahadur, the fugitive. Neither Alauddin Imad Shah nor Burhan Nizam could or did lift their little fingers to help him. As to Burhan Nizam Shah, he could not forget the humilitation which he had suffered at his hands, and therefore, it is not strange that moved by a spirit of sheer revenge, he instigated the Mughal Emperor Humayun to attack Gujarat. Never afterwards could Bahadur Shah poke his finger in the affairs of the Daccan, and thus was closed the chapter of relations between Ahmadnagar and Gujarat.

On his return Burhan Nizam Shah, devoted his attention to the civil administration of his country. On the advice of his wise minister Kunwar Sen, he reduced thirty forts belonging to the Maratha Rajas, who had neither paid due allegiance to him, nor the stipulated tribute. He enrolled them into his service gave them back their jageers on condition that they should supply fixed quotas of troops whenever required to do it.[109]

After Bahadur Shah had retired from the Daccan, Amir Ali Barid, attempted to tamper with the loyalty of Ismail Adil Shah's troops, which enraged the latter.[110] He therefore decided to make an end of him, because he had been intriguing to ruin him. Having assured himself of Burhan Nizam Shah's neutrality, Ismail Adil Shah assembled his army and laid siege to Bidar. Amir Ali Barid fled to Golkunda to seek the help of Qutb-ul-Mulk. He advanced twice and every time he was defeated by Ismail Adil Shah. Now Alauddin Imad Shah interceded on behalf of Ali Barid with Ismail, who refused to forgive his enemy. Upon this Alauddin Imad Shah marched to Udgir, where he was joined by Ali Barid. Ismail Adil Shah sent his minister Asad Khan Lari against them. The allies were defeated in a battle, and Ali was captured alive. The fort of Bidar was occupied by the Bijapuri forces; but soon after Ali Barid was pardoned and Kaliyani and Udgir were given to him on condition that he should swear fealty to Ismail Adil Shah and accompany him with three thousand horse on an expedition to recover Raichur, which he had lost to the Hindus of Vijayanagàra. After the capture of Raichur, Ismail Adil granted the government of Ahamadbad-Bidar to Ali Barid, provided he surrendared the forts of Kaliyani and Qandhar to him, to which the latter agreed. Now Ali Barid and Alauddin Imad Shah were allowed to return to their respective places. But once having gained the liberty, the wily old intriguer Amir Ali Barid refused to fulfil the promise he had made.[111]

In 1532 A.D. Ismail Adil Shah made preparations to enforce his demands at the point of the sword. Upon this Ali Barid solicited the assistance of Burhan Nizam Shah who had recently freed himself from the menace of Sultan Bahadur Shah of Gujarat. Instead of making an appeal to arms Burhan Nizam Shah thought it advisable to mediate the dispute peacefully. He wrote to Ismail Adil Shah to desist from the contemplated action, to which he sent a very haughty and insulting reply, telling him that he did not interfere with him when he had seized Mahur, then why should he poke his nose in his plans. He added that he was going to inspect his frontier posts of Naldurg and Sholapur and that he hopes that Burhan Nizam and his officers would not take alarm. Burhan Nizam was not the man to take the insult lying down. He sent an equally haughty reply to

Ismail Adil Shah. Thus the old dispute about the bounderies revived in all its bitterness. Ismail reproached Burhan saying, "Have you so soon forgotten your recent plight ? Why should you take pride in the tattered shreds of the king of Malwa ? Is it not rediculous ? Nor should you be proud of the title of Shah. After all it has been conferred on you by the king of Gujarat, whereas I derive by royal title from the line of the sovereigns of Persia and the descendants of the Prophet. I advise you to repent for your folly and eschew your arrogance, or otherwise I shall compel you to abandon your enjoyments in the Bagh-i-Nizam and have a taste of clashing of steel in the field of battle."[112]

Great was the mortification of Burhan Nizam Shah, when Ismail's words were reported to him. He began to burn with the spirit of revenge.[113] He left forthwith for Omrazpur,[114] where he stayed for a few days to assemble his troops. Accompanied by Ali Barid, and with 25,000 horsemen and a park of artillery he crossed the frontiers into the territory of Ismail Adil Shah. The latter also marched at the head of 20,000 horsemen, fought a battle with the enemy and inflicted on them a crushing defeat. Khurshid Khan and many other nobles of Burhan including 4000 men were slain in the battle, and much baggage fell into the hands of the victors. Burhan Nizam Shah retired to Ahmadnagar to shed tears on his humilitation; but henceforward he became more sober.[115]

**Burhan invades Bijapur (1531 A.D.)**

In 1532 A.D. the bitterness wore off and the erstwhile enemies became friends. They met at the frontiers of their kingdom, concluded a treaty of peace defining their respective spheres of authority. It was agreed that Ismail Adil Shah should be allowed to annex the territories of Telingana and Burhan Nizam Shah should be allowed to capture and annex Berar into his own country. But the plan proved to be still born, because of the sudden death of Ismail Adil Shah in 1534 A.D. which rendered the terms of the treaty inoperative.[116]

**Treaty concluded**

Burhan Nizam Shah devoted much of his time in the company of learned men who flocked to his court from the distant corners of India and other parts of the world. They would meet together very frequently to discuss various issues connected with the Islamic faith. It is not known if the followers of other religions were also allowed to participate in them, or were allowed to express their opinions as they did later on in the reign of the Mughal Emperor Akbar. The cosmopolitan outlook of Burhan Nizam Shah however, may lend support to the presumption that the Portugese, the Hindus, Muslims and others were allowed to hold discussions in his presence, though owing to the paucity of relevant historical material it is difficult to confirm the hypothesis. It may, however, be safely asserted that Burhan Nizam Shah was in this respect a precursor of Akbar. In the words of Sayyid Ali, "the main object of the king was to be able to discriminate the truth from error and to acquire the knowledge of God and an insight into the Holy Law in a way which might be a means of pleasing him." But differences in the opinions expressed, the bitterness and acrimony characterising the wide gulf between word and deed, confused the mind of the king in ever increasing measure. The larger the number of discussions held in his presence, the dimmer the light showing the right path to be followed.

**Establishment of Shia Religion.**

Shah Tahir also joined these discussions on religion and law, though under *Taqiah*, a practice among the Shias to conceal their exact religion. In his arguments he cited from the Shia authorities and attached much importance to them, which made a deep impression on the mind of the king. He sent for Shah Tahir in private and asked him what religion he professed, but he would not disclose it, because of the fear of persecution. At length, when the king became insistent, he told him that he was a Shia. Further Shah Tahir convinced his master that of all the sects of Islam the Shia Faith was the only right way to salvation.[117] To overcome the opposition of the Sunnis, the king advised Shah Tahir to argue his case in a general assembly.

Accordingly Shah Tahir initiated discussions with the theologians. Among them mention should be made of Maulana Pir Muhammad Sherwani, Shaikh Jafar, Maulana Abdul Awwal, Qazi Muhammad Niyata entitled Afzal Khan, Qazi Zainul-Abidin, Sayyid Ishaq the librarian and the Qazi Wilayat Ambar. In support of his arguments he cited quotations from al Hadith (an encyclopedia of seventy three sects of Islam) stressing the importance of the Shia faith as the only road to salvation. He vividly pointed out the basic differences between the four sects; his oratery carried conviction to the assembly. After that he quoted passages from the Sunni works, challenging the followers of it to point out if he had misquoted or misrepresented any passage in his discussion. He then sent for the work of al-Bukhari,[118] which the Sunnis regard as the most authentic collection of the traditions and pointed out from it the passages which confirmed his statements. Before the assembly dispersed Burhan Nizam Shah announced his conversion to the Shia Faith. He dropped the names of the four Caliphs from the Khutuba, and substituted those of the Imams; changed the colour of his standard and the canopy to green. Men were hired to move about in the lanes, market and the mosques of the city abusing the Caliphs, and declaring the Shia faith to be the religion of the state.[119]

After Burhan Nizam Shah, his son Prince Husain and other sons excluding Abdul Qadir, their mother Bibi Ameena and the entire inmates of the royal household both male and female turned Shias.[120] The religion of the king became the religion of the masses. Various Ulemas of the court, courtiers, Hindu slaves, Abysinian amirs, silahdars, menials, even sweepers, farrashs, keeper of elephants, including about 3000 of them, all became the followers of the Shia faith.[121] What Yusuf Adil Khan the *tarafdar* of Bijapur had failed to achieve owing to the bitter opposition of the nobles of the Bahmani kingdom, was achieved by Burhan Nizam very easily and peacefully.

Sunni theologians and their followers united to raise their voice against a change which to them was nothing short of heresy, but they were suppressed with an iron hand. Qazi Abrar and Maulana Abdul Awwal, the two staunch Sunnis who openly protested against the establishment of the new faith were subjected to severe torture.[122] The power of the sword joined to the penetrating intelect of Shah Tahir and the liberal attitude of the king, helped the establishment of the Imami Faith in the remotest parts of the kingdom.

But the embers of opposition flared up, when Pir Muhammad Sherwani, a stauch Sunni, and the tutor of Burhan Nizam Shah, remonstrated against the establishment of the Shia religion in the kingdom. He advanced with three thousand men and encamped outside the city of Ahmadnagar. He opened correspondence with the officers of the royal army and planned to force his way into court with 2000 men to seize and imprison the king and instal on the throne Prince Abdul Qadir, who had refused to accept the Shia faith, inspite of the persuation of his father, an attitude which had cost him paternal favour.

The rebels decided to surround the house of Shah Tahir, the chief instrument of the religious fermentation. They seized his sons and moved ahead with their plans. But Husain Abdul Rumi, king's master of horse and a friend of Shah Tahir informed Burhan of the impending trouble. For the moment much consternation prevailed in Ahmadnagar. Shah Tahir advised the king to attack the rebels, upon which he ordered that the gates of the city should be closed. Burhan Nizam Shah hesitated to take any drastic action against them. saying that he had taken a vow not to injure his tutor. But when the crisis began to deepen he had to fall in with the suggestion of Shah Tahir. He ordered Malik Ahmad Tabrezi and Khwaja Muhmud to attack the rebels. Meanwhile Maulana Pir Muhammad Sherwani had been deserted by his supporters. He took to flight, but was hotly pursued by the imperial forces, who took him prisoner. At the same time the king issued instructions to another officer named Zabit Khan to see that no harm befell his tutor. But when the rebel was produced before the king, he ordered him to be executed. But Shah Tahir interceded on his behalf, his life was spared, and was imprisoned in the fort of Pali.[123] He was released after four years at the suggestion of Shah Tahir. Maulana Pir Muhammad left the country and later went to the Mughal general Bairam Khan, who appointed him as librarian, and subsequently he became the tutor of Emperor Akbar.[124]

The change of state religion, created a corresponding change in the external relations of the kingdom. At the instance of Sultan Mahmud Shah of Gujarat, Muhammad Shah Faruqi I, Ibrahim Adil Shah and Alauddin Imad Shah formed a league to conquer Ahmadnagar and divide it between themselves. Burhan Nizam Shah despatched Rasti Khan to solicit Humayun's help. But as the latter was busy in dealing with Sher Khan, he could not respond to his call. The envoy returned to Ahmadnagar, disappointed Burhan Nizam Shah now resorted to diplomacy. He broke the confederacy by winning over Mahmud Shah the ruler of Gujarat and Muhammad Shah Faruqi I by offering them suitable presents. He then recruited into his service all the Foreigners who had been disbanded by Ibrahim Adil Shah and marched against him. He inflicted a crushing defeat on the Adil Shah and captured one hundred elephants, some pieces of cannons and triumphantly returned to Ahmadnagar.[125] When Shah Ismail Safavi, the ruler of Persia, heard that, Burhan Nizam Shah had embraced Shiaism and was propagating it, he sent Aga Salman Tehrani, alias Mehtar Jamal Chiragchi Baghi to congratulate him. He was accompanied by a slave named Shah Quli. They brought many presents for the King among which was a large and costly diamond and one sapphire on which was inscribed the name of the Caliph Mustasim Billah. Shah Ismail also sent a ruby ring for Shah Tahir on which was inscribed "God with you".[126]

When Mehtar Jamal arrived at Ahmadnagar, Burhan Nizam Shah accorded him a warm and cordial reception.

**Relations with Persian Monarch**

Letters and presents were exchanged, but soon after the immodest behaviour of the Persian envoy towards, Shah Tahir, estranged Burhan Nizam Shah, who forbade him audience. After some time, the king ordered him to return to his country, without any suitable presents or letters for the Persian monarch. But Shah Tahir was not the man to see the end of friendly relations with the outward world. He sent his son Shah Haidar, with presents, on his own behalf to the Shah and continued to remain in correspondence with him.[127]

Contact with Persia, brought in its train to the Nizam Shahi court Sayyids of noble parentage and religious leaders of fame. When Amir Sayyid Ali Shadghani Hussaini Madani, a person distinguished for learning arrived at Ahmadnagar, the king sent one of his courtiers to enquire as to what was the object of his visit. The Sayyid replied that he was desirous of offering prayers at his ancestor's tomb, and he wished to recite the evening prayers at the head of prophet's grave. Burhan Nizam Shah was so pleased to hear of the manner in which he replied that he gave him 12,000 huns and his daughter, Fath Shah Begam, in marriage to his son Sayyid Hasan.[128]

Another Sayyid who came to the Nizam Shahi court was Sayyid Muhammad Husain Wahdi, who was heartily welcomed by the king and his minister Shah Tahir. After staying for sometime, he returned to Iraq and there made a report to Shah Tahmasp, son of Shah Ismael, of all he had seen and heard of the Nizam Shahi king and his attachment to the Shia faith. This led to the opening of friendly communications between the two courts. It was fostered by Shah Tahir. In April-May 1542 Shah Tahmasp sent a royal firman to Shah Tahir, which infused joy in the hearts of all. Shah Tahir showed it to the king and represented that it would be advisable to send a reply, through an clever envoy, so that the bonds of ever lasting friendship with the Persian king may continue to be strong. Accordingly, Prince Shah Haidar the most learned and accomplished of his sons, was sent as envoy to the Persian court. Upon his arrival there he left no stone untruned to promote the friendship between the Safavis and the Nizam Shahis. In accordance with the time-honoured practice Shah Tahmasp sent Mir Nizammuddin Khur Shah to the Nizam Shahi court (April-May 1547 A.D.).

About the same time Mehtar Jamal again arrived at Ahmadnagar. He was soon found guilty of some foul deeds, and officers were sent to arrest him. But he escaped and took to flight. Burhan, however, sent a reply to the letter which he had brought from Persia in which he requested the Shah to send a contingent of troops to help him just to put down his rivals. Unfortunately, the distance, which lay between the two countries, prevented the suggestion to materialise. The preoccupation of the Safavid rulers with their neighbours and the Mughals, hardly left any time to them to remain in close touch with the Nizam Shahis; nor could the latter maintain diplomatic relations with them. And therefore, henceforward we do not come across any reference to Nizam Shahi-Persian relations.

Shah Tahir now began to play a vital role in the administration of the country, enjoy as he did much influence with his master. His reputation for piety and learning joined to the qualities of head and heart had made him an object of veneration for the masses and the classes alike. His cosmopolitan outlook, his learned discourses, his political accumen led his master to offer him the post of Wakil and Peshwa, which he accepted after much persuation, and took the reins of administration into his hands. His wise and benevolent reforms brought peace and prosperity to the country. To him goes the credit of having raised the cultural level of Ahmadnagar. His liberal gifts attracted the learned and the pious from distant lands. Every year ship loads of treasure, carpets, tents and other offerings were sent to Mecca and Madina, Najaf, Karbala, and other shrines of the infalliable Imams; and the gates of joy were opened before all the descendants of the Prophet". Thus Ahmadnagar became a centre of learning in the Daccan.[129]

With the establishment of peace and prosperity in the kingdom under the wise dispensation of his prime minister, Burhan Nizam Shah embarked upon the plans of territorial expansion. He marched against the fort of Galna which was held by Raja Bahar Jui of Balgana.[130] It was captured after a short siege. Next came the turn of Mulaher,[131] which was held by Bhirdra, a Hindu Raja. The victim of agression appealed for help to the Sultan Mahmud Shah who asked Burhan to spare his vassal. Upon this the Nizam Shah returned to his capital.[132]

**Minor Conquests**

On his way to Ahmadnagar, he was approached by Ratan Khan, who complained of the high handedness of his brother Fakhr-ul-Mulk Deccani entitled Khwaja Jahan, the chief of Parenda, which having been assigned to him after the partition of the defunct Bahmani Kingdom.[133] Khwaja Jahan, behaved as an independent prince and was loth to recognise the supermacy of either of the Nizam Shah or the Adil Shah. The quarrel between the brothers gave a handle to Burhan to push forward his scheme of aggrendisement. Alarmed at the approach of the Nizam Shahi army and considering resistence to be futile, Khwaja Jahan abandoned the fort and fled to Bijapur. It was occupied by Burhan Nizam Shah.

At Bijapur, Khwaja Jahan succeeded in persuading Ibramim Adil Shah to send a force with him to recover Parenda. Upon this Burhan despatched Husan and Daulāt with an army to fight the Khwaja, who was defeated and put to flight with heavy losses. The entire camp equippage falling into the hands of the victors, he escaped to seek refuge in Gujarat. Having remained there in exile for sometime, Khawaja Jahan felt homesick and he opened correspondence with some of the Nizam Shahi nobles, at whose intercession he was permitted to return to Ahmadnagar. He was admitted to the royal favour and as an earnest of good behaviour he married one of his daughters to Prince Miran Shah Haidar. After the nuptials had been performed Parenda was restored to him.[134]

During the time that Burhan Nizam Shah was involved in disputes with the Sultan Bahadur Shah, Ismail Adil Shah had annexed some of the frontier districts of Ahmadnagar. Burhan Nizam Shah asked for their restoration, but his demand was turned down. Luckily at this time the Adil Shahi court was witnessing a contest between two nobles Yusuf Turk and Asad Khan Lari. Ibrahim Adil Shah, being a minor, could not control the situation. Finding the ground uneven under his feet, Asad Khan retreated to Belgaum. But his enemy would not let him live in peace there. Failing in his attempts to remove him by poison or sword, he charged him with treason saying that he intended to surrender Belgaum to Burhan Nizam Shah, because he was dissatisfied with the establishment of Sunni faith in the kingdom. This encouraged Burhan Nizam to appeal to arms to gain his objective.[135]

**Burhan invades Bijapur**

Burhan Nizam Shah invited Amir Ali Barid to form a coalition on the pretext that he had been invited by Asad Khan Lari. He held out to him the promise that as the price of his support he would receive Belgaum.[136] Darya Imad Shah was also asked to participate in the campaign, which he did only half-heartedly for two reasons; firstly, because of the existing ties of matrimonial alliance between the Imad Shahi and Adil Shahi houses; and secondly, because of the moral improperiety of the invasion, the Adil Shah being a minor. But Burhan proved impervious to such considerations. Amir Ali Barid and Imad, though the latter very reluctantly marched[137] to Sholapur which was captured and placed in the hands of Khwaja Jahan Daccani. The next objective was Belgaum. Alarmed at the advance of the enemy Asad Khan Lari made frantic appeals to induce his master to fight the invaders. But his words fell on deaf ears. In the eyes of Adil Shah, he was a suspect and a traitor. Finding no way out, Asad Khan surrendered Belgaum to Burhan Nizam Shah and threw in his lot himself along with 6,000 men.

The way to Bijapur was now open and the allies arrived there in no time. In sheer helplessness Ibrahim Adil Shah retreated to Gulbarga. The fall of the capital being imminent, Imad Shah and Asad Khan Lari began to think out a plan to avert the disaster. They decided to desert Burhan Nizam Shah. The latter's position became so critical as to compel him to retreat to Bir. His erstwhile allies did not let him remain there even; they pursued him to his capital, which too he abandoned to their mercy, himself taking refuge at Daulatabad. Thus the tables were completely turned on Burhan Nizam Shah. To add to his misery, there occurred the sudden death of Amir Ali Barid. He now made overtures for peace with Bijapur. According to the terms of the treaty, he was compelled to restore the fortress of Sholapur and its five and half districts to Ibrahim Adil Shah, and to promise not to molest Bijapur again.[138]

In 1543, Ibrahim Adil Shah married the daughter of Darya Imad Shah, but soon after sharp disagreement arose between the two. To exploit the situation in his favour, Burhan Nizam Shah sent Shah Tahir to Jamshed Quli Qutb Shah, ostensibly to congratulate him on his accession to the throne, but really to induce him to form a league with Ram Raj, the ruler of Vijayanagara against Bijapur, and help him in recovering Sholapur and its five and half districts, which he had recently ceded to the Adil Shah.[139] Jamshed Quli Qutb Shah fell in with the proposal. He formed the confederacy and the allies attacked the Bijapur kingdom from three sides. Burhan Nizam Shah from the north, Jamshed from the east and Ram Raya from the south. In the face of this three pronged attack the fate of Ibrahim Adil Shah and his kingdom appeared to be doomed.[140] In this crisis Ibrahim sent for Asad Khan Lari and sought his advice.[141] The minister suggested to his master to isolate Jamshed Quli by restoring Sholapur, the bone of contention, to Burhan Nizam Shah and by offering presents and gifts to the ruler of Vijayanagara.[142] His suggestion was readily accepted and implemented. The confederacy went to pieces and Jamshed had to pay dearly for having played the game of Burhan Nizam Shah.[143] In another sense also the venture proved to be far-reaching in its implications. It gave a handle to the ruler of Vijayanagara to foster conditions of constant warfare among the succession states of the Bahmani empire, which he expected would exhaust their resources and curb their ambitions.

At the instance of Ram Raya, Burhan Nizam Shah revived the confederacy in 1546 and marched to reduce Gulbarga. Ibrahim Adil Shah moved forward to oppose him, but found him encamped on the eastern bank of the Bhima. It being impossible to effect a crossing, the rival armies faced each other for three months till the end of the rainy season. Ibrahim Adil Shah now crossed the river, delivered an attack on the enemy, who was defeated and put to flight, leaving to victor two hundred and fifty elephants, one hundred and seventy pieces of canon, the Mahi Miratib and other insignias of royalty. The credit for the success went to Asad Khan Lari who was lavishly rewarded by his master.[144]

Ibrahim Adil Shah now turned haughty and arrogant. He began to treat the resident ambassadors with contempt and behave tyrannically towards his subjects, putting to death many, and inflicting severe punishments on the leading nobles on the slight offences.[145] This occasioned some confusion, which Burhan Nizam Shah became keen to exploit to his advantage. He worked for the revival of the confederacy against Bijapur.[146] Accordingly he sent Shah Tahir to Ali Barid Shah I but the latter refused to join hands with him on the ground that it was his duty to support a Sunni ruler like Ibrahim Adil Shah, rather than a Shia. Barid's minister Khan Jahan insulted Shah Tahir, which deeply annoyed Burhan Nizam Shah who could neither bear the humiliation, nor the idea of a prospective alliance between Ali Barid Shah I and Ibrahim Adil Shah. Therefore, Burhan quickly changed his mind and resolved to punish Ali Barid Shah for his insolence.[147] He formed an alliance with the Adil Shah against Barid Shah and Vijayanagara. It was agreed between the allies that they would act individually; Burhan Nizam would attack Ali Barid and Ibrahim Adil Shah would march against Vijayanagara, whenever it should suit him. Burhan Nizam laid siege to the fortress of Ausa. He was joined by Darya Imad Shah. Upon this Jamshed Quli Qutb Shah marched to the relief of Ali Barid Shah I, but finding the enemy to be superior in numbers, he retreated and returned to his capital. Proving untrue to his plighted word Ibrahim Adil joined Ali Barid Shah I, the latter promising to cede to him the fort of Kaliyani. But Burhan Nizam Shah succeeded in defeating his enemy and capturing Ausa. He then marched to Qandhar which was jointly defended by Ibrahim Adil Shah and Ali Barid I, but they failed to avert the calamity and the fortress fell into the hands of the invader who returned in triumph to his capital Ahmadnagar.[148]

While Burhan Nizam Shah was still on the way to his capital, the representatives of a political faction of Bijapur met him to solicit his assistance in favour of Prince Abdulla, who had rebelled against Ibrahim Adil Shah I and had taken refuge with the Portuguese at Goa. Burhan Nizam Shah agreed to accede to the request and consequently with Jamshed Quli Qutb Shah marched against Bijapur.[149] He failed to seize the fort of Belgaum and was thrown back by the Bijapuri forces. He had no other course but to return to Ahmadnagar, there to mourn the death of his prime minister Shah Tahir, which occurred about this time. (1548 A.D.).[150] In his place Qasim Beg and Bhopal Rai were appointed as his chief advisors.[151]

In 1548-49 died[152] Asad Khan Lari, the minister of Ibrahim Adil Shah I, who held in his possession the fief of Belgaum. This encouraged Burhan Nizam Shah to make fresh efforts to recover the fort of Sholapur and its dependencies.[153] He succeeded in obtaining a promise of cooperation from Ram Raya, the ruler of Vijayanagara.[154] Professions of good will and presents were exchanged between the two. When this was reported to Ibrahim Adil Shah I, he insulted the resident ambassadors of Ahmadnagar and Vijayanagara, who in sheer fright fled from Bijapur to save their lives.[155] Upon this war was declared against Ibrahim Adil Shah I. Burhan Nizam Shah opened the campaign with the siege of Sholapur. But at the suggestion of Ram Raya he raised the siege and the joint armies converged on the fort of Kaliyani.[156] (1551 A.D.). When Ibrahim Adil Shah marched to its relief he was defeated and put to flight. The allies succeeded in cutting off the communication of the garrison of the fort of Kaliyani with outside, and reduced them to sore straits. Once more Ibrahim Adil Shah marched to relieve the garrison, and arriving in the neighbourhood of the fort he pitched his camp within the sight of the allies.[157] As Burhan was firmly determined to conquer the fort, he fortified his lines; but the Adil Shah detached light Maratha cavalry to harass the besiegers, by cutting off their supplies. Scarcity of supplies soon caused distress in the camp of the invaders. Burhan called a council of war, in which some nobles proposed that the siege should be raised and that they should withdrew to Ahmadnagar; while Shaikh Jafar and Qasim Beg suggested to launch a surprise attack on the enemy. The latter suggestion was seconded by Sadashiv naiyak and Bhopal Rai, who had been encouraged by the initial success they had gained over the Bijapuri forces. Accordingly on Shawwal I A.H. 958 (Oct. 2, 1551) Saifuddin Ain-ul-Mulk delivered a surprise attack on the Bijapuri army. Ibrahim Adil Shah who was taking his bath had hardly any time to dress himself. In sheer fright he fled towards Bir and thence towards Parenda. His troops were completely routed, and in the twinkling of an eye they dispersed helter skelter in all directions, leaving behind their tents, baggage etc.[158] The disaster which befell the Adil Shahi army alarmed the comandant of the fort of Kaliyani, and he sent a petition to Burhan Nizam Shah, offering to surrender on condition that his life and goods were spared. Burhan Nizam Shah granted the terms and the fort was surrendered.[159]

On the other hand no sooner did Ibrahim Adil Shah, appear before the fort of Parenda than he rushed into it giving no time to the Nizam Shahi Commander, Khwaja Jahan to close the gates. He then laid waste the surrounding country, levying heavy contributions from the people in order to divert the attention of the allies.[160] But when he heard of the approach of Burhan Nizam Shah he retreated towards Bijapur. While the Nizam Shahi troops were advancing towards that fort, one night the Daccani officer was disturbed in his sleep by some noise which he believed to be the sound of drums of the enemy who he thought had arrived at the gate, though in fact the cause of distraction was the buzzing of a mosquito. So struck with terror was he that he fled from the fort that very night.[611] The third day after his flight, the empty fortress of Parenda was occupied by Burhan Nizam Shah.[162]

The following year Ibrahim Adil Shah started preparations to recepture the fort of Kaliyani. Upon this Burhan Nizam Shah and Ram Raya met near the fort of Raichur and entered into a pact, according to which, the latter was to occupy Raichur and Mudgal, and help the former in seizing the fort of Sholapur. Accordingly Ram Raya left his brother Venkatadari to assist Burhan Nizam Shah in the achievement of his objective. They jointly attacked Sholapur which fell into their hands after a siege lasting for three months. In the mean while Ram Raya occupied the fortresses of Raichur and Mudgal (1552 A.D.)[163] and returned to Vijayanagara, and Burhan returned to Ahmadnagar.

**Burhan Nizam rocovers Sholapur (1552 A.D.)**

In 1553 A.D. to complete the conquest of Gulbarga, Burhan Nizam Shah once more allied himself with Ram Raya. He marched against Bijapur. In sheer alaram Ibrahim Adil Shah retreated to Panhala, leaving the capital to the mercy of the invaders. While the siege of Bijapur was going on Burhan Nizam Shah was seized with violent disorder in his bowels and was compelled to return to Ahmadnagar without achieving his object.[163]

**Abortive attempt to conquer Gulbarga (1553 A.D.)**

During his illness a war of succession broke out between his two sons, the eldest Miran Shah Husain and the second Abdul Qadir, both having been born of his favourite wife Ameena[165]. Originally Abdul Qadir was his father's favourite. He had the unique distinction of using the aftabgir and the umbrella. He was married to the daughter of Alauddin Imad Shah. Naturally his supporters looked to the prospects of his succession to the throne. But relations between father and son became strained, when Burhan Nizam Shah at the instance of Shah Tahir proclaimed Shiaism as the state religion, and Abdul Qadir under the influence of Pir Muhammad Sherwani refused to accept the new faith. Consequently, he was relegated to a secondary position in the court, being permitted to stand only near the throne. On the other hand, Miran Shah Husain accepted his father's faith and supplanted his younger brother in Burhan's favour, who assigned him a distinguished position in the court; he being permitted to stand immediately behind the sovereign. Naturally, Abdul Qadir became intensely jealous of him. In consideration of the principle of primoginature Burh an Nizam Shah declared his eldest son Miran Shah Husain to be his successor.[166]

**War of succession**

But the indefiniteness of the law of succession provided the urge for appeal to arms, which was further intensified by the existence of group politics in the Nizam Shahi court. The Foreigners and the Abysinians led by Qasim Beg Hakim supported Prince Miran Husain, whereas the Daccanis including the Hindus and Muslims advocated the cause of Prince Abdul Qadir. The gathering clouds alarmed the king and he ordered his sons[167] to proceed forthwith to their respective forts, an arrangement which he had made to prevent the outbreak of hostilities among them. Daulatabad had been assigned to Abdul Qadir, Junnar to Miran Shah Husain and Pali to Miran Shah Ali.

Miran Shah Ali complied with the royal instructions, but Abdul Qadir and Miran Shah Husain were reluctant to do it, each desiring the other to quit the capital first. But in the end Abdul Qadir was compelled to leave for Daulatabad. On the way he halted at Chamar Tiekri, where his supporters proclaimed him king. Soon after he was joined by his other brothers Shah Ali, Miran Khudabanda, Shah Haidar and Muhammad Baqiar, which further strengthened his position. This was a very serious development and Miran Shah Husain was not slow to take notice of it. He assembled his men, marched to Kala Chabutra, opened an attack on Abdul Qadir and routed him completely seizing his Umbrella and aftabgir as also his camp equipage. He fled to Berar to seek the help of his father-in-law.

After the battle was over, Prince Miran Shah Husain ordered his troops to refrain from pursuing the fugitives. Next morning he went to pay his respects to his father. While he was standing by the bed of the ailing king Qasim Beg related the incident, describing the struggle between the brothers and the triumph of the elder and the flight of the younger to Berar. But Burhan Nizam Shah was too weak to comprehend anything. He only stared at the face of his son and shed few tears. Soon the death closed his eyes (December 30, 1553 A.D.). He was buried in the Rauzah garden, the burial place for the Nizam Shahi family. Subsequently by the order of Husain Nizam Shah I, the late sovereign's remains were sent to Karbala where they were deposited in the earth near the shrine of Imam

**Death of Burhan**

Husain.[168] Burhan Nizam Shah died at the age of 50 years after a reign of forty three years.[169]

If Ahmad Nizam-ul-Mulk was the founder of the Nizam Shahi kingdom of Ahmadnagar, Burhan Nizam Shah may rightly be called the architect of its stupendous structure. His long reign of forty three years was full of constant struggle with the neighbouring states of Gujarat, Khandesh, Berar, Bidar and Bijapur. He measured his sword with every one of his contemporary rulers in the Daccan, though with varying success.

**Character of Burhan Nizam Shah**

He was fearless in the field of battle and shrewed in the art of diplomacy. Defeat hardly ever depressed him. On the other hand, it put on him on his mettle and spurred him on to fresh efforts. If by his warlike deeds he extended the territorial limits of his kingdom, he did not fail to promote the arts of peace. His faith in religion was unshakable; and his regard for justice unimpeachable. He was kind and generous towards masses and classes alike.[170] His indefatigeable energy, his uncommon physical strength, his keen and penetrating intellect, his pleasing manners, his love for scholarship made him the idol of his people. Even the contemporary Portuguese chroniclers speak highly of him, say, Burhan Nizam Shah, "was endowed with great natural and political sagacity, his court being hospitable resort of the best men of the time."

To canalise the ambitions of his nobles Burhan Nizam Shah started the practice of taking counsel with them on matters relating to peace and war. He did not make any office hereditary, but kept service open to talent.

He never missed the routine even in the field of battle. "Nothing escaped his eyes and no body could venture to be out of his place by a heir's breadth or to display any lack of vigilance." Himself being educated and learned, Burhan Nizam extended liberal patronage to the men of learning who flocked at his court from the distant lands of Persia and Arabia, Sistan and Khurasan, and other corners of the world. His minister Shah Tahir invited the Shia divines and scholars like Maulana Ismail Safvi, Khwaja Minuddin Shah Husain Anju, Shah Jafar, Mulla Shah Muhammad Nishapuri, Mulla Ali Gul Astrabadi, Mulla Rustam Jurjani, Mulla Ali Mazandarani, Ayub Abul Barka, Mulla Azizullah Gilani, Mulla Muhammad

Imami Astrabadi. They came to the Daccan and made Ahmadnagar an abode of learning. Inspite of his pre-occupation with the state affairs, Burhan Nizam Shah missed no opportunity of associating himself with these learned men. He was keenly interested in the propagation of Shia faith, which opened the contacts of the Nizam Shahi kingdom with the Safavid rulers of Persia. At the suggestion of Shah Tahir he constructed a magnificent building for a school and assigned a few villages for its expenses in terms of Altamgah grant. Residential quarters were also provided for the students and the teachers.[171]

---

*Notes and References*

1. Ferishta gives the chronogram Faiz Jawaid for the accession of Burhan Nizam Shah I. This gives the date of 914, A. H. (1508-9 A.D.) It has already been mentioned that this date is wrong. If we accept 1510 A.D. as the date of his accession to the throne, Burhan Nizam Shah I must have born about the year 1502-3; Burhan-i-Maasir (I. A. 1920) pp. 159; Ferishta ii pp. 102; Ferishta Briggs. III pp. 211; Muntakhab-ul-Lubab III, pp. 158; Tabqat-i-Akbari III, pp. 68;

2. Burhan--i-Maasir (I.A. 1920) pp. 160; Ferishta Briggs. III, pp. 212; Muntakhab-ul-Lubab III, pp. 158.

3. Burhan-i-Maasir (I.A. 1920) pp. 160; Ferishta ii, pp. 102; Ferishta, Briggs. III, pp. 212; Muntakhab-ul-Lubab III, pp. 158.

4. Ferishta Briggs. III, pp. 213.

5. It happened that the conspirators gained over to their interests Bibi Aisha, the nurse of young Burhan's mother, who enjoyed much of her confidence. It was decided that she would hand over Rajaji to the conspirators who would raise him to the throne and subvert the influence of the minister and his son, by deposing Burhan from power. Accordingly one day Bibi Aisha, dressed Rajaji in girl's clothes and carried him in her own palanquin towards the city. She was in the habit of taking the child to the city, where very often she stayed with him for two or three days. But on this occassion the motive was different. Fortunately, she had hardly gone a few paces when the mother of the child asked for him. Finding him missing, she sent officers to follow Bibi Aisha. Before the latter could enter the city, she was apprehended and brought to the palace. She explained her conduct by saying that she was doing nothing unusual. Though she was forgiven, the fact could not remain a secret for long. See, Burhan-i-Maasir (I.A. 1920), pp. 160; Ferishta, Briggs. III, pp. 212-13; Muntakhab-ul-Lubab III, pp. 158-9; A History of Maratha People, pp. 89.

6. Burhan-i-Maasir (I.A. 1920) pp. 160; Ferishta, Briggs. III. pp. 213; Muntakhab-ul-Lubab III, pp. 158-9.

7. Burhan-i-Maasir (I.A. 1920) pp. 160; Ferishta, Briggs. III, pp. 213.

8. Burhan-i-Maasir (I.A. 1920) 160; Ferishta, Briggs III, 214.

9. Ferishta has Rahauri, situated in 19° 22' North and 74° 40' East.

10. Burhan-i-Maasir (I.A. 1920) pp. 160; Ferishta, Briggs. III, pp. 214; Muntakhab-ul-Lubab III, pp. 159.

11. Burhan-i-Maasir (I.A. 1920) pp. 160; Ferishta Briggs. III, pp. 214; Muntakhab-ul-Lubab III, pp. 159.

12. Burhan-i-Maasir (I.A. 1920) pp. 160; Ferishta, Briggs. III, pp. 214 ; Muntakhab-ul-Lubab, III, pp. 159.

13. Burhan-i-Maasir (I.A. 1920) pp. 160; Ferishta, Briggs. III, pp. 214; Muntakhab-ul-Lubab, III, pp. 16.

14. Ferishta, Briggs. III, pp. 214; Muntakhab-ul-Lubab, III, pp. 160.

15. Basatin-ul-Salatin (pt. II) pp. 9.

16. Bahmanis of the Daccan, pp.

17. Burhan-i-Maasir (I.A. 1920) pp. 163-64; Ferishta mentions neither of these campaigns and according to him the first hostility between Ahmad Nagar and Berar, after the battle of Rahauri was that which resulted in the annexation of Pathri by Burhan Nizam Shah I in 1518 A.D.

18. Burhan-i-Maasir (I.A. 1920) 164.

19. Ibid pp. 164.

20. Burhan-i-Maasir (I.A. 1920) pp. 165; Muntakhab-ul-Lubab III, pp. 160.

21. Ferishta, Briggs. III. pp. 214-15; Muntakhab-ul-Lubab, III, pp. 160.

22. Ferishta, Briggs. III, pp. 215; Muntakhab-ul-Lubab, III, pp. 161; Tabqat-i-Akbari III, pp. 69.

23. Ferishta, Briggs. III, pp. 216; Muntakhab-ul-Lubab III, pp. 161.

24. Ferishta, Briggs. III, pp. 216; Muntakhab-ul-Lubab, III, pp. 161.

25. Burhan-i-Maasir (I.A. 1920) 161.

26. Burhan-i-Maasir (I.A. 1920) pp. 163; Muntakhab-ul-Lubab, III, pp. 162.

27. Burhan-i-Maasir (I.A. 1920) pp. 162.

28. Burhan-i-Maasir (I.A. 1920) pp. 163.

29. Burhan-i-Maasir (I.A. 1920) pp. 166; Ferishta, ii, 104-5; Muntakhab-ul-Lubab III, pp. 162-82; Tathkirai-Shorai-Dakhan, Vol. II, pp. 696; Tabqat-i-Akbari III, pp. 68; Maasir-i-Rahimi II, pp. 413-14.

In his work Khafi Khan states that according to one work Shah Tahir was a descendant of Ulvi Sayyids, while according to another, he is said to have been a descendant of Ismael Hussain, whose ancestors, according to the author of Mirat-ul-Jina and Habib-ur-Siyar, ruled in some western countries for about 266 years. It is related that he was amongst the Sayyids of Khudabanda and was considered to be a representative of that house. Whatsoever may have been his lineage it is certain that he was a Sayyid of pure blood and of the noble family, Muntakhab-ul-Lubab III, pp. 176.

30. Burhan-i-Maasir (I.A. 1920) pp. 166.

31. Burhan-i-Maasir (I.A. 1920) pp. pp. 166; Muntakhab-ul-Lubab III, pp. 176; Khafi Khan has Chaul.

32. According to Ṣayyid Ali, Ṣhah Tahir came from Bijapur to Gulbarga, and left the latter place with the intention of going to Macca. But on his arrival at Parenda, Makhduun Khwaja Jahan, the governor of the fort who had come to wait on him, requested him to postpone his departure, as the rains had set in, and the journey would become most troublesome. He also requested him to stay with him and give religious discourses to the people to which he agreed. See, Burhan-i-Maasir (I.A. 1920) pp. 166-7; Muntakhab-ul-Lubab III, Ferishta, ii. pp. 112.

It is also related by some of the modern authorities that Shah Tahir was sent by Shah Tahmasp, the ruler Persia to the Mughal court, in the early part of Humayun's reign to convert him to the shia faith and thereafter he entered the service of the Mughals. But it is very doubtful, if Shah Tahir ever went to the Mughal court. Humayun ascended the throne on 30th Dec. 1530 A.D. at the time when Shah Tahir was in the Daccan, at the court of Burhan Nizam Shah I. And the subsequent events in the Daccan show that, he never went to attend or join the Mughal court. The utmost that can be said is that he maintained close correspondence with Humayun in whose praise he wrote a few Qasidas also.

33. After the death of the Sultan Mahmud Shah Bahmani on the 17th Dec. 1518 A.D. though for all practical purposes the Bahmani kingdom had ceased to exist, Amir Barid remained powerful at the capital. He would have usurped the throne but he was discreet enough to realise that he would be no match for the great fief-holders at Bijapur, Ahmadnagar, Berar and Gol-

kunda; and therefore to save himself from the clutches, he raised Muhammad Shah's son Ahmad Shah to the throne (17th Dec. 1520 A.D.). Ahmad remained under the palms of Amir Ali Barid, who did not even allow him to leave the palace. He passed his time in drinking and debauchery till Mahmud Shah's death. Qutub-ul-Mulk, the governor of Telingana used to send considerable amount of money as tribute to the Sultan, but when he saw that he was too weak to administer the affairs of the state, which had been reduced to a few miles round the city of Bidar, and control the court, he too like others stopped sending the tribute. The Sultan was now compelled to break the ancient throne of the Bahmanis worth 15 lacs of rupees and sell the jewels in order to provide himself with the means of pleasure and enjoyment. Amir Ali Barid, when came to know of it, reduced him to sore straits until he was succeeded by his son Alauddin Shah on 28th Dec. 1520 A.D. who excused himself from playing any part in politics and was dethroned on 5th March 1526 A.D. Amir Ali Barid now enthroned another son of Sultan Mahmud Shah, Waliullah who soon after his accession tried to free himself from the dominance of the minister, for which the latter imprisoned him in his own Zanana and permitted him to live only on bread and clothes. When he protested against the harsh behaviour of Ali Barid, the latter poisoned him to death in 1526; and subsequently his brother Kalim-ul-llah was raised to the throne by that wily minister. He too like his few predecessors was closely guarded by him and to suffer the worst at his hands.

34. The Bahmanis of the Daccan, pp. 417-18.

35. Basatin-us-Salatin (pt. II) pp. 11; Ferishta, Briggs, III, pp. 216; Muntakhab-ul-Lubab III, pp. 162-63; Proceedings of the Indian History Congress session 1945, pp. 250-4;

36. Basatin-us-Salatin (pt. II) pp. 11; Ferishta, Briggs, III, pp. 216; Muntakhab-ul-Lubab III, pp. 163.

37. Sholapur is situated between 17$0^0$ and 18$0^0$ 22′ north latitude and 74$0^0$ 42′ and 76$0^0$ 15′ longitude. It is adjacent to Ahmadnagar in the north, to Bijapur in the south. The town is mentioned by different names in a number of old writings and inscriptions. Raghuvaka, the author of Sanskrit work, named Siddharma Purana, which deals with the life of one Siddharma; mentions him as an inhabitant of Sunnalapur, which is believed to be Sholapur. According to Ferishta, the name of the town was Sadlapur, while according to Burhan-i-Maasir, its name was Sundalapur. At another place, Sholapur has been given the name of Salapur. The earliest reference to the town is made in the 14th century, when it was a part of the Gulburga province of the Bahmani kingdom. The town has since then, a massive fort, in which there is a mosque and a temple, which are specimens of Hindu and Muslim architecture, generally found in the Daccan, belonging to the 13th and 14th centuries. However, it also shows that before the Muslim occupation of the country, the town Sundlapur had perhaps religious importance, during the age of early Chalukyas, eastern Chalukyas, Rashtrakutas, Chalukyas of Kalyani and Yadvas of Devgiri. Later on in 1314, during the reign of Alauddin Bahmani II, when his younger brother Muhammad in cooperation with Raya of Vijayanagara, rose in rebellion he made Sholapur as the base of his rebellions operations. After the rebellion had been supressed Sholapur was occupied by the Bahmani king. After the dismemberment of the Bahmani kingdom between (1490-1537) into five kingdoms Sholapur figures as bone of contention between the rulers of Bijapur and Ahmadnagar. It was in the beginning was annexed by Yusuf Adil Khan but after his death, in 1510 A.D. Ahmad Nizam Shah taking advantage of minority of Ismael Adil Khan, captured it and occupied the tract. But Kamil Khan, the Regent of Bijapur again recovered it from Zain Khan, the Nizam Shahi commander of the fort in 1511 A.D.—See, proceedings of the Daccan History Congress, 1945, pp. 230-32.

38. Basatin-us-Salatin (pt. II) pp. 11; Ferishta, Briggs. III pp. 216-7.

39. Ferishta, Briggs. III, pp. 217; Muntakhab-ul-Lubab III, pp. 163.

40. Basatin-us-Salatin (pt. II) pp. 11; Ferishta, Briggs. III pp. 217.

41. Basatin-us-Salatin (pt. II) pp. 13; Ferishta, Briggs. III, pp. 217 Muntakhab-ul-Lubab III, pp. 163-64.

42. Basatin-us-Salatin (pt. II) pp. 13; Ferishta, Briggs. III, pp. 217-18; Muntakhab-ul-Lubab III, pp. 164; Mirat-i-Sikandari pp. 160; See, also, Sir T. W. Haig, "The Faruqi Dynasty of Khandesh" (I.A. 1918) pp. 122-3; Baylay, "The History of Local Muhammedan Dynasties", pp. 340.

43. Mirat-i-Sikandari, pp, 160; Tabqat-i-Akbari III, pp. 68; Baylay, "The History of Local Muhammdan Dynastics," pp. 340.

44. Mirat-i-Ahmadi says that the Sultan had a hundred thousand horse and 300 elephants.

45. Mirat-i-Sikandari, pp. 161; Baylay, "The History of Local Muhammedan Dynasties," pp. 340-41.

46. Mirat-i-Sikandari, pp. 161; Baylay, "The History of Local Muhammedan Dynasties", pp. 341.

47. Mirat-i-Sikandari, pp. 161; Baylay, "The History of Local Muhammedan Dynasties", pp. 342.

48. Mirat-i-Sikandari, pp. 161.

49. Mirat-i-Sikandari, pp. 161; Baylay, "The History of Local Muhammedan Dynasties," pp. 342.

50. Mirat-i-Sikandari, pp. 161; Baylay, "The History of Local Muhammedan Dynasties", pp. 342.

51. Mirat-i-Sikandari, pp. 161; Baylay, "The History of Local Muhammedan Dynastics", pp. 342; Commassariat, "The History of Gujarat," pp. 321.

52. Mirat-i-Sikandari, pp. 161; Baylay, "The History of Local Muhammedan Dynasties," pp. 344.

53. Ferishta, Briggs. III, pp. 218; Mirat-i-Sikandari, pp. 162-43; Sir T. W. Haig, "The Faruqui Dynasty of Khandesh" (I.A. 1918) pp. 122; Muntakhab-ul-Lubab III, pp. 165; Bird's "History of Gujarat" pp. 237; Baylay, "History of Local Muhammedan Dynastics", pp. 344; Commissariet, "History of Gujarat", pp. 321-22.

54. Ferishta, Briggs. III, pp. 218; Muntakhab-ul-Lubab III, pp. 165; Baylay, "The History of Local Muhammedan Dynasties," pp. 344-5.

55. Ferishta, Briggs. III, pp. 218; Muntakhab-ul-Lubab III, pp. 165.

56. Ferishta, Briggs. III, pp. 218; Muntakhab-ul-Lubab III, pp. 165.

57. Ferishta, Briggs. III, pp. 219; Muntakhab-ul-Lubab III, pp. 165.

58. Ferishta, Brigs. III, pp. 219; Muntakhab-ul-Lubab III, pp. 165.

59. Ferista, Briggs; III, pp. 219; Muntakhab-ul-Lubab III, pp. 165.

60. Ferishta, Briggs. III, pp. 219, Muntakhab-ul-Lubab III, pp. 166.

61. Ferishta, Briggs. III, pp. 219; Muntakhab-ul-Lubab III, pp. 166.

62. Ferishta, Briggs. III, pp. 219; Muntakhab-ul-Lubab III, pp. 166.

63. Ferishta, Briggs. III, pp. 219; Muntakhab-ul-Lubab III, pp. 166; Tabqat-i-Akbari, III, pp. 68.

64. Ferishta, Briggs. III, pp. 219; Muntakhab-ul-Lubab III, pp. 166-67.

65. Ferishta, Briggs. III, pp. 219; Muntakhab-ul-Lubab III, pp. 167.

66. Ferishta, Briggs. III, pp. 220; Muntakhab-ul-Lubab III, pp. 167.

67. Mirat-i-Sikandari pp. 163; Muntakhab-ul-Lubab III, pp. 167; Baylay, "The History of Local Muhammedan Dynasties", pp. 345.

68. Ferishta, Briggs. III, pp. 220; Mirat-i-Sikandari, pp. 163; Muntakhab-ul-Lubab III, pp. 167; Baylay "The History of Local Muhammedan Dynasties", pp. 345.

69. Ferishta, Briggs. III, pp. 220; Muntakhab-ul-Lubab III, pp. 167.

70. Mirat-i-Sikandari, pp. 163; Balay "The History of Local Muhammedan Dynastics", pp. 345-46.

71. Ferishta, Briggs. III, pp. 220-21; Muntakhab-ul-Lubab, III, pp. 168; Bird's "History of Gujarat" pp. 238.

Sayyid Ali gives a different account of the whole affair. He has confused the sequence of events, and thus has failed to explain the circumstances which led to the invasions of the Daccan by Bahadur Shah of Gujarat. According to him after being defeated by Burhan at Valor, Imad-ul-Mulk fled and took refuge with Sultan Bahadur Shah of Gujarat. He painted to him an alluring picture for the conquest of the Daccan. Arriving at Daulatabad he, encamped before the fortress and upon the suggestions of his amirs and officers, opened its siege. Although the siege was prosecuted with vigour, there appeared little prospects of its reduction, for Manjhan Khan, son of Khairat Khan, the Kotwal bent all his energies to the defence. While these siege operations were in progress, Malik Barid wrote to Imad-ul-Mulk that he had acted unwisely in bringing a foreigner in the land and if Bahadur Shah conquered the Nizam Shahi kingdom, Imad Shah would not be left long to reign in Berar. He advised him to settle the dispute among themselves, so that the enemy might be induced to abandon his design of conquering the Daccan. Imad Shah accepted this suggestion, removed his camp at a distance from that of his ally and secretly sent a message to Manjhan Khan to remain firm and resist the besiegers, promising him ready assistance. Constant fighting went on for some time, whereafter Imad Shah convinced Bahadur Shah of the futility of continuing the siege, suggesting to him to abandon it, and bring Burhan into the open field and defeat him, which would be sufficient to cause the surrender of all the forts of the Daccan. As the latter was sick of the protracted operations, he consented, raised the siege and turned his attention towards the conquest of Bir.

After the Gujarati forces had withdrawn from the walls of the fort, Imad-ul-Mulk instructed Manjhan Khan to sally from the fortress, attack the rear guard and plunder the baggage. At the same time he sent a message to Burhan Nizam Shah to proceed with Ali Barid and attack the enemy saying that in the thick of the fight he would desert his ally, who anticipated his intentions, and withdrew with his army to some distance from the Gujarati camp. He then sent a message to Bahadur Shah informing him that he had already told him that if Malik Ali Barid and Burhan united themselves, the matters would take a serious turn. He had withdrawn from his camp, because he knew that his presence there would increase the resentment of the Daccanis more against the invaders. He advised Bahadur Shah to retire to Chanak Deo, when Bahadur Shah came to know that his ally had retired to his own country he also returned to Gujarat. See, Burhan-i-Maasir (I.A. 1920) pp. 177-80.

72. Burhan-i—Maasir (I.A. 1920) pp. 184; Ferishta, Briggs, III, pp. 221; Commissariat, "History of Gujarat", pp. 322; Baylay, "The History of Local Muhammedan Dynasties, "pp. 340-46.

73. Ferishta, Briggs. III, pp. 221; Tabaqat-i-Akbari, III, pp. 68; Muntakhab-ul-Lubab, III, pp. 169.

74. Ferishta, Briggs. III, pp. 221; Burhani-i-Maasir (I.A. 1920) pp. 180-81; Muntakhab-ul-Lubab, III, pp. 169.

75. Ferishta, Briggs. III, pp. 221; Muntakhab-ul-Lubab III, pp. 169; Sayyid Ali gives an imperfect account of Shah Tahir's reception. According to him before Shah Tahir arrived at the Gujarati court, Bahadur Shah had heard that he was the most learned man of his age and that even Emperor Humayun, used to seal his letter on the back of it, out of respect for him, and therefore he began to think about the manner in which he should accord him a grand reception. In the end, he decided to receive him unceremoniously while walking in the garden. After Shah Tahir had met Sultan Bahadur Shah, he was treated with highest honour consideration and since he took delight in his company, he did not give him leave, to depart. Thus Shah Tahir remained for three years with him and he even accompanied him in his expedition to Malwa—See, Burhan-i-Maasir (I.A. 1920) pp. 181.

76. Muntakhab-ul-Lubab III, pp. 169-70.

77. Ferishta, Briggs. III, pp. 222; Burhan-i-Massir (I.A. 1920) pp. 180; Mirat-i-Sikandari pp. 168; Muntakhab-ul-Lubab, III, pp. 170; Commissariat, "The History of Gujarat", pp. 322-23; Balay, "The History of Local Muhammedan Dynasties,", pp. 354.

78. Ferishta, Briggs. III, pp. 222; Mirat-i-Sikandari, pp. 168; Muntakhab-ul-Lubab, III, pp. 170; Baylay, "The History of Local Muhammedan Dynasties," pp. 354.

79. Mirat-i-Sikandari, pp. 169; Baylay, "The History of Local Muhammedan Dynasties", pp. 354.

80. Mirat-i-Sikandari, pp. 169; Baylay, "The History of Local Muhammedan Dynasties", pp. 354.

81. Ferishta, Briggs. III, pp. 222; Muntakhab-ul-Lubab, III, pp. 170; Tabaqat-i-Akbari, III, pp. 68; Mirat-i-Sikandari, pp. 169-70; Sayyid Ali, although has given a detailed account of the meeting between Burhan Nizam Shah and Sultan Bahadur Shah of Gujarat, but makes no mention about the title of Shah"—see, Burhan-i-Maasir, (I.A. 1920) pp. 181.

82. Ferishta, Briggs, III, pp. 222; Burhan-i-Maasir (I.A. 1920), pp. 181; Muntakhab-ul-Lubab, III, pp. 179..

83. Ferishta, Briggs. III, pp. 222.

84. Ibid.

85. Ferishta, Briggs. III, pp. 223; Muntakhab-ul-Lubab, III, pp. 172-6.

86. Ibid.

87. Ibid.

88. Ibid.

89. Burhan-i-Maasir (I.A. 1920) pp. 181; Ferishta, ii, pp. 107-8; Ferishta, Briggs. III, pp. 224; Muntakhab-ul-Lubab, III, pp. 172-6.

90. Burhan-i-Maasir (I.A. 1920) pp. 182; Ferishta, Briggs. III, pp. 224.

91. Ibid.

92. Ibid.

93. Ibid.

94. Ibid.

95. Ibid.

96. Ferishta, Briggs. III, pp. 224.

97. Ibid.

98. Ferishta, Briggs. III, pp. 225; Burhan-i-Maasir. (I.A. 1920) pp. 182; Maasir-i-Rahimi II, pp. 414; Brid's, "History of Gujarat", pp. 239; Baylay, "The History of Local Muhamedan Dynasties", pp. 354-55.

99. Burhan-i-Maasir (I.A. 1920) pp. 182; Ferishta, Briggs. III, p. 225.

100. Burhan-i-Maasir (I.A. 1920) pp. 183; Ferishta, ii, pp. 108. Ferishta, Briggs. III, pp. 225.

101. Burhan-i-Maasir (I.A. 1920) pp. 183.

102. Burhan-i-Maasir (I.A. 1920 ) pp. 183; Ferishta, Briggs. III, 225.

103. Burhan-i-Maasir (I.A. 1920) pp. 183; Ferishta, Briggs. III, pp. 225.

104. Ibid.

105. Ibid.

106. Ibid.

107. Ibid.

108. Ferishta, Briggs. III. pp 226; Burhan-i-Maasir (I.A. 1920) pp. 184.

This was the last meeting between Burhan Nizam Shah and Bahadur Shah, the king of Gujarat, but Bird in the "History of Gujarat" refers to one more meeting. According to him in 1534-35, Bahadur Shah, went to Mandu, by way of Mandsor, and soon after his arrival there he deputed Muhammad Shah Asiri, the ruler of Khandesh, with leading Gujarati nobles, to go against Nizam Shah, Muhammad Shah Asiri, after encountering the latter in the neighbourhood of the town of Bir, sent messengers to the Sultan for reinforcement. Accordingly 12000 horsemen, were sent to his assistance. Before their arrival, the opposite armies had already measured their sword, near Bir, and upon hearing of Sultan's advance, the Nizam Shah took to flight. After some time, Burhan Nizam Shah acknowledged his suzerainty, and came to meet him. Bahadur Shah, after having given him back his country, proceeded to Mandu. At this time Burhan Nizam Shah having accompanied the king of Gujarat several stages, obtained leave to return—see, Bird's "History of Gujarat".

It is doubtful if such a meeting ever took place between Burhan and Bahadur Shah, especially at a time, when the latter was hounded from place to place by the Mughal Emperor, Humayun.

109. Ferishta, Briggs. III, pp. 226.

110. Ibid.

111. Ferishta, Briggs. III, pp. 226-27; Basatin-us-Salatin (pt. II) pp. 20.

112. Ferishta, Briggs. III, pp. 227; Basatin-us-Salatin, pp. 20. Muntakhab-ul-Lubab, III, pp. 174.

113. Ferishta, Briggs. III, pp. 227.

114. Ibid.

115. Basatin-us-Salatin, pp. 20-21; Ferishta, Briggs. III, pp. 227. Sayyid Ali omits all mention of the events which followed after the meeting of Burhan with Bahadur Shah, perhaps because they do not reflect any credit on him.

116. Ibid.

117. According to Sayyid Ali, one evening after Shah Tahir had left him, Burhan went to his bed, and while asleep he saw in a dream Prophet Muhammad with Ali on his right, Hasan and Husain on his left, Muhammad Baqir and Shah Tahir were standing at a little distance from them, ready to carry out their orders, Burhan bowed to the Prophet. Upon this Muhammad Baqir told him, "The Prophet commands you that you should follow the guidance of Shah Tahir and stand fast to the faith of love of the Prophet and his descendants." The king was exceedingly delighted to receive this message and praised the Imam. Next morning he sent for Shah Tahir, related the dream which the latter had also seen and now decided to follow the shia faith—see, Burhan-i-Maasir (I.A. 1920) pp. 168.

According to Ferishta, Shah Tahir took advantage of the serious illness of Abdul Qadir, the son of Burhan Nizam Shah. He suggested to the king that if he professed the Shia faith the Prince would be cured. It was while the king was sitting by his son's bed that he saw a dream, in which Muhammad assured him that his son would recover from the illness and asked him to follow the teachings of Shah Tahir; Ferishta ii, pp. 112-13; see also, Muntakhab-ul-Tawarikh, Vol. I, pp. 625.

118. Al-Bukhari is a collection of the traditions of Muhamed Sahib. It was written by Al Bukhari who received the name from Bukhara, the place of his birth or chief residence. He was a famous lawyer, his name being Muhammad Ismail. He called his work Al-Salih eg. genuine because he separated the spurious traditions from those that were authentic. He says that that he selected 9,275 of the most authentic traditions out of 10,000. all of which he looked upon as true, having rejected 20,0000 as false. He died at Bukhara in the year 870 A.H. see, Oriental Biographical Dictionary, pp. 52.

119. Ferishta, Briggs. III, pp. 228-29; Muntakhab-ul-Lubab, III, pp 182-83.

120. Ferishta, Briggs. III, pp. 228.

121. Ibid.

122. Burhan-i-Maasir (I.A. 1920) pp. 187.

123. Ferishta, Briggs.III,pp.228; Burhan-i-Maasir (I.A.1920) pp.197

124. Ferishta III, pp. 228; Muntakhab-ul-Lubab III, pp. 182.

125. Ferishta III, pp. 228-29; Muntakhab-ul-Lubab III, pp. 183; Tathkiral-Shorai Dakkan II, pp. 709-10.

126. Ibid.

127. Ibid.

128. Fath Shah Begam performed pilgrimage with her husband, but when the latter wished to return to the Daccan, she refused to accompany

him, saying that she did not want to leave the Prophet's tomb for the sake of wordly pleasures. At length, she died there and was buried near his tomb. After her death, Sayyid Hasan returned to the Daccan, where he died and buried at Junnar—Burhan-i-Maasir (I.A. 1920) pp. 199.

129. Burhan-i-Maasir (I.A. 1920) pp. 197-98.

130. The fort of Baglana is situated in 20⁰ 46′ N. and 70⁰ 32′ East.

131. Mulhir is in Baglana, situated in 20⁰ 46′ and 74⁰ 4; East.

132. Sayyid Ali has wrongly mentioned here the name of Bahadur Shah. By this time he had died (14th Feb. 1537)—See, Burhan-i-Maasir (I.A. 1920), pp. 199-200; S. K. Banerji's "Humayun Badshah", pp. 170.

133. Burhan-i-Maasir (I.A. 1920) pp. 200.

134. Ibid pp. 201.

135. Sayyid Ali has baselessly charged Asad Khan Lari with instigating the invasion of Bijapur by Burhan Nizam Shah and he has misrepresented the circumstances in which it occurred. According to him Ibrahim Adil Shah had inveded Vijayanagar and was encamping there awaiting the army of Ram Raya. Asad Khan wrote a letter to Burhan Nizam Shah advising him to sieze the opportunity of recapturing his lost districts. The fact of the matter is that peace had already been concluded with the Raya, before Burhan invaded Bijapur, see—Burhan-i-Maasir (I.A. 1920)pp. 202; Basatin-us-Salatin (pt. III) pp. 9; Ferishta, Briggs, III, pp. 229.

136. Basatin-us-Salatin (pt. III) pp. 9.

137. Ibid. pp. 9-10.

138. Basatin-us-Salatin (pt. III) pp. 10-11; Ferishta Briggs. III, pp. 229-30; Proceedings of the Daccan History conference, 1945, pp. 233.

According to Sayyid Ali, Burhan Nizam Shah marched at the invitation of Asad Khan Lari, Ibrahim Adil Shah soon concluded peace with the ruler of Vijayanagar, whose country he had invaded, and returned to repel the invaders. Ali then wrote to Darya Imad Shah for assistance and the latter deserted his ally Burhan. Meanwhile discussions among the nobles of Burhan encouraged Ibrahim Adil Khan to proceed further and attack him. But as Darya Imad Shah wanted to solve the Sholapur issue peacefully, he asked him to desist. One right he entered Burhan's camp. bribed, Ain-ul-Mulk, by giving him 30,000 huns, promising an equal amount provided he deserted his master. Ain-ul-Mulk who had been resentful of Burhan's change of religion accepted the offer, left his camp with 3000 men and joined the enemy. Thus, the Bijapur forces having been strengthened, Ibrahim Adil wanted to attack the enemy. But Darya Imad Shah requested him to cede Parenda and its dependencies to Burhan Nizam Shah to which he agreed. Thereafter Burhan returned to his capital. Sayyid Ali has concealed the facts and has given a garbed version of what had taken place—see Burhan-i-Maasir (I.A. 1920) pp. 203-4.

139. Ferishta, Briggs. III, pp. 230; Basatin-us-Salatin pp. 11.

140. This action is recorded in "Narasabupalayami"—"He preserved the sapda (Adil Shah) in his kingdom on agreeing to pay him tribute and hand over Raichur and Mudgal, when the Nizam sought refuge with him, he begged him his help and established firmly in his kingdom"—see, S. K. Ayangar, "Sources of Vijayanagara History," pp. 224; Journal of Andhra Historical of Society, 1946-47, Vol. 17, pp. 189; R. Suba Rao's "A brief History of Vizianagara'.

141. Basatin-us-Salatin, pp. 11-12; Ferishta, Briggs. III, pp. 231.

142. Basatin-us-Salatin, pp. 12.

143. Basatin-us-Salatin, pp. 12-13.

144. Basatin-us-Salatin, (pt. III) pp. 13; Ferishta, Briggs, III, pp. 231; Journal of Andhra Historical Society, 1946-47, Vol. 17, pp. 189.

145. Ferishta, Briggs. III, pp. 95.

146. Ibid.

147. Ferishta, Briggs. III, pp. 231.

Sayyid Ali gives a different account of the whole affair. He says that Burhan Nizam Shah thought of recovering Sholapur which he had again lost.

Accordingly, he marched and encamped on the banks of the Godavari. Soon after arrived Darya Imad Shah with his forces and joined him. In order to organise a confederacy, Burhan sent Shah Tahir to Ali Barid to persuade him to join him with his forces immediately. Receiving the intelligence of the plans of the enemies, Ibrahim Adil Shah marched to meet them. But Ali Barid tried to play a treacherous role, by opening scret negotiations with Ibrahim and decided to desert to his side. Therefore, he sent his brother Khan Jahan and Bhopal Rai without giving any reply. Shah Tahir now advised Burhan Nizam Shah to put to death Barid Shah. While discussion on this matter was in progress, Ali Barid had to envoy of Imad Shah trampled to death, which enraged the latter, who prepared himself to take the revenge. But Burhan Nizam Shah advised him to wait, after which he would devote his whole attention to punish him. Ali Barid in fear retired to Bidar. Shah Tahir and Darya Imad Shah sent Ibrahim Adil Shah proposals of peace. The latter granted them on condition that Burhan Nizam Shah be allowed to seize Qandhar from Ali Barid., as compensation for the loss of Sholapur, to which Burhan Nizam Shah agreed. Accordingly he marched to Qandhar, laid siege to the fort and captured it and then returned to his capital—see Burhan-i-Maasir (I.A. 1920) pp. 1-3.

148. Ferishta, Briggs. III, pp. 231-32; Sayyid Ali places the siege of Qandhar first then the siege of Ausa and Udgir—see Burhan-i-Maasir (I.A. 1921) pp. 4;

Here mention should be made of an exaggerated account given by Hindu Chronicles. According to them Ram Raya, suspecting that the promoter of war waged against him by Adil Shah was Burhan Nizam Shah he resolved to take the revenge with the object of creating a rift between the allies leaving Ibrahim Adil Shah alone, he marched into the Nizam Shahi territory. To prevent the rulers of Golkunda and Bidar from coming to the rescue of the victim of his aggression, he split up his army into three divisions with the one under his personal command, he advanced towards Golkunda and the second under the command of his brother Triumla was sent against Bidar; while the third led by Hande Hammappa Nayadu of Sonnalpam, moved towards Ahmadnagar with the two fold object of punishing the ruler and occupying his capital. In the end these three divisions converged on a single point, when a bloody battle took place in which the three Muslim kings of the Daccan were signally defeated. Each of them fled towards his capital with the enemy in hot pursuit of him. Burhan Nizam Shah fell into the hands of Hande Hammappa Nayadu,[1] while Ram Raya seized Ahmadnagar razed it on the ground and sowed caster seeds there[2]—see Heras, "Arvidu Dynasty of Vijayanagara", pp. 27.

1. "Annals of Hande Anantpuram" and "Vasucharitram"—see, S. K. Ayangar "Sources of Vijayanagara History", pp. 179, 216.

2. Ramrajayamu, mentions that after this victory Ram Raya was given the title of "अहमद नगर सल भजनां" (Destroyer of the fortifications of Ahmadnagar) see, Ibid, pp. 183.

149. Ferishta, Briggs. III, pp. 232-33.

150. Shah Tahir left behind him three daughters and four sons. (i) Shah Haider, (ii) Shah Rafiuddin Hasan, (iii) Shah Abul Hasan, (iv) Shah Abu Turab. At the time of his death the eldest son, Shah Haider was in Iran at the court of Shah Tahmasp as the Nizam Shahi ambassador. Upon his return, according to the dying wishes of his father he was appointed as a peer of the kingdom—see, Tathkira-i-Shorai Daccan, Vol. II, pp. 718.

According to Tulgha-i-Sami, the Majlis-ul-Mumri and Tabeqat-i-Shahjehan, Shah Tahir died in 952 A.H. According to Burhan-i-Maasir, he died in 954 A.H. while according to Ferishta he died in 956 A.H.

See, Rieu, "Calalogue of Persian Manuscript in the British Museum Library", pp. 395.

151. Ferishta, Briggs. III, pp. 232.

152. Ferishta, Briggs. III, pp. 232; Burhan-i-Maasir (I.A. 1920) pp. 5.

Sayyid Ali has placed the date of Asad Khan's death in 1547, but has placed the event after the death of Jamshed Quli Qutb Shah, who died in 1550 A.D. Ferishta places this event after the death of Asad Khan Lari who died on 30th June 1549. A.D., but elsewhere he places the event after the death of Shah Tahir, who according to him died in 1549. According to Sir Wolesley Haig, the campaign occurred in 1551, but another campaign against Sholapur is mentioned in 1551, the two should not be confused. The fact of the matter is that this event took place after the death of Asad Khan Lari and Shah Tahir, but before the death of Jamshed Quli Q. Shah.

153. Ferishta, Briggs. III, pp. 232.

154. Ferishta, Briggs. III, pp. 232.

155. Ferishta, Briggs. III, pp. 232.

156. Ferishta, Briggs III, pp. 233; Basatin-us-Salatin pp. 11-13; Sayyid Sayyid Ali makes no mention of Ram Raya in this campaign against the Adil Shah, see Burhan-i-Maasir (I. A. 1920) pp. 5-6.

157. Ferishta, Briggs. III, pp. 233-34.

158. Ferishta, Briggs. III, pp. 233-34; Burhan-i-Maasir (I.A. 1921) pp. 6.

159. Ferishta, Briggs. III, pp. 234, Burhan-i-Maasir (I.A. 1921) pp. 6.

160. Ferishta, Briggs. III, pp. 234-35.

161. Ferishta, Briggs. III, pp. 234-35.

Hindu chroniclers give credit of the victory to the Hindus of Vijayanagara. According to them the fortress of Kaliyani was captured by Ram Raya, without mentioning the name of Burhan Nizam Shah. Ramrajyamu mentions that upon this victory Ram Raya, was given the title of "कल्यान नगर साधका" (ruler of the city of Kalliyani)—see, "Sources of Vijayanagara, History", pp. 183.

Padmeri grant of Venkatadari II also mentions the conquest of Kalliyani by Ram Raya—see, Epigraphica Indica XVI, pp. 293.

162. Ferishta, Briggs. III, pp. 235.

163. Ferishta, Briggs. III, pp. 235; Burhan-i-Maasir, (I. A. 1921) pp. 7-8.

164. Ferishta ii, pp. 119; Ferishta, Briggs. III, pp. 235; Burhan-i-Maasir (I.A. 1921) pp. 25.

165. Ferishta, Briggs III, pp. 235; Burhan-i-Maasir (I.A. 1921) pp. 26.

166. Burhan-i-Maasir (I.A. 1921) 26-28.

167. Burhan Nizam Shah had in all, six sons, Miran Husain and Miran Abdul Qadir by his favourite wife Aimna; Miran Shah Ali and Miran Muhammad Baqar by Bibi Maryam and Miran Khudabanda by another wife and Miran Shah Haidar.

168. Ferishta, Briggs. III, pp. 236; Burhan-i-Maasir (I.A. 1921) pp. 28; Muntakhab-ul-Lubab, III, pp. 186.

169 Ferishta, Briggs. III, pp. 236; According to Nizam-ud-din Ahmed, he reigned for forty eight years—Tabqat-i-Akbari III, pp. 68.

170. Burhan-i-Maasir (I.A. 1921) pp. 30.

171. Tathkira-i-Shorai Dakhan II, pp. 709-10.

## CHAPTER IV

# HUSAIN NIZAM SHAH I (1554-1565 A.D.)

Husain Nizam Shah was proclaimed king on February 9, 1554 A.D. (5th Rab-ul-awwal A.H. 961) at an auspicious hour selected by the astrologers of the court.[1] The Wazir, nobles, learned men and other officers of the state appeared in audience, paid their homage and made their obeisance to him. Largesses were distributed to small and great, high and low, poor and wealthy alike. General rejoicings took place in the city of Ahmadnagar. Qasim Beg was confirmed in the post of Wakil and Peshwa. To celebrate the occasion, he scattered coins among the populace like perfumed water.

**Accession to the throne**

Early in his reign the young king had to face numerous difficulties, which left him little time to devote his attention to and take interest in cultivating higher values of life. The first to distract his mind were his own brothers, who advanced their claims for the throne. It has already been noted that during the closing years of his father's reign Husain Nizam Shah had driven away all other claimants from the environs of the city. But he could not liquidate the existence of the parties. The Foreigners and the Abyasinians were interested in the cause of the king, whereas the Daccanis and others favoured Abdul Qadir, who after his defeat, had fled to Berar, to seek refuge with his father-in-law Darya Imad Shah.[2] Husain Nizam wrote to the latter reminding him of the friendly relations which had existed between the two houses and asking him to expel the rebel from his country. Upon the receipt of the letter, Darya Imad Shah asked the Prince Abdul Qadir to leave Berar and go wherever he liked.[3]

**Early Difficulties**

Prince Shah Ali and Miran Muhammad Baqr struck with fear had fled to their uncle Ibrahim Adil Shah I.[4] Another Prince Khudabanda fled to the north, and

Prince Miran Shah Haider in expectation of help from his father-in-law Makhdum Khwaja Jahan, the governor of the fort of Parenda took refuge with him. There he began to think of rising in rebellion against his brother. At the same time Nasir-ul-Mulk an influential noble, who had been confined in the fortress of Kondana, contrived to effect his escape in order to join Miran Shah Haider.[5] But Husain Nizam Shah took prompt steps to intercept him, before he could join hands with his brother. He directed his tutor Maulana Shah Muhammad to march at the head of a division of Khurasani troops and overtake Nasir-ul-Mulk.[6] The Maulana left Ahmadnagar by night and early next morning appeared before the enemy's camp. In sheer fright Nasir-ul-Mulk took to flight. He was hotly pursued, was captured and beheaded. Maulana Shah Muhammad returned to the court with the head of the rebel.[7]

Makhdum Khwaja Jahan neither sent any message of condolence to the Husain Nizam Shah, nor the customary presents on his accession. He was summoned to court to explain his conduct.[8] But being afraid of condign punishment at first he offered excuses, and after some time broke into open rebellion, supporting the cause of Miran Shah Haider. The king immediately took the field against him, but before he could arrive at Parenda, the rebels had fled to Ibrahim Adil Shah. Husain Nizam Shah opened the siege of the fort of Parenda and captured it by storming one of its walls. Then he returned to Ahmadnagar.[9]

In Bijapur Makhdum Khwaja Jahan strove hard to fan the fire of hostility between Husain Nizam Shah and Ibrahim Adil Shah I.[10] In the end he succeeded in inciting Ibrahim Adil to recover the fortress of Sholapur. Accordingly Ibrahim Adil Shah I concluded an alliance with Ram Raya, the ruler of Vijayanagara, and won over Saif-ul-Mulk, the commander-in-chief of the Nizam Shahi army in the time of Burhan Nizam Shah I, who in sheer fright had fled to Berar.[11] Adil Shah took up the cause of Prince Ali.

**Ibrahim Adil Shah I declares war against Ahmadnagar**

A compact was made with him according to which the ruler of Bijapur was to receive Kaliyani and Sholapur in lieu of his help to him in obtaining the throne of Ahmadnagar.[12] In accordance with a well-thought-out plan, a two-pronged attack was delivered on the Nizam Shahi Kingdom. Prince Ali having assumed the royal insignia marched to the frontiers of Ahmadnagar, whereas Ibrahim Adil Shah advanced to open the siege of Sholapur.

On receipt of the report of the invasion of his country, Husain Nizam Shah called a council of war to decide the future course of action. Qasim Beg Hakim advised him that he should first put to death the traitors in the camp who had brought about such an invasion. Accordingly, Farhad Khan, Khurshid Khan and Shujaāt Khan, who belonged to the Sunni party and had favoured the pretensions of Prince Abdul Qadir, were thrown into prison on the suspicion of treachery and were subsequently blinded.[13] After this the king sent Rafi-ud-din Husain, the son of Shah Tahir, as an envoy to the court of Darya Imad Shah to reestablish friendship with him and to persuade him to join him against Ibrahim Adil Shah I for two reasons; firstly, that the latter had given refuge to his brothers, and secondly, that he had invaded his dominions, in alliance with the ruler of Vijayanagara.[14] Unfortunately Rafi-ud-din Husain, who was a slave of passion, instead of carrying out his mission to a successful end, violently fell in love with a courtesan of Berar, who was a favourite mistress of Darya Imad Shah. Naturally Imad Shah was annoyed at the conduct of the envoy whom he sent back, even without receiving him in audience.[15] Husain Nizam Shah now sent Vishwas Rai, one of the Brahman officials of the court, who concluded the mission successfully.[16] Darya Imad Shah came to Ahmadnagar, and from there the allies marched to Sholapur to relieve it from the pressure of the enemy. A contested battle occurred in which the tide at first turned in favour of the invaders[17], but timely arrival of reinforcement from Ahmadnagar turned the tables on Ibrahim Adil Shah. Saif-ul-Mulk had to dismount from his horse and to fight on foot. The Adil Shahi forces thought that he was deserting to Husain Nizam Shah; overtaken by panic, they broke up, and fled, leaving their camp equippage as spoil for the victors.[18]

**Husain marches to repel the invasion.**

No sooner had Husain Nizam Shah shaken off the aggression caused by his brother than his attention was distracted by trouble in another quarter. When, towards the

**Rebellion of Dannaya Rai.**

end of his reign Burhan Nizam Shah was proceeding to cooperate with Ram Raya of Vijayanagara in besieging the fortress of Raichur, Dannaya Rai, the governor of the fort of Antur rebelled. The illness of the late king and the civil war at the capital allowed him fullest freedom of action. He declined to acknowledge Husain Nizam Shah as king. His example was followed by Raja Bharjui, the governor of the forts of Galna and Baglana. Husain Nizam Shah marched against them and within a short time captured the forts of Galna, Antur and Baglana, and reduced their chiefs to submission. (1555 A.D.)[19]

**Alliance with Ibrahim Qutb Shah.**

In 1558 A.D. when trouble arose in Bijapur after the death of Ibrahim Adil Shah I, Husain Nizam Shah was emboldened to snatch a small part of its territory.[20] Impressed with his rising power, his growing resourcefulness, Ibrahim Qutb Shah the ruler of Golkunda, thought it would be advantageous to him to enter into offensive and defensive alliance with him, against the kingdom of Bijapur. Accordingly, he sent one of his leading amirs Mustafa Khan, a shrewed diplomat and polished politician, to the Nizam Shahi court to lay before the king the proposal and conclude treaty with him.[21] The ambassador was cordially received at the court and was accorded a warm reception. Mustafa Khan succeeded in his mission and it was arranged that Ibrahim Qutb Shah should meet Husain Nizam Shah in front of the fortress of Gulbarga to ratify the terms of the treaty,[22] according to which the latter was to help the former in capturing the fortress of Bidar and Gulbarga.[23] The two kings marched from their respective capitals for the proposed meeting. After exchange of friendly professions and goodwill and taking of oaths of faithfulness they marched together, surrounded the fort of Gulbarga and opened its siege.[24] The garrison offered obstinate resistance, inspite of the superiority of the resources of the enemy. When driven to sore straits, they made frantic appeals for help to their master. To avert the calamity, Ali Adil Shah sought the help of the Raya of Vijayanagara, who asked Ibrahim Qutb Shah to withdraw, a request which the latter could not turn down, because of the obligation he felt to him for having given him asylum as Prince.[25] Moreover the Raya's army was now devastating his province of Pengal. In view of these considerations and on the advice of Mustafa Khan who had become fed up with war, Ibrahim Qutb Shah quietly deserted his friend and casting to the wind his plighted word, he returned to his capital.[26]

When the news of the withdrawal of his ally reached the ears of Husain Nizam Shah, he found himself in difficulty. He openly reprimanded Qasim Beg Hakim who had conducted the negotiations, and charged him with duplicity, treachery, and above all with the guilt of having instigated the Qutb Shahi monarch to raise the siege.[27] He was ordered to be imprisoned in the fort of Parenda, a step which led to the flight of many nobles from the royal camp.[28] One of them was Maulana Inayat-ullah Nayati, a learned and accomplished man of his age. He left to take refuge at the court of Ibrahim Qutb Shah of Golkunda[29]. Husain Nizam Shah returned to his capital and appointed Maulana Ali Mazandarani, who was distinguished for his learning, piety and had great command over rhetoric, to the office of Wakil and Peshwa.[30] Bhopal Rai, who had been formerly in the service of Ali Barid was appointed as Wazir. But the absence of Qasim Beg proved unbearable to the king. He was subsequently released and restored to his former post.[31]

It was now the turn of Ali Adil Shah to attack the kingdom of Ahmadnagar, to recover the forts of Kaliyani and Sholapur. To achieve the object, he sent his minister Kishwar Khan, and Shah Abu Taurab to the court of Ram Raya to form a league with him against Husain Nizam Shah.[32] Further to provide a *causus belli* for the invasion, he sent Muhammad Husain Siddiqi to the Nizam Shahi court to demand the cession of the two forts. The Adil Shahi ambassador was accorded a cordial reception at the court of Ram Raya who expressed his readiness to join the league.[33] But Husain Nizam Shah not only openly denounced the greedy nature and the jealous designs of Ali Adil Shah, but declined to show even the customary courtesy to the envoy, dismissed him without any reply,[34] and declared war against Adil Shah. Findidg himself too weak to encounter the enemy by himself all alone[35] and overcome

**Ali Adil Shah declares war against Husain Nizam Shah**

with unnerving fear, he left his capital and fled post-haste to Vijayanagara, where he was hospitably received by Ram Raya, who at the moment was in mourning, having lost his son.[36] To forget her grief, the Raya's wife adopted Ali Adil Shah as her son. After staying there for three days Adil Shah returned to Bijapur. Having cemented the bonds of friendship with Ram Raya,[37] he sent an expedition against Ahmadnagar justifying his action on two grounds viz, (i) Husain Nizam Shah had not fulfilled the custom of paying homage to him upon his coronation. (ii) that he had joined Tufal Khan and had created disturbance in the his country.[38] But before actually opening the campaign he sent a message to Husain Nizam Shah through Husain Anju, observing that, "the forts of Kaliyani and Sholapur belonged to his family by ancient right, though owing to the misfortunes of his father, they had passed into the hands of the Nizam Shahi government, but now he hoped, that they would be restored to him."[39] Husain Anju failed to persuade the Nizam Shahi ruler to give up either of the two places. Ali Adil Shah sent another envoy to Ahmadnagar, with a message to the effect that, "passion and obstinacy in the discussion of political questions of such importance do not make kings great and that to prevent evil consequences, he trustes that Husain Nizam Shah would see the justice in giving up the forts, which would increase the goodwill and amity between the two states ; otherwise he should expect the march of an army into his dominions which would lay it waste without mercy."[40] This was a direct challenge of Adil Shahi monarch, to the most sentimental, ambitious and powerful king of Ahmadnagar, who was ever ready to measure swords with his enemy. Annoyed at the tone of this message he sent a similar reply which touched Ali Adil Shah to the quick so that, "changing the colour of his canopy and standard from yellow to green by way of defiance, he challenged him to come and reclaim his honour."[41]

Husain Nizam Shah was not the man to take the insult lying down. To augment his resources and strengthen his fighting power, he immediately sent Maulana Ali Mazandarani with costly presents to Darya Imad Shah to conclude an alliance with him.[42] The Maulana succeeded in settling the marriage of Hussain Nizam Shah with Daulat Shah, the daughter of Darya Imad Shah. The parties met at Sonpat on the banks of river Beur, commenced the marriage festivities. At an auspicious hour the nuptials were performed, according to the rites of the Holy Law. The Amirs scattered largesses and offered felicitations on the occasion. At the end of the festivities the two kings met once more and they returned with great pomp to their respective capitals.[43] This closer alliance with Berar was an answer to the alliance between Bijapur and Vijayanagara.

Events now began to move to a climax. Ali Adil Shah was tired of waiting. He was joined by Ram Raya and Ibrahim Qutb Shah. The allies opened the offensive on Ahmadnagar by demanding the cession of Kaliyani and Sholapur as the price of peace.[44] Husain Nizam Shah's counsellors urged him to strike the bargain by the retrocession of Kaliyani, but he obstinately refused to listen to them.[45] The allies forced their way into the kingdom of Ahmadnagar and created a scene there. "Raya's army laid waste the country so thoroughly that from Parenda to Junnar and from Ahmadnagar to Daultabad, not a vestige of population was left. The infidels of Bijanaggar, who for many years were waiting for such an opportunity left cruelty unpractised. They insulted the honour of Musalman women, destroyed the mosques and did not respect even the sacred Koran."[46]

On the suggestion of Qasim Beg and Shaikh Jafer and other ministers, Husain Nizam Shah retreated with army to Paithan.[47] From there he sent envoys to Muhammad Shah I, the ruler of Khandesh, Ali Barid Shah I and to Darya Imad Shah, requesting each of them to come to his assistance.[48] But unfortunately Khan Jahan, the brother Ali Barid, was the conscience keeper of both Ali Barid and Darya Imad Shah.[49] He had been won over by Ali Adil Shah. He not only succeeded in dissuading Ali Barid and Imad Shah from extending a helping hand to the hard pressed Husain, but even obtained permission of Darya to attack the Nizam Shahi Kingdom. But his move failed, and he had to suffer the disgrace of defeat at the hands of a small detachment of Nizam Shahi horse under the command of Mulla Muhammad Nishapuri.[50] He felt so humiliated that he did not return to the court of Imad Shah but entered the service of Ali Adil Shah. Freed from the influence of Khan Jahan, Darya Imad Shah changed his mind and sent an army under the command of Jahangir Khan Deccani to the succour of his son-in-law Husain Nizam Shah.[51] Jahangir Khan marched to the borders of Bijapur and did good work in intercepting the supplies of the powerful allies.[52]

**Ahmadnagar plundered and devastated by allies.**

Meanwhile the allies had opened the siege of the fort of Ahmadnagar.[53] The Hindus began to plunder and destroy the houses of the poor masses and to persecute the Muslims. Ali Adil Shah and Ibrahim Qutb Shah laid waste the adjacent territory.[54] But with the advent of the rainy season the ground became slippery and soft. It impeded mobility of the allied army and their horses and other beasts of burden began to die for want of fodder. The Nizam Shahi troops now had the opportunity of harassing the enemy by delivering surprise attacks on their flanks, and slaying all on whom they laid their hands. Ram Raya ordered Sadashiv Nayaka to devastate the country as far as the Godavari.[55] To counter the activities of the enemy Husain Nizam Shah sent an army of Iraqi and Khurasani horse men under Maulvi Khan, Sanjar Khan and Satyu. A fierce battle occurred near the town of Jamgaon, in which Sadashiv's men were defeated, and it was with much difficulty that they could effect their escape.[56]

Ibrahim Qutb Shah soon grew tired of prolonged warfare. Foresight unmistakably pointed to the contingency that if Adil Shah was allowed to occupy the fort of Ahmadnagar, Golkunda would be the next objective of his ambition.[57] Moreover, the Qutb Shah was much distressed at the conduct of Hindus, who had demolished magnificent buildings and mosques, plundered and devastated the land, and insulted Muslim women. To stop this orgy of death and destruction, he secretly opened communication with the garrison and assisted them, by allowing supplies to pass through his lines.[58] Maulana Inayatullah Niyati, who had for a while been in the Qutb Shahi service proved to be a link between Husain Nizam Shah at Paithan and the garrison of Ahmadnagar.[59] The activities could not long remain a secret ; and when they leaked out, Ali

Adil Shah and Ram Raya asked for an explanation from Ibrahim Qutb Shah, who one night quietly retreated to his own country, leaving his camp standing in the field.[60] Inayatullah Khan Niyati now rejoined the service of his former master Husain Nizam Shah.[61]

Unable to bear the brunt of the harassing activities of Jahangir Khah the allies retired to Asthi, from where they sent an army to reduce Parenda and Ausa.[62] According to the changed plan, the siege of Ahmadnagar was to be resumed after the occupation of these forts and rehabilitation of supplies.[63] Meanwhile, Ali Adil Shah discussed with Ram Raya the scheme of the partition of the Nizam Shahi kingdom between them.[64] But when the Raya received the report of the defeat of Sadashiva Nayaka at the hands of the Nizam Shahi troops, he was much upset and began to wait for a pretext for coming to terms with the enemy. Husain Nizam Shah took the opportunity by the fore-lock and opend the negotiations to that end.[65] He sent Qasim Beg and Maulana Inayatullah Niyati to discuss the terms of a treaty with Ram Raya who proposed[66] :

1. that Husain Nizam Shah should cede the fortress of Kaliyani to Ali Adil Shah.[67]
2. that he should put to death Jahangir Khan, who commanded the auxiliary troops of Darya Imad Shah and who had been extremely active against the enemy.
3. that Husain Nizam Shah should submit to Ram Raya, pay him a visit and receive a, "pan" from his hands.

Husain Nizam Shah's hopes of decisive victory over the allies having completely faded out, he made the best of the situtation and to save his kingdom, he submitted to the terms dictated by Ram Raya. He was compelled to fulfil every letter of the conditions imposed upon him by the allies. Kaliyani was surrendered to the Adil Shah.[68] Jahangir Khan was put to death and the horses and arms which had been captured at Jamgon were duly restituted.[69] Finally, Husain Nizam Shah went to the camp of Ram Raya to wait on him and receive the pan.[70] On his arrival Ram Raya rose to welcome his guest, and took him by his hand. Being an orthodox Shia, he regarded the touch of a Hindu equivalent to pollution. He soon called for a basin and ewer to wash his hands. The humiliation of bowing before a Hindu proved galling to his pride and he offended Ram Raya by his conduct so much that the latter exclaimed, "Were he not my guest I would have cut off his hands and hung them round his neck."[71] But the meeting passed off without any further mishap. Husain Nizam Shah in mortification returned to Ahmadnagar, without calling upon Ali Adil Shah. The treaty was signed by Qasim Beg and Maulana Inayatullah Niyati an behalf of Husain Nizam Shah and by Venkatadari and Eltamraj on the part of Ram Raya.[72]

**Husain Nizam Shah Humiliated.**

Hardly had the ink on the paper on which the recent treaty had been written, been dry that Husain Nizam Shah in concert with Ibrahim Qutb Shah marched out of his capital to recover the fort which he had just surrendered.[73] Once more Ali Adil Shah invited Ram Raya to support him; and the two succeeded in weaning away the Qutb Shah from the side of the Nizam Shah Ali Barid Shah I was also invited to join the league. The allies met on the banks of the Krishna from where they marched towards Ahmadnagar ruthlessly plundering and devastating the country on the way. Considering resistance to be futile Husain Nizam Shah retreated to Junnar.[74]

**Husain attempts to recover the ceded forts.**

As on the previous occassion Ibrahim Qutb Shah proved to be a black sheep among the allies. He assured Husain Nizam Shah that he would do his best to avert the calamity and encouraged the garrison of the fort of Ahmadnagar to offer stiff resistance. The siege dragged on for two months and the besieged began to lose heart. Ibrahim Qutb Shah now won over the principal leaders of the Vijayanagara army, through whom he began to play upon the fears of Ram Raya, to whom they painted in dark colours the difficulties of retreat after the advent of the rains. But Ali Adil Shah tempted the Raya with the cession of the fort of Itgir and dwelt upon the advantage of pressing on the siege to the final conclusion. Thereupon Ibrahim Qutb Shah held out the threat of desertion. At the same time he offered the fort of Kondapalli to the

Raya. The effect of this double move proved to be very telling. The allies dispersed without doing any further harm to Ahmadnagar.[75]

Being still keen to recover the lost fortress, Husain Nizam Shah now decided to establish more intimate relations with Ibrahim Qutb Shah[76]. At the suggetion of his advisers Qasim Beg and Maulana Inayatullah Niyati, he agreed to marry his daughter Jamal Bibi to him.[77] The parties assembled in front of the fortress of Kaliyani, where the nuptials were celebrated amidst great festivities, after which they opened the siege of the fort.[78]

Once more Ali Adil Shah appealed to Ram Raya, who marched to his assistance. On the way he was joined by Ali Barid Shah I and Burhan Imad Shah, the ruler of Berar.[79] Upon the approach of the invaders Husain Nizam Shah sent his family in the fortress of Ausa, and himself with Ibrahim Qutb Shah advanced to meet the enemy with seven hundred pieces of canon and five hundred elephants.[80] Next morning it was reported to Ibrahim Qutb Shah that Ram Raya, taking advantage of his absence from the capital had detached his brother Venkatadari with Jagdev Rai and Ain-ul-Mulk at the head of 15000 cavalry and 30000 infantry to invade the Southern districts of his kingdom.[81] Ibrahim, therefore, with the consent of Husain Nizam Shah raised the siege of Kaliyani and returned to Golkunda. Realising the futility of continuing operations, Husain Nizam Shah also left for Ahmadnagar, losing almost his entire park of artillery.[82]

The allies marched in hot pursuit of him. In utter disregard of the peril to which he was exposed, Husain Nizam Shah one afternoon dismounted, and offered his prayers. Finding that he had done it with a golden girdle round his waist, which was unlawful, he repeated them once again. His behaviour deeply impressed the enemy who admired his presence of mind and devotion to religion and gave up the pursuit. Throwing adequate supplies into the fort of Ahmadnagar, Husain Nizam Shah retreated to Junnar.[83]

The allies once more opened the siege of the fort of Ahmadnagar.[84] The Hindus under Ram Raya again inflicted every type of indignity and atrocity on the persons and property of the faithful (Muslims) polluting the mosques and dishonouring the women". Though scandalised, Ali Adil Shah was unable to prevent them. He now advised Ram Raya to raise the siege and fight the enemy in the field. Husain Nizam Shah retreated into the neighbouring hilly regions, from where he sent Rustam Khan, Adham Khan Habashi and Sabaji Koli to hover round the camps of the invaders and to cut off their supplies.[85] Rustam Khan surprised the enemy at Canoor, and during the affrary Ali Adil Shah's uncle lost his life. But Rustam Khan was shortly after defeated and killed along with his three thousand followers, by the Adil Shahi army.[86] At the approach of the rainy season, the allies besieged Ahmadnagar. The army of Ram Raya encamped south of the fort, on the banks of the Sena river. Heavy showers in the hills caused unexpected flood which in the night swept off 25000 men of Ram Raya. The loss depressed him and he raised the siege, and took the road to the Karnatic.[87] Thereupon Ali Adil Shah moved towards Naldurg to put that fort in a state of defence. When the allies reached the town of Udgir, Ram Raya under the pretext of a foraging expedition plundered some of the frontier districts of Bijapur and Golkunda.[88] He compelled both Ali Adil Shah and Ibrahim Qutb Shah to cede some territories after which he retired to his capital.[89]

**Ahmadnagar again plundered, devastated.**

Having placed Murtaza Khan Anju in the command of of Naldurg, Ali Adil returned to Bijapur.[90] But his officers continued to make frequent incursions into the Sholapur district. Thereupon Husain Nizam Shah sent there a thousand loads of grain under a strong escort to enable it to sustain a siege. Murtaza Khan with a following of *bargis* intercepted the Nizam Shahi convoy between the forts of Sholapur and Parenda.[91] An action took place in which the Nizam Shahis were defeated with a loss of one hundred and fifty elephants. The *bargis* flushed with success began to plunder the Nizam Shahis. Murtaza Khan sent the elephants to Bijapur and himself retired towards Naldrug.[92] Meanwhile, the Nizam Shahis having learnt from one of their own soldiers, who had been made captive but subsequently released by Murtaza Khan, of the deplorable condition of his army, turned round surrounded the Bijapuri commander from all sides, made him prisoner and sent him to Ahmadnagar.[93] Soon after Hussain Nizam Shah sent another convoy of provisions to Sholapur. Sometime afterwards, he himself marched from the capital at the head of his tired and exhausted forces and succeeded in throwing into the fort two thousand loads of grain. This was followed by conclusion of peace between Bijapur and Ahmadnagar on condition of restitution of prisoners of war.[94]

The year 1564-65 was very important in the history of the Daccan. For the first time the Daccani states entered into close matrimonial and political alliances forgetting for a while their personal feuds, their clash of intrests, their religious and the racial differences, with the intention of ending the rise of the Hindu state of Vijayanagara which was struggling hard to gain the supremacy, a process stemming out of the local conditions in that region. Although the battle that followed did not entirely eliminate the existence of this state, the glory and the greatness, the splendour and magnificence, the power and the military superiority, which it had enjoyed so long faded away. It fell flat on the ground owing to its intrensic weaknesses and the aggressive foreign policy. It was its phantom which lingered on the political chess-board of the Daccan with its capital shifted first to Penugonda and later to Chandergiri ; but it could not recover from the fatal shock it received from its enemies. Its complete extinction was only the question of time.

According to Prof. Sherwani the only result of the battle fought in 1564-65 A.D. was that the political map of India was simplified. But the fact of the matter is that the defeat of the Hindu forces upset the balance of power among the various Muhamdan States of the Daccan. Their common enemy being relegated into the limbo of oblivion, they began either to fight among themselves, or otherwise the stronger amongst them began to corner the weaker ones. This created a very unhappy situation leading to the removal of the latter from the political map of the Daccan. It was not long afterwards that Bidar was annexed by Bijapur and Berar by the Nizam Shahi ruler of Ahmadnagar.

The Barid Shahi kings of Bidar had committed the most fatal error in inviting the ruler of Vijayanagara to intervene into the internal affairs of the Muslim kingdoms. Burhan Nizam Shah I followed the same path and solicited the assistance of the same Hindu ruler. The same thing was done by Ibrahim Adil Shah and the seed which the Nizam Shah and the Adil Shah had sown now bore disasterous fruits. Meanwhile the kingdom of Vijayanagara had extended its boundaries to the farthest limits with vast resources and the overwhelming military might. The ruler of Vijayanagara thereafter began to dream of not only crossing the natural frontiers and stepping into territories of the Muhamdan kingdoms, but also of incorporating their frontier districts into his far flung empire. But the varying personal equations of the successive rulers of that kingdom prevented the realisation of the dream of united Daccan under the single sceptre of a single authority. During the last few expeditions the armies of Vijayanagara had ravaged the territories of Ahmadnagar and had roused the sentiments of the orthodox Muslims. Wholesale destruction of buildings, stabling of the horses in the mosques, playing of music in them and outraging of the modesty of Muslim women poured oil on the ever burning fire of fanaticism.

**Causes which led to the battle.**

The Bahmanis had fostered the idea of Hindu Muslim unity. They had a considerate regard for the distinctions of caste and creed. They strove to encourage a cosmopolitan and the patriotic outlook. But in their lust of conquest, the successive states sought the alliance of the Hindu state of Vijayanagara, relegating into the background all the moral, ethical, and noble standards. Never before in the history of Daccan the Hindus had behaved toward the Muslims in such a callous manner. It may be stated in their defence that after all they were also the products of the same age, when in the flush of military success, the soldiers ceased to be human and inflicted terrible sufferings on the masses depriving them completely of wherewithall, setting fire to their smiling crops, perpetuating enormities, which in normal times could put the man to shame. Indeed, it was not religion which promoted such foul deeds, although worst sins were committed in the name of the religion. The Hindus of Vijayanagara perhaps laboured under the impression that they were avenging the enormities of Malik Kafur and his successors.

Incidentally it may be mentioned that the South was passing through a religious and the intellectual ferment, which might have provoked the Hindus to fight for independece. Whatever may have been the motives behind such attacks, it is almost clear that there were religious and political causes of the battle of 1556. Ram Raya had become haughty and arrogant, because of his recent successes over the Muslims. His inordinate thirst for power led him to acts of sacrilege. Nemisis was approaching slowly but steadily and the final storm swept him clean of existence.

Ibrahim Qutb Shah, the ruler of Golkunda was disgusted at the abominable conduct of the Hindu monarch. He never liked to see destruction of his neighbour, the ruler of Ahmadnagar. He always joined Ram Raya under duress, deserting him at the earliest opportunity, even at the most critical juncture. He was ever keen for peace and reconciliation, but in 1564 there was no room for it. The cup of his patience was full. Outwardly cordial relations had come to an end when Ram Raya despatched his brother Venkatadari along with Jagdev Rai and Ain-ul-Mulk to invade the Southern districts of Golkunda. It has already been related that Ibrahim Qutb Shah had to retire from Kalliyani and to send Mujahid Khan to oppose the aggressors. An action took place at Turkal which proved to be indecisive. As if this was not enough to antagonise the Qutb Shah, Ram Raya, sent Siddi Raya Timappa, the chief of Kondavidu against Kondapalli and Masaulipattam and his son-in-law, Yoltamraj against Dawarkunda and Inderkunda, while he employed his own forces in plundering the environs of Golkunda. Jagdev Rai compelled the Naikwaris of Pangal, Koyilkonda and Ganpura to surrender their forts to his master and Kashi Rao to deliver the keys of Indra-Konda. These expeditions reduced Qutb Shah to a miserable plight, breaking his backbone and making him an irreconcilable enemy of the ruler of Vijayanagara. The aforesaid occurrances shaped the foreign policy of Ibrihim Qutb Shah, who was thirsting to teach a lesson to Ram Raya. His prestige had suffered a blow, his territories had suffered a loss, his personality as well as his diplomacy had received a set back. How could he now remain silent spectator to what was happening in the Daccan. The gulf had so much widened that there was no question of its being bridged over.

In the other quarters also there was the feeling of resentment and dissatisfaction against the aggressive and the impolitic behaviour of Ram Raya. Ali Adil Shah the rular of Bijapur could not think better of his ally. His friendship with Ram Raya had brought misery and the humiliation to the Muslim population. Consciously or unconsciously an error had been committed by him, he thought, when he joined hands with Ram Raya to bring about the practical annihilation of the kingdom of Ahmadnagar. Although the kingdom had been humiliated, yet its total extinction was not so easy. It was still powerful enough to sustain the blows of the neighbouring states. Though, Ali Adil Shah might have repented his folly, but as he was a party to the Dual Alliance which he had concluded with him, he had to remain a silent spectator of all that occurred in Ahmadnagar. It is true that inexorable logic of facts had dragged him towards Ram Raya, but how could he be happy over the atrocities committed by the Hindu forces of Vijayanagara, in Ahmadnagar. However opposed he might have been to Husain Nizam Shah's pretensions and the claims over Sholapur, but he could not tolerate the heinous activities committed in Ahmadnagar, which outraged religion of the faithful, and invaders "singing and performing their worship in every mosque". When Ali Adil Shah asked Ram Raya's help against Husain Nizam Shah, he had made him promise that the army would not do any harm to the Muslim places of worship and would not touch the Muslim property. But all such promises were cast to winds. The behaviour of the Hindu soldiers was galling to Ali Adil Shah, but neither had he the means nor the power to stop it. To make the matters worse when the campaign was over there was a marked difference in the attitude of Ram Raya. He looked upon the Muslim kings with contempt, refused to accord to them or to their representatives the honour and the respect suited to their position in life. When they were admitted to his audience, they were not permitted to sit, besides being subjected to other forms of humiliation. On his (Ram Raya's) return from the last expedition to Naldurg, the officers and the soldiers of his army behaved towards the

Muslims insolently, using contempteous language. This brought to an end the friendly feelings of Adil Shah. He had to suffer further at the hands of his erstwhile ally, when the latter actually despatched his troops to the frontiers of Bijapur and compelled him to cede the districts of Bagalkot and Yadgir. Ali Adil Shah now began to think seriously over the consequences of his alliance with the Hindu ruler. He made up his mind that Ram Raya must be humbled. This was the idea which henceforward gripped his imagination and whetted his ambition.[95]

Thus it is absolutely clear that about this time Husain Nizam Shah, Ali Adil Shah and Ibrahim Qutb Shah who dominated the political stage of the Daccan, had seriously begun to think of suppressing the rising power and the prestige of the Hindu ruler of Vijayanagara. It must have occurred to them that if Ram Raya was allowed to materialise his aggressive ambitions, the day would not be far off when their own doom would be sealed and the Hindu empire in the Daccan would be re-established under one secptre of authority. They were dominated by one idea ie. to bring about the downfall of the Hindu kingdom of Vijayanagara, the only powerful kingdom of the far South. It was a struggle for survival, for existence and for establishing firmly the Muslim supremacy in the Daccan. In these circumstances and in this atmosphere of hatred and suspicion towards the Hindu state, isolation meant annihilation. The kingdom of Berar was on its downward path. The child Burhan Imad Shah was on the throne but the real authority lay with the minister Tufal Khan, who being forced by the circumstances formulated a foreign policy which aimed supporting the neighbouring powers against Ram Raya.

**Quintiple Alliance of Five Muslim Sultans of the Daccan.**

The fifth Bahmani succession state was ruled by Ali Barid, who had ceased to pursue an independant policy of his own. Situated at the eastern borders of the kingdom of Bijapur, Ali Barid always looked forward for assistance to the Adil Shah. Naturally Ali Barid seeing that his conscience keeper the Adil Shah was proposing to wage a war against Ram Raya, in collaboration with the sultans of other four kingdoms, must have joined the alliance. This is a matter of controversy for the scholars as to whether Tufal Khan, the regent of Burhan Imad Shah and Ali Barid, the ruler of Bidar were a party to the League of the Five Sultans. It is related that as Tufal Khan had been defeated by Ibrahim Qutb Shah recently, he did not join the League. Moreover there is no mention of any army from Berar in the context of the great battle which followed. Ferishta is explicit that Burhan Imad Shah did not join the battle. The other authorities also support the same contention. But taking into consideration the feverish activities taking place on the political chess board of the Daccan, how could Bidar or Berar remain isolated. It was but natural for them to sympathise with their neighbouring brothers and join in the event of war against Ram Raya of Vijayanagara. It appears that as only the three Sultans played the major part in the struggle the other two, which were not so much in prominence, might have escaped the notice of the contemporary writers. Besides, these Daccani Sultans, another extra ordinary personalty has been mentioned by the Telgu Kaifiyat of Gutti as quoted by Prof. H. K. Shervani, in his article "Telingana under Ibrahim Qutb Shah" (Journal of Indian History, Aug. 1957), which says that the Delhi Sultan also participated in the battle. This statement is also confirmed by the Bakhair of Ram Raja, which identifies the Sultan of Delhi with the Mughal Emperor Akbar, who is said to have been the rular of Jalnapur. Like the accounts of some of the foreign travellers, the village records on which such statements are based are less authentic in their information. They are based on the hearsay. Therefore little importance should be attached to the authenticity of either the Bakhair of Ram Raja or to the Telgu Kaifiyat of Gutti. It can safely be concluded that all the five Muslim Sultans of the Daccan actively took part in the battle and were members of the LEAGUE OF THE FIVE SULTANS.

Again it has always been a controversial matter as to who initiated the plan of forming the coalition of the succession states against the kigdom of Vijayanagara. The author of Burhan-i-Maasir, the historian of the Nizam Shahis, Sayyid Ali Tabatabai gives the credit of it to Husain Nizam Shah.[96] According to him, Husain Nizam Shah consulted his counsellors, Qasim Beg and Maulana Inayat-ul-llah, who pointed out to him the necessity of an alliance with Ali Adil Shah as a pre-requisite of success. But Husain Nizam Shah first approached Ibrahim Qutb Shah who was delighted with the suggestion and sent Sayyid Murtaza Khan to Ahmadnagar to discuss the plan. From the Nizam Shahi court the Qutb Shahi ambassador went to Bijapur to induce Ali Adil Shah to form a a league. The latter was convinced of the necessity for forming an alliance and undertaking a joint venture against Hindu ruler of Vijayanagara. The Poona Persian poem indirectly confirms the statement of Sayyid Ali when it mentions that it was the Sultan of Ahmadnagar, who alone fought and defeated the Hindu ruler.[97]

**Who Sponsored the Formation of the League against the Ruler of Vijayanagara ?**

But according to Ferishta and the author of Basatin-us-Salatin, it was Ali Adil Shah who resolved "to curb his (Ram Raya) insolence and reduced his power by forming a league of faithful against him".[98] Father Heras, taking a clue from Ferishta and Basatin-us-Salatin, also gives the credit for the origin of the scheme to Ali Adil Shah. It is related that Ali Adil Shah broached the matter with his advisers like Kishwar Khan Lari and Shah Abu Turab Shirazi and it was pointed out by him that the project was no doubt laudable but was impossible of accomplishment by him all alone. It was necessary to invite all the Muslim rulers of the Daccan because in military strength and the military resources, Ram Raya would be much more powerful and stronger to him which is evident from the fact that he ruled extensive territories and whose income from the flourishing ports and the towns and the districts was enormous.[99] Accordingly an envoy was sent to Ibrahim Qutb Shah to judge his reaction to the projected venture.

At another place, however, the same chronicler i.e. Ferishta says that Ibrahim Qutb Shah was the first to appreciate the significance of the threat involved in the frequent interference of Ram Raya in the affairs of the Muslim states of the Daccan, and that it was decided to organise a grand confederacy with the object of destroying his power completely or of curtailing it to the minimum. Accordingly he accredited Mustafa Khan to the Adil Shahi and the Nizam Shahi courts to ascertain the reactions of those sovereigns to the plan and to bring about a rapprochement between the two for its implementation.[100] Perhaps the variation in the two versions of Ferishta is due to the figure of Mustafa Khan, who played a very important role in the matter. It is not improbable either that the idea struck the mind of the three rulers almost one and the same time which can satisfactorily explain the readiness with which they accepted it.

The Bakhair of Ram Raja, though he does not throw light on the origin of this grand coalition yet refers to a notable incident which proved to be turning point in effecting a change in the relations of Bijapur with Vijayanagara. According to it, a Mahaldar arrived at Vijayanagara as envoy of the Adil Shah. He was accorded a grand reception and was accommodated in the Anand Mahal Palace. After he had been received in the audience by Ram Raya he was invited to witness the performance of the acrobatic feats by the troops and the Telgu Dambars. Highly pleased with the skill of the acrobatics, Ram Raya loaded them with all kinds of gifts and the presents, including two pigs. This offended the Adil Shahi envoy who expressed his resentment at it. Thereupon the Raya asked whether it was permissible for the Muslims to eat the fowls. The Mahaldar replied in affirmative. The Raya then ordered that a building should be vacated and the pigs should be installed in it for the night. Next morning when the envoy was taken there he found it stinking with filth. Now a number of fowls were put in it and by the evening the building became almost clean. The Raya now remarked, "Those who eat fowls should have a little justification to hold the pork eaters in contempt". This remark roused the temper of the Mahaldar who declined to stay any further in the court of Vijayanagara and obtained leave to return to his master.[101]

He appeared before Ali Adil Shah with his turban tied round his neck in token of his anger and humiliation. He tried to impress upon Ali Adil Shah the fact that the Muslim authority had come to an end in the Daccan and no muslim was likely to be respected so long as the kingdom of Vijayanagara remained in a position which it acquired. Failing to convince Adil Shah with the truth of his remarks he went to another quarter. He arrived at Jalna, where the three rulers of the Daccan were encamping and enjoying the hospitality of the Nizam Shah. He repeated his arguments before them and succeeded in rousing their feelings and their desire for action against Ram Raya. They sent an emissary to Adil Shah who refused to fall in with the proposals.[102]

The report of the discussion held at Jalna was sent to Ram Raya by his agent Timmaji Bhimji. It was further confirmed by the message received from the agent of Vijayanagara at the court of Adil Shah, that the ruler of Bijapur was determined to keep himself away from the proposed confederacy as the other Muslim rulers were keen to start the aggression. Therefore the Raya as soon as the Dashehra celebrations had come to a close, on the one hand issued instructions to his feudatories to assemble their armies and complete their preparations for the ensuing war ; while on the other, he sent his commander-in-chief Bislappa Nayaka to Bijapur with rich presents for Adil Shah. The Vijayanagara envoy was received with all honour and Adil Shan spared no efforts to express his feelings of friendship towards the Raya.[103]

All this was duly communicated to the Muslim Sultans by their agents in Bijapur. They sent another ambassador to point out to him the impropriety and the danger of the Muslim ruler being in alliance with the Hindu ruler. Further they warned him that if he failed to cooperate with them then they would march through his territories against his ally. As Bislappa Nayaka was still at Bijapur Adil Shah had to be very careful and cautious in his reply to the threat held out to him. He reminded them of the superiority of the resources of Ram Raya and the folly of taking any hasty action. Bislappa Nayaka returned with this information to Vijayanagara where he told his master that an invasion on his kingdom was in the offing. Upon this Ram Raya held a council of war, in which after much discussion it was decided to meet the enemy on the frontiers of the kingdom rather than to allow them to enter it.

It seems that there is nothing radically contradictory in

these accounts. As a matter of fact it was the realisation of the danger from that state on the part of the Muslim sovereigns which brought them closer than ever. The accounts given by the author of Burhan-i-Maasir, Ferishta, Basatin-us-Salatin and the Bakhair of Ram Raya, throw light on one single fact. The need of joint action was felt simultaneously by all the Sultans of the Daccan especially the three powerful ones. But it was Ibrahim Qutb Shah who acted as the intermediary between the warring kingdoms of Ahmadnagar and Bijapur. It is difficult to reconcile the various accounts given by the contemporary or the latter historians hence still more difficult to decide as to who was sponsor of the idea of a close political alliance.

But thanks however to the missionary zeal of Mustafa Khan and his persuasive genius that Hussain Nizam Shah stood like a rock to take revenge from the ruler of Vijayanagara, deciding to accept any plan which may bring about his reconciliation with Adil Shah.[104] What the clash of swords had failed to achieve was now easily achieved by diplomacy. To cement the bond of friendship, Husain Nizam Shah agreed to give his daughter Chand Bibi, the flower of his family, in marriage to Ali Adil Shah and the fort of Sholapur as dowery. In return it was arranged that the Adil Shah should give the hand of his sister Hadia Sultana to Murtaza the son of Hussain Nizam Shah. As if to complete the picture and cement the bonds of union, it is related by Diaego de Couto that Husain Nizam Shah gave his another daughter in marriage to Ibrahim Qutb Shah. This network of matrimonial alliances with the two powerful houses was intended to strengthen the mutual relations between the members of the projected League against Ram Raya.[105]

**Rapprochement between the Nizam Shah and Adil Shah, matrimonial alliance concluded.**

Mustafa Khan again went to Bijapur accompanied by the Nizam Shahi minister, Inayat-ul-llah Khan Niyati, where the terms of the treaties and the alliances were drawn up and confirmed on the most solomn oaths. Accordingly the double marriages were celebrated both in the cities of Ahmadnagar and Bijapur. At the end of the rejoicings the two princess left the same day to join their husbands. Sholapur was handed over to Ali Adil Shah but Chand Bibi was a more valuable prize than the number of the forts. Thereafter, it was decided that the three kings should assemble next year at Sholapur with their armies to devise the plan for the campaign against the kingdom of Vijayanagara. Then they would leave their respective countries to complete their preparations.[106]

Though arrogant, Ram Raya was not oblivious to the situation which was developing against him. He had long foreseen the contingency of a concerted attack on his capital by the Muslim rulers of of the Daccan. To meet it, he had constructed another bastion in the walls of the Vijayanagara fort under the supervision of Krishnappa Nayaka.[107] He had also fortified the hills of northern frontier in Bellary and Cuddapah districts by erecting the new forts and repairing the old ones, built in the time of Krishna Deva Raya. Now when he was definitely apprised of the intention of the Muslim rulers he lost no time in completing preparations to oppose them. He summoned, "all his dependents and the Rajas from the banks of the Krishna to the island of Ceylon."[108]

**Ram Raya makes preparations in advance.**

To find a pretext for breaking with Ram Raya the Adil Shah sent an envoy to his court demanding the restoration of Yadgir, Bagalkot, Raichur and Mudgal which the Raya had wrested from him at different times.[109] As was expected Ram Raya, "expelled the ambassador with disgrace. This proved to be a plea to the Muslim Sultans to hasten their preparations to crush the common enemy of of Islam."[110] The five Sultans,[111] with their respective armies met on the plains of Sholapur on the 14th December 1564 A. D. and after 12 days, on 26th Dec. 1564 they set out for the South. They first marched to Bijapur where they stayed for some time and then they marched towards the town of Talikota, which is 22 miles north of river Krishna. They halted at Talikota. Here Ali Adil Shah entertained his friends lavishly.[112] He was so pleased with his new friends that he frankly told them that as they were in his territory they should consider themselves as his guests and as host it becomes his duty to arrange for the further supplies for them, their armies and the attendants.[112] He issued instructions to his provincial governors to forward supplies of provisions to the camp with punctulious regularity.

Among the Muslim generals mention should be made of Mustafa Khan from Golkunda,[113] Maulana Inayat-ul-ullah from Ahmadnagar[114] and Kishwar Khan from Bijapur,[115] Rafat Khan who had been summoned from the south was also in the army of Golkunda.[116] Mustafa Khan whose real name was Kalal-ud-din Husain was a skilful general, a shrewd politician and a diplomat, besides being one of the foremost warriors of his age. Nor was the army composed exclusively of the Muslims. A number of Maratha leaders had also joined it e.g. Yashwant Rao, Bhoj Mal Naik, Dev Naik, Vishwas Rao and others the total strength of the allied forces was 50,000 horse, 30,000 elephants, and 3,000 foot.

**The strength of the Hindu Army**

On the other hand the Hindu army, according to Ferishta consisted of 70,000 horse, 90,000 infantry and 25,000 elephants.[117] The anonymous chronicler gives the respective figures as 10,000 horse and 300,000 infantry.[118] While according to Couto and Faria-i-Souza, the foot soldiers were more than 60,000. The author of Burhan-i-Maasir states that the Hindu army numbered about 44,000 horse, 3000 elephants and 41,000 foot.[119] Ram Raya and his two brothers held the command of this huge force. Though Ram Raya was an old man but was bubbling with energy and courage of a youth of thirty.[120]

Without either loosing patience or the presence of mind, Ram Raya threw himself into the task of organising the defence of his country and the dominions. The army which was mobilised and which now started northwards consisted of the mercenaries belonging to all the linguistic and racial elements, which went to form the Vijayanagara empire. There were the Konnadigas, Telgus, Mysorians, Malyalis, Tamils and the Muslims from the south. All this vast army, a hetrogenous body was under the Regent and under him and his two younger brothers Wenkatadari and Trimula.[120a] Thinking that the war with the Muslim sovereigns was inevitable, Ram Raya, took suitable measures to strengthen the defences of frontiers of his empire. For the purpose of

**Measures Finally Taken to Defend the Empire**

guarding the northern frontier, he sent his brother, Trimula with 20,000 cavalry, 100 elephants and 10,000 footmen to occupy the right bank of Krishna river, with instructions to keep a vigilant eye on every ford.[121] He also sent his another brother Venkatadari, with another equally large army consisting of about 25,000 horse, 20,00,000 foot and elephants.[122] He himself followed them by slow marches with the rest of the forces of his dominions besides, "horses, elephants, camels, stores, cattles, drink shops hunting materials, treasure chests and corn stores". All this were brought near to the royal camp. Every man in Vijayanagara was ordered to join the army. Marching across the river Ram Raya occupied the country otherside to a distance of sixty miles. Along the banks of the river he pushed forward the pickets and the advance posts almost up to the river Krishna and finally fixed his camp between the townlet of Tavenengiri and Krishnagiri, occupying the fords to prevent the entrance of the Muslim army into his dominions.[123] He took up his position near the villages of Raksas and Tangadi. Trimula and Venkatadari, who held the southern bank of the river threw up mud fortifications butressing them up with the cannon and the rockets. Soon after he was joined by his numerous feudatories.[124]

On the other hand the Muslim army under the command of their respective sovereigns and generals, having passed the town of Talikota took up their position in full view of the enemy. Incidentally it may be mentioned that the Muslim allies took too much time on the way from Sholapur and Bijapur to the borders of the Hindu empire. When they reached Krishna they found that all the known ferries and the fords had been occupied by the enemy who had even found time to build high ramparts on the other side of the river and mount cannons on them. They had started from Bijapur on 24th Dec. 1564 and had taken full four weeks to cover a distance of little more than 100 miles. The delay was due to the lack of mobility on the part of the huge army and over confidence on the part of the allies. Moreover the army which Ram Raya commanded was little less in the numerical strength and therefore he could reach the river long before his enemies. Apparently there may be another reason for this delay. The allies proceeded slowly to give enough time to the forces of Bidar and Berar to join them and reach the site of the battle in time.

**Actual Site of the Battle.**

It has always been a pressing problem for the historians of medieval India to decide as to where was actual site of the battle, which is usually called as Talikota situated 22 miles north of river Krishna. Nowhere it is recorded that the battle was fought on the grounds of Talikota. It may be remembered that the three Sultans of Ahmadnagar, Bijapur and Golkunda had assembled at Talikota to arrive at mutual understanding, to conclude a political alliance and to forget their past differences. After the meeting was over they returned back to their respective capitals to make suitable arrangements for the forthcoming struggle with the Hindu ruler. When all the military arrangements had been completed the armies started from their respective homes and shortly after were ordered to march southwards. Thus it is by convention that the battle is generally described as the battle of Talikota named after the village where the three Sultans had assembled to celebrate the matrimonial alliances. As regards our Persian chroniclers, they are not very clear on this point, but they are however unanimous on one point that the battle took place South of river Krishna. Nor there is great difference in their description of the earlier meeting of the allies.

According to J. A. Campbell, the author of Bijapur District Guzetteer, the battle was fought on the right bank of the river Krishna, about 30 miles from Talikota and six miles from Nalatwad. The ford which the allied army crossed was at Ingalgi on the left bank, while the remains of the earthworks erected by Ram Raya were then visible on the left bank near Tondihal village. The allies manoeuvered to cross the river by Dhanuri ford, ten miles higher up. They marched slowly on the northern bank westwards for three days in the direction of Dhanur and then marched back suddenly on Ingalgi ford and crossed.[125a]

Sewell thinks that the battle did not take place at Talikota, but many miles south of the river Krishna, probably ten miles from Ram Raya's camp, wherever that might have been, which he thinks was at Mudgal. In his opinion, the ford which the allies crossed was perhaps at the bend of the river at Ingalgi and the little village of Bayapur or Bhogapur on the road directly leading from Ingalgi to Mudgal.[125]b

Prof. Nilkanta Shastri and Dr. Venkata Ramanayya in their comprehensive work, "Further Sources of Vijayanagara History" have discussed the problem of the exact site of the battle. They have brushed a side the evidence of the Muslim historians who state that the battle was fought at Talikota. They think that the place of the battle is well described in the Hindu records like Ram Rajna Bhakair and the Kaifyats. The Bakhair of Ram Raj locates the camp of Ram Raya in the plains between the villages of Raksas and Tangadi. The Kaifiyats assert that Ramraja perished with all his army near the confluence of river Krishna and Malaprahari (the modern Malaprabha). The Kaifiyats of Nandiyala as quoted by Prof. Sherwani, says that the Muhamdans put Ram Raja together with his large army to death at Raksas Tangadi in the pargana of Honugunda near the confluence of the rivers Krishna and Malaprabha[125]c.

Patwardhan in his article, "The battle of Raksas Tangadi," Chanderker' in his article, "The destruction of Vijayanagara" and Father Heras in his, "Arvidu Dynasty of Vijayanagara," explicitly mentions that the battle was fought on the plains between the villages of Raksas-Tangadi[125]d.

The various sources hitherto mentioned contradict the accounts of the Muhamdan historians. This contradiction creates much confusion and with the result it becomes quite difficult to fix the actual site of the battle. Relying on the authority and the authenticity of Bakhair of Ram Raja and the other non-Persian and the Persian sources, one can conclude very easily that the battle must have been fought in between the villages of Raksas and Tangadi. But Prof. Sherwani in his article, "Telingana under Ibrahim Qutb Shah" has dealt with the problem of fixing the exact site of the battle and has thrown abundant light on the new facts discovered by him. He writes, "Talikota is situated on the river Don, 22 miles from the north bank of river Krishna. The land lying between the villages and the river is absolutely flat and there is still a curlway from it leading to the river and passing through the town of Nalatwad which is six miles from the nearest point on the southward curve of the river. Ingalgi is a village about half mile from the north bank practically on the straight line from the Talikota southwards. While Tondihal, where remains of earthworks were found by Campbell, is almost exactly opposite Ingalgi on the South bank. These earthworks are extended to a distance of about ten miles westwards. There is a local tradition that the battle was fought at the village called Islampur. The site of the battle indicated in the Survey of India map is three miles east of Islampur and quite at a distance from where the limits of the earthworks were seen by Campbell and it is not known why the site of the battle was shown there. If we suppose the Vijayanagara wall to commence at Talikota it would pass through Islampur, extend westwards to Dhanur ford about thirteen miles from Tondihal and a couple of miles from the Sangam of Malaprabha and the Krishna. Hukri river joines Maski, 12 miles south of Krishna which corresponds with the description as given by Ferishta. Bayapur or Bhogapur are names of the two district hamlets South-east of Ingalgi, on the road to Mudgal and are separated from each other by about a mile and half. In the same way Raksas Tangadi which are doubtless, are the real names of the villages mentioned in the Telgu documents as Rakasagi and Tangadi, are the two distinct places on the north or the left side of the river, both half a mile north of Krishna but seperated from each other by nine miles."

"Now if look at this topography objectively and picture to ourselves the probable movements of the troops it would appear that the invading army proceeded south from Talikota towards Vijayanagara territory, especially as it would then pass through the friendly town of Nalatwad and then reached the northern or the left bank of the river which is but six miles from it. On reaching Ingalgi, it would save the earthworks in the full view just 12 furlongs away on the southern or the right bank of Tondihal. These earthworks must have followed the present straight path from Tondihal to Dhanur and the Sangam of Malaprabha and the Krishna. The invading army adopted the ruse of leaving Ingalgi ford passed by Raksas to

Tangadiji, then it suddenly turned back and reached Ingalgi which is twelve miles distant from Tangadiji and crossed the ford where there was hardly any one to oppose it. It is possible that the same Vijayanagara troops were left to guard the place where Ilkal joines the Krishna which later on came to be known as Islampur and an eggagement took place between the opposing forces. As the main Vijayanagara army was at some miles away it must have been a walkover on the part of the allied forces and after this initial adavantage they must have moved on to the South till they had reached Banihatti on the confluence of the Maski and its southern tributary. There is no doubt that by this time the main Vijayanagara army had reached Banihatti as well as the two main armies should have waited at Tondihal and not taken advantage of the open ground to push forward".

Taking into consideration the historical, topographical and the documentary evidence, Prof. Sherwani arrives at an acceptable conclusion that the so called battle of Talikota or Rakasa-Tangadiji was fought twelve miles South of river Krishna probably at Banihatti on the Sangam of the Maski River and it sothern tributary.[125c] To disapprove the theories propounded by the different writers that the battle took place between the villages of Raksas and Tangadiji on the northern or the left banks of river Krishna, Prof. Sherwani says that "the protaganists of the theory are not certain of it". Ramrajna Bakhair on which the stand is taken is full of absurd details in regard to the battle and other matters to a certain extent. For instance, the Mughal Emperor is said to have taken part in the battle with his half a crore of foot soldiers, one lac elephants, two lacks camels and many others; the weight of the gun powder carried by the Vijayanagara troops is said to have been was near about ten crore of maunds; the number of cannon balls, reached the figure of ten thousand billions. Therefore it is difficult to put much reliance on such a document. Similarly highly exaggereted account of the battle is given in the Kaifiyat of Nandiyala as well as some Kaifiyats, where it is related that the Muhamdans who invaded the country met Ram Raya at Raksas Tangadiji. The invasion of Vijayanagara was only possible after the enemy had crossed the river Krishna. The place where the Vijayanagara army was routed was near the confluence of Malprabha and the Krishna and this confluence is on the southern bank of river Krishna. The distance between the villages of Raksas and Tangadiji is not less than nine miles and yet they have been "hyphenated" together as if they form one unit and placed near the Sangam. No doubt that the allies, according to Ferishta, left 40,000 soldiers at the farthest point they reached in the strategic movements westwards, which would have been near Tangadi and it is possible that some kind of rare guard action took place there, but not the actual battle. It could not have been a major action as the Hindu army had started in pursuit of the allied army which had marched southwards. Moreover there was no need on the part of Ram Raya to cross the river Krishna especially at a time when enemy secured the passage and had moved into Vijayanagara territory to give battle. Thus in the light of Prof. Sherwani's article, the old theories regarding the actual site of the battle should be discarded and it should be acknowledged that the battle was neither fought on the grounds of Talikota nor between the villages of Raksas and Tangadi but near Banihatti. Prof. Sherwani has given the name of the battle as the battle of Krishna, but as the battle was not fought on either banks of the river Krishna, how it could be named after it ? It would be better to call the battle as the battle of Banihatti, where it was fought and the issue was decided.

It has already been related that the allies took up their position in full view of the enemy, when they arrived near the northern bank of the river Krishna., which formed the boundary between the empires of Bijapur and Vijayanagara, they found that the route to Vijayanagara was completely blocked by the enemy. Ram Raya had already constructed

**Preliminary Operations**

huge wall having two or three gates in the length, along the whole water front of the river and mounted pieces of artillery on it, blockading almost all the formidable approaches of the allied army. The allies were greatly perplexed and there was great confusion for neither side had the courage to strike the blow first. All the information with regard to the military disposition of the Hindu forces continued to reach them. They shortly after realised that the only ford known to them was strongly defended by the enemy and it was not so much easy to cross the river even. Scouts were sent out to find any other ford which may be used for crossing the river Krishna.[126] After a good deal of search it was found that the only safe passage lay in front of the Hindu camp. Upon this the allies held a council of war in which it was decided that they should recourse to strategem ; that they should march to another part of the river to show the enemy that they intended to cross it there and thus induce him to quit his position which might give them a opportunity to turn back and throw a part of the army across the ford without any interruption. Accordingly the following morning the allies moved out of their camps upstream to a point farther than the fortifications put by Ram Raya. As the allied army marched westwards by the northern bank, they were followed by the Hindu forces on the southern bank. The commanders of the Vijayanagara forces were under the impression that the allies wished to cross the river beyond the earthworks erected by them. Whereas the allied armies marched slowly for two or three days. The plan created a desired impression, upon the mind of the enemy, who quitted their post and moved along the opposite bank of the river. On the night of the third day the allies suddenly stopped, left 40,000 soldiers to fight the rear guard if necessary, turned round and managed to cover the whole distance in a single night, when they reached the original ford which they found unguarded. They crossed the river without opposition. Husain Nizam Shah was the first to cross the river. The allies continued to march till they reached the Hukri river, situated 12 miles from the river Krishna.

The next morning Ram Raya was surprised to find that the enemy had crossed his territory. While the allies were within ten miles of his camp, he issued promptory orders to his brothers to fall back and join him. He also despatched an advance party of Rachibides under Bislappa Nayaka, Trivengallapa Nayaka and Kartik Virappa Nayaka for reconnoitering. This was met by the vanguard of the Muslim forces. They faced each other for three days, shooting volleys of arrows which occassioned heavy casualities on either side. In the end the Muslim forces were compelled to retreat a few paces. In the skirmish Ikhlas Khan opened the attack on the enemy with his Khurasani horses and slew a large number of Hindus. Ram Raya was having his dinner when he received the report that the enemy was in full advance and almost within the sight and that an engagement had taken place. In the words of Sayyid Ali when Ram Raya heard about it and of the crossing of the river by the Muslims "it seemed to him to be a passage of their success, he was much perturbed and alarmed.[128]"

Under these circumstances when the enemy was approaching fast like a calamity Ram Raya sent Divalai Gariappa and Jamadar Khan Pavadi to Adil Shah to point out to him, that it was not fair on his part that he should join the confederacy organised by the other Muslims rulers against him, who had brought him up like a son and had once provided the fortress of Raichur, Mudgal and Adoni for his milk and money.[129] In reply, Ali Adil Shah protested that he did not enter the war on his own hand but was compelled by the allies who had threatened him that they will attack the Hindu ruler by mobilising their forces through his territory. When the information of this correspondence reached the ears of the other Muslim sovereigns, they sent an ultimatum to Ali Adil Shah saying that "You joined us in the invasion against the Hindu ruler and now you are establishing the secret relations with him. If you do not adopt a more friendly attitude towards us and join us whole heartedly in the war, we shall declare the war against you as well."[130] While these transactions were going on, Ram Raya changed his head quarters to Banihatti. By this time he was joined by his brothers. Realising the determination of the Muslim rulers he entrusted the right wing of his army to his brother Trimula, the left wing to his younger brother Venkatadari and himself commanded the centre. He mounted his horse with juvenile agility and put his troops in the battle array.[131]

The allies also drew up their innumerable forces in the order of the battle. Ali Adil Shah took over the command of the right wing to oppose Venkatadari, the left wing was entrusted to Ibrahim Qutb Shah and Ali Barid to oppose Trimula, while the centre was commanded by Husain Nizam Shah. Ikhlas Khan a Nizam Shahi officer held the charge of the vanguard consisting of the mounted Khurasani horsemen. In each of the three divisions of the army, were planted twelve standards in the honour of the twelve Imams[132]. The allies did not open the attack on the enemy immediately after completing their prepartions but sent a message to Ram Raya that if he promised to return the territory which belonged to Bijapur and Golkunda then the allied forces would evacuate the Vijayanagara territory and retire to their respective kingdoms. It is doubtful whether Husain Nizam Shah was a party to such negotiations with the Hindu ruler. Ram Raya was too proud to accept these terms and therefore made preparations to face the enemy.

No sooner the reply was received by the allies than the gun carriages were fastened together with the strong chains and ropes and were drawn up in the front of Husain Nizam Shah's line[133]. There were 600 pieces of ordnance of varying size placed in three rows of two hundred each. In the first line were the heavy guns, in the second the smaller ones and in the third were Zamburaks or shivels.[134] The disposition and the supervision of the artillery was in the charge of Chlapi Rumi Khan, an officer of great distinction from Asia Minor, who had served in Europe.[135] The elephants were arranged not in an unbroken line but to fill in the gaps of the centre. Their tusks were equipped with sharp sword blades. To create consternation in the rank and the file of the enemy, two thousand foreign archers were thrown up in the front. They kept heavy discharge of arrows as the enemy approached forward.[136]

Before the arrow could be released from the bow and the drums could be beaten to declare the final attack, Trimula and Venkatadari tried to pursuade their brother Ram Raya to leave the supervision of the entire Hindu army to them. But he was adamant and firmly asked them to go back to their respective places. On one occasion he is said to have addressed his brothers and the generals in the field of the battle encouraging them "to make a resolute stand against the Muslims, remarking that he had attained the age of eighty without ever having disgraced himself and that he had no wish to be disgraced with cowardice towards the

**The last act of the Drama.**

end of his life. He said that if there was any body who was overcome with fear, he was at liberty to leave, while there was yet time to save his life." The Raya's brothers and their 30,0000 horsemen swore that they would fight until death.[137] Likewise two thousand elephants trained and armed and one thousand pieces of ordnance were disposed at various points along the front line. Ram Raya himself mounted on a state litter called Singhasan inspite of the remonstrances of his officers who felt that he would be safer on the horse back but he exlaimed that," there is no occasion for taking precautions against the children who would certainly fly on the first charge. This is not war."[138] In his pride and arrogance he issued orders to capture Ali Adil Shah and Ibrahim Qutb Shah so that he could keep them in the iron cages during the rest of their lives and also directed men to bring the head of Husain Nizam Shah to him.[139]

On the following day, Tuesday 23rd January 1565 A.D. both the sides having completed their preparations marched forward to measure their sword. The battle opened in the midday and soon the fighting became general. The bitter struggle continued for thirty-three days without any decisive result. On the last day, the battle lasted till the ninth hour of the night. On the same day the principal leaders and the princes of the Hindu army came to Ram Raya and pointed him of the futility of this kind of warfare. They suggested to him to divide the army into separate divisions, each of which was to fight against the coresponding divisions of the enemy's army. Ram Raya accepted the suggestion, directed his army to attack the separate divisions of the enemy. The Hindus now opened their attacks with volleys and the rockets and a terrific discharge of guns. Their left wing under the cammand of Venkatadari fell upon Adil Shah, inflicting terrible losses and finally compelling him to abandon his position. Likewise, Trimula who held the command of the right wing fell upon the combined forces of Ibrahim Qutb Shah and Ali Barid, mercilessly slaying hundred of Muslims in the field of battle. But soon the ranks of the army of Ibrahim Qutb Shah retuned and came forward, launched a severe attack on the enemy in which Venkatadari was driven away from the field. On Adil Shah's front, the Hindus suffered great losses by the sudden withdrawal of Trimula, who was blinded by an arrow.[140] The loss of the two greatest Hindu generals who commanded the key positions in the army of Ram Raya, decided the fate of the battle. The Muslim sovereigns readjusted their forces and delivered the final attack on the Hindu army.

When Ram Raya heard of the flight of Venkatdari and the withdrawal of Trimula from the field, he was terribly shocked. Although he knew that the ground was slipping and the game was lost even then he was not the man to lose heart. He came down from the state litter, mounted on the horse, repeatedly shouted "Gorid, Gorid", and fell upon the enemy.[141] He delivered such a terrific charge over the enemy that the right and the left wings commanded by Adil Shah and Qutb Shah and Ali Barid broke in the utter confusion.[142] Then he turned his attention towards the centre which was firmly led by Husain Nizam Shah.[143] Under the impact of Ram Raya's severe attack even Nizam Shah failed to hold the ground. He had to retrace his steps half a league with the loss of two thousand men. Thereafter holding the ground firm Nizam Shah once more came to the forefront and attacked Ram Raya. Seeing that their sovereign was amidst the grips of the enemy, the Rachevidu soldiers of the Hindu army hastened in that direction and slew large number of the Muslim forces.[144]

While Ram Raya was occupied in delivering death blows on the forces of Husain Nizam Shah, Ali Adil Shah and Qutb Shah returned to the battle field again, and began to fight with the enemy.[145] Meanwhile Husain Nizam Shah succeeded in rallying his men again and he marched post-haste to the relief of his allies. His forward move compelled the enemy to send several detachments to oppose him. When the Hindus had arrived within striking distance, Rumi Khan opened fire and Ikhlas Khan's archers, their volleys of arrows, carrying death and destruction in their ranks and file.[146]

At this stage, Husain Nizam Shah ordered that his camp be pitched in front of the enemy, in token of his determination to fight them to the end.[147] It was the last bid in the game, to win glory or die in the attempt. When Ram Raya saw Husain's camp, he was overtaken with a spirit of depression.

For once, he lost his nerve and became desperate. He dismounted from his horse and sat on a rich throne set with jewels, under a canopy of crimson velvet, embroidered with gold and adorned with pearls.[148] He placed round him heaps of money to distribute it in reward to his soldiers or to encourage them. Inspired by the generosity of their master and spurred by their fighting zeal, having recovered from the panic produced by the heavy fire from the enemy, the Hindus renewed their attack with greater vigour than ever before. The allies were once more thrown into confusion and were compelled to fall back with heavy losses.[149] Considering this to be the final retreat of the enemy, the Hindu army slackened their efforts and their leader Ram Raya stopped pressing any further the advantage so gained.[150] But Husain Nizam Shah remained firm in the centre. Chalapi Rumi Khan charged the cannons with bags of copper coins; and when he fired them on the enemy, about five thousand of them lay dead on the field before they could retreat.[151] Thus the tables were turned on the army of Vijayanagara which was overtaken by consternation and confusion. Kishwar Khan Lari pressed the advantage home and attacked the centre of the Hindu army. At this stage two Muslim generals of Ram Raya deserted him and came over to the allies. Treachery completed the discomfiture of Ram Raya.[152] The old king had been severely wounded and he mounted his litter to flee from the field. But at the approach of one of the furious elephants of the Nizam Shahi army, the bearers were struck with panic, ran away, abandoning their master in the midst of peril. Ram Raya now left his litter and fled on foot, but he was lifted by an elephant and handed over to the *Mahaut*. The prisoner was taken to Chalapi Rumi Khan who was going to kill him. But one Dalpat Rai, a Brahman general shouted, "Do not kill him, but carry him alive before Diwan Barid, for he is Sadashiv (Ram Raya[153]). Rumi Khan on hearing this, brought the prisoner before Husain Nizam Shah, who ordered that his head should be chopped. Immediately after, "his mischievous head was then severed from his foul body and cast beneath the hoofs of king's horse".[154] Thereafter Husain Nizam Shah had Ram Raya's head placed on the top of a long spear to announce his death to the enemy.[155]

(January 1565 A.D.)[156]

Upon the death of their leader, the Hindu army fled from the field in utter confusion, hotly pursued by their Muslim adversaries, who killed so many of them that, "the river was dyed red with their blood". After pursuing the fugitives for some distance the Muslim soldiers returned again to the battle field, where they halted for ten days.[157] They captured jewels, ornaments, furniture, camels, tents, camp equippage, drums, standard, maid-servants, men-servants, arms and ammunition of all sorts in such quantities that the whole army was enriched." So great was the plunder says Ferishta, "every private man in the allied army became rich in gold, jewels, tents, horses, and *slaves*; the kings permitting every person to retain what he had acquired, reserving the elephants only for their own use".[158] According to the Maratha account, the treasures Ram Raya had brought to the battle field, valued 12,357411 huns.

The battle of Banihatti wrongly known as the famous battle to Talikota, was one of the decisive and foremost battle which was ever fought on the Indian soil. The confederacy, organised by the most ambitious personalities of the age, viz., Husain Nizam Shah, Ibrahim Qutb Shah, Ali Adil Shah, Burhan Imad Shah and Ali Barid Shah I, broke for all the time, the back of the mighty power of Vijayanagara kingdom which had maintained for a century and half warfare on equal terms with the Bahmani kingdom and then with its offshoots, which had risen on its ashes.[159] The victory of the allies was due to superior manoeuvres, military tactics, artillary and the valour and bravery of their troops. Its implications were of far-reaching character. Free from the danger of the Hindu aggression, the rulers of the succession states heaved a sigh of relief. They now obtained much needed respite to consolidate their resources, to strengthen their power, utilising the vast economic resources which had fallen into their hands. The kingdoms of Bijapur and Golkunda whose frontiers ran contiguous to the boundaries of Vijayanagara, extended their territorial limits up to Kondikota and Gingee.[160] In a short time they acquired more extensive and richer lands than they originally had in their possession. But the hard pressed little kingdom of Ahmadnagar, unfortunately could not have a lion's share in the territories of the Hindu kingdom because of its geographical limitations. Nevertheless the victory added to the glory, greatness and fame of Husain Nizam Shah.

After staying for nearly six months in the city of Vijayanagara, the allies left the conquered city and started with their respective forces on their homeward journey. Perhaps their departure was hastened by some misunderstanding which had arisen among them and their generals.[161] They went together as far as Raichur, where they took leave of each other and then returned to their respective dominions. But before leaving the environs of the plundered and devastated city of Vijayanagara, the Muslim rulers deputed three of their generals Mustafa Khan, Maulana Inayatullah, and Kishwar Khan Lari to attack the forts of Raichur and Mudgal which were easily reduced and captured.[162]

**Death of Husain Nizam Shah (1565 A.D.)**

Husain Nizam Shah wended his way to the capital eating drinking and making merry all the time. On his entrance into the capital he was welcomed by holy sayyaids, saints, nobles, and above all by the masses, who came forth in numbers to greet and congratulate him and to pray for the long and prosperous life of their hero. After this ardous campaign the king needed rest and relaxation, and no wonder, therefore, that he took to drinking and enjoying the company of beautiful damsels and cheerful handsome wine cupbearers. Soon after his health gave way, he fell ill and he died on 6th June 1565 A. D. (Wednesday Zil-Qadat 7th A.H. 972). His death has been commemorated in the following chronogram:—

"The son of the Daccan has become obscured".

The short reign of Husain Nizam Shah was full of perennial warfare in which neither the king nor his subjects knew peace. His own lack of foresight and judgement can be held to be wholly responsible for it He was neither haughty nor arrogant, but was hasty in taking decisions. Even so he never failed to avert the dark clouds of strife and aggressive wars launched by the neighbouring states. True that he had to bow low, on one occasion, before the Hindu monarch due to the duplicity and faithlessness of his brother sovereigns, but no sooner had Ram Raya turned his back than he began to nurse in his heart the noble ambition of striking at him at the earliest opportunity in order to retrieve his honour. And when it came, he gave full proof of his bravery, intelligence and quick grasp of situation in the field of battle. He was a man of many virtues, brave and warlike, courageous and generous, learned and pious. Being a staunch follower of the Shia faith, he never failed to observe his prayers at stated hours. Under the shadow of his justice people lived happily and peacefully, while the learned and the pious were generously rewarded.

---

*Notes and References*

1. Ferishta, Briggs. III, pp. 237; Burhan-i-Maasir (I. A. 1921), pp. 73; Muntakhab-ul-Lubab III, pp. 187; Tabqat-i-Akbari III, pp. 187;
2. Burhan-i-Maasir (I.A. 1921) pp. 73;
3. Burhan-i-Maasir (I.A. 1921) pp. 73; Muntakhab-ul-Lubab, III, pp. 187;
4. Ferishta, Briggs. III, pp. 237-38;
5. Burhan-i-Maasir (I. A. 1921), pp. 73; Muntakhab-ul-Lubab, III, pp. 187;
6. Burhan-i-Maasir (I.A. 1921), pp. 73;
7. Burhan-i-Maasir (I.A. 1921), pp. 73;
8. Burhan-i-Maasir (I.A. 1921), pp. 73;
9. Burhan-i-Maasir (I.A. 1921), pp. 74-75; Farishta, Briggs. III, pp. 105; 238; Muntakhab-ul-Lubab, III, pp. 188;
10. Burhan-i-Maasir I.A. 1921), pp. 76; Ferishta, Briggs. III, pp. 105, 106; Muntakhab-ul-Lubab III, pp. 182-83.
11. Ferishta, Briggs. III, pp. 106, 107; Muntakhab-ul-Lubab III, pp. 188;
12. Ferishta, Briggs. III, pp. 106-107; Muntakhab-ul-Lubab III, pp. 188;
13. Burhan-i-Maasir (I.A. 1921), pp. 76;
14. Burhan-i-Maasir (I.A. 1921), pp. 76; Muntakhab-ul-Lubab III, pp. 189;
15. Ibid.
16. Ibid.
17. Ibid.
18. Burhan-i-Maasir (I.A. 1921), pp. 71; From Ferishta's version it appears that Darya Imad Shah himself did not accompany Husain Nizam Shah but sent 7,000 cavelry to assist him—Briggs. III, pp. 106-7; Muntakhab-ul-Lubab III, 189-90;
19. Burhan-i-Maasir (I.A. 1921) pp. 78; Muntakhab-ul-Lubab III, pp. 180-81;
20. Ferishta, Briggs. III, pp. 238;
21. Burhan-i-Maasir (I.A. 1921) pp. 101; Ferishta, Briggs. III, pp. 239;
22. Burhan-i-Maasir (I.A. 1921) pp. 101; Ferishta, Briggs. III, pp. 396;
23. Ibid.
24. Ibid.
25. Burhan-i-Maasir (I.A. 1921) pp. 102, Ferishta, Briggs. III, pp. 396;
26. Ibid.
27. Burhan-i-Maasir (I.A. 1921), pp. 102;
28. Ibid.

29. Ibid.
30. Ibid.
31. Basatin-us-Salatin (iv) pp. 16; Ferishta, Briggs. III, pp. 118-9'
32. Ibid.
33. Ibid.
34. Ibid.
35. Ferishta, Briggs. III, pp. 119-20; K.K. Basu's article "The Reign of Ali Adil Shah of Bijapur", Journal of Indian Culture, 1938-39, Vol. 5, pp. 5; Journal of Andhra Historical Research Society, 1946-47, Vol. 17 pp. 189;
36. Ibid.
37. Ibid.
38. K. K. Basu's article, "The Reign of Ali Adil Shah of Bijapur", Journal of Indian Culture, 1938-39; Vol. 5, pp. 52-53; Journal of Andhra Historical Research Society, 1946-47; 17; pp. 190;
39. Basatin-us-Salatin (Pt. iv) pp. 16; Ferishta, Briggs. III, pp. 120;
40. Ferishta, III, pp. 120;
41. Basatin-us-Salatin (iv) pp. 16; Ferishta, Briggs. III, pp. 120; Burhan-i-Maasir (I.A. 1921) pp. 102-3;
42. Ibid.
43. In this campaign against Ahmadnagar kingdom by Ali Adil Shah Ibrahim Q. Shah and Ram Raya, Sayyid Ali has concealed much that is to the discredit of Husain Nizam Shah I—see Burhan-i-Maasir (I.A. 1921) pp. 104-5; Basatin-us-Salatin (iv) pp. 16-17 Ferishta, Briggs. III, pp. 120;
44. Basatin-us-Salatin (IV) pp. 16-17; Ferishta, Briggs. III, pp. 120; K. K. Basu's article, "The Reign of Ali Adil Shah of Bijapur". Journal of Indian Culture, 1938-39, Vol. 5, pp. 53;
45. Basatin-us-Salatin (IV) pp. 17; Ferishta, Briggs. III, pp. 120;
46. Basatin-us-Salatin (IV), pp. 17; Ferishta, Briggs. III. pp. 120;
47. Ferishta, Briggs. III, pp. 120;
48. Ferishta, Briggs. III, pp. 240;
49. Ibid.
50. Ibid.
51. Ibid.
52. Ibid.
53. Ibid.
54. Burhan-i-Maasir (I.A. 1920) pp. 105;
55. Ibid.
56. Ferishta, Briggs. III, pp. 121, 240;
57. Ibid.
58. Ibid.
59. Ibid.
60. Ibid.
61. Ibid, pp. 241;
62. Ibid.
63. Ibid.
64. Ibid.
65. Ferishta, Briggs. III, pp. 241; Muntakhab-ul-Lubab, III. pp. 91-92;
66. Ferishta, Briggs. III, pp. 241. According to Sayyid Ali, Bhopal Rai, the commander of the fort of Kaliyani surrendered the fortress to the enemy, which compelled Husain Nizam Shah to sue for peace—see Burhan-i-Maasir (I.A. 1921) pp. 105;
67. Ferishta, Briggs. III. pp. 241;
68. Burhan-i-Maasir (I.A. 1921) pp. 106; Ferishta, Briggs. III, pp. 241; K. K. Basu's article, "The Reign of Ali Adil Shah of Bijapur, "Journal of Indian Culture, 1938-39, Vol. 5, pp. 53-54.
69. Ferishta, Briggs. III, pp. 241; Burhan-i-Maasir (I.A. 1921), pp. 106;
70. Ferishta, Briggs. III, pp. 241-42;

71. Ibid, pp. 242;
72. Ferishta, Briggs. III, pp. 242; Muntakhab-ul-Lubab, pp. 192.
73. Ibid.
74. Ferishta, Briggs. III, pp. 403, Muntakhab-ul-Lubab, III, pp. 192;
75. Ferishta, Briggs. III, pp. 404;
76. Basatin-us-Salatin Pt. (IV), pp. 18; Burhan-i-Maasir (I.A. 1921) pp. 141; Ferishta, Briggs. III, pp. 242-43;
77. Ferishta, Briggs. III, pp. 243; Basatin-ul-Salatin (III) pp. 18 Journal of Indian Culture, 1938-39, Vol. 5. pp. 54;
78. Basatin-us-Salatin (Pt. IV) pp. 18;
79. Basatin-us-Salatin (Pt. IV) pp. 18; Ferishta, Briggs. III, pp. 242;
80. Ferishta, Briggs. III, pp. 243;
81. Ibid.
82. Ibid.
83. Ibid, pp. 244;
84. Burhan-i-Maasir (I.A. 1921) pp. 141-42; Ferishta, Briggs. III, pp. 244; Basatin-us-Salatin (IV) pp. 28;
85. Ferishta, Briggs. III, pp. 244;
86. Ibid.
87. Ibid, pp. 245;
88. Ibid.
89. Ferishta, Briggs. III, pp. 245; Basatin-us-Salatin (IV) pp. 18; Sayyid Ali gives an entirely different account of the whole affair. According to him, no sooner had the allies laid siege Ahmadnagar and began to plunder and devastate the surrounding districts, than the Malika-i-Jahan, Malika-i-Humayun Bibi Aimna, the king's mother, who was in the fortress sent a message to Ibrahim Q. Shah saying that, "the whole of the land of Islam was groaning under the oppression of the idolators and that it ill became the Muhammedan sovereigns to instigate the idolators to persecute Muslims. "This message had the desired effect on Ibrahim, in stimulating his religious zeal and his enthusiasm for the faith. He resolved to retreat and to be no longer a party to the allied atrocities. With full knowledge of the fact that Husain Nizam would fail to face the allies in the field of battle, he recommended to the other participants to follow one of the three courses, (i) that, the expedition should be abandoned for that year to attain the object they had in view, or (2) that he himself be allowed to withdraw to his own country in order that he might reorganise his army and rejoin them when he had completed the task, or (3) if it was desired to press the siege, Adil Shah on whose behalf the expedition had been undertaken, should advance loans to the allies to enable them to reorganise their armies. Ram Raya and his brother approved these proposals; but Ali Adil Shah who was strongly in favour of the continuance of the siege did not react to them at all. Thereupon, next day, Ibrahim, with his army returned to Golkunda. Ram Raya too, who had also grown weary of the long compaign retired to Vijayanagara. Naturally Ali Adil Shah was compelled to retire without having attained the object.

It should be mentioned here that Ibrahim Qutb Shah joined Husain Nizam Shah rather than the allies, firstly because of the matrimonial alliance between the two and secondly, he bore bitter hatred towards the Hindu monarch, because of his atrocious policy towards the Muslims. Burhan-i-Maasir (I. A. 1921) pp. 142;

Father Heras has described the humiliation of Husain Nizam Shah, in the middle of this compaign, perhaps in disregard of the circumstances under which Ram Raya retreated to his capital. Evidently, the sequence of events is mistaken, because such humiliating terms could not have been implemented at a time when a part of the Hindu forces had been swept away by the fast current of the river. Ram Raya had no other choice but to withdraw to his capital; otherwise Husain Nizam Shah, could have surrounded him from all sides and have brought him to his knees. Thanks to the better judgement and right decision of the Hindu monarch, that he retired from the environs of Ahmadnagar kingdom, without further inflaming the revengeful spirit of Husain Nizam Shah—see Arvidu Dynasty of Vijayanagara, pp. 91;

90. Ferishta, Briggs. III. pp. 245;

91. Ibid, pp. 246;

92. Ibid.

93. Ibid.

94. Ibid.

95. Ferishta, Briggs. III, pp. 122-23; Basatin-us-Salatin (IV), pp. 20-22;

96. Burhan-i-Maasir (I.A. 1921) pp. 142;

97. As the most prominent part was taken by Husain Nizam Shah in the field of battle, Tarif-i-Husain Nizam Shahi, does not make any mention of other Sultans. According to the poet the army of Ahamadnagar only fought the battle and defeated Ram Raya, see, Poona Persian Poem.

98. Basatin-us-Salatin (IV) pp. 23; Ferishta, Briggs. III, pp. 123; the Mackenzie collection refers to the pretext for the commencement of the campaign against Ram Raya, the ruler of Vijayanagara:—

(i) Wilson says that "the Hindu records state that on going to an audience of the Ram Raya, the envoy of Ibrahim Adil Shah (here it should be Ali Adil Shah) passed on his way some swine intended to given to the menials of the court. As he expressed his abhorence of this unclean animal to the Raja, the latter treated his aversion with rediculas, asking him how he could hold them unclean when he fed himself upon fowls, which picked out grains from the ordure of the swine. He took an opportunity of showing him the fact, the insult roused Ali Adil Shah to arms—Mackenzie collection, pp. 268; Arvidu Dynasty of Vijayanagara, pp. 195 n.

(ii) According to Marathi M/s. "while Ram Raya was ruling, a Muhammedan Fakir came (to Angundi) and bathed in a sacred pool. When he was found doing so, he was arrested and produced before the ruler at whose commands he along with two others was severely beaten. All of them were subsequently let off. They went to Delhi (a word often losely used as Muslim) and represented that if Vijayanagara was not taken, Delhi ruler was no Musalman. In consequence of this incident preparations were made to march against Vijayanagara, which was captured—see, Taylor Catalogue, Raisonne III, pp. 691; Arvidu Dynasty of Vijayanagara, pp. 195 n.

99. Basatin-us-Salatin (IV) pp. 23; Ferishta, Briggs. III, pp. 123;

100. Ferishta, Briggs. III, pp. 412-13;

101. Bakhair of Ram Raj.

102. Ibid.

103. Ibid.

104. Basatin-us-Salatin (Pt. IV) pp. 26; Ferishta, Briggs. III, pp. 125-26; Burhan-i-Maasir (I.A. 1921) pp. 143-44;

105. Ferishta, Briggs. III, pp. 413;

106. Burhan-i-Maasir (I.A. 1921) pp. 144; Ferishta, Briggs. III, pp. 413;

107. Ferishta, Briggs. III, pp. 412-413;

108. Basatin-us-Salatin (Pt. IV) pp. 27; Ferishta, Briggs. III, pp. 126;

109. Ibid.

110. Ferishta, Briggs. III, pp. 126; Mirza Ibrahim Zubairi, the author of Basatin-us-Salatin, says that when the ambassador of Ali Adil arrived at the court of Ram Raya and delivered the message of his lord to him, the latter replied in a verse, "Do not move me so that the whole Earth might move with me; and I say it again and again." At the same time he turned out the Muslim ambassador from his court—(Pt. IV) pp. 27;

111. (i) Faria-i-Souza speaks only of three kings, Nizamula, Idalxa, and Gutubixa—see Faria-i-Souza II, pp. 432;

(ii) Burhan-i-Maasir also mention the names of the three Sultans (I.A. 1921) pp. 144;

(iii) The Maratha account of the battle gives the names of six sovereigns allied against the Hindu ruler on this occassion—see Chanderkar's article, "The destruction of Vijayanagara"—published in Bharat Itihas Samshodhak Mandal Poona, 1914, pp. 170;

(iv) Though Ferishta does not refer to the names of Sultan of Bidar, while describing the events relating to peace and alliance; but in a general way he remarks that Ali Barid Shah was making active preparations for the campaign against Ram Raya just as other Sultans were doing. See—Ferishta, Briggs. III, pp. 126, 246;

(v) Fedrick also mentions four, Dilcan, Zamaluc, Cotamaluc and Virdy—see Purchas X pp. 92;

(vi) Anquetil on Perron, like-wise states that, "Bishnagar was plundered by the four other kings of the Deccan and Concan, see Arvidu Dynasty of Vijayanagara, pp. 198;

(vii) Couto says that Izamaluco, invited four other kings to join the alliance, viz. Idalza, Heberache (Burhan Imad Shah); Cutubixa and Verido—Ibid pp. 198;

(viii) According to Basatin-us-Salatin the Sultan of Berar did not join the other Sultans on account of his hatred for Husain Nizam Shah—see, (Pt. IV) pp. 27;

112. (a) Basatin-us-Salatin (Pt. IV) pp. 27;
112. (b) See, Journal of Indian History, 1957 pp. 366.
113. Farishta, Briggs. III, pp. 414;
114. Ibid.
115. Ibid.
116. Ibid.
117. Ibid, pp. 127.
118. Ibid. pp. 414;
119. Burhan-i-Maasir (I. A. 1921) pp. 144;
120. Ferishta mentions that the age of Ram Raya was seventy years. According to Sayyid Ali he was eighty; the Portuguese authors like Couto and Feria-i-Souza who are supposed to be most reliable authorities, because of their close contacts with the court of Vijayanagara, state that he was in 90th years of his age—see, Ferishta, Briggs. III, pp. 129; Sewell pp. 203, The Arvidu Dynasty of Vijayanagara, pp. 201;

The Marathi account gives interesting details of the proceedings of Ram Raya on the eve of his departure from the capital. "He then went to his own harem, spent some time with Satyabhamabai, the chief Queen and presented many rich jewels to her. Then he went to another wife, named, Devachintamani Trivegal. Her company gave him much pleasure and he made presents to her. Then he came to the drawing room of his third wife, Mena Mohini Nijaswarupi. She tried to please him in different ways. He ordered sundry fruits from his orchards and presented them to his wives.........Then he visited the chamber of his mother Chandrasala. She waved many jewels over his head so that evil may be warded off. He then explained to her the state of affairs, how the four kings had made common cause in attacking him and how the temples, alms-distribution houses and the existence of the Brahmans was threatened. He, therefore, intimated to her the plan of repulsing and punishing the enemy. He then fell at her feet and then asked her leave. She did not like the idea and said, "We have not hurt the Muhammedans, but even then they are coming instead. It would be better to negotiate with them. Afterwards he took rest during the night in his chamber ? There he dreamt that somebody was depriving him of his ear-jewels and his throne and that he was being pulled down. At once he caused all the astrologers and fortune tellers of long standing to be summoned and related his dream to them. They consoled him saying that the enemy would be warded off and he would long live and rule his kingdom. He then presented them with costly clothes as well as coconuts. He also distributed 5,000 huns among the Brahmans." see, Chanderkar's article "The Destruction of Vijayanagara"; Bharat Itihas Samshodhak Mandal, Poona, 1914; pp. 171-2; Heras, Arvidu Dynasty of Vijayanagara" pp. 201; "Bakhair of Ram Raj", Proceedings of Indian Historical Records commission.

120 (a) See, H. K. Sherwani's article "Telingana under Ibrahim Q. Shah", J. I. H. (1957) Vol. 35, pp. 366-67.

121. Burhan-i-Maasir (I.A. 1921) pp. 144; Basatin-us-Salatin (Pt.) (IV) pp. 28-29;

122. Burhan-i-Maasir (I. A. 1921) pp. 144; According to Ferishta, the Hindu army consisted of (i) Right under Trimula, consisting of 20,000 horse, 20,000 foot and 500 elephants, (ii) centre under the command of Ram Raya himself, consisting 37,000 horse, 50,000 foot and 1,000 elephants, (3) left under Venkatadari, consisting of 25,000 horse, 20,00,000 foot and 500 elephants, and in all 82,000 horse, 90,c000 foot and 2000 elephants.

123. Basatin-us-Salatin (Pt. IV) pp. 29; Bakhair of Ram Raj.

124. Ibid.

125. See H. K. Sherwani's article "Telangana under Ibrahim Q. Shah" J. I. H. 1957, Vol. 35, pp. 367.

125 (a) Ibid.

125 (b) Ibid.

125 (c) Ibid.

125 (d) Ibid.

125 (e) Ibid.

126. Burhan-i-Maasir (I.A. 1921) pp. 145; Basatin-us-Salatin (Pt. IV) pp. 30;

127. Generally it is believed that the famous battle was fought near the village of Talikota, where the Muslim sovereigns had encamped. Burhan-i-Maasir and Basatin-us-Salatin only mention that the battle took place on the southern bank of the river Krishna. Ferishta says that "the armies united and marched to southward; they crossed the Krishna and encamped on the Hukery river, situated 12 miles from the former, which means that the battle took place 12 miles south, of river Krishna. But according to Sewell, the battle did not take place at Talikota, but many miles south of river Krishna and probably ten miles from Ram Raya's camp, wherever that might have been, which he thinks was at Mudgal. Moreover, according to him the ford crossed by the allies was perhaps at the bend of the river at Ingalgi and the little village of Bayapur or Bhogapur on the road directly leading from Ingalgi to Mudgal. But according to the Bakhair of Ram Raj, which makes the position more clear, the first camp of the Muhammedan allies, remained round the village Talikota, where no engagement took place. It was between the towns of Raksas and Tagdiji that the actual battle took place—see Ferishta, Briggs. III, pp. 127-8; Burhan-i-Maasir (I.A. 1921) pp. 145; Basatin-us-Salatin (Pt. IV) pp. 30-31; Patwardhan's article "The battle of Raksas Tagdi, published in Bharat Itihas Samshodhak Mandal, Poona, Vol. IV pp. 72; Chanderkar's article "Destruction of Vijayanagara", Bharata Itihas Samshodhak Mandal, Poona, 1914, pp. 196;

128. Burhan-i-Maasir (I.A. 1921) pp. 145-56; Bakhair of Ram Raj.

129. Bakhair of Ram Raj.

130. Ibid.

131. Bakhair of Ram Raj; Ferishta, Briggs. III, pp. 128; Basatin us-Salatin, pp. (IV) pp. 31-32; Burhan-i-Maasir (I.A. 1921) pp. 1 3;

132. Basatin-us-Salatin (Pt. IV) pp. 31; Ferishta, Briggs. III, pp. 128; Journal of Andhra Historical Research Society, 1946-47, Vol. 17 pp. 190-92;

133. Basatin-us-Salatin (Pt. IV) pp. 31; Ferishta, Briggs. III, pp. 128;

134. Ferishta, Briggs. III, pp. 248;

135. Ibid.

136. Ibid.

137. Burhan-i-Maasir (I.A. 1921) pp. 146; Basatin-us-Salatin (Pt. IV) pp. 31;

138. Ferishta, Briggs. III, pp. 128-29; Basatin-us-Salatin (Pt. IV) pp. 31;

139. Ferishta, Briggs. III, pp. 128-29; Basatin-us-Salatin (Pt. IV) pp. 31;

According to Sayyid Ali, Ram Raya and his brothers on the approach of the Muhamedan forces, "were terrified and decided not to fight on that day, but to make most of their last day of domination and power. They therefore, withdrew from the field and Husain Nizam Shah and other two sultans took advantage of their unwillingness to fight the enemies of Islam to allow time for repose, rested that night in anticipation of the merrow's battle—see Burhan-i-Maasir (I.A. 1921) pp. 145;

In an exaggerated way the Poona Persian Poem says that, "when infidel (Ram Raya) heard that the army (of Ahmadnagar) was approaching, the world became dark to his eyes See; Arvidu Dynasty of Vijayanagara, Appendix (a).

140. According to Tarikh-i-Qutb Shah, (1196) Venkatadari was killed at the hands of Ibrahim's officer, Sayedji. This is coroborated by Caesar Fredricik (Purchas X 93) referred to in Arvidu pp. 216; we however, find that it was Venkatadari who restored all the forts and parganas taken by his brother after this battle (for this see Ferishta, II p. 129). It seems possible while Venkatadari fled from the battle field and Timmraraja was struck in his eye, they were taken as casualities by the allied army. See H. K. Sherwani s article Telangana under Ibrahim Q. Shah, 1957; Vol. 35, pp. 379, n.

141. Arvidu Dynasty of Vijayanagara.

142. Ibid.

143. Ibid.

144. Ibid.

145. Bakhair of Ram Raj; Basatin-us-Salatin (Pt. IV) pp. 34;

146. Ferishta, Briggs. III, pp. 248; Burhan-i-Maasir (I.A. 1921) pp. 193; Basatin-us-Salatin, (Pt. IV) pp. 31-34;

147. It was the time honoured custom in the Daccan, that if a sovereign pitched his camp in the front of his enemy, it indicated that he would not quit the saddle till he had succeeded in his venture. It is also stated in Basatin-us-Salatin that Husain Nizam Shah had in his camp several of his wives, and concubines and at this point he placed eunuchs next to everyone of them, with special instructions to kill them, if the battle takes an unfavourable turn—see, Ferishta Briggs. III, pp. 129; Basatin-us-Salatin (Pt. IV) pp. 34.

148. Basatin-us-Salatin (Pt. IV) pp. 35;

149. Basatin-us-Salatin (Pt. IV) pp. 35-36;

150. Ibid.

151. Ferishta, Briggs. III, pp. 129, 248; Bakhair of Ram Raj.

152. This treason though neither recorded by Ferishta, nor by the author of Burhan-i-Maasir, explains satisfactorily the sudden termination of the battle. Fredricke who heard the account of the whole action, one year later, when he passed through Vijayanagara says, "These four kings were not able to overcome the cities and the king of Beezanaggar, but by treason. The king of Beezanaggar was a gentile, and had among all other of his captains, two of which were notable, and they were Moors an either of them in charge of three score and ten or four score thousand men. These two captains being of one religion with the four kings which were Moors wrought means with them to betray their own king into their hands. The king of Beezanaggar esteemed not the force of four kings his enemies, but went out of his citie to wage battle with them in the fields; and when the Armies were joined, the battle lasted but a while, not the space of four hours, because the two traitorous captains, in the chiefest of the fight

their companies turned their faces against their king and made disorder in his Armie that astonished, they set themselves to fight"– see Purchas Vol. X, pp. 92-93;

The treason is not recorded by Sewell, but has been mentioned by "Krishnamacharalu"—see "Origin Growth and Decline of the Vijayanagara Empire", Indian Antiquary L. II, pp. 11; The Maratha account mentions that the final cause of the defeat was the surprise attack on the Arvidu camp by the Sultans of Golkunda and Bijapur—see, Chandarker's article "Destruction of Vijayanagara."

Although the names of these two traitors are no where mentioned, but Father Heras thinks that one of them was Ain-ul-Mulk, whom the Raya used to call as his brother (see, Ferishta, Briggs. III, pp. 381); and at whose request Sadashivraya had granted the village of Bevinahalli to the Brahmans (see, Epigraphica Indica, pp. 231, vv, pp. 64-68). He seems to have come from the family of traitors, his father had been beheaded for treason at Bijapur in 1553 A.D. during the reign of Ibrahim Adil Shah; and it was perhaps that being offended at the conduct of the latter that his son left the Adil Shahi service and entered that Ram Raya—Ferishta, Briggs. III, pp. 381; Heras "Arvidu Dynasty of Vijayanagar", pp. 211-12;

153. Burhan-i-Maasir (I.A. 1921) pp. 193; Basatin-us-Salatin, pp. 103;

154. Burhan-i-Maasir (I.A. 1921) pp. 194;

155. Burhan-i-Maasir (I. A. 1921) pp. 194; Tabqat-i-Akbari III, pp. 69; This account differs from that given by Ferishta, according to whom Ram Raya did not mount the horse, but when he saw that the battle was going against him, he left his throne and re-entered his litter. One of Husain's elephants, named Ghulam Ali (Epigraphica Indo-Moslemica, 1931-38 pp. 7-8, Plate III (a) overthrew the litter and its bearer fled, leaving Ram Raya lying alone of the field. The driver again directed the elephant towards the jewelled litter, with a view to secure prize, when one of the Brahman of the Hindu king, came forward and said, "this is Sadashivaraya. Find a horse for him and he will make you one of the greatest lords of the kingdom. On having came to know who the captive was, the driver, caused the elephant to pick him and carried him to Chalapi Rumi Khan, who sent him on to Husain Nizam Shah, by whose orders he was beheaded, see Ferishta, Briggs. III, pp. 249;

The author of Basatin-us-Salatin has a different story to relate. He says that Nizam Shah was much pleased with the capture of Ram Raya, caused him to sit down before him and asked him, "How are you, and how do you feel ?" Ram Raya could not speak, but pointed out to his own head, saying that "this was destined". On this point Hakim Hasan Beg, who was one of the favourites of Husain Nizam Shah and his confident attendant, hastily came forward, told him that this was no time for conversation with the enemy and asked him to send him to the gallows of retribution, otherwise Adil Shah, who claims to be his son, will cause great disturbance and will snatch Ram Raya from his hands. Accordingly, Ram Raya's head was severed from his body—see Basatin-us-Salatin pp. 103;

While according to the Bakhair of Ram Raj, in the thick of the fight Ram Raya sent a messenger to Ali Adil Shah, requesting him to shoot him and kill him so that he could be saved from the hands of other Muslims. After some deliberations Ali Adil Shah agreed to do so and shot him dead.

The author of Basatin mentions that according to Ghulam Ali Astrabadi, the father of Muhammad Qasim Ferishta, the head of Ram Raya was sent to Burhan Imad Shah, who was not present in the battle—see Basatin-us-Salatin (Pt. IV) pp. 111; while according to Bakhair of Ram Raj, the bones of Ram Raya were sent to Benaras to be deposited in the Ganges.

156. As regards to the date of the battle, Mr. Sewell relying on the authority of Muhammedan Chronicles viz. the anonymous history of the Qutb Shahis and Ferishta's history, places in January 1565; the actual day being Tuesday 23rd Jan. 1565 A.D. whereas Ferishta mentions Friday the

28th of Jamad-us-Sani A.H. 972. According to Sayyid Ali, the victory was won on Friday Jamadi-ul-Akhair, A.H. 972 (Jan 4th 1565 A.D.). But the day given in the Bakhair of Ram Raj for the death of Ram Raya, in the year Raksakshi, the month of Visaka, 8th day, the dark night, Monday Sarvana Nakshatra corresponding to Monday or Tuesday the 5th May 1565 A.D. And if we accept as Mr. Swewell's dates, that the Muhamedan allies marched on 25th Dec. 1565, from the plains of Talikota towards the south, the final battle, could certainly have not (if the details given in the Bakhair be true) taken place on 23rd Jan. 1565 A.D. Moreover, neither Ferishta, nor the Qutb Shahi historian nor Sayyid Ali give details of the other engagements, as has been given in Bakhair and though the war began with firm determination on either side, it seems hard to believe that the fate of Ram Raya was decided in a simple engagement. But this date given by the Bakhair of Ramraj can not be accepted for the very reason that the Sultans stayed in the Vijayanagara territory after the battle was over, for six months. It was after the end of this period that the Sultans returned back to their respective kingdoms. It is related that after his arrival at Ahmadnagar, Husain Nizam Shah, gave himself to pleasure enjoyments and died on 6th June, 1565. This obviously shows that the battle ended in January 1565, not in May 1565 as mentioned in the Bhakhair of Ram Raj.

157. Ferishta, Briggs. III, pp. 414; Burhan-i-Maasir (I.A. 1921) pp. 194; According to Basatin-us-Saltin, the Sultan lived for 20 days in the field, see pp. 105-8;

158. Basatin-us-Salatin pp. 105;

159. The Vasucharitram states that, "the Nizam Shah (of Ahmadnagar) Kutupashi (Kutub Shah of Golkunda) and Sapda (the Adil Shah of Bijapur) fled to the forests before his march"—see, S. K. Ayanger's "Sources of Vijayanagara history" pp. 216;

While in Savaramalakalanidhi, it is stated that with his brother's aid, he (Ram Raya) "conquered all Parasikas (Muhamedans);? Ibid, pp. 190.

The British Musuemplates of Sadashivaraya state that "The dust raised by his amirs appears like the smoke that drives away those great" viz. Muslims. See, Epigraphica Indica, IV, pp. 3; Arvidu Dynasty of Vijayanagara, pp. 74;

160. Basatin-us-Salatin pp. 113;

161. Ferishta, Briggs. III, pp. 414-15; Burhan-i-Maasir A.D. 1921) pp. 194; Basatin-us-Salatin pp. 109-10;

162. Ferishta, Briggs. III, pp. 131, 414; Burhan-i-Maasir (I.A. 1921) pp. 196; Tabqat-i-Akbari III, pp. 69;

Husain Nizam Shah left four sons and four daughters. By Bibi Khwanjah Humayun, he had Murtaza Nizam Shah and Burhan Nizam III; Chand Bibi married to Ali Adil Shah and Bibi Khadijah was married to Jamal-ud-din Hasan Auju. By Surya, he had two sons Shah Qasim and Shah Mansur and two daughters, Aqa Bibi married to Mir Abdul Wahhab, son of Sayyid Abdul Azum and Bibi Jamal married to Ibrahim Q. Shah.

## CHAPTER V

# MURTAZA NIZAM SHAH I (1565-88 A.D.)

Prince Murtaza Khan commonly known in the Daccan history, as Diwana or madman was proclaimed king on sunday 15th July 1565 A.D. (16th, Zal-Hijjah. A.H. 972). But the coronotion ceremony was performed seven months after, on 26th Jan. 1566 A.D. (Sunday 5th, Rajab A.H. 973) at the time selected by the astrologers of the Nizam Shahi court. He assumed the style of Abul Muzaffer Ghazi Murtaza Nizam Shah I. The umbrella and the aftabgir were raised over his head. The officers of the state, the nobles and the people were admitted to audience to offer their homage to him.[1]

**Murtaza Nizam Shah ascended the throne.**

The new king was but a child of a few years and so the whole business of the state fell on the shoulders of his mother Khunzah Humayun,[2] a lady distinguished for her ability, talents and virtues. Early in her regency she made provision for the education and upbringing of her son. Her choice fell upon Maulana Husain Tabrezi, who was not only nobly connected but was famous for learning and piety. He was appointed as tutor to the boy-king. He instructed Murtaza in religion, holy law, Quran and Hadith and other subjects which formed the curriculum of study in those days. In short everything was done to train the mind of the boy into a healthy and wholesome way of life.

**Regency of Khunzah Humayun.**

The Queen mother appointed Qasim Beg Tabrezi as the Wakil and Peshwa of the kingdom,[3] but his advancing age rendered it difficult for him to perform the onerous duties of his office satisfactorily. He resigned and made room for Maulana Inayatullah, who had now returned from Raichur and Mudgal, where he had been left by the late king.[4] It appears that he could not put up with the interference of the regent; nor could he tolerate her inordinate partiality for her own kith and kin. Like his predecessor he too resigned and returned to the fortress of Lohgarh.[5] He was succeeded by Shah Rafiuddin Husain,[6] the eldest son of Shah Tahir but he too did not come up to her expectation and therefore was dismissed soon after.[7] The post was now jointly held by her three brothers Taj Khan, Ain-ul-Mulk and Itibar Khan, while she herself conducted the real business of the state, sitting behind the curtain in the open darbar.[8]

The political problems for the Nizam Shahis, both external and internal remained almost the same in their form and content as before. It is true that the battle of Banihatti had removed for all the time to come the danger of the Hindu aggression, but, whereas, so long it was there, there was the possibility of Muslim states combining together against the common enemy. Its disappearance intensified their mutual jealousies, whetted their territorial appetite and rendered political conditions in the Daccan worse confounded. The victors failed to arrive at an understanding with regard to the division of the spoils which led to the strained relations and perennial conflict among them.

During the interregnum which followed the death of Husain Nizam Shah I and the accession of the minor Murtaza Nizam Shah I, Ali Adil Shah seized some territory in the south, which formerly belonged to the Raya of Vijayanagara[9]. The existence of minority administration in Ahmadnagar encouraged him to prosecute his aggressive designs further. Trimula the late Raya's son, had after his father's death, established himself at Anegundi; and his uncle Venkatadari had established himself at Penukonda, a place beyond the reach of the victors. There was no love lost between the uncle and the nephew. Consequently, Ali Adil Shah decided to destroy both of them in detail and then to swallow up their possessions. In the first instance, therefore he took up the cause of Trimula and sent a large army to Anegundi.[10]

The threatened aggression compelled Venkatadari to appeal for help to Khunzah Humayun. It almost synchronised with a similar proposal from Ibrahim Qutb Shah, who was equally keen to curb the ambition of Ali Adil Shah, in regard to the southward expansion of his dominions. He sent an envoy to Nizam Shah to conclude an offensive alliance against Bijapur. The Queen mother not only fell in with the plan of Ibrahim Qutb Shah, but she also suggested him to invite the cooperation of Tufal Khan, the prime minister of Burhan Imad Shah. The allies accordingly advanced towards Bijapur.[11]

Plundering on the way, destroying and carrying off the crops, the allied armies reached the frontiers of Bijapur.[12] To avoid a pitched battle, Ali Adil Shah, who had withdrawn from Anegundi, fell back from place to place. Farhad Khan, Ghalib Khan, Kamil Khan, Mian Munjhu and Ramghar Khan, the Nizam Shahi officers carried fire and sword to very gates of the fort of Bijapur but the garrison resisted the enemy very stubbornly notwithstanding the serious deplection in their ranks.[13] Realising that Ali Adil Shah would not face the allies in the field, Khunzah Humayun accepted the terms which he had offered through intermediaries and after concluding peace the allies returned to their respective capitals.[14]

After the Nizam Shahi army had returned to Ahmadnagar, Ali Adil Shah resolved to wreak his vengeance on Tufal Khan who had joined Nizam Shah against him.[15] He therefore sent an envoy to the Nizam Shahi court to express his desire for meeting Murtaza Nizam Shah, so that the recent treaty between the two kingdoms might be renewed and that they might make common cause against their common enemies.[16] Considering it to be the most desirable policy, the Nizam Shahi court accorded a grand reception to the envoy and sent him back completely satisfied. The two kings set out from their respective capitals and met near the fortress of Ausa.[17] Here the treaty of peace was renewed. It was agreed to make war upon Tufal Khan, who had rebelled against his master, and had seized the administration of the kingdom of Berar. They decided to liberate the helpless Burhan Imad Shah from Tufal's domination and punish the latter for his failure to join personally the Muslim rulers in their struggle against Vijayanagara.[18] Accordingly, Frahad Khan from Ahmadnagar and Dilwar Khan from Bijapur were sent in advance towards Berar and in a few preliminary skirmishes, they scored victory against the enemy.[19] They were followed by the main armies led by their respective sovereigns. Upon the approach of the

**War declared against Tufal Khan.**

allies, Tufal Khan retreated to the fortress of Gawilgarh to stand a siege there.[20] While the operations were in progress, he secretly won over Ali Adil Shah, who not only suggested to his ally to raise the siege, but also persuaded him to lead a combined attack on the Qutb Shahi country.[21] Throwing to winds his professions of friendship, Adil Shah went to the length of making an unsuccessful attempt to seize the person of Murtaza Nizam Shah. His duplicity having been exposed, the alliance broke up, and each party returned to its respective capital smarting with resentment and dissatisfaction.

Now was the turn of Khunzah Humayun to form an alliance with Tufal Khan to avenge the treacherous conduct of the Ali Adil Shah and to recover the frontier districts of the Ahmadnagar kingdom which had been occupied by the latter's minister Kishwar Khan. With their joint armies they invaded the kingdom of Bijapur. Ali Adil Shah in sheer fright retreated and sent Kishwar Khan Lari to meet the enemy. The latter entered the fort of Ahsanabad-Gulbarga from where he led daily skirmishes on the besiegers. At length, his resources began to decline, but he was soon relieved of his anxiety because the allies were compelled to withdraw, after they had suffered heavy losses in a chance struggle.[23]

For varity of reasons the Queen mother Khunzah Humayun steadily became unpopular. Evidently, she had failed both as an administrator and as a politician. In fact her relations, her short-sighted schemes had occasioned grave dissatisfaction against her. To add to her consternation, Ali Adil Shah now became very keen to exploit in his favour, the state of affairs in Ahmadnagar. He seized Kondana and constructed a fort there, which he named Dharur (1569 A.D.).[24]

**Aggressive designs of Ali Adil Khan (1569 A.D.).**

Maulana Husain Tabrezi,[25] the tutor of the young king, in course of time, gained complete control over his mind. He began to aspire for the post of Peshwa and Vakil. To achieve the object he made his own plans of action. He impressed upon the king that kingship resembled Divinity and as such it did not admit any partnership. Further, he pointed to him vividly the evils flowing out, of the exercise of unlimited

**Regency Overthrown (1569 A.D.)**

powers by his mother.[26] Finally, he succeeded in persuading his pupil to deprive her of power, for which he hired some ruffians to seize her person.[27] But luckily the secret leaked out, Murtaza told her about it[28]. Whenupon the conspirators in sheer fright dispersed and fled. Among them were Khwaja Mirak Dabir,[29] subsequently entitled Changez Khan, and Sayyid Murtaza, who fled to take refuge at the court of Ali Adil Shah. But they were soon pardoned and readmitted into the royal favour.[30]

On September 1st, 1569 A. D.[31] the Queen mother Khunzah Humayun marched with her son to check the enchroachments of Kishwar Khan Lari, the Bijapur general.[32] Tej Khan and Ain-ul-Mulk, the Nizam Shahi officers encamped at the village of Jaichand,[33] at a distance of three or four leagues from the royal camp. Nursing malicious intentions against the Queen mother, they refused to obey her commands and to follow the main army. On the arrival of the royal army at Dharamgaon,[34] Murtaza Nizam Shah was again instigated by his friends and associates to bring about the fall of his mother from power. He now grasped the situation, made up his mind to liberate himself from her thraldom. Having gained over the principal nobles like Farhad Khan,[35] he asked Habsh Khan[36] to inform the Queen mother that, "it was his pleasure that she should no longer engage in public affairs, but lead a retired life like other princesses." Enraged at this message she summoned her men and throwing a veil over her face, came out of the palace, mounted a horse, armed with a bow, a sword and a dagger to put down the conspirators [37] Undaunted, Habsh Khan seized her and put to flight her attendants. She was then handed over to Itibar Khan[38] who escorted her to Daultabad. She was finally imprisoned in the fortress of Shivaner.[39] Khwaja Mirak was sent to arrest her brothers Ain-ul-Mulk and Taj Khan. But they took to flight. Ain-ul-Mulk took refuge with Ibrahim Qutb Shah, and Taj Khan with Raja Bahar Jui of Baglana.[40] After some time both of them returned to Ahmadnagar and lived in retirement, in their own jagirs.[41] The king Murtaza Nizam Shah now assumed charge of the affairs of his government. He honoured his tutor

**Fall of Queen Mother Khunzah Humayun (1st September 1569 A.D.)**

Maulana Husain Tabrezi with the title of Khan-i-Khanan, and put him in charge of administration.[42]

Murtaza now resolved to throw back the encroachment upon his territory, which had been made by the Adil Shah during the regency of his mother. He wrote to Kishwar Khan Lari, who was holding Dharur, to evacuate the fort, but the latter sent a very insulting reply. Upon this Murtza Nizam Shah marched against him and opened the seige of the fort. Adil Shah tried to divert the attention of the invaders by sending an army into the Nizam Shahi territory, but Murtaza Nizam Shah firmly held on. In the end when the walls of the fort had been breached, resistance by the garrison became impossible. Kishwar Khan was shot into his stomach by Changez Khan at close range and he fell dead. His head was put on the top of a spear and was paraded throughout the Nizam Shahi kingdom.[43] The fort of Dharur was captured and occupied.

**Adil Shahi invasion repelled**

Meanwhile Ali Adil Shah had sent an army under the command of Nur Khan, Ain-ul-Mulk, Ankas Khan and Zarif-ul-Mulk to the relief of Kishwar Khan Lari. But perhaps partly, because of their jealousy with the commandant of Dharur, but mainly because of their fear of Murtza Nizam Shah, they avoided meeting him in the open field. To draw him from Dharur they entered Nizam Shahi territory, but their hopes were not fulfilled. Having completed the operations at Dahrur, Murtaza Nizam Shah turned his attention to the Adil Shahi intruders and succeeded in repulsing them. In the course of action which followed, Ain-ul-Mulk, Firoz Khan and Zarif-ul-Mulk lost their lives.[44]

The king of Ahmadnagar now had every reason to be dissatisfied with Adil Shah and he was on the look out for an opportunity to wreak vengeance on him. Luckily, just about this time, arrived in Ahmadnagar an envoy of Ibrahim Qutb Shah to conclude a treaty of peace on behalf of his master.[49] The Prime Minister, Khan-i-Khanan pointed out to his master, the advantage of a friendly gesture towards Qutb Shah, particularly in his projected plan to humble the pride of Adil Shah.[46] He also impressed upon him thatthe moment was appropriate to implement

**Alliance with Qutb Shah against Ali Adil Shah.**

the plan, because Adil Shah had for some time been indifferent to repair the fortress of Bijapur,[47] which, if attacked, was certain to fall into the hands of the invaders, the more so when the Bijapur army was suffering from demoralisation caused by the death and discomfiture to Kishwar Khan Lari. The arguments of Khan-i-Khanan made an irresistable appeal to Murtaza Nizam Shah and he concluded an alliance with Ibrahim Qutb Shah,[49] who marched with his army towards Bidar, and persuaded Ali Barid Shah I[50] also to join the confederacy. The two met at the town of Wakdari[61] where they took oaths to stand by one another. Here it was agreed that they should march forthwith to attack the kingdom of Bijapur.[52]

But in an atmosphere of short-sighted selfishness and mutual distrust, the plighted word had little sanctity, especially among the Muslim rulers of the Daccan who united as readily as they unsheathed their swords to fight each other. Murtaza Nizam Shah, having instigated the invasion of the Adil Shahi country was the first to forget his own mission. Alarmed at the rapidity of the invader's advance, Adil Shah threw into prison Shah Abul Hasan,[43] the eldest son of Shah Tahir, whom he charged with complicity with the enemy. This action of Ali Adil Shah perturbed Sayyid Murtaza Sabzavari, formerly a noble of the Nizam Shahi court, but now a refugee in Bijapur and an intimate friend of Shah Abdul Hasan.[54] He importuned Ali Adil Shah to permit him to go as his emissary to Nizam Shah to persuade the latter to desist from aggression. But his real object was to secure the release of his friend.[55]

Relying on the clemency and generosity of Murtaza Nizam Shah, he set out from Bijapur at the dead of the night and reached the Nizam Shahi camp the next morning. Covering his head with a blanket, he made his way towards the royal enclosure.[56] Unable to obtain permission to enter it, he went to the Khan-i-Khanan and persuaded him to help him to have an audience of the king, without letting him know the objcet of his mission.[57] The audience having been granted, he placed his head on king's feet, vowing that he would not rise till His Majesty had promised to obtain the release of Shah Tahir's son, which was possible only if a

**Peace concluded and the camp of Qutb Shah plundered.**

treaty of peace was concluded with Ali Adil Shah.[58] Murtaza Nizam Shah who had a soft corner in his heart for Shah Tahir, readily consented to the proposal, on condition that Shah Abul Hasan be released and be sent as an ambassador to conclude the treaty.[59] Accordingly, Shah Abul Hasan was released and was sent with rich presents to the camp of the allies. During his stay there he succeeded in persuading the king, Murtaza Nizam Shah to attack Ibrahim Qutb Shah and Ali Barid, painting to him the rosy prospects of the reduction of Telingana and Bidar.[60] Murtaza Nizam Shah quickly reacted to the plan and gave orders to his army to surround the camps of his allies and to plunder them. Next morning while Ibrahim Qutb Shah was still asleep sudden uproar in his camp awakened him. Attacked as he was from every side, in sheer perplexity, he gave up the idea of offering any resistance whatsoever.[61] Abandoning his insignia of royalty, horses, elephants, tents, pavillion, handsome boy-slaves and beautiful slave-girls, not to speak of treasure-chests and jewels etc. he fled with a few of his courtiers towards his own country.[62] The Nizam Shahi forces now marched against the fortress of Udgir, besieged it and captured it by storming its wall. Thereafter Murtaza Nizam Shah returned in triumph to his capital.[63]

On his arrival at the capital, he associated Shah Haidar and Shah Jamaluddin Anju, who had connections with the royal house, by virtue of being the husband of Bibi Khadija, the daughter of Husain Nizam Shah I, with the administration of the state. Within a short time they brought to the notice of the king, the base actions of the Khan-i-Khanan, his having encompassed the death of Maulana Inayatullah; his ingratitude to Khunzah Humayun and his having counselled the plundering of Ibrahim Qutb Shah's camp. Murtaza Nizam Shah ordered him to be imprisoned in the fort of Jund.[64] After the disgrace and fall of the Khan-i-Khanan, the office of Wakil and Peshwa was bestowed upon Shah Haidar, and Shah Jamaluddin Anju was associated with him. But as the former neglected the administration of the state, he was removed. And the two offices were held by Shah Jamaluddin Anju.[65]

In November 1569 A.D. Murtaza Nizam Shah attacked the Portuguese because of their atrocious conduct towards the Muslim and Hindu population.[66] He opened the siege of Ravadanda, but was compelled to raise it. On his return from this expedition, the king reshuffled his ministry. Jamalludin Husain was banished ;[67] Frahad Khan and Ikhlas Khan being suspected of the treason in the recent campaign were thrown behind the bars. Khwaja Mirak Dabir entitled Changez Khan was appointed to the office of Wakil and Peshwa.[68] At the same time the Foreigners like Khudawand Khan,[69] Jamshed Khan Shirazi and many others were elevated to the ranks of amirs.[70] Murtaza Khan Sabzavari another Foreign noble was appointed to the office of Sar-Silahdar.[71]

Now was the turn of Ibrahim Qutb Shah to form a confederacy with Adil Shah and Barid Shah to take revenge from Nizam Shah. To forestall the contingency of Imad Shah joining Murtaza Nizam Shah, Qutb Shah sent an envoy to Berar to remind the regent Tufal Khan of the high handedness of Nizam Shah against his country. Tufal Khan readily accepted the proposal of joining the confederacy and as an earnest gesture of his intentions, despatched his son Shamsher-ul-Mulk to join Qutb Shah. The latter marched towards Bidar on the pretext of a hunting expedition. It was between Bidar and Kaulas that he was met by the Berar auxiliaries and Amir Ali Barid. With such a strong backing behind him he approached Ali Adil Shah with his proposal.[72] The latter not only responded to it with great enthusiam, but he even came to some secret understanding with some of the former ministers of the Nizam Shahi kingdom e. g. Shah Haidar and Jamaluddin Husain Anju, who were for some time in his service.[73] Still he was afraid of the incorruptibility of the new Wakil and Peshwa Changez Khan, who was honest and energetic.[74] To upset the apple cart which the allies had constructed, Changez Khan advised his master to march towards Bijapur and thus prevent an alliance between Adil Shah and Qutb Shah[75]. The trick succeeded beyond expectations. The two rulers came to terms and entered into a truce. The confederacy fell to pieces like a house of cards.

In great consternation the members retreated to their respective countries. While parting company, Ibrahim Qutb Shah advised Ali Barid to repair the fortress of Bidar, assuring him of full support in case of external aggression.[76]

Both Ali Adil Shah and Murtaza Nizam Shah being inspired by ambitious projects of territorial aggrendisement, agreed between themselves that Nizam Shah should have a free hand with regard to Berar and Bidar, whereas Shah should seize in the Carnatic territory an equal area to the two kingdoms. Accordingly the allies opened the siege of Bidar, but timely intervention of Ibrahim Qutb Shah upset their plans and they were compelled to withdraw. Murtaza Nizam Shah marched to complete the conquest of Berar and Ali Adil Shah moved south-ward in the direction of Vijayanagara, each agreeing to have in his court a permanent envoy of the other.[77]

**Dual alliance formed against Berar, Bidar & Vijayanagara (1572 A.D.)**

To overawe Qutb Shah into silence, Murtaza Nizam Shah sent a detachment of troops to plunder the environs of Golcunda, after which he marched towards Berar by way of Pathri.[78] Before actually opening the campaign he advised Tufal Khan, through Mulla Haider Kashi to hand over power to his master Burhan Imad Shah who had now come of age; but the suggestion was rejected outright.[79] Upon this Murtaza Nizam Shah occupied Pathri and its adjacent districts, which he assigned in jageer to his followers.[80] To save himself from the impact of the Nizam Shahi army and at the same time to distract its attention, Tufal Khan led a sort of counter offensive against the fort of Qandhar,[81] in the expectation of cooperation from Ali Barid Shah who was exposed to a similar threat of invasion by Nizam Shah. The move brought temporary relief to Tufal Khan, because Murtaza Nizam withdraw from Berar to save Qandhar.[82]

**Attempt made for annexation of Berar, failed**

But instead of returning to Berar, Tufal Khan marched Bidar and thus exposed that unfortunate kingdom to the Nizam Shahi invasion.[83] An indecisive skirmish between the rival forces followed, at the end of which Tufal Khan secretly escaped hotly pursued by Changez Khan who drove him out of Mahur and compelled him to seek refuge in the neighbouring hills.[84] Here too he was not allowed to stay long, and although on one occasion he inflicted heavy losses on the enemy, yet it did not deter them from following him close at his heels.[85] In the end, he took refuge with Miran Muhammad Shah II, the ruler of Khandesh, but the latter at the instance of Murtaza Nizam Shah, ordered him to leave his dominions.[86] The two rulers met on the banks of Purnadi, exchanged friendly greetings and promised to each other, amity and goodwill.[87] Though Tufal Khan was humiliated but Berar could not be annexed.

On his return to Berar, Tufal Khan shut himself in the fort of Narnala,[88] and sent his son Shamshir-ul-Mulk to protect Gavilgarh. He also appealed for help to Emperor Akbar, offering him to surrender Berar. But it was a far cry from Narnala to Agra, and before the Mughal Emperor[89] Akbar could respond, Nizam Shah simultaneously opened the siege of the fort of Narnala and Gavilgarh[90]. While these operations were going on, Qutb Shah attacked the Nizam Shahi troops on the borders of Qandhar. Murtaza Nizam Shah took prompt action, sent reinforcements to the threatened zone and compelled the enemy to retreat from Qandhar. (May 11, 1573 A.D.)[91]

Nizam Shah pushed on the siege of Narnala which dragged on for about a year.[92] He cleared the jungle and thus made the approaches to the fort more accessible to his army. He dragged the siege engines to the walls and battered them with incessant fire. But the garrison was equally dogged in its determination not to yield. Occasionally groups of soldiers sallied forth from the fort and fought the enemy courageously. The patience of the invaders was being sorely tried. They felt exhausted and tired. At this moment arrived, a directive from the Mughal Emperor asking Murtaza Nizam Shah to withdraw from Berar.[93] But the latter remained firm in his resolve, because his prestige was at stake.

At the same time Murtaza Nizam Shah received the news of the birth of a son at Ahmadnagar. For a while he thought of returning to his capital immediately, but his minister Changez Khan would not let him do it. To speed up the siege operations, he had recourse to a stratagem. He succeeded in introducing into the fort his own men, who created confusion there. On the one hand Tufal Khan was deserted by many of his officers, on the other Asad Khan,[94] the Nizam Shahi commander battered down most of the bastions of the fort.[95] It was now subjected to storming. Tufal Khan fled by the posterngate and the fort of Narnala was occupied by the Nizam Shahi army.[96] In course of his flight Tufal Khan was captured (April 12, 1574 A.D.) and he was thrown in prison along with his master Burhan Imad Shah and the other claimants to the Imad Shahi throne.[97] His title was conferred on his captor Sayyid Hasan.[98]

The news of the fall of Narnala and the imprisonment of his father Tufal Khan filled Shamshir-ul-Mulk with fear and alarm.[99] He agreed to surrender on condition that his life was spared. Thus Gavilgarh was also occupied and the property of Shamshir-ul-Mulk was confiscated.[100] This was followed by the occupation of other forts of Berar, which completed the conquest and annexation of the kingdom of Berar into Ahmadnagar. Undoubtedly it was a triumph of diplomatic and military skill of Murtaza Nizam Shah. His prestige stood high. He was now one of the leading potentates of the Daccan.

But Murtaza Nizam Shah's success created alarming reactions on the minds of his neighbours. Ali Adil Shah had helped him to achieve it, but he began to fear from the accession of the resources which the annexation of Berar had brought to the kingdom of Ahmadnagar.[101] As to Ibrahim Qutb Shah, he had all along been resentful. Now he positively became hostile. So did Miran Muhammad Shah II of Khandesh. They were finding in Murtaza Nizam Shah a powerful and ambitious rival at once bold and daring. The gravity of the situation became all the greater, because of the expansion and consolidation of the Mughal Empire in Northern India where the independence of Malwa and Gujarat had been completely wiped out. Add to this the decline and fall of the kingdom of Vijayanagara. This meant complete disruption of balance of power among the succession states of the Daccan. An era of fresh alliances and combinations dawned.

Murtaza made suitable arrangements for the administration of the newly annexed territory. It was assigned in jagir to Jamshed Khan, Kudawand Khan, Chand Khan, Bahri Khan Mirza Quli Khan, Shaikh Barraqi, Maqsud Aqa and others, who had distinguished themselves in the recent campaign. Khilat Khan Kashi was appointed as Commander-in-Chief, Bahram Khan Gilani was made the commandant of Gavilgarh and Sayyid Ali Zahir-ul-Mulk of Narnala.[102]

**Plan to conquer Bidar.**

Fully alive to the implications of his recent success in Berar which had roused the jealousy and envy of his neighbours, Murtaza Nizam Shah was reluctant to proceed further in his career of aggression and thereby aggravate the situation. But Changez Khan spurred on his ambition by pointing out to him that Ali Adil Shah was prosecuting his designs in the South, and hence it would be in the fitness of things for him to do the same. Accordingly plans were made for the conquest of Bidar.[103]

**Rebellions in Berar.**

But an outcrop of risings in Berar distracted the attention of Murtaza Nizam Shah and interrupted his plan of the conquest of Bidar. In fact this undertaking proved alarming as much as to Qutb Shah as to Muhammad Shah II.[104] Whereas Qutb Shah on the one hand professed friendship towards Nizam Shah and sent to Ahmadnagar, Sayyid Mir Zainal to strengthen the ties of amity and goodwill, on the other he suggested to Muhammad Shah II the ruler of Khandesh, to incite trouble in Berar for the conquest of which he promised his full support to the latter.[105] Such was the origin of trouble in Berar.

When Murtaza Nizam Shah arrived at Mahur on his way to Bidar, he received the report of the rising of Mirza Quli Khan who after slaying the Commander-in-Chief, Khairat Khan had left for Burhanpur.[106] It was further reported that the rebels had been pursued and defeated by Banu Khan[107]. But what proved to be a source of annoyance and anxiety to the Nizam Shahi King was the attempt of the Faruqi ruler to exploit the situation in his own favour. The latter sent his Commander-in-Chief, Zainuddin into Berar with instructions to expel the Nizam Shahis and instal there a scion of the Imad Shahi house who had taken refuge in Khandesh.[108]

Zainuddin entered Berar and spread out his forces there.

Upon this the Nizam Shahis withdrew to the outlaying districts and assembled forces at Elichpur to offer a united front to the intruder. But the Nizam Shahi Commander-in-chief Khurshid Khan did not approve this plan. He retreated to the fortress of Gavilgarh to stand a siege there.[109] The Faruqi army led by Zainuddin invested the fortress of Narnala.[110] Here he was attacked by Khurshid Khan, whom he defeated with heavy losses, pursued him up to the banks of Puranadi from where he escaped with great difficulty to the royal camp at Udgir.[111]

But Murtaza Nizam Shah was not to accept the situation lying down. He quickly marched with his army, entered Berar, expelled the Faruqi Commander Sayyid Zainuddin and then marched straight on Burhanpur.[112] In sheer fright Muhammad Shah II abandoned his capital to the mercy of the invader. Murtaza Nizam Shah entered it, sacked it and burnt the town.[113] The army plundered the rich and poor alike, seized the crown and the throne of the Faruqis and their hoards of treasure. After having satisfied their lust for booty, the Nizam Shahi army marched towards Asirgarh. On the way it fought a fierce battle with the Faruqi Commander-in-Chief Zainuddin, who was defeated with heavy losses.[114] Miran Muhammad Shah II, who was encamping outside the fort of Asirgarh was frightened out of his wits, and he abandoned his camp, fled post haste to the borders of the Mughal empire, being hotly pursued by the enemy.[115]

**Burhanpur invaded, sacked and besieged.**

Murtaza Nizam Shah opened the siege of Asirgarh and drove the garrison to narrow straits.[116] At length, Miran Muhammad Shah II sent the Khan Khanan[117] the former prime minister of Murtaza Nizam Shah, who had taken refuge in Khandesh to intercede on his bahalf and to purchase peace promising to pay 10,00000 Muzaffaris of Gujarat as *Nalbaha*,[118] (war indemnity) if the invader retired from Burhanpur.[119] When Changez Khan pleaded with his master for the Faruqi ruler, he accepted the terms which had been offered. As soon as the Nizam Shahi army had crossed river Tapti,[120] Muhammad Shah II fulfilled his promise to the very letter.

The decisive victory of Murtaza Nizam Shah over the Faruqi ruler created a wholesome effect on the mind of Ibrahim Qutb Shah, who pretended to have changed his attitude towards him. Now instead of attaching importance to the impending fate of Bidar, he expressed his greater keenness to check the ambitions of Ali Adil Shah who was prosecuting his territorial aggrandisement in the South. About the same time arrived an agent of Venkatadari offering to Murtaza Nizam Shah a sum of 90,000 huns as expense of war on Ali Adil Shah.[121] The coincidence of the similar demand from two distinctive quarters led Murtaza Nizam Shah to think and decide his future plans. But behind these scenes treachery was at work.

The Qutb Shahi envoy Sayyid Shah Mirza offered a bribe of six lac huns to Changez Khan as price for his advice to Murtaza Nizam Shah to desist from his aggression on Bidar.[122] But when the loyal minister rejected the offer with contempt,[123] the envoy began to pull other strings to win his object. He won over the king's favourite Husain Khan who had a grudge against Changez Khan and through him poisoned the mind of his master Murtaza Nizam Shah, who was led to believe that Changez Khan intended treachery, in so far as he wanted to seize Berar for himself.[124] The suspicion of the king was confirmed when he expressed his desire to leave Berar and Changez Khan respectfully disagreed, saying that it was necessary for a sovereign to remain for a while in the newly conquered land.[125] As an alternative the minister suggested that he should be permitted to remain there. Upon this Murtaza Nizam Shah became indifferent towards him.[126] This alarmed Changez Khan, and for the rest of life he stayed away from the court, on the pretext of indisposition.[127] His master's distrust deepened and at his instance, Hakim Muhammad Misri administered poison to the loyal minister who gave up the ghost in a spirit of dedicated service to the state.[128]

**Fall of Changez Khan**

After his death, some letters were found in the possession of Shah Mirza, which established the innocence of Changez Khan and when Murtaza Nizam Shah read them, he was overcome with grief and shame. He immediately expelled Sayyid Shah Mir from his camp.[129] Struck with feelings of remorse, he withdrew from state affairs saying that, God had withheld from him the faculty of discriminating between truth and falsehood and of executing righteous judgement. Still his infatuation for worthless Husain remained unchanged:[130]

Changez Khan's death closes an important chapter in the history of the reign of Murtaza Nizam Shah I. He was distinguished for his wisdom, resourcefulness, penetrating intellect and his ability to grasp the crisis in no time. He was a warrior in the field of battle, a diplomat and shrewed statesman at the enemy's court. Besides being a brave soldier, he was liberal, generous to the learned and the pious. During his short regime he left no stone unturned to highten the glory and fame of the Nizam Shahi kingdom to its zenith.

On his return to the capital, Murtaza Nizam Shah appointed Hakim Muhammad Misri as wakil and Peshwa, but he was dismissed after six months.[131] He was succeeded by Qazi Beg Tehrani.[132] Nor did the king ignore to carry out the dying wishes of his deceased minister. He appointed Sayyid Murtaza Sabzavari as Sar-i-Naubat.[133] Soon after he was raised to the office of Sar-i-Naubat of the right wing and then to the left wing and finally to the position of Amir-ul-umra and the Commander-in-Chief of Berar. Shah Quli, a Circassian youth of extraordinary gifts and capacities, who had been sent as a present to Husain Nizam Shah I by Shah Tahmasp, the Safvi ruler of Persia, was created a noble, and was honoured with the title of Salabat Khan II.[134] His ready wit and congenial temper had so much pleased the late king that he became his great favourite. In the new regime he was given the command of the left wing of the Nizam Shahi army and then of the right wing, a post which had fallen vacant owing to the promotion of Sayyid Murtaza Sabzavari. Other foreign nobles like Mirza Muhammad Taqi Naziri, Ain-ul-Mulk Nishapuri, Sayyid Sadi Beg Tehrani were also raised to high posts. Khudawand Khan Muwallid, Jamshed Khan, Bahri Khan Qizilbalash, Rustam Khan Daccani, Chagtai Khan Husain Turkoman, Tirandaz Khan Astrabadi, Sher Khan Tarshizi Khan, Chanda Khan Daccani, and Dastur Khwaja Sari, were given fiefs in Berar, and were sent along with Sayyid Murtaza. Perhaps to maintain a proper balance between the Daccani and Foreign factions, the king also showered favours on Sayyids, maulvis and learned men who were mostly Foreigners.

Add to this, the recruitment of *silahdars* and foreign soldiers, who were in the service of Changez Khan, which made the Foreigners most powerful at the court.[135]

At this stage a tragic fate overtook Murtaza Nizam Shah. Several factors combined to disrupt his mental equilibrium. In the first place, he could not get over the shock of the political assassination of his wise minister Changez Khan. His conscience constantly pricked and reminded him of the guilt. Secondly, perhaps the desire for the atonement of the sin made him indifferent towards the state affairs. The sense of frustration joined to the influence of Maulana Sadruddin Toligani turned him religious tending him to give more and more of his time to prayers, trying to seek refuge in God for the crime he had committed on this earth. Thirdly, his infatuation for Husain Khan affected his reason to the extent of madness. He retired to the Baghdad Palace, shut himself in it, forbidding everybody except his favourite to see him. In short, he became a complete mental wreck. Even so, be it said to his credit that with the full realisation of his mental and physical limitations, he handed over the charge of the government to Sayyid Qazi Beg, with whom he associated Ain-ul-mulk, Mirza Muhammad Taqi and Qasim Beg Hakim.[136]

Meanwhile, Firoz Shah a pretender of the Imad Shahi family raised the banner of revolt in Berar.[137] He styled himself as Imad Shah, collected the disbanded troops of Tufal Khan and defeated and drove out the Nizam Shahi officers posted in Berar. Sayyid Murtaza was transferred from Bir and was directed to deal with the insurgents.[138] At Jalanapur he was joined by Jamshed Khan and the joint forces proceeded towards Balapur.[139] The pretender Firoz Shah retreated to the fort of Amar-Charabi, whither he was followed, besieged, captured and put to death by the Nizam Shahi commanders.[140] It was perhaps to support his cause that the Gonds laid waste some of the border districts of Berar, but they were repulsed.[141]

Thus inspite of king's mental malady, the affairs of the Nizam Shahi kingdom ran smoothly and its fortune rose rapidly. But shortly after, dark clouds began to hover on the northern horizon of the kingdom. In 1575 the Mughal

Emperor Akbar demanded from Murtaza Nizam Shah the surrender of the fugitive Mirzas, who had taken protection in Ahmadnagar after the annexation of Gujarat to the Mughal Empire. But the demand received no favourable response, and it annoyed Akbar so much that he marched up to the banks of Narbada. This alarmed the rulers of Ahmadnagar and Khandesh who decided to offer united resistance to the aggressor. But fortunately the crisis did not develop any further. It ended with the establishment of friendly relations between the Mughal Emperor and Murtaza Nizam Shah, who accredited to the Mughal court his envoy Wafa Khan, who went there with costly presents. Shortly after Muhammad Husain Mirza rebelled in Berar. He was defeated and put to flight. He went to Khandesh, where Raja Ali Khan seized him and consequently surrendered him to the Mughal Emperor. Thus for the time being both the rulers remained amicable towards the latter.[142]

Murtaza Nizam Shah continued to shower his favours on Husain Khan whom he now styled as Sahib Khan. All of his relatives, friends and dependants were given lucrative jagirs and high ranks.[143] The quick rise in his fortune turned his head, and he began to meddle with the affairs of the state. He became instrumental in creating bad blood between the Daccanis and the Abyssinians on the one hand and Foreigners on the other.[144] He even impressed the king with the idea that the Foreigners intended to depose him. In sheer alarm most of them fled to Bijapur and those who remained behind were put to death at the instance of his favourite.

Sahib Khan's excesses began to increase day by day. Madly drunk, mounted on an elephant he would pass through the streets of Ahmadnagar, laying hands on handsome boys and beautiful girls, outraging their modesty. He forcibly seized the daughter of Mir Mahdi, a person of noble descent.[145] He poisoned the ears of the king against Qazi Beg, the Wakil and Peshwa, who was dismissed and exiled and this was followed by a second massacre of the Foreigners.[146] He was after the last drop of their blood and wanted to annihilate them to a man[147] But his evil designs were for the time being stopped by Sayyid Murtaza of Berar, with whom many of the victims of his intended coup had taken refuge. Feigning dissatisfaction, Sahib Khan fled to Parenda[108] refusing to be reconciled to his master.

He now dictated his own terms viz. firstly, the massacre of Sayyid Murtaza Khan Sabzavari and other foreigners who had taken refuge with him;[149] secondly, dismissal of Salabat Khan from the court;[150] and thirdly, the conquest and annexation of Bidar.[151] Murtaza Nizam Shah did not deem the first condition to be worthy of acceptance, because it was likely to weaken the military organisation of the state, and therefore he shelved it. But he removed Salabat Khan from the court and sent him to Bir. He then marched with his army to invade Bidar.[152] In this venture he obtained the support of Qutb Shah as well. It was only natural for Ali Barid Shah I, to solicit the support of Ali Adil Shah. But the rival armies did not fight for Barid Shah tendered his submission to Nizam Shah.[153]

The outcome of this venture did not prove to the liking of Sahib Khan who had fled from his master's camp and though every effort was made to conciliate him,[154] yet he dissimulated and retired to his jagir in Udgir,[155] where he began to nurse ambitious plans, refusing to respond to the royal summons. At length, at the insistence of his Wakil Asad Khan, who had succeeded Qazi Beg and the representations of other Foreigners, Murtaza Nizam Shah personally took the field against his imprudent favourite. Meanwhile, Sahib Khan courted the animosity of Bahri Khan Qizibalash by demanding the hand of his daughter.[156] On being refused he marched against him to gain his object by force. Bahri Khan fled to Jalna, where he joined Jamshed Khan Shirazi. At the instance of Sayyid Murtaza a few Foreigners marched to Sahib Khan's camp, succeeded in gaining entry into it where they strangled him to death. Information was sent to the king that Sahib Khan had attacked the royal troops and was slain during the combat.[156] Murtaza Nizam Shah was stricken with sorrow at the fate of his favourite.

The king marched from Udgir towards Qandhar where it was now reported to him that because of his withdrawal from the business of the state a rumour had been spread among the people that the king was dead. Consequently they had assembled at Lohgarh, where the Kotwal Jujhar Khan released Prince

Burhan from the prison, gave his daughter in marriage to him and taking him to Junnar declared him king. The two then advanced with their troops towards Ahmadnagar. This turn in the affairs alarmed Murtaza Nizam Shah, and he therefore, without making any delay turned towards his capital, sending Asad Khan in advance. He reached there just a day before the arrival of rebel Burhan.[157]

To silence the rumours of his death and to convince his subjects that he was alive Murtaza Nizam Shah soon after his arrival in Ahmadnagar rode in procession through the streets of the town. This encouraged the Foreigners who had been hiding in nooks and corners from fear of Sahib Khan. They now came forward and rejoined the royal service. Even their leader Salabat Khan was recalled. When, at length, Burhan advanced to join the battle with armies of his elder brother, his followers found that Murtaza was still alive, therefore they deserted him, (*May 27th* 1580 *A.D.*) almost to a man, and came over to the latter. In the course of conflict which ensued Jujhar Khan was killed and Burhan fled from the field and took refuge in Bijapur only to return to Ahmadnagar two years later in the guise of a darvesh.[158]

But nothing could restore to the king the equanimity of his mind. He could neither think nor could talk coherently. Sometimes he would experience a desire to abdicate, while at others of making pilgrimage to Macca.[159] Once he escaped to Humayunpur but was brought back to Ahmadnagar, where strict watch was kept on his movements.[160] He now replaced Asad Khan with Shah Haider who gathered all power into his hands to the exclusion of the Foreigners.[161] He ordered the latter to march to the frontiers of Burhanpur to protect the country from foreign incursions.[162] The motive behind this move was that no Foreigner should remain in Ahmadnagar.[163] Even Asad Khan was sent away to Daultabad.[164] Having thus freed himself from the fear of Foreigners, Shah Haider broke into excesses. He resumed the inam land of 400 bighas which had been granted to Shah Tahir,[165] and became indifferent to the royal commands though the king rebuked him times and again but to no effect.[166]

In sheer disgust Murtaza Nizam Shah left the palace on the pretext of a visit to the garden of the water course but made his way to Daultabad.[167] Here he was joined by Salabat Khan and many other nobles and officers. He held a darbar in which he once more offered the post of Peshwa and Wakil to Asad Khan, who insisted that he would accept it only on condition that he should be associated with Salabat Khan.[168] The king agreed, but he sounded a prophetic note in these words. "You are now making Salabat Khan a colleague of yours, of your own free will, but a day will come when you will repent on it and will taste the bitterness of collaboration with him."[169]

The king now returned to Ahmadnagar,[170] where he took up his residence in the garden of the water-course, passing most of his time in reading books in seclusion. Though he changed his old ways of living, but he did not concern himself directly with the affairs of the State. Asad Khan and Salabat Khan used to go daily to the vicinity of that garden where they decided cases, and if they found it necessary to obtain king's order, they approached him through a young eunuch, who was the only person allowed to see him.[171]

As had been foreseen by the king, Salabat Khan sooner than expected, gathered all power into his hands and pushed out of court his colleague and benefactor Asad Khan. He offended even Sayyid Murtaza Khan by his insolent and aggressive behaviour. In order to have a square deal for Asad Khan from the haughty Wakil, Sayyid Murtaza Khan marched with his troops to the capital. But Salabat Khan proved much too clever for him.[172] He won over Asad Khan with sweet words and induced him to persuade Sayyid Murtaza to return.[173] But the moment the latter turned his back from Ahmadnagar, Salabat Khan reverted to his old ways, which encouraged party strife at the court and threw the administ-ration out of gear.[174]

While, internally the condition of the Nizam Shahi kingdom was fast deteriorating, the demented king could not forget his ambition of reducing Bidar. He, therefore, asked Salabat Khan to finish the work which had been left in-complete on the previous occasion.[175] Having secured the alliance of Ibrahim Qutb Shah,[176] the joint armies numbering about 25,000 strong cavalry, under the leadership of Mirza Yadgar, styled as Khan-i-Khanan, Muhammad Khan Turkoman, Shah Vardi Khan, Ch gtai Khan, Chandra Ray, Samatya and Satya converged on Bidar and opened its siege.[177] In the hour of distress Barid Shah appealed as ever before to Adil Shah, who responded to the call, on condition that the two eunuchs, whom he had demanded before, were sent to him.[178] The condition having been fulfilled, the latter sent 10,000 horsemen to Bidar and himself marched to Sholapur where he struck his camp. Here he was murdered by one of the eunchs[179]

The assassination of Ali Adil Shah I brought about a change in the entire political situation. The position of the minor kingdom of Bidar become worst and the aggressive designs of Murtaza Nizam Shah created all the complications for minority administration in Bijapur. Ibrahim Adil Shah II, the successor of Ali Adil Shah was merely a child of nine. His guardian Chand Bibi though wise and valiant, was after all a woman. In the first instance, she chose Kamil Khan Daccani as the Regent, and when his behaviour and conduct dissatisfied her, she replaced him by Haji Kishwar Khan. The situation, however, did not improve. Party strife and mutual jealousy among the nobles became the order of the day. Add to this the persecution of the Shias which rendered confusion worse confounded.[180]

Troubles in Bijapur were Ahmadnagar's opportunity. Murtaza Nizam Shah hearing of the plight to which the kingdom had been reduced changed his mind, divided his forces into two and turned his attention towards Bijapur with a view to recover the fort of Sholapur. Immediately he entered into an offensive and defensive alliance with Ibrahim Qutb Shah, against the unhappy kingdom of Bijapur.[181] The handy pertext for such an invasion was found in taking revenge for the assistance which Ali Adil Shah had extended to Ali Barid Shah I. Thus the sin of the father was sought to be visited on his son.[182]

Having obtained the support of Ibrahim Qutb Shah, Salabat Khan organised a grand offensive. He assembled a large army composed alike of the Daccanis, the Abyssinians and Foreigners, which he placed under the command of a comparatively inexperienced officer Bihzad-ul-Mulk,[183] who marched towards Sholapur, plundering and laying waste the country on the way. He arrived at Naldrug and invested the fortress. Simultaneously, a contingent of troops was sent to lay siege to Bidar. To throw back this two-pronged attack Haji Kishwar Khan, the Regent of Adil Shah, despatched a contingent of troops under Ain-ul-Mulk Kirmani to the relief of Naldrug, and another under the command of Afzal Khan and others to relieve the garrison of Bidar and to drive out the invaders from that region.[184] In the conflict which ensued the Adil Shahis were the first to score a point when they succeeded in preventing the Qutb Shahi army to effect a junction with the Nizam Shahi army, which was defeated and put to flight.[185]

As if this initial mishap was not enough to damp the spirits of the Nizam Shahis, there was something worse to follow, because of the acute rivalry and misunderstanding between Salabat Khan and Sayyid Murtaza. The latter was reluctant to serve under Bihzad-ul-Mulk who was junior to him, both in rank and skill. Though Salabat Khan realising his error made an attempt to rectify the mistake by appointing Sayyid Murtaza to the supreme command, but it was too late. Bihzad-ul-Mulk was defeated by the Adil Shahis, and was covered with disgrace. Being afraid of meeting the same fate at the hands of the enemy, Sayyid Murtaza ordered a retreat, only to be ashamed of his conduct because shortly after a large number of troops from Bidar joined him and he found that the enemy had not pursued the fugitives. His pusillanimity discouraged those who were besieging Bidar, and they raised the siege of the fort.[186]

To retrieve his honour, Sayyid Murtaza reassembled the Nizam Shahi army and marched again towards Naldrug.[187] On the way he was joined by the Qutb Shahi contingent numbering 18,000 strong horsemen led by Sayyid Shah Mir.[188] The allies arrived before the fortress of Naldurg, where a desperate action took place in which the Adil Shahi forces were defeated and driven into the fortress. The invaders opened the siege but their efforts proved of little avail. Still the rapid deterioration in the politics of Bijapur encouraged them to further action and they seized some of the outlaying districts.[189] Their progress, however, came to a sudden halt because of the death of Ibrahim Qutb Shah on 6th June, 1580, whereupon the Qutb Shahi troops returned to Golcunda.

But Salabat Khan would not let the grass grow beneath his feet. He worked hard to bring round the new king of Golcunda to join him in the plan of invading Bijapur, and reopening the siege of Naldrug. Anxious to win laurels and to signalise his accession with a military venture, the young Muhammad Quli Qutb Shah threw his lot with Nizam Shah, and the allies arrived before the fortress of Naldrug. They pressed the siege with great vigour. Notwithstanding the distracted state of affairs in Bijapur, the commandant of the fortress and his garrison put up a gallant resistance, even though no relief forth came from the head-quarters. Failing in their military tactics, Sayyid Murtaza and Bihzad-ul-Mulk attempted to corrupt the loyalty and patriotism of the commandant Muhammad Aqa Turkoman. But he rejected with scorn all temptations of wealth and high rank which were held out to him. The impregnable defences of the fort, joined to the faithfulness of the garrison proved to be a source of despair to the allies, besides exposing them to severe losses.[190]

Now the Nizam Shahi generals hit upon another plan possibly in view of the threatened defection of Qutb Shah who was tired of protracted operations.[191] Sayyid Murtaza and Bihzad-ul-Mulk decided to lead a part of their army to make a dash to Bijapur which they hoped, would easily fall into their hands,[192] firstly, because of the sad state of party politics there and secondly, of its depleted resources in men and money and its in ability to put up resistance. The plan appeared to be plausible one, therefore Muhammad Quli Qutb Shah accepted it.

But unfortunately the secret leaked out and the enemy got an inkling of the designs of the allies. Accordingly the Adil Shahi army, the very same night left for Bijapur by a different route, and entered the city before the allies could arrive there.[193] The latter surrounded the fort from all sides. Soon reinforcements arrived under Ain-ul-Mulk and Ankas Khan who encamped near the Allapur Gate and kept the enemy constantly engaged. But owing to the heavy downpour of rain, twenty yards of the city wall fell down, which rendered the position of the besieged rather precarious. Since Ain-ul-Mulk and Ankas Khan were unwilling to make common cause with the Africans they remained outside the city. In the end, disgusted with the attitude of their opposite numbers in the city, they went over to Sayyid Murtaza. This unexpected accession of strength, prompted the allies to take the fortress by assault. But Sayyid Murtaza who did not see eye to an eye with Salabat Khan and Bihzad-ul-Mulk delayed the immediate implementation of the plan, which gave time to the garrison to repair the wall and reorganise the defence.

The defection of Ain-ul-Mulk and Ankas Khan, however, was an unmistakable pointer to the inability of the Africans to deliver the goods. But they rose equal to the occasion and furnished an unparalleled example of patriotism by tendering their resignation to Chand Bibi. Thereupon the Foreigners were called upon to take up the reins of administration. They summoned the Maratha and Canarese troops, skilled in guerilla method of warfare. Add to their activities, the attitude of Sayyid Murtaza, whose reaction to the advent of the Foreigners in Bijapur administration was very favourable. On the one hand, he suggested to Qutb Shah and Bihzad-ul-Mulk to withdraw from the Adil Shahi territory, on the other he induced Ain-ul-Mulk and Ankas Khan to return to their loyalty. Their arrival in the city proved to be a source of encouragement to the rank and file of the Foreigners. The internal state of affairs in Bijapur having considerably improved, the Maratha levies sallied out of the fort, intercepted the supply line of the besiegers, and inflicted untold hardships on them. The allies thereupon decided to separate from each other. Qutb Shah marched to Gulbarga while Sayyid Murtaza and Bihzad-ul-Mulk marched to open the siege of Naldrug. Such division of forces weakened the allies. The Nizam Shahi army was compelled to fall back. It returned to Ahmadnagar plundering and laying waste the districts of Kolhar and Miraj on their way.[194] Muhammad Quli Qutb Shah having left behind a detachment under his general Mustafa Khan to besiege Gulbarga, returned to his capital. After three months Mustafa Khan was defeated by an army under Dilawar Khan, sent from Bijapur and the Qutb Shahi troops were pursued up to the very gates of Golcunda.[195]

The inconclusive results of the preceding two campaigns goaded Salabat Khan to further action, and through Sayyid Shah Mir he succeeded in inducing Muhammad Quli Qutb Shah to make one more joint effort to seize Naldrug and other frontier districts of the Adil Shahi kingdom.[196] Accordingly towards the end of the month of Octobor 1581 the allies again encamped before the fortress. Sayyid Murtaza mounted batteries against that side of the fort where the moat had no water and opened its siege.[197] But Wazir-ul-Mulk the commander of the fort trusting in the invincibility of the defences and firmness of the garrison offered resistance which proved to be effective.[198] Sayyid Murtaza opened correspondence with him, offering him rank and service in Ahmadngar, but Wazir-ul-Mulk remained impervious to such temptations.[199] After a few more skirmishes the allies withdrew from Naldrug and encamped on Beora where they remained for nearly twenty days.[200] Here Muhammad Quli Qutb Shah, having got sick of fighting, at the instance of some of his senior officers decided to return to his country.[201] Sayyid Murtaza followed suit. Leaving a composite contingent of troops to guard the territories, which had been recently wrested from Bijapur, the allies separated from each other in the middle of Feb. 1582 A.D. and returned to their respective countries. Soon after the troops which had been left behind by them were forced by the Adil Shahi forces to withdraw.[202]

Military action having been found unavailing for the attainment of his objective, Salabat Khan II now made use of his diplomatic skill to take Sholapur from the kingdom of Bijapur. He proposed a matrimonial alliance between Prince Husain of Ahmadnagar and the sister of Ibrahim Adil Shah II.[203] The response from the other side being very favourable, Qasim Beg was sent as envoy to Bijapur to escort the bride to Ahmadnagar. She came there, accompanied by her aunt Chand Bibi, who was keen to pay a visit to her brother Murtaza Nizam Shah.[204] But the celebrations of the nuptials was delayed because of the non-fulfilment of the terms of the compact on the part of Bijapur; Adil Shah being reluctant to surrender the fort of Sholapur along with its five and half districts.

Serious rivalry now arose between Salabat Khan and his colleague Asad Khan.[205] The former persistently gathered power into his own hands by every means and attempted to deprive the latter of his prestige and influence, utterly forgetful of the gratitude, for all that Asad Khan had done for him. But Asad Khan had behind him the backing of the amirs of Berar, led by Sayyid Murtaza, who not only encouraged Jamshed Khan to destroy Salabat Khah by refusing to comply with his order to go to Bijapur with Qasim Beg, who was being sent to open negotiations for the marriage alliance betwen the Adil Shahi and Nizam Shahi house, but even instigated him to march with him into the capital and remove Salabat Khan from his post. Taken unawares as he was, Salabat Khan won over Asad Khan, and again averted the calamity.[206]

**Contest for Power**

Salabat Khan now began to think of other plans to break the back-bone of the support behind Asad Khan. To destroy the influence of Sayyid Murtaza in Berar, he, on the plea of improving the administration, sent there his own officers to collect the revenue from the Khalsa lands.[207] But Sayyid Murtaza refused to cooperate with them in the collection of revenue. His action was misrepresented by Salabat Khan to the king who ordered that Sayyid Murtaza should be immediately arrested. But thanks to the loyalty of his supporters that the warrant could not be executed.[208] Upon this Salabat Khan, in order to sow the seeds of dissension among the nobles of Berar, sent *khilats* directly to them with the object of winning them over to his side by impressing upon them, that they should look to him for the promotions and rewards rather than to Sayyid Murtaza.[209] But the trick worked only for a while. One of them, Khudawand Khan saw through his game and exposed his plan'. They assembled at Balapur and in a body reaffirmed their loyalty to their leader.[210]

In this way events began to move fast towards an open

clash between the rivals and Salabat Khan prepared to meet the challenge. In the first place he removed the king from Bagh-i-Hasht Bahisht to the Baghi-i-Farah-Baksh and from there to the Baghdad Palace,[211] where he was confined to pass his time in the company of Fath Shah,[212] and in sporting with the beauties of the harem and dancing girls of the city.[213] Secondly, he relegated Asad Khan completely into the back-ground, depriving him of every shred of power and prestige.[214] Thirdly, he assembled the nobles and appealed to them for their cooperation and support. So that even some of the avowed partisans of Asad Khan, perhaps under the stress of circumstances, professed to favour him, though they sent to Sayyid Murtaza secret messages promising him that they would come over to him on his arrival at the capital. But some of the nobles like Mirza Yadgar and Shahwardi Khan openly broke away from Salabat Khan and joined Sayyid Murtaza.

Sayyid Murtaza assembled his supporters at Balapur where he settled his plan of action, in consultation with them. The duty of protecting Berar was entrusted to Mirza Husain Ispahani and Chaghtai Khan. Having thus arranged for the security of the province, Sayyid Murtaza and his supporters advanced towards Ahmadnagar.[215] On the way they encamped at the Jeur pass, to pass the night (Dec. 1584) there. The attack was to be opened next morning.[216] Here they were surprised by Salabat Khan, who surrounded the hill from every side and closed the way of retreat upon the rebels. A contested battle ensued in which the nobles of Berar were defeated and put to flight, their leader Sayyid Murtaza being compelled to take refuge with Emperor Akbar.[217] Salabat Khan returned in triumph to the capital.[218]

The discomfiture of Sayyid Murtaza at Jeur Ghat completely demoralised the remnant of his partisans in Berar. Chaghtai Khan returned to his own jagir, where he was joined by Mirza Husain's brother and the two managed to escape to Burhanpur, where they were arrested by the nobles of Khandesh.[219] Salabat Khan now imprisoned Asad Khan in the fortress of Jond and appointed in his place Mirza Sadiq Urdubadi to look after the civil and revenue affairs.[220]

Thus was liquidated the opposition of the Berar faction, but it brought in its train more serious complications, the worst of them being the prospect nay the certainty of the Mughal intervention in the affairs of the Daccan.

Soon after a discontented faction brought the king's brother Burhan in guise of a holy man to the capital and conspired to raise him to the throne.[221] But the plot leaked out to Salabat Khan on the day, fixed for deposing the king Murtaza Nizam Shah.[222] Whereupon the conspirators dispersed and fled.[223] Burhan making good his escape fled to the Konkan (Baglana), from where he went to Kabiruddin Khan of Bidar. In the end he decided to seek asylum with the Emperor Akbar. On 21st March, 1585 on the occasion of the Nauroz festival, Sayyid Murtaza, Khudwand Khan and other amirs were introduced into the royal audience at Lahore.[224] Evidently conditions were ripe for a forward step in the Daccan. After the stormy spell of 1581 A.D. Northern India had settled down to peace and though the Emperor's mind was preoccupied with the affairs of the North-Western frontier of his empire, yet he could afford to look elsewhere.

**Burhan Nizam Honoured at the Mughal Court.**

Accordingly Khan-i-Azam Mirza Aziz Koka, the governor of the province of Malwa was directed to launch a campaign against the kingdom of Ahmadnagar with the help of discontented nobles of Berar and other officers.[225] Reinforcements were sent from the court to the Mirza. The imperial army marched to the town of Hindiya, situated at the junction of the frontiers of Malwa, Burhanpur and the Daccan, and encamped there.[226] It was given out that the Mughals had embarked upon the aggression to support the claims of Burhan in preference to those of King Murtaza Nizam Shah, who was mad.

**Early Mughal Invasions.**

The arrival of the Mughal army on the frontiers of the kingdom of Ahmadnagar stirred Salabat Khan to action. He despatched 20,000 troops under the command of Mirza Muhammad Taqi to the frontiers of Berar.[227] Another noble Mirza Husain was sent with a contingent of troops to Daultabad. Such were the arrangements made for the protection of the state, and it was expected that the cooperation of the Faruqi ruler would also be forthcoming.[228] The Mughal Emperor had already taken some precautions to prevent the alliance between the rulers of Khandesh and Ahmadnagar. He had accredited Shah Fathullah Shirazi to Asirgarh to obtain the loyalty of the ruler of Khandesh[229] Though the envoy was received with all honour due to him, but he was warned by the host, of the impending danger to his escort from the Daccanis, who had entered Khandesh.[230] In despair Fathullah fled from Asirgarh to Gondwana from where he went and joined Mirza Aziz Koka, who censored him for his craven-heartedness and sent him away to Gujarat.[231]

Khan-i-Azam Mirza Aziz Koka, left Hindiya, captured the fort of Gavaligarh from Nahar Rao,[232] a refractory Hindu, and undertook an expedition to Kherla which proved so disasterous for his horses and cavalry that he could not proceed any further. Meanwhile, the Daccanis overtook the imperial army, and Mirza Aziz Koka finding his position a little shakey, at the suggestion of Sayyid Murtaza and other amirs marched into Berar.[233] They arrived near Elichpur on a market day, plundered the merchants, burnt the place, levelling it to the ground, "in the twinkling of an eye, a city which had just before excelled Cairo and Damascus in population and prosperity. They seized women and children and made prisoners all whom they caught and bound them making no distinction between Musalman and unbeliever."[234] (20th March, 1586). Khudawand Khan proceeded to Malkapur and Rohankhed, which had been his jagir, collected his treasures and rejoined the imperial army. Thus Elichpur and Berar were attacked by the Mughals[235] but could not be completely occupied by them.

When the Daccani forces arrived at Hindiya they found that the imperial army had left for Berar. Therefore, they plundered and burnt the town and then marched post-haste on the trail of the enemy. Mirza Aziz Koka, finding himself pursued and his retreat cut off, gave up all idea of fighting the enemy and fled westward, leaving behind him heavy baggage and elephants to the mercy of the Daccanis. During the course of the retreat an action occurred at Chandur, in which the imperial troops seized some booty, but their leader

Abdulla Khan Kashghari was slain. The approach of the rainy season led Mirza Aziz Koka to give up the campaign. He returned to Ujjain and the armies of Ahmadnagar and Khandesh also marched back to their respective countries.[236]

The King's infatuation for the dancer Fath Shah increased to such an extent that he gratified every wish of hers, however unreasonable and high pitched it might be.[237] Her friends became recipients of lavish favours and gifts from her lover, over whose mind she had obtained complete control.[238] She created misunderstanding between him and his minister Salabat Khan, when the latter refused to pander to her desire to possess the costliest jewels in the royal collection.[239] The relations were further strained when in his fit of madness the king attempted to kill his son Prince Husain and whom Salabat Khan afforded the fullest protection.[240] The climex came when Salabat Khan refused to comply with the damand of Ibrahim Adil Shah II to celebrate the nuptials of his sister, or to send her back.[241] This occasioned a rupture between the two courts and Adil Shah was compelled to open the offensive against Ahmadnagar. Murtaza Nizam Shah was now completely estranged from Salabat Khan, who surrendered his post and voluntarily went into imprisonment in the fort of Dandarajpuri.[242]

**Fall of Salabat Khan II.**

Salabat Khan's regime forms a glorious chapter in the history of the kingdom of Ahmadnagar. True that Sayyid Murtaza's rivalry affected the fortunes of the kingdom, both externally and internally occasioning serious loss of moral and material prestige, in addition to the accentuation of the party strife. But these set backs were more than compensated by his good administration, by his efforts to expand his master's territories and by his schemes of public welfare, which were adopted during his regime. The kingdom made remarkable progress in trade and industry, arts and crafts, education and culture. The Maratha country was never so well governed as by Salabat Khan and ever, "since the days of Sultan Muhammad bin Alauddin Shah Bahmani such prosperity and administration were not heard of in the Daccan".[243]

After the imprisonment of Salabat Khan II, his favourite

Bihzad-ul-Mulk acted as the Wakil and Peshwa, jointly with Mirza Sadiq Urdubadi.[243] He attempted to follow in the foot steps of his predecessor, and very much like him attempted to gather power into his own hands to the exclusion of his colleague. When this was brought to the notice of the king, he threw Bihzad-ul-Mulk into prison and ordered Mirza Sadiq to hold the two posts conjointly.[244] Though his regime lasted for nine days only, he succeeded in removing Fath Shah and her followers from the side of the king and in freeing him from her and her friend's domination.[245] Now Murtaza Nizam Shah became accessible to the minister and other servants of the state.

On Monday, 18th Feb. 1587 A.D. the post of Wakil and Peshwa was conferred on Qazi Beg and that of Wazir on Mirza Muhammad Taqi.[246] Meanwhile Ibrahim Adil Shah II had advanced as far as Parenda and was speedily moving towards the capital. Murtaza Nizam Shah ordered Qazi Beg and Mirza Muhammad Taqi to conclude peace with the invader.[247] At the intercession of Qazi Beg, Adil Shah retired from Parenda. Prince Husain was summoned from Daultabad, and to celebrate his marriage, preparations were made for a splendid feast in the village of Patori.[248] At an auspicious hour the nuptials of Princess Khadija with Prince Miran Husain were celebrated with great splendour, pomp and magnificence.[249]

Not long after this event, the king becoming suspicious of his son, or perhaps at the instigation of some of the low born ruffians, resolved to murder him.[250] He was sent for, and was lodged in a room next to the royal bed chamber in the fort. One night while the Prince was asleep, the king set-fire to his clothes and closed the room so that he could die from suffocation.[251] But the Prince cried out for help which reached in time and he was saved. Thereafter he was secretly sent away to Daultabad.[252] After a few days the king came to the apartment to examine the ashes, but finding no traces of them there, he was very much excited. His suspicion fell on Fath Shah and his ministers whom he dismissed almost in a body.[253] Their places were filled with the sons of the old officers, who at one time or the other had been connected with the administration. Among the new comers mention should be made of Maulana Habibullah son of Maulana Inayatullah Niyati, Sultan Hasan son of Sultan Hasan Sabzavari, Wafa Khan and many others.[254] These men had hardly the capacity, or even the experience to run the administration. Nor could they receive any guidance or inspiration from their master who was completely demented. Confusion arose every where and the crisis came, when Habibullah arrested most of the nobles and the officers of the state especially the Foreigners like, Qasim Beg Hakim Misri, Mirza Muhammad Taqi, Aiu-ul-Mulk, Habib Khan, Shah Rafi-ud-din Husain, Mirza Muqim and sent them prisoners to the distant fortress.[255]

In Baglana, Narayan rose in rebellion against his brother Baharjui. The latter appealed to Murtaza Nizam Shah soliciting his assistance promising in return to pay indemnity and to acknowledge the suzeranity of the king.[256] Accordingly, a large army under the command of Farhad Khan was sent to the relief of the Raja.[257] But when it arrived on the frontiers of Baglana, it was much perturbed to learn that the Raja had been overpowered by his brother and there was none to be supported.[258] Upon this Farhad Khan asked for further instructions from the Wakil Habibullah, who being not sure of his position prevaricated and delayed[259] Soon after he was removed from his post and replaced by Mirza Khan[260], who recalled the army.

After the assumption of power Mirza Khan started his own game of duplicity. On the one hand, he flattered the favourites of the king, on the other secretly planned his deposition and the accession of Prince Husain. When Farhad Khan, Saif-ul-Mulk and others refused to be a party to his plans, he threw them into prison and confiscated their jagirs. He then won over Adil Shah, promising him the fort of Parenda in lieu of the support for the cause of his son-in-law; with the result that the regent Dilawar Khan led an invasion against Ahmadnagar.[261]

Murtaza Nizam Shah ordered Mirza Khan to take suitable steps to throw back the invasion. Mirza Khan assembled an army marched from Ahmadnagar and encamped near the town of Ranubari.[262] His conduct not only surprised Murtaza Nizam Shah but aroused his suspicions also and therefore he sent Ferishta to enquire into the matter.[263] Mirza Khan's duplicity was soon exposed. He fled to Daulatabad to bring Prince Miran Husain in order to elevate him to the throne. The deepening crisis pertubed the king who sought the advise of the historian Ferishta, who suggested to him two steps viz. to abandon his retirement[264] and march at the head of his body-guards against the rebels,[265] or to recall Salabat Khan.[266] But the importunities of Fath Shah joined to his own physical infirmity, prevented Murtaza Nizam Shah from implementing the first step.[267] He, however, issued immediate orders for the release and recall of Salabat Khan. But before he could arrive the game was up.

Desertion on a large scale occurred in the royal army. The soldiers flocked to the banner of Prince Husain at Daultabad.[268] Mirza Khan became stronger than ever before. Accompanied by his protege he arrived at Ahmadnagar and occupied the town. The Sultan was now completely isolated, all of his supporters with the exception of Fath Shah and others, having abandoned him in alarm or in disgust.[269] The Prince entered the fort at the head of 40,000 troops, putting to death all those who stood in his way.[270] At length he appeared before his father. But Murtaza Nizam Shah had neither any blood in his veins nor power at his command. He silently bore the insults which his infuriated son now hurled at him. He was seriously ill and would have died shortly after but Prince Husain had lost all patience. He shut his father in a bath room and lighted a fire underneath and the poor king died from sheer suffocation.[271] He was buried by his son Husain with honours which he had denied to him during the last hours of life.[272] Subsequently his mortal remains were transported to Karbala where they were interred in the family vault.

**Death of Murtaza Nizam Shah I (14th June, 1588)**

Murtaza Nizam Shah I has been described by the famous historian Sir Wolesley Haig as, "dissipated, self-indulgent young man, lunatic and mad, whose actions were blunders of a maniac, and whose daily life that of a licentious debauche". But the verdict is only partial, because it takes into account only the last phase of the king's life. Had he been insane or lunatic, would it have been possible for the kingdom to flourish under him ? Could he have remained on the throne for a

**Character of Murtaza Nizam Shah I.**

long period of more than twenty four years ? Taking the clue from the contemporary historian, Ferishta, none has to offer any words of praise for this monarch. It is Sayyid Ali Tabatabai the author of Burhan-i-maasir who has presented the other side of the picture. According to him Murtaza Nizam Shah was a highly sensitive person, of remarkable understanding possessing a well ordered mind. Evidently, the statement represents the other extreme.[273]

To have a correct appreciation of the man and his achievements and failures, it is necessary to analyse the circumstances in which he was called upon to play his role and the mysterious influences which shaped his line of thought and action. He had to face the rivalry of Ali Adil Shah and then of his successor Ibrahim Adil Shah II ; to put up with the wavering friendship of the Qutb Shah and the suspicions of the Faruqi ruler. And he was anxious to pursue his schemes of territorial aggrandisement and thereby to win for himself the status of unrivalled dignity among the kings of the Daccan. So long as he remained in possession of full bodily vigour, he worked ceaselessly to achieve his objectives undeterred by temporary failures, and equally unmoved by the transitory successes. His flight of imagination was very high, and so was his political ambition. When his brain began to soften, he entrusted authority to his ministers, whom he made and unmade according to the exigency of the situation. But though some of them strove hard to complete the mission of their master, none of them could maintain a balance between the rival factions, which in the end resulted in inviting the Mughal intervention. But for this, Murtaza was not to be blamed. By this time he had ceased to be his own master and to drown his fits of madness he had taken to a life of infatuation and drinking. There is yet another redeeming side in his character. He extended lavish patronage to the men of letters and learning, to authors and poets, who flocked to his court in ever increasing numbers.

Unlike many other Asiatic princes of his age, he and his predecessors did not lay pretensions to royal blood, but he missed no opportunity of drinking at the fountain of culture. He was an intelligent and gifted person ; read works on every subject especially theology and philosophy. He wrote a fine Nastaliq hand. In justice, valour and generosity he excelled all his predecessors. During his reign never ruthless hand was laid on the collar of any poor wretch. It is related by Sayyid Ali Tabatabai that once Sayyid Shah Jamaluddin Husain reported to the king that the whole of the treasury had been exhausted by his lavish generosity, and if he continued it, vessels and materials would also be sold out. The king did not speak a word but remained mum. In this context Sayyid Ali relates another story, "One day a Qalandar appeared before Shah Ismail Safvi of Persia, who promised to grant him anything he asked for. Emboldened by king's bounty the Qalandar begged to be made king of Persia for three days. The Shah granted the request. At the end of three days he asked the Qalandar to give back his kingdom". On hearing this Murtaza Nizam Shah exclaimed, "if he took back the kingdom from him again he acted ignobly for to take back what had been once given is not the part of a generous man."[274]

With the death of Murtaza Nizam Shah ends the story of the rise of the kingdom of Ahmadnagar. The glory had touched its zenith. For more than one reason his long reign of twenty four years forms an important episode in the history of Ahmadnagar. It witnessed an era of peace and prosperity, inspite of aggressive perennial campaigns, against the neighbouring states, party strife at the court and king's seclusion like a recluse. Thanks to the generosity of the king, the devoted service of the generals, diplomats and statesmen, and above all the valour of the soldiers, the work of the state did not suffer. The administrative machinery which had fallen out of gear in the preceding reign, the financial resources which had been completely paralysed by the consequences of the civil wars and strife, were renovated by the efforts of Changez Khan, Asad Khan, and Salabat Khan II, whereas successful wars resulted in the annexation of Berar and recovery of Sholapur and its dependencies. The territorial limits of the kingdom now comprised the greater part of Berar, Jalna, some districts of Khandesh, and Kaliyani in the Konkan and the whole area lying between Bankot and Bassien.

The last few years of the reign of Murtaza Nizam Shah

tended to accelerate the pace of the disruptive forces, which gradually gained momentum. The low born ruffians who had crept into the politics of the kingdom began to play the role of kingmakers. The foreigners and the Daccanis who saw the opportunity, did not lag behind. Thus commenced an era of chaos and confusion, of massacres and bloodshed, which ate into the vitals of the state, depleted its resources and worsened its power of resistance. Add to this the agonies of the party strife, the succession of weak and feeble monarchs on the Nizam Shahi throne. Thus was opened the way for the Mughals to follow with success their expansionist policy in the Daccan.

*Notes and References*

1. Burhan-i-Maasir (I.A. 1921) pp. 195-6; Ferishta, Briggs III pp. 250; Tabqat-i-Akbari III, pp. 69-70.
2. Burhan-i-Maasir (I.A. 1921), pp. 196, Ferishta, Briggs III, pp. 250.
3. Burhan-i-Maasir (I.A. 1921), pp. 196.
4. Burhan-i-Maasir (I.A. 1921), pp. 196; Ferishta, Briggs III, pp. 250.
5. Ibid.
6. Ibid.
7. Ibid.
8. Ibid.
9. Ferishta, Briggs III, pp. 251, Basatin-us-Salatin, pp. 113, According to Sayyid Ali, Ali Adil Shah at the instigation of Kishwar Khan, invaded the kingdom of Ahmadnagar. In this way he gives a false idea of the conduct of Ali Adil Shah, who was certainly not an aggressor—Burhan-i-Maasir (I.A. 1921) pp. 196.
10. Basatin-us-Salatin pp. 113-114; Muntakhab-ul-Lubab, III, pp.201
11. Burhan-i-Maasir (I.A. 191) pp. 196-97, Basatin-us-Salatin, pp. 114. Ferishta says nothing of Tufal Khan or Ibrahim Qutb Shah, having joined Murtaza Nizam Shah. According to Sir Wolesley Haig, it is most improbable that they did so, but if we evaluate and analyse the circumstances under which the campaign had been undertaken, it becomes almost clear that all of them joined the campaign to curb the power of Ali Adil Shah.
12. Burhan-i-Maasir (I.A. 1921), pp. 197; Basatin-us-Salatin, pp. 114-115;
13. Burhan-i-Maasir (I.A. 1921) pp. 197.
14. Burhan-i-Maasir (I.A. 1921) pp. 197. Unfortunately Sayyid Ali has not given the details of this campaign, perhaps to conceal the disgrace of the Nizam Shahi forces, which they met at the hands of the enemy. Whereas, the author of Basatin-us-Salatin, has painted a complete picture of the discomfiture of the Nizam Shahis, which compelled them to sue for peace and finally to retreat to Ahmadnagar. According to him when the allies reached the fort of Naldurg, Ali Adil Shah thought it prudent to avoid war. He came to Shahpur tank and encamped there. The allies were now free to besiege the fort of Bijapur. The defenders strengthened the walls of the fort, placing guards at every gate of the city, which were six in number. Kishwar Khan Lari, with about 6000 horsemen entered the city, took up his position in the centre of it, to assist the soldiers at every point. On the third day after the allies and entered the city of Bijapur, the guards fell upon

them. They retreated towards Mungalgate, where again they were attacked by the enemy. Hindia, one of the officers of Adil Shah advanced to drive them back. He successfully dispersed them and many of them took up their position near the Hauz of Allapur. The terrible heat of the day, the thirst for water, had exhausted them completely. No sooner than did they reach there than Kamil Khan, Nasir-ul-Mulk, Pir Muhammad, and Mukri Khan closed the way of retreat on them and opened an attack on them from all sides. The arrival of Kishawar Khan, made the conflict more bitter. Maulana Inayatullah, the former Wakil and Pashwa of the Nizam Shahi Kingdom, Jamaluddin, the treasurer besides many others were taken prisoners by Sherzada, the Bijapuri general. But soon after they were released by Kamil Khan, who had formerly been in the service of the Nizam Shahis and a close friend of Maulana Inayatullah. He sent a message to Murtaza Nizam Shah, asking him to return to his own country, whereupon the latter thinking it discreet, returned to his own capital—See, Basatin-us-Salatin pp. 115-117.

15. Burhan-i-Maasir (I.A. 1921) pp. 197.

16. Ibid.

17. Ibid.

18. Ibid.

19. Ibid.

20. Ibid.

21. While the siege of Gawilgarh was in progress Ali Adil Shah ignored his treaty with Murtaza Nizam Shah, broke his pact with him, entered into secret negotiations with Tufal Khan, from whom he received 100,000 horses and 50 elephants as a price of breach with his ally—Burhan-i-Maasir (I.A. 1921) pp. 198.

From Ferishta's account it appears that it was Khunzah Humayun, who proposed the alliance against Tufal Khan (Ferishta, Briggs III, pp. 132) which seems to be improbable, for more than one reason. The relations between Tufal Khan and Ali Adil Shah were more strained and hostile than with Nizam Shahis, firstly because, Tufal Khan did not join the Muhamedan alliance against Ram Raya personally, and secondly, because in the recent campaign he had joined the Nizam Shahis and Qutb Shahi's against Ali Adil Shah.

22. After having being bribed, Ali Adil Shah proposed that the suppression of Tufal Khan should be postponed and that they should attack firstly Ibrahim Q. Shah and thereafter devote their attention to Tufal Khan. The amirs of Ahmadnagar unware of Ali Adil's duplicity, fell in with the proposal, raised the siege, and with him retreated one day's march. Ikhalas Khan, Azizul Mulk and Ain-ul-Mulk, the Nizam Shahi officers were appointed to command the troops to be despatched against the Qutb Shahi kingdom. It happened that some of the Bargis and Adil Shahi officers attacked the baggage of the Nizam Shahi army. Fighting ensued in which Mansur Khan, the Nizam Shahi officer was killed. When Khwanzah Humayun learnt of the aggression of Bijapuris and death of Mansur Khan, her wrath knew no bonds and she determined to attack the enemy, who had appeared in the garb of a friend. But upon being advised by Mian Manjhu and other officers, she returned to Ahmadnagar, without causing further bloodshed—Burhan-i-Maasir (I.A. 1921) pp. 198; Ferishta, Briggs III pp. 251.

23. Burhan-i-Maasir ( (I.A. 1921) pp. 198; Ferishta, Briggs III, pp. 251; Basatin-us-Salatin, pp. 118.

24. Burhan-i-Maasir (I.A. 1921) pp. 207, Ferishta, Briggs III, pp. 132.

25. Burhan-i-Maasir (I.A. 1921) pp. 206.

26. Ibid.

27. Ibid. pp. 206.

28. Ibid. pp. 207.

29. Ibid. pp. 207.

30. Ibid, pp. 207.

31. Sayyid Ali gives the date 1562 (670 A.H.) which is wrong by seven years, perhaps owing to scribe's error.
32. Burhan-i-Maasir (I.A. 1921) pp. 207; Ferishta, Briggs. III, pp. 252.
33. Ibid.
34. Ibid.
35. Ibid.
36. Ibid.
37. Ibid.
38. Ibid.
39. Ibid.
40. Burhan-i-Maasir (I.A. 1921) pp. 208. According to Ferishta Ain-ul-Mulk fled towards Gujarat and was arrested on its frontiers while Taj Khan made good his escape to Golkunda.
41. Burhan-i-Maasir (I.A. 1921) pp. 208.
42. Burhan-i-Maasir (I.A. 1921) pp. 208.
43. Ferishta, Briggs III, pp. 253-4; Basatin-us-Salatin pp. 122. Sayyid Ali relates that when Murtaza Nizam Shah reached the gate of the fort, there he saw a bag full of nails, hanging. He asked what it meant and was told that Ali Adil Shah had written to Kishwar Khan, saying that he had built the fortress of Dharur and had ravaged the country round it, now he might return to Bijapur. But Kishwar Khan replied that he would neither return nor turn back, until he had captured Ahmadnagar, whereupon Ali Adil Shah had sent him these nails with the message that the nail's would be in the bag or for him, if he returned without taking Ahmadnagar—Burhan-i-Maasir (I.A. 1921), pp. 210.
44. Basatin-us-Salatin, pp. 122-23; According to Sayyid Ali, during the absence of Murtaza Nizam Shah, Adil Shah set out with his army to avenge the death of Kishwar Khan and to lay waste the Nizam Shahi country and to level to the ground all the buildings and dwellings—see, Burhan-i-Maasir (I.A. 1921) pp. 210; Ferishta does not say that Ali Adil Shah himself accompanied the force and it is improbable that he did so—See Ferishta, Briggs. III, pp. 133-34.
45. Burhan-i-Maasir (I.A. 1921), pp. 229; Ferishta, Briggs. III, pp. 428.
46. Burhan-i-Maasir (I.A. 1921), pp. 229; Ferishta, Briggs. III, pp. 254.
47. Burhan-i-Maasir (I.A. 1921), pp. 229.
48. Ibid.
49. Burhan-i-Maasir (I.A. 1921) pp. 229; Ferishta, Briggs III, pp. 428; Muntakhab-ul-Lubab III, pp. 210.
50. Sayyid Ali does not mention about Ali Barid Shah having joined the confederacy.
51. Burhan-i-Maasir (I.A. 1921) pp. 229; Muntakhab-ul-Lubab III, pp. 201.
52. Ibid.
53. Ibid.
54. Ibid.
55. Ibid.
56. Burhan-i-Maasir (I.A. 1921) pp. 229; Ferishta, Briggs. III pp. 428-29; 254.
57. Burhan-i-Maasir (I.A. 1921) pp. 229; Muntakhab-ul-Lubab III, pp. 201-2.
58. Ibid.
59. Ibid.
60. Burhan-i-Maasir (I.A. 1921) pp. 230, Ferishta, Briggs. III, pp. 429.
61. Burhan-i-Maasir (I.A. 1921) pp. 231; Muntakhab-ul-Lubab, III, pp. 202.

62. Ibid.

63. Burhan-i-Maasir (I.A. 1921) pp. 231; Muntakhab-ul-Lubab III, pp. 203-4.

64. Burhan-i-Maasir (I.A. 1921) pp. 231.

65. Burhan-i-Maasir (I.A. 1921) pp. 232; Ferishta, Briggs. III, pp. 254.

66. For the details see Chapter X.

67. Before raising the siege of Ravadanda Jamal-ud-din Husain Anju resigned his office of Wakil and Peshwa and returned to Ahmadnagar. On his return to the capital, Murtaza Nizam Shah banished him to Burhanpur and he entered the service of Akbar, in which he rose to the rank of Commander of 3000. Under Jahangir he attained the rank of Commander of 5,000 and received the title of Azud-ud-daulah—Burhan-i-Maasir (I.A. 1921 pp. 234, Ferishta ii, pp. 262.

68. Burhan-i-Maasir (I.A. 1921) pp. 234, Ferishta, Briggs, III, pp. 254.

69. His father was from Mashhad and his mother was an African.

70. Burhan-i-Maasir (I.A. 1921) pp. 234.

71. Ibid.

72. Ferishta, Briggs. III, pp. 429-30.

73. Ibid, pp. 430.

74. Ibid. pp. 430.

75. Ibid. pp. 430.

76. Ferishta, Briggs. III, pp. 430-31; Muntakhab-ul-Lubab, III pp. 304-5.

Sayyid Ali gives a different version of the events which preceded the conquest of Berar. According to him Ali Adil Shah heard that the forces of Nizam Shah had been demoralised in the late campaign against Chaul, therefore, he entered into an alliance with Tufal Khan against Ahmadnagar and thus violated the terms of treaty with Murtaza Nizam Shah. When the news of this alliance was brought to Changez Khan he advised the king to send an envoy to Tufal Khan to stop him from showing hostility to Ahmadnagar. He was advised by him to submit to Murtaza Nizam Shah and to refrain from meeting Ali Adil Shah or from entering into an alliance with him. Accordingly, Maulana Sadr was sent as an envoy to Tufal Khan. But as Tufal Khan had already entered into an alliance with Adil Shah, he refused to give audience to the Nizam Shahi envoy, which annoyed Murtaza Nizam Shah. It was now decided to crush Ali Adil Shah before he could join Tufal Khan. Murtaza Nizam Shah marched towards Bijapur laid waste the whole country so that no sign of habitation remained. Then the Nizam Shahi army turned towards Ausa, and encamped at village of Rui, Ali Adil Shah, having learnt of the approach of Nizam Shah, was perturbed, for he stood like an impenetrable rock between him and Tufal Khan. He marched to meet the Nizam Shahi forces, but before coming to grips he sent, Sayyid Mutbar Khan with rich presents to Murtaza Nizam Shah offering terms for peace. The latter responded to the message of Ali Adil Shah and appointed his minister Changez Khan to conclude the negotiations. Changez Khan met Ali Adil Shah before the fortress of Naldugg, where it was agreed that arrangements should be made for further discussions between the two kings. Accordingly the two kings met in the village of Kala Chutra where, the treaty was concluded. See—Burhan-i-Maasir (I.A. 1921), pp. 262.

77. Ferishta, Briggs. III, pp. 255; Basatin-us-Salatin, pp. 124-25; Burhan-i-Maasir (I.A. 1921) pp. 262; Muntakhab-ul-Lubab III, pp. 304-5.

78. Ibid.

79. Ibid.

80. Ibid.

81. Ibid.

82. Burhan-i-Maasir (I.A. 1921) pp. 263; Muntakhab-ul-Lubab III, pp. 205; Ferishta, Briggs III, pp. 255.

83. Burhan-i-Maasir (I.A. 1921) pp. 263-64; Muntakhab-ul-Lubab III, pp. 205, Ferishta, Briggs. III, pp. 255.

84. Burhan-i-Maasir (I.A. 1921) pp. 263-64; Muntakhab-ul-Lubab III, pp. 205, Ferishta, Briggs. III, pp. 255.

85. Burhan-i-Maasir (I.A. 1921) pp. 264-65; Muntakhab-ul-Lubab III, pp. 205, Ferishta, Briggs. III, pp. 255.

86. Burhan-i-Maasir (I.A. 1921) pp 266, Muntakhab-ul-Lubab III, pp. 206, Ferishta, Briggs. III, pp. 255.

87. Burhan-i-Maasir (I.A. 1921) pp. 266, Muntakhab-ul-Lubab III pp. 206; Ferishta, Briggs. III, pp. 255.

88. The fort of Narnala is situated in $20^0$ 15′ North and $75^0$ 4′ East on the southern most range of the Satpura hills. Burhan-i-Maasir (I.A. 1921), pp. 266, Ferishta, Briggs. III, pp. 255-56; Muntakhab-ul-Lubab, pp. 206.

89. Ibid.

90. Burhan-i-Maasir (I.A. 1921), pp. 266-67; Muntakhab-ul-Lubab III, pp. 206.

91. Ferishta, Briggs III, pp. 255; Muntakhab-ul-Lubab III, pp. 206.

92. Burhan-i-Maasir (I.A. 1921) pp. 267.

93. Burhan-i-Maasir (I.A. 1921), pp. 268, Ferishta, Briggs III, pp. 255, Muntakhab-ul-Lubab III, pp. 207.

94. When Changez Khan found that the king had grown weary of the protracted siege, he resorted to stratagem. An Afghan merchant, who had just arrived in the camp with horses and merchandise, from Lahore, represented to him that he had brought these in fulfillment of an order from Tufal Khan, and begged that he might be allowed to take them into the fort. Changez Khan granted the request on condition that after disposing off his merchandise, he should give up the trade and enter into the royal service. He also sent along with him his own agent, to bribe the officers of Tufal Khan and fortunately both of them succeeded in corrupting them. At length they informed Changez Khan that the task have been achieved. But the news leaked out. Tufal Khan was informed of their designs. He ordered Khawaja Muhammad Lari, to be imprisoned along with other Naikwaris, whom he suspected. This created great confusion inside the fort, many of his officers fled and all resistance paralysed—See, Burhan-i-Maasir (I.A. 1921) pp. 268; Muntakhab-ul-Lubab II, pp. 206, Ferishta, Briggs. III, 255-56.

95. Burhan-i-Maasir (I.A. 1921) pp. 268; Muntakhab-ul-Lubab III, pp. 207, Ferishta, Briggs. III, pp. 256.

96. Burhan-i-Maasir (I.A. 1921) pp. 277-78; Muntakhab-ul-Lubab, III pp. 207; Ferishta, Briggs. III, pp. 256.

97. Ibid.

98. Ibid.

99. Ibid.

100. Ibid.

101. Ibid.

102. Burhan-i-Maasir (I.A. 1921) pp. 279;

103. Burhan-i-Maasir (I.A. 1921) pp. 279; Ferishta, Briggs. III pp. 256; T. W. Haig's "Faruqi Dynasty of Khandesh" (I.A. 1918) pp. 142;

104. Burhan-i-Maasir (I.A. 1921) pp. 279; Muntakhab-ul-Lubab, III pp. 208, Ferishta, Briggs. III, pp. 256;

105. Burhan-i-Maasir (I.A. 1921) pp. 279; Ferishta Briggs. III, pp. 156; Muntakhab-ul-Lubab, III, pp. 208; T. W. Haig's, "Faruqi Dynasty of Khandesh" (I.A. 1928) pp. 142;

106. Burhan-i-Maasir (I.A. 1921) pp. 279-80; Ferishta, Briggs. III, pp. 256; Muntakhab-ul-Lubab, III, pp. 208;

107. Ibid.

108. Ibid.
109. Ibid.
110. Burhan-i-Maasir (I.A. 1921) pp. 280-81; Ferishta, Briggs. III, pp. 257;
111. Burhan-i-Maasir (I.A. 1921) pp. 281;
112. Burhan-i-Maasir (I.A. 1921) pp. 281; Ferishta, Briggs. III pp. 257;
113. Burhan-i-Maasir (I.A. 1921) pp. 281; Ferishta, Briggs. III, pp. 257; Muntakhab-ul-Lubab III, pp. 208;
114. Burhan-i-Maasir (I.A. 1921) pp. 281; Ferishta, Briggs. III, pp. 257;
115. Burhan-i-Maasir (I.A. 1921) pp. 281; Ferishta, Briggs. III, pp. 257; Muntakhab-ul-Lubab III, pp. 208;
116. Ibid.
117. Ibid.
118. Nalbaha is money paid to an invading army to induce it to abstain from plunder and devastation.
119. Burhan-i-Maasir (I.A. 1921) pp. 282-83; Ferishta, Briggs. III, pp. 257; Muntakhab-ul-Lubab, III. pp. 208;
120. Ibid.
121. Ibid.
122. Ibid.
123. Ferishta, Briggs. III, pp. 257; Muntakhab-ul-Lubab, III, pp. 208;
124. Ferishta, Briggs. III, pp. 257; Muntakhab-ul-Lubab, III, pp. 209;
125. Ferishta, Briggs. III, pp. 257-58; Muntakhab-ul-Lubab, III, pp. 209;
126. Ibid.
127. Ibid.
128. Ibid.
129. Ferishta, Briggs. III, pp. 257-58; Muntakhab-ul-Lubab, III, pp. 209; Ferishta and Sayyid Ali give different accounts of fall of Changez Khan. According to former, Mirza Shah Ispahani, the envoy of Ibrahim Q. Shah was the prime mover in the plot, against Changez Khan. He offered Changez Khan a bribe of 20,000 huns to dissuade his master from invading Bidar, but the latter refused the bribe saying that he was loyal to his master and that his intention was to overthrow the Sunni ruler of Bidar, in order that there might be only three shia kings in the Daccan who would live in amity and unity to oppose any aggression from Delhi. The attempt of Shah Mirza being foiled, he then turned his attention to the favourite of Murtaza Nizam Shah, telling him that Changez Khan intended to seize Berar for himself, there to establish himself as independent ruler. Husain Khan, lent a ready ear to these suggestions because the king had ordered Changez Khan to punish him for some insolence of which he had been guilty. Husain Khan, again reported to the king, Shah Mirza's accusation against Changez Khan, but the king paid no heed, telling him that he knew that he had a grudge against him, whereupon Husain Khan advised the king to make an enquiry directly from Shah Mirza. The king sent for him questioned him and he too repeated his accusations, and what followed thereafter has been mentioned above—see, Ferishta, Briggs. III.

While according to Sayyid Ali, Husain Khan conspired with some other courtiers to encompass the downfall of Changez Khan. He daily misrepresented his actions to the king until the latter was estranged from him. Among other things, he said, that the whole army regarded itself as the servant of Chengez Khan and would never appear at the court until Changez Khan was there. In order to prove this charge, Husain Khan and other courtiers raised a curtain of royal pavillion facing the king and enabled him to confirm the truth, since that day he became indifferent towards his wise minister, who becoming apprehensive of his life, withdrew from the court, soonafter he fell ill and died. See—Burhan-i-Maasir (I.A. 1921) pp. 321-22; Tabqat-i-Akbari III, pp. 70;

129. Ferishta, Briggs. III, pp, 258-9;

130. Ibid.

131. Burhan-i-Maasir (I.A. 1921) pp. 322, Ferishta, Brigs. III, pp. 260; Muntakhab-ul-Lubab III, pp. 210.

132. Ibid.

133. Ibid.

134. Burhan-i-Maasir (I.A. 1921) pp. 322, Akbar Nama III, pp. 820; Shaikh Chand Husain's article, "Salabat Khan II", published in the Proceedings of Indian History Congress, 1941, pp. 596-87; Islamic Culture, 1944, Vol. 18, pp. 187;

135. Ibid.

136. Burhan-i-Maasir (I.A. 1921) pp. 324; Ferishta, Briggs. III, pp. 260; Muntakhab-ul-Lubab II, pp. 210;

137. Burhan-i-Maasir (I.A. 1921) pp. 324;

138. Burhan-i-Maasir (I.A. 1921) pp. 324;

139. Ibid.

140. Ibid.

141. Ibid.

142. Burhan-i-Maasir (I.A. 1921) pp. 325-26; Ferishta, Briggs. III, pp. 261;

143. Burhan-i-Maasir (I.A. 1921) pp. 328; Ferishta, Briggs. III, pp. 261-62; Tabqat-i-Akbari III, pp. 69; Muntakhab-ul-Lubab, III, pp. 210

144. A quarrel arose between Husain Khan Daccani, the favourite of the king and Husain Khan Tuni, a foreign soldier, in the army of Sayyid Murtaza Sabzavari of Berar. The former sent to him an insolent message bidding him to change his title, and on refusing to do so attacked him with five or six thousand horse. Husain Khan Tuni withstood his enemy and compelled his rival to flee. He now pursued Husain Khan Daccani and his army. When the King came to know of the fight he summoned Husain Khan Daccani and gave him the title of Sahib Khan and gave the title of Sher Khan to Husain Khan Tuni. See Burhan-i-Maasir (I.A. 1921) pp. 328; Ferishta, Briggs. III, pp. 260; Muntakhab-ul-Lubab III, pp. 210; Tabqat-i-Akbari III, pp. 70;

145. Burhan-i-Maasir (I.A. 1922) pp. 29; Ferishta, Briggs. III, pp. 261; Muntakhab-ul-Lubab III, pp. 210-11;

146. According to Sayyid Ali a quarrel arose between Sayyid Murtaza and Sayyid Qazi Beg, the Wakil and Peshwa. The former approached Sahib Khan and gave him a large bribe to induce him to bring about the fall of his rival. Sahib Khan influenced the king, who first dismissed the Amir-ul-Umra, from the office of Wazir and then Qazi Beg. The latter was imprisoned in a fort and ultimately was banished across the sea to Jahrun—see, Burhan-i-Maasir (I.A. 1921) pp. 32-33.

Ferishta does not attribute the down fall of Qazi Beg to any intrigue between Sayyid Murtaza and Sahib Khan. He says that Qazi Beg was imprisoned on the charge of having embezzled 20,000 huns and jewels to the value of 10,000 huns from the royal treasury. Murtaza Nizam Shah refused to recover the money from him, released him from prison and sent him back to his own country.

147. Burhan-i-Maasir (I.A. 1922) pp. 30;

148. Burhan-i-Maasir (I.A. 1922) pp. 30; According to Ferishta, Sahib Khan was disgraced by Salabat Khan and fled to Bidar with two or three thousand horse and many elephants. There is no mention of his having gone to Parenda.

149. Burhan-i-Maasir (I.A. 1922) pp. 30; Muntakhab-ul-Lubab III, pp. 214;

150. Ferishta, Briggs. III, pp. 262; Muntakhab-ul-Lubab, III, pp. 214;

151. Ibid.
152. Ibid.
153. Burhan-i-Maasir (I.A. 1922) pp. 30-31; Muntakhab-ul-Lubab, III. pp. 215;
154. Burhan-i-Maasir (I.A. 1922) pp. 31;
155. Ibid.
156. Burhan-i-Maasir (I.A. 1922) pp. 32-33; Ferishta, Briggs. III pp. 262; Muntakhab-ul-Lubab III, pp. 262; Tabqat-i-Akbari, III, pp. 70;
157. Ibid.
158. Burhan-i-Maasir (I.A. 1922) pp. 31-32; On his return the king mounted on elephant and with a view to silence persistent rumours of his death, he rode through the city stopping at a druggist's shop asked the owner if he had any medicine for madness. The druggist replied that he had. Whereupon the king remarked that he did not know whether it was he, who had retained the crown or the royal title while living the life of a recluse or his brother, who was attacking him without a cause, was mad. The druggist replied that the king might let his mind at rest; he was not mad, for the affairs of the kingdom had been well-managed. The mad man was Burhan who had left a peaceful life to attack his generous brother. The king was much pleased and gave the druggist a purse of a hundred huns—see, Ferishta Briggs. III, pp. 262; Muntakhab-ul-Lubab, pp. 215-17; Tabqat-i-Akbari, III, pp. 75-77;
159. Burhan-i-Maasir (I.A. 1922) pp. 33;
160. Ibid, pp. 33;
161. Ibid, pp. 34;
162. Ibid, pp. 34;
163. Ibid, pp. 35;
164. Ibid, pp. 35;
165. Ibid, pp. 35;
166. Ibid, pp. 35;
167. Ibid, pp. 35;
168. Ibid, pp. 35;
169. Ibid. pp. 35;
170. Ibid, pp. 35;
171. Ibid, pp. 35;
172. Ibid, pp. 35;
173. Ibid, pp. 66;
174. Ibid, pp. 66;
175. Ibid, pp. 67;
176. Ibid, pp. 67;
177. Ibid, pp. 67;
178. Ibid, pp. 67;
179. At Sholapur, Ali Adil Shah was met by the envoy of Ali Barid Shah, who had arrived with the eunuch. After the meeting he sent one of them to a house, which had been specially prepared for him, and himself retired to his private apartments. When the night set in all the servants had retired and other attendants also had gone away, Ali Adil Shah approached the eunuch, who had concealed in his person a sharp dagger to avenge the insult which Adil Shah intended to heap upon him. He suddenly stabbed the king to death. The shrieks of the dying monarch were heard by a lamp bearer, who hastened to his master. But by the time he could reach there, the king was dead. He took the same dagger and killed the wretched eunuch, Burhan-i-Maasir (I.A. 1922) pp. 67-68;
180. Ferishta, Briggs. III. pp. 144; After the death of her husband Ali Adil Shah, Chand Bibi assumed the direction of the state affairs. She was a woman of great intelligence and activity. In the lifetime of her husband she accompanied him in his campaigns riding by his side in the field of battle. In times of peace, she conducted a large portion of public affairs, giving audiences and transacting business in open darbar. She was loved by all, not only for her courage, and boldness but for her justice and firm-

ness. No sooner Kamil Khan assumed power than he began to behave insolently towards that illustrious lady. According to the author of Futuhat-i-Adil Shahi his outrageous and brutal conduct went on increasing crossing all bounds of loyalty and devotion. His treacherous mind did not fail to plan molestation of Chand Bibi by a female slave of the royal seraglio. On another occasion, he ordered her to leave the palace and proceed to her ancestoral home. When she made a protest, Kamil Khan using indecent words exclaimed, "How dare you coerce me in the name of your brother Murtaza Khan ?" You will get such shoe beating that your teeth will come out". Humiliated and threatened, even then, this generous and high spirited women remained firm in her mind and actions.

At length, when the dominance of Kamil Khan became unbearable, she sought the help of Haji Kishwar Khan, another Daccani. She sent some cotton and spinning wheel to him with the message that, "evil has befallen us now. If you possess a grain of self-respect, you should consider the humiliation of your near relation as your own. Lo and behold ! I have been put into the sea of troubles by the arrogant Kamil Khan. Blow out his brains ! The ranks and dignity that he now possess was once enjoyed by your father and you, being the rightful heir, should receive it. Keep up the struggle, the well wishers of the royal family will be on your side. If not, put your hand to the cotton and Charkha"?

The Regency was no doubt overthrown, but no sooner Haji Kishwar Khan had succeeded Kamil Khan in the office, than he also begun to behave in similar manner by gathering sole power into his own hands and coercing the noble Queen.

181. Burhan-i-Maasir (I.A. 1922) pp. 69; Ferishta, Briggs. III, pp. 146; Muntakhab-ul-Lubab III, pp. 217; Tabqat-i-Akbari, III, pp. 71;

182. Burhan-i-Maasir (I.A. 1922) pp. 69;

183. Basatin-us-Salatin, pp. 160; Burhan-i-Maasir (I.A. 1922) pp. 69;

184. Ibid.

185. Ibid.

186. Burhan-i-Maasir (I.A. 1922) pp. 70-71; Basatin-us-Salatin, pp. 160-5; Ferishta, Briggs. III, pp. 152-53;

187. Burhan-i-Maasir (I.A. 1922) pp. 72;

188. Burhan-i-Maasir (I.A. 1922) pp. 72-73;

189. Bijapur was suffering from the miserable disease of party strife, which rendered confusion worse confounded and encouraged the allies to invade it. It has already been related that Chand Bibi had elevated Haji Kishwar Khan, to the office of the Wakil and Peshwa, after having brought about the fall of Kamil Khan. But the relations between Chand Bibi and the new minister, were not good from the very beginning owing to the latter's arrogance and high handedness. Chand Bibi was estranged from him, because of the murder of Sayyid Mustafa Khan. The quarrel between them reached to such a length that Kishwar Khan had her arrested and sent as prisoner to the fort of Satara on the false charge that she had invited her brother to invade Bijapur.

Kishwar Khan sent Mian Buddhu Daccani to threaten the amirs at Naldurg with imprisonment, if they slackened their efforts against the enemy. The message offended the African amirs like Ikhlas Khan, Dilawar Khan, and Hamid Khan, who arrested the envoy and marched on Bijapur with the object of deposing Haji Kishwar Khan. Ain-ul-Mulk Hamdani, Ankas Khan and other amirs retired to their estates. The murder of Mustafa Khan and the imprisonment of Chand Bibi, made Kishwar Khan very unpopular at Bijapur. He was openly abused as he rode thorough the city. When he heard that the African amirs were marching upon the capital, he took the young king out on the pretext of hunting excursion. On the way when he realised the futility of opposing the Africans, he allowed the king to return and himself took leave. He fled with 400 horse to Ahmadnagar, but being ill received there, he fled to Golkunda, where he was slain by

Ardistani, in revenge for the murder of Sayyid Mustafa Khan. Now Ikhlas Khan was made Prime Minister and Chand Bibi was recalled from Satara. She dismissed Ikhlas Khan and appointed Afzal Khan Shirazi in his place. But the former had his rival murdered. Resenting Chand Bibi's partiality for the Foreigners, he expelled Fathullah Shirazi, Shah Abul Qasim, Murtaza Khan Anju and other Foreigners from the city. The African amirs then summoned Ain-ul-Mulk Kamnani from his estates and as he approached the city, Ikhlas Khan, Hamid Khan and Dilawar Khan went out to meet him. Ain-ul-Mulk, treacherously seized them and put them into prison. Next day when he came to know that royal guards were ready to oppose him, he fled to his estates, leaving three prisoners behind him. Ikhlas Khan and his followers again resumed the affairs of the government. But this was followed by a period of great dissensions in Bijapur, which encouraged the neighbouring powers to prosecute their ambitious designs.

190. Ferishta, Briggs. III, pp. 151-52;

191. Burhan-i-Maasir (I.A. 1922) pp. 73; Ferishta, Briggs. III, pp. 151;

192. Burhan-i-Maasir (I.A. 1922) pp. 73, 125;

193. Basatin-us-Salatin pp. 165-70; Sayyid Ali gives an entirely different account of the fall of Haji Kishwar Khan—see Burhan-i-Maasir (I.A. 1922) pp. 125-29;

194. Burhan-i-Maasir (I.A. 1922) pp. 129; Ferishta, Briggs. III, pp. 151-4;

195. Ferishta, Briggs. III, pp. 151-54; According to Sayyid Ali the allies did not return to their respective capitals, but marched to Naldurg to renew the siege (I.A. 1922) pp. 129; but on page 131, he says again that Sayyid Shah Mir then convinced the king that it was necessary in the interest of the kingdom, that he should take the field with his army and join the Nizam Shahi army and Muhammad Quli Q. Shah, acting on his advice marched from Golkunda at the head of his army and joined the Nizam Shahi army." It appears that getting weary of the protracted siege of Bijapur, Muhamad Qutb Shah retired to Golkunda from where he marched to Naldurg as mentioned by Sayyid Ali.

196. Burhan-i-Maasir (I.A. 1922) pp. 199; Muntakhab-ul-Lubab, III, pp. 218;

197. Heavy Nizam Shahi canons like Nuhgazi Top, the Lailla Majnu Top, the Havai Top and others were arrayed against the walls of the fort.

198. Burhan-i-Maasir (I.A. 1922) pp. 199;

199 Ibid, pp. 199-200;

200. Ibid, pp. 200-201;

201. Ibid, pp. 201;

202. Burhan-i-Maasir (I.A. 1922) pp. 200; Ferishta, Briggs. III, pp. 154;

Before leaving for their respective capitals, the Nizam Shahis left Mirza Yadgar, Sher Khan and other amirs and the Qutb Shahis left Sayyid Mir Zainal and others, with troops under their command to guard the frontiers of their territory which they had taken from Bijapur. The Adil Shahi amirs, hearing of the departure of the allies collected their forces to recover the lost districts. Upon this Mir Zainal sent a messenger to Golkunda to inform the king, that the Adil Shahis were marching against him. Muhammad Quli Q. Shah, with a force marched to his relief. Meanwhile some of Mir Shah Mir's enemies at Golkunda, taking advantage of this opportunity to injure him, produced before the king a forged letter purporting to have been written by him to the Adil Shahi amirs, instigating them to fight with firmness and promising them the support of the foreigners of Golkunda. The device had the desired effect. The king was estranged from Sayyid Shah Mir and ordered his arrest without enquiring into the facts of the matter. This action created great confusion in the kingdom. The army was demoralised and large number of horses, elephants etc. were captured by the Adil Shahi amirs. When the arrest of that noble became known to Mir-Zainal and others, they fled without striking a blow on the enemy. The Adil Shahis defeated them and seized as much as they could. In this predicament Mirza Yadgar and other amirs of Nizam Shah too fled to Ahmadnagar—Burhan-i-Massir (I.A. 1922) pp. 201.

203. Muntakhab-ul-Lubab III, pp. 218;

204. Ferishta, Briggs. III, pp. 158, 281-282; Basatin-us-Salatin, pp. 190; Muntakhab-ul-Lubab III, pp. 218;

205. Burhan-i-Maasir (I.A. 1922) pp. 202;

206. Burhan-i-Maasir (I.A. 1922) pp. 202;

207. Ibid. pp. 235;

208. Ibid, pp. 235;

209. Ibid, pp. 235-236;

It had been a custom to send Khilats annually to the nobles of Berar and they were usually sent to Sayyid Murtaza who distributed them to the other amirs. But Salabat Khan now decided to send such robes of honour directly to the various nobles, with the object of gaining their loyalty and raising them against Asad Khan and Sayyid Murtaza. He therefore sent separate khilats to each amir, through a separate messenger and in this way each amir was led to expect promotion and favour from him. The amirs readily accepted the khilats, wore them and appeared before Sayyid Murtaza. The latter grew suspicious about their fidelity. But one of them Khudawand Khan, behaved differently. He hastened with the robe to his patron and placed his services at his disposal. His example was followed by other amirs also, who assembled in the town of Balapur, where they were invested with the royal Khilats by Sayyid Murtaza and then at the instance of Khudawand Khan, they renewed their ties with him, promising to join him against Salabat Khan II. The amirs returned to their jagirs to devise plans for the overthrow of Salabat Khan II.

210. Burhan-i-Maasir (I.A. 1922) pp. 235-36;

211. Sayyid Ali has again concealed the facts and says that the king being desirous to visit the buildings and gardens went for that purpose—Ibid, pp. 236;

212. Sayyid Ali has named Tulji. According to Abul Fazl she had been kept for sometime by a Sayyid named Mir Bahishti, Akbar Nama III, pp. 819; Maasir-i-Rahimi Vol. II, pp. 415; Muntakhab-ul-Lubab, pp. 219;

213. Burhan-i-Maasir (I.A. 1922) pp. 236; Tabqat-i-Akbari III, pp. 71;

214. Ibid.

215. Burhan-i-Maasir (I.A. 1922) pp. 237;

216. Ibid, pp. 237;

217. Burhan-i-Maasir (I.A. 1922) pp. 238; Maasir-ul-Umra, Vol. I pp. 816, Vol. II, pp. 318;

218. Burhan-i-Maasir (I.A. 1922) pp. 239;

219. Ibid, pp. 239.

220. Ibid, pp. 240.

221. Ferishta, Briggs. III, pp. 283; Muntakhab-ul-Lubab III, pp. 218;

222. Ferishta, Briggs. III, pp. 263; Muntakhab-ul-Lubab, II, pp. 218; Tabqat-i-Akbari III, pp. 71, 75, 76;

223. Ferishta, Briggs. III, pp. 263; Muntakhab-ul-Lubab, III, pp. 218;

224. Sayyid Murtaza received the rank of 1000 horse and fertile jagir (Maasir-ul-Umra II, pp. 318); Khudawand Khan received the rank of 1000; later on he lost favour. He was assigned a fief in Patan (Gujarat) where he remained until his death in 1588 A.D.—see, Burhan-i-Maasir (I.A. 1922) pp. 340; Tabqat-i-Akbari II, pp. 362; Vol. III, pp. 71; Maasir-ul-Umra I, pp. 816; Muntakhab-ul-Lubab, pp. 334; Akbar Nama III, pp. 401; (Elliot and Dowson Vol. VI) pp. 70-71; Muntakhab-ul-Lubab III, pp. 218;

225. Burhan-i-Maasir (I.A. 1922) pp. 240; Ferishta, Briggs. III, pp. 263; Tabqat-i-Akbari, Vol. II, pp. 383; Vol. III, pp. 76; Akbar Nama III, pp. 701; Muntakhab-ul-Lubab III, pp. 219;

226. Burhan-i-Maasir (I.A. 1922) pp. 240; Ferishta, Briggs. III, pp.

264; Tabqat-i-Akbari, Vol. II, pp. 383; Vol. III, pp. 76;

227. Burhan-i-Maasir (I.A. 1922) pp. 240-41; Ferishta, Briggs. III, pp. 264; Muntakhab-ul-Lubab III, pp. 219;

228. Ibid.

229. Burhan-i-Maasir (I.A. 1922) pp. 241;

230. Ibid.

231. Ibid.

232. Burhan-i-Maasir (I.A. 1922) pp. 241; Ferishta, Briggs. III, pp. 264; Akbar Nama III, pp. 739-40;

233. Akbar Nama III, pp. 739-40; Muntakhab ul-Lubab III, pp. 219;

234. Burhan-i-Maasir (I.A. 1922) pp. 241; Akbar Nama III, pp. 740;

235. Burhan-i-Maasir (I.A. 1922) pp. 241; Ferishta, Briggs. III, pp. 264;

236. Burhan-i-Maasir (I.A. 1922) pp. 241-42; Ferishta, Brigs. III pp. 264; Akbar Nama III, pp. 741-42; Tabqat-i-Akbari II, pp. 283-86; Muntakhab-ul-Tawarikh, pp. 272-73;

237. Burhan-i-Maasir (I.A. 1923) pp. 30; Ferishta, Briggs. III, pp. 264; Tabqat-i-Akbari III, pp. 71; Muntakhab-ul-Lubab, III, 219-20;

238. Burhan-i-Maasir (I.A. 1923) pp. 30; Muntakhab-ul-Lubab, III pp. 220;

239. Fath Shah asked the king for two necklaces which had been brought into the royal treasury from the plunder of Ram Raya's camp. They were made of valuable rubies and pearls. The king ordered Salabat Khan II to give them to her. But the latter was reluctant to see that such valuable stones were lost to the royal family, and therefore he substituted two strings of fake pearls in their place. After some time she discovered the substitution and complained to the king against his minister. Being offended at the latter's conduct the king ordered him to produce before him all the jewels for his inspection. The king then went with his lady love to have a look at them. But finding the particular jewel missing he wrapped all the jewels into a carpet and set fire to it. Thereafter he left the chamber for his own palace. No sooner did the Sultan leave the room than Salabat Khan II rushed to save jewels from the flame, but they had been completely damaged. Ferishta, Briggs. III, 264; Muntakhab-ul-Lubab, III, pp. 220;

240. Ferishta, Briggs. III. pp. 265; Muntakhab-ul-Lubab III, pp. 218-221;

241. Ferishta, Briggs. III, pp. 265; Basatin-us-Salatin pp. 191; Mutakhab-ul-Lubab III, pp. 221;

242. Ferishta, Briggs. III, pp. 265; Akbarnama III, pp. 820; Tabqat-i-Akbari III pp. 71; Muntakhab-ul-Lubab III, pp. 220-22;

According to Sayyid Ali, a firman was issued to Salabat Khan to go to the fortress of Darab and not to return till further orders. He went there, but returned without any orders. Again, he was ordered to go to Junnar and prepare a lofty throne for the king and await the arrival of the king in the village of Narangaon. After completing the task he again returned against the royal commands. After this a petition was submitted by Waghoji, the Naikwad of the fort of Shivanir, in which he preferred certain charges against Salabat Khan II. As this petition had been conveyed to the king, through the agency of the dancers, it carried much weight, with him. He was filled with much indignation towards Salabat Khan, who was ordered to go to Patori and set up a royal pavillion there, so that a court could be held there. Salabat Khan, as on all other previous occasions obeyed the commands of his master; but accidentally he fell ill and returned to Ahmadnagar without permission. He was summoned by the king to explain his conduct. A duel occurred between him and the king in which he was defeated. The king refrained from slaying him, but ordered that he should be imprisoned in the fortress of Parenda and then he was sent to Ausa—Burhan-i-Maasir (I.A. 1923) pp. 31-32;

243. Burhan-i-Maasir (I.A. 1923) pp. 32; According to Nizamuddin Ahmad after the fall of Salabat Khan II, Ismael Khan succeeded to the post of Wakil and Peshwa, Tabqat-i-Akbari III pp. 72;

244. Burhan-i-Maasir (I.A. 1923) pp. 32;

245. Shaikh Chand Husain's article "Salabat Khan II" Islamic Culture, April 1944, pp. 187;

246. Burhan-i-Maasir (I.A. 1923) pp. 32; Ferishta, Briggs. III, pp. 266; Muntakhab-ul-Lubab III, pp. 222;

247. Burhan-i-Maasir (I.A. 1923) pp. 32; Ferishta, Briggs. III, pp. 266; Basatin-us-Salatin pp. 191-92;

248. Burhan-i-Maasir (I.A. 1923) pp. 32; Ferishta, Briggs. III, pp. 266; Basatin-us-Salatin, pp. 191-92; Muntakhab-ul-Lubab III, pp. 222;

249. Burhan-i-Maasir (I.A. 1923) pp. 32; Ferishta Briggs. III, pp. 266; Basatin-us-Salatin, pp. 192;

250. Ferishta Briggs. III, pp. 266; Muntakhab-ul-Lubab, III, .pp 222;

251. Ferishta, Briggs. III, pp. 266; Muntakhab-ul-Lubab, III, pp. 222;

252. Ibid.

253. Ferishta, Briggs. III, pp. 266; Muntakhab-ul-Lubab III, pp. 222; According to Sayyid Ali when the King came to know the truth, that Prince had been saved by ministers, he removed Muhib Khan from the post of commandant of Daultabad; appointed Ahmad Khan giving him orders to put the Prince to death. But instead of doing so, Ahmad Khan, put another boy of the same age to death and the king was satisfied for the time being. When the real facts became known to the king Qasin Beg was dismissed and Habib Khan was appointed to the office—Burhan-i-Maasir (I.A. 1923) pp. 34.

254. Burhan-i-Maasir (I.A. 1923) pp. 34;

255. Ibid, pp. 35;

256. Ibid, pp. 35;

257. Ibid, pp. 35;

258. Ibid, pp. 35;

259. Ibid, pp. 35;

260. While the Nizam Shahi forces were at the distant frontiers of Baglana, Mirza Khan, one of the Daccani officers won over Ismael Khan the so-called brother of Fath Shah. He promised him to pay 10,000 huns if he enabled him to secure the office of the Wakil and Peshwa. He also presented 10,000 huns to Fath Shah to gain the support of her party of rif raffs and dancers. Soon after all of them began to support Mirza Khan unanimously and began to complain to the king about the incompetency of Habib-ullah. The king lent a ready ear to his favourites and removed him from the office and appointed Mirza Khan in his place—Burhan-i-Maasir (I.A. 1923) pp. 35; Tabqat-i-Akbari III, pp. 82; Muntakhab-ul-Lubab, III, pp. 223;

261. Burhan-i-Maasir (I.A. 1923) pp. 36; Ferishta, Briggs. III, pp. 267; Tabqat-i-Akbari III, pp. 72; Muntakhab-ul-Lubab III, pp. 223; Akbar Nama III pp. 820;

262. Ferishta, Briggs. III pp. 267; Sayyid Ali mentions Patori.

263. Ferishta, Brigs. III pp. 267; Mirza Khan knew of Ferishta's attachment for the king and he thought that if he discovered his plans, he will inform him. Therefore he bribed Fath Khan to obtain the king's order for Ferishta's recall and for the immediate advance of his army. Ferishta was in the camp. When Fath Shah arrived, she discovered the real designs of the minister, who had given orders for his return. Ferishta, escaped in the night, arrived at the capital and related the whole affair to the king who did not believe it.

264. Ferishta, Briggs. III, pp. 267; Muntakhab-ul-Lubab III, pp. 223-4;

265. Ibid.

266. Ibid.

267. Ibid.

268. Ferishta, Briggs. III, pp. 267; Akbar Nama III, pp. 820; Tabqat-i-Akbari III, pp. 82;

269. Ferishta, Briggs. III, pp. 267-68; Muntakhab-ul-Lubab III, pp. 224;

270. Ibid.

271. Ibid.

272. Ferishta, Briggs III, pp. 269; Muntakhab-ul-Lubab III, pp. 224; Tabqat-i-Akbari III, pp. 72; Sayyid Ali gives an entirely different account to conceal the humiliation and disgrace to which Murtaza Nizam Shah was subjected by his son Prince Miran Husain. According to him when the king heard of the approach of the Adil Shahi army towards the frontiers of his kingdom, he ordered Mirza Khan to assemble an army and face the invader. He himself marched from Ahmadnagar. But most of the loyal officers and Foreigners had been thrown into prison by the brother of Fath Shah and their followers. The king in State of helplessness sent a message to Adil Shah, promising him money, if he could terminate this quarrel by peaceful means. Mirza Khan was alarmed at the king's conduct. He induced the king's servants to let him go, so that he might persuade the amirs to cease their opposition according to the king's wishes. When he had been set free, instead of averting the danger, he went straight to Daultabad and offered his homage to Prince Husain. The royal camp now moved from the village of Patori to Malkari and thence back to the capital. At Daultabad Mirza Khan elevated the Prince to the throne and the latter entrusted to him all the affairs of the state and made him, his Wakil and Peshwa. Next day Mirza Khan brought the Prince into an open plain, where honour and ranks were distributed to the amirs. Thereafter the Prince and Mirza Khan with a large force marched to Ahmadnagar, Ismael Khan and his party streve hard to drive away the rebels, but failed. In fright the dancers and the dancing girls, dispersed in all directions. Ismael Khan too deserted the king and joined the rebels. On his arrival at the Capital the Prince halted at Kala Chabutra, in order to enter the town at an auspicious hour. Next day he was admitted to the royal presence, where he made obeisance to the king. He met his father and after a little while took leave to go. As the king's health was declining fast, the Prince sent him from Baghdad Palace to the bath of Haider Khan, where he soon after died—Burhan-i-Maasir (I.A. 1923) pp. 38;

According to Abul Fazl, Murtaza Nizam Shah I died on 2nd June, 1688. A.H. Akbar Nama Vol. III, pp. 821 (n) Ferishta gives the date of his death, 14th June, 1588 A.D. According to Oriental Biographical Dictionary, Prince Husain put his father into the heated bath on 15th June 1589, but does not mention the date of his death. It also mentions that according to the author of Jama-ul-Hind, Murtaza was poisoned by his son on 5th June, 1588 A.D.—see pp. 281;

273. The Portuguese historians have given a very wrong estimate of the character of Murtaza Nizam Shah. According to Diogo de Couto, "being affected of what he calls St. Lazarus malady i.e. leprosy and all the medical efforts to cure him having failed, was recommended by one of his physicians to bathe in children's blood. Accordingly large tank was filled with blood, but no result was achieved." The historian also tells that inspite of his leprosy, the king lived to an advanced age having reigned for a long period of 58 years.

While according to Cunha, the disposition of this king was not disimilar to that of Sultan Mohmad the king of Gujarat who like Mithriadates had accustomed himself to the use of Persian, to guard himself against being poisoned.

Faria-i-Souza, says that when any women happened to be near delivery, the king Nizam-ul-Mulk opened her womb to take out the foetus. And being out hunting one day accompanied by some of his women, he fell from his horse and was dragged by the stirrup, when one of his female companions bravely made up to his horse and cut the girth with a scimetar. In requital for this service, he killed her saying that, "a women of such courage was enough to kill him." It is also related that he was murdered by a page, in whom he had great confidence. "For tyrants" adds the historian", always die by the hands of those in whom they repose more trust.

274. Burhan-i-Maasir (I.A. 1923) pp. 259.

## CHAPTER VI

# ECLIPSE OF THE KINGDOM

After the death of Murtaza Nizam Shah I, prince Miran Husain aged 16 years was proclaimed king on 6th August, 1588 A.D. Mirza Khan was confirmed in the office of Wakil and also was appointed to the office of Commander-in-Chief, a post which was formerly held by Saif Khan. This considerably added to his power and influence.[1] The king promoted to high ranks several young persons like Akbar Khan and Yaqut Khan and made them companions in his round of pleasure and enjoyment.[2] Finding himself free from all restraints, young Husain threw himself headlong into a life of sensual debauchery. Reeling with intoxication he would ride through the streets of the city, accompanied by his drunken associates, trampling innocent persons to death and indulging in excesses of the most heinous character.[3] Naturally the control of the government passed into the hands of Wakil, who bagan to grind his own axe of ambition. In attaining the supreme position his ruthless hand first fell on the Foreigners. On more than one occasion Ismail Khan, the leader of the Foreign party attempted to counteract the high handedness of the minister but in vain. Salabat Khan II, was sent back into prison and Habib Khan was banished from the capital.[4]

**Husain Nizam Shah II proclaimed King (1588 A.D.)**

But the liquidation of the powerful Foreigners did not bring to end the anxiety of Mirza Khan. He now became an object of suspicion in the eyes of his own supporters, i.e., the Africans who informed the king that he was meditating treason, and intended to depose him and place on the throne his uncle Shah Qasim, whom he had sent for from the fort of Shivaneri.[5] But to clear his position and convince his master of his *bonafides* Mirza Khan offered to resign[6] suggesting at the same time that the working of the administration be handed over to Qasim Beg, Sayyid Miran Sharif Gilani and Sayyid Muhammad Samnani.[7] His suggestion was approved by the faineant king, who appointed these persons to the different posts. But they were not given sufficient powers to carry on the administration. On every issue they were required to consult Mirza Khan. Hence he continued to remain powerful. To convince his master of his loyalty Mirza Khan proposed to him that he should put to death all the surviving members of the royal house, and thus blood of fifteen princes was shed in one day.

Mirza Khan inspired by the ambition of playing the role of king-maker soon took steps to gain popularity among the masses. He made certain changes in the composition of the government. He promoted Sayyid Murtaza to the rank of *amir* and bestowed on him the jagir of Bir. Likewise Mirza Muhammad Salih, entitled Khan Khanan was appointed to the office of Sar-i-Naubat of right wing of the army. Farhad Khan, the African was released and restored to his former rank. Bahadur Khan Gilani was appointed Wazir. In effect, it meant the revival and reorganisation of the Foreign party, perhaps as a set off against the Daccanis, the favourites of the king.

As was expected, bitter hostility arose between the rival groups. Against Mirza Khan, the Daccains began to poison the ears of the king who two too became resentful towards him. Upon this Mirza Khan began to plan the deposition of King Husain Nizam Shah II. The latter sought the support of Ankas Khan and Ambar Khan who enjoyed his confidence.[9] This occasioned a game of mean and under hand manoeuvring in which Khan Khanan became the instrument of Mirza Khan's designs.[10] But the plan to kill Ankas Khan having failed, the latter began to work against Mirza Khan to pay him back in his own coins. He was almost caught in the trap but timely warning saved his life. On the pretext of stomachache Mirza Khan left the dinner party, which Ankas Khan had given at his house, and which was attended by the king and his nobles.[11] While he was leaving abruptly, he conveyed to Khan Khanan and Sayyid Murtaza about Ankas Khan's intended plot. Khan Khanan severely reprimanded Ankas Khan and taking Sayyid Murtaza with him repaired to the fort.[12] They waited out side till the arrival of Mirza Khan whom they sent for from his house. When he had joined him, a message was sent to the king, who was still at the residence of Ankas Khan, seeking his

**Hostility between the Daccanis and Foreigners.**

permission to admit Sayyid Murtaza to the royal hammam as he had been taken ill.[13] The permision was granted and the king directed Ankas Khan to look after the ailing noble.[14] Mirza Khan and Khan Khanan took Sayyid Murtaza into the fort, placing their own guards at the gates. When Miran Husain Nizam Shah II returned from Ankas Khan's house, they waited on him, informing him that Sayyid Murtaza was breathing his last.[15] Without the least suspicion of any foul play, the king entered the fort, but was immediately put into surveillance.[16] He was then removed to the Baghdad Palace and placed in solitary confinement, to brood over his follies and misdeeds.[17] Mirza Khan summoned Jamshed Khan, Ain-ul-Mulk, Shah Ibrahim and Mustafa Khan and the other amirs of the Daccani party and sent them to the fortress of Lohgarh to fetch the two royal princes, the sons of the king's uncle, Burhan Nizam Shah II, to choose one of them to elevate him on the throne.[18]

**Husain Nizam Shah II imprisoned**

It was three or four days after the imprisonment of king Husain Nizam Shah II, that Mir Tahir returned from Lohgarh with the two princes named Ismail and Ibrahim.[19] Mirza Khan now sent for Qasim Beg, Mirza Muhammad Taqi Naziri, Mirza Sadiq, Mir Azizuddin Astrabadi and the other foreignn obles, who were yet ignorant of what had happened inside the fort. After much consultation and discussion, their choice fell on Ismail.[20] Accordingly, on Monday 1st. April 1589 A.D. Ismail Nizam Shah was proclaimed king with the usual ceremonials.[21] Urgent orders were sent to the Sayyids, Qazis and learned men to repair to the court to pay their homage to the new king. While the ceremony was going on, the sound of a great tumult at the gate of the fort up-set the proceedings in the audience hall.[22]

**Ismail Nizam Shah proclaimed king (1589 A.D.)**

At the gates had arrived Jamal Khan, a military adventurer, at the head of large following composed of the Daccanis the Africans and the Abyssinians. He demanded to have an audience with Husain Nizam Shah II. But when he was told that Husain had been deposed and had been replaced by his cousin Ismail, to whom he and his followers would be

**Jamal Khan's opposition.**

shortly permitted to pay their homage, Jamal Khan publicly denounced the conduct of Mirza Khan and instigated opposition against him, appealing to the people that the Foreigners having formed cliques, had not only usurped power but were playing with the fortunes of the sons of the soil. This war cry proved very catching. A large number of soldiers flocked to the banner of Jamal Khan and the turmoil turned into a terrible revolt.[23]

As the fort had only a small garrison, Mirza Khan was much alarmed. He sent Lashkar Khan and Kishwar Khan to allay the strife, but the former was slain and the latter escaped with his life into the fort. In perplexity, he sent against Jamal Khan, his uncle Muhammad Said and Kishwar Khan with 150 sons of the Foreigners and 20 Daccanis and an elephant but they too were defeated. Seeing that the whole city was up in arms against him, Mirza Khan sent Jamshed Khan and Sayyid Hasan to arrange terms of peace, but Jamal Khan treacherously arrested them and put them in chains. After this Ismail was placed on the bastion of the fort, with the royal Umbrella spread over his head, but the Daccanis in their frenzy continued to shoot arrows at the fort, even wounding the young king.[24]

As a last resort Mirza Khan had Husain Nizam Shah II blinded and put to death. His head was placed on a spear and was planted on one of the bastions of the fort.[25] The mob was asked to disperse and to acknowledge the new sovereign who, it was proclaimed, would shower rewards on them, if they quietly returned to their houses. Quite a large number of the Daccanis were ready to return, but Jamal Khan vowed vengeance on the Foreigners whom he held responsible for the death of their late monarch.[26] An orgy of blood-shed followed in which Mirza Muhammad Taqi, Mirza Sadiq Urdabadi, Mir Izzuddin Astrabadi, Maulana Najmuddin Shustari and many other learned and accomplished men of the age lost their lives.[27] While Qasim Beg, Sayyid Sharif Gilani, Itimad Khan Shustari and Khwaja Abdul Salam Tuni managed to escape. In the end, Jamal Khan succeeded in forcing his way into the fort. Mirza Khan escaped to Junnar with some of his relatives like, Wali Khan, Ain-ul-Mulk Nishapuri, Khan

**Bloodshed and Massacres.**

Khanan, Sayyid Md. Samnani, Bahadur Khan Gilani, Mir Tahir Alvi, Aga Mir Sherwani and others, leaving behind hundred Foreigners who were slaughtered to a man.[28]

Jamal Khan now seated Ismail Nizam Shah on the throne. Not being content with recent orgy of blood, he issued a fresh order for the general massacre of the innocent Foreigners, "of every rank and occupation in the city, and for plundering and burning their dwellings. The soldiers and their followers, being once let loose, put to death indiscriminately the nobles, master, servants, the merchants, pilgrims, and the travellers and the strangers all alike. Their houses were set on fire. The heads of those lately exalted to the sky were brought low and trampled in dust, while the very females who from modesty concealed their faces from sun and moon were dragged by the hair into the assemblages of the drunken."[29]

Mirza Khan was seized near Junnar, and was brought before Jamal Khan. He was paraded through the streets of the city on an ass and then his body was cut into pieces, which were affixed on different buildings. His friends were also put to death, their bodies being put into a cannon and blown in the air. Within a week's time nearly a thousand more Foreigners were put to death. Very few of them escaped under the protection and with the connivance of the Daccanis and Abyssinian officers.[30]

**Jamal Khan's advent to power.**

No sooner did Jamal Khan find himself firmly in the saddle, than he assigned all jagirs formerly held by the Foreigners to Africans and the Daccanis, and gave liberal promotions to them.[31] Being himself a Mahdavi, he showed special partiality to the followers of that faith. Amjad-ul-Mulk a Mahdavi was made the Amir-ul-Umra of Berar and Khan-i-Malik was appointed Sar-i-Naubat of that province.[32] Nizam Khan Nishapuri and the other Mahdavis were enrolled in government service and were given posts according to their ability and merit.[33] Those who refused to conform to the Mahdavi faith were ruthlessly persecuted.[34] Shiaism was abolished as the state religion and in its place Mahdavi doctrines were openly propagated.[35] Within a short time a large number of Mahdavis flocked to

Ahmadnagar, which became a very important centre of their faith.[36] They acknowledged Jamal Khan as their Khalifa, swearing to sacrifice their life for him. In this way the administration of the Nizam Shahi kingdom fell into the hands of the Mahdavis.

In the first instance, Jamal Khan offered to Farhad Khan the post of the wakil and Peshwa.[37] He had returned to the court on hearing the death of Husain Nizam Shah II. But when he declined to accept the offer, he was arrested and sent to the fortress of Rajauri.[38] Now Yakut Khan was promoted to the rank of amir, was invested with the little of Khudawand Khan and was appointed wakil of the kingdom.[39] Jamal Khan betrothed his daughter to his son to strengthen the cordial relations with him. He also promoted to high rank Shah Abu Turab the maternal uncle of the king Ismail Nizam Shah.[40]

The propagation of the Mahdavi faith gave umbrage to the Daccanis, the Abyssinians and the Foreigners alike. It also excited the animosity of Adil Shah. In Berar it proved to be rallying cry for all those who bore a grudge against Jamal Khan. The spear-head of the revolt was Muhammad Khan, the former Sar-i-Naubat and the Amir-ul-Umra of Berar. He was supported by Bahri Khan, Ikhlas Khan, Ain-ul-Mulk, at whose instance he persuaded Sayyid Muzaffar Khan Mazandrani, to release Salabat Khan II, whom he was holding prisoner in the fort of Kherla. A large army was assembled and it converged on Ahmadnagar. On the way its ranks were further strengthened by the arrival of Bahadur Khan Gilani and other Foreigners. The report of the movements of the rebels alarmed Jamal Khan and what broke his confidence completely was the simultaneous attack by Adil Shah on Ahmadnagar. Faced with such a grim situation, he resorted to offering tempting promises to the followers of Salabat Khan in whose ranks desertions on large scale occurred. In the end the rebels broke and fled. Salabat Khan and Muhammad Khan escaped to Khandesh to seek refuge with Raja Ali Khan.[41]

Having disposed of the internal enemies, Jamal Khan marched to meet the external aggression. He came face to face with the Bijapur army at Asthi. The rival forces lay encamped there for fifteen days, without coming to any action whatsoever. As Jamal Khan was not strong enough to fight the Bijapuri forces in the field, he opened negotiations for peace, which was concluded on three conditions; firstly that Parenda and other adjacent forts should be ceded to Adil Shah; secondly, that Chand Bibi and Khadija Sultana should be sent back to Bijapur; and thirdly, that the Nizam Shahi government should pay two hundred and seventy five thousand huns as the war indemnity. The conditions having been fulfilled Ibrahim Adil Shah II, with his army retreated to Bijapur.[42]

On his return to Ahmadnagar Jamal Khan planned another blood bath for the Foreigners. But at the intercession of Khudawand Khan he spared their lives. Still his thirst for the blood of the Foreigners and for ruthless revenge continued unabated. He appointed a body of men to collect the Foreigners from every nook and corner of the city. He exiled many of them to Bijapur, Golcunda, Chaul and Malwa. Shah Rafiuddin Husain, Shah Haidar, Qasim Beg, Mir Sharif Gilani, Sayyid Muhammad Samnani and other leading and renowned personalities of Ahmadnagar kingdom were sent away to Mecca. And he filled these vacant posts by promoting and appointing his followers, who belonged to his own sect. It was a sad commentary on the Nizam Shahi politics, a development which boded sure and certain disaster.[43]

**Another Ruthless Massacre**

The outbreak of religious fanaticism in Ahmadnagar, the aggressive propogation of the Mahdavi faith and the consequent bloodshed, the mass deportations of the Foreigners, the flight of soldiers, politicians and men of letters from that kingdom, provided much food for thought to the Mughal Emperor Akbar. With his keen intellect, he analysed the situation both on the political and ethical level. Were not the state of affairs in Ahmadnagar a direct challenge to his broad principles of toleration ? Was not the disturbing politics there a potential danger to his province of Malwa ? Add to this the ideal of Chakravartin and his desire to achieve it. But at the moment his hands were full and he could not afford to divert his military resources towards the South, nor could he remain inactive and a silent spectator of all what was happening there.

The refugee Burhan Nizam II proved to be a ready tool for the prosecution of the ambitious schemes of the Mughal Emperor. He was sent for from his jagir at Bangash, and offerred the support of an army to enforce his rightful claims the throne of Ahmadnagar, which at this moment was held by his son.[44] But when he had convinced the Mughal Emperor of the disadvantages of being accompanied by a foreign army, which was likely to create more prejudices amongst his subjects against him than in his favour, he was allowed to go alone and try his luck in the Daccan. On the eve of his departure Burhan promised that in the event of success in the enterprise, he would acknowledge the suzerainty of the Mughal Emperor, who in his turn assigned him Hindiya in jagir and directed Raja Ali Khan, the ruler of Khandesh and Mirza Aziz Koka, the governor of Malwa to extend him the necessary assistance.[45]

**Mughal encroachments.**

From Hindiya, Burhan II wrote letters full of tempting promises to the nobles of the Nizam Shahi kingdom, asking for their support in this venture. Some of them responded to the call with alacrity and arrived in Berar via Gondwana.[46] Here they were joined by Jahangir Khan and other amirs. To meet the situation Jamal Khan sent Azmat-ul-Mulk and other amirs, directing them to prevent Salabat Khan from deserting to the invader.[47] But Salabat proved impervious to all temptations held out to him by Burhan.[48] Thereupon Burhan entered Berar but unexpectedly Jahangir Khan turned against him and attacked him. During the encounter one of the Mughal commanders Chaghtai Khan was killed. Burhan was defeated and he fled to Hindiya,[49] from where he went to Raja Ali Khan. Soon after he was invited by Jamal Khan to come alone to Ahmadnagar, but he declined to do it.

Burhan made another bid for the Nizam Shahi throne. On this occasion he had at his command a large number of the Nizam Shahi troops, and behind him the support of Ibrahim Adil Shah II and Raja Ali Khan. The former advanced from Bijapur towards Ahmadnagar and the latter met Burhan II at Burhanpur, and the two marched towards Berar.[50] Jamal

**Burhan's Second bid for the throne.**

Khan immediately collected his troops consisting of 10,000 Mahdavis, directed Sayyid Amjad-ul-Mulk of Berar to oppose Raja Ali Khan and Burhan, with his entire force on the northern frontier ; while he himself proceeded against the Bijapuris to prevent their junction with enemy.[51] He met the Bijapuris at the village of Kari-Naeri. Here he received report that Burhan had entered Berar and that the principal nobles of the province on whom he had relied had submitted to him. But, to prevent demoralisation among his men, he not only concealed the report but had the drums beaten announcing the defeat of Burhan. The very same night Abhang Khan, the African and other Nizam Shahi nobles fled to the Adil Shahi camp and thence to Berar, where they joined Burhan's army. Though Jamal Khan's force was depleted by this desertion, but he did not flinch from attacking the Adil Shahi army on the following day.[52]

**Jamal Khan Repels the Adil Shahi invasion**

Leaving Ibrahim Adil Shah II in the camp, Dilawar Khan marched to repulse Jamal Khan. While the two forces faced each other in the field of battle, Bahadur Khan Gilani and other Foreigners deserted their leader, joined Dilawar Khan, and opened the attack. In the thick of the fight Jamal Khan's troops broke and fled. Dilawar Khan emerged out victorious. He gathered the spoils and remained in the field. Meanwhile Jamal Khan collected his scattered forces, launched a surprise attack on the Adil Shahi commander Dilawar Khan and defeated him with heavy losses. Dilawar Khan escaped from the field with much difficulty, while his army fled to Naldurg, leaving behind their tents, camp equippage, baggage etc. which fell into the hands of the victor.[53]

Flushed with the recent success, Jamal Khan marched northward to Berar to fight Burhan II. Ibrahim Adil Shah II despatched the whole of his *bargi* cavalry, numbering about 90,000 under the leadership of Dilawar Khan to cut off his supplies. Jamal Khan relying on his Mahdavi followers rapidly marched to Rohankhed, notwithstanding the daily desertions among his ranks. On his arrival there, he found the pass occupied by the Adil Shahi and Burhan's forces, which had hemmed him in from all sides. His army found itself in great distress, owing to the excessive heat. Nor was it possible to move either forward or backward. Scarcity of water, compelled him to stop where he was.[54] Here he was attacked, defeated and killed by a musket shot. The leaderless army scattered in all directions. The eunuch Dastur Khan, who held the charge of the young king Ismail left the field. He was pursued by the enemy. Seeing that all chances of escape had been closed on him, he abandoned the king in a village. Ismail an innocent lad of twelve was over-taken, made prisoner and produced before his father Burhan II, who in affection kissed his forehead and forgave him. Later, the boy was kept in the fort of Bhakar. He ruled only for two years.[55]

**Battle of Rohankhed (May 7, 1591 A.D.)**

Having gained a decisive victory with the assistance of Raja Ali Khan, Ibrahim Adil Shah II and the moral support of the Mughals, Burhan Nizam bade his allies farewell and marched towards Ahmadnagar. On May 15th, 1591 A.D. (1st Shabaan A.H. 999) he ascended the Nizam Shahi throne in his advanced age, amidst great rejoicings at the capital. Instead of addressing himself to the task which lay ahead, like other feeble and incompetent monarchs, he too gave himself to the pleasure of wine, women and music, ill suited to his old age and dignity.[56]

**Accession of Burhan Nizam Shah II**

As the new king had gained the throne with the help of Raja Ali Khan, the ruler of Khandesh, he felt little obligation to the Mughal Emperor who had never extended any direct help to him. Therefore not only did he ignore the latter but openly opposed his policy of aggrandisement and forgot his promise of acknowledging his suzerainty. His deceitful conduct annoyed Akbar who sent Faizi and Aminuddin to Raja Ali Khan to ask him to warn his friend Burhan of the serious consequences of rank ingratitude.[57] Envoys were also despatched to the courts of Bijapur and Golcunda to persuade Adil Shah and Qutb Shah to acknowledge the Emperor as their overlord.[58] Whereas Adil Shah and Qutb Shah knowing as they did that the Mughal Emperor at the moment being preoccupied with the problems of the North western frontier, was not in a position to turn his attention towards them, sent replies, dismissing his envoys with polite words and presents. Burhan Nizam Shah II relying on the support of his neighbours, treated the Mughal envoy Aminuddin very clumsily, charged him with plundering some merchants and sent him back unceremoniously. His conduct annoyed Akbar, who soon after appointed Prince Murad as the viceroy of Gujarat and Shahrukh Mirza as the governor of Malwa, giving them instructions to prepare themselves to wage an aggressive war against the Daccan kingdoms at the earliest opportunity.[59]

Early in his reign Burhan Nizam Shah II, abolished the Mahdavi religion, put to death all those who professed the creed and reintroduced the Shia religion in the country.[60] The Foreigners who had been exiled during the hateful regime of Mirza Khan returned, and were restored to their former posts. Soon they recovered their former influence and ingratiated themselves into confidence of the king. Thus the new reign commenced with promising potentialities but Burhan unnecessarily provoked the hostility of Adil Shah by offering protection to Dilawar Khan the Abyssinian Regent of Bijapur, who had made himself unpopular there and therefore had been compelled to flee to Bidar and thence to Ahmadnagar.[61] The king enrolled him among his nobles and appointed him to reduce the fort of Sholapur.[62]

Ibrahim Adil Shah II immediately wrote to Burhan Nizam Shah II, protesting against the breach of diplomatic etiquette. Inspite of the fact that his position on the throne was still precarious, and that his people had not yet recovered from shock of the disaster which had fallen on them during the last two reigns,[63] Burhan Nizam treated the Adil Shahi envoys with contempt, and sent an insulting reply to his erstwhile benefactor.[64] The latter sent Mulla Inayatullah *Jharmi* to Ahmadnagar to demand restitution of 300 elephants which Dilawar Khan had taken with him. Burhan Nizam Shah instead of complying with the request, forgetting all that he owed to Adil Shah, at the instigation of Dilawar Khan declared war. He marched towards Bijapur, crossed the frontiers and laid waste the country.

**Burhan II declares war against Bijapur.**

In the course of onward progress he met with no opposition.[65] But on his arrival at Mangalwara, he began to suspect that the enemy was planning to draw him into the very heart of his kingdom. He would have retreated but for Dilawar Khan, who persuaded him to continue his advance as far as Bhima. He halted there and ordered repairs of the ruined fortress with the object of pushing forward the Nizam Shahi frontiers to the river Beora and conquering the fortresses of Shah Durg and Sholapur.[66] All this time Ibrahim Adil Shah II remained inactive and allowed Burhan and Dilawar Khan to put guns and provisions into the fortress. This having been done he commenced his own game. He enticed away Dilawar Khan, blinded and imprisoned him in the fortress of Satara. Having thus rid himself of his inveterate foe, he quickly assembled his army and opened the counter offensive. He sent his bargi leaders with 6,000 horse to cut off the enemy's line of communications. They were reinforced by Rumi Khan Daccani with 10,000 horse and Ilyas Khan with 3,000 more. They succeeded in the task assigned to them and harassed the Nizam Shahis with their surprise attacks. Burhan was compelled to cross river Bhima, and to fall back from one position to the other, until, he was completely vanquished losing one hundred elephants and four hundred horses.[67]

But the cup of Burhan Nizam Shah's humiliation and misery was not yet full. In his camp the Daccanis under the leadership of Kamil Khan conspired to depose him. Luckily for the king, the secret leaked out and the mischief was nipped in bud. In desperation he solicited peace from Ibrahim Adil Shah II, but the latter proved adament to all his appeals until Qutb Shah and Raja Ali Khan had interceded for him. He was asked by Ibrahim Adil Shah to demolish the fort which he had built on Bhima, and to save his skin, he complied with the demand.[68]

Hardly two years had passed since the recent venture Burhan Nizam Shah again embroiled himself in the affairs of Bijapur. He supported the cause of Ismail who had risen in rebellion against his brother Ibrahim Adil Shah II. But before he could advance beyond Parenda, the rebel had been defeated and killed. Thus he gave sufficient cause of annoyance to the ruler of Bijapur, who had forgiven him on a previous occasion. To provoke him further Burhan Nizam Shah allied himself with the Raya of Penukunda and sent an army to reduce Sholapur and Shah Durg. But the venture proved inconclusive.[69]

Burhan Nizam Shah II now fell ill, suffering from chronic dysentry, which made him irritable and weak, and confined him to bed. He sent for his elder son, Ibrahim whom he nominated as his successor, ordering that Ismail who was an enemy of the Shias and a strict Mahdavi and a friend of the Daccanis be put to death.[70] This occasioned great tumult. Ikhlas Khan Muwallid susppecting the hand of the Foreigners in the suppression of the claims of Ismail, spread a rumour in Parenda that Burhan Nizam Shah II was dead and that the Foreigners were in the danger of being massacred. Upon this, their leader Murtaza Khan Anju returned to Ahmadnagar but others like Khalifa Arab and Qazi Balash Khan fled to Bijapur in sheer fright. Ikhlas Khan accompanied by the Abyssinians and the Daccanis marched to the depose Burhan Nizam Shah II. But the latter in spite of his feeble health rode out against the rebels defeated them and put them to flight.[71] The strain of a campaign proved too much for him and he died on April 18, 1595 A.D. after a reign of four lunar years, four months and sixteen days.[72]

**Death of Burhan Nizam Shah II.**

Ibrahim Nizam Shah succeeded his father to the throne on 27th May 1595 A.D. In compliance with the dying wishes of his father, he appointed Mian Manjhu Daccani as his prime minister, who granted an amnesty to Ikhlas Khan and his party, and they returned to the city. It did not take long for the two leaders to come to loggerheads with each other. The cause of strained relations between the two was neither religious nor racial, but it lay entirely in the clash of their personal ambitions, each being keen to gain an upper hand of the other. Naturally they could not see eye to eye on political and administrative issues. A matter of immediate concern was the determination of the attitude of the Nizam Shahi State towards Ibrahim Adil Shah II, whose envoys had come to Ahmadnagar to condole with and congratulate the

**Accession of Ibrahim Nizam Shah.**

new sovereign. The mutual jealousy of Ikhlas Khan and Mian Manjhu made them blind to the consequences of their insolent behaviour towards Mir Safavi, the Bijapur envoy. To make the situation still worse the favourite of the Queen mother who was an Abyssinian, also hurled insults at the Mir.[73]

Ibrahim Adil Shah II had thus justifiable cause to be offended. His envoy had been treated with contempt and his friendly gesture had been deliberately spurned. On the pretext of liberating Nizam Shah, he left Bijapur at the head of a large army and after encamping for a while at Bahurnally, arrived at Shah Durg, still reluctant to proceed to extremities, which could be avoided by the offer of apologies on behalf of the offending party. Mian Manjhu was equally anxious for a compromise, but his master was in the hands of Ikhlas Khan who precipitated the conflict. In the initial stages success fell to the lot of the Nizam Shahis, but in the end Ibrahim Nizam Shah lost his life having been shot through his head. The death of the king decided the fate of the battle. Amidst great confusion the Nizam Shahi troops, with his body fled towards Ahmadnagar, to repent on the course of action he had followed. Ibrahim Nizam Shah's reign lasted only for four months. Its end was a signal for the forthcoming anarchy in the Nizam Shahi kingdom.[74]

Mian Manjhu arrived at the capital, occupied the fort, seized the royal treasury and summoned Ikhlas Khan and other nobles to consider the most advisable plan for conducting the government and for selecting their monarch. Meanwhile he sent for Ahmad,[75] a boy of twelve from Daultabad to seat him on the throne.[76]

**Party Politics.**

But his proposal was opposed by Chand Bibi who pressed the claims of the infant Bahadur, the only son of the late king.[77] She depended on the support of the Abyssinians, in carrying through her own plan of suppressing the internal troubles which had risen in Ahmadnagar, and of completing the preparations for withstanding the threatened aggression of the Mughals. But unfortunately, she was isolated, for her Abyssinian supporters were won over by Mian Manjhu. There after he and Ikhlas Khan joined and turned against her. Consequently Ahmad was proclaimed king on 6th August 1595

A.D., and the child Bahadur was seized from the hands of Chand Bibi and imprisoned in the fortress of Jond. She herself was placed under strict surviellance.[78]

But when the truth about the parentage of the new king had been revealed, Mian Manjhu and Ikhlas Khan fell out with each other, and the latter began to strive to depose Ahmad.[79] Thereupon Mian Manjhu left the fort with his Daccani followers and encamped at Kala Chabutra and sent his son Mian Hasan to disperse the mob which had collected under Ikhlas Khan.[80] But Mian Hasan was defeated and compelled to retreat into the fort which was besieged by Ikhlas Khan.[81] Meanwhile a rumour of king's death in the town led Ikhlas Khan to write to the governor of the fortress of Daultabad to release Abhang Khan and Habsh Khan.[82] They were released accordingly, but the commander of Jond refused to comply with the orders of Ikhlas Khan and declined to hand over Prince Bahadur to Abhang Khan.[83] It was a psychological moment for action. The mass support was behind Ikhlas Khan who promptly found the way out of the impasse. He secured a child of the same age as Bahadur gave him the title Moti Shah and proclaimed him king.[84]

The strength of Ikhlas Khan's followers and the progress they had made in the siege operations alarmed Mian Manjhu. Pressed by feelings of distress, he addressed appealing letters to Prince Murad, Abdur Rahim Khan Khanan and the governor of Malwa to come to the Daccan and restore peace and order there. Accordingly, orders were issued by the Mughal Emperor for the mobilisation of an army for the Daccan compaign and Raja Ali Khan of Khandesh was directed to afford all possible help in the enterprise.[85]

But even before these letters could have reached Prince Murad, the Abyssinian chiefs fell out among themselves on the question of distribution of offices. The dissensions in the camp of Ikhlas Khan were followed by desertions on a large scale; the deserters going over to Mian Manjhu in the fort. Taking advantage of the growing weakness of his enemy, Mian Manjhu marched on 18th September, 1595 A.D. (25th Muharram, A.H. 1004) to the Idgah, where he suddenly attacked and defeated the Abyssinians and completely routed them. Among those who were made captive was Moti Shah, the bazar boy[86] who had been proclaimed king.

Mian Manjhu now bitterly repented on the folly of having invited the Mughals. On the appearance of the latter, he threw up his mask and posed as a champion and saviour of the Nizam Shahi kingdom. Accordingly, he made out plans to resist the enemy and bar his progress towards the capital. He sent Saadat Khan an old noble belonging to the reign of Burhan Nizam Shah II, to Kolaba and Nasik districts, which he held in *muqasa*, from the Nizam Shahi government, to oppose the Mughals. But owing to the smallness of numbers, he could not make any head way and retreated homewards without offering any resistance. Face to face with the danger in all its nakedness, Mian Manjhu began to behave like a straw before the storm. He could neither trust to the loyalty of the Abyssinians, nor to the support of the Daccanis; nor in such a predicament he could come to a firm decision. His courage was failing and his confidence was shaking. His nerves were so shattered that he saw the ghost of the enemy everywhere. He was indifferent to the noble Chand Bibi, and still apprehensive of her. The nobles advised him to face the Mughals boldly, but in their advice he read sinister motives. He held a council of war and discussed the situation with Mujahiduddin, Shamshir Khan, and other Abyssinians. Shamshir Khan vehemently opposed the idea of taking to flight and demanded the control of the army promising to fight the invaders single-handed. And though Mian Manjhu made him the Amir-ul-Umra, but gave to him the command of Ahmadnagar troops only.[87]

**Mughals advance into the Nizam Shahi Territory**

Nor did the nobles, the Daccanis and the Abyssinians alike had faith in the words of Mian Manjhu. Some of them retired from active service. Others like Afzal Khan, Maulana Shamsuddin Muhammad Lari, the ambassador of Ibrahim Adil Shah II, Maulana Haji Isfahani, the envoy of Muhhamd Quli Qutb Shah, Habib Khan, Mubariz-ul-Zaman Rizvi Meshhadi and other Foreigners suspected treachery on the part of Mian Manjhu. In fact the latter had issued instructions to Safdar Khan to seize the Foreigners and kill them. Unable to bear the strain, in the last resort Mian Manjhu on the pretext of soliciting the assistance of Adil Shah and Qutb Shah fled to Ausa, taking Ahmad Nizam Shah with him and surrendering all the affairs of the state in the hands of Chand Bibi.[88]

The responsibility for the protection of the honour and dignity of her homeland, having devolved on her shoulders, the first concern of Chand Bibi was to set at rest the confusion which had arisen consequent upon the sudden flight of Mian Manjhu. She formed a composite council of action consisting the Abyssinian leaders, Mujahiduddin and Shamshir Khan, the Foreigners like Afzal Khan Barishi and Muhammad Zaman. The influential Daccani leader Muhammad Khan, was appointed Wakil, with the title of Amir-ul-Umra and the distinction of Naib. He was given the charge of entire administration. She appealed to all of them, to find out ways and means for averting the calamity. She dismissed Ansar Khan, formerly the commandant of Burhanpur, but who had lately gained favour with Mian Manjhu and been appointed to hold the charge of Ahmadnagar. Thereafter she proclaimed Bahadur Nizam Shah as the sovereign of Ahmadnagar.[39]

On 14th December, 1595 A.D. Prince Murad, with 3,000 Mughal and Rajput horses, in the company of Raja Ali Khan, Abdur Rahim Khan Khanan and other valiant generals appeared on the northern side of Ahmadnagar.[90] Upon his arrival in the vicinity of the Idgah a few shots were exchanged between the Mughal advance guard under Khan Khanan and the Nizam Shahi soldiers, who had been waiting for the enemy on the plains of Kala Chabutra. The Mughals retreated and encamped near the garden of Hasht-Bahisht (Old Kariz) awaiting further developments.[91] Murad endeavoured to win popular support for his enterprise. He sent his officers to Burhanabad with directions to treat the inhabitants with kindness, telling them that the Prince would safeguard their lives and protect them from high-handedness. With the advice of his engineers the Prince marked out the ground for the trenches against the fort, allotting to the various divisions of the army their

**Fort of Ahmadnagar besieged**

respective positions.[92] Soon Shamshir Khan and Mir Muhammad Zaman attacked the Mughals and broke their ranks in the plains of Kala Chabutra. But the sudden arrival of Mirza Shah Rukh, Shahbaz Khan, Sadiq Muhammad Khan, Sayyid Murtaza and other leaders with auxiliaries, saved the situation.[93]

Meanwhile one of the Mughal generals Shahbaz Khan, notorious for his tyranny over his troops and cruelty to all classes of inhabitants, left Burhanabad, in spite of Prince's orders and he encouraged his men to plunder. "In course of an hour the towns of Ahmadnagar and Burhanabad were completely sacked."[94] When the Prince heard of it, he flew into rage, ordered several miscreants to be publicly executed. But the inhabitants were so much alarmed that they no longer relied on Prince's assurances and promises and fled away in large numbers. Now, the Prince opened the siege of the fort of Ahmadnagar. (18th December 1595 A.D.).[95]

As if the Mughal invasion was not a calamity serious enough to ruin the fortunes of the Nizam Shahi kingdom, the disaffected Nizam Shahi generals who had fled to the different parts of the kingdom, now began to pursue their own individual ambition. Ikhlas Khan, Aziz-ul-Mulk, Bilail Khan and others hastened to Daultabad, won over the garrison of the fort and once more proclaimed a boy named Moti as Moti Shah and thereby unfurled the banner of opposition and independence.[96] Similarly, Mubariz-ud-din Abhang Khan, who was on the look out of a protege, hastened to Bijapur where he met Miran Shah Ali son of Burhan Nizam Shah II, a man of seventy, who was living as a refugee in Bijapur.[97] Abhang Khan raised the canopy over his head and with large number of his followers entered the district of Bid, whence he started for settling the affairs of the Nizam Shahi country and acquiring wherewith all, for the successful prosecution of his designs.[98] In such a state of unsettledness how could Mian Manjhu remain inactive. He marched to the borders of the Adil Shahi kingdom, encamped there and solicited the assistance of Ibrahim Adil Shah II.

From Daultabad Ikhlas Khan advanced at the head of 12,000 horse towards the capital with the object of wresting power from the hands of Chand Bibi and installing Moti Shah there. But his progress was interrupted by a Mughal army under the leadership of Daulat Khan Lodi, Sher Khwaja and Kamran Beg, who inflicted a crushing defeat on him on the banks of Godavari near Paithan. In the course of his retreat Ikhlas Khan sacked Paithan, stripping the inhabitants of their clothes even. His defeat and repulse however afforded only partial relief to Chand Bibi.[99]

To ensure united action against the invaders Chand Bibi now turned to Abhang Khan and sent confidential messages to him to come to terms with Mian Manjhu, and after which the two together should march to Daultabad and concert measures for the expulsion of the Mughals.[100] Accordingly Abhang Khan arrived at Daultabad where he was joined by 500 Abyssinian horsemen who had deserted Ikhlas Khan on his refusal to abandon the cause of Moti Shah. This unexpected accession to his fighting resources increased the confidence of Abhang Khan who made an effort to enter the fort of Ahmadnagar along with his followers on 21st December, 1595 A.D.[101]

By a strange coincidence, that very morning Prince Murad in the company of Khan Khanan, Shah Baz Khan, Shah Rukh Mirza, Muhammad Sadiq Khan, Sayyid Murtaza, Raja Ali Khan, Raja Jagganath and many other amirs inspected the surroundings of the fortress, marked out the ground for the trenches and distributed the commands. The eastern side which was the highway for traffic had been entrusted to the charge of Khan Khanan, who leaving the Namaz Gah (Prayer ground) retired to the garden of the Ibadat Khan. At the dead of the night, while his whole army was fast asleep Abhang Khan surprised them and cut his way into the fort along with Miran Shah Ali. But the forces which were coming behind him, with about 700 men was attacked by Daulat Khan Lodi and they were cut to a man.[102]

The success of Abhang Khan made Prince Murad more vigilant and cautious. Subsequently the fort was surrounded from all sides and vigorous efforts were made to move the trenches forward.[103] The Prince worked ceaselessly, spending all his time, supervising and inspecting the work of his men who were engaged in carrying forward the trenches, in filling the ditch, and in erecting batteries overlooking the wall of the fort.[104] But Shamshir Khan and his sons who had barricaded all the exits and entrances, occasionally sallied out to fight the enemy, till they rendered all the efforts of the imperialists useless.[105] Chand Bibi herself took an active part in the defence of the fortress, supervising the affairs of the army and handling the administrative problems with efficiency and foresight.[106] "By day she rested not from bestowing benefit and instructing those under her and by the aid of her own rare good fortune, in the night she slept not but weeping and wailing before the throne of God, praying for tranquility."

Inspite of the determined efforts of the Prince Murad, his followers could not make any headway, owing to the jealousy and rivalry between Sadiq Khan and Shahbaz Khan,[107] which proved to be a boon to the helpless Nizam Shahi kingdom in two ways; firstly, the garrison got the respite to put the defence in order and secondly, succour from out side friends became available.[108] Venkoji, a Koli chief and a supporter of Nizam Shah and an ally of Ahmad Nizam Shah and Mian Manjhu, arrived near the capital, opened surprise attacks on the besiegers, intercepting their line of communications with Gujarat and seizing their supplies of horses and camels.[109] Similarly, Saadat Khan cut off the communications of the Mughals between Sultanpur and Nandurbar. This was followed by indecisive skirmishes.[110]

The rising volume of opposition created a serious situation for the Mughals. The victory of Daulat Khan over Ikhlas Khan, the supporter of Moti Shah, drove the latter into the arms of Mian Manjhu, who was busy in organising a grand coalition of Bijapur, Golcunda and the Nizam Shahi nobles against the invaders.[111] At the same time Murad had to face the scarcity of provisions, caused by adandonment of their lands by the terror striken peasants.[112] Add to it, the treachery which was rampant in the Mughal camp. There was an old feud between Sadiq Muhammad Khan on the one hand and Shahbaz Khan and Khan Khanan on the other.[113] The last two were believed to be the partisans of Prince Salim who did not like the fall of Ahmadnagar, which might bring the glory to Prince Murad. At the instance of Khan Khanan, Sadiq Muhammad Khan was relieved of his command and the Prince himself arrived in the former's camp at Farah Baksh garden. He was so much captivated by the charms of this beautiful spot that for about a fortnight he completely forgot his mission, engrossed himself in a life of delightful licentiousness.[114] At the end of the interval, he once more awoke to his sense of duty for the performance of which he again became active and alert.

Meanwhile there had occurred a change in the affairs of Ahmadnagar. Mian Manjhu and Ikhlas Khan had become of one mind[115] and Adil Shah and Qutb Shah had been persuaded to send substantial help for the relief of the garrison, under the respective commands of Suhail Khan and Mehdi Quli Khan. Within a short time 70,000 troops assembled at Shah Durg, ready to march to Ahmadnagar,[116] and thanks to the friendly attitude of Raja Ali Khan, not only the communications between the garrison and the outside world were restored, but even substantial supplies both in form of provisions and arms could be smuggled into the fort whenever required.[117]

When Prince Murad learnt of the assistance which the rulers of the Daccan had extended to the unfortunate kingdom, he decided to launch a vigourous assault on the fort. At the same time when he came to know of the secret contacts between Raja Ali Khan and the garrison, he removed him from his charge, handing it over to Raja Jaggannath, with instructions to tighten up vigilance and intercept all communications between the garrison and their friends outside.[118] Raja Ali Khan was compelled by some of his officers to write a letter to Chand Bibi, asking her to surrender the fortress to Prince Murad and take in lieu thereof, any other fort or district of her own choice, otherwise there was a risk of losing reputation.[119] No doubt the garrison was alarmed on the receipt of such a letter from Raja Ali Khan, in whom they reposed great trust, but Afzal Khan wrote back an intelligent and firm reply, expressing his determination to defend the fort against the Mughals.[120] In a few days five mines were carried under the bastions on the one side of the fort. On 20th Feb. 1596 (1st Rajab A. H. 1004) at Prince's order they were filled with powder.[121] It was intended to explode them on the following morning and take the fort by storm. But during the night Khwaja Muhammad Khan Shirazi admiring the resolution of the besieged and reluctant to see that they should be sacrificed, managed to enter the fort, and informed the garrison of the danger which lay ahead.[122] The garrison immediately addressed itself to the task of undoing the work of the besiegers. They discovered one mine, removed the gun powder and filled it up with stone and earth. The digging of the second mine also started. Next morning it being Friday, Sadiq Muhammad Khan postponed the firing of the mines till the afternoon.[123] This helped the besieged, who succeeded in removing the powder from the other mines also and rendering them useless.

On the same day Prince Murad and Sadiq Muhammad Khan assembled the Mughal army at the foot of the fort and ordered that fire be set to the mines. But only one of them exploded, blowing about fifty yards of the wall. Others poured forth stones and earth hurling over the head of the Mughal soldiers standing by. Ready to rush into the fortress, they waited and waited, but no other mine exploded. Meanwhile the garrison had succeeded in throwing up the repairs to the breach which had been made in the wall. And although the invaders made desperate efforts to enter the fort but they were beaten back.[124]

While the garrison was suffering from excitement, suspicion and anxiety, ceaselessly working all the time to defend the fort, it occurred to some of the Foreigners and to the envoys of the kings of the Daccan to request Chand Bibi to be present on the spot to cheer up and inspire her people.[125] She promptly responded to the suggestion. Clad in glittering armour, mounted on an elephant she approached in full view of her army. A fresh wave of enthusiasm began to surge in the hearts of her soldiers, and they let loose a volly of arrows, granades and shots at the enemy.[126] Undaunted she moved forward in the thick of the fire which the Mughal guns were emitting, and addressing her people she said, "although to take one's own life is forbidden both by the commonsense and the divine law, yet I have brought a cup of posion to save myself from the indignity which the enemy would inflict on me. Martyrdom is certain from the wound of the enemy

**Chand Bibi's valour**

of the faith and state, how can I guard myself against such wounds ?"[127] Henceforward Chand Bibi became an object of universal admiration and conversation in enemy's camp. From that day the Regent who had been always called Chand Bibi now acquired the title of Chand Sultana.[128]

Prince Murad who was sorely disappointed at the failure, passed the whole night in anxiety, taking counsel with his amirs and leaders of the army as to the best means of reducing the fortress. Next morning he again held a review of his army, advanced to the breached wall of the fortress and decided to lead an attack personally. Dismounting from his horse at the very edge of the moat, he encouraged his men to fight the enemy desperately promising them rewards and promotions. He also requested Khan Khanan to cooperate with him but he excused himself from taking any part in the venture. The Prince's sense of honour being touched, he ordered his Ahadi troops, the choicest fighters of his army, to attack the besieged. Vigorous assaults were delivered by them, but the defenders, who were encouraged by the success of the previous evening, showered fire from the fortress, through *pak-bans*, guns and matchlocks. The Mughals showed the greatest valour, fought from the sunrise until the sun-set, but they found themselves striking against the walls of iron. After heavy casualities, much bloodshed, Prince Murad was compelled to withdraw to his camp disgusted and disappointed.[129]

At length the long drawn out siege exhausted the supplies in the fort. The people inside had to face helplessness and starvation. Realising the superiority of the Mughal army and the weakness of the defenders, Chand Bibi sent urgent letters to the allied armies to hasten for her relief. But all the time, she was suspicious of the intentions of Mian Manjhu, who, she thought, had formed the confederacy of the kings of the Daccan with the sole object of establishing the claims of his own nominee Ahmad Nizam Shah, which he would press after the retirement of the Mughals. By chance her letter was intercepted on the way by the Mughal Commander Sadiq Ali Khan who forwarded it to Suhail Khan, to whom it was addressed, adding a covering note of his own, asking the latter to speed up his advance to decide the issue finally.[130] Accordingly Suhail Khan advanced towards Ahmadnagar via Manik Duda hills.

The Mughals on their part were not finding themselves in an enviable position. They were tired and exhausted and were suffering from the scarcity of provisions. The approaching combined armies of Bijapur and Golcunda made Murad still more anxious, particularly when he realised that on their arrival Chand Bibi would meekly submit to them. He therefore, decided to open negotiations for peace and this work was entrusted to Sayyid Murtaza.[131] The Mughal plenipotentiaries included Khan Khanan, Mir Muhammad Zaman Rizvi Mashhadi, Shahbaz Khan, and Shah Bahram Astrabadi, whereas among the representatives of the Nizam Shahis mention should be made of Afzal Khan, entitled Changez Khan, Wakil and Peshwa of the kingdom.[132] The Mughals demanded the cession of Berar and Daultabad but after much discussion it was agreed that only Berar would satisfy the invaders.[133] Accordingly peace was concluded. The Mughals recognised the claims of Bahadur Nizam Shah as the ruler of the Nizam Shahi Kingdom under the suzerainty of the Emperor Akbar and Chand Bibi agreed to cede Berar. Prince Murad soon after the conclusion of peace raised the siege of the Ahmadnagar fort and retreated towards Berar without giving battle to the allied forces which had arrived near Ahmadnagar (19th March, 1596).[134]

**Peace concluded**

After the arrival of the allied armies of Bijapur Golcunda which encamped at Pathardi near Ahmadnagar, Chand Bibi found herself in awkward situation. Luckily for her Ikhlas Khan professed his loyalty towards her and joined her service along with his supporters and dependants, abandoning his protege Miran Shah Ali who fled to Bijapur again.[135] But Mian Manjhu had not yet given up his ambition or his projects. He pressed the claims of Ahmad Shah.[136] Upon this Abhang Khan closed the gates of the fort against him, sent for Bahadur from the fortress of Jond and proclaimed him king of the Nizam Shahi kingdom.[137]. Further, Chand Bibi obtained help from her nephew Ibrahim Adil Shah II in suppressing the commotion created by Mian Manjhu, who in the end was compelled to renounce the politics of Ahmadnagar and to retire to Bijapur.[138] In this way by sheer dint of her merit, diplomacy and firmness Chand Bibi succeeded in liquidating the influence of two prominent nobles and the claims of their respective proteges.

After peace had been restored, Chand Bibi appointed Muhammad Khan in whom she reposed all her confidence as Wakil and Peshwa of the kingdom.[139] But like many other of his predecessors, he too began to gather power into his hands, appointing his own relatives to high posts and excluding other competent persons from the administration. And when he put under arrest Abhang Khan and Shamshir Khan, the Regent, she in her helplessness and alarm again appealed to her nephew Ibrahim Adil Shah II for intervention.[140] The latter sent Suhail Khan to set the matters right in Ahmadnagar.[141] When he reached there, the Peshwa refused to allow him to enter the fort, which was soon after invested by the Adil Shahi forces.[142] In despair Muhammad Khan appealed for help to Khan Khanan, a step which made him odious in the eyes of the people and which resulted in his imprisonment.[143] Chand Bibi's authority was restored. She released Abhang Khan and appointed him Peshwa, whereafter the Adil Shahi army returned to Bijapur.

But Suhail Khan loitered in the Nizam Shahi country, in the hope of finding some pretext to measure swords with the Mughals. The new Peshwa Abhang Khan was equally anxious to recover Berar. But Chand Bibi restrained him, till at length, a cause of war with the Mughals had been found out. It was alleged that they had broken the terms of the recent treaty by making unauthorised enchroachments upon the Nizam Shahi territory. Adil Shah and Qutb Shah readily joined the anti-Mughal alliance and their armies encamped at Sonpat.[145]

But the Mughals, on their part, had their own grievances against Nizam Shah. His men had not evacuated Berar peacefully. On the contrary they had organised a force of about 10,000 horsemen to harass them. Indeed the Mughal position had been further weakened by the withdrawal of Shahbaz Khan to Malwa, without the permission of Prince Murad and the jealousy and rivalry rampant among the Mughal officers. Prince Murad became anxious when he saw the enemy encamped in full strength and ready to open the fight. He consulted his advisers and they told him to hold the ground in any case whatsoever.

Soon after, Muhammad Ali Beg, S. Daulat, Itibar Khan, Wafadar Khan, Afzal Tolaki, Shir Afghan, Mir Sharif Gilani Md. Khan, Ali Khan, Mir Nizam, Qadir Quli Khan Khokar, Islam Khan, with men 20,000 under the command of Shahrukh Mirza and Khan Khanan supported by Raja Ali Khan marched to fight the Daccanis.[146] They halted on the southern bank of the Godavari near the town of Sonpat. The rival armies faced each other for a fortnight during which minor skirmishes took place daily.[147] In this interval the Mughal officers obtained complete information about the disposition of enemy's forces and then they opened the attack on February 5th 1597 A.D. A grim battle was fought in the field of Asthi in which the Mughals suffered heavy casualities. Among them who died fighting was Raja Ali Khan the rular of Khandesh. In the evening the rival armies separated from each other in suspense and anxiety as what would follow next. At the night Suhail Khan renewed the attack, broke the right and the left wings of the Mughals and drove them towards Shahpur.[148]

**Battle of Asthi**

When Sadiq Muhammad Khan heard of the disaster which had befallen the imperial army, he decided to take away Prince Murad from the Daccan.[149] But Khan Khanan remained firm and resolved to attack the enemy again. Meanwhile the Daccanis plundered and seized much booty and with it retired to their strongholds. But Suhail Khan being puffed up with his recent success remained in the field. Next morning Khan Khanan was surprised to find himself face to face with the enemy, who commanded an army three or four times larger than his own [150] Khan Khanan in despair made overture for peace, but Suhail Khan declined and opened fire on the Mughals. A severe action took place and Khan Khanan was hemmed in from all sides.[151] The Mughals fought with great courage. Suhail Khan also displayed his prodigious valour in the field. But the battle took a sudden turn, when Suhail Khan was severely wounded and fell from his horse.[152] His followers took him away from the field towards Naldurg.

The flight of the Bijapuri general decided the fate of his followers who overtaken by panic fled. The Mughals were so much tired that no pursuit was made of the enemy. Khan Khanan now despatched a large part of his army to reduce the forts of Narlnala and Gawilgarh in Berar, while he himself encamped at Galna.[153]

In this way Khan Khanan succeeded in retrieving the honour of the Mughal army and making himself master of the situation. When Prince Murad asked him to propose a scheme for the reduction of Ahmadnagar, he declined to do it on the ground that it would be a folly to undertake the venture before consolidating the imperial hold in Berar. Thus the Mughal operations in the Daccan came to a stop because of disagreement between Prince Murad and Khan Khanan. Shortly after occurred the death of Sadiq Muhammad Khan. This was followed by the recall of Khan Khanan to the court at the instance of the Prince.[154]

The death of Sadiq Muhammad Khan and the recall of Khan Khanan was a blessing for the Nizam Shahis.[155] Although they maintained their pressure on the Mughal outposts, they lost the forts of Lohgarh, Gawilgarh, Mankar, Kherla, Nasik, Abugharh, Batiala, Taltam, Situnda and Mahur.[156] This was due to the lack of support from the headquarters, where serious rivalry had broken out between Chand Bibi and Abhang Khan.[157] She closed the gates of the fort on him, asking him to transact the state business from the outside. Soon after Ibrahim Adil Shah II sent Rafiuddin Shirazi to effect reconciliation between the two. But Chand Bibi remained firm in her attitude, refusing to admit Abhang Khan in the fort saying that she would prefer to be a slave of the Timurides rather than a dependant of Abhang Khan.[158]

The absence of any Mughal general of reputation and experience, encouraged Abhang Khan to start the offensive. Accordingly, he sent a detachment of troops to recover Bir from the Mughals.[159] Upon the approach of the Daccanis, the Mughal governor of Bir, Shir Khwaja marched 12 miles forward to oppose them. In the skirmish that followed, he was wounded, his party was defeated and he himself fled, and with great difficulty he reached Bir.[160] The Daccanis invested the place and Shir Khwaja appealed for relief to Abul

Fazl who immediately sent reinforcements to him.[161]

On Feb. 4th, 1598 A.D. died Abdulla Khan Uzabeg the terror of Central Asia, which relieved the Mughal Emperor and terminated his thirteen years of sojourn in the western provinces. Now he could turn his attention to the Daccan problem which had assumed serious proportions. After the recall of Khan Khanan, Abul Fazl had been sent to reorganise the affairs there, with instructions to send back Prince Murad and to submit a comprehensive report on the situation based on his personal observation.[162] When he arrived in the Daccan he found the ruler of Khandesh, Bahadur Khan, reluctant to support the Mughal cause and since the death his son Rustam Khan in Nov. 1598 A.D. to drown his grief, Prince Murad had taken to excessive drinking, which had brought on him an attack of epilepsy and chronic dyspepsia. Unable to bear the disgrace of having been recalled to the court, inspite of his serious illness Prince Murad setout to conquer Ahmadnagar. On his way he died on May 20th 1599 A.D. near Dihrni on the banks of Purna, forty miles from Daultabad.[163]

Abul Fazl applied himself whole heartedly to his work, without caring for the indifferent attitude of Bahadur Khan, the ruler of Khandesh and the laziness of the Mughal officers posted in the Daccan. He opened correspondence with Chand Bibi who, being much distracted by the affairs at the capital, had resolved to accept the Mughal suzerainty. He even intended to go personally to Ahmadnagar but learning that Shamshir Khan had entered Berar and that Prince Daniyal would arrive soon, he returned to his camp.[164]

On the suggestion and insistence of Abul Fazl, Emperor Akbar marched in person to the Daccan, in 1600 A.D. He occupied Burhanpur and then opened the siege of Asirgarh.[165] It having proved to be a long drawn out affair, he despatched Prince Daniyal and Khan Khanan against the fort of Ahmadnagar.[165] At this time Ahmadnagar had two governments. In the fort Chand Bibi ruled in the name of her nephew Bahadur Nizam Shah, while outside, it was Abhang Khan who managed the affairs. The latter, although many a time, had

**The fort of Ahmadnagar Besieged.**

tried to conquer the fort and seize the reins of administration from the hands of Chand Bibi yet had failed in his attempts.[167] In her distress Chand Bibi again had opened communications with Abul Fazl and had even agreed to surrender the fortress of Ahmadnagar to the Mughals on condition that they would allow her to occupy the fort of Bir.[168] But the ratification of these terms was possible only when the Mughals had driven away Abhang Khan.[169]

Upon the approach of Daniyal, Abhang Khan raised the siege of the fort and marched with 15,000 horse to check his advance by occupying the Jaipur Kotly Ghat. But the Prince took a different route, avoided the pass and marched through the village of Manuri. Finding himself outmanoeuvred and unable to resist the Mughals, Abhang Khan withdrew to Ahmadnagar. He now expressed the desire of coming to terms with Chand Bibi, but when she refused to listen to his overtures, in sheer disappointment he fled to Junnar.[170] The Mughals reached the fort without meeting any opposition, laid siege to it and commenced mining the walls.[171]

**Chand Bibi Murdered.**

Chand Bibi was fully aware of the inability of the garrison to withstand the Mughal onslaught, particularly when the Mughal Emperor himself was within a short distance. But still for several months the siege of the fort dragged on, even though she was ready to abide by the proposals she had made to Abul Fazl. But the officers in whom, she had faith were against peace and they wanted to stir up strife. In the last resort she turned for advice to Jita Khan or Hamid Khan, a eunuch and discussed the matter with him. The latter suggested that they should fight and defend the fort against the Mughals until their last breath. But she rejected the suggestion and decided to surrender the fortress to the enemy on condition that they guaranteed security of life and property of the garrison and allow her to retire to Junnar with the young king. Disagreeing with her, Hamid Khan ran into the streets of the city shouting and announcing that Chand Bibi was in secret league with the Mughals and that she intended to hand over the fort to them. The excited mob headed by him rushed into her private apartments and put her to death.[172]

Thus ended the life of a woman who in her life time had fought hard to save the honour of two kingdoms and two families. She was a contemporary of Queen Elizabeth, quite a match to her in ability and political talent. The kingdom was almost as large as England. She not only excelled in boldness, valour and courage, but in modesty, generosity and in beauty also. If the slave kings of Delhi were proud of their Raziah, the Mughals of their Nurjahan and Mumtaz Mahal, the Nizam Shahis could justifiably be pround of their Chand Bibi. "So great was the love she inspired that the peasants of the Western hills refused for many years to believe that she was dead. She had escaped they said, through an underground passage and was hiding in some deep fold of the Syhadri mountains. When the time will come, she would again reveal herself drive the Mughals across the Vindhyas and bring back once more the golden years of Ahmadnagar".

With her death, died the spirit of her troops. Confusion overtook the garrison which rendered resistence impossible. Hamid Khan with the help of Itibar Khan, Mir Baqi and Haji Muhammad Khan tried to defend the fort, but the Mughals by this time had completed the mines and filled up the ditch. On 18th August 1600 A.D. the mines were exploded. The Laila tower with seventy yards of the wall was blown up. Soon after, the Mughals delivered a vigorous assault, entered the fort, occupied and massacred, about 15,000 of the garrison, including young and old, women and children. The titular King Bahadur Nizam Shah was taken prisoner. Besides the treasures, valuable jewels, embroidered articles, a noble library fell into the hands of the victors.[173]

After the fort had been occupied, Bahadur Nizam Shah with all the children of both the sexes of the royal family, was sent to Emperor Akbar at Burhanpur, wherefrom he was escorted to Gwalior to be confined into the fort. His reign lasted for three years only and he passed the rest of his life behind the iron bars.[174]

Although the power and prestige of the Nizam Shahi kingdom of Ahmadnagar had gone to pieces, but in existence it did not completely disappear. The city no doubt lost its former glory and greatness, its splendour and magnificence in which it had once rivalled the famous cities of Cairo and Baghdad. Like other towns of Northern India it became an ordinary town and its capital constituted a separate suba of the Mughal empire. But the occupation of the fort did not mean the conquest of the Kingdom. It was still far from being completely subdued or wiped off from the political map of the Daccan. Most of it passed into the hands of ambitious, brave and daring, influential and powerful Nizam Shahi nobles, who wielded unlimited authority within their respective jursidictions and offerred stiff resistence to the Mughals even though there was no government, no king, no unity among them.

---

*Notes and References* :

1. Burhan-i-Maasir (I.A. 1923) pp. 160; Ferishta Briggs. III, pp. 270; Tabqat-i-Akbari III, pp. 72; Muntakhab-ul-Lubab, pp. 225;
2. Burhan-i-Maasir (I.A. 1923) pp. 160; Ferishta, Briggs. III, pp. 270-71; Tabqat-i-Akbari III, pp. 73; Muntakhab-ul-Lubab, III, pp. 225;
3. Burhan-i-Maasir (I.A. 1923) pp. 160; Muntakhab-ul-Lubab, III, pp. 225; Ferishta, Briggs. III, pp. 270-71;
4. Burhan-i-Maasir (I.A. 1923); pp. 160;
5. Burhan-i-Maasir (I.A. 1923) pp. 161; Ferishta, Briggs. III, pp. 271; Muntakhab-ul-Lubab III, pp. 225;
6. Burhan-i-Maasir (I,A. 1923) pp. 161; According to Ferishta Husain II imprisoned Mirza Khan on suspicion but released him and restored him to favour—Ferishta, Briggs. III, pp. 271; Muntakhab-ul-Lubab, III. pp. 271;
7. Burhan-i-Maasir (I.A. 1923) pp. 161;
8. Ferishta, Briggs. III, pp. 271; Muntakhab-ul-Lubab III pp. 226;
9. Burhan-i-Maasir (I.A. 1923) pp. 250; Tabqat-i-Akbari III, pp. 72-73;
10. Mirza Khan became intimate with Khan Khanan and asked him to cultivate friendship with Ankas Khan (Bangash Khan) to invite him to a dinner and put an end to his life, so that he might be removed from king's favour. Although Khan Khanan acted on his advice, but instead of putting him to death, passed the whole night in pleasure and gaiety with him. Being enraged at the foolish conduct of his friend Khan Khanan, Mirza Khan reported the whole affair to the king in order to gain his lost favour. But the king suspecting his evil designs, sent for Khan Khanan and enquired him of the truth. The silence of Khan Khanan confirmed the treacherous designs of Mirza Khan and henceforward bitter hostilities arose between them. Both Ankas Khan and Mirza began to endeavour to encompass each other's fall. Soon after, Ankas Khan was again restored to royal favour and became a tool of the king to put Mirza Khan to death.
11. Ferishta, Briggs. III pp. 272;
12. Ibid, pp. 272;
13. Ibid, pp. 272;
14. Burhan-i-Maasir (I.A. 1923) pp. 250; Ferishta, Briggs. III pp. 272; Tabqat-i-Akbari, III pp. 73;
15. Ibid.
16. Ibid.
17. Ibid.

18. Ibid.

19. Ferishta, Briggs. III pp. 272; Tabqat-i-Akbari III, pp. 73; Muntakhab-ul-Lubab III pp. 227;

20. Ferishta, Briggs. III pp. 272; Muntakhab-ul-Lubab III, pp. 227;

21. Ferishta, Briggs. III pp. 273; Muntakhab-ul-Lubab III, pp. 227;

22. Ibid.

23. Ibid.

24. Ferishta, Briggs. III pp. 273; Burhan-i-Maasir (I.A. 1923) pp. 252; Tabqat-i-Akbari III, pp. 73; Muntakhab-ul-Lubab III, pp. 227-28:

25. Akbar Nama III pp. 820; Tabqat-i-Akbari III pp. 73-74 Muntakhab-ul-Lubab III, pp. 228;

26. Ferishta, Briggs. III pp. 273; Tabqat-i-Akbari III pp. 75; Maasir-ul-Umra, I pp. 113-14;

27. Burhan-i-Maasir (I.A. 1923) pp. 254; Muntakhab-ul-Lubab III pp. 229;

28. Burhan-i-Maasir (I.A. 1923) pp. 254-55; Ferishta, Briggs. III pp. 274; Tabqat-i-Akbari III pp. 74; Muntakhab-ul-Lubab III, pp. 228; According to Abul Fazl, 3,000 Iranians and Turanians were put to death. Akbar Nama III pp. 821;

29. Ferishta, Briggs. III pp. 274; Tabqat-i-Akbari III, pp. 74; Muntakhab-ul-Lubab III pp. 229-30; Sayyid Ali has also related in a similar manner, the practice of general massacre. He says, "In those evil days the custom of general massacre and the general plundering became too rife in the city and kingdom of Ahmadnagar. That it was thought that peace and security had fled from the world; while those who had formerly held their heads as high as the heavens in their pride were humbled to dust and chaste virgins, who had never shown their faces to Sun or to the Moon were dragged by the hair of their head into the bazar among the drunken men. Buildings which stood erect to heaven, now bowed their heads as those ashamed and the palaces, buildings, and gardens of the foreigners were destroyed"—see, Burhan-i-Maasir (I.A. 1923) pp. 255;

30. Ferishta, Briggs. III pp. 275;

31. Burhan-i-Maasir (I.A. 1923) pp. 257; Ferishta, Briggs. III pp. 277; Muntakhab-ul-Lubab III, pp. 230;

32. Burhan-i-Maasir (I.A. 1923) pp. 257;

33. Ibid.

34. Burhan-i-Maasir (I.A. 1923) pp. 257; Ferishta, Briggs. III pp. 217; Muntakhab-ul-Lubab III, pp. 230.

35. Ferishta, Briggs. III pp. 277;

36. Ibid.

37. Burhan-i-Maasir (I.A. 1923) pp. 257;

38. Ibid.

39. Ibid.

40. Ibid.

41. Ferishta, Briggs. III pp. 278; Burhan-i-Maasir (I.A. 1923) pp. 258; Muntakhab ul-Lubab III pp. 231;

42. Burhan-i-Maasir (I.A. 1923) pp. 253; Ferishta, Briggs. III, pp. 278; Tabqat-i-Akbari III, pp. 83; Muntakhab-ul-Lubab III, pp. 231;

43. Ibid.

44. Ferishta, Briggs. III pp. 279; Tabqat-i-Akbari III, pp. 75-76; Basatin-us-Salatin pp. 200-201; Akbar Nama III pp. 821; Maasir-i-Rahimi II pp. 423; Muntakhab-ul-Lubab III pp. 232;

45. Ibid.

46. Ibid.

47. Akbar Nama III pp. 859;

48. Salabat Khan had begged permission from Nizam Shah to be allowed to proceed to his country, so that he could breath his last there. Jamal Khan granted his request, but at the same time requested Raja Ali Khan to persuade him to return to Ahmadnagar. While these negotiations were in progress Burhan II wrote to Salabat Khan II asking him to extend his sup-

port to him, but he preferred to remain loyal to the throne. At Ahmadnagar he was received favourably, with honour and dignity but being an old man of seventy he requested Jamal Khan to permit him to retire from the royal service, so that he may be enabled to finish uncompleted buildings at Tisgaon. Taking into consideration his loyal and devoted services, Jamal Khan complied with his every request and bestowed on him the town of Tisgaon. Henceforward, Salabat Khan, busied himself with completing the buildings and laying out the gardens for which he had an extraordinary aptitude. Some time after, he fell ill and his health began to decline rapidly . He came from there to the town of Bhinagar, repopulated it and 'breathed his last here in 1589 A.D. at the advanced age of seventy years. He was buried in the tomb, which he had built during his ministry on hills of Shah Dongar, lying to the South of Ahmadnagar.

In short it must be stated that Salabat Khan II was a born warrior, a general, a statesman, and an administrator, who left no stone unturned to introduce beneficial reforms in the kingdom and to improve the machinery of the Nizam Shahi government. Himself being a man of learning, he patronised poets, like Malik Qummni, Zahuri, Sairafi and many others. Like an accomplished scholar, he himself composed poems of no mean order. During his regime, education was promoted and a number of works were written. He has left behind him, the most eloquent, beautiful monumental pieces of architecture, which show his keen interest in architecture also—Burhan-i-Maasir (I.A. 1923) pp. 26; Ferishta, Briggs. III, pp. 279;

49. Akbar Nama III pp. 859; Tabqat-i-Akbari III, pp. 75;

50. Ferishta, Briggs. III pp. 279-80; Tabqat-i-Akbari III, pp. 76; Akbar Nama III pp. 891; Maasir-i-Rahimi II pp. 424; Basatin-us-Salatin pp. 201-4; Burhan-i-Maasir (I.A. 1923) pp. 287; Muntakhab-ul-Lubab III p.. 234;

51. Ferishta, Briggs. III pp. 280; Muntakhab-ul-Lubab III pp. 234;

52. Burhan-i-Maasir (I.A. 1923) pp. 287;

53. Burhan-i-Maasir (I.A. 1923) pp. 287; Ferishta, III pp. 28; Basatin-us-Salatin pp. 202-4; Akbar Nama III pp. 892; Tabqat-i-Akbari III pp. 76;

54. Basatin-us-Salatin pp. 204; Ferishta, Briggs. III pp. 280; Akbar Nama III pp. 892; Elliot and Dowson Vol. VI pp. 87; Muntakhab-ul-Lubab III pp. 234-35;

55. Burhan-i-Maasir (I.A. 1923) pp. 290; Basatin-us-Salatin pp. 204, 205, 210; Ferishta, Briggs. III pp. 280-81; Akbar Nama III pp. 892-93; Elliot and Dowson Vol. VI pp. 87; Tabqat-i-Akbari III, pp. 75-79; Muntakhab-ul-Lubab III, pp. 235-36; Oriental Biographical Dictionary pp. 185;

56. Burhan-i-Maasir (I.A. 1923) pp. 290; Ferishta, Briggs. III, pp. 283; Tabqat-i-Akbari III pp. 75. 776. 77; Muntakhab-ul-Lubab III pp. 236;

57. Akbar Nama III pp. 709, 882; Maasir-i-Rahimi II pp. 425; Muntakhab-ul-Tawarikh, pp. 390;

58. Akbar Nama III pp. 909, 982;

59. Akbar Nama III pp. 982; Elliot and Dowson Vol. VI, pp. 88, 91; Maasir-i-Rahimi II pp. 425; Muntakhab-ul-Tawarikh pp. 390, 403

60. Ferishta, Briggs. III pp. 284; Muntakhab-ul-Lubab III pp. 236,

61. Ferishta, Briggs. III pp. 284; Basatin-us-Salatin pp. 213-14; Muntakhab-ul-Lubab III, pp. 237;

62. Ferishta, Briggs. III pp. 284, 170; Basatin-us-Salatin pp. 213-14 Muntakhab-ul-Lubab III pp. 237;

63. Ferishta, Briggs. III pp. 284; Basatin-us-Salatin pp. 214; Muntakhab-ul-Lubab III pp. 238;

64. Ferishta, Briggs, III pp. 284; Basatin-us-Salatin pp. 214; Muntakhab-ul-Lubab II pp. 238;

65. Ferishta, Briggs. III pp. 171-71; Basatin-us-Salatin pp. 215; Muntakhab-ul-Lubab III pp. 238;

66. Ferishta, Briggs. III pp. 170-71; Basatin-us-Salatin pp. 215; Muntakhab-ul-Lubab III pp. 238;

67. Ferishta, Briggs. II pp. 171-72; Basatin-us-Salatin pp. 217; Muntakhab-ul-Lubab III pp. 238;

68. Ferishta, Briggs. III pp. 174-75; Basatin-us-Salatin pp. 218-19; Muntakhab-ul-Lubab III, pp. 239;

69. Ferishta, Briggs. III pp. 177-87, 286; Basatin-us-Salatin pp. 221; Muntakhab-ul-Lubab III pp. 242;

70. Ferishta, Briggs. III pp. 287; Basatin-us-Salatin pp. 227; Muntakhab-ul-Lubab III pp. 243;

71. Ferishta, Briggs. III pp. 287; Muntakhab-ul-Lubab III pp. 243;

72. Oriental Biographical Dictionary pp. 111; According to Abul Fazl, Burhan Nizam Shah II died on 6th April 1595 A.D. He also mentions that he was poisoned to death. Akbar Nama III pp. 1025; Badaoni says that he was put to death; Ferishta on page 287 wrongly mentions that Burhan died on May 5th 1594 A.D. after a reign of four months and sixteen days. Ferishta, Briggs. III pp. 287;

73. Ferishta, Briggs. III pp. 184; Basatin-us-Salatin pp. 227; Muntakhab-ul-Lubab III pp. 243;

74. Ferishta, Briggs. III pp. 184-186; Basatin-us-Salatin pp. 228-29; Akbar Nama III (Elliot and Dowson Vol. VI) pp. 91-92; Muntakhab-ul-Lubab III pp. 244-45;

75. According to Ferishta, after the war of succession which took place during the closing days of Burhan Nizam Shah I, his eldest son Husain Nizam Shah I ascended the throne; while his other brothers fled from the kingdom in fear and alarm. During the later days of Murtaza Nizam Shah's reign, Shah Tahir, an imposter appeared in Ahmadnagar giving out that he was the son of Khudabanda, the son of Burhan I who had died in Bengal. It being impossible to ascertain the truth and his free movements might cause trouble, Salabat Khan II imprisoned him in a fort, where he died, leaving behind him a son named Ahmad. Subsequently when the enquiries about Khudabanda were made from Burhan II who had taken refuge at the Mughal court, he said that his uncle Khudabanda died in his own house and that Shah Tahir was an imposter. As such his son Ahmad could have no claim on the throne—Ferishta, Briggs. III pp. 293-95 Muntakhab-ul-Lubab III pp. 246;

76. Ferishta, Briggs. III pp. 293; Basatin-us-Salatin pp. 233; Muntakhab-ul Lubab III pp. 246-47;

77. Ferishta, Briggs. III pp. 293; Basatin-us-Salatin pp. 223; Muntakhab-ul-Lubab III pp. 246-47;

78. Ferishta, Briggs. III pp. 293; Muntakhab-ul-Lubab III pp. 247;

79. Ferishta, Briggs. III pp. 295;

80. Ibid, pp. 296;

81. Ibid, pp. 296;

82. Ibid, pp. 296;

83. Ibid, pp. 296;

84. Ibid, pp. 296;

85. Ferishta, Briggs. III pp. 296; Basatin-us-Salatin pp. 223; Iqbalnama-i-Jahangiri pp. 439-40; Muntakhab-ul-Tawarikh pp. 416; Muntakhab-ul-Lubab III pp. 247;

86. Ferishta, Briggs. III pp. 297; Basatin-us-Salatin pp. 233; Muntakhab-ul-Lubab III pp. 247;

87. Burhan-i-Maasir (I.A. 1923) pp. 234;

88. Burhan-i-Maasir (I. 1898); Ferishta, Briggs. III, pp. 297; Muntakhab-ul-Lubab III pp. 248;

89. Ferishta, Briggs. III pp. 297-8; Muntakhab-ul-Lubab III, pp. 248;

90. Ferishta, Briggs. III pp. 297; Burhan-i-Maasir (I.A. 1923) pp. 280, 299; (I.A. 1898) pp. 236; Akbar Nama III pp. 1045-46; Iqbalnama-i-Jahangiri pp. 445-47; (Elliot and Dowson) Vol. VI, pp. 92-93; Mun takhab-ul-Tawarikh pp. 416; Muntakhab-ul-Lubab III pp. 248-49;

91. Ferishta, Briggs. III pp. 298; Burhan-i-Maasir (I.A. 1898) pp. 268-9; Muntakhab-ul-Lubab III pp. 249;

92. Ferishta, Briggs. III pp. 298; Muntakhab-ul-Lubab III pp. 249;

93. Burhan-i-Maasir (I.A. 1898) pp. 269; Muntakhab-ul-Lubab III, pp. 249;

94. Burhan-i-Maasir (I.A. 1898) pp. 269-70; Ferishta, Briggs. III pp. 298-99; Muntakhab-ul-Lubab III pp. 249;

95. Iqbalnama-i-Jahangiri pp. 448; Muntakhab-ul-Lubab III, pp. 249;

96. Ferishta, Briggs. III pp. 299; Muntakhab-ul-Lubab III, 250; Akbar Nama III pp. 1046;

97. Ferishta, Briggs. III pp. 299; Muntakhab-ul-Lubab III, pp. 250;

98. Burhani-i-Maasir (I.A. 1898) pp. 281; Ferishta, Briggs. III, pp. 299; Muntakhab-ul-Lubab III pp. 250;

99. Ferishta, Briggs. III pp. 299-300; Akbar Nama III pp. 1047; Iqbalnama pp. 447; Muntakhab-ul-Lubab III pp. 250-51;

100. Burhan-i-Maasir (I.A. 1898), pp. 281; Ferishta, Briggs. III, pp. 300;

101. Burhan-i-Maasir (I.A. 1898) pp. 281; Ferishta, Briggs. III, pp. 300; Basatin-us-Salatin, pp. 241-42;

102. Burhan-i-Maasir (I.A. 1898) pp. 281-82; Ferishta, Briggs. III, pp. 300; Basatin-us-Salatin pp. 241; Akbar Nama III, pp. 1046-47; Iqbal-nama-i-Jahangiri pp. 447; Maasir-i-Rahimi, pp. 582; Maasir-ul-Umra I pp. 54;

103. On the eastern side of the fort, the Prince himself remained with his special Gujarati forces. The southern side which was opposite the village of Shaitanpur and towards the Farah Baksh Garden, was entrusted to the charge of Khan Khanan. The western side of the fortress which as towards the city of Ahmadnagar and had the principal gate of the fortress, was given to the charge of Shahbaz Khan and Mirza Shah Rukh; while the northern side which as towards Burhanabad and Nimazgah was entrusted to Raja Ali Khan. From all the four sides the Mughal forces surrounded the fort and advanced batteries and entrenchments.

104. Burhan-i-Maasir (I.A. 1898) pp. 281;

105. Ibid.

106. Ibid.

107. Burhan-i-Maasir (I.A. 1898) pp. 282; Akbar Nama III, pp. 1045, 1046, 1070;

108. Burhan-i-Maasir (I.A. 1898) pp. 283; Akbar Nama III, pp. 1047;

109. Ibid.

110. Burhan-i-Maasir (I.A. 1898) pp. 284-85;

111. Ibid.

112. Ibid.

113. Ibid.

114. Ibid.

115. Burhan-i-Maasir (I.A. 1898) pp. 285; Ferishta, Briggs. III pp. 301; Muntakhab-ul-Lubab III, pp. 252;

116. Ibid.

117. Burhan-i-Maasir (I.A. 1898) pp. 285;

118. Ibid.

119. Ibid.

120. "It is surprising that with the perfection of your Highness's understanding and planning you should write such letters as this and endeavour to ruin this high dynasty. That you hastened to go forth to meet the Mughal amirs and brought them into this country is a fact which the kings of the Daccan will not forget. By the aid of God Almighty, the Mughal amirs will shortly be compelled to return, and your Highness will again be the subject to the kings of the Daccan, and take thought of your reputation and that of your kingdom"—Burhan-i-Maasir (I.A. 1898) pp. 286;

121. Burhan-i-Maasir (I.A. 1898) pp. 287; Ferishta, Briggs. III pp. 301; Akbar Nama III pp. 1048; Muntakhab-ul-Lubab III, pp. 253-54; Maasir-ul-Umra I pp. 54;

122. Burhan-i-Maasir (I.A. 1898) pp. 287-88; Ferishta, Briggs. III pp. 301-2; Muntakhab-ul-Lubab III pp. 253-54;

123. Burhan-i-Maasir (I.A. 1898) pp. 288; Ferishta, Briggs. III, pp. 301-2; Muntakhab-ul-Lubab III pp. 253-54;

124. Burhan-i-Maasir (I.A. 1898) pp. 288-89; Muntakhab-ul-Lubab III pp. 255;

125. Ibid.

126. Ibid.

127. Ibid.

128. Burhan-i-Maasir (I.A. 1898) pp. 289; Ferishta, Briggs. III pp. 303; Akbar Nama III pp. 1048; Muntakhab-ul-Lubab III, pp. 255;

129. Burhan-i-Maasir (I.A. 1898) pp. 290;

130. Burhan-i-Maasir (I.A. 1898) pp. 291; Ferishta, Briggs. III pp. 303; Iqbalnama--i-Jahangiri pp. 448; Muntakhab-ul-Lubab III pp 255;

131. Burhan-i-Maasir (I.A. 1898) pp. 291;

132. Ibid.

133. Ibid, pp. 291-94.

134. Burhan-i-Maasir (I.A. 1898), pp. 295; Ferishta, Briggs. III, pp. 303-4; Akbar Nama III, pp. 1048, Iqbalnama-i-Jahangiri, pp. 448; Maasir-ul-Umra I, pp. 54, Muntakhab-ul-Lubab III, pp. 255-56.

135. Ferishta, Briggs III, pp. 304; Muntakhab-ul-Lubab III, pp. 256.

136. Ibid.

137. Ibid.

138. Ibid.

139. Ferishta, Briggs III, pp. 305-6; Muntakhab-ul-Lubab III, pp. 256.

140. Ibid.

141. Ibid.

142. Ibid.

143. Ferishta, Briggs. III, pp. 307; Muntakhab-ul-Lubab, III, pp. 257.

144. Ibid.

145. Ferishta, Briggs. III, pp. 307; Iqbalnama-i-Jahangiri, pp. 450-51; Muntakhab-ul-Lubab III, pp. 257.

146. Akbar Nama III, pp. 1070, Muntakhab-ul-Lubab III, pp. 257.

147. Akbar Nama III, pp. 1070; Muntakhab-ul-Lubab III, pp. 257.

148. Ferishta, Briggs. III, pp. 308; Akbar Nama III, pp. 1070; Elliot and Dowson Vol. VI, pp. 95-96; Faizi Sarhindi's Akbar Nama (Elliot and Dowson) Vol. VI, pp. 131, Iqbalnama-i-Jahangiri pp. 450; Muntakhab-ul-Lubab III, pp. 257-58.

149. Ferishta, Briggs III, pp. 308; Akbar Nama III, pp. 1071.

150. Ferishta, Briggs III, pp. 309; Muntakhab-ul-Lubab III, pp. 159-60.

151. Ibid.

152. Ibid.

153. Ibid.

154. Ibid.

155. Akbar Nama III, pp. 1111, 1115, 1123, 1154, Elliot and Dowson Vol. VI, pp. 97, Iqbalnama-i-Jahangiri, pp. 1458; 460-488; Maasir-ul-Umra I, pp. 120.

156. Ferishta, Briggs III, pp. 310, Iqbalnama-i-Jahangiri, pp. 458, Maasir-ul-Umra I, pp. 54-56.

157. Ferishta, Briggs III, pp. 310; Muntakhab-ul-Lubab II, pp. 260;

158. Ferishta, Briggs III, pp. 310, Basatin-us-Salatin, pp. 238;

159. Ferishta, Briggs III, pp. 310.

160. Ibid.

161. Ibid, pp. 311.

162. Akbar Nama III, pp. 1142-43; Iqbalnama-i-Jahangiri, pp. 458; Maasir-ul-Umra I, pp. 119-20.

163. Ferishta Briggs III, pp. 311; Akbar Nama III, pp. 1126; Elliot and Dowson Vol. VI, pp. 96-97; Muntakhab-ul-Tawarikh Vol. II, pp. 391-92; Tuzuk-i-Jahangiri (R & B), Vol. I, pp. 34.

164. Iqbalnama-i-Jahangiri, pp. 465.

165. Ferishta, Briggs III, pp. 311; Akbar Nama III, pp. 1146, 1163; 1168; 1191; Muntakhab-ul-Lubab III, pp. 260-61.

166. Basatin-us-Salatin, pp. 254; Akbar Nama III, pp. 1143-44; Tuzuk-i-Jahangiri (R & B) Vol. I, pp. 89; Maasir-ul-Umra I, pp. 56; 120.

167. Ferishta, Briggs. III, pp. 312.

168. Akbar Nama III, pp. 1144.

169. Ferishta, Briggs III, pp. 312; Akbar Nama III, pp. 1157; Muntakhab-ul-Lubab III, pp. 262.

170. Ferishta, Briggs III, pp. 312; Akbar Nama III, pp. 1157;

171. Ferishta, Briggs III, pp. 312; Muntakhab-ul-Lubab III, pp. 262. Describing the siege of the Ahmadnagar fort, Manucci says, "Akbar went against Princess Chand Bibi, "Lady Moon." She also was a Muhamedan she defended herself with great vigour, but was obliged to surrender the fortress for want of provisions, she was so grieved at seeing herself depoiled of her dignities that she made up her mind not to allow her wealth to fall into the hands of Akbar. With this idea, she gave orders that all the gold she had, should be melted and made into the cannon balls. Upon this she had words engraved to the effect that the ball belong to any one who found it, that no one had the right to take it, by force from the finder, adding other words of malediction against him who acted otherwise. The cannons were loaded with these balls and they were discharged in all directions". Storia de Mogor, pp. 122.

The author of "A new history of the East Indies", wrongly states that "Akbar enrolled her (Chand Bibi) in the number of his wife; he treated her always as a Queen or rather he considered her for a long time as the favourite of the Sultaness", See pp. 190.

172. Ferishta, Briggs III, pp. 312; Manucci, while mentioning the Deccan campaign refers to Chand Bibi. He says that "After the fortress was taken, Akbar fell in love with her beauty and transferred her to his own palace". Such a statement can not be believed—See, Storia De Mogor.

173. Ferishta, Briggs III, pp. 313, Akbar Nama III pp. 1157. Elliot and Dowson Vol. VI, pp. 99-100, Faizi Sarhindi's Akbar nama (Elliot and Dowson) Vol. VI, pp. 195; Iqbalnama-i-Jahangiri pp. 465-70.

174. Ferishta, Briggs III, pp. 313; Akbar Nama III, pp. 1161; while praising the noble Queen, Meadows Taylor writes, "Few in England know that the contemporary of our Queen Elizabeth, in the Deccan kingdom was a woman of equal ability of political talent, of equal, though in a different sense, educated and accomplished, who ruled over a realm as large a population as large and rich as England, a women who surrounded by jealous enemies preserved by her own personal valour and endurance, her kingdom from destruction and partition, who through all temptations and exercise of absolute power, was at once simple, generous, frank and merciful as she was, Chaste, virtuous, religious and charitable—one who among all the women of India, stands out as jewel without flaw and beyond price", See Gribble "History of the Dakhan", pp. 222-23.

## CHAPTER VII

# REVIVAL OF THE KINGDOM

Although the fort of Ahmadnagar, the districts adjacent to the fort of Daultabad and Berar had been occupied by the Mughals, strictly speaking the Nizam Shahi kingdom was still far from being annexed into the Mughal empire. It took almost another forty years to complete its extinction. The more did the imperialists mobilise their forces into the hilly and rugged soil of the Daccan, the greater became the enthusiasm of the Daccanis to repel them. Urged by the spirit of local patriotism, the Marathas and the Muslims joined hands to throw back the tide of Mughal aggression. The ensuing struggle represented an attempt on their part to preserve their autonomy in particular and the separate political entity of the Daccan in general. Equally keen was the urge of the invaders who were actuated by the desire of ruling the entire peninsula from the Himalayas to the Cape Commorin.

The idea of offering opposition to the Mughals gained ground under the leadership of Malik Ambar, an Abyssinian adventurer of the Nizam Shahi kingdom. Very soon he gathered round his person the Marathas and the Muslim alike, formed them into an organic body, trained them in a new method of warfare, infused in them a new spirit and arrayed them against the enemy. This was the happy beginning of his chequered career and the history of the next twenty years of the Nizam Shahi kingdom, may be said to be a record of the heroic activities of one individual, who rose equal to the occasion, fought valiantly against the enemy and restored and revived the almost effete Nizam Shahi kingdom.

Ambar Chapu, Ambar Jui and Malik Ambar as he was commonly known in the Daccan was born in an obscure Abyssinian family about the year 1549 A.D.[1] Like Qutbuddin Aibak, Iltutamish and Ghyasuddin Balban, who played heroic roles on the political stage of India and who were purchased in the famous slave markets, Malik Ambar

**Early life of Malik Ambar**

was also brought by his poor perents to Baghdad to be sold to Khwaja Mir Baghdadi, commonly known as Mir Qasim, one of the famous merchants of that town. Mir Qasim treated him like his own child with utmost generosity and kindness[2] Although contemporary historical material does not throw much light on his early life, parentage and education etc., it is clear enough that his fortunes took a decisive turn after his generous patron had brought him to the Daccan, which in those days was a land of luck for the venturesome. Malik Ambar was again sold to Malik Dabir styled as Changez Khan, the famous and the loyal minister of Murtaza Nizam Shah I, who had already a thousand slaves to maintain his position at the court, which was rent with party strife.[3] Chivalrous and intelligent as Malik Ambar was, within a short time he gained prominence among the other slaves of his master. Under the patronage of his wise and able benefactor, who then controlled the gear of the Nizam Shahi politics and wielded much influence at the court, Malik Ambar gained an insight into the details of military and civil administration. The death of Changez Khan proved a great shock to him, because it retarded the growth of his fortunes. He then entered into the Nizam Shahi army in the capacity of a soldier where he had another opportunity to watch closely the dark clouds gathering on the political horizon of the kingdom[4] He was enabled to visualise at close quarters the consequences of civil war and party strife. In course of time the negation of all the principles of politics shook the pillars of the kingdom and let loose the disruptive forces, which overwhelmed the integrity of the state. Add to this the constant danger of the Mughal invasion which rendered confusion worse confounded. In such circumstances Malik Ambar had to be content with a small salary which he drew by serving changing masters in various capacities.

With the outbreak of another storm in the kingdom consequent upon Mughal invasion, Malik Ambar, perhaps being disgusted and disappointed by the deplorable state of affairs in the Nizam Shahi kingdom, left for Golcunda in the hope of attaining prominence there. He then went to Bijapur entered in the Adil Shahi army, in which he held a minor rank.

Having failed to get any recognition, his surging ambition brought him back to Ahmadnagar in company of some other brave and warlike Abyssinians, who were coming to seek their fortune in the troubled atmosphere there[6]. (1596 A.D.)

At this time the Nizam Shahi kingdom was a target to the deadly blows of the party strife, bitter rivalries of the nobles and a prey to the pressure of the Mughals. Its condition had deteriorated considerably more than what it was when Ambar had left for Bijapur. Abhang Khan the Abyssinian leader who had refused to acknowledge Bahadur Nizam Shah, the candidate of Chand Sultana as king, was now in open rebellion. In order to strengthen his party and to press the claims of his protege, Ahmad Shah, he extended patronage to his tribesmen. Malik Ambar also joined his standard and was made commander of 150 horsemen.[7] He served his new master with all his ability and intelligence. On the arrival of the Mughal forces, on the invitation of Abhang Khan, Malik Ambar with his master withdrew to Junnar. But during the siege of the fort of Ahmadnagar by the invaders, he displayed much valour, by cutting off their supplies and intercepting their line of communication. When Abhang Khan agreed to join hands with Chand Sultana in offering opposition to the enemy, Malik Ambar also went with him into the fort. But during the confusion which followed, he left the fort. He gathered round him a large following and harassed the Mughals from all sides. After the conclusion of peace he was left with no other alternative but to choose a different line of action. When Khan Khanan and Prince Daniyal opened the siege of the fort, he again entered the field to harass them. He marched to the Mughal frontiers and frequently led incursions into their territory, plundering and devastating everywhere. This enhanced his military reputation. By reducing highwaymen to narrow straits he compelled them to give up their profession and enrol themselves under his banner.[8]

The fall of Ahmadnagar fort created a very favourable atmosphere for him. To secure better obedience of the local population and to strengthen his own position in the face of the Mughal aggression, he succeeded in discovering a Prince of the Nizam Shahi family in the person of Prince Ali, son of

Shah Ali and the grand son of Burhan Nizam Shah I who was living at Parenda. As Shah Ali was an old man of eighty, Malik Ambar preferred to elevate his young son to the Nizam Shahi throne. He requested Ibrahim Adil Shah II, with whom the Prince had taken refuge, to allow him to accept the crown. But Shah Ali had no faith in Ambar's words. He hesitated to comply with his proposal, refusing to stir out of Parenda, inspite of all promises of safety. To inspire confidence in the old man, Malik Ambar promised Shah Ali, to marry his own daughter to Prince Ali.

**Murtaza Nizam Shah II raised to the throne (1600 A.D.)**

Accordingly Prince Ali, came from Bijapur and the marriage was celebrated amidst pomp and magnificence and he was raised to the throne under the title of Murtaza Nizam Shah II (1600 A.D.). Malik Ambar became the Prime Minister and Wakil-ut-Saltanat of the kingdom and Parenda was fixed as the temporary capital. In a short time, by dint of his ability experience and courage Malik Ambar re-established the administration and restored law and order in those parts over which he wielded influence. Conditions thus returned to normal, which enabled the masses and the classes to live in peace and tranquility.[9]

While Malik Ambar was harassing the Mughals with his surprise attacks in one part of the kingdom, one of his future rivals named Raju Daccani or Raju *paulad* gained prominence in another quarter.

**Raju's early life.**

He was the adopted son of Munna Daccani, the Mahaldar of Saadat Khan, the Hindu minister of Burhan Nizam Shah II.[10] After the death of his father, Raju succeeded to the post of his father. Within a short time he became the chief or head of all the Mahaldars. Thereafter he was promoted to the office of Wakil and Madur-ul-Maham.[11] As chaos and confusion began to prevail in Ahmadnagar after the death of Burhan Nizam Shah II, Raju too like Malik Ambar took to wandering along with his master in the hilly tracts. While the Mughals were besieging the fort of Ahmadnagar, Saadat Khan and Haibat Khan began to deliver surprise attacks on them, harassing them by cutting off their communications. In these ventures Raju must have also helped his master.[12]

It has been related that Saadat Khan with about 3,000

horsemen cut through Khan Khanan's lines who was then supervising the siege and attempted to enter into the fort.[13] But Chand Bibi refused to allow him in, whereupon Saadat Khan retired to his jagir which was situated in Nasik and Trimbak.[14] Upon this, his followers gave up his cause and joined the Mughal service.[15] In this way the entire territory lying between Nasik and Trimbak passed into the hands of the Mughals. Saadat Khan apprehending that his property would also be seized by the enemy deemed it discreet to join them. Handing over to Raju a slice of his jagir he went over to Khan Khanan.[16] The latter enrolled him in his service. After some time, Sadat Khan requested Prince Daniyal to allow him on behalf of the imperialists, to conquer and annex the territories adjoining his jagir, which were still in the possession of the Nizam Shahis.[17] His proposal was accepted but when he marched with the Mughal forces in that direction, he was opposed by Raju who had in the meanwhile been incited by Abhang Khan to seize the territories of his master who had once been a slave of Burhan Nizam Shah II. Abhang Khan also promised to elevate him to the rank of amir at the Nizam Shahi court, if he harassed the Mughals by plundering them, saying that the, "reward to fidelity to salt is greatness. Guard carefully the territory and the forts now in your possession and try to increase them."[18] Being allured by the hopes of receiving high favours at the Nizam Shahi court Raju soon assembled eight thousand horsemen and began to harass the enemy. He compelled the Mughal army under his former master and Fathullah to retreat in disorder.[19]

On the accession of Murtaza Nizam Shah II, Raju secured a promise of safety and went to pay homage to him. On his arrival at the court, he presented to the king one elephant, twelve Turki horses and 40,000 huns in cash and kind.[20] He was enrolled into the Nizam Shahi service and for some time served as Khawas (standing behind the Nizam Shah holding a handkerchief in his hand). Being dissatisfied with the post he held, he returned to his own country. But upon his arrival there he found that his army had turned against him, and therefore, he came back to the Nizam Shahi court. After some time he complained to the king that his suspicion

**Rivalry between Raju & Ambar.**

was that Ambar was instigating the royal forces against him, with malicious intentions. Seeing a rival in the person of Raju, Malik Ambar thought it prudent to reduce his potentiality. Therefore he went to Raju's territories, won over the garrison of the several forts and occupied them. This was bitterly resented by Raju, who again turned to the king to help him against the designs of his rival. But when he came to the court, Malik Ambar arrested him in order to remove him from his way. But, soon after, Raju effected his escape recovered his jagirs and became the sworn enemy of Malik Ambar.[21]

Realising his intentions and in full appreciation of the situation Malik Ambar decided to adopt a different line of action. Raju was now openly hostile to him.[22] The pressure of the Mughals in the Daccan was increasing fast and the rulers of Bijapur and Golkunda were waiting to swallow the remanents of the fallen Nizam Shahi kingdom, unmindful of the fact that the same fate lay in store for them. In such circumstances it is not strange that Malik Ambar turned to the Mughals to exploit his friendship with them to advance his own interests. Khan Khanan took a liking for him and extended to him a helping hand, perhaps with the idea that rivalry between him and Raju would enable him to have a free hand in the Daccan. Malik Ambar came to Abul Fazl offering to be enrolled in the imperial employ but he had to return disappointed because Raja Harbans expressed doubts with regard to his future fidelity.[23]

When bitter rivalry arose between Raju and Malik Ambar, Prince Daniyal made up his mind to strike a blow at both of them. He appointed Khawajgi Fathullah to recover the territories of Saadat Khan from the hands of Raju Daccani. When Khawahgji arrived near Nasik, the Mughal forces deserted him and went over to Raju, who now became so strong that he marched towards Daultabad and seized the country up to the fort Jalna. Upon this, Prince Daniyal despatched Abul Fazl to retrieve the situation. Leaving Mir Murtaza, Wafadar Khan and Mir Hazar to protect the Mughal frontiers against the incursions of Malik Ambar, the Shaikh marched to deal with Raju. Upon the advance of the imperial army Raju fell back and Jalna was again captured by the Mughals.[24]

While the Shaikh was preoccupied with Raju, Malik Ambar made a dash into Telingana, defeated Bahadur Gilani, the Mughal commander, who had been left there with a small contingent.[25] But on the appearance of Shaikh near Jalna, he too withdrew and reappeared before the fortress of Ahmadnagar. Ali Mardan Bahadur with a contingent of Telingana troops hastened in that direction to assist Sher Khwaja, the commander of the fort of Ahmadnagar. But at Pathri he was defeated and taken prisoner by Ambar's men.[26] On receiving the report of Ambar's success over the imperial troops, Khan Khanan thought it necessary to send another contingent of troops against him. Accordingly he issued instructions to S. Abdul Rahman, the son of Shaikh Abul Fazl to leave Berar with a strong army and annex Malik Ambar's territory on the Telingana border. Abdul Rahman proceeded towards Nander to implement the order.[27]

Malik Ambar appointed Farhad Khan to lead the Abyssinian and the Daccani troops to oppose the Mughal advance and himself crossed the Godavari near Nander. He moved on further till he arrived near the river Manjiera where he laid out his camp. On the way Abdul Rahman was joined by Sher Khwaja and the combined forces arrived near Malik Ambar's camp. The rival armies took up position ready to join issues. Malik Ambar commanded the centre of his army, while Farhad Khan and Mansur Khan Habshi respectively commanded the right and the left wings. The action began after mid-day on Sunday 16th May 1601 A.D. After a severe contest the imperialists came out victorious. Ambar lost four hundred men, besides those who were wounded.[28] After this defeat Malik Ambar sued for peace. He agreed to release all the Mughal prisoners and in return was confirmed in the possession of the Sarkars of Ausa, Dharur and a part of Bir (3rd Jan. 1602).[29]

**Battle of Nander**

While Malik Ambar was busy in recuperating from the losses he had sustained in his recent defeat, Raju Daccani again appeared before the Mughals. He marched through Daultabad plundering Satara and other places which fell in his way. Abul Fazl, who was hotly chasing him, overtook him with 5,000 Mughal horsemen, defeated and put him to flight. After some time he reappeared again to plunder the Mughal camp but was again put to flight. But on this occasion 500 horse of his were seized by the victors. This drove him into wilderness for a while but he never missed an opportunity to harass the Mughals.[30]

After having reorganised his army Malik Ambar marched at the head of seven to eight thousand cavalry to recover Telingana.[31] He surprised Hamid Khan, Baz Bahadur and Bahadur-ul-Mulk and inflicted on them a crushing defeat at Manjana. It was with great difficulty that Bahudur-ul-Mulk could cross the river and effect his escape. Hamid Khan and Baz Bahadur were captured[32]. The fertile tracts of Telingana thus again passed into the hands of Malik Ambar. He now sent Farhad Khan with a contingent of troops against Sher Khwaja to wrest the fort of Ahmadnagar from him. Khan Khanan, who was then in the fort was compelled to come out and call Abul Fazl to his assistance. Upon this Farhad Khan retreated after making a few night attacks on the enemy.[33] Meanwhile Malik Ambar had collected his troops, entered the hilly region of Ausa and thence he made a dash to Bidar. Malik Barid sent his general Ibrahim against him. In engagement which followed Ibrahim was defeated and put to death; fourteen elephants fell into the hands of Malik Ambar which added much to his strength and power.[34] He then went towards Naubilas, fought with the Qutb Shahi forces and captured a few more elephants and compelled Qutb Shah to pay a large sum of money. Thereafter he returned to Telingana. As Mir Murtaza had no strength to resist Malik Ambar, the latter entered into the fort without any opposition, took possession of some districts and then despatched a body of troops to occupy the other parganas of Berar. Meanwhile Malik Barid had sent him money and made peace with him.[35]

**Telingana subdued**

Having failed to cope with Ambar and Raju, Prince Daniyal divided the conquered Mughal territory into two provinces of equal size. Khan Khanan was appointed to hold Berar, Pathri, Telingana and was entrusted with the duty of suppressing Malik Ambar; while Abul Fazl was given the charge of Ahmadnagar and the duty of putting down

Raju Deccani and other rebels.[36]

Khan Khanan in shame and anger despatched his able son Mirza Iraj with a select body of 5,000 horse to retrieve the honour.[37] Meanwhile Malik Ambar had reduced Mir Murtaza in Nander and Sher Khwaja at Jahri to utter helplessness. Mirza Iraj on his arrival effected a junction with Murtaza and Sher Khwaja and planned to attack Malik Ambar. On hearing their advance the latter retreated to Dantur and from there proceeded to Qandhar and then turned towards Nander. Farhad Khan joined him on the way with two or three thousand horse. A severe action took place between the rival armies. Malik Ambar was completely routed and wounded. He would have fallen into the hands of the enemy but for gallantry of some of his attendants who safely carried him away from the field (1602 A.D.).[38]

This heavy disaster gave a severe shock to Malik Ambar. It unmistakably pointed to the fact that his failure was the direct outcome of his rivalry with Raju Daccani. They fought between themselves and Khan Khanan reaped the advantage. Nevertheless he continued to harass the Mughals as he did with his surprise attacks in the region situated between the Telingana border to within a few miles of Bir and Ahmadnagar and forty miles west of Daultabad to within striking distance of the port of Chaul, in which he wielded popularity and influence. Similarly his rival Raju Daccani was making himself troublesome to the enemy in another part of the country, lying between Daultabad and few miles of Ahmadnagar to the frontier of Gujarat. Inspite of the fact that he repeatedly got a hammering he did not give up his activities. It is true that he was a rival of Malik Ambar but by keeping the Mughals preoccupied, he inadvertently paved the way for latter's success. In fact the rivalry between the two proved very distracting to the imperialists. It prevented them from concentrating their attention on one without affording to the other an opportunity to retrieve his lost position.[39]

Even so, it was difficult to counteract the Mughal pressure. No doubt that from the very outset Malik Ambar had posed as the saviour of the fallen Nizam Shahi kingdom but the role was not so easy to play. Internally, neither had the country as yet recovered itself from the ravages it had suffered at the hands of the enemy; nor were his resources strong enough to repel the attacks. Again, there was a group of discontented nobles which had been completely demoralised by the invaders by their military superiority and by their lavish distribution of gold. Generals, soldiers and even the common man deserted the cause of the homeland, throwing in their lot with the new comers. Their attitude was not altogether unreasonable. They had been exposed to the misery of mal-administration, religious persecutions and above all to the evil consequences of the party strife. In quest of peace and security a vast bulk of population had fled to take refuge either with the rulers of Bijapur and Golcunda or had migrated to the north. The sense of local patriotism had completely died down. Herculian efforts were needed to revive it. The task of Malik Ambar was rendered all the more difficult because his own Abyssinian followers presented a picture of a house divided against itself. Those who had a few soldiers and a little territory dreamt of establishing a small independent principality. Precisely for this reason the civil administration had gone to pieces and the military organisation had been completely shattered.

Nor was the external position in any way better. Both Bijapur and Golcunda had purchased peace with the Mughals by offering valuable presents through their ambassadors. How could they be expected to extend cooperation to the fallen Nizam Shahi house, whose existence was slowly being wiped out? On the top of it they looked upon Malik Ambar as a mere adventurer, who had yet to establish his *bonafides* and convince Qutb Shah and Adil Shah of his worth and his earnestness in favour of the fallen house.

In the midst of these conditions it is not surprising that inspite of their rivalry, Raju and Malik Ambar saw for a while eye to eye with each other. Their field of activity lay in the same region and they were exposed to the same peril and their objective was the same viz. to prop up Murtaza Nizam Shah II, to whom both of them were professing allegiance. They agreed upon to give the fort of Ausa for the king's residence and the revenue of few adjacent villages for his maintenance. They were keen to put a check on the Mughal enchroachments and to prevent the total annihilation of the kingdom. Both of them tried to harass the invaders on all sides by plundering their stores, cutting off their means of communications and raiding their territories. But this was a temporary phase. The community of objective between the rivals was merely a passing attitude. Each worked for the outwardly common cause with a mental reservation, being on the look out for an opportunity to gain the upperhand over the other. Such a disposition proved to be a source of unending misunderstanding and disputes between the two, which blurred their vision and made them forgetful of the supreme cause, namely the revival of the Nizam Shahi glory. It proved fruitful in producing one crisis after the other in quick succession. And even the reverses, which each had to suffer in his turn, failed to impress them with the desirability nay the necessity of united action.

But Malik Ambar believed in ceaseless activity. He was anxious to retrieve the losses he had sustained and no sooner did he recover from his wounds than he began to collect troops and within a short time succeeded in raising about 20,000 soldiers. He freely recruited the Marathas, trained them in the guerilla method of warfare, inspired them with confidence and satisfied them by giving them high ranks in the army and thus he marshalled their energies into a single channel. Nor did he fail to raise the morale of the people by his just and impartial behaviour and by assuring them security of life and property. His growing propularity bring as it did the consolidation of his striking power, but it alarmed Khan Khanan, who found himself face to face with new military tactics to which his soldiers were almost strangers. Secondly, he was not certain of the support of his own colleagues and followers who were torn with discord and dissensions. Thirdly, he visualised to himself the possibility of Bijapur and Golcunda extending secret support to the Abyssinian adventurer, who, it was patent enough, would be able to suppress Raju Daccani and occupy Nasik and Trimbak. How to stem the tide was a problem which began to agitate the mind of the Mughal Commander-in-Chief ?

On the other hand, Malik Ambar inspite of his growing resources and increasing popularity, was also not unaware of the weakness of his own position and of the risks involved in the bid he was making. What would happen in case his counter-offensive against the Mughals failed? Would it not shatter his dreams to pieces? Would it not strengthen the hands of his rivals like, Raju Daccani, Patang Rao, Farhad Khan and Sandal, who were conspiring against him? Would it, therefore, not be wise to come to terms with the Mughals and deal with the internal enemies first? At the moment Raju was very active.

In short, Malik Ambar was as much keen to come to terms with the Mughals as the latter with him. Therefore, when Khan Khanan sent proposals for peace, he heartily accepted them. To cement the bonds of friendship with personal contacts, he marched to Jinapur where Khan Khanan accorded to him a fitting reception. The parties concluded a treaty whereby their respective boundaries were demarcated. Soon after, Khan Khanan was advised by his councillors to make an end of Malik Ambar but he rejected the proposal forthwith. On the contrary, he showered favours on him trusting to his goodwill.[40]

**Peace concluded with Khan Khanan**

But such treaty could be no more than a truce or temporary cessation of war, stem as it did from the selfish interests of either party. The rising power of Malik Ambar, organisation of a strong army, his enthronment of a Nizam Shahi Prince and his ambitious designs threatened the Mughal position in the Daccan. The Mughal aggression and the constant distractions caused by the enemy would have rendered his task more difficult, almost impossible. Khan Khanan was swayed by the idea that by winning over Ambar he would be able to exercise a restraint on his anti-Mughal activities, which would add a feather in his cap. Whereas Malik Ambar thought that friendship with the Mughals would n t only bring him immunity from the external danger but would also give him a status in the eyes of the neighbouring states and his rivals and enemies would be demoralised, which would be a preliminary step towards their total annihilation. Indeed this treaty represents the first stage in the trial of diplomatic skill between the Mughals and Malik Ambar.

After the conclusion of the treaty, Malik Ambar was free to tackle his rivals in the kingdom. The conspirators Patang Rao, Malik Sandal, Farhad Khan and others joined the king at Ausa and instigated him to take up arms against Malik Ambar. Murtaza deciding to oust him from regency detached a force against him. Malik Ambar took up the challenge, speedily marched to Ausa, met the conspirators, gave them a crushing defeat, making Patang Rao a prisoner. Thus, the discomfited king on the advice of Farhad Khan and Malik Sandal concluded peace with the victor on the following day.[41]

As Malik Ambar had long cherished the design of obtaining possession of Parenda, he proceeded with the king in that direction. But Manjhan Khan, the Abyssinian commander who had been holding the fort for the last twenty years, opposed him on the pretext that he was in league with the Mughals. In fact it was the commander who was in league with Ambar's enemies and extremely keen to bring about his fall. All attempts of Malik Ambar to convince Manjhan Khan of his loyalty to Nizam Shah, having failed and in order to prevent the boy king from going over to conspirators, he put him under surveillance. Upon this Farhad Khan and Malik Sandal deserted Malik Ambar, entered the fort and made common cause with the garrison. Ambar opened the siege of Parenda, which dragged on for a month. It was a sheer accident which enabled him to gain possession of the fort. Sona Khan, the son of Manjhan Khan, kidnapped the wives and daughters of some of the inhabitants of the place, consequently the garrison rose in revolt against him and put him to death. Apprehending his safety Manjhan Khan fled from the fort accompanied by Farhad Khan and Malik Sandal to Bijapur. The garrison of the fort, held out for some time longer. But when Malik Ambar removed all the restraints which he had imposed upon Murtaza Nizam Shah II, the gates of the fort were opened for him and he occupied it.[42]

**Parenda Captured**

Shortly after, the Mughal envoy Asad Bag, then on his way to the Adil Shahi court arrived at Balaghat.[43] While he was at Burhanpur, he had been requested by Khan Khanan to effect a reconciliation between Hasan Ali Beg, the governor of Bir and Malik Ambar. As Asad Beg had brought a royal firman for the latter, he directed him to receive it in the customary manner.[44] This was truely a heaven-sent blessing for Malik Ambar. It meant an honour to him and more than that, it gave him an opportunity to cement further his alliance with the Mughals. He marched out to a distance of a *karoh* to pay homage to the royal firman and to receive it formally. He was happy to renew his acquaintance with the Mughal envoy and escorted him to his house, where a grand reception awaited him. The formalities being over, "the two (Malik Ambar and Hasan Ali Beg) retired into privacy and cleared their misunderstanding in a heart to heart chat. Fresh promises were made and each party was satisfied." Hasan Ali Beg presented an elephant and a horse to Ambar and the two parted as friends. Then the Mughal envoy Asad Beg was escorted by malik Ambar's brother to the Adil Shahi frontiers.[45]

Asad Beg performed his duties with courage, prudence and much common sense. Having achieved the object of his mission, he started on his homeward journey. At Mangalbir he found himself in a rather awkward situation. He was distracted by the lukewarm attitude of Mir Jamaluddin Anju who, perhaps had incited the Bijapuris to refuse to move any further. Add to this, the rumours of a raid by Malik Ambar which led to the flight of the Bijapuri troops and the return of the general who was escorting the palanquin of Begam Sultana. But Asad Beg relying on the friendship of Ambar asked his men to stay where they were. Just at this moment arrived Khwajgi Inayatullah, who was going to the Adil Shahi court on an ambassadorial mission from the Mughal court. He informed Asad Beg that reinforcements under the command of Mirza Iraj and other Mughal officers would be arriving soon. Thus Mir, together with the palanquin was escorted safely to Ahmadnagar.[46]

Prince Daniyal marched from Burhanpur towards Ahmadnagar by the route of Daultabad and Nasik to receive the hand of the daughter of Ibrahim Adil Shah II, in marriage.[47] He expected that Raju would appear before him and would pay him respects and acknowledge his authority in the Daccan, as Malik Ambar had already done. But Raju refused to wait upon the Prince, even when he was asked to do it.[48] On the other hand when challenged to a fight he sent a haughty reply saying that, "if I oppose your army and any harm befalls it, Emperor Akbar will send ten times more troops against me; but if some harm befalls me I have nothing to fall back upon. I shall be annihilated and from whom shall I seek justice ? Rest assured, I shall be at your service, if it be near Agra. So long as I live I shall not fail to do it. The source of subsistence and the greatness of my army depends upon your Sarkar and I shall continue to indulge in my activities".

Though Raju did not come out in the open, he constantly harassed Daniyal's army with his light cavalry and compelled him to send for reinforcements from Jalna. Khan Khanan made a forced march with five thousand cavalry and joined Daniyal, which compelled Raju to withdraw. But it appears that Raju's raids subsequently had a demoralising effect on the Mughals and compelled them to come to terms with him. He was permitted to rehabilitate such districts as had been plundered by him and their revenue was to be divided equally between the two parties. Henceforward, in every village and town there were to be two *amils*, one representing Raju while the other representing Prince Daniyal.[49]

As Patan was not included in the agreement, Raju demanded a loan of thirty thousand huns from its merchants, who being certain of the Mughal protection refused to comply with the demand.[50] This enraged Raju, who made a forced march to the town, besieged it, seized the leaders and extorted three or four lacs huns from them. Henceforward whenever his men approached a village or town the inhabitants from sheer fear readily submitted to his extortion.[51] His high-handedness alienated his followers; they went over to Malik Ambar, who received them with open arms and assigned to them villages. Encouraged by this accession of strength Malik Ambar attacked Raju and besieged the fort of Patan, which contained Saadat Khan's treasures. He occupied it but could not hold it for long.[52]

Malik Ambar's alliance with the Mughals, offended

Murtaza Nizam Shah II, who sent messages to Raju, complaining of the treatment he was receiving at the hands of his regent. Considering it to be an excellent excuse to fall upon his rival, Raju responded to the invitation. He arrived at Parenda without meeting any opposition. He saw the king and promised him his unbounded loyalty and cooperation. When Ambar heard it, he marched to oppose Raju. The rival forces encamped near the fortress of Parenda and for a month several indecisive skirmishes took place. Malik Ambar being hard pressed by his rival, solicited help from Khan Khanan. The latter issued instructions to Hasan Ali Beg Turkman, the commander of Bir and Bahadur-ul-Mulk to proceed immediately with 3,000 cavalry to the assistance of Malik Ambar. Upon the arrival of the Mughal reinforcements, Ambar attacked Raju, defeated him and drove him towards Daultabad. But the struggle between the two continued and Raju succeeded in seizing a large portion of the Nizam Shahi territory and in collecting 20,000 bargis and Maratha soldiers round him. Whenever the imperial forces arrived in the Daccan, Raju would fall upon them, intercept their line of communication and seize their supplies and compel them to retreat. But during the absence of the imperial forces the rivals would fight between themselves.[53]

In April 1604 A. D. Prince Daniyal died. Khan Khanan therefore went from his cantonment at Jalna tc Burhanpur to take up charge of office of the viceroy of the Daccan. The death of the prince and the absence of the Mughal general from Jalna offered Malik Ambar splendid opportunity for aggrendisement. Accordingly, he collected his troops and marched against Daultabad, where he inflicted a crushing defeat on Raju. The latter's position became so untenable that he was unable to offer any resistance. In despair, he appealed for help to Khan Khanan. In response to his call Khan Khanan personally marched towards Daultabad. After his arrival there, to the surprise of both Ambar and Raju, he began to act like an impartial umpire, refusing to extend his support to either of them. Thus for six months he prevented the two rivals from attacking each other. In the end when

**Ambar concluded peace with Raju.**

Malik Ambar realised that Khan Khanan was well disposed towards Raju, he deemed it prudent to yield to the suggestion of the Mughal Commander-in-Chief, concluded a treaty with his rival and retired to Parenda. Thereafter Khan Khanan returned to Jalna.[54]

The attitude of Khan Khanan perplexed Malik Ambar who began to analyse his motives. If he really meant to stick to the spirit of peace which he had previously concluded with him, why did he respond to Raju's call ? And then why did he compel him to come to terms with Raju ? But Khan Khanan had his own reasons for the attitude he had adopted. On the one hand being well aware of the real motives and intentions of Malik Ambar, he was loth to purchase his hostility for the sake of Raju, on the other, he deemed it to be in his interest to prevent Malik Ambar from gaining undisputable sway and unrivalled mastery in the Nizam Shahi kingdom. This is why he contrived to maintain a balance of power between the two ; their constant rivalry being a source of strength and advantage to him. For the time being Malik Ambar remained quiet.

In October 1605 A. D. died Emperor Akbar and his son Prince Salim, succeeded to the throne at Agra with the lofty title of Nuruddin Muhammad Jahangir Badshah Ghazi. Soon after occurred the rebellion of Prince Khusaru (April 1606 A. D.) and Qandhar (1606-7 A. D.) was besieged by the Persion king Shah Abbas Safvi, which diverted the attention of the Mughal Emperor towards the north-west. With the result that the imperial pressure on the Daccan relaxed. This gave an opportunity to Malik Ambar to avenge the loss of Ahmadnagar. He launched an offensive against the Mughals, moving in quick succession from one place to the other, conquering all places through which he passed. So that within a short time not only did he recover all the lost territory but he reduced the Mugal Commander-in-Chief to a miserable plight. Khan Khanan began to smart with the sense of defeat and gross humiliation.

**Ambar Recovers the lost territory**

Having thrown back the Mughals, Ambar transferred the capital of the Nizam Shahi kingdom from Parenda to Junnar, on account of its strategic importance and nearness to Daultabad.[55] Moreover it offered him greater facility to carry on his campaigns against his rival Raju. He now exerted all his energy in subverting his power completely. Fortunately for him Raju's position at the moment was at the lowest ebb. He had alienated the sympathies of his soldiers and subjects alike, who deserted him in large numbers, went over to Malik Ambar, complaining against his oppression and high-handedness. Malik Ambar received the deserters with open arms and gave them ranks and honour according to their merits. Having thus strengthened himself, he marched with a large army against Daultabad. Raju offered a gallant resistance, but owing to discord and dissensions in his own ranks, he could not fight in the open for a long time. He retired into the fort to stand a siege. But here too treachery lay in store for him and he was compelled to surrender. He was arrested and imprisoned and the fort was occupied by Malik Ambar. His territory was annexed to the Nizam Shahi kingdom. For four years, Raju remained as prisoner in Junnar. When Malik Ambar found that some of the Daccanis and the Marathas were contriving to rescue him, in order to put a stop to the future troubles he brought about his end.[56]

**Raju's fall and his death**

Thus Malik Ambar removed the most troublesome and powerful of his internal opponents and obtained possession of a large slice of land with the important and strategic fortress of Daultabad which inspired him with a feeling of security, such as he had never experienced before. He was now free to canalise his whole power and resources to fight the external enemy against whom he again and again launched successful campaings.

The failure of Khan Khanan in the Daccan roused the anger of the new Emperor Jahangir, who summoned him to explain the cause thereof. But that astute politician who had spent most part of his life in the service of the Mughals and in the Daccan did not fail to impress the sovereign with sweet words and encouraging promises. He succeeded in persuading him to send him again to the Daccan with a reinforcement of 12,000 cavalry and ten lacs of rupees for restoring the imperial prestige there.[57]

The report of Khan Khanan's advance towards the Daccan caused serious concern to Malik Ambar. He had broken the terms of the pact which he had concluded with the Mughal Commander-in-chief, who would not now spare him. He had only recently started his work of recovering, for the Nizam Shahis, the lost territories and therefore any interference at this stage would not only hamper his progress, but give a blow to his rising reputation, besides causing a set back to his plan. Therefore urged by consideration of personal security as much as by the desire of protecting the gains he had made, he sought the assistance of Ibrahim Adil Shah II, who in the past had helped the Nizam Shahi kingdom, or whenever it suffered at the hands of the internal or external enemies. He wrote to the ruler of Bijapur that, "it is my design to fight the Mughal troops so long as life remains in this body. May I through your Majesty's daily increasing fortunes succeed in expelling the Mughals from the Daccan". Secondly, he requested Adil Shah to hand over to him the fort of Qandhar, which the Adil Shahis had wrested from the hands of the Nizam Shahis, and thirdly, he proposed to bring the two states together into a close bond of union by matrimony.[58]

**Ambar seeks assistance from the ruler of Bijapur**

In full appreciation of impending Mughal aggression Ibrahim Adil Shah II readily responded to the request of Malik Ambar. He immediately sent ten thousand horse-men to render military assistance to him. The fort of Qandhar was also given to him for the residence of his family and for storing provisions. A matrimonial alliance between the two states was also contracted in so far as Ambar's son Aziz-ul-Mulk, commonly known as Fateh Khan was married to the daughter of an influential Abyssinian noble of Bijapur, namely, Yaqut Khan who enjoyed the highest confidence of the king. The occasion was celebrated with great rejoicings and festivities which continued for forty days. Ibrahim Adil Shah II, himself took keen interest in the ceremony, provided from the state exchequer a handsome dowry for the bride and spent 20,000 huns (20,000 rupees) on fireworks alone. After the elebration of the nuptials on 5th

**Cordial Relations with Bijapur**

Feb. 1609 A.D. Fateh Khan and his bride left Bijapur for Junnar.[59] Thus Malik Ambar succeeded in achieving his twofold objective. He had obtained the backing of Adil Shah in his forthcoming struggle with Khan Khanan and secondly, he had improved his social and moral stature. Some time afterwards, again at his request Adil Shah sent another force of three to four thousand cavalry for his aid.[60] He seized the fort of Antur from the hands of the Mughals and put the entire garrison to sword.[61]

**Failure of Khan Khanan to retrieve the situation. Prince Parvez sent to the Daccan**

Upon his arrival in the Daccan Khan Khanan did his best to improve the Mughal position there. But thanks to the recurrent jealousy and discord among his officers, it became utterly impossible for him to take either concerted action or pursue a uniform policy against the enemy. The Commander-in-Chief could neither control the situation nor secure obedience of his orders. Within a year it became absolutely clear that success was as remote as ever. In fact condition for the Mughals was going from bad to worse, in so far as Malik Ambar was consistently scoring against them. Having collected a large force Malik Ambar attacked Jahangir Beg, the Commander of Patan. On hearing of the attack, Darab Khan went to Jahangir Beg's help and succeeded in escorting him safely to Jinapur. On receiving the report of attack on Patan, Khan Khanan immediately despatched his son Shah Nawaz Khan to afford relief to Jahangir Beg. Meanwhile Malik Ambar having gained his object at Patan encamped with a large force near Jinapur. Here he was attacked by Shah Nawaz Khan who compelled the enemy to fall back. After this Shah Nawaz Khan marched to Jinapur where he joined Darab Khan and Jahangir Beg. But Malik Ambar did not let the grass grow under his feet. He reorganized his forces and advanced to deliver fresh attack on the enemy. He successfully surrounded the Mughal camp at Jinapur and compelled Khan Khanan to retire to Burhanpur. He then occupied Jinapur and sent his men in pursuit of the Mughals. Having failed to cope with the situation, owing to the inadequate forces, Khan Khanan in his distress, repeatedly requested the

Emperor for further reinforcements.[63] Emperor Jahangir appointed Prince Parwez to the supreme command with Asaf Khan as his adviser and guardian.[64]

The Prince arrived at Burhanpur early in 1610, and though he also strove hard, he could not effect any change for the better. Malik Ambar's star was in the ascendant. He was inflicting humiliation and defeat on his enemy. At one stage the situation became so alarming that Asaf Khan suggested to the Emperor to come over personally to the Daccan. Emperor Jahangir gave serious thought to the proposal but he was dissuaded by his courtiers from accepting it. He sent his favourite Khan Jahan Lodi to the Daccan with sufficient reinforcements under the command of the valiant generals like Raja Bir Singh Deo, Raja Vikramajit, Shujat Khan, Saif Khan Barha and others.[65]

Khan Khanan had in the meantime devised an elaborate plan for delivering surprise attacks upon Malik Ambar during the rains in 1610 A.D. Accordingly, even against the better judgement of his own followers, he made a dash from Burhanpur into the Nizam Shahi territory. Up to this stage the move worked according to the expectations; but it was to end in tragic disaster for more than one reason. Firstly, because the Mughal Commander-in-Chief had not the unanimous support of his officers who did not extend unstinted cooperation to him; secondly, because the rainy season was not suitable for military operations in that region; and thirdly, because he did not equip himself with an adequate supply of provisions.

**Failure of the attempt.**

Malik Ambar avoided pitched battles. But his light Maratha cavalry harassed the invaders who were lured into the rugged hills and narrow passes of Balaghat. Here the Mughals found themselves exposed to severe suffering; their supply of provisions having been exhausted, it could not be replenished from the local sources. Famine conditions began to prevail in the army, taking a heavy toll of men, horses and beasts of burden. The officers began to denounce the commander-in-chief accusing him of rashness, treachery and inefficiency. Driven to despair and in sheer disgust Khan Khanan was compelled to conclude a dishonourable peace with Malik Ambar and return to Burhanpur.[66]

After subjugating the environs of Ahmadnagar, Malik Ambar's forces opened the siege of the fort itself. The Mughal commander Khwaja Mirza Safi, a relation of Shah Tahmasp of Persia who had been in charge of it since its conquest by Akbar, made every effort to defend it. But Malik Ambar cut off the garrison's communications with the outside, and intercepted the supply of provisions. In distress Khawaja Mirza appealed for help to Khan Khanan. But latter was licking his own wounds, having been defeated by Malik Ambar at Jalanapur. The news caused great consternation among the garrison who forthwith decided to evacuate the fort. Khwaja Mirza tried to pacify and encourage them, but to no purpose and in the end he was compelled to leave the fort on the promise of safe passage to Burhanpur.[67]

**The fort of Ahmadnagar Besieged.**

Such were the state of affairs when Khan Jahan Lodi arrived at Burhanpur. The recent reverses had eclipsed Khan Khanan's prestige. In fact he had become an object of ridicule. Ever since the arrival of the Prince, there had formed a clique against the Commander-in-Chief. Its members took a malicious delight in his humiliation; they persistently misrepresented him to the Emperor. And this clique was now joined by Khan Jahan, who succeeded in persuading the Emperor to order the recall of Khan Khanan so that he may direct the affairs in the Daccan single-handed and thus claim for himself the glory of success; where his predecessor had miserably failed. He promised to complete the conquest of Ahmadnagar and Bijapur within the brief period of two years, failing which he said he would never show his face to him. Upon this, the supreme command was vested in Khan Jahan Lodi and Khan Azam was sent to assist him. Mahabat Khan was commissioned to go to the Daccan with instructions to investigate into the causes of the recent reverses which had befallen on the imperialists and to escort Khan Khanan to the court. It was believed that this simple process of changing the commanders would yield the much expected results but this was not to be.[68]

With an imposing array of 2,000 ahadis, 10,000 horsemen

experienced generals like Khan Alam, Faridun Khan Birlas, Yusuf Khan, Ali Khan Niyazi and others and a sum of Rs. 3000,000, Khan Azam joined Khan Jahan Lodi. But the situation did not change for the better. The Mughals were unable to face the guerilla warfare. As usual they indulged in mutual recriminations more than in meeting the enemy. And though Khan Jahan Lodi exerted himself to the utmost, he could not prevail against the superior tactics of Malik Ambar which brought his inevitable fall.[69]

Murtaza Nizam Shah II did not play his role according to the expectations of Malik Ambar. Instead of acknowledging the debt of gratitude to his benefactor, who had raised him almost from the dust, he constantly intrigued against him and formed factions against him, thus impelling the security of the state and the popularity of the man who was rebuilding it. It was Murtaza who had instigated the rebellions of Patang Rao, Farhad Khan and Malik Sandal. Besides this, he had been found to be in league with Raju Daccani. Such duplicity could not be tolerated by Malik Ambar. But before resorting to any drastic step, he consulted Ibrahim Adil Shah II who disapproved the plan of deposing Murtaza. He intervened on the latter's behalf and restored good relations between him and his minister.[70] But in 1610 A. D. misunderstanding cropped up again, which became more serious than ever. It happened that the king's first wife who was fair complexioned and of Persian extraction, taunted Malik Ambar's, daughter saying that she was a slave girl, merely a concubine of the king and that her father was a rebel. The latter being offended complained about it to her father, who made up his mind to depose the king. Although once more Adil Shah exerted himself to remove the misunderstanding, but he failed, perhaps because Malik Ambar was now finding himself much stronger than ever before, or he could trust his master no further. Accordingly, he won over the King's secretary Mir Abul Fateh, who poisoned him to death and proclaimed a minor Prince of the royal house as king under the style of Burhan Nizam Shah III (1610-1630.A. D.).[71]

**Murtaza Nizam Shah II deposed and poisoned**

While Khan Jahan Lodi was devising plans to hem in

Malik Ambar from all sides with a view to crush him for all time, the latter continued to recover the lost territories step by step. He was now the unrivalled master of the entire kingdom from Bankot to Bassien, to the frontiers of Bijapur in the South; to Bidar on the south east and Khandesh on the north. His possessions also included Balaghat or southern Berar. His successful and glorious campaigns against the Mughals had not only enhanced his power and popularity but had restored the fallen prestige of the Nizam Shahi kingdom. Now he was looked upon not as a rebel of mean repute but as the leader of an independent country, with a trained and organised military force behind him. His work of consolidation and expansion, defence and offense, retrocession and aggression went hand in hand. In 1610 he transferred his capital from Junnar to a more strategically important fort of Daultabad, whose isolated position, strength and hilly protection offered an extremely satisfactory protection against the sudden aggression of the enemy.[72]

Mailk Ambar had just heaved a sigh of relief, when the Mughals became active again. Like his predecessor Khan Jahan Lodi also failed to remove the feelings of jealousy and supineness from the hearts of the Mughal officers and nobles and as such he too could not make any headway against the enemy. The situation increased the anxiety of the Emperor and he concerted the "Grand plan of 1610". It envisaged a two pronged invasion of Ahmadnagar. Abdullah Khan was to march in the direction of Nasik and Trimbak and was to keep in touch with the armies which were to advance under Khan Jahan Lodi, Man Singh and Amir-ul-Umra from the sides of Berar and Khandesh. The success of the plan depended on unity of action, which did not materialise at any stage whatsoever.[73]

**"Grand Plan of 1610 A.D."**

Urged by the ambition of monopolising to himself the entire credit for the prospective victory against Malik Ambar, Abdullah Khan made an impetuous dash into the Nizam Shahi territory, disregarding the dire need of coordinating his movements with those of his other colleagues. With their normal tactics of avoiding pitched battle and harassing the invader with guerilla warfare, the Daccanis succeeded in luring the enemy into the hilly regions, all the time hovering on his flanks and intercepting his line of communication and creating scare among its ranks by throwing rockets at frequent intervals. When at length Abdullah Khan arrived at Daultabad he found himself in a state of utter isolation. His troops were almost exhausted and demoralised, whereas his enemy's ranks were constantly swelling. Moreover he had no information about the movements of his other colleagues. This was a heaven sent opportunity for Malik Ambar, who delivered a heavy attack on the Mughals compelling, Abdullah Khan to order a humiliating retreat, losing on the way many soldiers and officers like Ali Mardan and Zulfiqar Beg. He was hotly pursued by the Daccanis. It was with difficulty that he could escape to Gujarat. Thereafter Malik Ambar returned to Daultabad.[74]

On receiving the report of the disaster which had befallen Abdullah Khan, the Berar and Khandesh divisions of the Mughal army also retreated and joined Prince Parvez at Adilabad near Burhanpur.[75] They justly threw the blame for the failure of the plan on Abdullah Khan, accused him of rashness and dereliction of duty, in so far that he had not carried out the instructions of the Emperor and disregarded all canons of sound judgement and precaution. But while conceding all this, it can not but be stated that there were some basic draw-backs in the "Grand Plan of 1610". It did not take note of the new tactics which Malik Ambar had developed, nor did it take into account the age long impossibility of ensuring harmonious and concerted action on the part of the imperial generals in the Daccan. Abdullah Khan, Khan Jahan Lodi, Amir-ul-Umra and Man Singh were of equal status and none of them was ready to subordinate himself to the other. In other words, their earnestness was no match to that of Malik Ambar.

When the news of the defeat of the Mughals in the Daccan reached the ears of Emperor Jahangir, he in his indignation raprimanded all the officers, especially Abdullah Khan. He once more thought of taking the field in person, but again gave up the idea. He held a council to consider the problems in which every one realised the difficulties which the imperial generals had to face in the Daccan. In this context Khwaja Abul Hasan remarked, "no one had a firmer grasp of the Daccan problems and no one is better fitted to solve them, than the old Mughal general Khan Khanan who had unjustly been accused of treachery.[76] Accordingly, the Emperor invested the latter with the supreme command in the Daccan, promoted him to the rank of 6,000, conferred on him a dress of honour, a jewelled dagger, a special elephant and an Iraqi horse. He also promoted his sons Shah Nawaz Khan, Darab Khan and Rahmandad Khan to high mansabs. Khan Khanan with his sons and other commanders like Abul Hasan and Razzaq Vardi Uzbeg arrived in the Daccan in 1612 A.D. to pursue a cautious policy and to recover his lost prestige. Luckily he found the field clear and the atmosphere favourable for pushing his own line of action. Some of his bitter enemies like Asaf Khan, the Amir-ul-Umra, and Raja Man Singh had died. Khan-i-Azam was subsequently transferred to the Mewar front in 1613 A.D. He therefore addressed himself to the task of removing some of the internal drawbacks before turning to Malik Ambar.[77]

**Khan Khanan again sent to the Daccan.**

Just at this time dissensions broke out among a section of Daccanis. The disgusted Rajputs conspired to assassinate Malik Ambar. They placed themselves in an ambush and at an opportune moment surprised him and inflicted a wound on him but the injury proved to be only slight. His attendants overpowered the conspirators, killed them and carried him safe to his quarters. To add to his consternation, some of the influential nobles of the Nizam Shahi kingdom like Jadhav Rao, Babaji Kayath, Uda Ram, Adam Khan and Yaqut Khan, who had rendered invaluable services to him, fell an easy prey to the Mughal gold, deserted his cause and went over to the opposite camp. They proceeded to the camp of Shah Nawaz Khan at Balapur, where they were received by the Mughal general with honour and cordiality. He gave to each of them money, an elephant, a horse and dress of honour according to his rank and position. He now opened the offensive against Malik Ambar and

**Conspiracy against Malik Ambar**

marched towards his new capital Khirki.[78]

To avert the crisis Malik Ambar formed an alliance with Adil Shah and Qutb Shah who responded to his call for help. Adil Shah sent twenty thousand horse under Mulla Muhammad Lari and Qutb Shah detached five thousand under Mir Musa.[79] Thus reinforced, Malik Ambar decided to remain at Khirki with forty thousand horse and despatched fifteen thousand horse under the command of Mahaldar Khan, Dilawar Khan, Atish Khan Bijli Khan and others to check the progress of the enemy who was moving fast towards the capital.

As Shah Nawaz Khan advanced beyond Jalna, the Daccanis began to hover on his flanks and harass him. But his superior numbers proved too much for them. They were always repulsed and beaten back. The Mughals thus steadily advanced towards Khirki. On receiving the reports of the reverses suffered by his men, Malik Ambar left his capital to give battle to the enemy. He arrayed his forty thousand soldiers at Roshangarh, which was situated between Khirki and Samvate.

Shah Nawaz Khan too arranged his men. He himself assumed the command of the centre ; to Darab Khan was entrusted the charge of the van ; the left flank was placed under Raja Maha Singh and the right flank under Khwaja Beg Safvi. The battle opend in the afternoon with a volly of fire from cannons and rockets. Darab Khan with his colleagues like Bir Singh Deo, Raja Chand, Ali Khan, Jahangir Quli Beg Turkman attacked the vanguard of the Daccani forces, which was commanded by Malik Ambar. A fierce contest ensued which lasted for two hours. The Daccanis failed to stand to the Mughal pressure. Soon they lost confidence, broke and fled. Malik Ambar retreated, being hotly pursued by the victors till sun-set, after which the latter returned in the thick of night to their camp with rich spoils (Feb. 1616 A.D.).

In this battle Malik Ambar suffered very heavy losses. A large number from amongst his soldiers were either slain or taken prisoner and those who managed to escape were panic striken, disunited and scattered. His entire park of artillery, elephants, horses and the camels laden with rockets fell into the hands of the Mughals. Likewise the Bijapuri and Golcunda forces also suffered heavily ; many of their soldiers having been made captives. Of them mention should be made of Ambar Bijapuri, Musnad Ali and Bijili Khan. The last two, besides innumerable soldiers were put to death. Malik Ambar abondoned Khirki which was ravaged and destroyed by the Mughals.[80]

No doubt Khan Khanan had attained a glorious victory and had partially retrieved the lost prestige of the Mughals in the Daccan but Ambar was still far from being crushed. Indeed, the Mughals could not annex even a small slice of the territory, not to speak of the extensive possessions of the Daccanis.

As soon as the enemy retired from Khirki, it was reoccupied by Malik Ambar, who began to rehabilitate his position. With the help of Ibrahim Adil Shah II, he brought back to his side Adham Khan, Jadhav Rao, Babaji Kayath, and Uda Ram, who had deserted him and joined the Mughals.[81] But though they had returned to their former loyalty, they became a source of trouble for Malik Ambar. They secretly organised a party against him with a view to bring about his fall. But Malik Ambar was not slow to react to their machinations. He imprisoned Adham Khan in the fortress of Daultabad and finally put him secretly to death. Babji Kayath and Uda Ram unsuccessfully attempted to escape to Bijapur. The former was betrayed by his own followers, whereas the latter gallantly opposed Malik Ambar's forces and defeated them. But realising that his stay in the Nizam Shahi territory would not be safe, he went over to the Mughals at the time when Prince Khurram arrived in the Daccan.[82]

Emperor Jahangir, who was passing his days in pleasure and enjoyment at Ajmer was disappointed at the developments in the Daccan which inspite of the change of commanders and pouring in of fresh reinforcements showed no sign of improvement. He was now convinced of the incompetence of Prince Parvez and the inability of Khan Khanan to deliver the goods. A bold decision had to be taken and the Emperor rose equal the occasion, particularly because the recent success in Mewar had buoyed up his spirits. Both Parwez and Khan Khanan were removed from the Daccan to make room for Prince Khurram, the rising star of destiny. And Jahangir himself moved to encamp there, to be available for advice and guidance in the projected operations in the Daccan.[83]

On 6th October 1616 A.D. Prince Khurram left Ajmer with an imposing array of generals like Abdullah Khan Firoz Jang, Raja Suraj Singh, Dayanat Khan and a host of others. With rapid marches he arrived on the banks of the Narbada, where he was met by Khan Khanan, Khan Jahan Lodi and Mahabat Khan. Without halting there he moved straight for Burhanpur, where he arrived on 6th March 1617 A.D. Here he married the daughter of Shah Nawaz Khan who pledged his full support to him, which augered well for securing unity of action among the imperial officers. The presence of the Emperor at Mandu gave further confidence to the Prince. He now opened negotiations with Adil Shah and Qutb Shah and Malik Ambar through reliable and trustworthy messengers like Afzal Khan and Raja Vikramajit. He offered them definite proposals of peace viz. that they must relinquish their right over the territories which they had seized from the Mughals and that they must acknowledge the Mughal suzerainty by agreeing to pay tribute.

**Prince Khurram sent against Malik Ambar**

The extensive preparations of the Mughals, the innumerable army which they were ready to pour into the Daccan, the rising prestige of Prince Khurram, the persence of the Emperor at Mandu with the avowed object of solving once for all the Daccan problem, unnerved Adil Shah and Qutb Shah, and recognising discretion to be the better part of valour, they succumbed to the unprcedented and unexpected pressure exercised upon them. Adil Shah personally waited upon the Prince with costly presents in cash and kind. He was dignifed with the title of Farzand or son. Qutb Shah did the same and tendered submission to the Mughal Emperor.[84](b)

Malik Ambar was now completely isolated. His position became very precarious. Never before did he find himself with such overwhelming odds arrayed against him in the north and the south at one and the same time. Uptil now he had always come out successful, even in the midst of the most perplexing and desperate circumstances. In adversity both Adil Shah and Qutb had always rendered their assistance to him. But now they had not only fallen at their knees before the Mughals, but Adil Shah was pressing him to bow before the inevitable. In sheer helplessness he had to purchase peace by ceding Ahmadnagar together with the adjacent districts, as also the parganas of Balaghat which he had seized from the Mughals. It was a heavy and humiliating price which he had to pay but the choice lay between the annihilation and a temporary lease of life. Prudence counselled him to accept the latter alternative in the hope of retrieving his losses at the earliest. Indeed basically his position was still unimpaired and he considered the present treaty to be no more than a mere scrap of paper.[85]

**Peace concluded**

After the conclusion of the treaty, Prince Khurram made the necessary arrangements for the defence and administration of the Daccan provinces. Khan Khanan was appointed governor of Berar, Khandesh and Ahmadnagar. His eldest son Shah Nawaz Khan was stationed in the ceded territory with 12,000 cavalry. Ahmadnagar was placed in the hands of Khanjar Khan. Trustworthy officers were appointed to other posts. Leaving 30,000 horses and 7000 musketeers in the Daccan, the Prince retired from Burhanpur with remaining 25,000 horse and 2,000 gunners and most of the principal officers like Khan Jahan Lodi, Abdullah Khan, Mahabat Khan, Darab Khan and others, arriving at Mandu on 12th October 1617 A. D. Apparently he had won a resounding success, but in effect the situation in the Daccan was no better than at the end of 1605 A.D.[86]

In sullen resentment Malik Ambar patiently waited for two years, till he found an opportunity to strike at the enemy again. Prince Shahjahan was preoccupied with the siege of Kangara in the Punjab and Emperor Jahangir was having a delightful time in the vale of Kashmir. Thanks to their absence from the hub of affairs, the Mughal officers in the Daccan as usual fell a prey to mutual dissensions and petty jealousies. Malik Ambar once more formed an alliance with the rulers of Bijapur and Golcunda and opened the offensive. He called up his light Maratha bands, recruited 60,000 fresh troops, organised and trained them and made a surprise attack on the Mughal territory in Ahmadnagar. He conquered all the places through which he passed and at length compelled Khanjar Khan, the commandant of the fort to retire into the fort. Leaving a contingent of the Daccani troops to besiege the fort, Malik Ambar with his main army marched further extending once more the Nizam Shahi territory to the frontiers of Berar. The Mughal commanders in sheer terror fled to Darab Khan, who had succeeded his brother Shah Nawaz Khan as governor of Berar and Ahmadnagar. The Marathas hotly pursued them. Although two or three pitched battles occurred between the Deccanis and the Mughals, but the latter inspite of their success in them could gain nothing, because as soon as the battle was over, the Marathas would gather again, deliver surprise attacks upon the imperialists and reduce them to extremities. Within three months all the outposts were lost by the Mughals one after the other and the major portion of Berar and Ahmadnagar passed into the hands of Malik Ambar.[87]

**Ambar recovers what he had ceded**

Malik Ambar now took up his position at Mehkar, from where he directed his activities against the enemy. He harassed them from all sides, plundering their camp, cutting off their supplies and devastating the surrounding country. He compelled the Mughal officers to retreat from Balaghat through the pass of Kishangarh to Balapur, where they hoped to have some measure of safety. But there also, the Daccanis appeared, reduced them to distress by plundering and devastating the environs of Balapur. The imperialists now contrived to lure the Daccanis into the open and inflicted a severe defeat on them. Malik Ambar's camp was plundered and many of his men were either made captive or were slain in the field of battle. Laden with rich spoils, the victors turned towards their camp. But the moment they turned their back, Ambar's men reassembled and began to attack them from different sides. The Marathas gave them a hot pursuit as far as Balapur. It was only after a loss of several hundred men and with

**Ambar's ceaseless activities; Mughals driven to bay**

much difficulty that the imperialists were able to reach their camp. Balapur now became the target of Malik Ambar's activities, which were so devastating that desertions on a large scale occurred in the Mughal camp, the deserters going over and swelling the ranks of the enemy. Scarcity of provisions joined to the loss of hope of speedy relief alarmed the Mughal officers. They abandoned their stand at Balapur and marched towards Burhanpur. But Malik Ambar would not spare them. He chased them up to the fort of Burhanpur, plundering and devastating the country on the way. He even opened the siege of the fort (1620 A.D.). Within a short time the surrounding country passed into the hands of the Daccanis, who boldly crossed the Narbada and penetrated into the very heart of Malwa, burning and plundering the environs of Mandu and its adjacent villages. For another six months the Mughals remained subject to harassment, till at length the reinforcements arrived from the north. Malik Ambar reduced them to sorry plight, struck terror into their hearts and showed to them the superiority of the Daccani forces, the patriotic feelings of the common inhabitants and their zeal in repelling and driving away the enemy from the Daccan.[87](a) In no circumstances did he desire to remain under the Mughal suzerainty. He had now thrown off the mask. His ambitions soared high, for, he had completed his plan of expansion. He was now the master of not only the portions lying within jurisdiction of Ahmadnagar, but of many parganas of Berar and Khandesh including those which lay across the Narbada.

Great consternation arose in Burhanpur and in other Mughal possessions in Ahmadnagar and Balaghat, where the lives of the Mughal generals were in peril. They had neither the courage to remain in the Daccan, nor resources to fly to the north. Misery and tears formed their lot. Khan Khanan in rank despair had more than once appealed to the Mughal Emperor for speedy relief. He even threatened to commit suicide to obtain eternal deliverance from the difficulties. Every day he passed in anxiety and every night from fear of the Daccani forces. In his last despatch he compared his position to that of Aziz Kokah in Gujarat in the reign of Emperor Akbar and he pathetically called upon Emperor Jahangir to save him, as his father had saved his foster brother.[88]

When the tragic state of affairs was reported to the Emperor he decided to send Prince Shahjahan again to retrieve the position in the Daccan. As on the former occasion, the Prince was accompanied by a galaxy of officers and generals and had at his command a very large army. From Ujjain he sent reinforcement under Abul Hasan and Bairam Beg to Mandu where the Commander Muhammad Taqi[89] stood in hourly fear of the Daccanis. On the receipt of the report that relief was speedily comming, the latter came out of the fort, fell upon the enemy and put them to flight. Subsequently, in conjunction with Abul Hasan he drove them to Akbarpur. In this way the Maratha pressure was completely neutralised and the Prince arrived at Mandu. Here he received a despatch from Khan Khanan, asking him to stay where he was and not to attempt to proceed to Burhanpur where he had been couped up by the enemy. The Prince rejected the suggestion and carefully planned his bold offensive, taking every possible precaution against the unexpected movements of the Daccanis.

**Prince Shahjahan again sent against Malik Ambar (June 1621 A.D.)**

He left Mandu on 25th March, 1621 A. D. and marched towards Burhanpur. He personally commanded the centre of the Mughal army; while Abdullah Khan, Raja Vikramajit and Abul Hasan respectively held the charge of the van, the right and left wings of the army. They easily crossed Narbada on 14th April, 1621 A. D. The Prince succeeded in getting to Khan Khanan in Burhanpur. But the Daccanis took no notice of him, sticking fast to their outposts round the city. Upon this Shahjahan held a council of war in which various suggestions were put forward. Khan Khanan and others advocated postponement of further operations till the end of rains, but the Prince stood for swift action, because it would deprive the enemy of all chance of strengthening their position. Moreover, it was the only way of taking advantage of the superiority of numbers. To augment his army further Shahjahan asked such Jagirdars whose lands had been seized by the enemy to raise levies and place them at his disposal.

Every detail of the plan having been worked out with

meticulous care and elaborate instructions having been issued to the commanders, Shahjahan ordered the imperial army to advance. It made its way to Balaghat inspite of the interruptions caused by the Daccani Commander Yaqut Khan, who constantly hovered over the rear, delivering surprise attacks, reassembling his men after reverses and repeating his exploits over again. From Balaghat, the Mughals marched towards Khirki, fighting the Daccanis all along the way. Malik Ambar abandoned the capital, removed Nizam Shah to Daultabad, followed him there and took up his position outside the fort. Khirki was once more occupied by the Mughals and was subjected to the most barbarous vandalism.[90]

Shahjahan was not the man to give any quarter to Malik Ambar. He left Khirki on 5th May 1621, A.D. to hound him out of Daultabad. But on the way the imperial army was subjected to repeated surprise attacks from the enemy, which exhausted their patience, broke their morale, so much so that the Prince had to abandon his attempt on Daultabad. He now turned his attention towards Ahmadnagar which was closely invested by the Daccanis. As usual, the progress of the imperial army was interrupted by the enemy who would appear all of a sudden, give battle and disappear with equal speed.

Thus fighting their way the Mughals moved on to find themselves caught up in a net. They had pushed too far into the Nizam Shahi country and their retreat was cut off. The weather was tiresome and the rainy season was approaching fast. To create a diversion in favour of his own men, Shahjahan directed Muhammad Taqi to recover Berar and Khandesh. He succeeded in driving away the enemy from those two provinces. But this did not improve the position of the imperial army in Balaghat where the Daccanis made their appearance again. But Muhammad Taqi quickly occupied all the strategic points in that region and restored the line of communication. To counteract this move Malik Ambar sent Atish Khan but he was defeated and put to flight.

Even so the pressure of the Daccanis on Ahmadnagar could not be relieved. Shahjahan now resorted to another plan and sent an army to Nasik and Sangamnir. But the venture proved to be stillborn. The scarcity of provisions owing to the devastations in the surrounding country, the spectre of complete starvation of the army, the apprehension of the surprise attacks from the Daccanis, began to work heavily on the mind of Prince Shahjahan and he began to think how to extricate himself from such an impossible situation with dignity and grace. As to Malik Ambar, he was in no better frame of mind. He could perceive the inferiority of his resources in a struggle with the mighty ruler of the Northern India. He was brave and indefatigable no doubt but this could not compensate the paucity of numbers at his command. Defeat and destruction once more began to stare him in the face. To save his skin, he opened negotiations for peace, entirely ignorant of the distress his enemy was suffering from.

Malik Ambar's representative met Raja Vikramajit at Patan where he was staying with the main army. He offered to surrender the territories once held by the Mughals in the Daccan but had been wrested by him during the last two years; secondly, he promised to abondon his right over fourteen kos of the adjoining territory and thirdly, he contracted that fifty lacs of rupees would be paid as indemnity by the rulers of Bijapur, Golcunda and Ahmadnagar. But the Raja declined to listen to anything till Malik Ambar had withdrawn his men from the environs of Ahmadnagar, and let the convoy of provisions which was sent to the garrison pass freely. Malik Ambar readily complied with these demands. Thus satisfied with his conduct and behaviour, the Mughals concluded peace with him. Shahjahan, thereafter returned to Burhanpur.[91]

**Ambar submits**

It need hardly be noted that this humiliating treaty was the result of the pressure exerted on Malik Ambar by the rulers of Bijapur and Golcunda, who used him as safety valve against the Mughal aggression, but withdrew their support whenever they found that the situation had become irresistable or their own interests stood in serious danger. In this way they played a double role, helping Malik Ambar, whenever it suited their interests, and professing their loyalty to the Mughal Emperor whenever it became inevitable to do it. Even so an enforced peace like this could not be lasting.

It made Malik Ambar more resentful towards his neighbours than towards the Mughals.

A year after the conclusion of peace, an event took place which was symbolic of new development which had taken place in the Nizam Shahi kingdom in the hour of its struggle with the Mughals. A number of Maratha chiefs had made their way to high ranks and positions. They were ambitious and jealous of each other, a state of affairs which in the long proved to be a running sore to the integrity of the kingdom.

**Desertion of Jadhav Rao—rivalry between Jadhavs and Bhonsles**

One day at the close of the audience, the elephant of a Maratha noble Khandagale got out of control and trampled down several men. Jadhav Rao's son Dattaji ran out to control the elephant. Misunderstanding the intentions of Dattaji, Vithoji's son Shambhuji, Kheloji, and Shahji too advanced to save their friend Khandgale from the hands of Dattaji. In the struggle which ensued Jadhav Rao's son Dattaji was killed. Jadhav Rao in revenge killed Shambhaji and wounded his son-in-law Shahji. On hearing of the incident, Burhan Nizam Shah III arrived on the scene and separated the two combatants. But he was so disgusted with the power and pride of Jadhav Rao that he began to plan to oust him with the help of the Bhonsles. At length because of the intense rivalry with Kheloji Bhonsle and his brothers, who supported Nizam Shah against him, Jadhav Rao with all his adherents left Daultabad and joined the Mughal service. He was recipient of honours there, and was given the Mansab of 2400 Zat and 15000 Sawars. His relatives who had accompanied him were also elevated to high posts. His desertion was a serious loss to the Nizam Shahis because henceforward the Maratha nobles in expectation of high ranks and mansabs frequently deserted the cause of their master and joined the Mughals.[92]

By a singular irony of fate, Prince Shahjahan who had won glory in the Daccan and had humbled the pride of Malik

**Rebel Prince Shahjahan solicits Ambar's assistance**

Ambar had to appear as a suppliant in the very region, where he had once dictated commands to the high and mighty. He had rebelled against his father and had been hounded out of northern India and, was compelled to cross the Tapti on 10th September 1623 A. D. He sent Afzal Khan to Malik Ambar to solicit his help, but the latter was in no mood to listen to the request. How could he forget the humiliation which he had received at the hands of the rebel Prince ? Moreover, he was the last man to court disaster at the hands of the imperial army which was moving fast at the heels of the fugitive. And finally, he had to settle scores with Adil Shah, an objective which he could only achieve with the help of the Mughals. Nor did Afzal Khan fare better at the Adil Shahi court and thus Shahjahan had to leave the Daccan disappointed.[93]

As Ahmadnagar and Bijapur were contiguous states, frequent disputes used to occur between them, mostly for the possession of border lands. In an hour of distress in the affairs of the Nizam Shahi kingdom, Ibrahim Adil Shah II had annexed Sholapur and its adjoining territories in 1600 A.D. The process of aggrandisement once begun, continued unabated. The rise of Malik Ambar and his unrelenting efforts to revive the fortunes of the fallen house, added further to the distraction of Adil Shah. But refugees like Farhad Khan who had come to Bijapur, after deserting Nizam Shah and courting the animosity of Malik Ambar, whetted the territorial appetite of the ruler of Bijapur. Moreover the Adil Shahi nobles were equally anxious to see the fall of Ambar in the vain hope of partitioning out his lands among themselves. On the other hand Malik Ambar had his own plans of recovering such territories as had been seized by Adil Shah. When Mahabat Khan arrived in the Daccan, he received overtures from Malik Ambar as well as from Ibrahim Adil Shah II. Each in his anxiety to obtain the Mughal alliance offered better terms than the other. But Mahabat Khan kept both of them in suspense, till Shahjahan had left the Daccan and then he decided the issue in favour of Adil Shah, hoping that the ensuing struggle between the two would bring about the security of the Mughal position in the Daccan. In compliance with terms

**Rupture with Bijapur**

**Adil Shah II and Malik Ambar apply to Mahabat Khan for assistance**

of the pact, Adil Shah despatched a contingent of 500 troops under Mulla Muhammad Lari, which safely arrived at Burhanpur.[94]

Taking no notice of the movements of the Bijapuri contingent, Malik Ambar left Khirki, removed the Nizam Shahi family to Daultabad, and himself moved towards Qandhar on the borders of Golcunda, with the avowed intention of realising the subsidy from Qutb Shah, but in reality to form an alliance against the new coalition. Shortly after, Mahabat Khan and Prince Parwez left Daccan to meet Shahjahan's threat in the north.[95] This was the signal for Malik Ambar's move against Adil Shah.

**Ambar enters into an alliance with Qutb Shah**

Having concluded an offensive alliance with Qutb Shah, Malik Ambar marched towards Bidar which had been in the possession of Ibrahim Adil Shah II since 1619 A.D. He attacked the Bijapuri forces, took them by surprise, routed them completely and plundered the city of Nauraspur. After seizing much booty he marched towards Bijapur, plundering and devastating in the way. Ibrahim Adil Shah II being unable to fight him in the open, retired into the fort which was besieged by Malik Ambar.[96] Ibrahim Adil Shah now recalled Mulla Muhammad Lari from Burhanpur, and appealed for help to the Mughal governor Sarbuland Rai. It was only after the latter had received three lacs of huns from the Adil Shahi general and an order from Mahabat Khan that he started mobilising his troops. Having arranged for the security of the imperial possessions in the Daccan Sarbuland Rai allowed Mulla Muhammad Lari to return to Bijapur along with a contingent of the Mughal troops. The coalition alarmed Malik Ambar and he importuned the Mughals to stand aside and let him settle the score with Adil Shah. But the Mughal officers paid no heed to his appeals and remonstrances. They pushed forward and compelled him to raise the siege of Bijapur.[97] He retreated northward, hotly pursued by the allies. He crossed the Bhima at Taligaon and took up his

**Battle of Bhatvadi 15th June 1625 A.D.**

position at Bhatvadi, ten miles from Ahmadnagar. Here the rival parties arrayed their forces and fought a contested battle in which Malik Ambar inflicted a crushing defeat on the allies. On this occasion he was supported by a host of Maratha officers, like Shahji, Sharofji, Kheloji, Maloji Mambaji, Nagoji, Parsoji, Trimbakji, Kakoji, Hambir Rao Chavan, Madhji. Narshinghraja, Ballela Tripul, Vithalraj Kavata, Dattoji Naganath, Narsingh Pingle, Sunder Jagdev etc.[98]

**Ambar's prestige rose high**

Success at Bhatvadi saved the Nizam Shahi kingdom from extinction. It raised the prestige of Malik Ambar and increased his self-confidence. It humbled the pride of the Mughals as well as of Adil Shah. It revealed the superiority of the military tactics of Ambar and his unique skill as a general. His achievements on this occasion may aptly be compared to those of Rana Pratap at Haldighat and Sher Khan at Surajgarh. Mulla Muhammad Lari was slain in the field of battle and the Mughal Commander Khanjar Khan had to pass the rest of his life in prison at Daultabad. It was a sad commentry on the diplomacy of Mahabat Khan who had befriended Adil Shah as against Malik Ambar.

The report of the disaster at Bhatvadi created much consternation at Burhanpur where Sarbuland Rai grew apprehensive of the safety of Mughal possessions. Indeed Malik Ambar embarked upon the counter-offensive, with his zeal redoubled. He laid siege to the fort of Ahmadnagar, marched to Bijapur which he had invested, occupied the territories up to Balaghat and captured Sholapur by storming it on 15th June 1625. His general Yaqut Khan invested Burhanpur. Verily the network of Malik Ambar's activities now covered a larger area than ever before. He was in a position to strangulate the Mughal supremacy in the Daccan. (1625 A. D.)[99]

At such a psychological moment arrived Shahjahan, who after a brief spell of success in Bengal and Bihar had again been expelled from Northern India to seek asylum in the Daccan. And when he solicited Malik Ambar's friendship, the latter received him with open arms. The prince

**Burhanpur Besieged**

agreed to play the game of his host, forsaking all loyalty to the empire which he was looking forward to rule. At Malik Ambar's instance, he laid siege to Burhanpur, but it was stoutly defended by Sarbuland Rai. And when at length Mahabat Khan arrived again in the Daccan, Shahjahan and Yaqut Khan were compelled to withdraw from Burhanpur. Shahjahan soon after tendered his submission to his father who allowed him to remain unmolested in the Daccan.[100]

The events now moved fast at Mughal court. Mahabat Khan's growing influence and his attachment to Prince Parwez excited the jealousy of Nur Jahan, who after having humbled the pride of Shahjahan, truned her attention towards her life-long foe. Mahabat Khan was recalled from the Daccan and was sent away to Bengal. Subsequently charges of embezzlement and breach of court etiquette were levelled against him. He arrived at the court to offer his explanation and succeeded in making the king and his consort prisoner. But Nur Jahan not only managed to escape; but she also succeeded in rescuing her husband. Tables were thus turned on Mahabat Khan, and in sheer desperation he unfurled the banner of revolt. The preoccupation of the imperial army in dealing with the outbreak and want of competent officers to control the situation there, offered an excellent opportunity to Malik Ambar to complete his plan of expelling the Mughals completely from the Daccan. But before he could embark upon his project, he was snatched away by the cruel hands of death on 14, May 1626 A. D. at the age of eighty. He was buried at Amarpur or Ambarpur.[101]

**Death of Malik Ambar**

Bhimsen the author of Nuskha-i-Dilkusha says that "although Malik Ambar was dead, but his sweet fragrance still remained behind", Pieter Van den Broecke the famous Dutch traveller gives a vivid description of the personality of Malik Ambar. He writes that, "this Malik Ambar is black kafir from Abyssinia or Prester John's country. He has a stern Roman face and strong body with white glazed eyes which were very unbecoming".[102] While according to Ravesteyn,

**His Personality**

"he is a substantial man in body and limb, of more than middle height, black as Moor".[103] Echoeing the same view, Prof. Saksena remarks,"he was dark complexioned and tall; having long and tapering arms, broad chest, narrow waist and a stout and thick set neck, like that of a lion. Every limb of his body betokened vigour, and vitality; boldness appeared from his face, determination from his lips, and farsightedness from his eyes. Indeed he was gifted with all the qualities befitting a leader of men".[104]

In the midst of adverse condition and beset by vicissitudes of fortune, Malik Ambar by sheer dint of skill, undaunted courage and rare genius, like the few renowned Sultans of the Slave dynasty, rose from poverty to affluence and impressed the annals of the Daccan with the hall mark of his personality. Early in life, he was able to secure the patronage of a generous and noble minded man like Changez Khan which proved of great advantage to him. But he could hardly enjoy the spell of peace for any considerable time, because the death of his patron threw him into the depth of sorrow and helplessness. Nevertheless he fought against heavy odds, and his ambition never faltered even when distress and disappointment stared him in the face. He was not the man to lose his mental poise even in conditions of gloom and despair. His energy was indefatigable, his strength uncommon and his intelligence extraordinary. He was charming in his manners, dignified in his behaviour, and firm in his resolve. His one mission in life was to throw back the tide of the Mughal aggression in the Daccan and revive the drooping fortunes of the Nizam Shahi house, which the providence had handed over to his charge. He pursued it with single-minded devotion gathering all the available resources and constantly improving his striking power. His perseverence was proverbial, instead of being perplexed by serious reverses, he felt encouraged for fresh ventures. He waged a relentless struggle against the enemy for about a quarter of a century, perfecting his own methed of offence and defence, and changing his tactics from time to time. Nor did he depend on the strength of his sword alone. He roused the patriotic feelings of the population, which began to look

**Saviour of the Nizam Shahi House**

upon him as their saviour. He was respected and loved by Hindus and the Muslims alike. His achievements form a noble example of how a mighty power can be resisted with the popular support. In the interregnums which occurred between the series of invasions, he remodelled the civil and military administration of the Nizam Shahi kingdom, made roads safe from the highwaymen and robbers, introduced a new system of land revenue, which made the people happy and prosperous.

His claim to greatness rests both on his genius as a general and an administrator. As a military leader he was unrivalled in his age. He reorganised the militia on a new pattern; initiated a new system of warfare called, "bargigiri" or predatory warfare, which was suited as much to the physical features of the country as to the nature of local population. He collected them, recruited them, trained them, and infused in them a new martial spirit. The essence of his tactics lay in avoiding pitched battles, hovering on the flanks of the enemy, cutting off the stragglers, intercepting the supplies, and attacking their camp in the night. He made full use of the light Maratha cavalry and laid the foundation of the future Maratha nation. He also trained a corps of Habshi slaves to act as guards and shock-troops and he developed the spy system so efficiently that he never failed to obtain the minutest information with regard to the movements of the enemy. He was not only a master of the predatory warfare but was equally at home in the pitched battle. In the field of Bhatvadi he proved the superiority of his military skill to that of the Adil Shahis and the Mughals. He knew when to strike the blow on the enemy, or to wait for a suitable opportunity. In 1624 A. D. when the Bijapuri forces chased him hotly from the environs of Bijapur, he retreated and repeatedly negotiated for peace, but when his efforts failed, he chose his ground, waited for an opportune moment for general action, used his superior military tactics and inflicted a crushing defeat on them.

**Ambar as a General**

It was beyond the power of his enemies to catch up his tactics. His speedy mobilisation of troops from one field to another, caused headache to the Mughals, and exposed the bankruptcy of their military skill. He subjected them to continuous harassment, reducing them to miserable plight. He more than once carried war into the very heart of their territory, laying siege to their capital in the Daccan. It was his daring personality, which inspired his soldiers to penetrate successfully into Malwa and levy contributions from the inhabitants of Mandu and create fresh problems for the enemy by plundering and devastating the surrounding country. It is true that Shahjahan scored twice over him, but his success was more showy than real. It did not touch the basic reservoir of his resources. Each time no sooner did the Prince turn his back than Malik Ambar started counter-offensive, driving the enemy back across the Narbada. Even Mutmad Khan the author of Iqbalnama-i-Jahangiri, who never, omitted to abuse, Malik Ambar as dark-faced, ill-fortuned Abyssinian speaks in glowing terms of his achievements as a general and statesman. According to him "Ambar was a slave but an able man. In warfare, in command, in sound judgement and in administration he had no equal or rival......History records no instance of an Abyssinian slave arriving at such eminence".[105] Emperor Jahangir was himself forced to admire the greatness of Malik Ambar. He writes "in the art of soldiering Ambar was unique in his age. He put down the disorderly elements in his country and spent his whole life honourably".

**Ambar an astute Politician**

As an astute politician Malik Ambar stood far above his contemporaries. With his sound judgement and extraordinary tactfulness he was able to save the Nizam Shahi kingdom from total extinction. His keen insight quickly diagnosed the malady which had eaten the body politic of the Nizam Shahis and he promptly addressed himself to the task finding out the suitable remedies. He believed in internal peace and external security. He was the biggest opportunist of his age, who liked to wait rather than to purchase unnecessary disgrace by hasty action. He fought when necessary, and yielded when inevitable. In that atmosphere of political fludity, war and peace had no fixed values in his eyes. He used them to further his own ends. He befriended Khan Khanan or Adil Shah when it suited him; he turned against them when he found them crossing his objectives. He spurned the advances of

Shahjahan when he arrived in the Daccan as a rebel for the first time; but subsequently received him with open arms when he found him ready to play his game. In short neither the military superiority of the Mughals nor their diplomatic skill could ever break his bone completely. He always emerged out victorious, preserving the existence of the Nizam Shahi kingdom.

He could clearly perceive that it was impossible to live in isolation or to face the Mughal aggression all by himself. Therefore, he made it the cardinal principle of his policy to seek the support and cooperation of other Daccani states. He formed offensive and defensive alliances with the rulers of Bijapur, Golcunda and Bidar, which were driven into his arms, from the sheer consideration of self-protection, see as they did the misfortune which had befallen Khandesh. Naturally, they could repose more faith in Malik Ambar than in the aggressive Mughals. Though occasionally compelled to acknowledge the Mughal suzerainty, they never falied to help Malik Ambar secretly with men and money. It was Ambar's genius which enabled him to keep them together for two decades, and to present, with their cooperation a strong opposition to the Mughals. It was during the latter part of his life that the bitter hostility between him and Adil Shah threw the latter into the arms of the Mughals.

**Protector of the Daccani States**

But Ambar was great not only as general or politician, he was a successful administrator also. Even in the midst of a stormy life, he spared no efforts for devising a suitable system of administration. With an iron hand he crushed all factious strife, turbulence and lawlessness. Being convinced of the fact that unless the government has for its basis the goodwill of the people, it can not survive long, he impregnated his policy with due regard for impartiality, affection and justice. Thus he earned not only the gratitude of his people but also their undying reverence.

**Ambar as administrator**

True to the Nizam Shahi tradition Malik Ambar followed a policy of religious toleration. His hands never fell upon the Hindu temples. Hindus and Muslims had full freedom to

**His Liberal outlook**

follow their faiths. Like Akbar he threw service open to talent. Many posts of high distinction were filled up by Hindus like Shahji, Sharofji, Vithalraj and Jadhav Rao, who rendered valuable services in the civil and military departments. Muslims, Hindus, the Portuguese[106] and the Dutch worked in complete harmony and in the interest of the Nizam Shahi kingdom.

Malik Ambar possessed a highly developed sense of justice as is testified by contemporary historians and foreign travellers.[107] All classes of people lived in contentment under his regime, and his fame as the upholder of law spread far and wide. Khafi Khan has narrated a story bearing upon this aspact of his character. After the battle of Bhatvadi, when the Mughal and the Bijapuri amirs were produced before him, he scolded them for their cowardice which prompted them to take to flight from the field of battle. He ordered that each of them to be punished with one hundred stripes. Among the prisoners was a poet, and a mansabdar of five hundred. When he was brought to receive the punishment, he exclaimed, "I have heard that Malik Ambar is a just and upright man, but it was a mistake for me to think so. Would it be just to punish the mansabdar of 3000 and 2000 in the same manner ?" Malik Ambar was highly pleased to hear these remarks, and excused him. Since then his fame as bestower of justice became by word in the Mughal and Bijapuri camps".

**His sense of Justice**

Throughout his life, Malik Ambar was engaged in the military campaigns against the Mughals in defending and reviving the tottering kingdom of his master. Though he had little leisure, he did not fail to devise means for the welfare of his people in general and the peasantry in particular. Taking into account the exhausted financial resources of the kingdom, he worked hard to improve them by introducing a new system of land revenue which has immortalised his name in every village of that region. It was based on the pattern adopted by the great financier Raja Todar Mal in Northern India, and which was prevailing in some

**Malik Ambar as a financier**

parts of Gujarat and Khandesh. It was modified to suit the requirements of the situation. Very much like its counterpart in Northern India, it took into account the correct knowledge of land under cultivation and money value of the crops. Further more the land was classified according to its quality, and the assessment of the government demand was made accordingly.

In introducing the new system of land revenue administration Ambar had three objects before him; firstly, to promote the interest of the peasantry which formed the bulk of local population; secondly, to promote agriculture and thereby enhance the income of the Government; and thirdly, to eliminate, as far as possible the middle agency. Keeping these objects in view he started with the abolition of the farming system. According to the prevailing practice the settlement of land revenue was made with the hereditary revenue superintendents and accountants i.e. deshmukhs and deshpandes. The high handedness of the big and wealthy landholders which had ultimately resulted in the neglect of cultivation and led to the poverty of the cultivators, in the rural areas, was too well known to Malik Ambar. He, therefore, decided to establish direct relation with the peasants. With one stroke of his pen he did away with the intermediaries. He made the village headman or the *patil* and the revenue officers hereditary and made them responsible for the realisation of the government dues. Each *patil* was required to collect the revenue of the entire village under his jurisdiction, and to remit it directly to the Government. Similarly each petty land holder was required to pay the full share of his rent to the *patil* of his village.

To determine and fix the government demand, Ambar adopted Todar Mal's method of surveying and classifying the arable land. About his survey it is stated that, "the areas were fixed not by measuring, but by a glance estimate Nazar Pahani". He seems to have divided the land into good or bad, without aiming at so elaborate a classification as was intended in Todar Mal's scheme. In his system the word 'bigha' stood not for any measurement, but it only indicated the amount of rent which a holding could bear. No wonder, therefore, that in some cases even though a cultivator held twice as much of the less fertile land than another holding the bigha of more fertile land, the demand in either case was same. Thus the bigha indicated the crop yielding powers of a particular area.

In his experiments to fix the average yield of the different plots of village land he took only arable lands into account. Hill lands were not included. When the whole arable land of a village had been ascertained, it was divided according to the ancient practice into two classes; (1) Baghyat or garden lands, (2) Zirayat or corn lands. The corn lands were further divided into four classes, the first, second, third and fourth (Avval, Dum, Som, and chaharim) while the uplands were classified in a general way.

For the sake of government revenue, the arable lands were divided into Khalsa or lands which yielded revenue to the government, and Inamat or lands whose revenues had been alienated through royal favour or in return for some service. After deducting the latter from the total area, the Khalsa land (the land which paid rent to government) was entered as including so much garden (Baghiat) and so much corn land or Ziriat. In the accounts, first came the alienated lands which were distinguished, dumla or two ownered *inam*, held by the Vatandars and wholly *inam* which were assigned to mosques, temple and village servants. After the entries regarding the rent alienated lands, were entered the details of the assessment of the rent paying or Khalsa lands. Lastly, there was an entry of the cesses, some of them fixed while others varying, which were levied on craftsmen, shop keepers and village servants.

It is not known what portion of the produce Malik Ambar took as government share ? According to Captain Robertson "Malik Ambar probably adopted Todar Mal's plan and fixed the rent at one-fourth of the yield". While according to others he fixed two fifth of the produce of the land in kind as state share. It is also stated that when grain payment was commuted into cash payment, it represented about one-third of the yield in 1614 but in 1618 he doubled the government demand. As regards the conversion rates, they did not vary with the fluctuations in the price of the grain and from their extreme lowness were probably at the time when they were introduced greatly below the actual prices. It appears that the average normal payment called *tankha* was fixed for each plot of land and surveyed, in every village. The actual collections varied from year to year in accordance with the conditions of crops. The main determining factor was the harvest. If the season was bright, the actual collections increased vice versa. Undoubtedly the assessment made on such elastic and sympathetic basis was up to the full satisfaction of the peasant. Similarly the "principles of adaptability and moderate demands" gave a new impetus to agriculture. It also enabled the *patils* to give out the waste lands at low rates to the cultivators to till them. In this way all the barren and waste lands were transformed into cultivable fields.

Instead of making the state to be the sole landowner, Malik Ambar sought to strengthen the government by giving the people a definite interest in the soil they tilled. He made a considerable portion of land private property. And the land of the village was considered as joint property of the townships. The fallow land was common for the pasture of the cattle and the ploughed land was either the property of the individual villagers or it was tilled by the headman's tenants who received a portion of the crop. It appears to have been a principle of his wise administration, to encourage the possession of private landed property as a means of attaching the cutlivators to the soil. In fact these excellent measures served two objects of Malik Ambar; firstly, they satisfied the people and thus strengthened the government; and secondly, they led to the cultivation of lands which might have otherwise been neglected and must have certainly deprived the government a share of revenue. His system combined two great merits; firstly moderate and permanent demand; secondly, inculcation of a new spirit in the cultivators to till the soil.

But unfortunately this system was not without its drawbacks. The land was never carefully surveyed, the practice of glance-estimate was extremely defective, because it did not help in arriving at a correct assessment of the produce. Moreover, as the settlement was made with the village headman or *patil* (who was made hereditary), instead of individual cultivators, it gave an opportunity to the former to use his power and influence for his own advantage. Though the first defect did not attract attention of Malik Ambar, he did attempt to remove the second to a certain extent. He entrusted the management and superintendence of revenue to the persons of different nationalities, each serving as a check upon the growing power of the other. The administration of land revenue was entirely in the hands of Brahmins, but they had to work under the supervision of Muslim officers who acted as a check on their high handedness. This measure of Malik Ambar proved to be of great advantage to the cultivators. His personal supervision and close vigilance prevented the officers from becoming greedy and selfish. No wonder during his regime agriculture began to thrive, the country became populous, and the finances of the state became stable. This was by no means a small achievement.

Malik Ambar's revenue reforms not only yielded rich dividend in terms of money, they added considerably to his reputation. Within a short time his name became a household word in every family of the Daccan. He earned the gratitude of the producing classess by looking after their interests and providing them impetus for working harder and for reclaiming waste lands. Naturally the revenue of the government increased. So much so that in spite of heavy military expenses the Nizam Shahis under him had never to face financial crisis.

Ambar was also a great builder. He founded the town of Khirki in 1605 A.D., the memorable year of the Gun powder plot in the English History and called it after his son Fatehnagar, which latter on came to be known as the famous city of Aurangabad. Here he built many mosques and palaces, planted gardens and dug canals. The most remarkable feat of his engineering skill was the ingenious system of water supply, which he provided to the city. A deep underground channel brought the water to the new capital. Among his buildings the traces of which still remain in Aurangabad are Bhadkal Darwaza, Nakhuda Mahal and Kalachabutara (which is now in ruins, but consisted of five Zanana buildings, a Diwan-i-Am, a Diwan-i-Khas, big grounds, cisterns and many baths). He also built for the Christians a church (of which only a solitary wall exists now) which

**Great Builder**

shows his respect for that Faith and which testifies to his liberal attitude towards the different religious sects.[108]

**Promoter of Learning**

He was also a patron of learning and of learned men. Scholars flocked to his court from the distant lands of Arabia. One of the greatest among them was Shilli *Hadrani*, whose work, "Iqd-al-Jawahar" contains biographical sketches of great men, who flourished in the 11th century Hijra. Shilli records that poets who flocked to Ambar's court, read eulogistic verses and were handsomely rewarded. There were many other Persian scholars at his court, which shows that he was a fairly cultured man who loved the society of the learned and pious. At Khirki he built a "Chitkhana" or house of learning, where Hindu Pandits, learned men and scholars gathered and prosecuted their studies in different branches of learning.[109]

Ambar was famous for his charity and benevolence, which induced Asad Khan, the author or Waqiyat-i-Asad Beg to praise him in these words, "Verily if the virtues of the tree of Universe were to be set down, even in part, it would require a chapter, nay an entire volume to do it". He was never oblivious of his duties towards the people whose imagination he had captured by his plain living and high thinking. He was very punctilious in observance of the tenets of his religion. In his camp every night 12000 men recited the Holi Quran. He offered his prayers along with the common people, whose number was never less than a thousand. His charities are beyond description. In his piety he is compared to the pious Bilal, the disciple of Prophet Muhammad.[110] In short, it may be remarked that he became neclues of the revival of the cultural traditions of the Nizam Shahi kingdom.

---

*Notes and References*:

1. According to Dr. D. R. Seth, Ambar's original name was Shambu see, "Life and times of Malik Ambar", Islamic Culture, April, 1957, pp. 142; Iqbalnama-i-Jahangiri places his death at the age of eighty on 31st Urdibahist, 1035, A.H.—Iqbalnama, pp. 607; Khafi Khan also says that Malik Ambar died in the year 1035 A.H. at the age of eighty years—see Muntakhab-ul-Lubab I pp. 376; Shiva Bharata gives the date of his death, as 1548, saka era, which also comes to the year 1035 A.H. The author of Basatin-us-Salatin also places the date of his death in the same year;

pp. 274; Therefore it may be justly inferred that Malik Ambar must have, been born about the year 1549 A.D.; see also, Ghulam Ahmad's article "Rise and Decline of the city of Aurangabad"—Proceedings of Daccan History Conference, 1945, pp. 220;

2. According to the Dutch traveller Pieter Van Den Broecke, Malik Ambar was a slave and was sold in Mocha for 20 ductas—see, Journal of Indian History, 1932 pp. 146; Also see, Islamic Culture, April, 1957, pp. 142;

3. Futuhat-i-Adil Shahi pp. 267; For Marathi translation of Futuhat-i-Adil Shahi, see, "Shiv Charitra Vrita Sangraha" part III, Persian section of the Bharata Itihas Samshodhak Mandal, Poona, Quarterly, Vol. 20 1930; Islamic Culture, April 1957, pp. 142; Epigraphica Indo Moslemica 1931-38, pp. 22-3;

4. Futuhat-i-Adil Shahi, pp. 262;

5. Futuhat-i-Adil Shahi, pp. 262; An interesting story is narrated by the author of Tarikh-i-Shivaji about the advent and rise of Malik Ambar. According to it, Malik Ambar came from Bijapur to Daultabad as a Faqir and while he was sleeping in a shop on the road-side with his legs raised, Shahaji Annant, then an influential Nizam Shahi noble, happened to pass by that road. His eyes fell upon the soles of the feet of Malik Ambar and he discerned in them marks of his rising fortunes. It occurred to him that he was either a chieftain or his son. Therefore Shahaji awakened him and took him to his house, honoured him and made him the naik of the kingdom. The story seems to be a myth rather than a fact; see, Tarikh-i-Shivaji, Modern Review, Vol. I Jan. to June, 1907;

6. Futuhat-i-Adil Shahi, pp. 262; Marathi translation, pp. 3; Bharat Itihas Samshodhak Mandal Quarterly, Vol. 20. 1939; Islamic Culture, April, 1957, pp. 142;

7. Ibid.

8. Futuhat-i-Adil Shahi pp. 267-68 (a) Marathi Translation pp. 3 (Bharat Itihas Samshodhak Mandal, Poona) Quarterly, Vol. 20, 1939.

According to the Dutch Traveller Pieter Van Den Broecke, after the death of his master (Changez Khan) Malik Ambar won over his widow who had but little property because the king of the country usually seizes the property of great men, so that he had to turn to theft and robbery. In this he was successful and he obtained a large following, so that eventually he came to command more than 5,000 horsemen. He maintained himself and robbers in an impregnable place where the king of Ahmadnagar could do nothing for many years, but because the king was at war with the great Mughal, who wanted to make himself master of the whole Daccan, he summoned Malik Ambar and offered to employ him on a good salary against the Mughals. The Malik refused this offer and persisted in his activities so that eventually he collected a force of over 8,000 horse and gained many partisans. Seeing this, the king again offered terms of peace and suggested that if the latter married his daughter and made her as Queen, he would serve him faithfully against the great Mughal, and would always be his subject. The king with the approval of his counsellors agreed to proposal and married Malik's daughter with great pomp and magnificence. Whereupon the Malik came to the court with 8,000 well mounted horsemen, was cordially welcomed and provided with 4,000 additional horsemen making 12,000 in all and he rose to high favour with the king—see, Journal of Indian History, 1932, pp. 146-7; see also, "Travels of Pietro Della Valle" Vol. II pp. 144-46;

9. Ferishta II pp. 164; Futuhat-i-Adil Shahi, pp. 269 (b) and 270; Basatin-us-Salatin, pp. 261; Akbar Nama III pp. 1173; Elliot and Dowson, Vol. VI pp. 101; Iqbalnama-i-Jahangiri pp. 268; Maasir-i-ul-Umra, Vol. I pp. 534-5; Oriental Biographical Dictionary pp. 283; See, Ghulam Ahmad's article, "The Rise and Decline of the city of Aurangabad," Proceedings of Daccan History Conference, 1945, pp. 220; also see Dr. D.R. Seth's article, "Life and Times of Malik Ambar", Islamic Culture April, 1957; pp. 143; Maasir-i-Rahimi, wrongly mentions that Muhammad Husain, the

son of Shah Quli Bahri was raised to the throne—see, Maasir-i-Rahimi, Vol. II pp. 511; Similarly Khafi Khan also has made a mistake in mentioning that Shah Ali, the son of Burhan Nizam Shah I was raised to the throne and Bidar was fixed as temporary capital of the Nizam Shahi kingdom see, Muntakhab-ul-Lubab III, pp 264;

10. Maasir-i-Rahimi Vol. II pp. 501; Futuhat-i-Adil Shahi pp. 268 (a) Marathi Translation, pp 3; According to Dr. D. R. Seth, Raju was a Sayyid and not a Hindu as Grant Duff in his "A History of Marathas"; has wrongly mentioned see; Vol. I pp. 93;

11. Maasir-i-Rahimi Vol. II pp. 501; Akbar Nama, III pp. 1047;

12. Maasir-i-Rahimi Vol. II pp. 502; Akbar Nama, III pp. 1047;

13. Maasir-i-Rahimi, Vol. II pp. 502; Akbar Nama, III pp. 1047;

14. Maasir-i-Rahimi, Vol. II pp. 502; Akbar Nama, III pp. 1047;

15. Maasir-i-Rahimi, Vol. II pp. 502; Akbar Nama, III pp. 1047;

16. Futuhat-i-Adil Shahi (Marathi Translation) pp. 4; Maasir-i-Rahimi, Vol. III pp. 502-3;

17. Akbar Nama Vol. III pp. 1047;

18. Futuhat-i-Adil Shahi (Marathi Translation) pp. 4;

19. Akbar Nama Vol. III, pp. 1185; Futuhat-i-Adil Shahi (Marathi Translation) pp. 4;

20. Futuhat-i-Adil Shahi pp. 270.

21. Ibid, pp. 271 (a)

22. Ferishta, Briggs. III pp. 315;

23. see, Dr. Banarsi Prasad Saksena's article, "A few unnoticed facts about the early life of Malik Ambar" Proceedings of Indian History Congress, 1941; p. 601;

24. Akbar Nama III pp. 1187, Iqbalnama-i-Jahangiri, pp. 474-5;

25. Akbar Nama III pp. 1178; Iqbalnama-i-Jahangiri, pp. 274-5;

26. Akbar Nama III pp. 1181; Iqbalnama-i-Jahangiri, pp. 475;

27. Akbar Nama III pp. 1181; Iqbalnama-i-Jahangiri pp. 475;

28. Ferishta, Briggs. III pp. 315; Akbar Nama III pp. 1186; Maasir-ul-Umra Vol I pp. 535; Takmilai-i-Akbar Nama (Elliot and Dawson Vol. VI) pp. 105;

29. Iqbalnama-i-Jahangiri pp. 479; Islamic Culture, April, 1957 pp. 144;

30. Akbar Nama Vol. III, pp. 1193; 1194; 1125; 1200. Iqbalnama-i-Jahangiri, pp. 477; Maasir-ul-Umra Vol. I pp. 122;

31. Akbar Nama Vol. III pp. 1194;

32. Akbar Nama, Vol. III pp. 1194; Iqbalnama-i-Jahangiri, pp. 478;

33. Akbar Nama, Vol. III, pp. 1195, 1197;

34. Akbar Nama, Vol. III, pp. 1209;

35. Akbar Nama, Vol. III pp. 1209; Iqbalnama-i-Jahangiri pp. 481; Islamic Culture, April, 1957 pp. 144;

36. Akbar Nama, Vol. III, pp. 1209-10; Iqbalnama-i-Jahangiri, pp. 478;

37. Ferishta, Briggs. III, pp. 315-16; Akbar Nama, Vol. III pp. 1212; Iqbalnama-i-Jahangiri pp. 478-79; Muntakhab-ul-Lubab III pp. 255; Islamic Culture, April 1957, pp. 144-45;

38. Ferishta, Briggs. III, pp. 315-16; Akbar Nama, Vol. III pp. 1212; Muntakhab-ul-Lubab III, pp. 255; Iqbalnama-i-Jahangiri, pp 484; Islamic Culture, April, 1957, pp. 145;

39. Ferishta, Briggs. III pp. 315;

40. Ferishta, Briggs. III pp. 136; Maasir-i-Rahimi Vol. II pp. 502; Muntakhab-ul-Lubab III pp. 265; Islamic Culture, April, 1957. pp. 145;

According to Fizuni Astrabadi, the author of Futuhat-i-Adil Shahi, Malik Ambar even met the Mughal Emperor Akbar, a fact which is only a myth. It is not mentioned by any historian of Akbar's reign. See, Futuhat-i-Adil Shahi pp. 271 (a); Marathi Translation, pp. 4;

41. Ferishta, Briggs. III pp. 316;

42. Ibid. pp. 317;

43. Waqiyat-i-Azad Beg (Elliot and Dowson) Vol. V. pp. 152-53;167;

44. See, Dr. B. P. Saksena's article, "A few unnoticed facts about the early life of Malik Ambar" Proceedings of the Indian History Congress, 1941, pp. 601;

Emperor Akbar had sent Mir. Jamaluddin Anju on a mission to Bijapur to conclude a treaty with the ruler and to fetch his daughter, Begam Sultana, who had been promised in marriage to Prince Daniyal. But the Mir instead of bringing the mission to an early termination, overstayed there. This caused great anxiety to the Mughal Emperor, who wanted to see the Bijapur affairs settled as soon as possible. He was well aware of the Mughal position in the Daccan and the rising fortunes of the Daccani adventurer Malik Ambar and therefore he deputed Asad Beg, the author of Waqiyat-i-Asad Beg to escort the Mir and fulfil the task.

45. The Mughal envoy describes in the following lines the reception which was given to him by Malik Ambar, "All the amirs, members of the government, men of letters, religious leaders, and saints formed an assemblage, even one tenth of which was rarely to be seen at one place in India; religious discourses and recitals from the Quran were held on a scale only to be witnessed in the holy town of Mashhad. Verily, it was good luck (to be there) and heavenly joy.........Between the prayers a magnificent dinner was held, which in the Daccan dialect is called "Khanduri". A large tent was pitched in an open square and around it were erected shamiyanas decorated with figures and fish woven in covering. In every corner were placed, brass and silver vessels, each filled with dainty eatables. Every item of food was tastily cooked, sprinkled with a profusion of spices. There were numerous varieties of dilicious puddings, sweets, cakes, unleavened bred, all beyond praise, description or exaggeration."—Ibid.

Mentioning the charming manners of Malik Ambar the French Traveller, Francois Pyrard, who was in India between 1601-1608, writes, "The reigning Prince of Chaul is called Malique (Malik) and is a vassal of the great Mughal. The Malik has a large number of elephants. When he dines, he sends for many handsome women, who sing and dance, during the meal. Then some of them cut pieces of cloth called Tafety into bits so minute that they have no other use than that of being carried away by the spectators, who stick them over their breasts as if they wear so many medals, when the specticle is over. The King remains alone in his palace, his mind absorbed in the contemplation of variety and uncertainty of life, until he goes to sleep at last".

46. See, Dr. B. P. Saksena's article, "A few unnoticed facts on early life of Malik Ambar"—P. I. H. C. 1941. pp. 601;

47. Akbar Nama, Vol. III pp. 1239-40; Ferishta, Briggs. III pp. 318-9;

48. Futuhat-i-Adil Shahi (Marathi Translation) pp. 4;

49. Ibid.

50. Ibid.

51. Ibid, pp. 5;

52. Ibid, pp. 5;

53. Ferishta, Briggs. III, pp. 318;

54. Ibid, pp. 319;

55. Basatin-us-Salatin, pp. 270; Ferishta, Briggs. III, pp. 319-20;

56. Ferishta, Briggs. III, pp. 319-20; Maasir-i-Rahimi Vol. II, pp. 511;

57. Khan-i-Khanan stated in writing, "If I do'nt complete this service in course of two years, I shall be guilty (of fault) on the condition that in addition to the force that had been allotted to that subah, 12,000 more horse with Rs. 1000,000 should be sent with me. "Tuzuk-i-Jahangiri (R & B) pp. 149-153; Iqbalnama-i-Jahangiri, pp. 522; Muntakhab-ul-Lubab III, pp. 259; Maasir-i-Jahangiri (A.U. M/s) pp. 116; Basatin-us-Salatin pp. 261; Maasir-ul-Umra Vol. I pp. 56; Islamic Culture, April 1957, pp. 147;

58. Basatin-us-Salatin pp. 263-65; Futuhat-i-Adil Shahi (Marathi Translation) pp. 6;

59. Basatin-us-Salatin pp. 263-65;

60. Basatin-us-Salatin, p. 263-65;
61. Ibid, pp. 261;
62. Maasir-i-Rahimi, Vol. II, pp. 513;
63. Ibid, pp. 516;

64. Tuzuk-i-Jahangiri (R & B) Vol. I pp. 155-57; Iqbalnama-i-Jahangiri (A. U. M/s) pp. 119-21; Muntakhab-ul-Lubab Vol. I, pp. 26; Massir-ul-Umra, Vol. I pp. 54-56; Early Travels in India (William Finch—1608-11) pp. 131; Islamic Culture, April, 1957, pp. 147;

65. Tuzuk-i-Jahangiri (R. & B) Vol. I pp. 161-63; Iqbalnama-i-Jahangiri, pp. 525-26; Maasir-ul-Umra Vol. I pp. 54-56;

66. Tuzak-i-Jahangiri (R & B) Vol. I pp. 178, 179, 183; Iqbal-nama-i-Jahangiri pp. 525; Maasir-i-Jahangiri (A.U. M/s) pp. 131; Basatin-us-Salatin pp. 267; Muntakhab-ul-Lubab, Vol. I, pp. 261-62; Maasir-ul-Umra, Vol. I, pp. 57; Futuhat-i-Adil Shahi (Marathi Translation) pp. 6; Purchas and His Pilgrims (William Finch) Vol. IV pp. 39; Islamic Culture, April, 1957, pp. 148;

67. Tuzuk-i-Jahangiri (R & B) Vol. pp. 181-82; Maasir -i-Rahimi, Vol. II, pp. 514, 516, 518; Basatin-us-Salatin pp. 27; Muntakhab-ul-Lubab, Vol. I pp. 262; Early Travels in India, pp. 130-31; Travels of William Finch, pp. 24-25; Islamic Culture, April 1957, pp. 148-49;

69. Tuzuk-i-Jahangiri (R & B) Vol. I, pp. 183-84; Muntakhab-ul-Lubab, Vol. I pp. 262;

68. Tuzuk-i-Jahangiri (R & B) Vol. I pp. 179-80; Iqbalnama-i-Jahangiri, pp. 525; Maasir-i-Jahangiri (A. U. M/s) pp. 132; Muntakhab-ul-Lubab Vol. I pp. 262; Travels of William Finch, pp. 25;

70. Ferishta, Briggs. III, pp. 319-20;

71. John Briggs. and Col. T. W. Haig, whose lists of the Muhammedan dynasties of the Daccan are by far the most reliable and complete have omitted the name of Burhan Nizam Shah III. They have apparently confused his reign with that of Murtaza Nizam Shah II. The historians who have followed them, have committed the same mistake. But the name of Burhan Nizam Shah III is preserved in Basatin-us-Salatin (pp. 286) where it occurs in connection with the events of the reign of Muhammad Adil Shah (1628-58). Maasir-i-Rahimi clearly mentions that Malik Ambar administered poison and got rid of Murtaza Nizam Shah II (Vol. II pp. 516, though Baqi Nihawandi has used the words, "God only knows" Shri Jogindra Nath Chaudhery, has considered it "as an invented Bazar gossip." But in a series of inscriptions in the Antur fort dated 1610, Burhan's name is given as that of the reigning king. It is likely that Malik Ambar set up Burhan III as king and deserted the cause of Murtaza Nizam Shah II, whose period has been fixed by Sir Wolesley Haig between 1603-1630. On the contrary Basatin-us-Salatin mentions the name of Murtaza Nizam Shah II only up to the year 1610, which confirms the contention that he was removed from the throne in that year. Henceforward, the name of Burhan Nizam III is mentioned until Mahabat Khan's expedition to conquer the fort of Daultabad in 1631 (See pp. 270). In this connection Basatin also records that Burhan III either died a natural death or was killed by Fateh Khan who subsequently placed the crown on the head of deceased king's son Husain Nizam, then only seven years old. Khafi Khan has also mentioned the death of Nizam-ul-Mulk at the hands of Fateh Khan in 1040 A.H. (1630) which also supports the fact that Burhan III died in 1630 A.D.

No historian has clearly mentioned the circumstances in which Malik Ambar dethroned Murtaza Nizam Shah II. But the Dutch traveller Pieter Van den Broecke, clearly mentions, that "later it happened that king's first wife, who was white Persian women, reproached Malik Ambar's daughter with bitter words saying that she was only a slave girl and the concubine of the king and that her father was a rebel. The daughter told her father who was so angry that he determined to have the king killed and at last he gained over king's secretary, Mir Abdul Fateh, who poisoned him with a drink of which he died, leaving a minor son. Malik Ambar at once took charge of the minor son, made himself master of the whole country. The son is now above 12 years old, and was only five when his father died. The Malik goes in person twice a week to pay his respects. The boy king is named Nizam Shah. The Queen, who was the cause of the whole quarrel was also poinsoned, after her husband's death"—Journal of Indian History 1938, pp. 147;

The following inscriptions in the Antur Fort give the name of Burhan Nizam Shah III :—

(i) the second gateway, apart from Bhairav Darwaza, has a long inscriptional tablet 6 ft. x 2 ft. 3 inches fixed on the outside mentions :—

......In the reign of the just king and accomplished ruler......the Sultan Burhan Nizam Shah (May God perpetuate his kingdom) and majesty and may God pour his (lofty king's) blessings and benevolence over the world. This lofty gateway was built by the exalted Khan, the Chief of the nobles...... Nasir Farhad Khan,......by the order of the devoted servant of the lord of the land and sea, the supporter of the kingdom of Malik Ambar......in the year 1035 A.H. of the era of migration of Prophet...... see, Epigraphica Indo-Moslemica, 1913-20; Plate VIII pp. 12-13.

(ii) Inside the fort of Antur there is another inscription of Burhan III, set in the prayer-niche of a mosque on the western end of the large tank.

"In the glorious and auspicious reign of (the king) shadow of God, Burhan Nizam Shah, Ismael Husain in order to secure reward of both the worlds built this mosque in 1024 A.H. (1625 A.D.)—see, Ibid, pp. 13, Plate VII (a).

(iii) To Burhan's reign belongs another inscription in the fort dated 1019 A.H. It is carved on a basation on the north-west wall of the fort:—

"The royal bastion was built during the reign......Burhan Nizam Shah, by the order of...........Malik Ambar, on the 19th Rajjab, 1019 A. H. (1611 A.D.)—see, Ibid, Plate VII (B) pp. 14;

(iv) Another inscription, on the pillar of the Hamani Maszid, on the Shivaneri hill, gives the name of Burhan Nizam Shah III. It reads :—

"That the mosque's are Allah's therefore call not upon any one with Allah......The messenger of Allah, may Allah bless Nizam Shah, the son of Murtaza Nizam Shah, Shahur San 1025......secure in the favour of Beneficent, Ambar, Adil & Changez Khan Mian Birbad"—see, Ibid, Plate XIII (a) pp. 22-3;

(v) Another inscription, on the pillar of the Hamani Maszid gives the same of Burhan Nizam Shah III—see, Epigraphica Indo-Moslemica—1931-38, Plate XII (c) pp. 22;

72. Basatin-us-Salatin pp. 270;

73. Tuzuk-i-Jahangiri (R & B) Vol. I pp. 219; Iqbalnama-i-Jahangiri pp. 525-27; Maasir-i-Jahangiri (A.U. M/s) pp. 168-8; Maasir-ul-Umra, Vol. I pp. 185;

74. Tuzuk-i-Jahangiri (R & B) Vol. pp. 219-21; Iqbalnama-i-Jahangiri pp. 533; Muntakhab-ul-Lubab I, pp. 273-6; Maasir-ul-Umra Vol. I I pp. 98, 99, 185, Travels of William Finch pp. 25;

75. Tuzuk-i-Jahangiri (R & B) Vol. I pp. 219-221; Maasir-i-Rahimi Vol. II pp. 520; Iqbalnama-i-Jahangiri pp. 533; Basatin-us-Salatin, pp. pp. 271-72; Muntakhab-ul-Lubab Vol. I pp. 273-6; Maasir-ul-Umra Vol. pp. 98, 99, 185;

76. Tuzuk-i-Jahangiri (R & B) Vol. I pp. 221; Maasir-i-Jahangiri (A.U. M/s). pp. 168; Travels of William Finch, pp. 35;

77. Tusuk-i-Jahangiri (R & B) Vol. I pp. 21-22; Iqbalnama-i-Jahangiri pp. 533; Maasir-i-Rahimi Vol. II pp. 527; Maasir-i-Jahangiri (A.U. M/s) pp. 167, 174, Basatin-us-Salatin pp. 262-63; Muntakhab-ul-Lubab, Vol. I, pp. 276;

78. Tuzuk-i-Jahangiri (R & B) Vol. I pp. 275; 312; Iqbalnama-i Jahangiri pp. 539-40; Maasir-i-Rahimi Vol. I pp. 282; Muntakhab-ul-

Vol. I pp. 282; Futuhat-i-Adil Shahi (Marathi Translation) pp. 8;

79. Basatin-us-Salatin pp. 263; Travels of William Finch pp. 39-40; Cambridge History of India Vol. IV wrongly states that at this period neither the rulers of Golkunda nor Bijapur concerned themselves with the important struggle in the north-west of the Daccan, otherwise by supporting Malik Ambar by pecuniary contributions—pp. 261;

According to Pieter Van Den Broecke, Malik Ambar had 80,000 horses, in all including 600 from Golkunda, 10,000, horse and foot from Bijapur and 12,000 of his own Maratha auxiliaries which makes it clear that both Golkunda and Bijapur did not confine themselves to pecuniary assistance alone—see Journal of Indian History 1938, pp. 140;

80. Tuzuk-i-Jahangiri (R & B) Vol. I pp. 313-14; Maasir-i-Rahimi Vol. II pp. 523-31; Maasir-i-Jahangiri (A.U. M/s) pp. 229-30; Iqbalnama-i-Jahangiri pp. 539-40; Muntakhab-ul-Lubab Vol. I, pp. 282-85; Futuhat-i-Adil Shahi, Marathi Translation (B. I. S. M. Q.) pp. 10;

81. Maasir-i-Jahangiri (A.U. M/s) pp. 229;

82. Tuzuk-i-Jahangiri (R & B) Vol. I pp. 398-99;

Van Ravesteyn, the Dutch traveller who travelled from Masulipatam to Surat and back between May 1615 and January 1616, records that, "Malik Ambar's camp was in confusion, because the Chief officers both Hindu and Moslem who had been sent against the Mughals, rebelled and proposed to set up another king, three days later the rebels submitted but the camp was still disturbed", Journal of Indian History, 1938, Vol. 17, pp. 142;

83. Tuzuk-i-Jahangiri (R & B) Vol. I pp. 337, 340; Iqbalnama-i-Jahangiri pp. 541-42; Muntakhab-ul-Lubab Vol. I pp. 288; Maasir-i-Jahangiri (A.U. M/s) pp. 240-44; Basatin-us-Salatin, pp. 272; Maasir-us-Umra Vol. I pp. 57;

84. Tuzuk-i-Jahangiri (R & B) Vol. I pp. 368, 387-88; Iqbalnama-i-Jahangiri pp. 545; Maasir-i-Jahangiri (A.U. M/s) pp. 248-54; Muntakhab-ul-Lubab Vol. I pp. 290-292; Maasir-ul-Umra, Vol. I pp. 57-58; Futuhat-i-Adil Shahi, Marathi Translation (B. I. S. M. Q) pp. 10; Roe, pp. 340-41; 359-60, 365; Islamic Culture, April 1957, pp. 149;

84. (a) Shiva Kalin Patra Sar Sngraha Vol. I pp. 28 (no 120)

85. Tuzuk-i-Jahangiri (R & B) Vol. I pp. 390; Iqbalnama-i-Jahangiri pp. 545-46; Maasir-i-Jahangiri (A.U. M/s) pp. 254; Muntakhab-ul-Lubab, Vol. I pp. 291; Maasir ul-Umra, Vol. pp. 58; Islamic Culture, April, 1957, pp. 149.

86. Tuzuk -i-Jahangiri (Elliot and Dowson) Vol. VI pp. 376-78; Iqbal-nama-i-Jahangiri pp. 568-9; Maasir-i-Jahangiri (A.U. M/s) pp. 294; Islamic Culture, April, 1957, pp. 149;

87. Tuzuk-i-Jahangiri (R & B) Vol. I pp. 393-95; Iqbalnama-i-Jahangiri pp. 546; Muntakhab-ul-Lubab Vol. I pp. 292-93; Maasir-ul-Umra Vol. I pp. 58;

87. (a) Travels of William Finch, pp. 30-31; 39-40;

88. Tuzuk-i-Jahangiri (R & B) Vol. II pp. 155, 157; 188, 190, 206; Waqiyat-i-Jahangiri (Elliot and Dowson) Vol. VI pp. 377; Iqbalnama-i-Jahangiri pp. 574; Muntakhab-ul-Lubab Vol. I pp. 304-5; 3074; Maasir-ul-Umra, Vol. I pp. 58-59; For dislocation of trade see, "Foster's" English Factories in India (1618-21 A.D.) pp. 207, 210, 211, 217, 218, 231, 231, 240, 243, 259, 287, 296;

89. Iqbalnama-i-Jahangiri pp. 274-75; Shiva Kalin Patrasara Sangraha Vol. I pp. 30 (no. 131).

90. Tuzuk-i-Jahangiri (R & B) Vol. II, pp. 190-206-8; Iqbalnama-i-Jahangiri pp. 575; Muntakhab-ul-Lubab Vol. I pp. 315-21; Islamic Culture, April, 1957 pp. 150;

91. Tuzuk-i-Jahangiri (R & B) Vol. II pp. 208; Maasir-i-Jahangiri (A.U. M/s) pp. 296-309; Iqbalnama-i-Jahangiri pp. 575-76; Muntakhab-ul-Lubab Vol. I pp. 322; Shiva Kalin Patrasara Sangraha, Vol. I pp. 35 (no. 146, 152, 153), Islamic Culture, April, 1957, pp. 150;

91. (a) Shiva Kalin Patrasara Sangraha, Vol. I pp. 35 (no. 146).

92. Tuzuk-i-Jahangiri (R & B) Vol. II, pp. 218; Iqbalnama-i-Jahangiri pp. 578; Muntakhab-ul-Lubab Vol. I pp. 325; Shiva Bharata, Chapter IV, sloka 1-3; Foster's "The English Factories in India" Vol. I (1618-21) pp. 330-33;

93. Tuzuk-i-Jahangiri (R & B) Vol. II pp. 290; Maasir-Jahangiri (A.U. M/s) pp. 322-26; Islamic Culture April 1957 pp. 150 Shiva Kalin Patrasara Sangraha Vol. I, No. 175; 183; 186, 189, 192, 193, 194, 197; throw light on the rebellion of Shahjahan and his activities.

94. Tuzuk-i-Jahangiri (R & B) Vol. II pp. 296; Iqbalnama-i-Jahangiri pp. 589; Muntakhab-ul-Lubab Vol. I pp. 343-44; Islamic Culture, April, 1957 pp. 151.

95. Iqbalnama-i-Jahangiri pp. 589; Maasir-i-Jahangiri (A.U. M/s), pp. 348; Muntakhab-ul-Lubab Vol. I pp. 347;

96. Iqbalnama-i-Jahangiri 592; Basatin-us-Salatin pp. 273; Muntakhab-ul-Lubab Vol. I. pp. 347-48; Futuhat-i-Adil Shahi, Marathi Translation (B. I. S. M. Q.) pp. 10; Shiva Kalin Patrasara Sangraha, Vol. I (no. 217).

97. According to Futuhat-i-Adil Shahi, an epidemic broke out among the horses of Malik Ambar's forces, and 500 of them died each night, which compelled him to raise the siege—see Dr. D. R. Seth's article, "The Life and Times of Malik Ambar," Islamic Culture, April, 1957.

98. Iqbalnama-i-Jahangiri pp. 595; Basatin-us-Salatin pp. 273-74; Tarikh-i-Shivaji pp. 76; Shiva Bharata, Chapter IV slokas, 10, 66; Futuhat-i-Adil Shahi, Marathi Translation (B.I.S.M.Q.) pp. 11-12; Muntakhab-ul-Lubab Vol. I pp. 348-49; Islamic Culture April, 1957, pp. 152-53;

Pietro Della Valle, referring to the battle of Bhatvadi, mentions that, "on October the one thirteenth (1624) news came to Goa, that Malik Ambar, who for a good while successfully warr'd Adil-Sciah, at length in a victory had taken one Mulla Md., General of Adil-Schiah's army and much favoured by him; who by his ill demeanor towards the said Malik (even so far as to endeavour to get Malik's chief intent was to revenge himself on the said Mulla Md. whom being thus taken, they say, he beheaded and caused him in that manner to be carry'd about his camp with this proclaimation; that this Traytor Mulla Md, the cause of the warr and present discords between Adil Sciah and Nizam Sciah (to whom this Malik is the governor, otherwise Friends and allies, was thus in the name of this lord Adil Sciah, as Traytor and disturber of public peace, put to death. By which act Malik meant to signifie that he had no evil intention against Adil Sciah but only took up Arms for the mischiefs done by Mulla Md, whom he desired to remove from the govt of Adil Sciah and from the world. Yet it was not known how Adil Sciah received this action, and what end the business would have.

In this warr, they say, the Mogol favoured Adil Sciah against Malik and supplied him with 20,000 horse, but, be that how it will, Adil Sciah hath hitherto always gone by the worst and some times been in great danger; Malik who is a brave Captain, having over-run all the State almost to the Gates of Vidhiyapor, which is the Royal City of Adil-Sciah where he hath sometimes been forced to shut himself up as if it were besieged. A few months before Adil Sciah put one of the principal wives to death, for conspiracy which she was said to hold with Malik, and for having been a party in promoting this warr, out of design to remove Adil Sciah from the Government as become odious, to his own people, either through his covetousness, or inability.........See The Travels of Pietro Della Valla in India, Vol. III pp. 442-3.

99. Iqbalnama-i-Jahangiri pp. 595-96; Muntakhab-ul-Lubab, Vol. I pp. 350; Elliot and Dowson, Vol. VI pp. 416;

100. Iqbalnama, pp. 296-97; Maasir-i-Jahangiri (A.U. M-s) pp 376-380; Muntakhab-ul-Lubab Vol. I pp. 356-57.

101. Maasir-i-Jahangiri (A. U. M/s) pp. 390; According to Sir

Wolseley Haig and P. N. Patwardhan, Malik Ambar was buried at Rauza and his tomb stands there; see, B. I. S. M. Q. Vol. 20, part II (1939) pp. 20; Haig's "Historical Landmarks of the Daccan" pp. 57;

102. Journal of Indian History, 1938, pp. 146;

103. Ibid, pp 145;

104. Dr. B. P. Saksena's article, "Malik Ambar", Quarterly Journal of Hindustani Academy, Vol. 3 P. IV, Oct. 1933;

Pitro Della Valle, has given an interesting account of "Malik Ambar'. It is not fully reliable, for it is based on hearsay. But still, a general view of the towering personality of this great warrior, shrewd statesman, polished diplomat and enlightened financier, of the Nizam Shahi Kingdom has been recorded by the traveller: He writes :—

"The Nizam Sciah now reigning, is a boy of twelve years old, who, therefore, doth not govern it, but an Abyssinian slave of the Moors and that with such authority that at this day this territory is more generally known and called by the name of Malik's country, than the kingdom of Nizam Sciah. Nevertheless Malik Ambar governs not fraudulently and with design to usurp, by keeping the king shut up, *as I have sometimes heard*; but according as I have better understood since from persons informed nearhand, he administers with great fidelity and submission towards the young king to whom nevertheless they say, he hath provided or already given to wife a daughter of his own; upon security that himself shall be governor of the whole state as long as he lives." Writing further the traveller remarks", This Malik Ambar is a man of great parts and fit for government, but as they say, very impious addicted to sorcery whereby is thought that he keeps himself in favour with his king, and that for works of Inchantments, he hath with certain superstitious is in these countries, committed most horried empieties and cruelties, killing hundred of his slaves children and others; and offering them as in sacrifice to the invok'd Devils, with other abominable stories which I have heard; but because not seen by myself, I affirm not for true."

105. Iqbalnama-i-Jahangiri pp. 607;

106. There were many Portuguese in his employ, one of them was Mansur Khan, a Portuguese convert to Islam, who held the rank of 6,000 and jagir of Qandhar—W.H. Moreland's article "From Gujarat to Golkunda" in the reign of Jahangir"—Journal of Indian History, 1938, Vol. 17, pp. 141;

While at another place, Pieter Van Den Broecke, says that, "there were many Portuguese in his service, all of whom had become Moslems, some commanded 1000 horse, others 3000 and 5000"—see, Ibid pp. 148;

107. Muntakhab-ul-Lubab Vol. I pp. 349-50; Maasir-ul-Umra, Vol I pp. 536;

Pieter Van Den Broecke says that, "the Malik maintains good laws and administration in his country. He punishes thieves very severely so that you can safely travel with gold through his country. If any one gets drink, he promptly had melted lead poured down in his throat. No body on pain of death offer strong drink for sale or even travel (with it) through the country......" see, Journal of Indian History, 1938, pp. 147-48;

Similarly Ravesteyn, the Dutch traveller says "I understand there is very good justice here, and he is greatly respected by every one;——Ibid pp. 145;

108. Maasir-ul-Umra Vol. I pp. 536; Ghulam Ahmad's article "Indian History Congress, 1945, pp. 221-5; Dr. D. R. Seth's article "Malik Ambar (an Estimate)", Islamic Culture Vol. 20, Oct. 1945, pp. 348; see, also, his article, "The Life and Tunes of Malik Ambar", Islamic Culture, April, 1957, pp. 154;

109. Islamic Culture, April, 1957, pp. 154;

110. Maasir-ul-Umra Vol. III, pp. 79; Islamic Culture, April, 1957 pp. 155;

## Chapter VIII

# EXTINCTION OF THE NIZAM SHAHI KINGDOM

Malik Ambar left behind him two sons, Fateh Khan and Changez Khan. The elder Fateh Khan succeeded him as the regent of the Nizam Shahi kingdom. He was extremely haughty incompetent, imperious and blood-thirsty-[1] He had neither the ability nor the courage to put down the mutual dissensions among the Nizam Shahi nobles at home and the aggression of the Mughals abroad. Early in his regime he committed a blunder by invading the kingdom of Bijapur, shortly after the death of Ibrahim Adil Shah on 12th September, 1627 A.D. and the accession of his minor son Muhammad Adil Shah. It alienated his friends and associates from him.[2] Henceforward he delegated his authority to Yaqut Khan, an Abyssinian slave whom he appointed as Commander-in-Chief. Unable to handle the gear of Nizam Shahi politics, he at the instance of his master and at the instigation of the nobles at Jalnapur opened negotiations with Sarbuland Rai offering allegiance to the Mughal Emperor.[3]

**Fateh Khan**

Khan Jahan Lodi who had succeeded Mahabat Khan to the supreme command in the Daccan, in view of the failing health of the Emperor and the consequent complications in affairs at the court, avoided military entanglements with the Daccan states, and endeavoured to bring some sort of settlement with the Nizam Shahi ruler, in order to prevent the likelihood of latter's alliance with Shahjahan or Mahabat Khan. He therefore readily accepted the offer of Yakut Khan, and wrote to him in warm and assuring terms, directing at the same time his own officers and the amirs to receive him with all hospitality and to escort him to Burhanpur. No sooner the olive branch of high favour and rank was extended to him than Yakut Khan deserted the Nizam Shahi service and joined the Mughals.

**Policy of Khan Jahan Lodi towards the Daccan States**

The departure of Yaqut Khan was signal for confusion in the Nizam Shahi politics, in the midst of which Hamid Khan, the Abyssinaian favourite of Burhan Nizam Shah III rose to prominence by making himself popular among the masses and classes alike. He was able no doubt, but like others unscrupulous. He married a woman who was serving in the royal herem, and the two together contrived to gain control of the king's mind by catering to his baser instincts. They encouraged Burhan in his licentiousness, and gratified his passions by procuring young girls for sexual satisfaction, sometimes even the daughters of nobles and by plying him with wine. Making a puppet of him they persuaded him to declare war against the Mughals.

**Rise of Hamid Khan to Power**

Being gratuitously provoked, Khan Jahan Lodi opened the campaign against the Nizam Shahi kingdom with all his vigour and ability. He placed Lashkar Khan incharge of Burhanpur and marched towards Khirki. No sooner did the report of his advance arrive at the court, than Hamid Khan's wife sent her husband three lacs huns to purchase peace by bribing the invader. Khan Jahan Lodi fell an easy prey to gold and not only agreed to withdraw, but also restored the entire district of Balaghat and the territory as far as the fortress of Ahmadnagar, to the Nizam Shahi king. He also issued instructions to the commandants of various forts asking them to surrender their forts to the Nizam Shahi officers and return to the headquarters forthwith. All obeyed except Sipehdar Khan the commandant of the fort of Ahmadnagar, who refused, saying, "occupy the rest of the country for it belongs to you, but I will not surrender the fort without the royal firman'. Though the Nizam Shahi officers tried their best to win him over, but in vain. On the contrary he collected the necesssary provisions and put the fortress in a state of defence, upon which the Nizam Shahi officers laid siege to it. The news of Jahangir's death, however, occasioned a sudden change in the affairs of the

**War declared against the Mughals**

**Khan Jahan Lodi cedes the Mughal territory to the Nizam Shahis**

Daccan (29th October, 1628 A.D.).[4]

On the 6th Feb. 1628 A.D. Shahjahan, the ablest of the sons of Emperor Jahangir ascended the throne.[5] He confirmed Khan Jahan Lodi in the supreme command of the Daccan, even though like a traitor he had reduced the Mughal authority there only to the fort of Ahmadnagar. He directed him to recover the lost territory and called upon the Nizam Shahi king to surrender what had been ceded to him without proper authority. Thus began the last chapter in the history of the Nizam Shahi dynasty.

**Shahjahan ascended the Mughal throne**

The minister Fateh Khan tried to play the double game. Outwardly he expressed his readiness to restore the disputed territory but secretly he instigated his officers to resist the Mughals. The result of it was most disastrous. Innumerable Mughal forces under able generals entered the Daccan. Shahjahan secured the neutrality of Bijapur by offering to Adil Shah a slice of the Nizam Shahi territory. In November 1628 A.D. the Mughal viceroy marched to take possession of the fort of Bid. Fateh Khan despatched Shahji and a party of *silahadars* with 6000 cavalry to raid eastern Khandesh and thus create a diversion in the rear of the Mughals. Darya Khan a Mughal officer who held a big jagir in Banswara, attacked the raiders, slew many of them and expelled them from the region between the river Tapti and Purna.[6] In this way the campaign against the Mughals which had been undertaken by Fateh Khan to establish superiority over Hamid Khan went against him. Add to this, his failure in the administration which further aggrevated the dissatisfaction of the king Burhan III, who at the instance of his favourites became keen to get rid of him. The violent and reckless behaviour of the regent rendered the task all the easier. He was charged with failure in apprehending Khan Jahan Lodi, with covering himself with disgrace at the hands of the Mughals, and above all his incompetence in suppressing the dicordant elements in the internal politics of the kingdom and arresting the Mughal pressure. He was arrested at the instance of Hamid Khan

**Mughal advancement**

**Fateh Khan imprisoned**

and imprisoned in the fortress of Khaibar in Junnar. But Fateh Khan bribed the guards and escaped to Sipehdar Khan, the Mughal commander of Ahmadnagar fort, who welcomed him. He soon gathered a large following and proceeded to fight Burhan Nizam Shah III, but was defeated and captured. This time he was imprisoned in the fort of Daultabad. Now Burhan Nizam Shah III appointed Muqarrab Khan as Commander-in-Chief and Ikhlas Khan as the Peshwa of the kingdom.[7]

With the exit of Fateh Khan, the king was also relegated into the background and the strings of power fell into the hands of Hamid Khan and his wife, who jointly administered the kingdom. The Nizam Shah was thus kept under the control like a bird in a cage, outdoors by the Abyssinian and indoors by his wife.[8] This gave an excellent opportunity to Adil Shah to take advantage of the chaotic and deplorable state of affairs of the Nizam Shahi kingdom. He sent a large army towards the frontiers of that kingdom to seize some parts of it. It was considered as an open challenge by Hamid Khan's wife, and she readily accepted it. She mobilised a large army under her personal command, fought a decisive battle, inflicted a crushing defeat on the invader and returned to the capital in triumph. In this respect she even excelled Chand Sultana.[9]

**Hamid Khan's wife repels the Adil Shahi invasion**

Meanwhile when it was reported to the Mughal Emperor that Khan Jahan had failed to recover the ceded territory he was summoned to the court to explain his conduct. Khan Azam, the son of Mahabat Khan was appointed to supersede him.[10] During his stay at the royal court he conducted himself insolently, and fearing some severe punishment he took to flight. He was hotly pursued by the imperialists under the command of Khwaja Abul Hasan, who hounded him from the north and compelled him to take refuge with Burhan Nizam III.

**Khan Jahan's failure to recover the lost territory His rebellion**

The arrival of his former friend brought a fresh chain of hopes to Burhan Nizam Shah. He thought that with his cooperation he would be able to stem the tide of Mughal aggression, and strengthen his hold on his own country. He therefore, extended him all possible hospitality, brought him into his palace and honoured him by offering a seat in the centre of the masnad. In expression of his sincerity and to gain his unstinted loyalty, he also assigned him the pargana of Bid and granted money for his personal expenses. At the same time every one of his followers was treated well and was given suitable rank and jagir. Thus Burhan Nizam III began to espouse the cause of a rebel of the Mughal empire. But such an unwise step instead of improving the affairs of the kingdom proved to be a source of ruin to it, for it excited the wrath of the Mughal Emperor, who determined to sap its foundations and destroy its existence. The Mughal nobles in the Nizam Shahi employ made confusion worse confounded by playing a double role. They professed loyalty to their new master, but secretly favoured the cause of the Mughal Emperor and did everything to undermine the power and prestige of Nizam Shah and Khan Jahan Lodi. Though they, in the first instance helped the Daccanis to drive out the Mughal generals from the Nizam Shahi territory, but they also precipitated the crisis.

**Khan Jahan Lodi honoured at the Nizam Shahi court**

The Mughal prestige in the Daccan stood now at the lowest ebb. The cordial and hearty welcome extended to Khan Jahan Lodi by Burhan, and the strained relations with the kingdoms of Bijapur and Golcunda presented two fold problem to the Mughal Emperor. He, therefore, ordered Abul Hasan to march to the Daccan to fight the rebel, prevent the allies from going to extremes and recover the lost territory. As it was expected that the Daccan war would take a serious turn, Shahjahan also sent Shir Khan, the governor of Gujarat to the assistance of Abul Hasan. Subsequently, Asaf Khan the Wakil of the Mughal Empire was also sent to infuse vigour in the army and coordinate the plans of different Commanders. But the Emperor did not stop here. He knew that neither the change of governors will improve the Daccan affairs, as had happened in the past, nor the prolonged operations and negotiations would ever

**Mobilisation of Mughal forces against the Nizam Shahi kingdom**

solve the problem. All this had been tried before, but in vain. He was fully aware of the fact that in maintaining such a strong opposition, Nizam Shah was always assisted by the neighbouring powers. The former knew how to bow before the storm, but his power had never been finally broken, inspite of the grand plans of the imperialists and their superior military resources. The kingdom of Ahmadnagar had the unique capacity of facing the worst. Shahjahan's long stay in the Daccan had convinced him of the futility of protracted operations, as also of the impossibility of securing unity among the generals entrusted with the task of reducing that region to submission. Bearing these considerations in mind, he decided to go there personally. He, therefore, left Agra on 3rd Dec. 1629 A.D. Without halting at Mandu, he marched straight to the Narbada, which he crossed at Akbarpur. On the frontiers of Khandesh he reviewed his army and on 12th Feb. 1630 A.D. Azam Khan welcomed him at Burhanpur.[11]

The Nizam Shahi kingdom at present included the entire province of Aurangabad, Jalna, Baglana and the district of Kaliyan in the Konkan from Bankot to Bassien. Without waiting any further the Mughal Emperor mobilised his multitudious army in the hilly region of Balaghat, where he planned a simultaneous attack on all the strategic points in the Nizam Shahi kingdom to offset the advantage which the physical features of the country and the guerilla method of warfare gave to the enemy. He sent an army with Khan Azam to enter Balaghat and overpower the rebel Khan Jahan; Abul Hasan was sent with another force to plunder and occupy Nasik and Sangamnir; while a third contingent of troops was sent under Nasiri Khan towards Telingana.[12]

Meanwhile an ugly incident took place which gave a blow to the prestige of the Nizam Shahi kingdom. A severe famine began to stalk the land causing appalling mortality and scarcity of food and fodder. It not only retarded the progress of the Mughals, but suspended their activities altogether. Shahjahan now found his task more difficult than ever. While keeping the show of military operations, he started underhand intrigues in the councils of the Nizam Shahi king. Lakhoji Jadhav Rao, who had once joined the Mughals now returned to the

**Murder of Jadhav Rao**

Nizam Shahi service. But finding the atmosphere there too hot for him, owing to the party strife and confusion in the kingdom, he thought it prudent take to flight. Having come to know about his intentions the Mughal Emperor gained him over by supporting him secretly and instigated him to make the confusion worse confounded at the Nizam Shahi court. Soon he became a menace to the safety of the Nizam Shahis, against whom he started his activities from his seat at Sindhkhed, which proved to be a source of much anxiety to the former. At length the Nizam Shahi king consulted his nobles like Hamid Khan and Ikhlas Khan as to the course of action to be taken against him. He decided to place him under surveillance unmindful of the consequences which were to follow. On the pretext of deciding some political issue the king called the entire body of Jadhav chiefs for an interview in the fort of Daultabad on 25th July, 1629 A.D. He suddenly withdrew from the audience hall and according to a preconcerted plan Farhad Khan, Safdar Khan and Moti Khan fell upon Jadhav Rao and his son Achlaji. A gruesome struggle occurred in which Jadhav Rao lost his life and his sons Achlaji and Raguji and his grand-son Yash-want Rao were wounded. Lakhuji Jadhav Rao's wife Girja Bai and his brother Jagdev Rao and his son Bahadur Ji, besides many other members of the family escaped to Sindhkhed.[13]

The treacherous murder of their chief alienated the sympathy of other Marathas towards Nizam Shah. Shahjahan exploited the situation to his best advantage. Upon his arrival in the Daccan he honoured the Maratha chiefs like, Maloji, Kheloji, Uda Ramji Daccani and others who had already been in the imperial service. He liberally conferred upon them high sounding titles and ranks with the object of of tempting the others to desert the Nizam Shahi service and increase the strength of his army. Now arrived the relatives of Jadhav Rao like, Jagdev Rao, who was honoured and was given the rank of 4,000 Zat and 3,000 Sawar; Telang Rao received the rank of 3,000 Zat and 1,500 Sawar while Yashwant Rao and Vithoji were given the mansabs

**Desertion of the Marathas from the Nizam Shahi service**

of 2,000 Zat and 1,000 Sawar respectively. Not only did the Maratha nobles give up the cause of the Nizam Shahis, Muslim officers like Saadat Khan, Khudawand Khan, Yaqut Khan and Shirza Khan also joined the Mughal service and made the matters worse for the Nizam Shahis. Local patriotic feelings on which rested the power and prestige of the kingdom disappeared; loyalty and fidelty were replaced by defection and desertion. There was neither any capable leader who could assure the masses and classes their safety of life and property; nor was there any general of high repute who could infuse fresh vigour into the veins of the demoralised soldiers. This gave an splendid opportunity to the Mughals to launch vigorous campaigns into the very heart of the Nizam Shahi kingdom.[11]

Azam Khan the Mughal general opened his offensive by pressing upon the centre of the Nizam Shahi kingdom, with the double object of putting down the rebel Khan Jahan Lodi and recovering the lost territory. He pursued the rebel in the hilly tracts of Bid, and subsequently drove him out of the country. During the pursuit of the rebel the imperialists revaged the Nizam Shahi country. Famine began to prevail round the city of Daultabad which added much to the misery of the people. At the same time differences arose between Nizam Shah and his friend Khan Jahan Lodi. The former now regretted to have invited all these troubles in vain, while the latter had grown weary of the protracted campaign against the Mughals. He now sought safety in flight with the object of trying his luck in the north. Accordingly he left Daultabad for Malwa (Nov. 1630 A.D.) Burhan Nizam Shah did not at all feel sorry at his departure for the expectations he had entertained of him had not been fulfilled.[15]

Nizam Shah now found himself face to face with another enemy Shahji, the son-in-law of Jadhav Rao, who had by now acquired great prominence amongst the Marathas. He had risen into rebellion against him, for he considered himself unsafe in the face of wanton murders, which had created a feelings of repulsion and disgust among his kith and kin. Shahji started from his impregnable fortress of Parenda on a plundering expedition. Firstly, he strengthened his seat at Poona and then opened his depredations both in the Nizam

Shahi and the Adil Shahi territories taking forcible possession of the country around.[16] Upon this Adil Shah despatched Murar Jagdev Pandit with a large army to punish Shahji. He captured Poona and Indapur and set fire to the towns and destroyed all that was there. He then built a fort on the Baleshwar hill, named it as Daultmangal and appointed Aba Rao its commandant. Finding himself pressed from all sides Shahji retreated to Shivaneri, opened negotiations with Shriniwas Rao, the Sar Naik and the famous noble of Junnar and took refuge with him.[17] Soon after, he repaired the fort of Pemgarh and renamed it Shahgarh, collected a force of 6,000 horse, left his family there and chalked out a plan to save himself from the clutches of Nizam Shah and Adil Shah. Having been a partisan of Khan Jahan Lodi, he thought it proper to throw himself to the mercy of the Mughal Emperor, by obtaining a promise of pardon for his past offences and agreeing to enter the Mughal service and thus save his little jagir of Poona. He, therefore, opened correspondence with Azam Khan who forthwith sent information to the Mughal Emperor. The latter was well aware of the bravery and intrepidity of Shahji and therefore he welcomed him, to make him a tool in the subsequent annihilation and annexation of the Nizam Shahi kingdom. With two thousand horsemen Shahji went to have a personal interview with Azam Khan. He was honoured and was given the mansab of 5,000 horse, a robe of honour and two lacs of rupees. At the same time his son Shambhaji and other relations and dependents were honoured and taken into the imperial service. Henceforward the Bhonsles began to work for the Mughals in digging up the foundations of the Nizam Shahi kingdom.[18]

While the Maratha chiefs were thus active in seizing the territories of the Nizam Shahi kingdom and adding them to the Mughal Empire, Shahjahan threatened the ruler of Bijapur and obtained armed assistance from him in seconding his military operations. On the one hand, Adil Shah sent contingents of troops under Randola Khan and Kanhoji Jedhe the Maratha Deshmukh of Kari to assist the Mughals ; on the other he sent Raja Chander Rao More and Baji Valvale with troops to conquer the country up to the port of Dabhol. They seized Mahad, Chodegaon, Nizampur and few other places from the hands of the Nizam Shahi officers. Siddi Mirjan, the Subedar of Talkonkan marched out of Chaul to oppose the Adil Shahi forces, but he was defeated and slain and Chaul fell into the hands of the Adil Shahis. But this victory of the Maratha chief was followed by the rout of Baji Valvale who was defeated and slain at Kolar by Siddi Saba Ambar Khani, who had been reinforced by the troops of Ikhlas Khan from Daultabad. Chaul was recovered along with other places in the Konkan which the Adil Shahi generals had forcibly seized from the Nizam Shahis.[19]

No sooner did Khan Jahan Lodi leave the Daccan than the Mughals found themselves free to concentrate their attention on the Nizam Shahis. Azam Khan who was encamping near Dharur, directed Multafit Khan and others to attack the town on the market day. After taking possession of the town both of them opened the siege of the fort, which was a place of strategic importance on the road across Balaghat. Within a short time the imperialists reduced the number of musketeers among the garrison by shooting them through loopholes and subsequently the chance fall of a gun from the bastion discouraged the defenders still further. A party of the assailants succeeded in scaling the fortifications by means of ladders and nooses. The commander Siddi Salim lost heart and capitulated. The fort was occupied and all the treasures including jewels etc. fell into the hands of the imperialists. The family of Siddi Salim and his brother and Malik Badan were made prisoners.[20]

**Fall of Dharur Monday 23rd Jumadi II 1040 A.H.**

The fall of such an important fortress alarmed Nizam Shah. He could depend only on his meagre resources to save himself from the imperial onslaughts. He now quitted his camp which was 20 karoh from that place, and moved towards Qandhar to create trouble for Nasiri Khan, the Mughal commander who was besieging that fortress.[21] The imperialists closely pursued him all along the way and compelled him to take shelter into the fortress of Daultabad. Famine prevented the imperialists from opening the siege of the fortress. To divert the attention of the enemy, Burhan Nizam Shah sent one contingent to besiege the fort of Taltam which was held by the Mughal commander Sipehdar Khan, and an other force under the command of Muqarrab Khan to open negotiations with Randola Khan, the Adil Shahi commander who was deputed by Muhammad Adil Shah to march to the frontiers of the kingdom and protect the Mahalls from the depredations of Nizam Shah.[22]

Azam Khan resumed the pursuit of the Nizam Shahis under Muqarrab Khan. Arriving at Shahgadh, he asked Randola Khan to prevent the enemy from crossing Balaghat. But the latter excused himself on the ground of paucity of numbers and replied that he was going to Naldurg to obtain reinforcements, and to wait there for further instructions of his master. Realising that the imperialists were not giving up his trail, Muqarrab Khan wrote to Randola Khan to save the Nizam Shahi house by entering into an alliance with the king and promised to cede the fort of Sholapur as the price of assistance against the Mughals. Fortunately by this time the influence of Mustafa Khan at the Bijapur court had almost declined and misunderstanding had cropped up between him and Khawas Khan, which enabled Randola Khan to persuade the latter to accept the terms of Muqarrab Khan. Azam Khan repeatedly reminded him of the agreement which Adil Shah had entered into with him, but the general remained obdurate. He allowed Muqarrab Khan to proceed to the Ghat of Manik Dudah and thereby showed his favourable attitude towards him. Finding a smooth passage Muqarrab Khan moved towards the fort of Parenda, left his extra baggage there and then moved towards Talab Kukrala where Randola Khan was staying in order to conclude a treaty with him.[23]

The attitude of Randola Khan alarmed Azam Khan and he requested the Emperor for reinforcements. Shortly after, he received orders from Asaf Khan to secure safe passage for Shaikh Muinuddin and Muhiuddin who were coming with presents from Bijapur and Golcunda respectively. Azam Khan thought that if he pressed the Nizam Shahis near Nander, they would certainly change their course and move towards Ausa, Bhalki and Jitkopa near Bidar and interrupt, the two Shaikhs. He, therefore, decided to press on to Parenda, to arrange for its reduction and keep the enemy

**Siege of Parenda**

busy till the arrival of the reinforcements, thinking that in the meanwhile he would be able to confirm the news of the alliance between the two enemies. Accordingly he despatched Jai Singh and Multafit Khan to plunder the suberbs of Parenda. They marched thither dismantled the walls of the town, plundered the inhabitants and succeeded in reaching up to the moat of the fort. Two shots were fired from the fort from a big cannon weighing one and a half maunds each; one of which fell upon the imperialists, reducing them to ashes. Soon after Azam Khan arrived there and obtained much booty and elephants.[24]

The sack of Parenda and close proximity of the imperial forces distracted Muqarrab Khan and his followers. He now again appealed to Randola Khan for assistance, representing to him the miserable condition to which the Nizam Shahi kingdom had been reduced. He wrote that the kingdom had ceased to exist, as the entire country was in the hands of the Mughals. Nasik and Sangamnir had been plundered and seized by Abul Hasan; Junnar, Chakan and Poona were in the hands of Shahji now an ally of the Mughals; the fort of Qandhar was on the verge of capitulation and a severe famine was raging round Daultabad. He added that if Parenda was allowed to pass into the hands of the enemy, the extinction of the Nizam Shahi kingdom would be complete which, he warned Randola Khan, would pave the way for the subjugation of Bijapur.[25]

Azam Khan who was continually receiving reports of the correspondence between Muqarrab Khan and Randola Khan, was now fully convinced that the peace had been concluded between them, and that the latter had been asked by Khawas Khan to assist the Nizam Shahis. The policy of Adil Shah towards the Mughals was now clear. He therefore decided to capture the fort of Parenda and opened its siege without waiting any longer for reinforcements. The fort was invested on three sides, and commands were distributed to various officers. After a contested fight an approach to the moat was secured and the enemy began to fill it up. The garrison was reduced to sore straits and was compelled to appeal for help to Muqarrab Khan, Bahlol and Vithoji.

Muqarrab Khan sent Vithoji to fall upon the imperialists, but he was repulsed.[26]

Constant campaigning exhausted the supplies of the Mughals and it became necessary to send out foraging parties to the districts situated at a distance. This gave an opportunity to the Daccanis to harass them. On one occasion, when Multafit Khan and Khudawand Khan were returning with convoy of provisions, Muqarrab Khan and Bahlol organised a surprise attack and fell upon them. The timely arrival of Azam Khan with Raja Jai Singh and Jujhar Singh saved the imperialists. Muqarrab Khan and his party were driven into the hills with heavy losses. His rear was looted and 600 camels and 200 horses and many bullocks were seized by the imperialists.[27]

Conditions made it difficult for the Mughals to continue the siege of Parenda any longer. They found themselves in the grips of severe famine and scarcity of provisions. They were harassed by the Daccanis from all sides. The strength of the Nizam Shahis had been doubled by the assistance which they were enabled to secure from Adil Shah. This compelled Azam Khan to raise the siege of the fort and retreat towards Dharur. Next day when the imperialists left Patarah, the Daccanis appeared under the command of Vithoji and fell upon their rear. Yaqut Khan and Multafit Khan fought with them and killed many of them. Shortly afterwards the Daccanis again attacked the van of the imperialists at Ghat Bansi. Azam Khan sent Raja Jai Singh, Pahar Singh and other Rajput generals to its succour along with Multafit Khan and two thousand horsemen. The Daccanis were put to flight and the imperialists easily crossed the Ghats and encamped on the banks of river Manjira where Yaqut Khan, Maloji and Kheloji joined them. Meanwhile, Muqarrab Khan, Bahlol, Vithoji and other Nizam Shahi chiefs in cooperation with Randola Khan and his father Farhad Khan alone with the Adil Shahi forces appeared in the field to check the advance of the Mughals and to harass them. Azam Khan sent Yaqut Khan against them. He attacked them and dispersed all of them. Next day the imperialists ravaged and plundered the town of Bansi passed through it and arrived at Manduah and Dharur, after suffering severe hardships in the way.[28]

After taking a little rest at Dharur, Azam Khan renewed his campaign against the Nizam Shahis. According to the report of the spies, the Adil Shahis and Nizam Shahis were encamping separately on the banks of river Manjira, at a distance of four Karoh from each other. He led surprise attack on the Nizam Shahi general Bahlol, who was defeated with heavy losses. The Mughals seized 600 horses 200 camels with many bullocks and then moved towards Ambajui Kahi which was in possession of Tanaji Duniya, a trusted follower of Nizam Shah. It was captured and plundered. Next day it was reported that the allies were marching to Qandhar to distract Nasiri Khan the Mughal general who was besieging that fort. To intercept the allies Azam Khan marched towards the pargana of Darnal and Rajauri. Meanwhile the Mughal general Sipehdar Khan laid the siege to the fort of Talbain. The troops soon came to terms with the Mughal general and entertained a body of the imperial troops inside the fort. The Governor of the fort was taken by surprise and the fort was captured.[29] Then he marched to the fort of Sitwandah and laid siege to it. The garrison having been reduced to distress the commander Siddi Jamal sued for terms, surrendered the fort and entered the imperial service.[30]

It has been mentioned above that Nasiri Khan had been despatched to subjugate Telingana. Ever since his arrival there, he had concentrated his energies in capturing the fort of Qandhar, which was held by Sadiq, son-in-law of Yaqut Khudawand Khan.[31] He had distributed commands to Raja Bharat and Shahbaz Khan. Sarfaraz Khan, the Daccani Commander of that region attacked the imperialists fought a bloody battle, but was repulsed with heavy losses. The Mughals captured the neighbouring town along with 500 horses, making five to six thousand prisoners including women and children. They now started the work of laying mines beneath the fortifications. They succeeded in charging six out of twenty one mines which had been completed. Bahlol and other Nizam Shahi generals tried to distract Nasiri Khan, but were always put to flight. After the arrival of Azam Khan three of the mines which were kept in reserve were fired. One failed, but the other two destroyed the outer earth-work of a bastion. The garrison maintained a constant volley of rockets,mortars, stones and grenades, but the storming party pressed on and a fierce conflict continued from mid-day till sun set. The breach proving not negotiable, the assailants were compelled by the defenders to retire. In the night, again the trenches were carried forward and preparations were made to fire the other mines. The Adil Shahis and the Nizam Sahis assembled and delivered joint attacks upon the imperialists, but they were defeated and put to flight. The garrison continued to defend the fort vigorously, but realising that no relief was forthcoming from any quarter and the fall of the place imminent, they capitulated on terms and the imperialists occupied the fort on May 7th 1631 A.D. after having besieged it for four months and ninteen days. The commander of the fort Sadiq entered into the imperial service.[32]

The army which had been sent to Nasik and Berar under the command of Abul Hasan and Wazir Khan, strove hard to gain an upper hand of the Nizam Shahis. Wazir Khan quickly drove the Daccanis from Berar and returned to Burhanpur. But Abul Hasan's task did not prove so easy as it appeared to be. According to the orders of the Emperor he deputed his subordinate officers to plunder the Mahalls of Jalna and Pātori. Burhan Nizam Shah III sent Mahalldar Khan and Dada Pandit to oppose the enemy, but they were defeated and pursued by them up to Sangamnir. Abul Hasan, soon after occupied both Nasik and Sangamnir. After giving over the charge of Nasik to Shahji, Abul Hasan marched to the assistance of Nasiri Khan at Qandhar, in accordance with the royal instructions. The reduction of Dharur and Qandhar, Nasik and Sangamnir completed the first phase in the final extinction of the Nizam Shahi kingdom.[33]

**Nasik and Sangamnir occupied**

While these extensive operations of the Mughals were ruining and devastating the country, and famine was taking a heavy toll of life, a revolution broke out at the Nizam Shahi court which finally sealed the doom of that unfortunate kingdom. On the one hand, the murder of Jadhav Rao, the rebellion of Shahji, the desertion of the Marathas, the alliance of Bijapur with the Mughals had created an unprecedented crisis in that affairs of that unfortunate kingdom; on the other hand constant drain of man power and material resources broke the back-bone of its resistence. Faced with such a dismal situation Burhan Nizam Shah threw himself at the mercy of his nobles like Safdar Khan, Ikhals Khan and Farhad Khan and asked them to think out a plan of saving the dying kingdom. In doing this he ignored the services of Muqarrab Khan who had so valiantly resisted the enemy. He had disapproved his anti-Mughal policy at a time when the Mughals and the Bijapuris were endeavouring their best to swallow up the kingdom. Again, he was constantly pressed by his mother[34] to release her brother Fateh Khan who she said, would bring about a change for the better. To please her, Burhan Nizam Shah III set Fateh Khan free and raised him once more to the dignity of Wakil and Peshwa, asking him to protect his life and the kingdom like his father.[35] But instead of infusing any vigour into the operations against the Mughals, his advent to power brought the matters to a standstill. Muqrrab Khan, the leader of anti-Mughal movement was much annoyed by his promotion. He approached Azam Khan and through him entered the Mughal service. He was honoured with the rank of 6000 zat and 6000 Sawar and was given the title of Rustam Khan.[36]

**Revolution at Nizam Shahi court**

The desertion of Muqarrab Khan and the death of Hamid Khan cleared the way for Fateh Khan. No sooner did he obtain control of the state of affairs, than he won over the sympathies of his fellow Abyssinians and made them friends.[37] He could not forget the humiliation inflicted on him by Burhan Nizam Shah, nor could he be sure about his own future. He felt that he had been released under necessity, and that he would be imprisoned again as soon as the purpose had been accomplished. What aggravated his apprehensions against the king was his desire to follow a policy of making friends with the Mughals, in which he was opposed by most of the nobles. Therefore, he sought the earliest opportunity of seizing and imprisoning his master, as his father, Malik Ambar had done before. Luckily for him, Burhan was seized with insanity. Upon this Fateh Khan removed him from the palace and took to his own house (formerly the

**Burhan Nizam Shah III put to death (Feb. 1632 A.D.)**

mansion of Salabat Khan) on the pretext of treatment. He then opened secret negotiations with Asaf Khan, soliciting favour of the Emperor and expressing his readiness to tender allegiance to him.[32] He received an encouraging reply and was asked to give proof of his sincerity by putting his captive to death. Moved by the spirit of revenge, and in order to convince the Emperor of his bonafides, he poisoned the imbecile Burhan Nizam Shah III giving it out that he had died a natural death (Feb. 1632 A.D.)[39]. In his place, Fateh Khan raised to the throne his son, Husain Nizam Shah III, a boy of ten years.[40]

With the murder of Burhan Nizam Shah III, and accession of Husain Nizam Shah III began the second phase in the extinction of the kingdom of Ahmadnagar. The provincial governors and the commandants of different forts refused to obey the king-maker and his crowned prisoner. As the nobles had no faith in the sincerity of Fateh Khan, they deserted him and went over either to the Mughals or to Adil Shah, as it suited them. Shahji Anant, Sewaji Pandit, Shakharam and other Maratha and Hindu officers went over to the Mughals.[41] Similarly, Muslim nobles also deserted the cause of the Prime Minister reducing him to a miserable plight. In these circumstances the Emperor raised his demands still further. He asked Fateh Khan to surrender the jewels and elephants belonging to Nizam Shah, before he could extend protection to him.[42] This created suspicion in the mind of Fateh Khan with regard to the genuineness of the professions of the Mughal Emperor. It was confirmed by the warm welcome accorded to men like Muqarrab Khan and other sore enemies of Fateh Khan. As such the latter turned to Bijapur and Golcunda for help.

**Fateh Khan's submission**

For a little while, the prospects appeared to be favourable for Fateh Khan. Shahji bitterly resented the transfer of some districts to the latter which had originally been assigned to him. He deserted the Mughals and even took up arms against them. The ruler of Bijapur had his own grievances against the imperialists, and the relations between the two were getting strained. Lastly, Qutb Shah was also resentful of the aggression, and perhaps was not in a position to feed the monetary hunger of the Mughals, because heavy rains and flood had destroyed the crops in his kingdom. Moreover, the fortress of Daultabad was still in the hands of Fateh Khan which inspired him with confidence and hope of throwing back the invaders. Such were the reasons which induced him to show an attitude of indifference to the demands of the Mughal Emperor.

But Shahjahan was not the man to be toyed with. He despatched Wazir Khan and Muqarrab Khan, Jansipar Khan and Bithal Das to conquer the fort of Daultabad.[43] The advance of the imperial army alarmed Fateh Khan, and he sent his son Sayyid Abdul Rasul, to apologize to the Emperor for his conduct. On his arrival at the court, Abdul Rasul presented to the Emperor 30 elephants, nine horses, and jewellery worth eight thousand rupees.[44] The Emperor restored to Fateh Khan jagirs which he had confiscated earlier and had assigned to Shahji, thereafter Fateh Khan recited the Khutuba and struck coins in the name of the new suzerain. Upon being satisfied, Shahjahan left Burhanpur on March 6th. 1632 A.D. after appointing Mahabat Khan to the viceroyalty of the Daccan. Khan Zaman was ordered to officiate till the arrival of his father.[45]

Shajahan had no doubt suppressed the rebellion of Khan Jahan Lodi, recovered Balaghat and had restored the Mughal prestige in the Daccan but the sparks of resistence and disaffection were still alive there. After the return of the Emperor, Shahji found his position to be rather precarious. He was as much dissatisfied with the Mughals as Fateh Khan. He, therefore, chalked out for himself an independent line of action. He strengthened the fort of Pemgiri, raised a large army, and once more began to plunder and devastate the adjacent country. Soon he extended his authority over the territory from Poona-Chakan to the Konkan, from Junnar and Sangamnir to the environs of Daultabad and Ahmadnagar. He seized Nasik and Trimbak from the hands of the imperialists and recovered a large part of the Nizam Shahi territory. He found a scion of the Nizam Shahi house, who had been confined in a fort, raised the umbrella over his head and proclaimed him as the rightful ruler of Ahmadnagar. He now felt stronger than ever before. Now he

**Shahji's bold stand.**

had a cause to support and a mission to accomplish.[46]

After Fateh Khan had put to death Burhan Nizam Shah III Muhammad Khan the commandant of the fort of Galna repudiated his authority and put the fort in a state of defence. Shahji succeeded in persuading him to deliver the fort to him. But when Khan Zaman came to know of it, he wrote to Mir Qasim Haravi the commandant of the fort of Alang, which was near Galna, asking him to win over Muhammad Khan by promises of imperial favour. The move proved successful, the commandant dismissed Shahji's men and the fort of Galna passed into the hands of the imperialists (7th Oct. 1632 A.D.).[47]

**Fort of Galna surrendered**

Disgusted with the treacherous conduct of Fateh Khan and taking advantage of his growing unpopularity amongst his subjects, Shahji opened negotiations with Murari Pandit, the Adil Shahi minister with the object of impressing upon the latter the desirability of an immediate attack and capture of the fort of Daultabad.[48] His proposal was accepted and Muhammad Adil Shah sent a large force to serve under his command. The joint efforts of Shahji and Adil Shahi general and the disaffection of his own officers alarmed Fateh Khan, who in sheer fright appealed to Mahabat Khan to save him and the fort from the hands of the enemy. Mahabat Khan soon responded to his call and sent his son Khan Zaman to his succour.[49]

**Fateh Khan seeks assistance of Mahabat Khan**

Having arrived within one stage of Khirki, Khan Zaman arranged his forces, crossed the valley of Phulanbari[50] where it was reported to him that Shahji was blocking the way with seven or eight thousand men, and that the Adil Shahi general, Randola Khan had not yet effected a juncture with him. Finding a suitable opportunity the latter suddenly fell upon the Mughal right wing led by Murtaza Khan. But the timely arrival of Khan Zaman saved the situation. The Bijapur army was put to flight and was pursued up to five or six karohs. Shahji, however, continued to hold his ground on the heights of valley. But Diler Himmat compelled him to retreat, pursuing him up to the Khirki tank. He captured his drums and other war equipment, and struck his camp at Sanki (two karoh from Khirki) to watch the movements of the Daccanis.[51]

Unable to check the advance of the imperialists Randola Khan opened negotiations with Fateh Khan.[52] He warned him of the consequences of surrendering the fort of Daultabad to the Mughals. It would mean the complete extinction of the Nizam Shahi house, and it would also bring the Mughal aggression within striking distance of Bijapur and Golcunda. He assured him of the whole hearted support of Adil Shah, in case he agreed to give up his claims on Sholapur and its five and a half districts. Further he held out to him the temptation of three lacs of huns in addition to the supply of provisions and other equipments to stand the siege of Daultabad.[53] The offer was too alluring to be resisted, and Fateh Khan succumbed to it. Accordingly he admitted Randola Khan's uncle Khairat Khan with 600 men and started preparations for defending the fort.

**Fateh Khan incited by Randola Khan against Mughals**

When at Zafarnagar, Mahabat Khan was apprised of the treachery of Fateh Khan, he directed his son Khan Zaman to intercept the communications between him and Randola Khan ; to disperse the Adil Shahi army and Shahji's men who were encamping at Nizampur to smuggle the supplies into the fort, and directed him to open the siege of the fort.[54] Accordingly, Khan Zaman despatched Maloji, Bikhoji, Kheloji, Yashwant Rao to attack the Daccanis. The latter gave good fight, but on the appearance of Khan Zaman they took to flight and were hotly pursued for three karohs. Many of them were killed in the skirmishes which followed on the way.[55] After this Khan Zaman opened the siege of the fort of Daultabad and commenced laying mines and digging trenches.

After having completed the arrangements for the regular supply of provisions, Mahabat Khan left Burhanpur and arrived at Daultabad on 1st March, 1633 A.D. Next morning he rode out with his son to inspect the defences of the fort and took up his residence in the house belonging to the Nizam Shah at Nizampur. Fresh dispositions were made and the fortress was surrounded from all sides ; batteries

**Daultabad surrendered**

were established at strategic points and the siege was pressed with great vigour. Fateh Khan removed Husain Nizam Shah to Kalakot (a citadel in Daultabad which was considered to be impregnable) himself took post at Mahakot and strengthened Amberkot and other fortifications of Daultabad by distributing command and installing guns at vital points.[56]

At this stage Yaqut Khan, who had formerly been in the Nizam Shahi service but had deserted to the Mughals began to play foul. He attempted to smuggle the provisions into the fort but vigilance of the imperialists foiled his efforts. His men were caught red-handed and put the death. Therefore he fled to the Bijapuris, followed by Kheloji and other Maratha leaders. To add further to the distraction of the Mughals, Randola Khan and Shahji succeeded in joining hands. They led surprise attacks both individually and collectively and attempted to intercept the Mughal line of communications but they were repeatedly defeated and put to flight.[57]

The siege of Daultabad now resolved itself into a titanic struggle. Shahji and Adil Shahis on the one hand making frantic efforts to throw the supply of provisions into the fort; the imperialists on the other, equally determined to prevent them from doing it. In the skirmishes which followed every time the Daccanis were put to flight but they made themselves a source of perpetual distraction to the Mughals. The alertness of the enemy forced the garrison to starve but the threat of surprise attacks kept the Mughals in a state of suspense. On one occasion when Turkman Khan was bringing provisions from Zafarnagar, he was suddenly attacked by the Daccanis led by Yaqut Khan, Bahlol Khan, and Farhad Khan. It was only the timely arrival of Khan Zaman which saved the situation, and enabled the convoy to reach its destination.

Disappointed at the failure of his allies outside, to convey into the fort supply of provisions, in sheer desperation Fateh Khan resolved to give a fight to the enemy in the open. Accordingly, he sent out three elephants with some forces from Patan and Khirki gates, with the object of removing the mines which had been laid by the enemy in the fortifications.[58] But the attempt proved to be futile. He was

**Ambarkot fell into the hands of Imperialists**

compelled to retreat into the fort after losing many of his men. Khan Zaman now became more active than ever and he pressed the siege of Ambarkot with great vigour, making extensive preparations for the final assault. And although a mine was exploded before the time fixed for it, the besiegers rushed into the breach under a heavy fire of rockets, bullets and arrows. The defenders led by Khairat Khan Bijapuri fought valiantly, but in the end had to yield in the face of the superior numbers. Ambarkot fell into the hands of the Mughals, which raised their spirits and added to their fervour.[59]

Undeterred by their repeated failures Randola Khan and Shahji planned once more to throw provisions into the fort where the garrison was now subsisting on boiled skins of the dead animals.[60] To divert the attention of the besiegers and intercept their line of communication, Yaqut Khan, Bahlol Khan, Kheloji and Farhad Khan set out to raid Telangana and Berar; whereas Randola Khan and Shahji advanced towards the fort with 3000 loads of grain which they despatched under an escort of 3000 Carnatic musketeers. To counteract the trick of the Daccanis, Mahabat Khan despatched Khan Zaman, Rao Karan and Chatrasal against Yaqut Khan and others, and he directed Nasiri Khan to fall upon the convoy of provisions and seize it.

After driving away the Daccanis from the environs of Daultabad, Khan Zaman returned and joined the main army. Mahabat Khan now opened the siege of Mahakot. His men succeeded in laying a mine in the fortifications, which so

**Mahakot Besieged**

alarmed Fateh Khan that he removed his wives and children to Kalakot. But he could not ameliorate the distress of the garrison who were suffering from the scarcity of food, so that some of the Bijapuris like Datunak Khan, Tanaji Duniya approached Mahabat Khan through Maloji to solicit permission to escape to their master. Their request having been granted, they came out of the fort with two hundred men. Maloji presented them to Mahabat Khan who treated them kindly and allowed them to go with a message from him to Adil Shah.[61]

As usual the Daccanis spared no efforts to reduce the pressure on Mahakot and to distract the besiegers they adopted the normal tactics of intercepting their line of communication, seizing their convoy of provisions and raiding Berar. But the alertness and agility of Khan Zaman foiled their efforts. Meanwhile arrived Murari Pandit with fresh reinforcements from Bijapur which increased the activities of Randola Khan and Shahji between Khirki and Daultabad. The Daccanis now planned to engage Mahabat Khan and his assistants separately and defeat them in detail. But they were not destined to win success. Khan Zaman put them to flight and his father inflicted a crushing defeat on Murari Pandit[62].

By this time the besiegers had carried a mine into the fortifications and Mahabat Khan decided to fire it.[63] Fateh Khan lost all courage and sent Tuko Pandit to request the Mughal Commandar-in-Chief to postpone it. As an earnest of his faith Mahabat Khan asked Fateh Khan to send his son to the Mughal camp, but when the latter temporised and delayed, fire was set to the mine. It exploded, demolishing one bastion and eighteen yards of the fortifications. The imperialists led an assault through the breach thus created and occupied Mahakot.[64]

**Mahakot occupied**

Almost simultaneously Mahalldar Khan, the commander of the fort of Nabli near Jalna offered submission to Mahabat Khan. The latter asked him to give proofs of his sincerity by falling upon Shahji's men and seizing his treasury which he had installed at Baizapur. Mahalldar successfully seized Shahji's treasure of ½ lacs huns together with his wife and children, in addition to numerous horses. Mahabat Khan then asked him to come to Daultabad, after leaving the family of Shahji in charge of Jafar Khan of Jalna.[65]

**Shahji's family reduced**

The fall of Mahakot, the failure of Murari Pandit to relieve the sufferings of the garrison, the fall of Jalna, the terrible famine and scarcity of provisions reduced Fateh Khan to a miserable plight. The Mughal diplomacy had weakened the morale of the Daccanis, and many Bijapuris had taken shelter with them, which added much to his troubles.

**Daultabad fort surrendered by Fateh Khan**

The outbreak of epidemic rendered further resistence out of question. In despair, disgust and utter helplessness, Fateh Khan sent his son Abdul Rasul to apologize on his behalf to Mahabat Khan for his recent treacherous conduct and to obtain a week's time to evacuate the fort. Mahabat Khan acceded to his requests and even advanced one and half lac of rupees to enable him to arrange his departure from the fort. He placed at his disposal, elephants, camels and other means of transport. Fateh Khan left the fort in a week's time and the imperialists occupied it on 17th June, 1633, A.D. Enormous quantities of war material fell into their hands. The occupation of the fort of Daultabad symbolised the signal triumph of Mahabat Khan. Verily he had achieved the impossible.[66]

Leaving the fort in charge of Nasiri Khan, Mahabat Khan proceeded to Zafarnagar. The earlier treachery of Fateh Khan had made him more suspicious, and therefore soon after his arrival at Burhanpur, Mahabat Khan placed upon him strict guard.[67] Shahjahan, who was extremely delighted to hear of the conquest of Daultabad, ordered Mahabat Khan to send the captive Fateh Khan and Husain Nizam Shah III to the court under the escort of Islam Khan who was going to the north from Gujarat.[68] Fateh Khan and Nizam Shah were led into audience before the Emperor at Agra on 21st Sep. 1633 A.D. Shahjahan passed over the crimes of the wretched Fateh Khan, restored his jagirs to him and fixed an allowance of 2,00,000 rupees per annum for his expenses.[69] But the fate of the poor, helpless and innocent Husain Nizam Shah III was different. He was handed over to Sayyid Khan Jahan to be imprisoned in the fort of Gawalior, where Bahadur Nizam Shah was passing his days behind the bars.[70]

**Husain Nizam Shah III imprisoned**

The fall of Daultabad, the submission of the Fateh Khan the imprisonment of the king Husain Nizam Shah III, did by no means complete the subjugation of the kingdom of Ahmadnagar. Some of the Nizam Shahi officers refused to acknowledge the new dispensation and asserted their own authority in their respective jurisdictions. The commanders of the two strategic hill forts of Udgir and Ausa, were not prepared to yield without a struggle. The western districts including Junnar, Poona, Chakan and Konkan were witnessing a new upsurge in the rise of the Marathas, who, under the impact of religious renaissance were in the process of forming themselves into a powerful instrument of aggression under the leadership of Shahji Bhonsle. Siddi Rihan in Sholapur, Siddi Ambar in Danda Rajpuri and Siddi Saba Saif Khan in Kalyan assumed independence, but subsequently tendered submission to Adil Shah. Shriniwas Rao of Junnar, however, could not make up his mind whether to join Bijapur or to go over to the Mughals. In short, the dying state presented a picture of conflicting intrests, seething with discontent and utter political confusion.[71]

In the midst of this turmoil, Shahji decided to strike a bold line of action by reviving the pretensions of independence of the Nizam Shahi state by setting up a puppet and proclaiming him king. He established his capital at Pemgiri. It was a clever move on his part; thereby he thought that he would be able to rally round his banner the floating mass of Ahmadnagar soldiery and to exploit local patriotism by playing upon the resentment of the populace against the Mughals. He then turned to Adil Shah and impressed upon him the necessity of joining hands with him in the task of giving a fresh lease of life to the Nizam Shahi kingdom, which was not difficult in view of the fact that out of eighty four forts of the kingdom only one was in the hands of the imperialists. The argument proved so convincing that Muhammad Adil Shah sent five to six hundred troops under the command of Ambar Khan to the help of Shahji. This was a welcome addition to his army which numbered 8000 (September 1633).[72]

**Shahji's attempt to revive the fallen Dynasty**

But much to the consternation of Shahji, the Muslim nobles of the defunct Nizam Shahi kingdom were reluctant to recognise the puppet Nizam Shah as their sovereign. One of them Siddi Saba Saif Khan after surrendering his territories to Shahji, while retaining the remaining forts into his hands, set out to join Adil Shah. This proved intolerable to Shahji and he marched to lay siege to the village where the Khan was encamping. But the intervention of Murari

**Difficulties in the way**

Pandit saved the latter and enabled him to go to Bijapur. Similarly Siddi Rihan of Sholapur after resisting the Mughal pressure, surrendered the fort to Adil Shah.[73] The Mughals now attempted to conciliate Shahji through his cousin Maloji, but he proved impervious to their overtures.

Within a short time Shahji captured all the territory in the Konkan and Talkonkan, seized few districts of Khandesh, brought the rebellious jagirdars to submission and won over the support of the Hindu nobles, who being actuated by patriotic feelings and religious fervour, joined hands with him to fight Mughals.[74] Even Shriniwas Rao, the chief of Junnar who had refused to acknowledge the new king, had to bow before the storm. The fall of Junnar, and Shivaneri was followed by that of Jivadhan, Sunda, Bhirgadh, Parsagadh, Hansgadh, Maholi, Khej and other forts. The boy king Murtaza Nizam Shah III was brought to Shivaneri, which now became the seat of further operations.

Shahji obtained immense booty in these conquests, which enabled him to employ 12000 horsemen who had been discharged after the capture of Daultabad. He now plundered and devastated the environs of Ahmadnagar, Daultabad and Bidar. His success so much alarmed the Mughals that they sent Khawas Khan with 3000 horse men towards Ahmadnagar to drive him away. Though the Mughals devastated Chamargunda, the home of the Bhonsles, yet they failed to circumscribe the sphere of Shahji's activities. (Dec. 1633). Mahabat Khan appealed to the Emperor to send men and money and at the same time sent agents to Muhammad Adil Shah, requesting him to withdraw support from Shahji, so that he could inflict on him an effective blow. But he did not succeed and died of a broken heart in Oct 1634 A.D.[75]

The death of Mahabat Khan proved to be a heaven sent blessing to Shahji to accomplish the task he had set before himself. Hardly any competent leader was left there to check the ambitious designs of the Daccanis or strike terror in their heart. Mustafa Khan the governor of Daultabad and Allahvardi Khan of Painghat found it hard either to dislodge Shahji or to defend the forts against the latter. Both of them found the ground slipping from beneath their feet.

When Khan Dauran heard of the crisis in the Daccan he

marched from Burhanpur, and thence to Daultabad arriving there on 27th January, 1635 A.D.[76] He found that the Daccanis had retreated to Ramduda ; therefore he stayed there to watch further developments. On the next day, he marched with Raja Jai Singh and others to punish Shahji's men. Near Panganga, he received the news that the Daccanis were moving towards Shivgaon.[77] He overtook them, but they soon broke up and fled. He pursued them closely up to Amrapur,[78] seized their camp, and thence marched towards Junnar via Manik Duda, intending to cross Balaghat by Kotal Mohri.[79] On the way he plundered their camp again, seized about 8000 bullocks laden with grain and made about 3000 men captive. He then marched towards Ahmadnagar.[80] He equipped the fort with copious supply of provisions and fodder. Shortly after, he was informed of the arrival of Khan Zaman in the Balaghat and of his march towards Daultabad. When he received orders of appointment as governor of Painghat, he left Ahmadnagar and went to Burhanpur.[81] Shahji however continued to hover round the imperialists. He ravaged and plundered the Mughal territories as ever, being assisted in his activities by Adil Shah.

**Shahji's activities**

Shahjahan realised the gravity of the situation in the Daccan. The rebellion of Jujhar Singh and the mobilisation of the imperial forces in Bundelkhand, and the consequent decline of the imperial prestige in the south, had left the ground clear for Shahji. Shahjahan found that it was beyond the means of Khan Zaman to handle the state of affairs. Therefore, he left Agra on 21st Sep, 1635 A.D., with the three-fold object ; firstly, securing unity among his officers campaigning in Bundelkhand, secondly, visiting Daultabad and completing the subjugation of the Ahmadnagar kingdom, and thirdly, obtaining the allegiance of the other two kingdoms. From Hindiya he despatched his envoys to Adil Shah and Qutb Shah to warn them of the disastrous consequences, if they attempted to interrupt or refused to co-operate with him in an attempt to restore peace in the country annexed by him. He crossed the Narbada on January 4th,

**Shahjahan's arrival in the Daccan**

1636, celebrated his birthday at Burhanpur and from thence he went to Daultabad.[82]

Here he chalked out a grand plan of operations against Shahji. He divided his army into three sections ; one division of 12000 led by Khan Dauran and Raja Jai Singh, was sent to Qandhar and Nander to watch the frontiers of Bijapur and Golcunda, to be ready to march to the relief of threatened points and to reduce the forts of Ausa and Udgir. They were also instructed that in case Adil Shah endeavoured to help Shahji, they should punish him by ravaging his territory.[83] The second division, of 12000 strong was placed under the command of Khan Zaman who was to be assisted by Bahadur Khan Rohilla, Sayyid Shujaat Khan, Shah Beg Khan, Rao Chatrsal and others. He was asked to go towards Ahmadnagar to seize Shahji's mahalls; to reduce the entire Konkan and wait for further orders regarding attack on the Adil Shahi country.[84] While the third division consisting of 6000 horsemen was placed under Shaista Khan, who was to work in cooperation with Allahwardi Khan, Yaqut Khan, Taj Khan, Shaikh Farid and Raja Sangram. They were to capture Junnar, the seat of Shahji's power and to occupy Sangamnir, Nasik and Trimbak.[85]

**Grand Plan against Shahji**

Shaishta Khan opened his campaign by despatching Allahwardi Khan with 20,000 troops to the north to reduce various forts in that region.[86] Of those in the district of Chandore and Dharab, six were in the hands of Bhojir, a rebel. Shahji's men were not ready to surrender the forts. Allahwardi Khan advanced rapidly towards them and captured the forts of Ramsej and Kherdurg, and from there marched towards the fort of Chandore and laid siege to it.[87] Being pressed from three sides, Shahji began to move to and fro between Junnar and Sangamnir. He made Mahauli as his headquarter and kept Murtaza Nizam Shah there. He was constantly encouraged and supported by the Adil Shahi commander Randola Khan. When it became apparent to Shahjahan that Adil Shah would not refrain from assisting Shahji and would not submit to his authority, he sent Khan Zaman with 10,000 men to punish him. He was to act in concert

**Shahji closely pursued**

with the other three generals, who were directed to converge upon Bijapur from three distinct directions, to punish Randola Khan and to prevent his junction with Shahji, and to ravage and devastate Bijapur country. The new disposition of the imperial forces alarmed Shahji and took wind out of his sails.

Meanwhile Allahwardi Khan closely invested Chandore and occupied it. This served as warning to other Maratha chieftains, who meekly submitted to the Mughal authority. Soon after Khanjanah, Manjanah, Rola, Jola, Ahwant, Kol, Dewhbar, Achlakar and many other forts of Konkan fell into the hands of the imperialists. In one of these forts which was held by Raja Deohir, were some members of the Nizam Shahi family. Likewise the fort of Dharab held by Bhojil was also captured and its commandant was taken into imperial service.[88]

Shaishta Khan drove Shahji's men from Sangamnir towards Nasik and sent Shaikh Farid in that direction to check their activities in that region. At the same time Ahmad Khan Niazi was sent to Dundan Ahdad to capture its fort, and Mahmud Khan to Ankolah to encourage the people to take to agriculture and save them from rebels and assure them of security of their life and property. Upon the approach of Shaikh Farid, the Daccanis retreated towards Konkan. Within a short time Shaishta Khan seized Junnar and strengthened the Mughal position in the western districts of Ahmadnagar.[89]

To turn back the tide of the Mughal invasion Adil Shah ordered that the whole country for twenty miles round Bijapur be desolated so that, "not a blade of grass or a drop of water could be obtained by the enemy". This rendered the task of the invaders difficult, rather impossible, and compelled them to conclude peace with Adil Shah. According to the terms of the treaty Adil Shah was to pay an annual tribute of twenty lacs of rupees and to acknowledge the suzerainty of the Mughal Emperor; secondly, that he had to treat the Nizam Shahi kingdom as defunct; and its territory was to be divided between him and the Mughals. He was assigned the area comprising Sholapur, Wangi Mahalls, the parganas of Bhalki,

**The fate of the Nizam Shahi kingdom sealed**

Chitkopa and the Konkan which included the districts of Poona and Chakan; thirdly, Shahji should not be taken in the Bijapur service, or even allowed to enter into the Adil Shahi territory until he had surrendered Junnar, Trimbak and the whole country he held in his possession. The treaty was concluded and ratified by the Mughal Emperor in May 1636 A.D. which sealed the fate of the Nizam Shahi kingdom, a part of which had been successfully recovered by Maratha leader Shahji.

After the submission of Muhammad Adil Shah, Shahjahan returned from Daulatbad leaving Prince Aurangzab as viceroy of the Daccan. There was still much to occupy the attention and absorb the energy of the Mughals.[90] The forts of Ausa and Udgir were in the hands of the Nizam Shahi officers, who refused to surrender them inspite of the fact that they were promised full freedom to remove their families and seek their fortune wherever they liked. When conciliation and persuation failed, Khan Dauran marched to Udgir and invested the fort on 19th June 1636 A.D. He occupied the adjacent town, ran the trenches beneath the fortifications charged them with mines. One of them was fired, but the breach did not prove to be negotiable. He did not wish to explode the other mines lest during the general assault harm should befell the grandson of Ibrahim Adil Shah II, who was inside the fort. At length the garrison lost heart and Siddi Miftah, the Abyssinian commandant of the fort opened negotiations for surrendering the fort. But he put forward impossible terms, and therefore the siege was pressed with greater vigour. Another mine was fired which blew off the entire earthwork with its guns and other armaments. Siddi Miftah now surrendered the fort to the imperialists on 28th Sept. 1636 A.D. and entered into their service.[91]

**The fort of Udgir captured**

Similarly the fort of Ausa was also invested by Rashid Khan. The fall of Udgir created terror in the hearts of the defenders. Bhojraj, a Rajput commandant kept up a ceaseless fire from the fort on the besiegers, but when the trenches had been run and mining completed, he lost heart and gave up the fort to the imperialists on 19th Oct. 1636 A.D. and entered

**The fort of Ausa captured**

into the imperial service.[92]

Aurangzeb now sent Khan Zaman to reduce Shahji, who by now had become stronger than ever. He marched to Junnar, left a contingent of troops to invest that fort and himself moved to dislodge Shahji from Poona.[93] Soon after he was joined by the Bijapuri troops under Randola Khan and Kanhoji Jedhe. Upon their approach Shahji fled to the hills of Kondana and Torna. The allies found it difficult to contact him owing to heavy rains. At the close of rains, he was pursued closely by Khan Zaman. He was complelled to retreat to Dandarajpuri, from where he came to Moranjan. Here Khan Zaman gave a crushing defeat to him. Leaving behind all his baggage, he proceeded to Mahauli where he resolved to take the final stand against the Mughals. Khan Zaman after another forced march through mire and mud, seized the village at the foot of the fort with its store of provisions. The joint forces of Adil Shah and the Mughals besieged the fort. Kanhoji Jedhe opened secret correspondence with Shahji. When the provisions of the fort were exhausted and the people began to starve, Shahji offered to surrender the fort and the puppet Nizam Shah, on condition that he should be allowed to serve Adil Shah and that the Nizam Shahi territory lying to the south of the river Godavari be given to to him in lieu of his services. These terms were reported to Adil Shah, who ratified them. After it, Shahji surrendered to the Mughals the puppet Nizam Shah along with Mahauli and six other forts of Trimbak, Tringalvadi, Harshgadh, Jivdhan, Chaund and Hadsar. He joined the Adil Shahi service and Adil Shah, assigned to him Poona and Supa in jagirs.[95]

**Shahji surrendered the Nizam Shah to the Mughals**

While going to the north in 1637 A.D. for his marriage with Dilras Banu Begam, Aurangzeb took with him the last of the Nizam Shahi kings, Murtaza Nizam Shah III. The unfortunate king of Ahmadnagar, like others who had preceded him was confined in the state prison at Gawalior.[95] Thus came to an inglorious end, a kingdom which was once the pride of the Daccan. But it took forty years for the Mughals to reduce it completely and annex it into their empire, inspite of the

**Last Phase**

superiority of their resources, both in man power and in money. The carcass was duly partitioned. The districts of Nasik and Khandesh were joined together to form the new suba of Aurangabad, while the territory between Bhima and Nira was handed over to Adil Shah whose age-long territorial greed was thereby satisfied.[96] Apparently the annexation of the kingdom of Ahmadnagar signalised a great achievement for the mighty Mughal Empire, but in reality it marked the beginning of the political malaise which in the end proved fatal.

*Notes and References :*

1. House of Shivaji, pp. 36.
2. Ibid, pp. 36.
3. Iqbalnama-i-Jahangiri (Elliot and Dowson) Vol. VI, pp. 432.
4. Iqbalnama-i-Jahangiri, pp. 384; Elliot and Dowson, Vol. VI, pp. 433-34; Muntakhab-ul-Lubab, Vol. I, pp. 383-85;
5. Qazwini (Elliot and Dowson) Vol. VIII, pp. 6; Shiva Kalin Patrasara Sangraha, Vol. I (No. 200).
6. Lahauri, Vol. I, pp. 251.
7. Basatin-us-Salatin, pp. 286; Maasir-ul-Umra, Vol. I, pp. 532.
8. Iqbalnama-i-Jahangiri, pp. 611; Elliot and Dowson, Vol. VI, pp. 433.
9. Iqbalnama-i-Jahangiri, pp. 611; Basatin-us-Salatin, pp. 286; Tuzuk-i-Jahangiri (R & B) Vol. I, pp. 416.
10. Lahauri, Vol. I, pp. 199-257;
11. Lahauri, Vol. I, pp. 293-94 Shiva Kalin Patrasara Sangraha, Vol. I, pp. 308.
12. Lahauri, Vol. I, pp. 293-94.
13. Basatin-us-Salatin pp. 287, Qazwini (Elliot and Dowson) Vol. VII, pp. 10-11, Lahauri, Vol. I, pp. 293.
14. Basatin-us-Salatin, pp. 283, Qazwini (Elliot and Dowson) Vol. VII, pp. 11; Lahauri, Vol. I, pp. 293-310.
15. Basatin-us-Salatin, pp. 283; Qazwini (Elliot and Dowson), Vol. VII, pp. 11, Lahauri, Vol. I, pp. 293-310.
16. Basatin-us-Salatin, pp. 287.
17. Basatin-us-Salatin, pp. 287.
18. Basatin-us-Salatin, pp. 287-88; Qazwini (Elliot and Dowson), Vol. VII pp. 15; Shiva Kalin Patrasara Sangraha, Vol. I (No. 332).
19. Basatin-us-Salatin, pp. 288.
20. Qazwini (Elliot and Dowson) Vol. VII, pp. 20, Lahauri Vol. I, pp. 339-43.
21. Lahauri, Vol. I, pp. 344.
22. Lahauri, Vol. I, pp. 344; 347.
23. Lahauri, Vol. I, pp. 345; 346; 347; 355; 356; Qazwini, pp. 214 (a), Muntakhab-ul-Lubab, Vol. I, pp. 450-51.
24. Lahauri, Vol. I, pp. 356-58; Muntakhab-ul-Lubab, Vol. I, pp. 452.
25. Lahauri, Vol. I, pp. 358-9.
26. Ibid, pp. 359-60.
27. Ibid, pp. 360.
28. Ibid, pp. 360-63.
29. Lahauri, Vol. I, pp. 367-68; Muntakhab-ul-Lubab, Vol. I, pp. 454.
30. Lahauri, Vol. I, pp. 368; Qazwini, pp. 229 (a), Elliot and Dowson, Vol. VII, pp. 25, Muntakhab-ul-Lubab, Vol. I, pp. 454.

31. Lahauri, Vol. I, pp. 374-6; Qazwini, pp. 229 (a); Elliot and Dowson, Vol. VII, pp. 25-26; Muntakhab-ul-Lubab, Vol. I, pp. 454-56.

32. Lahauri, Vol. I, pp. 477; Qazwini, pp. 229; Muntakhab-ul-Lubab, Vol. I, pp. 455-56.

33. Lahauri, Vol. I, pp. 367-68; Muntakhab-ul-Lubab, Vol. I, pp. 454-5.

34. This is very knotty point which is difficult to clarify. There is sufficient historical evidence to establish the fact that Murtaza was done to death at the instance of Malik Ambar. According to Pieter Van Den Broecke, he left behind a minor son who was raised to the throne, who according to the inscriptions in the Autur Fort, assumed the style of Burhan Nizam Shah III. As such the lady who secured the release of Fateh Khan was the mother of the Nizam Shah rather than his wife, a fact which is confirmed by the author of the Maasir-ul-Umra (Vol. I, pp. 532). But other historians, particularly, Mughal, call her the wife of the Nizam Shah. This error perhaps is due to two facts viz. (i) that they failed to take notice of the change of rulers which had been effected by Malik Ambar, who had his own son-in-law Murtaza poisoned and (ii) that the Mughal historians could not distinguish between Abul Fateh who poisoned Murtaza Nizam Shah II and Fateh Khan, who poisoned Burhan Nizam Shah III.

35. Muqarrab Khan proceeded with his forces to join Azam Khan. The latter sent his son Multafit Khan to receive him and himself too went forward to welcome him. Muqarrab Khan was honoured with the rank of 6000 Zat and 6000 Sawar and given a robe of honour, four horses, two elephants and one lakh rupees. Besides 200 horses and 70 Khilats were given to his followers—Lahauri Vol. I, pp. 378; Muntakhab-ul-Lubab, Vol. I, pp. 457.

36. Lahauri, Vol. I, pp. 277-78; Qazwini (Elliot and Dowson) Vol VIII pp. 27; Basatin-us-Salatin, pp. 289-90; Maasir-ul-Umra Vol. I, pp. 532-33.

37. Lahauri Vol. I, pp. 402; Qazwini, pp. 237-9, Muntakhab-ul-Lubab, Vol. I, pp. 461; Maasir-ul-Umra, Vol. I, pp. 533.

38. Lahauri Vol. I, pp. 402; Qazwini pp. 237-9; Muntakhab-ul-Lubab Vol. I, pp. 461-62;

39. Basatin-us-Salatin pp. 295; Lahauri, Vol. I pp. 409-10; Qazwini (Elliot and Dowson) Vol. VII, pp. pp. 27; Muntakhab-ul-Lubab, Vol. I pp. 462; Maasir-ul-Umra Vol. I pp. 533;

40. Basatin-us-Salatin mentions the age of Husain Nizam Shah III, seven years only. Lahauri Vol. I pp. 402; Qazwini pp. 239; Maasir-ul-Umra. I, pp. 533;

41. Basatin-us-Salatin pp. 304; Lahauri Vol. I pp. 442; Qazwini, pp. 237-239, 241;

42. Lahauri, Vol. I 409-10; Qazwini pp. 241-42; Muntakhab-ul-Lubab Vol. I, pp. 462;

43. Lahauri, Vol. I, pp. 409-10; Qazwini pp. 241-42; Muntakhab-ul-Lubab Vol. I pp. 463;

44. Lahauri Vol. I, pp. 422; Qazwini pp. 242-45; Muntakhab-ul-Lubab Vol. I pp. 467;

45. Basatin-us-Salatin pp. 295; Lahauri, Vol. I, pp. 426; Qazwini pp. 246-9; Muntakhab-ul-Lubab Vol. I pp. 468;

46. Basatin-us-Salatin pp. 304; Lahauri Vol. I pp. 442-43; Muntakhab-ul-Lubab Vol. I pp. 471;

47. Lahauri Vol. I pp. 442-43; Qazwini pp. 254-56 (a); Muntakhab-ul-Lubab Vol. I pp. 471;

48. Lahauri Vol. I pp. 497; Muntakhab-ul-Lubab Vol. I pp. 477;

49. Lahauri Vol I pp. 497-98; Qazwini pp. 279;

50. Lahauri Vol I pp. 498; Qazwini pp. 279;

51. Lahauri Vol I. pp. 498-9; Qazwini pp. 279;

52. Lahauri Vol I pp. 500; Qazwini pp. 280; Muntakhab-ul-Lubab Vol. I pp. 477;

53. Lahauri Vol. I pp. 500; Qazwini pp. 281; Muntakhab-ul-Lubab Vol. I, pp. 477;

54. Lahauri Vol. I pp. 500-1; Qazwini pp. 281; Muntakhab-ul-Lubab Vol. I pp. 477;

55. Lahauri Vol. I pp. 501-2; Qazwini pp. 281; Muntakhab-ul-Lubab, Vol. I pp. 477;

56. Lahauri Vol. I pp. 502-3; Qazwini pp. 281; Elliot and Dowson, Vol. VII pp. 38; Muntakhab-ul-Lubab Vol. I pp. 477;

57. Lahauri Vol. I pp. 504-511; Qazwini pp. 281-87;

58. Lahauri Vol. I pp. 510; Qazwini pp. 287;

59. Lahauri Vol. I pp. 510-12; Qazwini pp. 288; Muntakhab-ul-Lubab Vol. I pp. 479-82;

60. Lahauri Vol. I pp. 515; Qazwini pp. 289-81; Muntakhab-ul-Lubab Vol. I 483.

61. Lahauri Vol. I pp. 515-16; Qazwini pp. 290-91; Muntakhab-ul Lubab Vol. I 283;

62. Lahauri Vol. I pp. 516-20; Muntakhab-ul-Lubab Vol. I pp. 284-85;

63. Lahauri Vol. I pp. 525-26; Qazwini pp. 296; Muntakhab-ul-Lubab Vol. I 487;

64. Lahauri Vol. I pp. 526; Qazwini pp. 296;

65. Lahauri Vol. I pp. 526; Qazwini pp. 296; Muntakhab-ul-Lubab Vol. I pp. 487;

66. Lahauri Vol. I pp. 528-31; Qazwini pp. 297; Muntakhab-ul-Lubab Vol. I pp. 487;

67. Lahauri Vol. I pp. 531; Qazwini pp. 299; Muntakhab-ul-Lubab, Vol. I pp. 491;

68. Lahauri Vol. I pp. 540;

69. Lahauri Vol. I pp. 541; Qazwini pp. 303;

70. Basatin-us-Salatin pp. 300-301, Lahauri Vol. I pp. 541; Qazwini pp. 303; Muntakhab-ul-Lubab, Vol. I pp. 487;

71. Basatin-us-Salatin pp. 302-3; Lahauri Vol. II ppl 33;

72. Basatin-us-Salatin pp. 306; Lahauri Vol. II pp. 36; Qazwini pp. 332;

73. Basatin-us-Salatin pp.306;

74. Basatin-us-Salatin pp. 307; Lahauri Vol. II pp. 36;

75. Lahauri Vol. II, 36-45; Qazwini pp. 325-332;

76. Lahauri Vol. II, pp. 68; Qazwini pp. 335-36; Muntakhab-ul-Lubab Vol. I pp. 496;

77. Lahauri Vol. II pp. 68; Qazwini pp. 335-36; Muntakhab-ul-Lubab, Vol. I pp. 508;

78. Lahauri Vol. II pp. 68; Qazwini pp. 335-36; Muntakhab-ul Lubab Vol. I pp. 508;

79. Lahauri Vol. II pp. 68; Qazwini pp. 335-36; Muntakhab-ul-Lubab Vol. I pp. 508;

80. Lahauri Vol. II, pp. 68; Qazwini pp. 335-36; Muntakhab-ul-Lubab Vol. I pp. 508;

81. Lahauri Vol. II pp. 68; Qazwini pp. 335-36; Muntakhab-ul-Lubab, Vol. I pp. 508;

82. Lahauri Vol. II pp. 135; Qazwini pp. 360-61;

83. Lahauri Vol. II, pp. 136; Qazwini pp. 364; Muntakhab-ul-Lubab Vol. I pp. 520;

84. Lahauri Vol. II pp. 136; Qazwini pp. 364; Muntakhab-ul-Lubab, Vol. I pp. 521;

85. Lahauri Vol. II, pp. 136; Muntakhab-ul-Lubab Vol. I, pp. 521;

86. Lahauri Vol. II, pp. 139; Qazwini pp. 366; Muntakhab-ul-Lubab Vol. II pp. 523;

87. Lahauri Vol. II pp. 139-40; Muntakhab-ul-Lubab Vol. I pp. 523;

88. Lahauri Vol. II pp. 141; 146; 148; Muntakhab-ul-Lubab Vol. I pp. 523-24;

89. Lahauri Vol. II pp. 149;

90. John Frayer writing about the last days of the Nizam Shahi Kingdom says, that the king held the Mughals play for a long while, though by degrees the latter, "from without and the perverse remissness of his own sect at home, reduced him to that part of the Daccan; the entire conquest of which the present Aurangzeb finished......The reward which gratified him was the Extirpation of the Royal Race of the Nizam Shaws, whose Destruction, the remaining two may at lieusure repent being thereby incapacitated to made head against the Mughal, mangre all their forces where before Nizam Shah alone could withstand the even defeat his most peeissant Armies; but since his down fall they have enough to do Guard themselves." —see, "A New Account of the East Indies and Persia", Vol. II pp. 49-50;

91. Lahauri Vol. II, pp. 217-18; Muntakhab-ul-Lubab Vol. I pp. 538-39;

92. Lahauri Vol. II pp. 218; Muntakhab-ul-Lubab Vol. I pp. 539;

93. Lahauri Vol. II pp. 225-28; Muntakhab-ul-Lubab Vol. I pp. 539;

94. Lahauri Vol. II pp. 229-30; Qazwini pp. 398-400.

95. Qazwini, pp. 407; Muntakhab-ul-Lubab Vol. I pp. 542;

96. Shiva Kalin Patrasara Sangraha.

CHAPTER IX

# THE NIZAM SHAHI-PORTUGUESE RELATIONS

While the founder of the Nizam Shahi kingdom, Ahmad Nizam Shah was ceaselessly endeavouring to carve out an independent principality for himself, out of the rapidly declining Bahmani kingdom, the Portuguese made thair appearance on the Western coast of India. The original motive of the Portuguese adventurers was mainly religious, for,"they were keenly desirous of bringing Christianity to the vast tribes lying under the wrath of God, and join hands with Prester John the fabled Christian Prince of the East with a view to wash out the very existence of Islam from the very face of the earth." Their success in bringing to an end the Muslim rule in Spain and setting up an Inquisition in the Peninsula had inspired them with the ambition of propagating the Faith by any means, even at the point of the sword. And to this religious motive was closely linked the objective of attaining wealth and power by carrying on trade in spices and other articles, abundantly found in the East.

Vasco da Gama rounded the Cape of Good Hope, and was piloted to the Indian shores by the Muslim sailor Abdul-Majid, arriving at Calicut on 20 May, 1495 A.D. Once the route to India by sea, having been discovered, larger and stouter sailing crafts began to move from the West to the East. As the Daccan and the south India were then in great turmoil, the new adventurers found a splendid opportunity of laying the foundations of a political Empire based both on religion and commerce.

On their arrival on the Western coast, the Portuguese found themselves in close competition with the Muslim merchants, who had monopolised all the indigenous and foreign trade. Inspired by religious fervour and fired by crusading spirit the Portuguese sought to oust with their stronger vessels the Indian or the Arab sailing crafts, because they could better face the mild storm and rough weather, mount heavy guns, the fire of which proved devastating. They attacked the Muslim traders and their crews, inflicted heavy losses on them and obtained foothold on the Western coast of India. In the beginning they contented themselves with establishing factories in the territories of the Zamorin of Calicut or in those of the Raja of Cochin avoiding establishment of possessions on the land. But the factories were soon turned into fortresses and open contest for maintaining supremacy on the sea and the land commenced between a handful Portuguese adventurers and the Muslim traders. The first stage of this adventure came to an end in 1505, when Dom Francisco de Almeida was appointed as the political head of the Portuguese dominions in the East. Early in January 1508, the Portuguese received a heavy blow at Chaul at the hands of Amir Hasan, the admiral of Qansuh-el-Ghuri, the king of Egypt, and Malik Ayaz, the commander of the Gujarati fleet.[1] But they soon recovered their strength and defeated the Egyptian fleet at Diu in February 1509 A.D.[2] Having concluded a treaty with Malik Ayaz, the Viceroy Dom Francisco de Almeida returned to Cochin and on his way, he made Ahmad Nizam Shah a friend to the crown of Portugal.[3] He at first demanded of him immediate payment of 30,000 Cruzodos and an annual subsidy of 10,000 Cruzados, perhaps for the reason that he had allowed the Muhamedan forces to deliver a surprise attack on the Portuguese in his kingdom, which they had never expected of him. Having been intimidated by recent victory over the Egyptian fleets Ahmad Nizam Shah thought it prudent to enter into friendly relations with them. He placated the Viceroy by paying 2000 Cruzados and the latter remained satisfied with that amount (April 1509 A.D.)[4]. According to Duarte Barbosa, a factor was appointed at Chaul by the Portuguese in 1514 A.D.[5] The port had a Portuguese settlement on the coast, but the city and its adjacent villages remained in the possession of the Nizam Shahi kings till the year 1625 A.D. and served as one of the biggest commercial and industrial centres of the Nizam Shahi kingdom during the sixteenth and seventeenth century of the Christian era.[6]

Dom Francisco de Almeida was succeeded by Alfonso Albuquerque (1509-1515 A.D). As new governor, he realised that the power and strength of the Portuguese could only rest on their occupation of strategical points all along the

Western coast, where they could maintain their naval supremacy, he captured Goa in 1510 A.D. and made it the political centre of the Portuguese possessions in India. He was succeeded by Lopo Soares in the year 1515 A.D. The latter partly taking advantage of the minority of Burhan Nizam Shah I, who had succeeded his father in 1510 and partly with the intention of remaining on friendly terms with him obtained his permission for establishing a big factory at Chaul in order to have a freer access, than the Portuguese hitherto had, to this important harbour.[7] This was the happy beginning of the friendly intercourse between the two powers whose strength and stability depended on mutual support.

In 1521 war broke out between Burhan Nizam Shah and Bahadur Shah, the king of Gujarat. As the relations between the Gujaratis and the Portuguese were bad, Burhan Nizam Shah deemed it advisable to exploit the situation by joining the latter with a view to thwart the rising power of the common enemy. Accordingly he gave permission to Fernao Camello, the Portuguese factor, who had succeeded Joao Fernandes to erect a fort on the site of Ravedanda, where they had already built a house, called factory (1516 A.D.)[8]. Being enraged at the conduct of Adil Khan, the commander of the Dabul fleet, which in an attempt to drive out the Portuguese from the Indian waters, had burnt the city of Chaul, Burhan Nizam Shah sent Latif Khan to the Portuguese governor Diogo Lopes de Sequeira to persuade him to erect the fort immediately and to concert measures against the Gujaratis by drawing up an agreement or treaty between the two parties.[9] Meanwhile the governorship of the city of Chaul fell vacant and the dispute for it arose between the two brothers namely, Shaikh Ahmad and Shaikh Mahmud. Diogo Lopes Sequeira did not fail to take advantage of such an splendid opportunity.[10] He entered into a treaty with Burhan Nizam Shah I and immediately commenced building the fort on the northern margin of the creek, about half a league to the south, for it was a most convenient site for warlike purposes.[11] Among the stipulations of the treaty was the one concerning the importation of horses for the use of Burhan Nizam Shah who agreed to assist the Portuguese against the Gujaratis.[12] Being terrified by the constant success of the Portuguese

Burhan Nizam Shah sent his ambassador to the Portuguese governor to a renew his former treaty of peace. ( 1530 A.D. ) The same year at the request of the Portuguese governor, Burhan Nizam Shah entered into peace with Bahadur Shah, the Sultan of Gujarat and agreed to assist him against the Mughals.

The very same year misunderstanding arose between the Portuguese and Burhan Nizam Shah. The latter inspite of his amicable relations with them showed his unwillingness to cede to them more ground at the Chaul creek. It seems to have originated from the defeat of the Captain of Chaul, Francisco Pereira Barreto, who at the request of Burhan Nizam Shah had been sent with a detachment to fight Bahadur Shah but was defeated and driven back. Thereupon Burhan Nizam Shah changed his attitude towards the Portuguese which shows that the friendship he bore towards them was dictated by self-interests alone. However the differences between the two were soon healed up and peaceful relations were restored.[14]

While Bahadur Shah was engaged in war with the Mughals, Burhan Nizam Shah thought the moment an opportunity to strike a heavy blow on him, to avenge the disgrace he had met at his hands. He, therefore, decided to take possession of the fortresses of Sangaca and Carnala ( Sankri and Karnala ? ) held by the subjects of the Sultan of Gujarat on the frontiers of that kingdom. Accordingly, he marched against them, attacked and captured them.[15] The previous owners being anxious to recover their possessions sought the assistance of Dom Francisco de Menezes, the Captain of Bassien, promising to hold them in the name of the Portuguese. Being tempted by the offer, Dom Francisco marched with three thousand Portuguese and a part of the native troops. He scaladed the walls of the fortresses, stormed them, recaptured them for their lawful owners, but installed in them the Portuguese garrison. The hostile conduct of the Portuguese Captain once more aroused the wrath of Burhan Nizam Shah who sent a force of five thousand men to devastate the entire adjacent country. It ruinned the two districts, and compelled the commandants of those fortresses to abandon them. Resigning their title in favour of the Portuguese Captain, they withdrew to Bassien, from where

Menezes sent supplies and relief. Upon this Burhan Nizam Shah despatched an additional force of six thousand men, of whom one thousand were musketeers and eight hundred were well equipped horsemen, to attack the fort of Sangaca. The Nizam Shahis opened the siege, led assaults against it twice but they were repulsed with heavy losses. Hunger and fatigue tired out the patience of the invaders compelling the parties to conclude truce. But Dom Francisco de Menezes's arrival there with 160 Europeans, twenty horsemen, some Naiks and 2000 native soldiers, led the Nizam Shahis to renew the attack, though they were compelled to raise the siege and take to flight, leaving behind a large quantity of arms and amunition. Dom Francisco after throwing in the forts, sufficient supplies of stores and amunition returned to Bassien.

After the battle was over, the governor Dom Estavao da Gama happened to arrive at Chaul. Being of the opinion that these forts were of little value to the Portuguese and that Burhan Nizam Shah was their ally, he ordered that they be handed over to him in lieu of an additional subsidy of 5000 pardos in gold, to the regret of Dom Francisco de Menezes who by his skill and ability had captured and maintained them. Dom Francisco in the first instance was reluctant to carry out the instructions of the governor but in the end was compelled to do it.[16]

In 1547 A.D. serious complications arose between the Portuguese and Ibrahim Adil Shah,[17] the ruler of Bijapur, which compelled the former to conclude treaties with the Raya of Vijayanagara[48] and Burhan Nizam Shah I (6th October 1547). This treaty strengthened the bonds of friendship between the Nizam Shahi ruler and the Portuguese. In accordance with its terms, "there were to be friendship between him (Burhan Nizam Shah) and the Portuguese, who were to help each other, when necessary against all the kings of India with the exception of the king of Bisanaga (Vijayanagara). The Portuguese governor of Indian possessions also bound himself not to make peace with the Adil Shah without previously giving notice of the same to Iniza Moxa (Nizam Shah)".[19] In 1548 the Portuguese Viceroy Dom Joao de Castro received the envoys from the "Zamorin, Canara, Nizamaluco, Cotamaluco and other Princes", who wished to ratify the former treaties of peace.[20] This is a clear proof of the rising power of the Portuguese on the Indian soil and the influence they had begun to wield over the rulers of the Daccan peninsula. But during the entire period lasting from 1510 A.D. to 1555 A.D. the Portuguese and Burhan Nizam Shah I enjoyed the blessings of peace and prosperity, inspite of the set backs they experienced at the hands of their bitter enemies. Burhan Nizam Shah frequently employed the Portuguese in his service and went to the length of including among his courtiers, Simao Peres a Portuguese renegade. He was held in great esteem by the king who appointed him as one of his ministers and general of his army. While Burhan Nizam Shah was breathing his last, he commanded his son and successor Husain Nizam to be considerate towards this faithful servant and Peres executed all his duties with fidelity and loyalty. But early in the reign of Husain Nizam Shah I, Peres losth is life in a struggle between his master and Ali Adil Shah.[21]

In 1557 A.D. the Portuguese governor Francisco Barreto being informed of the death of Burhan Nizam Shah and being not quite sure of the friendly treatment at the hands of his son, decided to secure the promontory of Karole or Karleh and fortify it into an outwork of defence for the city of Chaul,[22] which would compensate the drawbacks of the fortress in the face of the threat of Egyptian agression and the likelihood of all the Muslim states of the Daccan aiding and abetting it, with the object of throwing out the Portuguese from their eastern possessions. But before completing the project it was necessary to submit the Plan for the approval of Husain Nizam Shah.[23] Accordingly an ambassador was sent with presents to the Nizam Shahi court. But the young king regarded the proposal as an insult to his dignity and an attempt on the part of the Portuguese to undermine his power and influence. He rightly perceived that such project was merely to levy duties on merchandise leaving or entering the port and deprive him of this important item of revenue.[24] Therefore, he not only refused to comply with the request but made the Portuguese ambassador prisoner and sent his general Farhad Khan along with Rumi Khan, and Maulana Shah Muhammad Ustad with 30,000 men with the instructions to build as early as possible an impregnable fortress there on his own account.[25] At the same time he also instructed his general, not to show hostility towards the Portuguese in the fort, nor to those settled in the city. Being alarmed by the activities of the Nizam Shahi general, Garcia Rodgues de Tavora, the governor of the fortress of Chaul made representations to the Portuguese Viceroy,[26] and obtained a fleet under the command of Alvaro Peres Souto Mair to blockade the port, till he arrived to stop the progress of the work begun.[27]

Soon after Francisco Barreto, the viceroy arrived in person with a numerous and well manned fleet consisting about 4000 Portuguese troops, besides the natives. His men opened a continuous discharge of bullets on workmen, and prevented their progress in the construction of the fortifications. Husain Nizam Shah with the desire to stop the conflict, sent his envoy with the following message:—

"that he was a friend to the king of Portugal, having inherited that feeling from his predecessor who had given them a place where they had already built a citadel, a gift which he certainly never thought of revoking but that he had reasons to apprehend that by allowing them to build a new fort, would eventually lead them to place them under his yoke and deprive him of the custom duties which belonged as hitherto to him alone as sovereign of the place."[28]

The Portuguese Viceroy found the argument convincing and he agreed to conclude peace on the condition that the construction of the fort would proceed no further, and that Karole should remain as it was before.[29]

The phenomenal success of the Muhamedan powers of the Daccan against the Hindus of Vijayanagara infused in them a new vigour and so they decided turn their alliance against the Portuguese, who had by now become a great menace to their safety. Accordingly, negotiations were opened with Zamorin with remarkable secrecy, by the rulers of Ahmadnagar and Bijapur.[30] It took five years to form a coalition of the Daccani powers against the common enemy. The rulers of Bijapur and Ahmadnagar were to be assisted by the Zamorin with the object of inflicting a fatal blow on the Portuguese and drive them out of the Indian seas.[31] The allies were so much confident of their success, that they also settled a plan for the distribution of their expected conquests. According to it, the Adil Shah was to have Goa, Onor and Barcelor; Murtaza Nizam Shah I would occupy Chaul, Daman and Bassien; and the Zamorin would have, as his share, Cannanore, Mangalore, Cochin and Chale. Adil Shah went a step further in so far as he also assigned posts at Goa to his principal officers. The allies then persuaded the king of Achin to deliver an attack on Malacca, to create a diversion in the resources of the Portuguese. In accordance with the scheduled plan Adil Shah marched to open the siege of Goa and Murtaza Nizam Shah I marched to Chaul in utter disregard of the existing treaties of the peace between them and the Portuguese (1570 A.D.)[32].

In the face of this threat, the Portuguese Viceroy gave proof of his undaunted courage. He was advised to abandon Chaul for greater security of Goa, but he rejected the suggestion saying that he would not let the enemy have anything. He immediately despatched Dom Francisco de Mascarenhas with 600 men in four galleys and five smaller vessels to relieve Chaul and himself left Goa with many other soldiers about the end of September 1570 A.D.[33]

Unfortunately, from the very beginning the members of the grand coalition displayed lack of mutual trust, though all the time they made a show of it. Inspite of their solemn oaths for concerted action every one of them was loth to strike the first blow, apprehending that his ally would not second his efforts. Even Murtaza Nizam Shah who was so anxious to get rid of the Portuguese by driving them out of Chaul and seize their possessions as a part of his spoil, refrained from taking the initiative in opening the siege of Chaul until Adil Shah had commenced the invasion of Goa.

Farhad Khan the Nizam Shahi Commander left towards the end of December to besiege the fortress of Chaul.[34] His army consisted of about 25 elephants, 8000 cavalry and 20,000 infantry. His soldiers were men of courage and willing to fight, but were wanting in discipline. They marched into the environs of the city amidst the beating of drums and sounding the instruments of war. Four thousand horsemen were despatched towards the north to cut off the supplies of the enemy and prevent the arrival of reinforcements from Bassien and from the small fortress of Karanja, which had but a small garrison of forty men under the command of Estevam Perestrelo.[35] The numerical superiority of the invaders did not alarm the Portuguese. They ramained steady in their determination to fight and to behave in the same manner as their brethren were behaving at Goa amidst exactly similar conditions.[36]

While Goa was facing the onslaught of the Adil Shahi forces, Luiz Ferreira de Andrade, an able officer and the Commandant of Chaul was striving to repel the blows of the Nizam Shahi soldiers, who had opened the siege of the place. Although he did not possess an adequate supply of provisions to stand a prolonged siege, but even then he spared no efforts to make the best of the situation.[37] He erected fortifications and put together the available supplies. To ensure the mobility of troops, he pulled down such gardens and houses of his countrymen as appeared to obstruct the same or whose owners were thwarting his plans at the cost of honour of their nation. Shortly after, arrived reinforcements under the command of Dom Francisco Mascarnhas who brought 600 men in four galleys and five small vessels.[38] More of them came subsequently under the command of Ruy Goncalvez and Dom Luis de Menezes Borche.[39]

Immediately after his arrival, Farhad Khan set his artillery and elephants in battle array.[40] Being informed that Adil Shah had opened the campaign against Goa, without waiting for the orders of Murtaza Nizam Shah to join him, he issued orders that assault be delivered on Chaul. His forces were repulsed with great loss after a fight lasting for three hours. Undeterred Farhad Khan and his men marched to invest the town. Thereupon Luis Ferreira de Andrade pulled down the houses which stood near the fort and which afforded protection to the invaders.[41] In the beginning of January 1570 A.D. Murtaza Nizam Shah arrived with the remainder of his army which now numbered 34,000 horse; 100,000 foot; 16000 sappers; 4,000 smiths and other artisans; 360 elephants and an infinite number of buffaloes and oxen; forty pieces of cannon etc. Thus a huge array of well armed men encamped before a town which was protected by a single wall and which had a much smaller number to defend it.[42] Farhad Khan now took up his position near the adjoining church of "da Madra de Deos" with 7,000 horse and 20 elephants; Ikhlas Khan with 6,000 horsemen took up his position near the house of Diogo Lopes and Zamiri Khan between that spot and upper Chaul with 2000 horsemen so that the city was surrounded from all sides.[43] The flotilla of boats which had been sent by Zamorin to assist Murtaza Nizam Shah was directed to engage the Portuguese in the port. The king himself ascended the top of one of the mosques to watch the progress of action but had to bear the shock of the defeat of his Malabarese allies in whom he had placed more dependence than in his own army. He had already despatched 4000 horse to plunder and devastate the territories of Bassien.[44]

When the report of the investment of Chaul reached the ears of the Portuguese inhabitants of the town, they rushed to defend it, and within a short time their number swelled to 2000.[45] They decided to defend the monastery of Sao Francisco, the command of which was entrusted to Alaxandre de Sousa. While Nuno Alvarez Pereira, Dom Goncalo de Menezes and Nuno Velho Pereira were directed to defend some of the houses.[46] In view of the superiority of numbers under the command of the enemy, it was once more suggested to the Viceroy to abandon Chaul but he rejected the proposal forth with. In his decision he was supported by Fernando de Sousa de Castello-Branco. From Goa he sent Dom Duarte de Lima and Fernando Telles de Menezes with two galleys and some men in four other ships to reinforce the garrison at Chaul.[47]

Before the arrival of the above reinforcements, Zamiri Khan who had promised Murtaza Nizam Shah that he would be the first to enter the town, opened a vigorous attack on the position entrusted to Henrique de Betancor and Fernando Pereira de Miranda. But both of them bravely held their ground and upon receiving relief they repulsed Zamiri Khan with a loss of 300 men. The Nizam Shahi commander now turned his guns on the monastery of Sao Francisco, where there was some artillery in the charge of Alaxendre de Sousa. The action lasted for a while but in the end, the Nizam Shahis were again beaten off. This enraged Murtaza Nizam Shah, who the very same night renewed the attack on the monastery. The struggle continued for five hours, but the invaders fared no better. They were again repulsed with a loss of 300 men, who were slaughtered in the action.[48]

Next day the Nizam Shahis again opened the attack with great vigour. This time the struggle lasted for five days but the invaders had to meet unbending courage on the part of the enemy, who often sallied out against them and covered the field with the dead. It was an unequal contest and the Portuguese had to give it up. The Nizam Shahis now occupied the fort and the monastery of Sao Francisco. But when they attempted to capture some houses they failed and were beaten back with a loss of four hundred men.[49] But the ranks of the defenders had been considerably thinned and they sent Ruy Goncalvez de Camara to Goa to bring men and provisions with which he returned in two galleys.[50]

The attack of Chaul synchronised with that of Bassien. But the Nizam Shahi army was defeated and thrown back at Acarim and Daman, after which it lay encamped before Karanja, which was then commanded by Estevam Perestrelo with a garrison of only forty men. Soon there arrived Manoel de Lima with thirty men, which added much to the strength of the garrison. Losing no time, Eatevam Perestrelo fell upon the Nizam Shahis. After a contested battle, the field was covered with dead bodies and the remainder of the Nizam Shahi troops took to flight leaving behind their cannons and much arms and amunition.[51]

At Chaul the Nizam Shahis continued to bombard the place furiously with seventy pieces of cannon for a month, using about 160 cannon balls every day. The fire caused much consternation among the people; it took a heavy toll of human life besides demolishing many houses. At length guns were turned against the Bastion of the Cross where Pedro Ferreira and Mem de Ornelas were posted. The bastion was soon levelled to the ground and the Portuguese troops marched out boldly against the enemy's battery and captured many of them. Hearing that Chaul was in danger, Joao Alvarez Soares, a revenue officer fitted his own fleet and sailed with soldiers and rendered valuable assistance in the defence of the place.[52]

The Nizam Shahis then attacked several houses but were repeatedly repulsed. However at length they succeeded in planting their banner on Heytor de Sampayo,[53] whereupon a contested fight took place. As the house had been mined and during the struggle when some fire reached it, the powder blew up, killing about 42 Portuguese soldiers.[54] The Nizam Shahis escaped unhurt. Soon after, they captured Xira.[55] Zamiri Khan, the same night made a surprise attack on the Bastion of the Cross with 600 men, but Fernando Pereira and Henrique Betancor drove them back capturing their five standards which they had planted upon their works.[56]

Although the month of April had set in, still then Murtaza Nizam Shah was not the man to give up the fight. He resolved to remain before Chaul during the rains, and therefore erected new earth works there. Alexandre de Sousa and Dom Goncal de Menezes made an attack with 200 men, fought the enemy and drove them from their earthworks, which they destroyed.[57] Though the reverse for a little while perplexed Murtaza Nizam Shah, but he did not lose courage. He assembled his army and delivered a general assault, simultaneously on all points held by the Portuguese. But the invaders were again beaten back. To add to their consternation the enemy received fresh reinforcements from Goa, Diu, and Bassien, but this did not relieve their anxiety because fresh dangers arose for them. An epidemic broke out at Chaul, which enfeebled men and beasts alike, and secondly, Murtaza Nizam Shah began to approach other states for help.[58]

Murtaza Nizam Shah requested the king of Sarceta and some rebels of Cambay to attack the Portuguese and thus prevent them from despatching relief to Chaul. But there was no response to his proposals. Realising that he would have to depend upon his resources alone, Murtaza Nizam Shah opened bombardment on the house of Dom Nuno Alvares Pereira which continued for twenty days, whereafter he assaulted it with 500 men. Though the defenders were less in number, they easily drove away the invaders again. Once more the Nizam Shahis attacked this house but they were again beaten-back. At length the Portuguese captain decided to blow it up. After the Portuguese had abandoned the house, the invaders rushed in; but just at the moment, when they were planting their colours on the roof, a mine which had been placed in it caught fire and exploded, hurling death and destruction.[59]

The summer was drawing to a close but Murtaza Nizam Shah could'nt find himself nearer the goal. He now started preparation for continuing the operations during the ensuing winter. Upon this, struck with terror more than 200 Portuguese fled from the town, but the arrival of three hundred men from Goa improved the position of the defenders. On 11th April 1571, Ruy Goncalvez de Camara attacked 500 Nizam Shahis who were encamping in an orchard and killed all of them with exception of five, who succeeded in effecting their escape.[60] Enraged at the tragedy, the Nizam Shahis opened fire and continued it until a chance shot hit one of the galleys which sunk with all the goods worth 40,000 ductas. Next day they were attacked by the Portuguese led by Fernando Teles, who defeated them killing a large number from amongst them, seizing their arms and amunition. Murtaza Nizam Shah, who was witnessing the action from a distance, now mounted his horse to join the battle. But when he heard that his men had been defeated, he took a whip in his hand and began to beat the soldiers scolding them for their cowardice.[61]

The Nizam Shahis now put up more earthworks and began to lay mines under the houses. Dom Joao de Lima, Francisco de Sa and Dom Muro Alveres went out to sweep the mines the enemy were laying, and coming upon a party engaged in the work, they attacked them and put them to sword. But this did not stop the operations of the Nizam Shahis in pursuance of their plan.[62]

When preparation for continuing the siege of Chaul had been completed, Farhad Khan secretly made overtures of peace with the Portuguese without bringing it to the knowledge of the king[63] On suspicion that Farhad Khan had accepted bribe, Murtaza Nizam Shah arrested him, though he himself was keen to conclude peace after having unsuccessfully besieged the town for seven months and lost 7,000 men. Nor were the Portuguese averse to the proposal, they too having lost 700 of their own men besides the native soldiers. But all hopes of peace ended with the imprisonment of Farhad Khan. Upon this Jorge Pereira Coutinho went forth with his fleet and burnt three of the ships belonging to Nizam Shah.[64]

In the beginning of June, Murtaza Nizam Shah reopened the attack with his usual vigour. The target was the house defended by Dom Nuno Alvares, which was soon captured. The Portuguese though tried to recapture it, but they failed in their attempt. The Nizam Shahis then occupied the monastery of S. Domingos, where they put many of the Portuguese to sword. Dom Goncalo de Menezes defended this place with courage, but in the end the enemy's fire began to prove telling. Murtaza Nizam Shah at this stage decided to effect a large breach to enable his entire army to pass through it. On 28th June, a number of soldiers mounted on elephants appeared before the wall and the whole army waited for a signal to advance. But the signal did not come, because the Portuguese cannon had killed a Nizam Shahi officer of high rank, which the king considered to be inauspicious, and therefore postponed the attack for the next day. This gave an opportunity to the six Portuguese soldiers, who drew the enemy with in the distance of a gunshot and killed 118 of them, wounding 500 men.[65]

On 29th June 1571 A.D. about noon Murtaza Nizam Shah gave the signal for the attack. The whole force advanced amidst the sound of drums and other instruments.[66] Ikhlas Khan attacked Diogo Soares de Albergaria, Joao de Silva Barreto, Rodrigo Homen da Silva and Lourenco de Brito in their respective positions. Farhad Khan (who had been released) and Shujaat Khan advanced against Misericordia and Misnarao, the Captain guards, and fell on the position commanded by Ruy Goncalvez. Dom Francisco, the Portuguese Commander-in-Chief after having sent his men where they were badly needed took up his position with the remaining troops, opposite the king. A furious and contested battle took place. "The days were darkened by the smoke of the guns and the nights illuminated by the flames of burning buildings, the slaughter and confusion being great on all sides".[67] Although the Nizam Shahis were able to plant their banners on the Portuguese works, but they were soon cast down or thrown away along with those who had placed them there. The drunk elephants being burnt and wounded, ran madly in the field making confusion worse confounded. The battle continued until sun-set, up to which time the Portuguese maintained their position steadfastly slaying about 3,000 of the enemy. After suffering heavy losses both parties showed their readiness to sue for peace, but none of them was willing to take the step first in that direction. Soon, however negotiations for peace were begun. Farhad Khan, and Asaf Khan were appointed to act on behalf of Murtaza Nizam Shah and Pedro de Silva e Menezes and Antonio de Teyoe for the Portuguese Commander-in-Chief, and Dom Francisco de Mascarenhas for the Captain of the city of Chaul. The treaty established an offensive and defensive alliance between Murtaza Nizam Shah and the king Sebastiao of Portugal. At the end of June 1571 A.D., after making great rejoicings and exchanging the presents, Murtaza Nizam Shah returned to Ahmadnagar.[68]

It may be mentioned here that the grand coalition organised by Daccani powers received a decisive blow at the hands of the Portuguese owing to the inherent weaknesses in it. Zamorin, who was to attack the Portuguese by the sea and to render assistance to his two other allies, performed his part only half-heartedly. Moreover, both Farhand Khan and Ikhlas Khan, the Habshi leaders of the Nizam Shahi army played a dubious role throughout, for they had been bribed by the enemy, especially with supply of wine and they connived at smuggling the provisions in the fort. Another noble Jamshed Khan, though a commander and statesman, took no active part in operations, and abandoned himself to pleasures. Being tired of his behaviour, the king sounded him a warning through Mirak Dabir entitled Changez Khan, which offended his rival Shah Jamal-ud-ddin Anju, who resigned the office of Wakil and Peshwa, and before the siege was raised, he returned to Ahmadnagar. In these circumstances Murtaza Nizam Shah had no other choice but to purchase peace. Shortly after his arrival at the capital, he banished Shah Jamal-ud-ddin Anju to Burhanpur, wherefrom he went to the court of Emperor Akbar. He was taken into imperial service and was made the commander of 3,000 horse. While Farhad Khan and Ikhlas Khan, the two faithless nobles were thrown behind the bars.[69]

Success against the Daccani powers helped the Portuguese in establishing their sway on the Western Coast. Their trading stations now extended from Diu to Hanover, including the others like, Daman, Bassien, Chaul, Cannanore, Cochin, Salsette, Dabhol, Karanjah, Bardes island, Cucllu, Verunda, Manglore, Karanganore and Quilon. But in 1580 when Portugal had been annexed to Spain, her commercial and political policy underwent a change in so far as it began to be dominated by the Spanish point of view, which was more religious and less commercial. Proselytisation became the order of the day and the Portuguese engaged themselves in converting the Indians to Christianity. Their activities were marked by ruthless cruelty, and violence, which was bitterly resented by the native rulers and their oppressed subjects, who never failed to take up arms against their oppressors. In the years which followed, deadly struggles occurred between the Indians residing on the Western coast and the Portuguese. But the latter were not prepared to give up their missionary zeal, until at length the arrival of the English and the Dutch gave a blow their dominence.[70]

During the interregnum between the conclusion of treaty of the 1571 and 1592 A.D. stirring events occurred in the Nizam Shahi kingdom. The prevailing chaos and confusion afforded little opportunity to the weak and feeble Nizam Shahi rulers and their incompetent advisers to give a blow to the Portuguese power, not to speak of crushing them. Burhan Nizam Shah II was almost compelled to fight them. At this time a ship named "Husaini" which was coming from Macca to the port of Mustafabad Chaul with a large number of Muslim pilgrims was plundered by the Portuguese near Vaisi which was in their possession. Fatim Khan the governor of that district endeavoured to recover what had been seized by them, but failed to achieve any success. Thereupon he reported the matter to Burhan Nizam Shah II. The latter sent for him enquired of him about the physical features of the that region and ordered him to prepare a plan of the village of Ravadanda, Chaul and the hill of Korla. He then decided to build a fort on the hills of Korla, overlooking the sea, between Chaul and Ravadanda, with a view to strike terror into the hearts of the Portuguese, by demolishing their dwellings and closing the way of their supplies. Accordingly a fort named Korla was built there, but the Portuguese obtained their supplies from the other ports and did not refrain from harassing the Muslim population by their night attacks. On every such occasion, hundreds of the Daccanis lost their lives. The king showed great concern at the tragedy which was occurring at Chaul.[72]

He decided to put down the Portuguese in contravention of the terms of the peace of 1571 A.D. In utter disregard of the fact that all the troops had been sent to Berar, for, it was rumoured that Prince Murad was marching to invade the Nizam Shahi territory, and ignoring the strained relations with Ibrahim Adil Shah, he declared a holy war against them.[73] He gave a robe of honour to Farhad Khan and appointed him to command the expedition. Itimad Khan, the Sar-i-Naubat of the left wing was raised to the office of Sar-i-Naubat, was appointed as master of the Nizam Shahi forces and was ordered to assist Farhad Khan. Other famous nobles like Shujaat Khan, Taj Khan, Bijli Khan, Bahadur Khan, Nasir-ul-Mulk, Ane Rao, Kamail Khan, Mustafa Khan, and Shaikh Farid Raja, who commanded all the Silehdars and Havaldars and officers of the army, were sent on the fore-said expedition.[74]

Thus a large army numbering about 10,000 horsemen marched under the command of Farhad Khan. Shujaat Khan was soon after ordered to reinforce the fort of Korla and defend it.[75] As the king expected the arrival of reinforcements for the enemy from Bassien, he appointed Bahadur Gilani as governor of the fortress of Korla, ordering him to blockade Ravan-danda.[76] The vigilance of the Nizam Shahi soldiers prevented the Portuguese from delivering surprise attack on them. After some time, when the Portuguese attacked on Ravadanda they lost one hundred Europeans and two hundred natives. Daulat Khan, Ane Rao, Dost Adil Muwallid successfully cut off their supply line at Ravadanda, and reduced the besiegers to sorry plight, compelling them to capitulate on terms. When Burhan Nizam Shah II heard of the success of his officers, he began to take fancy for the foreign boys and girls and seized handsome women both married and unmarried. In his lust he gave up all sense of proportion. Hearing of the beauty of Shujaat Khan's wife he sent his officers to bring her to his presence. Shujaat Khan refused to send her. Whereupon he imprisoned him seized his wife and brought her in his palace. But when he saw her, he was so much disappointed at her ugly appearance that he ordered her to go back. Being unable to bear the insult, Shujaat Khan stabbed himself to death.[77] This caused great consternation in the army. Farhad Khan and other officers resenting the misbehaviour of the king, neglected all their duties and looked for an opportunity to return to the capital, to save the honour of their families and to depose the king. This gave a chance to the Portuguese to throw the supplies into the fort. Fortunatly at this time a fleet consisting of sixty vessels full of men and provisions, managed to pass Korla in the night and anchored safely in the harbour of Ravadanda. Here landed four thousand men, who on the next morning proceeded to deliver attack on the fort of Korla. On the approach of the Portuguese, the Nizam Shahis fled in confusion towards the fort, whither they were so closely followed by the invaders who gained entrance into it, put 12,000 of them to sword and set fire to it, destroying it completely.[78]

After this Fatim Khan the governor of that district, who was well acquainted with the physical features of that region was appointed to assist Farhad Khan and his army in besieging the fort of Chaul. Bakhtiyar Khan was appointed as the commander of the infantry, the gunners, the archers and the spearmen. Asad Khan the former Wakil and Peshwa, who was unrivalled in the art of conducting siege operations was associated with Rumi Khan, and directed to press the siege of Chaul very vigorously with the object of expelling the Portuguese from the borders of the kingdom. Arriving before the fort in April 1592 A.D. the Nizam Shahis opened the siege. Their foraging parties plundered and devastated the environs of Chaul and Bassien. While the heavy artillery was pounding the walls of the fort, the Portuguese sallied out and surprised the besiegers killing nine officers and making two of them captives. Fatim Khan was seriously wounded. He shortly after died to be succeeded by Rnmi Khan, who too did not live long to conduct the operations.[79] He was succeeded by Farhad Khan. He gave no respite to the Portuguese day and night, and continued the bombardment ceaselessly. The arrival of Dom Alvaro de Abranches with an additional force of 300 from

Bassien and 200 from Salsette raised the strength of the garrison to 1500 men.[80] The Portuguese now delivered an attack on the Nizam Shahi army. A severe battle took place in which the latter were defeated with heavy losses and many of them were slain in the field of battle. The Nizam Shahi nobles, who having learnt that Burhan Nizam Shah II was enticing their wives and daughters at the Capital, betrayed their trust and refrained from putting in their best. Naturally the prestige of the Nizam Shahi kingdom suffered.

In 1594 A.D. Burhan Nizam Shah II again assembled a large army of foreigners to attack the Portuguese, but the rebellion of Prince Ismael Adil against his brother Ibrahim Adil Shah II at Bijapur compelled him to postpone his plan, because he wanted to support the rebel. But before he could reach beyond Parenda, Ismael was defeated and slain, and Burhan had to return to his capital. After his death in 1594 the kingdom of Ahmadnagar was practically engaged in factious strife, civil war, palace revolutions, religious fanaticism and ruthless persecutions. In these ciruumstances the Portuguese were left free to pursue their own course on the Nizam Shahi soil. In 1600 the pressure of the Mughals on the Daccan placed the ruler of Ahmadnagar as much as the Protuguese in critical position. Both of them sought safety in mutual help. Apprehending danger to their dominions in the east,[82] and to withstand the expected onslaughts of the Mughals, the Portuguese decided to form a coalition of the Daccani powers. But the plan did not materialise, because of the perpetual discord prevaling among the latter, which blinded them to the fate which lay in store for them. But the Mughals did not fail to exploit the situation in their favour. When they stepped in the territory of Nizam Shah and laid siege to the fort of Ahmadnagar, the Portuguese for their own selfish interests secretly helped the besieged (1600-1 A.D.) by supplying them, with men, money, and amunition.

The occupation of Ahmadnagar fort by the Mughals did not finally destroy the Nizam Shahi kingdom. It obtained a fresh lease of life at the hands of Malik Ambar. He proclaimed Murtaza Nizam Shah II as the sovereign but retained all powers in his own hands. When he came in touch with the Portuguese, he could not ignore the past history of their relations with the Nizam Shahis or their recent attitude towards the Nizam Shahi kingdom. As to the Portuguese their position in commerical and political set-up had undergone a radical change. It is true that for certain reasons, Akbar the Great Mughal had befriended them, but southward expansion of the Mughal empire could not be looked upon with equanimity by them. Moreover by the beginning of the 17th century other competitors had also entered the field. The English and the Dutch were seriously threatening their life line on the sea and their dominence on land.

In fact after 1600 A.D. the Portuguese power began to decline because of their corrupt officers, heavy drain of wealth and man power from their nation, their lack of character and want of moral discipline in them. As has been mentioned earlier that the port of Chaul was controlled by the Portuguese from the adjoining hillock which was in their possession and near it lay the Nizam Shahi port of Ravadanda, which now afforded the point of contact between them and Malik Ambar (in 1601 A.D.)[83] Guided by the instincts of self preservation the Portuguese openly sought with him an alliance [84] The relations between the two remained very cordial till 1604, when the Portuguese obtained from the Regent the right of collecting half of the land revenue in the vicinity of Chaul. But unfortunately they behaved in a high-handed manner towards the rayots subjecting them to rack-renting, violence and bloodshed. Striken with terror and unable to bear the atrocities any further, traders as well as peasants fled, abandoning their homes and seeking refuge in Ravadanda, Dabhol and the other adjacent villages. When Mamur Khan, the local officer brought the matter to the notice of Portuguese captain, he readily agreed to return the excess revenue realised from the peasants. After the conditions had become normal, Malik Ambar assured safety to the people, and repopulated the deserted and desolated country. In 1605 A.D. while the Regent was engaged with the Mughals, the Portuguese again wrought great havoc near Chaul. They once more made forcible exactions from the rayots, seized their bullocks and seeds and sold them against their wishes, rendering them homeless, with the result that trade and commerce received a set-back. Unfortunately, it is not recorded what action was taken by Malik Ambar to protect the peasantry of Chaul and its vicinity from the future ravages of the Portuguese and how their activities were checked and peace and tranquility was restored in that region. But disgusted at their obnoxious behaviour and their brutal conduct Abdul Karim, the provincial governor of Chaul with the assistance of the Dutch fitted out a fleet of thirty sails to cruise against the Portuguese in 1609 A.D.[85] They plundered all the Portuguese ships which came in their way. Then the allies pursued Jorge Henrique, killed him and seized his wife and two daughters.

This act of violence incensed Portuguese inhabitants of Chaul, who advised Rolim to take steps for avenging the affront. As he had only a few men and had no instructions from the Viceroy to commence war he showed some reluctance. But in the end he had to yield. One night he sent out two officers with sixteen men who discovered the enemy near the temple of Ranaceyra. He put to death many of them and then retreated. Another officer, Pedro Corenjo with 30 men started and fell upon the village of Tal, killed the inhabitants, burnt their houses and sunk two vessels which were in the port. To stop the aggression of Abdul Karim the Portuguese decided to punish him. Accordingly Dom Francisco Rolim marched to upper Chaul with 350 men in three bodies; one led by himself; another by Machael de Abrew and the third under Calleyros. Abrew pushed into a narrow street which led to a open place, where the Muslims were drawn up in a battle array. They opened fire on him and killed him. Soon after arrived Rolim on the scene, who killed a large number of the Muslims and put the rest to flight. He then set fire to the house of Abdul Karim and devastated the surrounding country.

Thus open war now began at Chaul. To wage it on a larger scale, both the sides made full preparations. Several skirmishes took place in which the Portuguese always gained the upper hand. Their strength increased further after the arrival of Dom Francisco de Sotomayor with northern fleet, and he left three vessels for their support. With this reinforcement Rolim took the field and marched against the Muslims, but the latter too gave him some hard knocks, and the struggle between the parties remained indecisive. Both of them, therefore, became anxious to come to terms, mainly because of the impending campaign of Khan Jahan Lodi in the Daccan which created a problem as much for the Nizam Shahis as for the Portuguese. So peace was concluded by them.

Between 1609 and 1615 the Portuguese not only avoided direct conflict with Malik Ambar, but they remained very friendly to him. Upon hearing of the reverses which Malik Ambar suffered at the hands of the Mughals, the Portuguese directed all their energy to knit the Daccani powers into close bond of friendship with a view to create strong bulwark against the common enemy. For this purpose they opened negotiations with Adil Shah and Murtaza Nizam Shah II to ratify and confirm the alliance which they had formerly entered into.[86]

Nevertheless minor incidents did continue to occur. Trouble arose at Chaul in 1612-13 A.D. which for a little while threatened to disrupt the peaceful relations existing between the Nizam Shahis and the Portuguese.[87] The *thanadar* of Chaul, to avenge the losses he had sustained at their hands in the preceding year, hired some Muslims of Karanja, to assassinate Balthsar Rabello de Almeida, the commander of the fort.[88] The assassins surprised him, while he was taking his supper, killed him and his sister-in-law and shut themselves in the fort. The Portuguese opened the gates, and put all the Muslims to sword. Thereupon Abbas Khan, a general of the Nizam Shahi army marched with a body of troops to Karanja to avenge the death of his co-religionists. The Portuguese were unable to stop him from entering the town which was subjected to plunder and bloodshed. But while the Nizam Shahis were busy in collecting their booty, Simao Rangel with 17 Portuguese suddenly fell upon them. At the very same time Ferdinao de Sampayo de Cunha also arrived surrounded the enemy, defeated and put every one of them to sword. After this Cunha ravaged the whole country adjacent to the town and made three hundred men captives. This enraged Nizam Shah who decided to embarrass the Portuguese by attacking their strongholds at Salsette, Bassien and Agashi.[89] Upon this, Ruy Freire de Andrade, who was cruising off the coast with a squadron sailed in that direction, and arriving near the village between Karanja and Thana, sent some ships to relieve his countrymen at Agashi, which was besieged by the Nizam Shahis. But the defenders were attacked by 2000 Muslims and were compelled to take refuge in the monastery of St. Francisco.[90]

The Nizam Shahi soldiers who had opened the siege of the Portuguese fort of Manora, were driven away from there by Freire de Andrade.[91] The latter now marched to the relief of his countrymen at Thana. Upon this Malik Ambar sent more troops against Agashi. The Portuguese were now reduced to a miserable plight there. Had Freire de Andrade not reached there in time and escorted them safely to Bassien, all of them would have been put to sword. At Bassien, Andrade was joined by the cammander of the fort, men of the north and by the Diu fleets. Thus strengthened, he revenged himself on the inhabitants who had risen up in arms against them.[92]

No sooner did Andrade find himself free from the threat of Muslim forces, than he was called to Daman, where the king of Sarceta had sent his men to drive away the Portuguese inhahitants. The enemy destroyed the crops and took away forcibly what they could seize from its Portuguese inhabitants. Freire de Andrade with about 200 men from Daman and Tarapor fell suddenly upon the plunderers and put many of them to death. After the conditions had become normal, the Portuguese for their own safety, came to a sort of truce with Malik Ambar and thereby also obtained a respite to recoup their losses.

In 1615 the Portuguese, Burhan Nizam Shah III and Adil Shah concluded a treaty of peace among themselves (9th October 1615) ratifying the terms of the treaty of 1571 A.D. [93] But as Malik Ambar entertained friendly relations with the Dutch and the English an additional condition was incorporated in it.[94] It was laid down that in the Nizam Shahi, territory the English and the Dutch should be forbidden to settle down and its ruler should never extend any sort of assistance to them.

Sometime afterwards Malik Ambar and Wafa Khan the envoy of Adil Shah incorporated other condition in the above mentioned treaty, viz., that the disputes among the officers and rayots of Nizam Shah and Adil Shah and the Portuguese, should be avoided at Ravadanda and Chaul; but if they did occur in connection with the possession of gardens and coconut groves, they should be referred to a board of arbitrators composed of two persons, one representing Nizam Shah and the other representing the Portuguese Viceroy. The arbitrators were required to scrutinise the claims on the basis of legal documents, which, if found to be in order, possession was to be restored forthwith to the rightful owner. Otherwise a decision as regards to the ownership was to arrived at after full and complete enquiry and investigation. It was for the board to fix the price of the gardens with the consent of the owners and written deeds should be executed in case they were purchased. This document of the treaty was stamped with the seals of Nizam Shah, Malik Ambar, Antoni Matier and Wafa Khan. On the 1st January 1617 A.D. when it was laid before the Viceroy and Captain General of the Portuguese, Dom Jeromymo' Azevedo at Goa by the Nizam Shahi envoys, Kashi Pandit and Samshir Khan, he ordered his secretary to read it out to him. After its perusal the Viceroy willingly signed it and informed that the treaty would be observed by the Portuguese so long as Nizam Shah and his descndants do not violate its terms.[95]

Though outwardly Malik Ambar was bound by the terms of the treaty with regard to the Dutch and the English, in reality he remained friendly towards them. In 1617, Pieter Van den Broecke, the Dutch traveller obtained a passport from him to ensure his safety in the territories of the Nizam Shah. When he went to meet Malik Ambar, he offered him presents consisting of a Japanese sword and costly Javan crease. The Dutch traveller writes—

"He (Malik Ambar) was highly pleased with the sword but not with the crease, because the Devil was engraved on it; he gave it back to me with a firman for the wounded men (who had been attacked by the Marathas) we had left behind. He was gracious towards men and put on me two Shwals, one of gold, the other of Camel's hair, which is the greatest honour that can be paid to any one. Further he offered to give me a guard of soldiers to escort me to Golkunda".[96]

We know that in 1620 Malik Ambar, with the help of

his allies embarked on a war against the Mughals, and drove them to Burhānpur, invested closely their Viceroy in that city, crossed the Narbada and carried out daring raids into the Mughal territory. His success in giving an effective blow to the Mughals may partly be attributed to the alliance which he had entered into with the Portuguese and other Daccani powers. Though Ambar was friendly towards the Dutch and the English, Mansur Khan a Portuguese renegade of the Nizam Shahi army plundered near Mandu an English mercantile caravan (March 15th 1621) bound for Burhanpur from Agra.[97] Negotiations for compensation were opened by Mr. Jafferies, who was deputed to conduct them. Malik Ambar consulted his interpreter Jasper Gomes, a Portuguese, with regard to the amount of compensation. Although Mr. Jafferies appealed to him through Jasper Gomes to allow him to meet him personally to explain the facts, the regent refused to do so, very likely because of his obligation to observe the terms of the treaty which had only recently been concluded.[98]

During the next five years the Nizam Shahis seem to have remained friendly with the Portuguese. It was in June 1625 A.D. that the latter broke the terms of the treaty by disturbing the peace of Chaul. Upon which in the same year the port of Dabhol was annexed by the Nizam Shahis whereafter it appears that the Portuguese must have certainly come to a sort of truce with the Nizam Shahi resident of that place. (10 June 1625).[99] But after the death of Malik Ambar when the political fabric of the Nizam Shahis began to crumble to pieces and when the Mughal advance began to imperil the safety of the Portuguese, they remained steady in their policy of helping the states of the Daccan against the imperial power of northern India.

---

*Notes and References*:

1. History and Antiquities of Chaul and Bassien, pp. 22-31, Duff. Vol. I pp. 73-4;
2. History and Antiquities of Chaul and Bassien, pp. 31-32, Duff. Vol. I pp. 74;
3. History and Antiquities of Chaul and Bassien, pp. 32; Duff. Vol. I pp. 74;
4. Danvers "The Portuguese in India" Vo. I, pp. 141-42;
5. Describing Chaul, Durate Barbosa, writes, "leaving the kingdom of cambay, along the coast towards the south at eight league's distance, there

is a fine large river and on it is a place called Chaul—not very large, of handsome houses, which are all covered with thatch. This place is one of the centres of great commerce in merchandise, and in the months of Dec. Jan, Feb. and March, there are many ships from Malabar country and all other parts which arrive with cargoes. That is to say, those of Malabar laden with coconuts, arecas, spices, drugs, palm, sugar emery, and there they make their sales for the continent and the kingdom of Cambay; and the ships of Cambay come there to meet them laden with cotton stuffs and many other goods, which are available in Malabar, and these are bartered for the goods which have come from Malabar country. And on return voyage they fill their ships with, wheat, vegetables, millets, rice seasome, oil of seasome, of which there is much in the country and these Malabarese also buy many pieces of muslin for women's head-dress and many beyranies (!) of which there are plenty in the kingdom. A large quantity of copper is sold in this port of Chaul and at a high price, for it is worth twenty ductas the hander weight, or more because in the interior money is made of it and it is also used throughout the country for cooking pots. There is also a great consumption of quick-silver and vermilion for the interior and for the kingdom of Gujarat, copper quick-sliver and vermilion, is brought to this place by Malabar merchants, who get it from the factories of the king of Portugal and they get more of it by way of Makkah, which comes there from Diu. These people wear the beyranies put on for a few days nearly in the raw-state and afterwards they bleach them and make them very white and gum them to sell abroad and thus some are met with amongst them which are torn. In this port of Chaul, there are few inhabitants, except during three or four months of the year, the time for putting in Cargo, when there arrive merchants from all the neighbourhood and they make their bargains during this period and despatch their goods and after that to return their homes, until the next season, so that this place is like a fair in those months. *There is a Moorish gentleman as governor of this place, who is a vassal* of the king of the Daccan, and collects his revenues and accounts to him for them. He is called Xech and does great service to the King of Portugal and is great friend of Portuguese and treats very well all those who go there and keeps the country very secure..." Barbosa's "Description of the Coasts of East Africa and Malabar"; Translated by Hon. Henry, E. J. Stanley, London, 1866, pp. 69; Also see, "The Voyage of John Huyghan Van Linschotten to the East Indies Vol. I pp. 63-65. Early Travels in India, pp. 13-14 by Ralph Fitch (1583-91) pp. 58-63; Purchas His Pilgrims, Vol. X pp. 169-70, "A Description of the coasts of East Africa and Malabar" pp. 69-70;

6. History and Antiquities of Chaul and Bassien, pp. 34;
7. History and Antiquities of Chaul and Bassien, pp. 35;
8. History and Antiquities of Chaul and Bassien, pp. 35;
9. History and Antiquities of Chaul and Bassien, pp. 35;
10. Ibid.
11. Ibid.
12. Ibid, pp. 36 (n).
13. Ibid pp. 40.
14. History and Antiquities of Chaul and Bassien, pp. 40; Faria-i-Souza, Pt. I pp. 26-27;
15. History and Antiquities of Chaul and Bassien, pp. 42;
16. Faria-i-Souza, Pt. I, pp. 26-28; History and Antiquities of Chaul and Bassien, pp. 43; Danvers, "The Portuguese in India", Vol. I pp. 452-53; Historical Inscriptions of South India, pp. 248;
17. In 1544 A.D. Burhan Nizam Shah at the instance of Ram Raya besieged Gulbarga, but was defeated by Ibrahim Adil Shah and was driven from the environs of the kingdom. Once more Burhan tried to form a confederacy, but Ali Barid refused saying that it was his duty to support the sunni ruler rather than the Shia and he insulted Shah Tahir, the Nizam Shahi envoy. In order to avenge the disgrace hurled on his loyal minister, Burhan Nizam Shah invaded Bidar. Although Ali Barid was assisted by his

ally Ibrahim Adil Shah, Burhan was able to capture the fortresses of Ausa, Udgir and Qandhar. Ibrahim Adil Shah attributed these reverses to the trachery of his own officers and put many of them to death. Enraged at the conduct of their king some of the nobles entered into a conspiracy to depose him and raise his brother Abdullah to the throne. Asad Khan, who having fallen a prey to the suspicions of his master, had retired to his fief at Belgaum, opened communications with Burhan Nizam Shah, Jamshed Quli Qutb Shah and Dom Gercia de Castro, the Portuguese factor at Goa, with a view to enlist their support in raising Abdullah to the throne. While these negotiations were going on Ibrahim Adil Shah discovered the plot and put many of the conspirations to death. In utter fear Abdullah fled to Goa, where he was welcomed by the Portuguese factor, who agreed to espouse his cause on condition that Konkan was ceded to the Portuguese.

But when according to the scheduled plan Burhan and Jamshed Quli marched towards Bijapur, Asad Khan refused to join them; fearing that after their success they would divide the kingdom between themselves. Upon this the two rulers retired to their respective capitals, and the Portuguese also withdrew their support from the pretender. But the Konkanese resented the annexation of their country by the Portuguese and rebelled against Ibrahim Adil Shah. The latter crossed the Ghats with a large army and put down the rebellion.

Fearing lest the conspiracy should again revive against him, Ibrahim Adil Shah offered the lands of Salsette and Bardes to the Portuguese on condition that Martin Affonso de Souza, the Portuguese governor should deliver Abdullah to him. Martin Affonso agreed; whereupon Ibrahim Adil Shah fulfilled the promise. Abdullah was sent away to Cannonore so that he could no longer disturb the ruler of Bijapur. But shortly afterwards Martin Affonso again brought him back to Goa. Meanwhile in addition to handing over Salsettle and Bardes to the Portuguese, Ibrahim Adil Shah, gave him the vast treasures, which Asad Khan had collected to carry through the rebellion. But no sooner did he realise that he had been befooled by the Portuguese governor than he pressed him to hand over Abdullah to him or to restore what had been ceded to him. The latter attempted to refrain from complying with the demand. He sent Joao Ferdnandes de Negreires as an envoy to the Adil Shahi court to deal with the matter. But Ibrahim Adil Shah seized him, together with all the Portuguese who had accompanied him, and imprisoned them, retaining them as hostages until the fulfilment of his demands. In this way Martin Affonso was compelled to comply with his legitimate demands. In utter helplessness he assured him that soon-after the end of the rainy season he would send Abdullah to Mallaca, instead of handing him over to him.

But before he could fulfill his promise, Martin Affonso had to hand over the charge to Dom Joao de Castro, the newly appointed governor. Naturally the entire situation changed. A few days after the departure of Martin Affonso, Ibrahim Adil Shah opened negotiations asking the new governor to honour the contract his predecessor had made with him. But the new governor declined to do it. Upon this Ibrahim broke off the friendly relations with the Portuguese. But as the governor feared that, the affair might take a serious turn, he prepared for war, which cowed down Ibrahim Adil Shah, who made a peace with the Portuguese (26th Feb. 1546). But in the treaty no condition was incorporated regarding Abdullah Khan and the surrender Salsette and Bardes to the king of Portugal, Ibrahim Adil Shah constantly sent expeditions against them to recover the ceded places. This compelled Joao de Castro to enter into a close alliance with the Nizam Shah and the Raya of Vijayanagara.

Faria-i-Souza, Pt. I, pp. 133; Danvers "The Portuguese in India", Vol. I, pp. 464-64 and 474-78; F. C. Danvers "Report to the Secretary of State for India in council on the Portuguese Records relating to East Indies"—Tratados T. I. pp. 50; 120; Historical Inscriptions of South India, pp. 248;

18. Faria-i-Souza, Pt. I pp. 133; see, F. C. Danvers "Report to the Secretary of State for India in Council on the Portuguese Records relating to East Indies", pp. 50; The Portuguese in India Vol. I, pp. 478;

19. "The Portuguese in India", Vol. I, pp. 478; Historical Inscriptions of South India. pp. 251; History and Antiquities of Chaul and Bassien, pp. 44;

20. Faria-i-Souza Pt. I, pp. 133; Danvers "The Portuguese in India", Vol. I, pp. 484-85;

21. History and Antiquities of Chaul and Bassien, pp. 44;

22. Faria-i-Souza, Pt. I pp. 188; History and Antiquities of Chaul and Bassien, pp. 44-45;

23. Burhan-i-Maasir (I.A. 1920) pp. 103; Faria-i-Souza, Pt. I pp. 188; History and Antiquities of Chaul and Bassien pp. 46;

24. History and Antiquities of Chaul and Bassien, pp. 46;

25. History and Antiquities of Chaul and Bassien, pp. 46;

26. Ibid, pp. 46;

27. History and Antiquities of Chaul and Bassien, pp. 46; Danvers "The Portuguese in India," Vol. I pp. 510;

According to Sayyid Ali, when the Portuguese heard of the approach of the Nizam Shahi forces, they repented their move and sought pardon from Husain Nizam Shah. Accordingly they sent envoys to Husain Nizam Shah, who pardoned them for their offensive conduct. See, Burhan-i-Maasir (I.A. 1920) pp. 103-4;

28. Burhan-i-Maasir (I.A. 1920) pp. 104; Ferishta, Briggs. III, pp. Danvers, "The Portuguese in India" Vol. I, pp. 510; History and Antiquities of Chaul and Bassien, pp. 46;

29. History and Antiquities of Chaul and Bassien, pp. 46-47;

30. Faria-i-Souza Pt. I pp. 281; Danvers, "The Portuguese in India, Vol. I, pp. 560; History and Antiquities of Chaul and Bassien, pp. 47;

31. History and Antiquities of Chaul and Bassien, pp. 47;

32. Faria-i-Souza, Pt. I, pp. 281; Danvers "The Portuguese in India", Vol. I, pp. 551; Historical Inscriptions of Southern India, pp. 256;

33. Faria-i-Souza Pt. I pp. 281-82; Danvers "The Portuguese in India", 'Vol. pp. 551-554;

34. History and Antiquities of Chaul and Bassien, pp. 48; Danvers says that Farhad Khan invested the fortress of Chaul on the last day of November 1569 A.D. see, "The Portuguese in India", Vol. I pp. 560;

35. Faria-i-Souza, Pt. I pp. 283; History and Antiquities of Chaul and Bassien, pp. 48;

36. Faria-i-Souza Pt. I pp. 286-312; History and Antiquities of Chaul and Bassien, pp. 49; Danvers, "The Portuguese in India", Vol. I pp. 560;

37. History and Antiquities of Chaul and Bassien, pp. 48; Danvers, "The Portuguese in India", Vol. I, pp. 561;

38. History and Antiquities of Chaul and Bassien pp. 48; Danvers, "The Portuguese in India, Vol. I pp. 562;

39. History and Antiquities of Chaul and Bassien, pp. 49; Danvers, "The Portuguese in India," Vol. I pp. 562;

40. History and Antiquities of Chaul and Bassien, pp. 49; Danvers, "The Portuguese in India", Vol. I pp. 561;

41. History and Antiquities of Chaul and Bassien, pp. 49; Danvers, "The Portuguese in India", Vol. I pp. 561;

42. History and Antiquities of Chaul and Bassien, pp. 49; Danvers, "The Portuguese in India", Vol. I pp. 561;

43. History and Antiquities of Chaul and Bassien, pp. 49; Danvers, "The Portuguese in India", Vol. I pp. 561;

44. History and Antiquities of Chaul and Bassien, pp. 49; Danvers, "The Portuguese in India," Vol. I pp. 561;

45. History and Antiquities of Chaul and Bassien, pp. 49; Danvers,

"The Portuguese in India", Vol. I pp. 561;

46. History and Antiquities of Chaul and Bassien, pp. I pp. 561-2;

47. History and Antiquities of Chaul and Bassien, pp. 50; Danvers "The Portuguese in India", Vol. I, pp. 562;

48. History and Antiquities of Chaul and Bassien, pp. 50; Danvers "The Portuguese in India", Vol. I, pp. 562;

49. History and Antiquities of Chaul and Bassien, pp. 50; Danvers "The Portuguese in India", Vol. I, pp. 562-63;

50. History and Antiquities of Chaul and Bassien, pp. 52; Danvers "The Portuguese in India", Vol. I, pp. 563;

51. History and Antiquities of Chaul and Bassien, pp. 52; Danvers "The Portuguese in India", Vol. I, pp. 563;

52. History and Antiquities of Chaul and Bassien, pp. 52; Danvers "The Portuguese in India" Vol. I, pp. 563;

53. History and Antiquities of Chaul and Bassien, pp. 52-53; Danvers "The Portuguese in India," Vol. I, pp. 564;

54. History and Antiquities of Chaul and Bassien, pp. 53; Danvers, "The Portuguese in India", Vol. I, pp. 564;

55. History and Antiquities of Chaul and Bassien, pp. 53; Danvers, "The Portuguese in India", Vol. I, pp. 564;

56. History and Antiquities of Chaul and Bassien, pp. 53; Danvers "The Portuguese in India", Vol. I, pp. 564;

57. History and Antiquities of Chaul and Bassien, pp. 53; Danvers, "The Portuguese in India", Vol. I, pp. 564;

58. History and Antiquities of Chaul and Bassien, pp. 54; Danvers, "The Portuguese in India", Vol. I, pp. 564.

59. History and Antiquities of Chaul and Bassien, pp. 54; F Danvers, "The Portuguese in India", Vol. I, pp. 564-65;

60. History and Antiquities of Chaul and Bassien, pp. 54; Danvers, "The Portuguese in India", Vol. I, pp. 564-65;

61. History and Antiquities of Chaul and Bassien, pp. 54; Danvers, "The Portuguese in India", Vol. I pp. 565-566;

62. History and Antiquities of Chaul and Bassien, pp. 54; Danvers, "The Portuguese in India", Vol. I, pp. 566;

63. History and Antiquities of Chaul and Bassien, pp. 54; Danvers, "The Portuguese in India", Vol. I, pp. 566;

64. Danvers, "The Portuguese in India", Vol. I, pp. 566;

65. History and Antiquities of Chaul and Bassien, pp. 55; Danvers, "The Portuguese in India", Vol. I, pp. 566;

66. History and Antiquities of Chaul and Bassien, pp. 55;

67. Ibid, pp. 55.

68. History and Antiquities of Chaul and Bassien, pp. 55-56; Danvers, "The Portuguese in India, Vol. I, pp. 567-68;

69. Burhan-i-Maasir (I.A. 1921) pp. 232-34; Muntakhab-ul-Lubab, III, pp. 204-5; Ferishta ii pp. 134-35;

70. History and Antiquities of Chaul and Bassien, p. 60;

71. Burhan-i-Maasir (I.A. 1923) pp. 291; Ferishta ii pp. 154; Muntakhab-ul-Lubab III, pp. 240;

72. Ferishta, Briggs. III, pp. 284;

73. Burhan-i-Maasir (I.A. 1923) pp. 291-92;

74. Ibid, pp. 293;

75. Ferishta, Briggs. III, pp. 285;

76. Ferishta, Briggs. III, pp. 285;

77. Muntakhab-ul-Lubab III, pp. 239-40;

78. Ferishta, Briggs. II, pp. 286;

79. Danvers, "The Portuguese in India", Vol. II, pp. 89;

80. Ibid, pp. 89;

81. Burhan-i-Maasir (I.A. 1923) pp. 292; Ferishta, pp. 155-56; Muntakhab-ul-Lubab III, pp. 240; History and Antiquities of Chaul and Bassien, pp. 61-62; Denvers, "The Portuguese in India", Vol. II, pp.

88-90; Historical Inscriptions of Southern India, pp. 286;

According to the Portuguese historian, Fari-i-Souza, in this battle, Farhad Khan was taken prisoner along with his entire family. His wife was ransomed and his daughter was converted to Christianity and was sent to Portugal. Farhad Khan soonafter died.

Ferishta does not refer to it. But according to Abul Fazl, Burhan Nizam Shah II seized Farhad Khan's wife, who felt ashamed and made terms with the Christians. The Portuguese attacked the Nizam Shahis and drove them back; many Muslims were killed and Asad Khan was made captive. See, Akbar Nama III, pp. 1024;

But as a matter of fact Farhad Khan continued to live up to the year 1035 A.H. (1625 A.D.) for his name is recorded in one of the inscriptions inside the fort of Antur. See, Archaeological Survey of India Reports 1920-21, pp. 38;

82. Diogo de Couto, writes, that, D. Panto de Lima, Captain of Chaul......was soon apprised of all these kings and comprehending fully well, how much evil it would be if the Mughals set their foot in the kingdom of Verar (Berar) because it would be very easy for them to conquer the whole of the Daccan, sent an express messenger to Khalabat Khan (Salabat Khan) with a letter to......arrange the defences of the Kingdom of Ahmadnagar...... and that he should assemble other kings of the Daccan that all should join to oppose the Mughals for if they were to pay no heed, he as an older and more experienced Captain would tell them that Mughals would render him self master of these kings......and that if for the defence of the kingdom (of the Nizam Shah) his favour......and help were needed, he would immediately start with Portuguese"—see, Panduranga Rao Pissunlecar's article, "The Extinction of the Nizam Shahi kingdom", published in Sardesai Commemoration Volume, pp. 27 (n).

83. This contact is recorded in the following letter of Philip III of Spain to the Viceroy Ayres de Saldenha, dated Lisbon 25th Jan. 1601 A.D.:—

"And though the Coude (de Vidiguera) writes me that Akbar is already an old man, distrusting his eldest son and fearing to be poisoned by him (on account of that) he had stopped the war, he was waging against the kingdom of Mellique yet since that King is very powerful and sagacious and desirous of approaching to that island of Goa; I recommend you to keep your eyes open on his designs and intentions to prevent them with the necessary remedies" (Ibid).

84. In another letter dated 23rd March 1604, the King writes, "The circumstance of the relations between Akbar and his eldest son, as related by you are most suitable for the welfare of that state and since we know the purpose of that king, I wish that the discord between them would last until his death; for after his demise it is understood that war will ensue in all his kingdom. The precautions taken by the Mellique to defend himself from him, as you told me must be appreciated and I thank you for the pains you are taking to induce and incite him to do so—(Ibid).

85. History and Antiquities of Chaul and Bassien, pp. 63; Danvers, "The Portuguese in India", Vol. II pp. 149-51;

86. (1) In a letter addressed to the Viceroy, Rui Lourenco de Tavora, the king of Portugal wrote on 29th Oct. 1609 A.D. "The Archbishop, governor of this state wrote me about the conquest of the Daccan, which was something to be feared about, for although the Mughal Emperor showed himself a friend and was sending a new ambassador (Muqarrebe Khan) who was waiting, he believed that his affairs did not mean anything good and from the place where he was and up to the walls of my fortress of the north, there was nothing to oppose him and he only found some resistence from Adil Khan, who had sent some ambassadors to the Malik and Cotta Mulk, king of Masulipatam and Venkata Naik, (of Ikri) that all of them may unite; however they and all the Dacanis were in great terror and he, the governor, had requested them all to defend themselves. And because this matter is of great importance and as you know, for the Mughal is so powerful king that should he be

in the vicinity of the said fortress, he would give them much to do and everything would run danger. I recomend you to do all that is possible in order to unite these princes against him, helping them in all that be needful, not only to reward them for the good done on the occasion of the rebellions but also for the great advantage of this state. However it should be done, with such secrecy that the Mughal may not be apprised of it. You should rather honour him with all the possible demonstrations to preserve his friendship and understanding so that in case you be fevered to declare yourselves for any of the parties, it must be that of the neighbouring kings" see, Panduranga Rao Pissunlecar's article, "Extinction of the Nizam Shahis", published in Sardesai's Commemoration Volume, pp. 29;

(ii) In another letter written to Viceroy Rui Lourenco de Tavera, on the 11th March 1611, he mentions that, "I recommend you to maintain with him friendly intercourse, making him favours, that he may be encouraged against the Mughals." Ibid.

87. Ibid, pp. 30;

88. History and Antiquities of Chaul and Bassien, pp. 63; Danvers "The Portuguese in India", Vol. II, pp. 158.

89. History and Antiquities of Chaul and Bassien, pp. 64; Danvers, "The Portuguese in India", Vol. II, pp. 158-9;

90. Danvers, "The Portuguese in India", Vol. II, pp. 159.

91. Ibid, pp. 159-60;

92. Ibid, pp. 159.

93. On the occasion of the conclusion of the treaty, Adil Shah and his Prime Minister assembled in the royal palace at Nauraspur on the 9th Oct. 1615. A.D. In this assembly Shah Nawaz Khan the Adil Shahi envoy was also present. Here came Kashi Pandit, the Nizam Shahi envoy, who showed a letter of Malik Ambar, bearing his seal and date of 19th September 1615 A.D. which read "whatever agreement is entered into by Ibrahim Adil Shah and Shahnawaz Khan (Adil Shahi) with the Viceroy shall be signed by our ambassador, Kashi Pandit, and this will be observed by us". Similarly Antoni Matier, who had been deputed by the Portuguese Viceroy, to grace the occasion came and showed the orders of the Portuguese king dated 13th May 1615 A.D., which authorised him to sign a treay on behalf of the Portuguese crown promising to observe the terms of it. See, B. G. Tamashkan's article, "Malik Ambar and the Portuguese" published in the Journal of Andhra Historical Research Society Volume XVI (July 1945 to April 1956) pp. 106-8; Panduranga Rao Pissunlecar's article, "The Extinction of the Nizam Shahis" published in Sardesai Commemoration Volume pp. 31-32; F. C. Danvers "Report to the Secretary of state for India in the Council, on the Portuguese Records, relating to East Indies" pp. 51.

94. In a letter dated 18th May 1611 to Sir Henry Middleton, Lawrance Fernel and John Wittans, it is mentioned that "Every day we receive kindness from Malik Ambar Nahuda of the Great ship."

In reply to which Sir Henery Middleton wrote "I percieve you are beholden to Nahuda Malik Ambar, to requisite part thereof. I have sent him a good sword blade and another to his Kaiclso and for the rest I acknowledged myself indebtor" (Letter No. 55).

While expressing his hearty thanks for the presents Malik Ambar in a letter dated 19th may 1611 (Letter No. 59) to Sir Henry Middleton writes:—

"Malik Ambar being glad to hear of your worship's welfare *salutes* you. Your letter with a sword blade, I have received, returning you many thanks for your kindness and will be ready to require your courtsey upon any occasion if your worship make use of me; whereof I prey doubt not what hath been sent both into your worship and people ashore, was not with expectation and recompense, but in token of *goodwill* partly to manifest my love, I bear for you. I doubt not but within these eight days answer will come from Basha with order of your people's deliverence. If any letter will pleasure you for any part of India you propose to go unto, you may command me as I also desire the like from you for my safe passage if I should meet with army of your countrymen in my way. I dare warrant you if you would go into Dabul your entertainment would be friendly and bracement of trade greatfully accepted......yours loving and assured friend" Malik Ambar, Nahuda of Great ship—See, East India Company Records, Vol. II (1613-15).

95. See, B. G. Tamashkan's article, "Malik Ambar and the Portuguese" Journal of Andhra Historical Research Society, Vol. X VI.

96. Journal of Indian History, 1938 Vol. 17 pp. 145-46;
The Dutch Traveller Van Ravestyn, writes, that on reaching the camp of Malik Ambar, "he presented a letter of introduction to Mir Abdul Fateh, who introduced him to Malik, "who talked to us very freely about the sea war between the Portuguese and the English; he seemed to be very well inclined towards us, and gave us a letter authorising us to cross the frontier......"

97. Journal of Indian History, 1938, pp. 236-36; Shiva Kalin Patrasara Sangraha Vol. I pp. 33; No. 139, 140, 141, 142, 143; 144, 145;

98. See, B. G. Tamashkan's article, "Malik Ambar and the Portuguese", published in the Journal of Andhra Historical Research Society Vol. XVI; Foster, "English Factories in India (1608-21) pp. 315-18;

99. Journal of Indian history 1938, pp. 12;

CHAPTER X

# POLITICAL INSTITUTIONS AND CULTURE

The available contemporary historical records yield very little information with regard to the administrative and cultural institutions of the Nizam Shahis. In fact the rulers of this unfortunate kingdom were constantly engaged in the ceaseless struggle against their neighbourers, with the twofold object of maintaining their own individuality and balance of power in the Daccan. It did not give them adequate time to enable them to turn their attention to the development of the higher values of life. They did not evolve any new institution for the welfare of their own subjects. They readily adopted the administrative system of the Bahmanides, infused new vigour into it, imparted a fresh colour to it, and shaped and remodelled it according to their own needs and the needs and the people in terms of local tradition.

The theory of kingship during the Nizam Shahi rule appears to have passed through few stages in the course of its evolution. The founder of the Nizam Shahi kingdom, Ahmad Nizam Shah although did not belong to any ruling house, but his ambitions raised him to the status of a sovereign. Henceforward, the same kingly dignity which finds eloquent expression in the coins and in the titles of the independant rulers of Malwa and Gujarat, of Bengal and Khandesh or of the slave kings of Delhi or in the pages of Abul Fazl, according to Sayyid Ali Tabatabai, was adopted by and maintained by the enlightened despots of the Nizam Shahi kingdom of Ahmadnagar. The Nizam Shahi kings were regarded as, "the candle of the family of Khilafat", "the Sulaiman of the Age", "the lord of the world and mankind" and "born in the family of Dara" etc. Such hyperbolic expressions used for the glorification of their kingly dignity and authority, illustrate the hectic zeal of the historian of the Nizam Shahis to sustain the theory of royal absolutism. In theory as much as in practice the Nizam Shahi king was supreme and

**Nizam Shahi Theory of Kingship**

absolute. He was a worthy representative and the vicegerent of God and in pomp and magnificence equal to the renowned Parsian king Darius. In theory he was always liable to explain his conduct to the Muslim theologians, but in practice he was responsible to no body.

The Nizam Shahi state being a monarchy, the entire administrative machinery derived its momentum from the king whose status had a religious sanction behind it. He was the source of all administrative law. His political powers were unlimited and supreme. He was the head of the military organisation and being the custodian of the welfare of his subjects, he held in his hands the reins of the executive and the judiciary.

**The daily routine of the King**

To handle smoothly the gear of administrative machinery, the Nizam Shahi king followed a fixed routine, which he strictly adhered to whether in the camp or in the capital. He led a strenuous life like the Mughal Emperors. And very much like them, he clearly apportioned his time for the business of the state and amusement. After the morning prayers the jesters appeared before him and would amuse him. They were followed by the Mahaldars who stayed till the arrival of the councillors. The Privy Council meeting being over, the king would mount his horse to go forth to inspect the elephant stables, horse stables and Karkhanas (workshops). On his return he ate his breakfast, followed by some amusements. After it, he transacted the business of state, decided the cases, enquired into the administrative and revenue matters, and discussed the questions of law with the help of the learned. In the open court, religious discussions often took place in the presence of the king, in which he took keen interest. It was at this time that he would issue necessary instructions to the provincial governors and to the state officials who laid their representations before him. After this gathering the king retired for his lunch and for mid-day nap and prayers.

When he awoke, he would send for the musicians and singers of "Hindustan and Khurasan" to listen to their songs. Then he would rise for his afternoon prayers. After having performed them, he would sit with his nobles until the fourth hour of the night, all the time discussing and deciding the affairs of the state.

After the conclusion of the state business, the ladies of the harem would come in and would converse with him for some time. Often the camp boys were also brought in, and were asked to wrestle to the delight of the king and his consorts. He would retire to bed about one or two in the night and with the dawn of the next morning would again begin the usual daily routine of duty and pleasure.

**Principles of Succession**

Succession to the throne was though hereditary in principle, but it went by royal nomination, election by the nobility and personal accomplishments of the princes. Ahmad Nizam Shah nominated his son Burhan Nizam Shah I to the throne during his own life time. But during the latter part of Burhan's life a war of succession between his sons gave strength to the principle of survival of the fittest. After a short but bloody contest, the ablest of his sons, Husain Nizam Shah I ascended the throne. Like his grandfather he maintained the principle of hereditary succession and nominated his eldest son Murtaza Nizam Shah I to the throne. But when the health of Murtaza Nizam Shah declined there arose much uncertainty. Mirza Khan, the Wakil and Peshwa of the Kingdom, challenged the authority of the old king and even during his lifetime raised his son Miran Shah Husain to the throne. The bitter opposition of Jamal Khan compelled Mirza Khan to depose and slay his puppet. He then elected and elevated Ismael Nizam Shah to the throne. Thus the principle of election by the nobility came into vogue. Like his predecessors Burhan Nizam Shah II too nominated his son Ibrahim to the throne. In the period which followed, various claimants were supported by the ambitious and powerful nobles, with a desire to wrest the political power. The state of confusion prevailing in the capital, provided a suitable opportunity to Chand Bibi to proclaim Bahadur Nizam Shah, the son of Ibrahim Nizam Shah as king. But when after the murder of the queen, and the fall of Ahmadnagar fort, the unfortunate king became a prisoner in the hands of the Mughals, Malik Ambar elected and elevated Ali, the son of Shah Ali to the throne under the title of Murtaza Nizam Shah II. Finding him incompetent, he put him to death and raised his son Burhan Nizam Shah III to the throne. Fateh Khan who had succeeded his father as Prime Minister, put Burhan Nizam Shah III to death and raised his son, Husain Nizam Shah II to the throne. Tragic was the fate of the last scion of the Nizam Shahi house who was handed over to the Mughals to be imprisoned in the fort of Gawalior.

The foregoing survey makes it clear that in the matter of succession both the principles of election by the nobility and the nomination by the king were observed and they in their turn were influenced by the personal equation of the individual princes. If his personality was strong, his deter mination firm, his judgement sound, his succession did not stand in doubt. But a feeble prince could neither wield power nor fit in with the requirements of the situation. He could be no better than a puppet in the hands of his factious nobility. In such cases, the administration used to go out of gear and the prestige of the sovereign used to fall to the lowest ebb.

**The Regency**

Often provision was made for the smooth administration of the kingdom during the minority of the crowned head. On such occasions either the Queen mother or the noble who was best acquainted with the state affairs and who enjoyed popularity at the court and country alike became the Regent. Mukammal Khan, the Wakil and Peshwa of Ahmad Nizam Shah was appointed by the latter as the Regent of his son Burhan Nizam Shah I. Both Malik Ambar and Fateh Khan, though they were self-made Regents, acted for Murtaza Nizam Shah II and Burhan Nizam Shah III and Husain Nizam Shah II. Instances there are, when the Queen Mothers also became Regents of the minor kings. Khunzah Humayun was the Regent of her son Murtaza Nizam Shah I, while Chand Bibi was appointed by the nobles as the Regent of Bahadur Nizam Shah. Both of them administered the kingdom with utmost ability and political foresight.

One of the Arabian proverb is that, "the bravest of men require arms and the wisest of the kings need ministers". Like wise the Nizam Shahi sovereigns too took the advice of their ministers in all the political and religious matters. Although the Nizam Shahi rulers unlike the great Mughals, had no

**The King and his Ministers**

regular council of ministers, but for the purpose of taking counsel, they used to appoint them. Neither their number was fixed nor the tenure of their office. So long as they enjoyed the confidence of the king, they remained in his attendance; when they lost it they were dismissed. Though the prime minister was the highest officer of the state below the king, the ministers in no sense were his colleagues. They were definitely inferior to him and should aptly be called secretaries rather than ministers. Their work was liable to revision by the prime minister, and the royal orders were transmitted to them through him.

When the king held private consultations, other high dignitaries, advisers and ministers attended the meeting along with the Prime Ministers. Often the political issues and some important matters were decided by the king and the Prime Minister alone, without the knowledge of the other ministers. But the king had full liberty to accept or reject the advice of Prime Minister or of other ministers.

Ahmad Nizam Shah was in the habit of taking connsel with the ministers on the political issues.[2] We know that soon after the death of his father, Ahmad had to face the Bahmani forces many a time. On one occasion when Shaikh Muaddi advanced against him, he immediately called his adviser Nasir-ul-Mulk Gujarati to advise him, as to how the enemy should be repelled. With his consultation a definite plan was chalked out and the rebel forces were driven to bay.[3] There is another instance, when Ahmad Nizam Shah altogether avoided to consult his minister. When the ruler of Khandesh sought his assistance. he started at once with his army to Burhanpur, and "refrained from consulting Masnad-i-Ali Nasir-ul-Mulk Gujarati who was accustomed to be consulted in all the matters of importance."[4]

Burhan Nizam Shah I, being the chip of the old block, followed the customs and precedents set up by his father. He too was in the habit of taking counsel with the amirs, ministers and officers of the state, before entering upon any enterprise and in all the matters of administration and religion. His most intimate counsellors were Kamil Khan, Miyan Raja, Partab Rai, Shah Tahir and many others. If any one of these happened to be absent, when any matter was discussed, that discussion was again repeated at the king's commands in his presence by the other counsellors, and he was called upon to express his opinion.[5]

When Husain Nizam Shah I ascended the throne, the same Privy Council, which had been constituted by his predecessor, continued to play its role. He too like his father, used to discuss with his ministers, matters of utmost importance,[6] though very often, he would differ from their opinions. Among his chief counsellors mention should be made of Qasim Beg and Maulana Inayatullah.[7]

Murtaza Nizam Shah I too realised the necessity of consulting his ministers. Although, he ascended the throne during minority, he never failed to lend a ready ear to the nobles or the ministers. It was on the suggestion and advice of the nobles or the ministers like, Shah Jamaluddin Anju, Qasim Beg and other counsellors that he permitted that the regency of his mother Khunzah Humayun should terminate.[8] But no sooner than the regency had been overthrown, than the ministers began to play a dominant role in the political affairs of the court and the country as well.[9] At length the king was relegated into the background and reins of administration passed into their hands. With the death of Murtaza Nizam Shah, it appears that the Privy Council ceased to exist.

**Wakil and Peshwa**

The Prime Minister or the Wakil and Peshwa of the Nizam Shahi kingdom was the highest officer in the central structure of the Nizam Shahi administration. Unlike the Prime Minister of the present day, he was neither the elected representative of the people nor the representative of the body of king's advisers. He was directly appointed by the king, and hence was responsible to him alone for his actions. So long he enjoyed his confidence he had no fear of losing his office or authority. His position was like the wazir of the Caliphs. He acted like a secretary, bound to carry out the instructions and orders of his master, but when the latter was weak and feeble, he stepped into his place and became the real source of power.

The title of Wakil and Peshwa was an honorific title

during the Nizam Shahi rule, which did not imply the charge of any particular branch of administration. On the whole, he had to look after the working of the different departments and had to supervise them. When he found himself unable to carry his duties alone, upon his request another influential noble was appointed and associated with him in his office.[10]

On the basis of contemporary historical records, it may be stated that the central government of the Nizam Shahis was split up into several departments, falling under two broad divisions; civil and military, each presided over by a minister. The following were the main departments on the Civil side:—

1. Department of Revenue and Finance.
2. Department of Law and Justice.
3. Department of Public Works.
4. Department of Endowments and Trusts.
5. Department of Royal Mints.
6. Political Department.

The head of the department of Revenue and Finance was the Wazir, who was in charge of revenue and expenditure of the kingdom. He had under him a Diwan, whose principal duties were to formulate rules and regulations for the revenue settlement and to fix the rates of other kinds of revenues and to examine and control disbursements. All official records were sent to his office for his perusal and were kept by him. He had to scrutinise all transactions and payments. All the matters pertaining to any department whatsoever emanated from and passed through him. He imprinted his seal on all papers which thereafter were countersigned by the Wakil and Peshwa of the kingdom without which no order was considered as valid.

The Diwan under the Nizam Shahis did not enjoy that wide range of powers and discretion as the Mughal Diwan, because the former was under the strict vigilance of the Wakil and Peshwa. To assist him in his task, Nazirs (Superintendents) were appointed. All the revenue of the kingdom was collected at his office, known as Diwan-i-Mal. The entire amount was then remitted to the public treasury which was under the direct control of the Wakil and Peshwa.

Although the historical material available to us does not tell us much about *the department of law and justice*, but it appears that the Nizam Shahis inherited it from the Bahmanides. They organised and remodelled it after the injunctions of Shariat which were enforced in consultations with the chief Qazi.

The Nizam Shahi rulers were famous for their sense of justice. Being the head of the judiciary at the centre, they daily heard civil and criminal appeals and dispensed justice with the help of the Qazis and Muftis. We do not know, if there was an institution like the high court at the centre, headed by a Sadr. Perhaps the Qazis and the Kotwal decided the civil and criminal cases at the capital.

Although Ahmad Nizam Shah found no time to introduce any judicial system but his justice was famous. One of his merciful benevolent practices, related by Sayyid Ali the historian of the Nizam Shahis is, that if any person charged with some offence was produced before him in the court of justice, he would ask him if he had committed the crime or not. In case he confessed, the king would say, "Tie your turban again" and would set him free. This clearly shows that Ahmad Nizam Shah wanted to supress the criminal instinct of the offenders not by inflicting severe punishment on them, but by reforming them with kindness and love.[11]

His successor Burhan Nizam Shah adopted a different policy. He was very severe in punishing the criminals. But he never acted hastily or without careful consideration in giving his decision.

It was Murtaza Nizam Shah I, who ordered that, "a chain of justice should be hung in the plains of Kala Chabutra".[12] This was definitely a new innovation, which was later on adopted by Emperor Jahangir. He also established a high court at Ahmadnagar, where several leading officers of the state and jurists sat to hear the cases brought before them and to dispense justice to the people.

*The department of endowments and trusts* was one of the most important department of the state headed by the Wazir. During the Nizam Shahi regime, ministers and public spirited men created a large number of endowments and trusts for the benefit of the public. The management of these public charities was actually in the hands of Mutwallis who were under the supervision of Wazir.

Another department known as the *department of Royal Mints*, does not seem to have flourished before Salabat Khan II. It was he who had established royal mints at Ahmadnagar, Burhanpur and Daultabad, where gold, silver and copper coins were struck in the name of Nizam Shahi ruler. These mints continued to flourish up to reign of Burhan Nizam Shah II, under the supervision of either the Wazir or the Prime Minister.[13]

Then there was the department of *Public Works*. This department was presided over by a Wazir or minister, assisted by a state engineer. All the public works were carried out at the suggestion of the latter and in accordance with his advice. He had under him a band of trained architects who prepared plans for all buildings. An inscription on the Mangalwar Gate near the Municipal office at Ahmadnagar speaks of the buildings which Nimat Khan Samnani had constructed for the public. They included a house of charity, a mosque, and cisterns full of running water.[14] While another inscription mentions that he had constructed a *Caravan sarai*, hammam (bath) which were situated in the bazar named Panjshambah, in Ahmadnagar. It is also related in the same inscription that he also cultivated portions of Nami Bagh, situated in the village of Sarar, for the Namiyyah Masjid, and running conduits in the latter for the welfare of the people, so that their income may be utilised for essential repairs, for the carpets, and lighting of the mosque and for the conduits. (1564 A.D.).[15] The public works department also looked after canals and waterways that supplied water to the city of Ahmadnagar. The following canals were laid out in the time of Nizam Shahi rulers:—

(1) *Kapurwadi Channel*:—Its aqueduct was built by three nobles, Ikhtiyar Khan, Qasim Khan, and Siddi Shamshir Khan, who were in the court of Ahmad Nizam Shah. On the overthrow of the Nizam Shahi dynasty this channel fell into ruins.[16]

(2) *Nagabai Channel*:—It had its source about a mile below the Kapurwadi channel. It too was built in the reign of Ahmad Nizam Shah after the construction of the fort of Ahmadnagar.[17]

(3) *Shendi Channel*:—It was built by Salabat Khan

Gurji, during the reign of Ahmad Nizam Shah.[18]

(4) *Bhinagar Channel*:—The Bhinagar Channel originally called as Farah Baksh Garden conduit was one of the chief sources of water supply to the city. This channel was constructed in the reign of Burhan Nizam shah I, by two of his nobles Salabat Khan Gurji and Nimat Khan Daccani. According to the tradition, on finding that king had become tired of the garden of Hasht Bahisht, the two nobles planned to lay out a new garden. Thus came into being the Farah Baksh garden (Bagh-i-Farah Baksh) and along with it the conduit and a part of new octagonal palace. But the king did not like this design, and the plan remained unfinished.[19]

(5) *Nagapur Channel* :—this channel was built by Changez Khan during the reign of Burhan Nizam Shah I.[20]

(6) *Varulvadi Channel* :—this channel was built by Murtaza Khan Fikiti and Farhad Khan Daccani in the reign of Husain Nizam Shah I.[21]

During the reign of Murtaza Nizam Shah I, Salabat Khan II took keen interest in the working of this department. As Wakil and Peshwa, he constructed many tanks, water ways and channels. The Bhatodi Talao was constructed by him, which is still in a good condition. It was perhaps his design to carry water from the above lake to the town of Tisgaon, which was founded by him. He also constructed the Shahpur Channel which has its source at the foot of the hill known as Shah Dongar. This Channel joins Farah Baksh channel, which was dug by Salabat Khan's state engineer, Nimat Khan Samnani, with a view to supply water to the Baghi-Farah Baksh.[22]

An important section of the public works department was the department of public gardens, which was under the direct supervision of a Superintendent. The Nizam Shahi kings were very fond of planting gardens and maintaining them.[23] After his signal victory over the Bahmani forces on 19th June 1490 A.D., [24] to commemorate this event Ahmad Nizam Shah laid out a garden. His successor Burhan Nizam Shah I possessed a refined taste. He also laid out many gardens. Among them mention should be made of the beautiful garden of Old Kariz or underground water course, which was afterwards known as Bagh-i-Hasht Bahisht (garden of eight heavens). It was completed by the state engineer Malik Ahmad Tabrezi.[25] Like his predecessors Murtaza Nizam Shah I could not remain indifferent to the beauties of nature. He appointed Nimat Khan Samnani to the post of Chashnigiri (Superintendent of gardens) with the title Nimat Khan.[26] Within a short time he became a favourite of the king, who ordered him to lay out a garden. Accordingly in 1574-5 A.D. a splendid garden was laid out with a fascinating garden house known as garden of Farah Baksh. But it is related that the nobles who had personal grudges against the architect, incited the king against him by representing that the design of the garden house consisted of a series of triangles, whereupon the latter ordered for it demolition. Sometime later the king entrusted its reconstruction to Salabat Khan II.[27] Accordingly Salabat Khan II pulled down the building on which an immense sum of money had been spent and constructed another in its place. Shah Ahmad Murtaza Anju, composed the following chronogram :—

"Inform the dancers and singers 'O' king.
Visit the Farah Baksh garden 'O' king.
For the date of its reconstruction, expel,
Ni' mat Khan from the Farah Baksh Garden, O ! king".[28]

The art of gardening was brought to a perfection under the Nizam Shahis. Thanks to the refined tastes of Salabat Khan II, who is said to have planted a number of flowers and fruit trees in Ahmadnagar. According to Ferishta, he planted no less than five lakhs mango and lemon trees in Ahmadnagar.[29]

The most important department of the state was the *military department*, which was under the direct control of Wakil and Peshwa. It was this department which recruited the soldiers, trained them and supervised the work of Karkhanas, where arms and amunition were produced. Mention should be made of numerous pieces of cannons which were manufactured in the Nizam Shahi factories, and which can still be seen (1) A canon on the rampart of the Udgir fort, named Sher Bachacha. Its length is seven feet and diameter of the bore is nine inches. On the other bastion of the same fort there is another cannon measuring eleven feet in length, the diameter of the bore being nine inches. Its shape is like a crocodile.[30]

(2) There are a few cannons in the fort of Ausa e.g. the Nizam Shahi, Bahattari, Karak-bijli, Sher Dahan, Lam Gharki, etc. The Nizam Shahi cannon measures eight feet in length and has ten inches diameter bore. It contains the following inscription,

"Abul Ghazi Shah Nizam. The work of Ustad Muhammad Husain Rumi".[31]

(3) The most famous piece of cannon was Malik-i-Maidan, which is now lying in the fort of Bijapur. It has been described by European writers as the largest peace of ordnance in the world.[32]

The Nizam Shahi rulers also invented some cannons, which were loaded with copper coins and when discharged they caused destruction like machine guns in the enemy's camp.[33]

The Nizam Shahi rulers had to keep a well organised and efficient army, for, they had to wage incessant wars against the neighbouring rulers of the Daccan on the one hand; while on the other hand had to ward off the danger of attack from either the Portuguese or the Muslim states of the north. Their history of one hundred and forty six years is a record of their struggle for the maintenance of independent existence, which was constantly assailed by deadly wars. The supreme attention given to the army imparted a military character to their administrative machinery, and this was in consonance with the spirit of the age.

**Military Organization**

The physical features of the country, and the limited resources at their disposal did not allow them to keep a large standing army. Therefore every time, when they went to war they assembled troops from far and near. The army consisted of two types of soldiers. Firstly, the Bergis, who were in the regular service of the state, recruited individually, paid directly by the Government and secondly, those troops which were maintained and equipped by the Silehdars, who were paid annually a lump sum by the central government according to the number of troops maintained by them.

This army was divided into four main branches, the cavalry, the infantry, the artillery and the navy. On account of its mobility in the hilly regions of the Daccan, the cavalry was always thought to be more important than the other three.

Moreover, the peculiar mode of guerilla fighting which the Nizam Shahis had developed for the purpose of offence and defence both, the cavalry was deemed to be most useful. But for assaulting the forts and mining the fortifications, the infantry was absolutely necessary and due attention was paid to its maintenance. Elephants were also used for purposes of war. The navy also formed an important arm of the Nizam Shahi military organisation, because of the necessity of protecting an extensive sea-coast. It was for the first time used in the reign of Burhan Nizam Shah II, for waging the war against the Portuguese. Malik Ambar too was well aware of the necessity and advantages of a strong fleet with which to protect his commerce with the Persian Gulf. For this purpose they had created a strong naval base on the rocky island off the Konkan coast, named as Janjira, about twenty miles west of Rajgadh and he entrusted the command of warships to the Abyssinians.

The command of the entire army was vested in the Commander-in-Chief, who was the had of the military department. He was appointed either by the Prime Minister or by the King; but he received his orders directly from the former and was bound to obey them. He was assisted by a number of subordinate officers who held the charge of various sections of the army.

One of the greatest advantage, to the Nizam Shahi rulers was the existence of several important strategic hill forts in their state. They formed the bulwark of protection and defence. Sufficient attention was paid to maintain in them adequate garrisons and provisions. They were controlled by able and trustworthy officers, who were appointed and paid directly by the central government. They were subjected to close vigilance on the part of the Prime Minister. The chief officer of a big fort was called Kotwal or Sar-i-Naik who had assistants like Nazir (store keepers), Subnis (accountant) etc. The smaller forts were controlled by district officers who were mostly Marathas, Kolis, and Dhongars. The charge of strategic forts was reserved for the Muslim commandants or Qiladars.

## PROVINCIAL ADMINISTRATION

In the heyday of its glory, the entire Nizam Shahi dominions extending over greater part of Berar, the subsequent suba of Aurangabad, Jalna and some other districts in Nasik and Khandesh and the district of Kalyan in the Konkan from Bankot to Bassien, was divided into provinces, the basis of division being geographical and natural limits. It is difficult to indicate the exact number of Subas or provinces, but perhaps the chief of them were Bir, Berar, Junnar, and Chaul. Each of these provinces was under a provincial governor, who as the head of the province commanded a large force. He was the representative of the king, and was directly appointed by him. Like the Bahmani Tarafdar, the Nizam Shahi provincial governor was chosen from amongst the most capable military officers, gifted with executive ability. He was expected to be a man of influence and character. His tenure and promotion depended upon the will of the king.

The governor was responsible for the welfare of the subjects of his province and was required to perform three-fold functions. As a civilian, he was the executive head of the entire administration of the province; as a judicial authority he heard appeal from decisions of the Qazis, and decided the criminal cases. He was to maintain peace and order in the country and to punish the disaffected and recalcitrant. As a military officer he was required to maintain proper quota of troops and discipline among them, and had to exact obedience from them. He had the full power of appointing and dismissing his subordinate officers, besides the power of recruiting the soldiers.

Although nothing is on the record with regard to the officers subordinate to a provincial gavernor but there must have been quite a number of them, arranged in proper gradation and holding charge of separate departments.

Each province was further sub-divided into a number of districts (Sarkars). Probably every district had a Faujdar, a Qazi, a Kotwal, a treasurer and a revenue collector. The Faujdar had to perform threefold duties. He was to maintain peace and order in his jurisdiction, to keep roads safe from robbers and thieves, and to enforce the imperial orders. Being a military officer he was required to maintain local militia and was expected to assist the collector of the revenue in the work of the realisation of the revenue.[34]

Each district was divided into subdivisions, which was

generally known either by the Persian names viz, pargana, Kuryat, Simt, Mahal, the taluka or sometimes by the Hindu names of prant, and desh. The hilly west was generally managed by Hindu officers. In the parganas, the civil suits relating to land were generally referred to the panchayats; while the hereditary revenue superintendents and accountants who were known as deshpandes realised the revenue and looked after the administration.[35]

## LITERATURE

In human race there is always a passion for self expression. The dawn of a new era is always accompanied by the birth of great literary and artistic movement. The age in which the Nizam Shahi rulers flourished was favourable to the growth and development of literature, art and architecture. For not only at Ahmadnagar, but in other independent kingdoms of the Daccan, there was a genuine desire on the part of generous and bounteous kings and their wise and able nobles to promote different aspects of culture. They were intent upon harmonising the indigenous and foreign traits and thus creating a new atmosphere for fresh appreciation of the aesthetic values.

Educated as Nizam Shahi rulers were, in accordance with the traditional pattern of the Muslim educational system, they were keen to extend patronage to the learned and pious. Inspite of all the horrors of political chaos and confusion and perpetual warfare with the neighbours, the Nizam Shahi rulers did not forget to promote Indo-Muslim culture. Their court became a famous rendezvous for men of euridition and learning from all the quarters of the Islamic world. "Poets and writers, historians and biographers, reciters of Quran and theologians, jurists and law givers, politicians, statesmen and administrators, warriors and swordsmen, all of these received munificent rewards according to their worth."

In the short but eventful reign of Ahmad Nizam Shah, unfortunately we do not find the name of any poet or writer of fame in Persian, but the reasons for it were obvious.

Burhan Nizam Shah I, the son and successor of Ahmad Nizam Shah proved himself to the greatest patron of learning in his age. Indeed those who were patronised by him made copious contribution to the growth and development of the Persian language and literature.

The foremost scholar was Shah Tahir Husaini, surnamed Daccani, who was well versed in all branches of learning. He was a great warrior, a statesman, and a successful administrator. Apart from his multifarious social, political and religious activities, Shah Tahir was a prolific writer. Besides his voluminous Diwan of Persian and Arabic verses he has left behind a large number of other works as well. Among them mention should be made of the following:—[36]

(1) Sharhu'l-Babil-Hadi Ashara a commentary of Hasan b. Yusuf al-Hilli's (1325) work on the Principles of Religion.

(2) Sharh'l-Ja'faria, a commentary on al-Karki's (1538) work on the Imamiya method of prayer.

(3) Hashiyatu'la Anwari't-Tanzil, a commentary upon Baidawi's famous work. It tries to interpret it in Imamiya style.

(4) Al-Hashiya 'ala'l-Muhakamat, a gloss of Muhukamat of Qutubu'd Din ash-Shirazi (1310) which discusses the controversial points arising between the commentaries of Tusi and Razi on the Ishrat of Ibn Sina.

(5) Al-hashiya alat-Majisti, a gloss on Tusi's commentary on Poelemy's Kitabu'l-Majisti.

(6) Hashiyatu ala Sharhil-Ishrat, a super commentary upon Tusi's commentary upon the Ishrat of Ibn Sina.

(7) Hashiyatu-sh-Shifa, a gloss on the fourth and the last part of Ibn Sina's (1036) encyclopedic work dealing with Metaphysics.

(8) Hashiyatul-Mutawwal, a commentary on Taftazais (1390) al-Mutawwal on Qazwini's treatise on rhetoric called Takhlisul-Miftah.

(9) Sharh-i-Gulshan-i-Raz, a commentary on Mahmud Shabistari's famous mystical poem. Both according to Ferishta and Burhan-i-Massir, this work is attributed to Shah Tahir, but according to the author of the Nataiju'l-Afkar it is the work of Shaikh Mahmud Shabistari himself. The author of Tadhkira-i-Shura-i-Dakan attribute it to the Khwaja Ahmad Fani. (see Vol. II,p. 887).

(10) Risala-i-Palki.

(11) Insha-i-Shah Tahir (a volume of letters).

(12) Tuhfa-i-Shahi, a super commentary upon Ali al-Bakhshi's commentary upon Tusi's Tafridul-Kalam.

(13) Fath-Nama. It gives an account of the conquest of Sholapur by Burhan Nizam Shah I.

Another poet patronised by Burhan Nizam Shah I was Ghulam Ali Hindu Shah Astrabadi. He was a man of learning, who came to Ahmadnagar probably in his reign. He was a good poet, and wrote in Persian and Arabic. Ferishta has given the following chronogram, which is believed to have been composed by his father:—[37]

Three kings expired at one time,
On account of whose justice India was the abode of peace,
First, Mahmud (III) The Emperor of Gujarat,
Who was as young as his fortune;
2nd Islam Shah (Suri) the Sultan of Delhi;
Who was in India, the Master of Felicity,
3rd was the Nizam, the Bahri king,
Who was in Daccan possessed of royal insignia,
Why do you ask me the date of the deaths of these kings ?
It was the "fall of the kings" A.H. 961 (1553 A.D.).

In the short reign of Husain Nizam Shah I, who was himself an accomplished man of his age, there were a few poets in his court. The most famous among them is Ali Niwadi. He was a pupil of Shah Tahir. Nothing more is known about him except that he came to India from Persia and was patronised by Husain Nizam Shah I. It is related that for sometime he fell in disgrace with his patron, and therefore he changed his takhallus or the poetical name from Niwadi to Na Ummedi (or hopeless). He died in 1567 A.D. at Ahmadnagar.[38]

The long and prosperous reign of Murtaza Nizam Shah I formed a glorious epoch in the history of the Nizam Shahi kingdom. The king being himself learned and educated patronised poets and writers. In the second half of his reign as has already been related, he took to retired life, reading the finest gems of Persian literature. His magnificent library at Ahmadnagar was a patent proof of his interest in promoting learning and poetry. Among the poets contemporary to him, are the following.

**Sayyid Qasim Arsalan:**[39]

He was a native of Mashhad. He came to India during the reign of Emperor Akbar, at whose court he remained for some years. Then he came to Gujarat and took service in the king's court at Ahmadabad. After some time he left for Ahmadnagar, where he was honoured by Murtaza Nizam Shah, who also persuaded him to stay at his court for ever. But he did not stay there and went to visit Bijapur court. From Bijapur he went to visit Golkunda where Qutb Shah received him most respectfully. From there he returned to Ahmadabad where he died in the year 1606-7 A.D.

Arsalan was known for his poetry and distinguished himself in calligraphy and in composing chronograms. The following is a specimen of his composition:—

Ah-i-dilam gar athari dashti,
Sham-i-ummidan sahari dashti,
Gird-i-sarat gashti wa kardi tawaf,
Ka' ba agar bal-o-pari dashti;

Translation:

If the sighs emnating from my heart had any effect,
The evening of my hope would (perforce) have had a dawn;
If the Kaba had wings and feathers,
It would have hovered over your head, and circumam bulated round it;[40]

**Malik Qummi**

He originally belonged to Qum. From his early childhood he was deeply interested in poetry and spent his time in the company of poets. He went to Kashan and from there to Qazwin where he remained for four years. In 1579 he left Qazwin for Ahmadnagar. Both Murtaza Nizam Shah I and his minister Salabat Khan II and Burhan Nizam Shah II patronised him. After some time he migrated to the Adil Shahi court, where he was patronised by Ibrahim Adil Shah (1580-1627). Here he composed the best of his works either with the help of his son-in-law Zuhuri or by himself alone. He was assassinated along with his son-in-law in the course of a Daccani rising in 1616 A.D.[41]

Besides a poem in the praise of Bagh-i-Farah Bakhsh of Ahmadnagar, he wrote a number of poems in Persian. Of them mention should be made of the following:—

(i) A mystical mathnavi in the style of Sanai's Hadiqa which begins with:[42]

Eeen Tarab Saz hum nigarendeh
Ham Nigari dahem-o-ham nigarendeh

(ii) Another mathnawi begins with:—[43]

Banam ankah dar dil ha watan Saakht
Sanam ra kibla gahe Bar ḥaman Saakht.

(iii) Manwa-ul-Anhar, a mathnawi divided into 17 nahrs. Sprenger ascribes it to Malik Qummi but Ethe (Catalogue of Persian Manuscripts in the India office Library pp. 821) ascribes it to Zuhuri on the ground that the author of Khulast-ul-Kalam, gives extracts from the mathnawi under Zuhuri's name. According to Mr. Shaikh, the poet might have united the work of Zuhuri and Malik Qummi.[44] It begins with:—

Bismillah al rahim ul rahim
ahdad na alsara ata-al-mastak bim.

(iv) Asrar-i-Aimna, is another mathnawi which Mr. Shaikh Chand Husain has discovered in the Manuscript copy of Malik Qummi's Kulliyat, no. 851 of the Hyderabad Asafia Library. Its first part according to him, seems to be missing but in the concluding lines the name of the poem is given thus:[45]

Eeen daftar ra tamam kardam
Israr Ammah nam kardam

The most notable, farfamed and the greatest of all the

**Zuhuri**

poets and writers who flourished at the Nizam Shahi court was Mulla Muhammad Tahir Nuruddin, often known as Maulana Haidar, but was famous as Zuhuri. He was a native of Tarshiz in Iran. After completing his education, Zuhuri took to the profession of Katib, and it is related that he copied no less than a hundred copies of Rauadat-us-Safa. Inspite of his hard work he suffered from poverty. In utter helplessness, he left his native town in search of livelihood. He first came to Ahmadnagar and resided as the guest of Malik Qummi, who married his daughter to him. When Faizi came to Ahmadnagar on a political mission, he found Zuhuri and Malik Qummi at the head of all the court poets. He has also paid a glowing tribute to their poetical telents,in his letter to the Mughal Emperor. At Ahmadnagar, he also enjoyed their company and became their intimate friend. They used to correspond with each other and exchange their compositions when they were ready.[46]

During the Mughal invasion of Ahmadnagar, when Malik Qummi migrated to Bijapur, Zuhuri also accompanied him. For some time he remained as guest with the court physician Mirza Muhammad Yusuf. He was much entertained by the latter and was introduced by him to Ibrahim Adil Shah. Adil Shah was much impressed by his poetical talents and it was under his patronage that Zuhuri produced the finest works of Persian poetry and prose.[47]

Although as a writer he is credited with elegance and grace, the fame of Zuhuri rests on the "classical and laboured style and Ciceronian expression." He possessed wonderful talent in the art of poetry and his writings are noted for their "sweet rhythms and graceful euphones". Among some of the enchanting and thrilling lines of the poet, which reveal the anguish of the ailing and afflicted soul, striving after communion with the Lord are:—[48]

Oh beloved. (Referring to God) dost thou wish me to roam as a vagrant (in search of they love).
Or thou, desireth that I should detach my love from thee;
Dost thou desire that I should retain my letter of servitude to thee,
Or that, I should tear it up in fragments;

Among his famous works, which enjoy the same popularity now as they did in the past, are (i) Mina Bazar (ii) Gulzar-i-Ibrahim, composed in partnership with his father in-law Malik Qummi at the order of the Adil Shah. (iii) Khwan-i-Khalil was written at the King's order and in collaboration with Malik Qummi. (iv) A Diwan of Ghazals, qasidas and Rubiyat etc. (v) Saqi Nama which is considered to be the best of its type in Persian Literature. The work was dedicated to Burhan Nizam Shah II, who sent elephants fully loaded with valuable presents to Zuhuri as a reward for his poem. (vi) Ruqaat, a collection of his letters and (vii) Abdaliya. Zuhuri was killed in the Daccan in 1616 A.D.[49]

**Abul Qasim Muhammad Bin Gulam Ali Hindu Shah**

Of the most famous and important of the literary personages who flourished at the Nizam Shahi court was the historian Abul-Qasim Muhammad Bin Gulam Hindu Shah, generally known as Ferishta. He was born about the year 1570 at Ahmadnagar and was educated under the direct tutorship of his father Gulam Ali, who was appointed as tutor to the Prince Miran Husain by Murtaza Nizam Shah I. Ferishta started his career as a soldier and soon rose to a high post in the reign of Murtaza Nizam Shah I. During the period of anarchy which followed after the death of Murtaza Nizam Shah, he left Ahmadnagar for Bijapur in 1589 A.D. There he was warmly welcomed by Adil Shah who entrusted him the work of writing his famous and monumental work, ' The History of India". He also wrote a work on medicine, entitled as, "Ikhtiyarat-i Qasimi or Dastur-ul-Attibba". According to Briggs, Ferishta died at Nauraspur.[50]

The king's Minister Salabat Khan was himself a poet, and extended patronage to poets and men of letters. Both Zuhuri and his father-in-law Malik Qummi were recipients of favours at his hands. Another poet to attain fame under his patronage was Mualana Salahuddin Sairafi. He originally belonged to Sawa, but had come to India with his father. He stayed for a few months in Gujarat, but soon left for Lahore where he lived a life of Darvesh, probably getting a stipend from the Mughal Emperor Akbar. He came to Ahmadnagar with Faizi and decided to remain there.[51]

Sayyid Ali Tabatabai mentions him among the renowned poets of Ahmadnagar, who had assembled to sing the praises of the Bagh-i Farah Baksh on the occasion of its opening ceremony, which Salabat Khan celebrated in a grand manner. The function was attended by the nobles and courtiers, poets and writers. Sairafi also brought a Qasida of his own composition to recite it before the assemblege. But when Malik Qummi recited his qasida, Sairafi feeling that his own was inferior to it, tore into pieces the roll on which it was written. When Salabat Khan heard of it, he sent for him and rebuked him for his action. Sairafi died in 1590 A.D. at Ahmadnagar. The following lines bear testimony to his poetical talents:—[52]

(I) Gulfarush-i-man ki khawahad gul be bazar award
Bayad awwal tab-i--gha wagha-i-kharidar awarad.

Translation :

My florist who desires to bring roses into the market,
Must needs prepare himself to endure the tumlet of purchasers:

(II) Ba tu ashkam kushadu bi tu judai, chi kunam ?
Mi kasham inha ma az didan-u-na-i-didan-i-tu;

Translation :

In thy company my tears kill me; without thee separation, what shall I do ?
I have to put up with all this in seeing and in not seeing thee.[53]

Another poet who was patronised by Salabat Khan II, was Mirza Sadiq Urdubadi. Besides being a warrior and an administrator, he was also an excellent *munshi*. He was the right hand man of Salabat Khan who raised him to posts of honour and responsibility. After the dismissal of Asad Khan Turk, he was appointed by his benefactor as his deputy.[54]

During the anarchy which prevailed in Ahmadnagar in the short reign of Husain Nizam Shah II (1589) Mirza Sadiq was put to death by the orders of Jamal Khan Madhavi.

Ferishta, who was his contemporary and intimate friend has praised the exeellence of his accomplishments as poet and Munshi in the following lines:—[55]

(i) Ai rahzan-i-karwan-i-Zuhdu parhiz
Bid'at nih-i-dusti-i-khasmi amiz,
Dar ku-i-tu az hazum-i-nazzaragian
Na ja-i-Sitadan ast na pa-i-guriz;

Translation :

O ! Highway robber of devotion and piety,
O ! Innovator of friendship, adulterated with hostility
Due to the overcrowding by spectators in the lane,
There is neither place for standiug nor scope for escape

(ii) Shukhi ki ba Sadagi azu Kardam Sabr
Akun khatash az ghubar-darad Sar-i-jabr
Gar Suz-i-man az khatash fuzun Shud Chi 'ajab
Suzi n datar ast aftab-az-tah-i-abr.

Translation :

That impudent person whom I simply tolerated.
Her downs have now the obession by tyrnnising me on account of malice
There is no wonder if my burning increased owing to her downs,
For the sun gets more scorching from under the cloud.

(iii) Man masaf-i-aqdas-i-muqad das kisham
Man haikal-i-alwi-i-qada andisham

Khawhi zi zamana chashm-i-zahmat na rasad;
Ta'widh-i-tu am juda makun zi khisham.

Translation :

I am the holy scripture of the divine religion,
I am the celestial form of Destiny's idea,
If you desire immunity from world's injuries,
Remove me not fiom yourself, for I am your amluet;

(iv) Ai rawshani-Chashm zi hiran bidar
Ai wasl-i-tu marham i-darun-i-i-afghar,
Az hijran-i-tu bi qarar ast dilam.
Yak lahza kinar-i-khatiram gir qarar;

Translation :

O ! Thou art the light of the eye that has remained wakeful in separation,
O ! Though union with Thee acts like ointment to the wounded heart;
My heart is restless in separation from thee,
Pray, rest a while in my heart's embrace.

Last to be mentioned in the list of the poets, who flourished during the regime of Salabat Khan II was *Shah Ahmad Murtaza Anju*,[56] who composed fine chronograms. Although very little is known about his poetical talents, but the chronogram which gives the date of the completion for the second time of the Bagh-i-Farah Baksh makes us beleive that he was a good poet. This chronogram has been mentioned by all the historians.

Although Burhan II was preoccupied with turning political tides which were furiously advancing against his kingdom, but in accordance with the cultural standards set by his predecessors he also extended patronage to poets. The prominent among them were Khwaja Ahmad Fani and Mirza Hayati,

**Khwaja Ahmad Fani and Shirazi**[59]

He was a native of Shiraz. He completed his education in his native place and then came to the Daccan where he entered the service of Ali Adil Shah (1558-59). He succeeded in persuading his master to send for his tutor Shah Fathullah Shirazi. Accordingly Shirazi was brought to the Adil Shahi court at an expense of 40,000 huns. On the death of Ali Adil Shah, Fathullah joined the court of Akbar.

Fani was a man of deep learning, with a pronounced inclination towards mysticism. He left Bijapur and came to Ahmadnagar, where Burhan Nizam Shah II gave him the post of Nazir-i-Sultanat (Superintendent of Political Department). During his stay at Ahmadnagar he became a great admirer of Mulla Shaikh Ahmad Najafi with whom he had studied the traditionalistic and rationalistic books. He now turned a Sufi. He spent his last days in retirement, in contemplation and mystic pratices.

Among his works which deserv notice are (i) A gloss of Jalim's Nafhatul Uns (ii) Sharh-i Gulshan-i-Raz. (iii) Faslu'l-Khitab. (iv) Sharh-i-Khutuba-i-Bayan. (v) and a Diwan of poems.

Fani died at Ahmadnagar at the age of sixty nine in 1607 A.D. the following are the two specimens of his poetry:—

(i) Yak jura ki az harif-i-mastat birasad,
Pas chashini-*i-dam-i*-alastat birasad.
In jam nihada and bar taq-i-baland,
Pa bar sar-i-khesh nih ki dastat birasad.

Translation:—

If a drought comes to you from the intoxicated friend,
You will, indeed, then have a relish of the breath of, "am I not?"
They have placed his cup on the high arch,
Put therefore your feet upon your head so that yon might be able to reach it.

(ii) Dar aina khal-i-pusht ar bini,
Yak Chashm ba pushi wa ba digar bini,
Khurat binad har anki binad zi qifa
In ast mithal-i-khair-o-sharr gar bini.

Translation:—

If you can see in the mirror the mole on the back of your eye
You will then close one of your eyes and see with the other.
He who sees you from behind considers you a blind
This is merely an illustration of good and bad only if you realisé it.

Another famous poet beloging to the reign of Burhan Nizam Shah II was *Mirza Hayati*,[58] a native of Kashan. In the early part of his career he was a rationalist, therefore he busied himself in rationalistic pursuits. Later on, he was declared as heretic. To save his life, he left Kahsan in the company of a goldsmith's son, of whom he was very fond of and arrived at Qazwin. Here he passed his time among such people as well known for their heretic inclinations. He was arrested along with his other companions, who were produced before Shah Tahmasp, who cast them into prison. When after two years he was released, he went to Shiraz. In 1578 he returned to Kashan abandoning his heretic beliefs altogether. Then he come to the Daccan and was welcomed by Burhan Nizam Shah II. Here he passed his time in much happiness. Within a short time his fame as a poet reached the ears of the Emperor Jahangir who invited him to his court. He left Ahmadnagar for Agra.

In 1610 when Amir Khusaru's Tughlaq Nama was brought to the notice of the Emperor Jahangir, he was deeply impressed with it. But as a chapter was missing from the poem, the Emperor ordered the court poets to complete it. Hayati's composition surpassed those of others, and the emperor had him weighed against gold. It is related that six bags containing in all 6,000 gold asharfis were equal to Hayati's weight and the entire amount was given to him as a reward for his poem.

Hayati died about the year 1643 A.D. the following are the best examples of his poetical talents:—

(i) Dar dil-i-man dard afzudi wa mi gui manal,
Atish-e-dar dilam afgandi wa mi gui masoz;

Translation:—

You have added to my heart's pain and yet you say "do not cry",
You have set fire in my heart and yet you say "do not burn".

(ii) Khak-i-Kui-tu zi sail-i-maza purnam kardim
ta ghubari batu az rahgudhar-i-ma na rasad.

Translation:—

We have made the ground of your lane wet with the stream of tears;
So that the dust from our passage might not come to you.

## ARCHITECTURE

Nor did the Nizam Shahi rulers and their nobles lag behind in extending patronage to architecture. They constructed beautiful and imposing monuments, "which have withstood the ravages of time and destiny and are today are everlasting testimony to the greatness of their creators". It must be noted here that these rulers were more interested in laying out gardens round the buildings rather then beautifying them with elaborate carving etc. They perhaps believed more in simplicity than in ornamentation. Again, it may also be noted that most of the buildings were constructed by the nobles and ministers, and as such they are devoid of that grandeur and magnificence which is associated with the architectural developments in Bijapur and Golcunda. Even so the style as a whole has an individuality of its own. It is marked by the use of small pieces of stones, slim towers, semicircular domes and low arches.

Soon after the conquest of the fort of Daultabad, the founder of the Nizam Shahi kingdom, Ahmad Nizam Shah determined to erect a fort in his capital at Ahmadnagar. Accordingly, he ordered the surveyors and architects to lay its foundations in an auspicious hour. With in a short time the fort was completed.

"The fort is oval in form, one mile and eighty yards in circumference. From the outside a steep wooded or glacis, with a broad top or covered way, hides the walls nearly to the top. Inside the bank runs a great dry ditch, eighty-five to one hundred and eighty feet wide and fourteen to twenty feet deep, whose outer side is an unbroken perpendicular wall four feet thick. The cut stone masonary walls of the fort, said to have been built from the rock hewn out of the ditch, are massive throughout, the parapets being five feet thick and lower masonary of gradually increasing strength."[59]

In the interior of the fort, according to Sayyid Ali, Ahmad Nizam Shah had constructed "dwelling houses and other buildings; gardens were laid out and planted with fruit trees; flower gardens were planted with herbs and flowering plants and fine palaces with arches and domed roofs with coloured and latticed walls like the mirror of the satin sky, red and yellow with floors paved with turquise lapis lazuli; the courts were like the gardens and their fountains like the springs of Paradise."[60]

Of the old buildings, in the fort constructed during the reign of Ahmad Nizam Shah, of greater interest, in the centre and still in good order, is the palace of Ahmad Nizam Shah, which was afterwards repaired by Husain Nizam Shah I. Of the palace, the most notable part, is the public room about ninety feet long, twenty two feet broad and eighteen feet high. The roof has a series of domes. From inside they had been adorned by rich embossed stucco work.[61]

Close inside to the outer gate on the left hand side is the tomb of a holy man Sayyid Bagh-i-Nizam, who was buried about 1490 A.D.[62]

Then there are the remains of Chand Bibi's Palace, which are still sufficient to show that when in their original splendour they were a fine pile of buildings. "The gothic arches and ceilings are very highly finished; the quartering of the ceilings into a variety of angles and curves has a very pretty effect and some paintings in a minaret adjoining the palace are very well executed. Suites of room may be traced, running parallel from the minaret. In front are some fountains which still throw up water conveyed by aqueducts from a distance of two miles or more. The bathing place for the women of the harem is easily known by its having only sky light on the top in the middle of the roof to admit light and leaden pipes run in different directions through the wall of the room,"[63] writes John B. Seely.

The next building inside the fort, which drew the attention of John B. Seely, was the Qilahdar's House, in which there is an irregular range of apartments. On the ground and the upper floors, the rooms are commodious and have communication with each other by galleries, but they "partake much of that heaviness which we often meet in the Asiatic buildings". In front of them is a little garden, at the farther end of which and in front of one of which is a fountain. As that is beneath one of the best apartments and at the end of the avenues that lead through the garden having a few cypress trees, writes Seely, "It gives a pleasing appearance to the scenery."

The two storyed building was built in the beginning of sixteenth century during the reign of Ahmad Nizam Shah by Qasim Khan. The centre hall entered by a long flight of steps is a stately room. The ceiling is supported on large stone-pillars of black stone, similar to the pillars in Rumi Khan's mosque. The ceiling of the side room is formed of domes elaborately carved.[64]

**Qasim Khan's Palace**

Bagh-i-Rauza the garden of Shrine where lay the remains of Ahmad Nizam Shah is one of the finest building in Ahmadnagar. It is of black stone, about forty feet square and roofed by a dome and inscribed inside with texts from the Quran in golden letters. In the centre of the building with other tombs on both sides, stands the tomb of Ahmad Nizam Shah. To the south east of the main building is a small square domed building, believed to be the vault, wherein, previous to its being carried to Karbala, the body of Shah Tahir was laid. The gateway to the south is also domed and also contains some graves.[65]

**Bagh-i-Rauza**

Immediately to the left is a stone and masonary platform about ten feet high and eighteen feet square. It is partly canopied by a square slab supported by a number of stone pillars. It is said to be raised on the place where lies buried the body of elephant Ghulam Ali, which captured Ram Raya in the famous battle of Krishna. Near it also stands the tomb of the driver of that elephant.[67]

**Bagh-i-Hasht Bahisht**

We know that Ahmad Nizam Shah was very fond of gardens. Thus according to the advice given by Salabat Khan Gurji, he built a palace and a garden generally called as Hasht Bahisht or the Eighth Paradise, though in the beginning it was known as Faiz Baksh or the gain giver. Inside the garden in the middle of a large pond, was built an eight sided two storeyed palace representing the eight gates of Paradise, which according to Muhammedan belief has eight doors. The water for the pond was brought by a ditch from the village of Vadgaon and Shendi, and on the banks of the pond another high palace without houses was built. Burhan Nizam Shah named it Hasht Bahisht and made in it eight flower beds watered by a canal from the Sena and enlivened with singing birds. Murtaza Nizam Shah had a special attraction for it, and he often retired into it to play chess with a Delhi singer. The central eight sided palace is now in ruins. Between this garden and the city there are seventy domes and four mosques which are said to have contained the tombs of many royal favourites.[68]

**Rumi Khan's or Makka Mosque**

This building was constructed in the reign of Burhan Nizam Shah I, by Rumi Khan, the famous caster of the great Bijapur gun Malik-i-Maidan. The mosque is built of trap and lime masonary. It is about forty feet long, north and south, by about thirty feet broad east and west, and on its eastern front has an enclosure surrounded by a mud wall about seven feet high. The mosque has two floors, the ground floor was intended for a rest house, while the upper for the place of worship. The flat roof of the mosque rests upon four round polished stone pillars, two in each row like the pillars used in Qasim Khan's palace. Each pillar is about three feet round and eight feet high and of black marble. The pillar are said to have been brought from Macca hence it was named after it. Over the pillars, two rows of three arches run north and south and on the arches rests the roof.[69]

**Illahdad's or Kali Mosque**

It was built by Syyiad Illahdad Khan Dakhni who was administrator general of Burhan Nizam Shah I.

**Shah Tahir's Palace and Mosque**

Although no trace of these buildings are now left, but they had been constructed in the reign of Burhan Nizam Shah I by Shah Tahir, the Shia minister and one of the most talented and interesting characters of the Nizam Shahi history.[71]

**Chobin Mosque**

It was built by Sayyid Jalal Daccani in the reign of Burhan Nizam Shah I.[72]

**Husain Mosque and College**

It was built by Sayyid Husain Mashhadi in the reign of Burhan Nizam Shah for the spread of the Shia faith. The mosque is a original building with a large centre dome and is said to be designed on the model of a mosque at Mashhad in Persia. It is surrounded by a number of buildings.[73]

**Kotla Mosque**

The mosque has a walled enclosure with out-houses. It was built by Burhan Nizam Shah in 1537 A.D. on the advice of Shah Tahir and it was intended to be a charitable institution and College. Except the outer wall, little of the old building is left. The enclosure which is about 300 feet square is surrounded by a wall about fifteen feet high built of dressed trap and lime. It has two entrances on the east and south. The east and main entrance is about seven feet high and four feet wide. In front on either side of the entrance were travellers resting places with two feet square stone pillars and covered with stone archways set in lime. The central part of the west enclosures wall forms the back of the mosque. On either side of the mosque along the enclosure line are said to have been sheds for the scholars. In the centre of the enclosure is a large cistern.[74]

**Rumi Khan's Tomb**

It is also called Pila Gumbad or yellow dome. It is a square tomb surmounted by a dome. The tomb is eighteen feet square inside and including the dome is forty feet high. The walls are four feet thick. It has been made into a dwelling by introducing a floor which divides the tomb into an upper and lower room.[75]

**Farah Bagh**

About two miles south east of the city are the ruins of the Farah Bagh, a fine building in the middle of which was a lake. The palace was begun for Burhan Nizam Shah by Changez Khan and finished by Niamat Khan. When he came to see it Burhan Nizam Shah disliked the design and instigated by Shah Tahir who was the bitter enemy of Niamat Khan, ordered it to be pulled down and rebuilt. The work was entrusted to Salabat Khah I who died while it was in progress. It was finally finished by Salabat Khan's nephew the famous Salabat Khan II in 1583 A.D.[76]

The palace is a two storeyed octagonal structure, with a flat roofed upper storey. The central hall has a dome of about thirty feet high, including an outer platform all round, about twenty five feet wide. The building is about two hundred and fifty feet in diameter and is built of rough stone and lime masonary plastered inside and outside with stucco. Round the palace lies a dry pond which was fed by Bhinagar aqueduct. About five hundred yards round the pond the ground had beautiful garden.

**Changez Khan's Palace**

It was built by Changez Khan in the reign of Husain Nizam Shah I. It is a fine doule storeyed building.[77]

**Farhad Khan's Mosque**

It was built by one Farhad Khan in 1559-60 A.D. The mosque is raised on stone plinth, but has no architectural beauty. The front is of pointed arches and the roof has six domes resting on the central eight sided pillars. At the east end of the mosque stands the tomb of Farhad Khan. Attached to it is a rest house which is in a separate court-yard surrounded by a verandah and supported on pointed arches.[78]

**Sarje Khan's Palace and Mosque**

Both these buildings are in a state of ruin. Close to the mosque is Sarje Khan's tomb which is covered with an elegant cut stone rectangular canopy surmounted by a dome and supported on open arches. The mosque is locally known as the Dobootika Chira Masjid. Both the palace and mosque were built in 1561 A.D.[79]

**Tora Bibi's Mosque**

Another simple building belonging to the reign of Murtaza I is Tora Bibi's mosque. It was built by Tora Bibi one of the maids of Chand Sultana.[80]

**Niamat Khan Palace and Mosque**

Both the buildings are in now in ruins, but still they speak of the grandeur and magnificence of the reign of the Murtaza Nizam Shah I. Both the palace and mosque were designed by Sardar Farah Baksh and were finished by Niamat Khan Daccani, in 1579 A.D.[81]

Mention should be made here of other minor and simple buildings which although possess little architectural beauty, still draw the attention of the local inhabitants. The most famous of them are Kamani mosque, built by Asad Khan Rumi;[82] Muntakhabuddin's Mosque, built by Muntakhib-ud-din in 1585 A.D.[83] and Sadru-ud-Din's Mosque and tomb built in 1576 A.D.[84]

**Damadi Mosque**

It is said to have been built in 1567 A.D. by a noble of the Nizam Shahi Kingdom named Sher Khan. This small piece of architecture is notable for its elaborate carving and unusually large stones. Close to it about a mile to the east of the city is Jamal Khan's mosque which was built by the famous minister Jamal Khan Ghair Mahdi in the reign of Murtaza Nizam Shah I.[85]

**Salabat Khan II's Tomb**

It stands on the Shah Dongar Hill. The greatest contribution in the field of architecture was that of Salabat Khan II. It was he who founded the city of Shahpur and built a mosque there. By the simple contrivance a stone terrace is built about twelve feet high and hundred yards broad and the tomb seems to rise with considerable dignity from the centre of an octagon. The building is plain but the eight sided platform the three tiers of pointed arches and the dome have all beauty in form.

"A few steps from the terrace lead into the vault which contains the tomb. The name of Salabat Khan has been forgotten and the tomb is locally known as Chand Bibi's Mahal", writes Campbell, "The tower is about seventy feet high and the base about twelve feet wide, while the galleries are about twenty feet broad. A narrow stair case runs round the tower hidden inside the wall which separates the tower from the galleries. The top storey of the tomb is said to be unfinished." It is difficult to say whether an outside dome was intended as a finish or the building was meant to be carried higher by adding additional galleries of smaller size. According to one account, Salabat Khan meant to carry up the tower till from the top of it he could see his beloved Daultabad.[86]

In order to glorify the architectural traditions of the kingdom, this wise minister during the reign of Miran Husain Shah II founded the town of Tisagaon and named it after him as Husainabad. He beautified it by constructing a number of buildings as is clear from the fact that he had to take a special Qaulnama from Jamal Khan to complete those buildings which he had left incomplele. Of these, there are the five gates which were perhaps entrances to the town and a Sarai, which still stands.[87] As regards the other mounments, only a few traces of them have remained to this day to speak of the architectural taste of the minister. He also built the gateway[88] of the Taltam fort in 1581 A.D.[89]

With the death of Murtaza Nizam Shah and later on of his wise minister Salabat Khan II, disappeared that spirit which had inspired them to construct monuments and edifices and to lay out beautiful gardens. But with the revival of the Kingdom under Malik Ambar, the old tendency was revived once more. Mention has already been made of the architectural contributions of Malik Ambar to the Nizam Shahi kingdom.

## PAINTING

The land of the Daccan had played in the past a conspicous part in the development of the pictorial art of India. The attractive frescoes of Ajanta and Ellora, which were in the Nizam Shahi kingdom had not only exercised great influence on the western School of Painting in Gujarat, but also over the far lying countries of Bengal, Nepal, Burma etc.'[90] Unfortunately nothing is known about the state of pictorial art under the Bahmanides. But with the dismemberment of their empire three main schools of painting sprung up in the Daccan i.e.

the Nizam Shahi School of painting at Ahmadnagar; the Adil Shahi School of painting at Bijapur, and the Qutb Shahi School of painting at Golcunda. As regards the Nizam Shahi School of painting very little is known. But it is certain that the art of painting did flourish under the loving care of the Nizam Shahi monarchs.

Nothing is on record about the artistic tastes of Ahmad Nizam Shah and his successor Burhan Nizam Shah I. Husain Nizam Shah I seems to have patronised the artists. It appears that after the fall of the Vijayanagara kingdom writers and men of the letters, artists and the painters, who flourished at the Hindu court sought new masters. The Nizam Shahi rulers extended a hearty welcome to them and thus founded the Nizam Shahi School of painting. Here the Islamic art of Persia was harmonised with the indigenous art and with the Hindu art of Vijayanagara. The Tarif-i-Hasain Shahi an illuminated historical manuscript which can be dated 1565-68, now at Poona, bears sufficient testimony to the art of painting which developed at the Nizam Shahi Court. Its miniatures show the tall and stately females as appear in the Rangmala series which was perhaps produced at Bijapur and a similar mixture of "blue orange and yellow, with pink".[91] Unlike Husain Nizam Shah I, his brave and cultured daughter, Chand Bibi besides being a linguist was also well versed in the art of painting.

Unfortunately again history is silent about the patronage of painting under Murtaza Nizam Shah I and his successors. But there is enough material to show that in common with Bijapur and Golcunda, Ahmadnagar in the closing years of the 16th century enjoyed a distinctive school of portrait painting marked by its verile draughtsmanship and strong colour tones. The most famous portrait painter who flourished at the Nizam Shahi Court was Nur Muhammad, who after the capture of Ahmadnagar by the Mughal troops in 1600 A.D. was patronised by the famous Rajput, Rai Singh of Bikaner. It is related that Nur Muhammad harmonised the Daccan style of painting with that of Rajput style. For instance, in the portrait of Rao Bhoj Rathore, the uncle of Rai Singh, instead of following the Daccan style in employing "a cool monochrome background", he has combined with it the

Daccan style "arched arabesque".[92]

Another famous portrait painter whose reference we find is Mir Hashim, who belonged to the Daccan School of Ahmadnagar, but some time afterwards went to the Mughal Court where he became one of the most notable artists of the Jahangir-Shahjahan period.[93] At the Mughal court, Mir Hashim did not continue to paint in the earlier typical Daccani idiom.[94]

The portraits of Malik Ambar and Abhang Khan, published in "Lalit Kala" bear sufficient testimony of the fact that Mir Hashim was amongst the top ranking painters of this school. In short it may be stated that the Daccan School at Ahmadnagar has also its importance, although contemporary history is quite silent about it.

The brief survey of the political and cultural institutions of Ahmadnagar thus clearly brings out that though the contributions of the Nizam Shahi did not in this field were equal to those either of the Adil Shahis or of the Qutb Shahis, they had atleast an individuality of their own. Situated as the kingdom was on the high road between the north and the south, it succeeded in assimilating all qualities associated with these two regions without finding adequate time to mature or harmonise them. Architecture painting and literature associated with this kingdom had a variety and originality, but it was characterised by immaturity and instability.

---

*Notes and References*:

1. Adverting to the subject of succession to the throne in the Daccan, John Frayer writes "Lords of the Daccan are Born Princes, assume Honour from their lands, have as a perfect right to them as the king to the kingdom and descend from father to son, by inheritence, whereupon they grow indolent and stubborn and are not easily Bribed; as the ruler is arbitrary and are only restrained from Raising men, in king's name and for his use; but these make peace and war, built forts and fallout one with another and with their sovereign too at their own pleasure and hardly unite through a common necessity require, may many times side with the enemy—" see, "A new account of East Indies and Persia", pp. 53-53;
2. Burhan-i-Maasir (I.A. 1920) pp. 87;
3. Burhan-i-Maasir (I.A. 1920) pp. 87;
4. Burhan-i-Maasir (I.A. 1920) pp. 125;
5. Burhan-i-Maasir (I.A. 1921) pp. 30;
6. Early in his reign when Ibrahim Adil Shah, taking up the cause of Miran Shah Ali, advanced against Husain Nizam Shah, the latter called the members of Privy Council, along with Qasim Beg, the Wakil and Peshwa. It was at the suggestion of the council that traitors like Farhad Khan, Shujat Khan, and Khurshid Khan, who had instigated the rulers of Bijapur to in-

vade, were thrown into prison and were blinded—see, Burhan-i-Maasir (I.A. 1921) pp. 76, 105, 143.

7. Burhan-i-Maasir (I.A. 1921) pp. 143;

8. Ferishta, Briggs. III pp. 252; Burhan-i-Maasir (I.A. 1921) pp. 207-8;

9. Burhan-i-Maasir (I.A. 1922) pp. 34;

10. Asad Khan was requested to undertake the office of Wakil and Peshwa, now he declared that he would not be able to perform the duties of such a responsible post alone, and suggested that Salabat Khan II should be associated with him in the office. Accordingly, the king agreed and Salabat Khan II was appointed Sarupa of the office of Wakil. see, Burhan-i-Maasir (I.A. 1920) pp. 35;

11. Burhan-i-Maasir (I.A. 1920) pp. 158-159;

12. Burhan-i-Maasir (I.A. 1921) pp. 323;

13. See, Plate V (a) Epigraphica Indo-Moslemica, 1931-38, pp. 10-11;

14. See, Plate V (b) Epigraphica Indo-Moslemica, 1931-38, pp. 11; see, also, Plate XXV (a) pp. 37-38;

15. see, Shaikh Chand Husain's article, "Salabat Khan II", published in Islamic Culture, April, pp. 187;

16. Ahmadnagar District Gazetteer;

17. Ibid.

18. Ibid.

19. Ibid.

20. Ibid.

21. Ibid.

22. Burhan-i-Maasir (I.A. 1921) pp. 328, see, Shaikh Chand Husain's article, "Salabat Khan II", published in Islamic Culture, Vol. 18,April, 1944, pp. 187;

23. Ibid.

24. Ferishta, Briggs. III, pp. 197; Muntakhab-ul-Lubab III, pp. 29;

25. Burhan-i-Maasir (I.A. 1921) pp. 29;

26. Ibid. pp. 328;

27. Ferishta ii pp. 142-143; Burhan-i-Maasir (I.A. 1920 ) pp. 328;

28. Epigraphica Indo-Moslemica, 1933-34, Plate VI (a) pp. 11-12,

29. Ferishta II, pp. 143;

30. see, Zafar Nadvi's article, "The use of cannon in Muslim India", published in Islamic Culture, 1938, Vol. 12, pp. 405;

31. Ibid.

32. Describing it, Pietro Della Valla, says, "of strange things they relate that that Nizam Shah, hath I know not where in this country a piece of ordnance so vast that they say it require 15000 powder to charge it, that the ball it carries almost equal the height of a man, that the metal of the piece is about two spaces thick and that it requires, I know not how many thousand Oxen, besides elephants to move it, which therefore is useless for war and serves only for vain pomp. Nevertheless the king so esteems it that he keeps it naturally covered with rich cloth of gold and once a year comes in person to do it reverence almost adoring it, and, indeed, although these kings are moors but they still retain much of ancient idolatory of the countries wherein Muhamatism is little or not yet universally settled", see. "Travels, of Pietro Della Valle, Vol. III, pp. 144-7; Shivaji the Great, pp. 74-75;

33. see, Sayyid Abu Zafar's Nadvi's article "The use of Cannon in Muslim India," Islamic Culture, 1938, Vol. II 12, pp. 405;

34. Bombay District Gazetteer.

35. Ibid.

36. see, Shaikh Chand Husain's article "some Literary Personages of Ahmadnagar" published in the Bulletin of the Deccan College Research Institute, Poona, Vol. III.

37. Ibid.

38. Ibid.

39. Ibid.

40. Ibid.
41. Ibid.
42. Ibid.
43. Ibid.
44. Ibid.
45. Ibid.
46. Ibid.
47. Ibid.
48. Ibid.
49. Ibid.
50. Ibid.
51. Ibid.
52. Ibid.
53. Ibid.
54. Ibid.
55. Ibid.
56. Ibid.
57. Ibid.
58. Ibid.
59. Ahmadnagar District Gazetteer pp. 693.
60. Burhan-i-Maasir (I.A. 1920).
61. Ahmadnagar District Gazetteer, pp. 594;
62. Ibid, pp. 694;
63. see, John B. Seely's "Wonders of Ellora".
64. Ibid.
65. Ahmadnagar District Gazetteer pp. 697;
66. Ahmadnagar District Gazetteer pp. 702; Epigraphica Indo-Moslemica, 1931-38, Plate XXX (c) pp. 43;
67. Ahmadnagar District Gazetteer. pp. 702;
68. Ibid, pp. 704;
69. Ibid, pp. 696;
70. Ibid, pp. 697;
71. Ibid, pp. 638;
72. Ibid, pp. 698;
73. Ibid, pp. 700;
74. Ibid, pp. 701;
75. Ibid, pp. 702;
76. Ferishta, ii pp. 142-43; Ahmadnagar District Gazetteer, pp. 703-4; Archaeological Survey of India Reports, 1921-22, pp. 15;
77. Ahmadnagar District Gazetteer, pp. 699;
78. Ahmadnagar District Gazetteer, pp. 699; Epigraphica Indo. Moslemica, 1931-38, pp. plate II (9).
79. Ahmadnagar District Gazetteer, pp. 698;
80. Ibid, pp. 700;
81. Ibid, pp. 698;
82. Ibid, pp. 700;
83. Ibid, pp. 700;
83. Ibid, pp. 700;
84. Ibid, pp. 700;
85. Ibid, pp. 703;
86. Describing this building, John R. Seely, writes "another novelty is a large hollow stone edifice of an octagon figure, standing upon a high hill in the rear of the fort. It was intended to commemorate the memory of Salabat Khan II, who built it as sculpture for himself. Having incurred the displeasure of the Sultan, by his exactions, while in charge of the country about Ahmadnagar, he poisoned himself having first asked his wife, if she would die with him. Her good sense, the relish for the pleasure of this world, made her decline her husband's proposition. But one of his favourite concubines immediately coincided with his wishes and they are said to have died at nearly the same hour; their tombs are in a vault underneath the

buildings. One of these tombs belongs to a female—a similar tomb which stands outside and which is supposed to contain the remains of the obdurate and unaccommodating wife."

"The steps by which one proceeds to the roof of the building, wind up through the wall; spaces being left between the stones. They are very steep, are 72 in number and two places they finish, leading out by apertures or doors to two stone gallaries, with large windows, which encompass the building on the inside. The stones which form the lower part of the frames of the windows are at least 14 yards long and of immense thickness. Omitting the gallaries and proceeding up to the stone stair case, between the walls on entrance, which leads to the roof, "From this part the view is delightful and very extensive, embracing a complete prospect of the town and fort of Naggar, a few villages, a number of Muhamedan buildings of various descriptions, some fine rich tracts of cultivations, the river Sena, and many water courses, which give the scenery a very interesting and lively appearance"—see, "Wonders of Ellora", pp. 535; Ahmadnagar District Gazetteer, pp. 705;

87. Archaeological survey of India Reports, 1920-21; pp. 43;

88. The two inscriptions on the gateway of the Taltam fort give the name of its builder and the date, when it was built:—

(i) "In the reign of Shah Murtaza, the gateway of the Taltam fort was built by Shihab Khan (entitled) Salabat Khan".

(ii) "The date of the building from the Hijra of the Prophet Muhammad) nine centuries had passed and eighty nine years over that 989 (1581 A.D.)".

See, Epigraphica Indo-Moslemica (1931-38) Inscriptions at the Taltan fort—Plate XII (a and b) pp. 20-21;

89. Taltan fort is situated ten miles west of Ajanta, in the same range of hills which contain Ghololkach (janjala) caves. The fort has three gateways defended by large number of bastions. The names of the gateways are (i) the Baitalbari Darwaza—facing the East (ii) the Jinjala Darwaza —facing South and (iii) Jermadi Darwaza—facing west. The area inside the fort is not very large and the buildings situated therein are in a depleted condition.

90. See, Moti Chandra's article "Some Unpublished paintings from Bijapur, in Prince of Wales Museum of Western India, Bombay". Journal of Bombay Historical Society, 1940, Vol. 6, pp. 34; A survey of Paintings of the Daccan, pp. 117-119, 137-138;

91. See, Basil Grey's "Treasures of Indian Miniatures in the Bikanir Palace Collection" pp. 8;

92. Ibid pp. 14;

93. See, Lalit Kala Vol. I and II (1955 March 1956) pp. 30.

94. Ibid pp. 30.

## BIBLIOGRAPHY

### (A. Assessment of the Source Material)

When I undertook to write the history of the Nizam Shahi kings of Ahmadnagar, I was struck by the paucity of historical material, for the obvious reason that, unlike the Mughal Emperors, the earlier Nizam Shahi Kings never cared to employ historians to write about their success in their struggle to maintain the independence of the region over which they ruled. Another problem which made me anxious was, as to what exent one could depend upon "Burhan-i-Maasir" of Sayyid Ali b. Azizullah Tabataba, the only work which chiefly deals with the history of the Nizam Shahi kings. After tracing the exact position of the Nizam Shahi kingdom on the political map of the Daccan and its relations with the neighbouring powers of the Daccan and the north, it became easier for me to collect historical material and complete the history of the Nizam Shahi kings. There is abundant material in Persian and non-Persian sources. This entire mass of historical material can be divided into Persian and non-Persian and then subdivided into two broad catagories viz; works chiefly dealing with the history of the Nizam Shahi kings and those which only give the names of Nizam Shahi kings in the context of events.

In the first category comes only Burhan-i-Maasir which primarily deals with the history of the Nizam Shahi kings. Its author was Sayyid Ali b. Azizullah Tabataba, a native of Samnin in Perisa. He mentions nothing about his early life and activities. He came to India from Iraq and entered the service of Ibrahim Qutb Shah (1550-60). It appears that he was present at the siege of Naldurg in 1581 and thereafter quitted Qutb Shahi service and entered the service of the Nizam Shahis. He was a contemporary of Ferishta and like him a noble at the Nizam Shahi court.

Burhan Nizam Shah II, who had lived at the Mughal court for some time and where he must have seen the compilation of official history, brought with him this idea, and therefore after ascending the Nizam Shahi throne, ordered Sayyid Ali to write an account of his predecessors. Sayyid Ali started writing in 1592, as the title of the work suggests, and completed the work on 17th November 1594. Beginning from the foundation of the Bahmani kingdom, Sayyid Ali recalls the glorious past, the rising fortunes ef the Nizam Shahi kings and continues the narrative right up to the siege of the fort of Ahmadnagar by the Mughals and the conclusion of peace between Chand Bibi and Prince Murad on 14th March, 1596. His style is bombastic, prolix in the extreme, and in language is interpersed with pompuous phraseology. Regarding the authenticity of the work, Sir Wolseley Haig remarked, "the value of the work as historical document is much impaired by its partiality" and "unscrupulous partiality" for the Nizam Shahi kings. This may be true a limited extent because the author was quite conscious of his limitations. Since he had to please his royal patron, he could not present an objective and trustworthy account of the Nizam Shahi kings. Ignoring the evidence available to him, he continued to applaud their actions. Thus very often his pen took him far away from the realities. Though it was a well known fact that Malik Hasan Bahri was a converted Muslim, yet like other historians of the medieval period he conceals the fact and tries to trace the lineage of the Nizam Shahi kings from the male line of the Bahmani kings. Likewise he has given a fictitious account of the defeat of Sultan Mahmud Shah Bageda at the hands of Ahmad Nizam Shah fighting in the defence of mythical Mahmud Shah of Khandesh. But these solitary examples, in no way minimise the value of the work. Again, though his chronology is mostly inaccurate and the accounts of the various campaigns, confused yet his narrative on the whole is reliable. Since he himself was an eye-witness to many of the events of his day, he was in a position to furnish a first hand account. His version of the negotiations for peace between the representatives of Chand Bibi and the Mughals and of the Nizam Shahi-Mughal conflict is not only trustworthy but valuable. Burhan-i-Maasir thus contains much information which is not to be found elsewhere. It is the primary as well as the foremost authority for the history of the Nizam Shahi kings. The portion which deals with the Nizam Shahi kings was abridged and translated by Sir Wolseley Haig and published in the Journal of Indian Antiquary.

Coming to the second category, I could find large number of works. Sayyid Ali's contemporary, Muhammad Qasim Hindu Shah, surnamed Ferishta, wrote, "*Gulshan-i-Ibrahimi*", which is a general history of Muslim rule in India. Ferishta has been called the Prince of the Muslim historians of the medieval period. He was born in Astrabad in Iran in 1552 and died at Bijapur in 1623. His father came to the Daccan, entered the Nizam Shahi service and was subsequently appointed by Murtaza Nizam Shah I as tutor of Prince Husain. Ferishta also joined government service, took to military career and held the post of personal bodyguard of Sultan Murtaza Nizam Shah I. A revolution in court politics drove him into wilderness. After the death of Murtaza Nizam Shah I, when there was confusion in the Kingdom of Ahmadnagar, Ferishta moved to Bijapur to try his luck there. He entered the Adil Shahi army but later changed his profession and took to pen.

At the request of Sultan Ibrahim Adil Shah II he started writing the history of the Muslim rule in India and completed his work within five years. He presented the work to Ibrahim Adil Shah in 1606 in a complete form, but subsequently enlarged it, bringing the narrative down to 1609. The number of authorities he consulted, the broad perspective which forms the backgroud of his narrative, the range of his subject, the length of the period he selected, his lucid style and his impartial account of events, gives "*Gulshan-i-Ibrahimi*" a unique place in historical literature. As he passed his life in the Daccan, he was an eye witness of many events. His work has been looked upon as reliable, authentic and trustworthy. So far as the history of the Nizam Shahis is concerned, his account is concise but accurate. It is true that he has omitted details at places but still his work is commendable. "*Gulshan-i-Ibrahimi*" is a good supplement of "*Burhan-i-Maasir*" and the two taken together complete the account of the Nizam Shahi kings. This entire work has been abridged and translated into English by John Briggs under the title, "History of the Rise of the Muhameden Power in

India". At places however the translation is neither reliable nor literal.

As the Nizam Shahi kings could not afford to live in isolation, they, compelled by the exigencies of the situation, maintained relations with the neighbouring powers. The independent works dealing with the history of the provincial kingdoms of Gujarat, Bijapur and Golkunda thus alo mention about the Nizam Shahi kings. Sikandar Manjhu Gujarati's "*Mirat-i-Sikandari*" mentions the relations of the Sulatans of Gujarat with the Nizam Shahi rulers and their interest in the politics of the Daccan. Likewise *Basatin-us-Salatin* of Mirza Ibrahim Zubairi and *Futuhat i-Adil Shahi*, which are the general histories of Bijapur supply ample information on the Nizam Shahi-Adil Shahi relations, the wars and campaigns between the rulers of the two kingdoms, the Mughal activities in the Daccan, the early activities of Malik Ambar and the efforts of the rulers of the two kingdoms in repelling the Mughal invasions. These two works are of much help. Certain portions of "*Futuhat-i-Adil Shahi*" have been translated into English by Mr. S. K. Basu and published in the Journal of Bihar and Orissa Research Society, 1938. As I could not get the manuscript, I utilised these extracts.

For the period from 1600 to 1636, there is no dearth of material. The trustworthy account of the Mughal campaigns as directed against this unfortunate kingdom was written by the official historians of the Mughal court, whose number is fairly large. Shaikh Abul Fazl's monumental work, "Akbar Nama" which brings the political narrative down to 1602 gives details of the Mughal activities against the Nizam Shahi kingdom. "*Takmīlai Akbar Nama*" of Shaikh Inayat-Ullah mentions the activities of Malik Ambar during the last three years of Akbar's reign. "*Akbar Nama*" of Shaikh Illahdad Faizi Sirhindi, though based on Nizam-ud-din Ahmad's "*Tabqat-i-Akbari*" and Abul Fazl's "*Akbar Nama*", describes the affairs of the Daccan during Akbar's reign under the titles "Victories of the Daccan" and "Conquest of the Daccan". Some extracts from this work have been translated into English and published in Elliot and Dowson's "History of India as told by her own historians", Vol. IV. Nizam-ud-din Ahmad's "*Tabqat-i-Akbari*", though comes under the title "general history", for the narrative begins with the times of Ghaznavides and ends with the thirty eight year's of Akbar's reign (1593), yet this work has its own value. The autor not only mentions abut the Mughal activities in the Daccan but also gives a concise account of the history of Nizam Shahi kings up to the year 1590 when Burhan Nizam Shah II was reigning. Equally important is Asad Beg's "*Waqaya i-Asad Beg*". Asad Beg was a native of Qazwin. He arrived in India, entered the service of Abul Fazl and served him for 17 years. After the murder of his patron, he joined the imperial service where he secured distinctions, rewards and honours. Emperor Jahangir honoured him with the title of "Peshru Khan." He died in the early part of Shahjahan's reign. "*Waqaya-i-Asad* Beg" is an interesting memoir of the author. It contains information about some of the political events of the later part of Akbar's reign which is not to be found elsewhere. For instance, the author tells us about the relations of Malik Amber with the Mughals, his keenness to join the Mughal service and his friendly attitude towards the Mughal government. In this respect this work is useful. Emperor Jahangir's own memoirs, "*Tuzuk-i-Jahangiri*", gives detailed account of the struggle of the Mughals with Malik Ambar and the Emperor's anxiety to curb his power and keenness to retrieve the lost prestige. Muhmmad Abdul Baqi Nihawandi's "*Maasir-i-Rahīmi*" throws a flood of light on the Mughal wars is the Daccan. Muhammad Abdul Baqi Nihawandi, who was in the service of Abdur Rahim Khan Khanan and who had received a jagir from him in the Daccan, did not fail to present an authentic account of the campaigns waged by his patron Khan Khanan and his sons against Malik Ambar up to the year 1611. He has also mentioned about early activities of Raju Daccani against the Mughals. Mutmad Khan's "*Iqbalnama-i-Jahangiri*" and Kmghar Husaini's "*Maasir-i-Jahangiri*", also narrate the story of the struggle between the Mughals and Malik Ambar in a lucid and simple style without concealing and distorting the facts. No one could more vividly describe the process of extinction of the Nizam Shahi kingdom than Qazwini the author of "Padshah Nama" or Abdul Hamid Lahouri the author of "Padshah Nama.".

Both of them furnish ample details relatng to Mughal campaigns against Nizam Shahis, the peculiar conditons caused by famines, the reduction of the Nizam Shahi state to sorry plights, the gradual occupation of the country, submission of Fath Khan, suppression of the rising power of Shahji Bhonsle, and the completion of the process of subjugation and annexation of the Nizam Shahi kingdom into Mughal Empire. Khafi Khan's "*Muntakhab-ul-Lubab*" though merely a repitition of the above-mentioned story is better in the sense that it mentions about all the Nizam Shahi kings.

From 1600 onwards, large number of Mughal nobles were sent to the Daccan to fight, conquer and consolidate. Their names and a record of their activities find place in "*Maasir-ul-Umra*". This work is a biographical dictionary of eminent persons, who lived from 1500 to 1780. It was written by Shah Nawaz Khan and his son Abul Hasan. Although written in the early 18th century it is based on authentic records. In it are to be found biographical sketches of nobles like Abdur Rahim Khan Khanna, Abdullah Khan Firoz Jang, Abdul Fath Khan, Abul Fazl, Raja Vikramajit and many others who fought against the enemy.

There is also copious material in non-Persian sources. Unfortunately, as yet, no contemporary historical work in Marathi, dealing with the history of the Nizam Shahis, has come to light. The scanty material which is available, mostly belongs to the period after the Nizam Shahi kingdom, had ceased to exist. In the material so far published by the *Bharat Itihas Samshodhak Mandal, Poona*, there are very few references of the Nizam Shahis. "*Shiv Kalin Patrsara Sangraha*" which gives extracts and gists of the few state papers, mentions a few political events. A few articles on the Maratha nobles, as have appeared in "*Shiv Charitra Nibhandhavali*" and in the Quarterly Journal of Bharat Itihas Samshodhak Mandal, Poona, are of some use for completing the account of the Nizam Shahi kings.

"*Shiva Bharat*" of Kavindra Parmananda written in Sanskrit, about the year 1670, in form of a dialogue between the poet and the Brahmans of Banaras, gives details of the battle of Bhatvadi. Since it gives the names of Marathas who participated in the battle, it enables us to know the part which they played on this occasion.

The foreign travellers, who visited India from 15th to 17th century have also described summarily the economic conditions prevailing in the kingdom of Ahmadnagar, a few political events, and some other matters. Some of them have recorded the facts on the basis of their personal observation, while others have reproduced only what they had heard and as such have committed many errors. One has to be very cautious in accepting their versions. *Durate Barbosa*, chiefly supplies information on social, political and economic conditions of South India. He speaks very little of the general economic conditions prevailing in the Nizam Shahi kingdom except in so far as he talks of trade and commodities produced in this part of the Daccan and the articles imported or exported from the Nizam Shahi ports of Chaul and Dandarajpuri. *Caesar de Frederick*, the Italian traveller who visited India in 1563, has left for us an interesting account of his visit. Two years after the battle of Krishna, he visited the ruined and devastated city of Vijayanagar. He presents a gripping description of what he saw there, and on the basis of what he heard, he relates the way in which the Sultans of the Daccan organised the league and won battle against the Raya. He also writes that Raya was defeated only because of the desertion of the two Muslim generals. He also tells us about the death of Raya and the fate of the kingdom after him. His account of the battle of Krishna has been publishsed in extenso by Purchas in his, "*Purchas and His pilgrims*". Likewise *Sir Thomas Roe's* account of his presence at Ajmer, of his visit to Burhanpur, the headquarters of Prince Parvez, who was then conducting the Mughal operations against Malik Ambar, and his subsequent visit to the Mughal court, is also very useful. Although his journal has been regarded as the principal source for the history of Jahangir's reign, nevertheless, for our purposes his account is important because of two reasons. Firstly, it refers to Mughal wars in the Daccan and secondly, he clearly mentions that court politics hampered the progress of the Mughals in the Daccan.

The diaries of Ralph Fitch and William Finch, who visited India in 1583 and 1608 respectively, throw very little light on the political condition of this kingdom. But their accounts are important from the economic point of view. Both of them mention about trade and the commodities which were produced of manufactured in this part of the country and the commercial importance of Chaul, an important port in the Nizam Shahi kingdom. In a similar way the accounts of John Huyghem Van Linschotten, who came to India in 1584 and lived at Goa for five years mention about the trade, which flourished at Bassien and Chaul, the dismemberment of the Bahmani kingdom and the manners and customs of the Daccanis.

Amongst the Dutch travellers who visited India and have mentioned little or more about the Nizam Shahi kingdom Pieter Van Den Broecke and Van Ravestyn are the most important. Little is known about the latter, whereas the former was known to be a very outstanding figure in the early history of the Dutch East India Company, which he served from 1613 onwards. In 1617 he arrived in India to establish a factory at Surat. He however suffered many reverses in life got two extensions in the appointment at Surat and then after sixteen years of service, returned to his country. There he sat down to write an account of his voyages. His diary tells us very little of his nine years' residence at Surat, and it is precisely for this reason that, Moreland writes" as a diarist Van Den Broecke was unsatisfactory, left some incidents half told and began others in the middle ; sometimes he would record trivial matters at length, while at others he would omit all mention of occurrances of real importance and his jottings must be taken as it is ; the hurried jottings of a busy man certainly not meant for publication." Still his description of certain events has its own merit. For our purposes he has given a lucid and interesting account of Malik Ambar's early life, of his camp, which, according to him was, at Karka (Khirki), the military assistance which the rulers of Bijapur and Golkunda extended to him, the dethronement of Murtaza Nizam Shah II and the elevation of Burhan Nizam Shah III to the Nizam Shahi throne, the conquest of Dabhol and the other political events of great historical importance. He also gives an estimate of Malik Ambar's personality, popularity and liberality. On the whole his account can be relied upon. The manuscript of his diary is preserved in the library of the

University of Lydon, from which, Mr Moreland has taken few passages and translated them into English. These extracts have been published in the Journal of Indian History. Since I could not procure the manuscript, I have made use of the extracts.

Pietro Della Valle, who arrived in India in 1623 and visited Cambay, Ahamdabad, Chaul, Goa and many other places, has left a very interesting account of his travels. For our purposes he has mentioned the manner in which independent kingdoms were established in the Daccan. He also talks of Nizam Shah who derived his title from the post he held under the Bahmani Sultan ; the battle of Bhatvadi, of Malik-i-Maidan ( the famous cannon ) and of the assistance which Adil Shah and Qutb Shah gave to Nizam Shahis and a little of the early life of Malik Ambar.

The most voluminous writer amongst the European travellers of the seventeenth century is *Manucci* ( 1653 ), the author of "*Storia da Mogor*". But he has mentioned very little about the Nizam Shahi kingdom. His statement regarding Chand Bibi can hardly be accepted. In the long line of foreign travellers, the last name to be mentioned is that of *John Frayer*, the author of "*A new account of East Indies and Persia*". He arrived in India in 1672, paid visits to the western coast and South India. In his account, the chief points of importance for us are, his description of the last phase of the Bahmani kingdom, the birth of the independent kingdoms, the hostile feelings which ran amongst the rulers of these kingdoms, the extinction of the Nizam Shahi kingdom and the principles of succession in the Daccan etc. etc. No one can afford to ignore the original letters of the English residents in India written on behalf of the East India Company to their masters in England. These letters are found in Sir William Foster's, "*English Factories in India*". They throw some light on the dislocation of trade, due to the incessant wars of the Mughals against Malik Ambar, during the siege of Burhanpur by Malik Ambar, and the desertion of the Nizam Shahi nobles like Jadhav Rao to the Mughals etc. etc. The volumes of "*English Factories in India*" covering the period from 1628 to 1633 have been consulted and their references have been given in their proper places.

## (B. List of Various Sources)

*Persian Sources*:


| | | |
|---|---|---|
| 1. | Abul Fazl | Akbar Nama, translated by H. Beveridge. (Bibliothica Indica, Asiatic Society of Bengal, Calcutta, 1897) |
| 2. | Astrabadi, Fizuni | Futuhat-i-Adil Shahi (a few passages of it translated in Quarterly Journal of Bharat Itihas Samshodhak Mandal, Poona) |
| 3. | Badaoni, Abdur Qadir | Muntakhab-ul-Tawarikh, vol. II, translated by Ranking, Lowe and Haig, 3 Vols (Bibliothica Indica, Asiatic Society of Bengal, Calcutta) |
| 4. | Gujarati, Sikandar Manjhu | Mirat-i-Sikandari, translated into English by Sir E. Clive Baley under the title, "Local Muhamedan Dynasties-Gujarat. (W. H. Allen Co. London, 1886.) |
| 5. | Ferishta, Muhammad Qasim Hindu Shah | Gulshan-i-Ibrahimi alias Tarikh-i-Ferishta, translated into English by John Briggs under the title, "Rise of the Muhemden Power in India," (London, 1829) |
| 6. | Husaini, Mirza Kamghar | Maasir-i-Jahangiri (Allahabad University manuscript). Extracts in Elliot & Dowson, Vol. VI. |
| 7. | Inayatullah | Takmilai Akbar Nama. Extracts translated into English and given in Elliot & Dowson Vol. VI. |
| 8. | Jahangir | Tuzuk-i-Jahangiri, translated into English by Rogers and Beveridge (Royal Asiatic Society, London, 1909) |
| 9. | Khan, Abdul Jabbar | Tazkira-i-Shorai Dakhan. |
| 10. | Khafi Khan | Muntakhab-ul-Lubab (Biblio- |

thica Indica, Asiatic Society of Bengal, Calcutta, 1869)

11. LAHAURI, ABDUL HAMID — Padshah Nama (Bibliothica Indica, Asiatic Society of Bengal, Calcutta. 1867).

12. MUTMAD KHAN — Iqbalnama-i-Jahangiri (Bibliothica Indica, Asiatic Society of Bengal, Calcutta).

13. NAHAWANDI, ABDUL BAQI — Maasir-i-Rahimi (Persian Text) (Bibliothica Indica, Asiatic Society of Bengal, Calcutta, 1924).

14. NIZAMUDDIN, AHMAD — Tabqat-i-Akbari translated into English by B. De (Bibliothica Indica, Royal Asiatic Society of Bengal, Calcutta, 1913).

15. QAZWINI, MUHAMMAD AMINAI — Padshah Nama (Persian Text) (Bibliothica Indica, Asiatic Society of Bengal).

16. SHAH NAWAZ KHAN — Maasir-ul-Umra translated by H. Beveridge (Bibliothica Indica, Asiatic Society of Bengal, Calcutta, 1911)

17. TABATABA, SAYYID ALI-IBN AZIZULLAH — Burhan-i-Maasir translated and abridged by Sir Wolseley Haig, Journal of Indian Antiquary.

18. ZUBIRI, MIRZA IBRAHIM — Basatin-us-Salatin.

*Secondary Sources* : (English)

1. AYYANGAR S. KRISHNASWAMI — Sources of Vijayanagar History (University of Madras, 1919)
2. AYYANGAR, S. KRISHNASWAMI — South India and her Muhamedan Invaders (London, 1921)
3. BRIGGS JOHN — History of the Rise of Muhamedon Power in India (R. Cambray & Co, London, 1910).
4. BIRD, JAMES — History of Gujarat.
5. BROWN, PERCY — Indian Painting (Y. M. C. A. Publishing House, Calcutta, 1947).

6. BETHAM, R.M. — Maratha and the Daccan Musalmans (Simla, 1908)

7. BEVERIDGE AND ROGERS — The Memoirs of Jahangir (See under Jahangir)

8. BROWN, C. J. — Coins in India (Association Press, Calcutta, 1922).

9. BAYLAY, EDWARD CLIVE — The Local Muhamedan Dynasties (Gujarat) (W.H. Allen & Co. London, 1886).

10. BEVERIDGE, HENERY — Comprehensive History of India.

11. BEALE — Oriental Biographical Dictionary (Baptist Mission Press, Calcutta, 1881).

12. BHANDARKAR, R. G. — Early History of the Dakhan (Calcutta, 1928).

13. BURNELL, ARTHER COKE — The Voyage of John Huyghem Linschotten to the East Indies (Hakluyt Society, 1884).

14. COMPOS, J.A.A. — History of Portuguese in Bengal.

15. COMMISSARIAT, M.S. — A history of Gujarat (Orient Longman Green & Co, Bombay, 1938).

16. DA CUNHA, J. GERSON — Notes on the History and Antiquities of Chaul and Bassien (Bombay, 1876).

17. DAMES, MANSEL LONGWORTH — The Book of Durate Barbosa, translated & edited by, (Hakluyt Society, 1918).

18. DANVERS, F. C. — Report to the Secretary of State for India in Council on the Portuguese Records, relating to the Indies, contained in Archivo Da Torre Do Tombo and Public Libraries at Lisbon and Evora. (London, 1892)

19. DANVERS, F. C. — The Portuguese in India (London, 1894).

20. DELLA VALLE, PIETRO — The Travels of Pietro Della Valle in India, ed. by E. Grey (Hakluyt Society London, 1891).

21. DUFF, JAMES GRANT — A History of the Marathas (R. Cam-bray & Co, Calcutta, 1921).

22. ELLIOT AND DOWSON — History of India as told by her own Historians. (London, 1862-77).

23. ELIPHINSTON — History of India (London 1916).

24. FRAYER, JOHN — A New Account of East Indies and Persia. Ed. by William Crook (Hakluyt Society, London, 1909).

25. FITCH, RALPH — England's Poineer in India, Burma etc. Edited by J. A. Railey.

26. FREDERICK, CAESAR — Travels (in Purchas and His Pilgrims, vol. I, London, 1905).

27. FINCH, WILLIAM — Early Travels in India, edited by Foster.

28. FOSTER, WILLIAM — English Factories in India, in eight Vols. (Owford 1910).

29. FOSTER, WILLIAM — The Embassy of Sir Thomas Roe to India (1615-19) (Oxford University London, 1896).

30. GRIBBLE, J.D.B. — A Histoy of the Daccan (Luzac & Co London, 1896).

31. HAIG, T. WOLESLEY — Cambride History of India, Vol. VI (Cambridge, 1937).

32. HASAN, AGHA MAHDI — The Rise and Fall of Muhammad bin Tughlaq (Luzac & Co. London, 1938).

33. HERAS, REV HENERY — The Arvidu Dynasty of Vijaynagar. (B. G. Paul & Co, Madras, 1927).

34. HERMANN, GOETEZ — The art and architecture of Bikaner state.

35. KINCAID, C. A. — A History of the Maratha People (Oxford, 1922).

36. LAL, K.S. — The History of the Khaljis

(Indian Press, Allahabad, 1950).

37. LINSCHOTTEN, VON JOHN HUYGHEM — See under Arther Coke Burnell.

38. MANUCCI, NICCLAO — Storia Do Mogor translated into English by William Irvine. (Indian Text Series, London 1906).

39. MUKERJI, RADHA KUMUD — The Fundamental Unity of India.

40. PYRARD, FRANCOIS — The Voyage of Francois Pyrard de Lavel to the east Indies, translated & edited. by Albert Grey (Haklyut Society 1887-89).

41. PIETER VAN DEN BROCKE — Travels of Pieter Van Den Broecke, See, Journal of Indian History Vol. XI. 1932.

42. PRASAD, ISHWARI — The Qarunah Turks (Indian Press, Allahabad, 1936).

43. PRASAD, BENI — History of Jahangir (Indian Press Allahabad, 1922).

44. PURCHAS, SAMUEL — Purchas and His Pilgrims (Hakluyt Society, London, 1905).

45. RANADE, M.G. — Rise of the Maratha Power (Bombay 1900).

46. ROW, B. SURYA NARAYAN — A short history of Vijayanagara.

47. RAWILSON H. G — Source Book of Maratha History (Bombay 1929).

48. SAKSENA, B.P. — Shahjahan of Delhi (Indian Press, Allahabad, 1932).

49. SARKAR JADUNATH, — House of Shivaji (M.C. Sarkar & Sons, Calcutta, 1955).

50. SARKAR JADUNATH, — Shivaji and His Times (M.C. Sarkar & Sons, Calcutta, 1929).

51. SARKAR JADUNATH, — A History of Aurangzeb. (M. C. Sarkar & Sons, Calcutta, 1921).

52. SHASTRI, NILKANTA — A History of South India (Oxford Univesity Press, 1955)

53. SEWELL, ROBERT — A Forgotten Empire (London, 1900).

54. SEN SURENDRA NATH — The Administrative System of the Marathas (University of Calcutta, 1925).

55. SARDESAI G.S. — New History of the Marathas (Bombay, 1946).

56. SHERWANI, H.K. — The Bahmanis of the Daccan.

57. SHERWANI, H.K. — Mahmud Gawan (Kitab Mahal, Allahabad, 1942.)

58. ST. HARAMICH — A Survey of the Painting of the Daccan.

59. SHARMA, S.R. — Mughal Empire in India (Karnatic Publishing House, 1940).

60. SMITH, V. — Akbar the Great Mughal (Oxford 1917).

61. SIDDIQI ABDUL MAJEED — History of Golkunda.

62. TRIPATHI, R.P. — Rise and Fall of the Mughal Empire (Central Book Depot, Allahabad, 1956).

63. TIKEKAR, SHRIPAD, R — Sardesai Commemoration Volume Edited by (Bombay, 1938.)

64. VENKATARAMANCHARYA, — The Early Muslim Expansion in South India (Madras, 1942).

65. WHITEWAY, R.S. — The Rise of the Portuguese in India (London, 1899).


*Marathi Sources* :


1. SHIVA CHARITRA NIBANDHAWALI
2. SHIVA KALIN PATRASARA SANGRAHA

} Published by Bharat Itihas Samshodhak Mandal, Poona.


*Hindi Sources* :


1. DAS, BRIJ RATNA — Masir-ul-Umra.
2. JAHURBAKSH ADHYAPAK — Musim Mahila Ratna.
3. VARMA RAM CHANDRA — Akbari Darbar

*Sanskrit Sources* :

1. PARMANANDA KAVINDRA Shiva Bharat (see under Rawilson).

*Journals and Gazetteers* :

1. Journal of Indian Antiquary.
2. Journal of New Indian Antiquary.
3. Journal of Andhra Historical Society.
4. Islamic Culture.
5. Bulletin of Daccan College Research Institute, Poona.
6. Journal of Indian History.
7. Proceedings of the Indian History Congress.
8. Proceedings of the Daccan History Conference.
9. Proceedings of the Indian Historical Records Commisson.
10. Archaeological Survey of India Reports.
11. Journal of Bihar and Orissa Research Society.
12. Journal of Bhandarkar Oriental Research Institute.
13. Bharata Itihas Samshodhak Mandal's Quarterly Journal.
14. Epigraphica Indica.
15. Epigraphica Indo-Muslemica.
16. Bombay District Gazetteer.
17. Poona District Gazetteer.
18. Ahmadnagar District Gazetteer.

# GENEALOGICAL TABLE OF NIZAM SHAHI KINGS OF AHMADNAGAR

- Bhairon
  - Timma Bhat (Malik Hasan Bahri)
    - Ahmad Nizam Shah (I)
      - Burhan N. Shah I (2)
        - Shah Haidar
        - Mir Muhammad Baqar
        - Miran Shah Ali
          - Ali (Murtaza N. Shah II) (10)
            - Burhan Nizam Shah III (11)
              - Husain N. Shah III (12)
        - Miran Husain N. Shah I (3)
          - Shah Qasim
          - Murtaza Nizam Shah I (4)
            - Husain Nizam Shah II (5)
          - Shah Mansur
          - Burhan Nizam Shah II (7)
            - Ibrahim Nizam Shah (8)
              - Bahadur Nizam Shah (9)
            - Ismael Nizam Shah (6)
        - Abdur Qadir
        - Miran Khudabanda
      - Raja ji

# INDEX

C.

## F.



## G.



## H.

## J.

N.

S.

T.



U.



V.

## ERRATA

| Page | line | has | should be read as |
|---|---|---|---|
| 4 | 30 | adventures | adventurers |
| 8 | 28 | reponse | response |
| 12 | 16 | remnent | remnant |
| 12 | 33 | became and | became the |
| 13 | 29 | patetnal | paternal |
| 16 | 40 | deput | deputy |
| 20 | 11 | adventure | adventurer |
| 27 | 18 | supressed | suppressed |
| 32 | 11 | surpirse | surprise |
| 35 | 29 | Mirza Gulbarga | Miraj Gulbarga |
| 37 | 10 | had done | had been done |
| 38 | 16 | greenees | greenness |
| 58 | 5 | refuge | refugee |
| 59 | 10 | had become | had not become |
| 61 | 16 | discreation | discretion |
| 62 | 4 | acquained | acquainted |
| 79 | 5 | rediculous | ridiculous |
| 79 | 7 | derive by | derive my |
| 90 | 4 | withdrew | withdraw |
| 91 | 11 | alaram | alarm |
| 115 | 9 | affrary | affray |
| 118 | 6 | 1556 | 1565 |
| 136 | 31 | pursuade | persuade |
| 151 | 4 | coronotion | coronation |
| 153 | 9 | Ramghar Khan | Kamghar Khan |
| 157 | 5 | discomfiture to | discomfiture of |
| 160 | 34 | withdraw | withdrew |
| 160 | | Attimpt | Attempt |
| 214 | | susppecting | suspecting |
| 219 | 27 | Burhan Nizam Shah II | Burhan Nizam Shah I |
| 223 | 38 | posion | poison |
| 389 | | beloging | belonging |